① investigate hampered use of [...]
② Few personal rewards? Dead [...] warnings rate?
③ How first became aware.
④ In other countries as prevalent?
⑤ Links with CIA, FBI, — technology?
   technology?

SPOOKS

The Haunting of America—
The Private Use of Secret Agents

by Jim Hougan

SPOOKS

DECADENCE

SPOOKS

The Haunting of America— The Private Use of Secret Agents

by JIM HOUGAN

WILLIAM MORROW AND COMPANY, INC.

NEW YORK   1978

Library of Congress Cataloging in Publication Data

Hougan, Jim.
    Spooks.

    Includes index.
        1. Detectives—United States. 2. Espionage—United
States. 3. Intelligence service—United States.
I. Title.
HV8088.H68   363.2′092′2   78-8182
ISBN 0-688-03355-5

BOOK DESIGN   CARL WEISS

Printed in the United States of America.

2   3   4   5   6   7   8   9   10

FOR DORIS DALY EDWARDS HOUGAN,

CAROLYN, DAISY, & MATT

CONTENTS

              Bobby Hall's fall . . . and a Jewish pornographer
              from Shanghai . . . and Howard Hughes too . . .
              and Vesco . . . Muhammed Ali?   243

  IX   THE MASTER SPOOK
              Robert Aime Maheu, his origins . . . Aldo Icardi
              . . . and the Nixon/Burger war against Onassis   259

   X   HOWARD'S MAN
              Rogue agents and the Amityville horror . . . bad
              scene at the Boom Boom Room . . . Howard
              Hughes, an American Dracula   307

  XI   INTERTEL
              "Tradewinds" . . . the Acid Angel . . . two all-
              beef-patties-special-sauce-lettuce-cheese-pickles-onions-
              on-a-sesame-seed intelligence agent   377

 XII   IT STARTED WITH THE PRINCE
       OF PHONES, PERHAPS
              Sosthenes Behn and Milo Minderbinder . . . Aramco
              struggles . . . and those of other multinationals   419

XIII   CAVIAR'S LOCUSTS
              Dan the Man and the Bagmen . . . agents of
              influence . . . Kodama . . . America's *kurumaku*
              . . . a "*Domestic* Agents Registration Act"?   439

       ACKNOWLEDGMENTS   465

       INDEX   467

INTRODUCTION

IT SEEMS FITTING THAT IN A COUNTRY WHERE PEOPLE ASPIRE TO TWO of everything—cars, kids, and homes—we should have two histories as well. And so we do: a public chronicle, or "Disney version," so widely available as to be unavoidable . . . and a second one that remains secret, buried, and unnamed. Lately, Americans have come to suspect the existence of this second history; the Watergate affair, with all its resonances, and subsequent snippets of CIA malpractices have disinterred a part of the times. *Spooks* is an effort at further excavation in an area that has long been identified as *terra incognita*: the private use of secret agents by multinational corporations and the rich.

Our subject, then, is not the CIA—but "Mission Impossible" agencies whose clandestine expertise is available to the highest bidder. As we'll see, agents from the federal intelligence community have entered private practice by the tens of thousands, impinging invisibly, but profoundly, on current events and our perception of them. The specter they raise is one of a country "haunted" by its wandering spooks, much as Japan was formerly haunted by itinerant samurai cut loose from baronial service. The prospect this presents is an unhappy one in which the federal bureaucracy is compromised by its own veterans, intelligence agents working in behalf of what threatens to become a multinational raj—a world whose borders are marked not by loyalties but by the secret transits of company spies, the ebb-and-flood of laundered currencies. Preventing that prospect from becoming a reality is predictably a matter of full disclosure: light has always been the most dependable means of exorcism. So it is that the haunting of America will end only when our secret history becomes public knowledge. *Spooks* is a mere beginning in that process of illumination, but the task is likely to be pursued. It is, after all, *literally* intriguing, and the subjects of our reportage quite worthy of fiction. Consider, for instance, Allan Bell:

Sitting behind his desk in the Virginia headquarters of Dektor Counterintelligence, Inc., Colonel Bell explains the significance of the Chinese "fighting wand" awarded to him twenty years before. It's a baleful baton: sixteen inches of petrified wood with knobby skulls carved in either end. One skull is white, the other black, alluding to some lethal metaphysic of the Orient. Bell earned it in Korea, where, he says, he became "the first Western black belt in Kung Fu." There's no reason to doubt him. The walls of his office are hung with mysterious memorabilia: photos of Bell instructing King Constantine in the nuances of karate, a samurai sword, examples of Oriental calligraphy, and other exotica. On the desk in front of him is a switchblade that he uses to open mail, a bundle of tape cassettes, three Uher tape recorders, and a pile of charts made with the Psychological Stress Evaluator (PSE), an invention of his and two other former Army intelligence officers. Across the hall is an office filled with locks of every conceivable kind, and, three doors farther down, is a room packed with state-of-the-art countersurveillance devices. All the offices at Dektor are equipped with metal blinds whose purpose is not so much to soften the lighting as it is to counter eavesdroppers. Allan Bell is a spook.

So is Robert Maheu. Dressed like a French banker, Maheu radiates *presence*—that combination of authority and *savoir-faire* associated with great actors and a handful of world-class gangsters and tennis players. Entering a Washington restaurant at Maheu's side is like arriving in the jungles of New Guinea: the ordinary clamor of the place stiffens to a sudden silence; you can feel the stares pressing on your back, the whispers washing around you. At a nearby table, a woman mentions the names "Onassis, Hughes, and Niarchos" to her companion. Waiters approach like tentative bushmen, half bowed in their anxiety to please. A bottle of vintage wine arrives, compliments of the restaurant's owner (who begs to be remembered but "doesn't want to disturb"). Operating in a milieu that places an extravagant value on anonymity, Bob Maheu is that strangest of things: a clandestine celebrity, a spook with solid-gold cuff links.

Mitch WerBell doesn't wear cuff links, but if he did, they'd probably contain explosives. The cane he carries conceals a small, but serviceable, sword; his swagger stick doubles as a rocket launcher. When he's on a business trip, his attaché case is neatly fitted with the tools of his trade: a featherweight submachine gun nestled in deep velvet beside a specially designed silencer. Together they're capable of squeezing off eight hundred rounds of ammunition in a minute of almost perfectly preserved quiet. WerBell is a spook who specializes in the crafts of assassination and the free-lance *coup d'état*. He loves his work.

So did Bobby Hall love the work *he* did—until, if you can believe the wavering testimony of a somewhat dubious cop, a Jewish pornographer from Shanghai put an end to it. A corrupt private investigator, drug dealer and wiretapping specialist, Hall was a man obsessed with intrigue. Blackmailing Robert Vesco and playing middleman in a bizarre burglary of Howard Hughes's inner sanctum, the Hollywood spook came to a Raymond Chandler ending on a hot summer night in 1976. Found on the floor of his kitchen with three Bing cherries in his mouth and a .38 slug in the back of his head, Hall left a legacy to his family of incandescent tape recordings that police have sworn to burn.

Another piece of America's secret history is held by a reporter who formerly covered the news for *The Washington Post* (and currently works for another news publication). As we'll see, he played an instrumental and witting role in a conspiracy mounted by Richard Nixon against one of the world's wealthiest and most glamorous men. With CIA officers, free-lance secret agents, and others at his command, the reporter shuttled between European capitals on his "silent mission," while spooks at home supported his operations with calculated smears, surveillance teams, and an explosive wiretap in New York. The identity of that reporter/spy will be revealed in subsequent pages. So will his statements laying the operation at the feet of a man who is currently one of this country's most powerful and prestigious public officials. Suffice to say here, however, that the operation I've referred to was an affair of profound historical resonance, a prelude to Watergate in which future political shocks might

easily have been divined—had only we known at the time the degree
to which both history and the public are subject to the spooks' manipulations.

Nixon, of course, has always had an affection for intrigue (and a
propensity for getting caught at it). The effect of this has been to
make the former President seem unique, a political aberration. In
fact, however, Nixon's intrigues were complemented in full by his
more likable counterparts in the Democratic Party. As we'll see in
subsequent pages, the Kennedys also had an affection for spooks and,
according to sources in and out of government, used White House
discretionary funds to establish an "archipelago" of private intelligence agencies designed to further their political ends.

Bob Peloquin, president of International Intelligence, Incorporated (Intertel), is no stranger to intrigue either, presiding over a
private apparat whose ranks are filled with trade-craft specialists and
executive spies culled from the highest echelons of the federal intelligence community. Nicknamed "The Needle," the lean and
lawyerly Peloquin operates in a milieu of pulp dimensions, a world
of billionaires, hydrofoils, seaplanes, baccarat, and listless casuarina
trees.

Jack Holcomb is another spook, one who tried to sew up the tiny
island of Anguilla but saw his needlework undone by a battalion
of British paratroopers. He could take solace, however, in his realization of another dream, the creation in Ft. Lauderdale, Florida,
of the National Intelligence Academy and Surveillance City. The
latter is an enormous scale model of an average American community upon which teams of apprentice agents practice the gray
arts of electronic eavesdropping, dedicated to a vision of Total Surveillance. Leaning over the tiny streets in quiet conversation, they
deploy batteries of mini-mikes, cameras, and laser devices across a
spectrum of unlikely places: sewers, drainpipes, streetlamps, etc.

And then there's John J. Frank, a/k/a "John Kane," the former
CIA officer whom no one seems to want to talk about except to ask,
"When does he get out?"

Bell, Maheu, WerBell, and the others—they seem implausible,
characters from the cheapest sort of fiction. Where else but in a
James Bond novel would one find someone with the skills of Allan
Bell? An archetype of the master spy, Bell is certifiably lethal with
his hands, a master of Chinese knife fighting, a crack shot, brilliant
interrogator and legendary inventor of spy-tech. To add that he is
also something of a mystic, interested in ESP and the dharma, is to

tempt credulity too far. Yet Robert Maheu is drawn with an equally broad brush. Who else but Ian Fleming would create a spook whose "Mission Impossible" agency (for such is what it was) would earn him more than a half-million dollars per year in his role as alter ego to a cadaverous and demented billionaire who was, for his part, determined to rule the world from a dark and malodorous hotel room in Las Vegas? And WerBell: like a man in love with death, he has spent his life courting it. A specialist in the development of assassination devices, he moves from one world capital to another arrranging *coups d'état* while flogging the most murderous devices he can invent to fugitive millionaires and Third World fascists alike. It's all legal, whatever its morality, and if the weapons filter down to the commandants of political death squads—men whom WerBell admits he "probably" knows—it's none of his affair . . . so long as his papers are in order and his clients' politics are Right.

Spooks.

The word is gray and vaguely mocking, filled with grammatical twilight. There's an ambiguity about it, a lack of definition. On the one hand, it denotes nothing more than someone skilled in the practices of intelligence. On the other hand, depending on the circumstances, it may suggest an elusive mixture of force, deception, and intrigue. Black humor too. Dirty tricks, after all, are a part of the trade; and no matter how dirty, they're still "tricks." The lethal light bulbs and exploding telephone receivers dreamed up by the B. R. Fox Company are, in essence, practical jokes—albeit of a deadly kind. And "spooks," the word itself, moving in and out of fashion, interchangeable with "players" and "swingers," is the source of so many in-jokes that one would rather not do without it. Norm Casper, for instance, the Tums-popping private eye who uncovered Richard M. Nixon's secret bank account in the Bahamas, is, in deference to the word, referred to by colleagues as "the friendly ghost." And there is humor too, although of a special kind, in the person of John P. Muldoon. A sepulchral giant with a slate-gray flattop, Muldoon retired from the CIA in 1972 at the age of thirty-four, ending a career of overseas service that saw him posted from Scandinavia to Germany, Laos, Thailand, Vietnam, and Korea. Chain-smoking Lucky Strikes and drinking Budweisers serially in a small restaurant near the White House, Muldoon recalls with a chuckle his work for *The Washington Post*'s liberal publisher, Katharine Graham. During the 1975 Pressmen's strike, the John P. Muldoon Detective Agency, comprised almost exclusively of ex-CIA officers from the Clandestine Services, was hired by The Wackenhut Corporation to provide security for Mrs. Graham and other executives at the *Post*. About twenty of Muldoon's spooks were given plainclothes assignments that placed them round the clock in the execs' living rooms. "It was uncomfortable," Muldoon remembers, pointing out the awkwardness of the situation. "These were really nice homes," he says. "The family would eat dinner, the kids would be playing—and there, sitting on the couch, would be me or some other guy from the agency—big, you know, and checking his gun. It was sorta tense. We didn't really fit in. I'll tell ya: some of those people were real shits about it. Katharine Graham wouldn't even let us in. She wanted my man to sit outside on a cot in the cold all night. I wouldn't let him. I mean who the hell does she think she is?" The pressmen bothered Muldoon even more. Coming home one morning, he found his car filled with garbage, and a threatening message painted on his hood. Infuriated, he "called a friend in New Jersey who's very well connected to both the unions and, well, organized crime. And I told him that I had a list of twelve union leaders here in Washington. If anyone fucked with me or my family or anything of mine, I was going to take out three of the bastards at the *exact same time*. As a warning. If anything else happened, I was going to hit the other nine—all at once. I told him I didn't care if those guys were responsible or not. I was *holding* them responsible and he'd better get the word out. I was not bullshitting either. I would have done it. I know guys inside the Agency, and guys who'd left, who could do that. And they would, too. I offered, as a demonstration, to abduct three of the union people and hold them for an hour—just to show that I was serious. But he took the hint. Nothing ever happened after that." Muldoon smiles and admits that the abduction, had it taken place, would have been embarrassing to the *Post*'s publisher. But then he shrugs. "What the hell? If they can hit my car, they can hit my family."

Applied equally to Norm Casper, Bob Peloquin, and John Muldoon, "spooks" refers to an almost incongruous mixture of personalities. Nevertheless, the word is apropos: America has become a haunted place as its intelligence agents move from the federal campus to the more profitable private sector. Bringing burn-bags, bugs, scramblers, covers, conduits, and codes to an array of business activities ranging from labor negotiations to mergers and sales, the spooks are making a financial killing while transforming the way business is done, American style. Their clients are the *premier cru* of the financial establishment—Hughes, Hunt, Rockefeller, Getty, Ford,

Niarchos, Graham, Mellon. Institutional clients have also piled up: Exxon, IBM, ITT, Chase Manhattan, General Motors, American Express, Northrop, Bell Telephone, the Marriott Corporation—indeed most of the *Fortune* 500 can be said to "swing." Even the McDonald's hamburger chain has become a "player," putting Intertel on retainer: behind the billowing costume and the playful visage of the Ronald McDonald clown is the expertise of some sixty spooks whose apprenticeship at the FBI, CIA, and National Security Agency (NSA) allows them to command fifty dollars an hour per agent for their services. Elsewhere, the Lockheed Corporation entered upon an espionage bender, hiring Manchurian spies, Ivy League bagmen, and even a Japanese assassin to help sell its planes. Nor are the spooks' clients uniformly conservative in their politics. Employing The Wackenhut Corporation, which boasts of its sophisticated "strike service," the liberal Katharine Graham found herself in very strange company. An enormous private intelligence agency-*cum*-guard service, Wackenhut was founded by retiring FBI agents whose conservatism was immediately apparent. For years, Wackenhut relied upon the dossiers of the Church League of America, a right-wing think tank whose "intelligence files" on the Left undoubtedly include volumes about Mrs. Graham herself. Neither is the *Post*'s publisher the only liberal to realize the value of an investment in spooks. Stewart Mott, eccentric angel of the American Left, was for years the secret partner of Mitch WerBell, financing the paramilitarist's development of assassination devices in Georgia. Mott, strangely enough, is a director of the Fund for Peace and explains his involvement with silencers and submachine guns in "environmental" terms —an explanation that will be elaborated in later pages.

What's happened is that private CIA's-for-hire, established after World War II, have metastasized across the landscape. Whether it's computers, hamburgers, newspapers, or jets, America's paladin spooks are increasingly likely to have a hand in it (and sometimes a strong arm as well). Occasionally their work benefits the public, though only incidentally. More often the public is their target and, even when no laws are broken, justice is often undone. Subverting federal agencies and the courts with the promise of future jobs and the exploitation of "contacts," industry's intelligence agents often labor in a moral vacuum: profit, rather than patriotism, is their assignment. And, not infrequently, laws *are* broken: smears, bag jobs, bribes, wiretaps, deception operations, currency scams, industrial espionage, tax frauds, and even assassination programs have been planned and carried out by contract agents of the business world.

The dimensions of the phenomenon are difficult to gauge—it's like measuring the perimeter of an expanding fog. But there are indications. Senator William Proxmire, for instance, has pegged the number of employees in the *federal* intelligence community at 148,000. It's from these ranks that the shock troops of the *private* intelligence agencies come, though Proxmire's number is itself a conservative one. The "intelligence community" is officially defined as including only those organizations that are members of the U. S. Intelligence Board (USIB); a dozen *other* agencies, charged with both foreign and domestic intelligence chores, are not encompassed by the term. Nor are tens of thousands of "contract employees" and "agents" working under cover (or otherwise unsalaried) included in the Senator's estimation. The bustling community described by Proxmire is in fact no more than a suburb of a much larger metropolis that may be compared to a secret Pittsburgh in our midst. The number of intelligence workers employed by the federal government is not 148,000, but some undetermined multiple of that number. And if to this elusive figure we add those spooks who are privately employed as in-house or contract agents and investigators, it becomes apparent that the intelligence fraternity is enormous, whatever its exact size may be.

There are in the United States some 32,000 licensed private investigators working outside government, and more than 4,200 registered firms specializing in "security work" of various kinds.* The number of *un*licensed detectives would swell those figures considerably: not only is the enforcement of licensing laws lax in many states, but an even dozen have so far failed to impose any form of regulation whatsoever. In any case, a minority of spooks choose to call themselves detectives, viewing the licensing laws as an unnecessary bother and the image as a burden. Their services are often more sophisticated than a mere investigator can provide, and as a result many prefer to incorporate under a more general rubric; Intertel, for instance, can be found in the *Yellow Pages* under "Management Consultants." They are, however, spooks par excellence.

Of these 4,200 firms, five account for more than half the revenue earned in the field. At least they're said to; the truth is that no one can be certain how much money is involved, if only because many

---

* James S. Kakalik and Sorrel Wildhorn, *Private Police in the United States*, 5 volumes, a Rand Corporation publication.

private apparats shun written agreements, preferring oral contracts "for security reasons." This book, however, is not concerned with the majority of these firms,* their income deriving primarily from rent-a-guard and armored-car services. (Nevertheless, it's worth pointing out that in-house and contract guards number more than 250,000 and are part of an industry that grosses in excess of five billion dollars annually.) Nor is this book concerned with those private detectives (for example, Julian ["J.J."] Armes) who deliberately create an unjustified aura of mystery about themselves and their work. The accouterments of intrigue are, for them, a commodity that proves useful in selling themselves to the credulous and easily impressed. In fact, most private investigators are engaged in thoroughly banal activities: skip tracing, the search for guru-struck teen-agers, marital espionage, and so forth. Such matters are of only incidental account.

Surveillance, of course, *is* a concern of this book. Saber Laboratories president Leo Jones is correct when he declares that "Society today is on a surveillance binge," citing the fact that for every bugging device in the hands of government, there are *three hundred* in the private sector. Indeed, surveillance has become such a routine of Western life that we pay it hardly any attention. In the banks, supermarkets, department stores, and airports *we're watched*—sometimes by kindly eyes, always by hidden ones—and have become accustomed to it. The technology and methods used in this effort have in many cases been developed by the intelligence community and its graduates. But it isn't only in the streets and stores that we're overseen and monitored. Security agencies such as Fidelifacts often place undercover agents in offices and on the assembly line, there to report to management upon their "co-workers'" behavior, attitudes, "loyalty," and performance. (To this day General Motors' Lordstown, Ohio, workers don't realize that they were up against Intertel, as well as GM, during their 1972 strike.) Should we apply for credit or a job, the Metropolitan Bureau of Investigation, Inc., Uffinger's, or Mitchell Reports may well be hired to conduct a covert "background investigation" in addition to the usual checks we've come to accept from credit-reporting services. Meanwhile, at home our telephones are "monitored" at the absolute discretion of the Service Observance Bureau (SOB), a section of the Bell System; with literally

---

* The "Big Five" are Pinkerton's, Inc.; William J. Burns International Detective Agency; The Wackenhut Corporation; Walter Kidde & Company's Globe Security Systems; and Wells Fargo Guard Services (a division of Baker Industries).

millions of wiretaps in unregulated operation (125,000 in Manhattan alone during a single year), SOB's network of former FBI agents and others sometimes works in close liaison with police and private individuals who have, on occasion, traded and sold information obtained from the taps. By no means finally, the psychiatric invasion of our privacy can be accomplished almost anywhere by means of the Psychological Stress Evaluator (PSE), a lie-detecting device available from Dektor Counterintelligence, Inc. Developed for CIA and Army intelligence units, the PSE requires neither contact with nor the consent of the subject; stress and truthfulness can be measured *remotely*, using tape recordings made *without the subject's knowledge*. And if an individual has cable television (which usually relies on the existing wiring of the phone company), an *optical wiretap* can be installed to observe his actions in the home. Presumably, Ma Bell's Service Observance Bureau will find reason to monitor the *movements* of selected customers, just as it monitors their speech. With the exception of some wiretapping equipment, the tools of surveillance are as near as the local Radio Shack or Christmas catalog: a "parabolic microphone," capable of recording "songbirds" a half-mile away, is available from Edmund Scientific (Barrington, New Jersey) for $299; an "infinity transmitter," billed as an anti-burglary device, can be had from Law Enforcement Associates, Inc., also of New Jersey—ask for the "Tele-Ear" (about $400). The state of the eavesdropper's art, moreover, is such that private conversations and movements in the home can be recorded aurally and optically *without breaking the law*: all one needs is the wherewithal to rent the services of spooks to operate sophisticated equipment, lasers, and other devices, unforeseen by antiquated legislation. What's happened is that the technology of surveillance has outraced the evolution of laws designed to regulate it, subordinating our rights of privacy to mere suspicion and the quest for private advantage.

It's not my intention to suggest that all of us are monitored most of the time. We aren't. Nor do I mean to imply that we've arrived at a state of affairs resembling a corporate police state. We haven't. The technology needed to realize Orwell's worst nightmares is available, poorly regulated, and widely abused, but so far the United States has escaped its full potential. Elsewhere, particularly in such totalitarian laboratories as Paraguay, Nicaragua, and the Philippines, *1984* is a *fait accompli*. What's preserved the United States from the fate of some small nations is, of course, its democratic institutions and a cantankerous public jealous of its rights. A great deal of attention has understandably been paid to the federal government's malpractices in the areas of intelligence and surveillance, especially to the activities of the FBI and CIA. Indeed, a President and his advisors have been shamed from office, and reforms within the intelligence community are said to have begun. Very little, however, is known about the commercial sector, whose internal operations are regarded as "privileged" and which are easily hidden from view.

The dangers inherent in that privilege are many, and we pay for them every day.

- The businessman pays when his trade secrets are stolen by spies and when his reputation is ruined by artful rumor.
- The taxpayer pays when spooks use their government "contacts" and offshore "connections" to undermine legal proceedings against their clients, or to enable those clients to evade taxes.
- The union member pays when corporate spies bug collective bargaining sessions, subjecting the union's position to the scrutiny of a PSE, betraying the union's bargaining position and the "bottom line" of its demands.
- The consumer pays when, without knowing it, he's brainwashed by commercially exploited propaganda techniques developed by spooks working in psychological-warfare laboratories.
- The job applicant pays when he's blackballed on the basis of politically oriented dossiers compiled by industrial sleuths with an axe to grind and a quota to fill.
- Everyone pays when his workplace is infiltrated by management spies.
- The investor pays when a rival firm obtains contracts through bribery, foisting inferior products on the marketplace and destroying investments that deserved to be rewarded.
- And, of course, we all pay when elections are stolen, when due process is undermined, when our privacy is compromised, and when U. S. foreign policy becomes a slave to corporate intrigues.

Sometimes the threats posed by the paladin spooks are subtle, but occasionally they're obvious. When Mitch WerBell, David Sterling, or a clique of Dade County sheriff's deputies separately set out to invade or subvert another country on behalf of their clients—would-be dictators and ideologues—it's clearly not in the public interest. Moreover, when the private sector provides guns and money to mercenaries and rebels, American foreign policy is unlikely to be furthered. No less dramatic an example of the spooks' abuses is their involvement in activities that may well be criminal: for example, the plots of private investigator Bobby Hall and and some British mercenaries to kidnap Robert Vesco, and John McCone's grotesque attempt to place a million-dollar contract on the regime of Salvador Allende. This isn't to say, however, that the affairs of spooks and their employers are always black or white. Occasionally, as billionaire Nelson Bunker Hunt learned, a corporation's internal-security apparat can turn against its master with terrible consequences. Convinced that the family's secret agents were embezzling from family coffers, Hunt directed a corporate counterintelligence operation that led not only to the indictment of some crooked spooks, but to his own indictment on charges relating to wiretapping as well. Compounding what amounted to a storm of Texas intrigue, one of Hunt's intelligence targets, an ex-FBI agent on the family payroll, leveled a series of allegations against his boss. According to the spook, the right-wing Hunt planned to terrorize the American left by means of a paramilitary "killer force" he's supposedly established in Southern California. Stung by that allegation, and others of equal seriousness from the same source, Hunt denied all and told this writer that his nemesis was actually a CIA operative who'd infiltrated the family firm! Angered . . . But that's for later.

Plots to murder, kidnap, and invade—the "small wars and demolitions" of free-lance secret agents—are perhaps the least threatening activities of the spooks and their employers. Wiretapping, bribery, and industrial espionage are more threatening, precisely because they're more commonplace. The most dangerous activities, however, are those that are usually the least visible. For instance, in the pages that follow, it will be seen that U. S. intelligence officers working for the CIA and other agencies have fattened their wallets by moonlighting for the private apparats. The practice is a dangerous one, dividing the officers' loyalties and often bringing them into direct conflict with their own agencies' goals. In one case, agents of the Drug Enforcement Administration (DEA) were hired to debug secretly the home of a criminal under investigation by the DEA for smuggling heroin; in another case, a CIA officer assisted a large aircraft firm in evading an embargo imposed by the United States, thereby enabling the firm to obtain a multimillion-dollar contract paid for by the People's Republic of China.

Yet another practice of interest is the use of former intelligence agents to penetrate the federal bureaucracy, relying upon their colleagues to obtain privileged or classified information. Virtually epidemic in Washington, the practice of leaking secrets to the special interests frequently neutralizes the judiciary, regulatory bodies, and even the legislative branch. And there are variations on the practice. Some firms—Intertel and ITT are two examples that are poles apart in size—promise lucrative jobs to government agents with access to the most sensitive dossiers in federal files. Not occasionally, bureaucrats working for the Internal Revenue Service, CIA, or other government agencies will, with the knowledge that they'll someday be employed by a particular firm, act in their future employer's interest while supposedly serving the public. In one such case, a CIA officer provided deliberately falsified "intelligence" data concerning Stavros Niarchos to State Department officials in Morocco —a month later, embassy employees who'd acted on that data were infuriated to find the spook had joined Niarchos' payroll. A paper bag filled with twenties is one way to bribe an official; a more discreet way is merely to offer him an executive position at triple his government salary one or two years hence. The *quid pro quo* needn't be spelled out. Everyone understands.

The abuses, then, are legion. And it becomes clear that the problem is not merely one of "surveillance" but of "operations" as well. As we'll see, those operations can be disastrous. Establishing what Lockheed calls "foreign intrigue channels" to set up conduits and fronts for bribery and kickbacks, the multinationals subordinate value to influence in the marketplace. Inevitably, the quality of products declines, inflation results, and honest competitors are driven from the market. Moreover, the bribery of foreign officials has created a national security problem of unprecedented dimensions. Because the targets of the multinationals' spooks are the most influential officials and citizens of America's allies, political blackmail results. Suborning NATO officers and government ministers, the spooks accomplish overnight what the KGB and NKVD have been trying to do for decades: render these same people susceptible to being "turned" if they want to protect their wealth and reputations.

And there are even larger, albeit more subtle, dangers. In some countries the intelligence budgets of the multinationals exceed that of the CIA's. In Venezuela, for instance, the Agency has physically merged its offices with those of an Exxon subsidiary, recognizing the time and money to be saved by doing so. In Saudi Arabia and some other nations, the U. S. intelligence community has become *an instrument of multinational corporate policy*, reversing the natural order of things, with the result that American objectives are distorted in those areas. Americans, having long ago separated Church and State, are today confronted with the need to separate State and Industry. If we fail to do so, we'll find ourselves increasingly bewildered at the direction of current events being influenced by men and women working in the shadows.

Without further anticipating the material that follows, I'd point out that *Spooks* has to do with the *milieu* of intelligence. Many of the individuals and firms discussed have relationships with one another—it's an incestuous universe. Edward Bennett Williams, Robert Maheu, Mitch WerBell, the spooks at Intertel and the Hughes organization—their paths crisscross in what amounts to a plenum of secret agentry. After a while, it becomes apparent that there's a game going on in the United States but that very few people know it's being played. Or where. The action shifts from Caribbean resorts to Washington bars, from New York law offices to executive suites in Houston, arsenals in Georgia, ruined mansions in Costa Rica, casinos in Atlantic City, and grand hotels in Tokyo. *Spooks*, then, is meant to be a map, *and* a scorecard.

I

SIONICS, QUANTUM & MAC

"HALLO! ZHEEEM? THIS IS . . . UHH, YOU RECOGNIZE MY VOICE?"

Mmmmn. Andrew St. George, bearded and portly, is the only person I know whose accent transforms my first name into a manifestation of fog-shrouded alleys in prewar Budapest. With the cynical wit of a courtier, fulminating intelligence, and the manner of a spook in high dudgeon, St. George is a European television correspondent whose career has roller-coasted through a series of ups and downs dating back to Castro's initial skirmishes in the Sierra Maestra. And yet, while I like him enormously, he stimulates a kind of defensive reserve—perhaps because he gives the impression that he's playing three-dimensional chess, even, or especially, when he seems to be relaxing.

"Of course, Andrew. What's going on? Where are you?"

"Fine, fine . . . here, in Washington, on the shores of the Potomac. But listen: I have a favor to ask. If you don't want to do it, just tell me. But, Zheeem, there may be something in it for you, something that you'll like. A surprise, you see!"

"Uhh . . . favors, yes. Surprises . . . what kind of surprise?"

"I'm here with a friend (goddamn him) and I think you'd like to meet him."

"Who is it? What friend?"

"Can you meet me at the Key Bridge Marriott? Do you know where it is, Zheeem?"

"Yeah, I suppose so. What friend?"

"In forty minutes?"

"I guess so, Andrew, but—"

"And perhaps you'll be free for a few hours tonight?"

"Uhh—"

"I can't tell you any more about it right now, *telecommunications being what they are,* but—you have your car?"

"Of course."

"Where do you want to go?"

"Not now, not now. We'll have dinner in a nice restaurant. A bottle of wine. There are some things I want to talk to you about."

"Okay. When?"

"As soon as you can get here. Tell Carolyn not to expect you until late tonight. And, Zheeem?"

"Yeah?"

"Don't tell anyone where you're going."

"That's easy, Andrew. I don't know where I'm going."

"Of course. Very good. I'll meet you in the bar."

I got to the Key Bridge Marriott an hour later, having told my wife that, if I wasn't home by midnight, she should . . . well, worry. Inside, Andrew was standing up to his ankles in wall-to-wall, nervously trying to look composed while hotel guests bound for Georgetown nightclubs swirled around him and through the revolving doors.

"Zheeem! Come with me. We have to talk for a moment." I followed him to a long plastic couch in the lobby and we sat down amid a hiss of air from the cushions.

"*Qué pasa?*" I asked. He looked furiously nervous.

"Shit! I will tell you *que pasa.* But first, maybe you don't want to go through with this?"

"I didn't know we were going to 'go through with' anything, Andrew. I thought we were going for a drive, have dinner."

"All right, listen. Inside"—his eyes darted toward the bar—"is a man I know you want to meet. He needs to get to an airport. To-night."

"No problem. National's ten minutes."

"No. It cannot be National. It must be Baltimore . . . or Rich-mond. Richmond would be best."

"That's a couple of hundred miles. I don't want to—who is this guy?" A suspicion was beginning to dawn.

Andrew looked around, and then he nodded. "Mitch," he said. "He's finally got himself completely fucked. The federal attorney's office will indict him tonight and—"

"Jesus," I said. "He's not trying to escape, is he?"

"Not so loud! You will get us all in the soup!"

"That's from an old movie, isn't it, Andrew?"

He ignored the question. "He isn't trying to escape. We're trying to get him on a plane to Atlanta. There, with Hildegaard and his attorney, Marger, he can surrender himself and get yet another mortgage on The Farm and make bail and—" Andrew sighed heavily and sank back on the couch. "We're witnessing the end of an era. He's not the same man."

I was touched by Andrew's genuine unhappiness at his friend's situation, but I wanted to know what, if anything, I was getting into. "What is it? Another machine-gun rap?"

"No. This time it's much worse. This time he is *fucked*. Dope. They say he was part of a conspiracy to fly tons of marijuana into the States with his plane."

"He's got a plane?"

St. George nodded.

"Well . . . is he innocent?"

"I don't know. Who knows if he's innocent in *any* sense."

"Well, what's *he* say?"

"You know, the CIA defense. 'I did it for my country.' Marger is going to make a fortune. He is going to become the world's greatest expert on the CIA defense. All he has to do is stick with WerBell, and before long he'll be able to write a book on the CIA defense. I need a drink."

We got up to go to the bar—I was eager to meet the notorious Mitchell Livingston WerBell III—but Andrew grabbed my arm. "You'll go to Baltimore?" he asked.

"Yeah," I said, and we started walking again. Then I took Andrew's arm and stopped him. "On one condition."

"What?" he asked.

"That he isn't armed."

Andrew shook his head. "He isn't armed," he said, but then his features settled into a look of uncertainty.

"I mean, I don't want to get into a Bonnie and Clyde thing at the airport just so he can go out in a blaze of glory."

"He isn't armed," Andrew repeated, but it sounded like a prayer.

The object of all this consternation was slumped in darkness in one of those ersatz easy chairs that pretentious hotel bars adore, the kind with the automobile upholstery and the baseball-sized silver casters.

I didn't recognize him at first. The pictures I'd seen showed WerBell with a huge handlebar moustache. Inevitably, he was depicted in battle dress, paratrooper boots, and an Australian bush hat. Usually, he had an Ingram M-10 submachine gun cradled in his arms, and as often as not the silencer was smoking.

WerBell was nothing like his photos, though. His moustache was gone, he'd allowed his hair to reach an almost normal shortness, and he was wearing a suit that, unless I'm very mistaken, was hand-tailored and cost in the neighborhood of five hundred dollars. What's more, he was shorter than I'd expected, and thin. Sickly thin.

We introduced ourselves.

"Get yourself a drink," he said. "And me too. The bitch cut me off an hour ago." He snapped his fingers loudly, but the waitress ignored him. "Janet! Hey, Janet! Get your ass over here."

"You see," Andrew said, speaking to me but meaning it for Wer-Bell, "*this* is what he's come to. *This* is how he acts inconspicuously . . . bellowing . . . like a frog. He'll get us all arrested."

WerBell smiled and stared at St. George.

"Do you know what he did before?" Andrew said, still talking to WerBell through me. "He insulted a Senator. He called him a crook. He told him to go fuck himself. *Strangely enough, the man was trying to help him.*"

WerBell chuckled.

"Is that the action of a sane man? Is that the way you treat your friends?" Andrew was getting worked up. "And do you know what else the great WerBell did? He got us kicked out of my hotel—"

"The Francis Scott Key?" I asked.

"Yes, my hotel, the same hotel I've been staying at for years, with its convenient location, its ambiance, its reasonable rates—a hotel I will never be able to return to again—got us kicked out, after wandering the halls in his blue kimono with everything hanging out, insulting the maid, and finally got us kicked out, as I said, when he made an outrageously obscene suggestion to the switchboard operator . . . who, as you know, is a rather heavy woman, but very nice and—" Andrew puffed mightily and then stood up. "I have to make some phone calls," he said. "I'll see that the waitress brings you a drink."

"He *was* a crook," WerBell said. "They're *all* crooks."

"Who?" I asked.

"The Senator. Politicians. Worse'n the Mafia. What'd you say your name is?"

"Hougan."

WerBell nodded and then noticed Andrew walking out of the bar. "ST. GEORGE! ST. GEORGE!" Andrew ignored him, doubling the pace of his exit. Other customers looked nervously at WerBell and then returned to their own conversations.

"I think he's calling the airport," I said.

"I'm not going to any goddamn airport."

"Uhh . . . to get a reservation for a flight to Atlanta. So you can get back home. To The Farm, the kids, the—"

"I'm not going to Atlanta."

"You aren't?"

He shook his head. "I'm staying here. They aren't gonna run Mitch WerBell out of town. Besides, I want to see my girl friend. You ever meet her?"

I shook my head. Arguing with WerBell would obviously be a waste of time, and I figured that Andrew, probably his oldest friend, could handle him.

"So," I said, changing the subject, "how do you like our little town? Treating you all right, are they?"

He smiled. "They're trying to pin my balls to the wall, and you ask me if they're treating me—"

"Who is?"

"The Company," he said. "Who else? The C . . . I . . . A."

"Why?"

"They wanta shut me up. They tried it in 'seventy-four with that phony fucking summachine-gun rap, and that didn't work, and now they're trying to frame me on a dope charge. Can you imagine? Me? Dope? Who's gonna believe that? Well, it ain't the first time."

"What isn't?"

"It ain't the first time they've tried to frame this old Watusi, and it ain't the first time I've told the Senate to go fuck itself. It'll pass." The waitress arrived with a tray full of beers. "Thank you, honey," WerBell said. "You're all right. Now just keep 'em coming."

I knew what WerBell meant about the Senate, and while we sat there talking, I thought back to his first encounter with the men on the Hill, and I thought also about who WerBell was and what he'd come to. After all, there was a time when he'd been called (and here one has to hold one's breath, such is the gall of Andrew St. George's imagery) "The Wizard of Whispering Death." It wasn't a bad description either.

1 / THE CBS INVASION

In August, 1966, Mitch WerBell was a good deal more sober than he was the night I met him. He was also richer and, if there is any certainty in life, he was happier. A veteran of OSS operations in Indochina, he'd maintained friendships with Clandestine Services officers who'd gone on to high positions in the CIA and the Defense and State departments. He had a top-secret security clearance, of which he was proud, and he let it be known that he was well connected with those who worked on the darker side of the planet's conservative governments. Among those whom he counted as friends, for instance, was Lucien Conein, an archetypal CIA spook who, as the expression goes, "knows where the bodies were buried." Another friend was Colonel David Sterling, founder of Britain's notorious "Tan Berets," a commando elite which, as the Special Air Services (SAS) Regiment, has waged counterinsurgency battles against the Mau Mau in Kenya and dissidents in Malaya, Borneo, Cyprus, Aden, Oman, and, most recently, Northern Ireland.* Others who sat down to WerBell's table from time to time included Watergate burglar Frank Sturgis; the commander-in-chief of the Royal Thai Armed Forces; Walt Mackem, a former CIA officer and expert in the international narcotics trade (currently for hire); right-wing Texas millionaire Bennett Bintliff, described by one former WerBell aide ("Kip" Smithers) as "a real wisp of smoke—no one knew where he came from, and no one knew where he went; as spooky as they come"; the infamous Cuban exile leader Rolando Masferrer; international arms dealers such as Anselmo Alliegro and Ken Burnstine, both from below the Mason-Dixon Line and each with a record of criminal indictment; adventurer Colonel Robert K. Brown; Martí

---

* The SAS, which eschews uniforms, the use of last names, and badges of rank, is a Top Secret regiment skilled in *both* unconventional warfare and intelligence operations. Accused of using assassination and torture (notably sensory-deprivation techniques) against the Irish Republican Army (IRA) and others, SAS veterans have long been available to Colonel Sterling for service in paramilitary adventures of an *ad hoc* sort and have served widely as mercenaries under various leaders and banners.

Figueres, son of Costa Rica's Number One national hero, "Don Pepe"; various high-ranking officers in the intelligence services of Latin America and the Far East; international smugglers, mercenaries, gunrunners, petty hoodlums, private detectives, fanatics of various persuasions, and aides to part-time liberal angel and full-time Magic Christian Stewart Mott.

It was a salon, of sorts, and a heady one at that. By all accounts the conversation floated on a lagoon of expensive Scotch through a kaleidoscope of bloody topics: the Communist Menace, the Black Menace, the Student Menace, techniques of assassination, the relative utility of torture in interrogation, the merits of the "destroyer" carbine, Scandinavian grease guns, Israeli submachine guns, and silencers. And, ineluctably, there were storied exploits recounted with hilarity or despair, depending, and anecdotes about the consequences of monumental drinking bouts in Manila, Bangkok, and Singapore (all centers of the war surplus—and international arms—trade). Conversations too about which spook had been sent to dry out where, who'd cracked up when, and which dealers were no longer reliable and why.

These conversations tended to last long into the Georgia night, until either the booze was exhausted or the people were. They took place in the elegant surround of The Farm—sixty acres of rolling beauty-in-the-boondocks, located near Atlanta in Powder Springs. It might be thought that a lack of imagination gave The Farm its name, but that isn't so. One says "The Farm" in much the same way that Bela Lugosi might say "The La-bor-a-tory"; the name's emptiness is meant to hint at clandestine activities incapable of bearing the weight of sunlight. And, more specifically, it's meant to hint at (and even be confused with) the CIA training facility at Camp Peary, Virginia, also called The Farm.

And like its government counterpart to the north, WerBell's Farm was not known for its contributions to agriculture or animal husbandry. It was instead devoted to perfecting the tools and techniques of sniping, counterinsurgency, and the *coup d'état*. Weapons, men, and tactics of war were all tested on the elaborate shooting range that substituted for a garden.

In retrospect, of course, WerBell's preoccupations may seem eccentric, and perhaps they were. Nevertheless, it was a time in which the talk of war was everywhere. Vietnam had heated to a melting point. The campuses were afire with the rhetoric of revolution. Cuban exiles still dreamed of finessing Fidel from power. And militant blacks mau-maued about a domestic rebellion that would include the establishment of an all-black republic, "somewhere in North or South Carolina." All these things worried those who passed through The Farm, and because they tended to be men of action, they plotted antidotes to what they thought was America's drift toward "anarchy and appeasement."

In August, 1966, then, WerBell was in his element. The son of a Russian cavalry officer, he'd prospered as an international arms dealer and parlayed his considerable talents and contacts into a successful "public relations—private detection" business. When he went to the airport to meet a visiting general or traveling spook, he rode in the back of a forty-thousand-dollar Mercedes-Benz cabriolet —"one of only four in the world," he bragged, dying to tell you who had the other three—or drove a classic Porsche.

And yet it was at about this time, when everything was going famously, that things began to fall apart. In the spring of 1966, Wer-Bell was part of a bizarre military operation led by Cuban and Haitian exiles. The intent of what came to be called "the CBS Invasion" was to overthrow the regime of "Papa Doc" Duvalier, establish a paramilitary base in Haiti, and use it as a staging area for subsequent invasions of Cuba. As with any private war, financing was central: weapons and transportation had to be arranged, safe-houses established, mercenaries paid, and military instructors hired. A consultant to the would-be invaders, WerBell confided details of the plot to his friend Andrew St. George. Recognizing the filmic possibilities, St. George approached the Columbia Broadcasting System (CBS) with plans for a documentary. CBS was appropriately enthusiastic. In clandestine meetings in executive suites and fashionable Manhattan restaurants, a production team and budget was put together with great secrecy and code-named "Project Nassau." Immediately, filming began, with sequences of gunrunning, training exercises, and interviews with WerBell, the exiles, their leaders, and assorted mercenaries who'd convened in Florida for the secret war. The footage was dynamite, but, of course, there was a price tag on it. The Caribbean exiles were not engaged in a charitable exercise: CBS had to pay them for the film that it took, and as it happened, the money received by the exiles was being used partially to finance the very invasion CBS was filming. And, while that television network has lately received some notoriety for its excursions into "checkbook journalism," Project Nassau was an especially egregious abuse.

The incidents being filmed were in many cases staged at the network's convenience, and the operation itself was wholly illegal, a blatant violation of U. S. "neutrality laws." CBS, then, appeared to be creating the news, using its financial resources to enable newsworthy crimes to be committed in front of its cameras and microphones. It paid for the invaders' local transportation, leased boats to be used in the invasion, disbursed various sums to the exile leaders (using St. George and WerBell as conduits), helped in the creation of a staging base on a small island off Haiti, and paid fifteen thousand dollars to a Cuban exile blinded in a "training sequence." In return, it was promised "exclusive rights" to everything, including the hanging of President Duvalier. "Even that," swore one exile leader, "shall you have exclusive!"

It wasn't all smooth sailing, of course. Using CBS equipment, WerBell secretly recorded incriminating conversations with Haiti's consul general in Miami, intending to blackmail him. The hope was that the consul would persuade Papa Doc to fork over $200,000, in return for which the invasion would be canceled. As WerBell later admitted, the blackmail attempt nearly cost the consul his life—but that was business as usual.

Indeed, duplicity and double crosses were so much a part of the CBS Invasion that it was doomed to failure from the start. WerBell himself was bugged by CBS technicians, virtually all the principals were informing the CIA of the planned invasion, and Andrew St. George narrowly escaped assassination when Rolando Masferrer—"El Tigre"—grew angry at the journalist's handling of CBS monies. Shortly before the invasion was to occur, St. George was nearly killed by a bone-cracking explosion in the hold of a boat belonging to the invaders. He was catapulted unconscious into the water, and his life was saved by WerBell, who swam out to the burning craft and paddled his wounded friend to safety. Shortly thereafter the invasion was crushed on the beaches of Florida, when the Coast Guard intervened as the exiles were setting sail for the beaches of Haiti.

2 / THE SILENCER

"Zheeem! I have made the reservation. We can have one more drink, and then we must go." Andrew returned to the Marriott's bar and sank, sighing, into a chair. With an ambiguous wave of the hand, index finger corkscrewing clockwise, then counterclockwise, he instructed the waitress to bring us another round. "But we must hurry," he added.

WerBell smiled carnivorously, a lupine grin. "I'm not going anywhere," he pronounced.

Andrew unsheathed his I-haf-been-in-the-Sierras-with-Fidel stare, glaring across the table with such intensity that I was afraid he'd ionize the air, creating an electrical storm in the bar. WerBell's grin became impossibly large. His teeth were pulled apart by it.

"You!" Andrew declaimed, nodding rhetorically. "You! How do you intend to stay here? With what? You haven't got a penny. You lost it all. In a hallway somewhere! In a phone booth! How will you pay for your room? Your booze? With what? Beads? Autographs? Military advice?"

WerBell continued smiling. Finally he broke the silence. "I could kill you with one hand," he said. "Without getting up from this chair."

Andrew started to say something but thought better of it. Wer-Bell's reply reminded me of old confrontations on the playground. On the other hand, there was some truth in what he said, though I thought he'd probably have to get up.

As we waited for the drinks, the silence became embarrassing. I asked WerBell about the small pin in his lapel.

"Soldier's Medal," he said. "The only one of my medals that I wear. Very few of them around."

"What's it for?"

"You get it for . . . you have to save someone's life at risk to your own. Right, Andrew?" The question was rhetorical, but pointed. Unless I was mistaken, WerBell was reminding St. George of his mishap in the Caribbean. "Right, St. George?"

Andrew nodded impatiently, refusing to listen or speak with his friend. The drinks arrived, and I asked WerBell about the Military Armaments Corporation.

"They really steamrollered me," he said. "Wanted to leave the old Watusi holding the flag—bag, I mean."

"Is that what the indictment's all about?"

WerBell shook his head morosely. "The Senate wants me to testify against my friends. But, then again, *They* don't want me to testify about anything. That's why They got this trumped-up dope indictment. Happens every time. Happened the *last* time—with that fat-faced Vesco."

"They?"

"The Cuban Invasion Agency. The C . . . I . . . of fuckin' A. They're trying to shut me up."

"Is that what the hearings are about? Vesco?"

"No. Mike Morrissey. Lou Conein. Fox. You know about that?" I nodded.

"Well, the Senate says 'Talk,' and the Company wants me to shut up, so they say I'm conspiring to fly tons of *pot* into the country. It's a joke." Mitch chuckled.

"Yes," Andrew said, "it's very funny. They have your balls in a vise."

"Agh . . ." WerBell brushed his hand at imaginary flies.

I knew what he meant when he referred to Morrissey, Conein, and Fox. The matter involved an alleged plot to assassinate international narcotics traffickers, using electronic booby traps, foreign criminals, and a dozen ex-CIA officers secretly attached to the Drug Enforcement Administration (DEA). The scheme was supposed to be the "final solution" to the so-called War on Drugs, and WerBell was believed to have been the plot's point man. It was he, along with his friend Lou Conein, who'd put the "Dirty Dozen" together with the B. R. Fox Company, designer of the exotic explosive devices, establishing a safe-house for the federal spooks in the Washington offices of WerBell's private detective agency.

Just when the Senate was preparing to question WerBell about its discovery of the plot, the Georgian was indicted, effectively preventing him from answering questions on Capitol Hill. Maybe it *was* a frame. WerBell has lately had a habit of getting indicted at strategic times and then, somehow, getting off. Following the CBS Invasion, for instance, he'd been charged with Masferrer and others for having conspired to violate the Neutrality Act. It seemed a reasonable charge—and yet the indictment was quickly dropped. Indeed, it's fair to say that it was "mysteriously dropped"; when congressional investigators inquired about the reasons for withdrawing charges against WerBell, Justice Department attorneys could only scratch their heads. They'd been trying to find out for three years, but so far no one would comment. And then, too, when the Senate subpoenaed WerBell to testify in 1974 about his involvement with archfugitive Robert Vesco, testimony WerBell would have been *delighted* to provide in view of his hatred for the man, WerBell suddenly found his son, his partner, and his company (Defense Services, Inc.) named as defendants in a criminal case alleging the illicit sale of automatic weapons. The circumstances surrounding *that* indictment were so strange that the Senate investigating committee itself gave credence to WerBell's complaint that he'd been "set up" in order to silence him. Not only had the indictment come down within *hours* of the Senate subpoena, but the case was obviously the result of a pseudo-investigation built with haste upon a foundation of naked entrapment. Alleging that the defendants sought to make an illegal transfer of submachine guns to undercover agents, the federal case was ultimately laughed out of court.

Because the feds had chosen to indict his son and namesake, however, WerBell felt betrayed by the Agency: as he put it, "When they start fucking with my family, it's a whole new ball game." Accordingly, his attorney filed a motion for dismissal, which threatened to uncap a CIA plot of explosive dimensions. According to the motion, WerBell's legal difficulties stemmed from his role in a conspiracy among the CIA, Robert Vesco, and various corporations to finance "clandestine guerrilla activities" in Latin America.*

We'll return to that (and to the activities of Morrissey, Conein, and the B. R. Fox Company) in subsequent pages. But for now it would be best to modify the impression conveyed of WerBell by accounts of the CBS Invasion and his seeming disintegration at the Key Bridge Marriott Hotel. The man from Georgia is a lot more than a hard-drinking braggart: he's a genius. Indeed, in some (admittedly rarefied) circles, Mitch WerBell is known as the Thomas Edison of silenced weapons.

3 / SIONICS & THE SILENCER

In 1967, after his failure to seize Haiti for the Cubans, WerBell returned to The Farm, but not to rest. His most important project was about to reach fruition, and it seemed to him that he was on the brink of millions. The project involved a firm he owned—SIONICS, Inc. It sounded, somehow, like an electronics business, but the deadly nature of its product line was hinted at by the corporation's heraldic

---

* Document of U. S. District Court, Northern District of Georgia, Atlanta Division, in criminal case No. CR74-471A, entitled "Memorandum of Law and Argument in Support of Motion to Dismiss."

insignia and the meaning of the acronym that was its name. The emblem was a "cobray"—half cobra snake and half moray eel. The acronym stood for "*Studies In the Operational Negation of Insurgents and Counter-Subversion*." It was, of course, a workshop in assassination.

Its most significant product, developed under Mitch's guidance, was a weapons system so lethally and even beautifully efficient that it made Ian Fleming's paraphernalia obsolete.* It consisted of a submachine gun and a silencer (or "suppressor"), each made for the other, and each representing a giant step forward in the state-of-the-art of killing.

The suppressor was WerBell's invention, and according to David Truby, perhaps the foremost authority on this arcane subject, its pressure-relief valve represented "the greatest modern contribution in the history of silencers." † Not only did it transform BANGs into *phyyyt*s, but it improved the accuracy of marksmen using the gun by reducing barrel vibration; even more surprisingly, the silencer actually *increased* the weapon's penetrating power—an unheard-of development. As if this were not enough, WerBell's invention also served to inhibit fouling of the weapon, stifle gas from the breach, and smother the powder flash. This last improvement made it ideal for snipers, assassins, and practitioners of the ambush. As it happens, there are not one but two sounds made by a weapon's firing. The first is that of the powder exploding; the second is the sonic boom that results when a high-velocity shell exceeds the sound barrier. WerBell's suppressor (resembling a sawed-off black baseball bat) virtually eliminated the first noise. The second sound could also be prevented: all that was necessary was for the shooter to lower the velocity of his bullet by using less powder than usual. This done, the weapon made less noise than a cap pistol and, with the powder flash smothered, rendered the sniper less visible than ever before. (Soldiers in Vietnam, however, found that the sonic boom had its own utility: because the bullet moved faster than the speed of sound, those being ambushed heard the shot only as it moved away from them. As a consequence their first reaction was to retreat into the direction from

---

* Indeed, even Hollywood recognized its dramatic appeal. Moviegoers who saw *Three Days of the Condor*, *McQ*, or *Killer Force* will remember the silent weaponry as virtual stars. The submachine gun and silencer used in those films were the same one under discussion here, having been invented for SIONICS.

† David Truby, *Silencers, Snipers, and Assassins*, Paladin Press, p. 108.

which the shots had actually come—*walking backward into the same ambush.**)

And the silencer was cost-effective too. According to WerBell, his suppressors, used on Army sniper rifles, "killed nineteen hundred V.C. in six months. Those V.C. took only one-point-three rounds per kill. Twenty-seven cents apiece they cost Uncle Sam. That's the greatest cost-effectiveness the Army's ever known." Former Green Beret officer Robert K. Brown, citing congressional hearings on the matter, points out that fifty thousand rounds of ammunition were expended for each enemy killed in Vietnam by conventional methods. At almost a nickel a round, that works out to about $2,300 a body. WerBell's method accomplished the same end for about a quarter. Clearly, it was a devastating technological "advance."

Doubly devastating, that is, because it was expressly designed for use with automatic and semi-automatic weapons, guns that had formerly resisted silent operation. And the particular gun that Wer-Bell had in mind, the other half of the weapons system, was the super-sleek Ingram M-10/M-11 LISP (Lightweight Individual Special Purpose) "machine-pistol."

Developed at SIONICS by Gordon Ingram, a bashful "pure scientist" who insists, "I'm only a technician doing a job for money—I'm not interested in the higher politics," the M-10 makes killing easier than ever. Consider: capable of firing 700 rounds per minute at an effective range of two hundred fifty to three hundred yards, it is ideal for use with either .45-caliber or 9-millimeter ammunition. Weighing less than seven pounds, the M-10 submachine gun combines the firepower of an automatic weapon with the convenience of a pistol; and with its stock telescoped, the weapon is less than a foot long.

Even smaller and more advanced is the Ingram M-11. Weighing less than four pounds, it fires 850 rounds per minute (fourteen shots per second) and utilizes .380-caliber ammo—a subsonic cartridge. Fitted with a precision Starlight scope for evening assignments, it is the Ferrari of clandestine weapons systems.

And at Volkswagen prices: introduced in 1969, the silencer-*cum*-Ingram could be purchased for slightly less than one hundred dollars.

---

* It's curious that no one seems to have mentioned this characteristic in connection with the John F. Kennedy assassination, in which both the number and direction of shots fired are still debated. If a silencer was used in combination with another, *un*silenced rifle, witnesses located in different parts of the caravan and Dealey Plaza would have heard the shots coming from different directions. Unanimity would have been impossible on the subject of the gunfire's origin.

One might think, therefore, that the M-10 or M-11 would be strapped to the hip of every anti-Communist grunt from Bangkok to Brunei. But it isn't. The international arms trade is a behavioral sink of spooks and bureaucrats, corrupt officials and megalomaniacal generals. The "open marketplace" is mined with industrial espionage agents, bagmen, con men, and influence peddlers. Whom one knows, or owns, is often more important than what one has to sell, and the best submachine gun doesn't always win.

"SIONICS," WerBell says, "was vastly underfinanced." A factory needed to be built, salesmen hired, and so forth. To raise the required capital, WerBell took to the skies in a private jet, searching out (ad)venture capitalists, carrying a hand-tooled leather attaché case with prototypes of the silencer and M-11 inside.

The selling point was simple. Not only did the arms package have marvelous applications for snipers and assassins, but, more importantly, the gun itself might actually *replace* the ancient .45 and serve in support of the standard M-16 rifle. Generally, America's Vietnam ground-combat strategy was one of saturation fire. If a swatch of jungle looked hostile, if something moved, or, God knows, if someone was actually shooting, GI's would put their guns on "rock 'n 'roll" and empty clip after clip into the area. And, of course, if you take the five minutes necessary to pour four thousand rounds per soldier into a space the size of a department store, something or someone's bound to fall. But what about the soldier in support—the cook, the driver, the orderly, the seven or so guys who must support each man at the front? They couldn't be lugging M-16's wherever they went, and, in fact, they didn't. Which is to say, most GI's were, most of the time, unarmed. And, because insurgents preferred to hit and run, sap and split at unexpected times and inconvenient hours, the unarmed soldier was always at hazard. What he needed, WerBell theorized, was a small, lightweight *machine*-pistol—an M-10—loaded with hard-hitting .45-caliber ammunition and capable of withering automatic fire. The sort of thing you could wear in the kitchen, the latrine, the movie, and the hospital. And so it seemed that for every M-16 sold, more than half-a-dozen Ingrams could be flogged. Having a patent on the Ingram, then, should have been equivalent to holding debentures on the golden goose.

The pitch proved persuasive. In 1970, when investors were being sought, Wall Street was bullish on counterinsurgency, and to many financiers it looked as if a killing could be made. As one investor put it, "Can you imagine having gotten in on the ground floor with

Colt? You'd have had a piece of every war since 1850. Well, that's what it seemed like with WerBell. It was a tremendous package. Truly revolutionary!"

Indeed, it seemed a perfect package, especially in combination with WerBell's flair for paramilitary dramatics. When he was not aloft in a private Lockheed Jetstar, he might be found demonstrating the weapons system's efficiency in any of several inappropriate places. In expensive hotel suites and in the offices of staid investment bankers such as Brown Brothers, Harriman, prospective shareholders would watch with bated breath while WerBell solemnly attached the silencer to the M-11, slamming a clip into place. Sipping from an icy tumbler of single-malt Scotch (imported from the Isle of Islay), he'd arrange a stack of telephone directories on the floor and then, with only a twinkle betraying his amusement, fire a few silenced rounds into the phone books. Those outside the room, bellhops or secretaries, would prove oblivious to the gunfire nearby. The sibilant *phyyyt* of the bullets ripping into the *Yellow Pages* was softer and less disturbing than the noise made by the opening of a pop-top can.

Even more persuasive, however, were demonstrations carried out at The Farm. Urged to try the gun themselves, investors were invited down to WerBell's estate in Powder Springs. There, amid the magnolias, honeysuckle, counterintrusion devices, attack dogs, and booze, they'd be led to a quiet grove of trees strung with red balloons. Except for the spray cans of red paint littered across the forest floor, it looked like a garden party, albeit one presided over by Death himself. While the millionaires and their advisors, carpetbaggers in the Louis Vuitton mold, milled in anticipation of what was to come, WerBell paraded back and forth in a paramilitary uniform of his own devising. Across one breast was emblazoned the name WERBELL; across the other, sharing the background of khaki camouflage, SIONICS. Clamped between his lips was the stub of a fat cigar. And neatly symbolizing the Prussian context of the afternoon, a monocle, lightly fitted over WerBell's right eye. Swinging a sword cane with a casual air, he gave the appearance of a boulevardier who was accustomed to stepping over corpses in the course of his strolls.

Suddenly, WerBell would check his "wrist chronometer," clear his throat, squint upward, and make a chopping motion with his hand. "Now," he'd whisper, riveting the millionaires' attention. And one by one, yet rapidly, indeed almost simultaneously, the balloons would be torn to pieces by—by nothing! and drip from the branches of the trees. The spray cans, minerally still on the ground, would inexplicably leap into the air, seemingly on their own, spin wildly, and explode in bursts of thick red.

It took a few seconds, and there was no other sound beyond the popping of balloons, the muffled *whhhuck!* of the cans as they crunched. A whirring noise, perhaps. The hum of flies, swaying in the southern air. But then the balloons and the spray cans would be *dead*, and the New York financiers popeyed with glee. Two hundred yards away, a sharpshooter called "Daniel Boone" would drop from his sniper's nest in the limb of a tree and, almost sheepishly, accept the standing ovation of America's financial elite. While drinks were passed around, the millionaires would be led to WerBell's private firing range and permitted to test the gun themselves. It was a Walter Mitty affair, with stockbrokers, economists, and heirs removing two-thousand-dollar watches from their wrists as they queued for the privilege of blasting away in silence at paper silhouettes in the distance.

Not surprisingly, WerBell found his investors—twenty-nine of them who collectively chipped in seven million dollars. Forming a holding company called Quantum Ordnance Bankers, Inc. (later changed to the less revealing Quantum Corporation), the moneymen submerged WerBell's SIONICS into a newly established manufacturing subsidiary, the Military Armaments Corporation (MAC), placing WerBell in overall command of the firm's operations. He was the logical choice for the job: not only had he invented the suppressor, but he'd worked closely with the guns' designers and had excellent contacts among international arms dealers, Third World police/intelligence services, and Pentagon officials. Almost as importantly, WerBell seemed to enjoy the high profile that went with the job—whereas Quantum's other investors were determined to remain anonymous.

4 / DEATH MERCHANTS & LIBERAL ANGELS

"I don't know whether you know it or not, but we've got a fat-assed Jewish community here in New York that's selling America down the drain to the Communists. People like Javits and Kennedy. *No*, goddamnit, I *won't* tell you who Quantum's stockholders are, but I assure you that every one of those twenty-nine individuals is in *Who's Who* and you'd recognize each name. If I said Nelson Rockefeller—you'd recognize *that* name, wouldn't you? Well, that's the caliber of men we're talking about!"

"I see."

"You're goddamn right! Now listen: I'm not ashamed of being a patriot. But I promised those people that their names would be kept secret. I raised that seven million as a patriotic American citizen and—and I'll tell you something else. They're a bunch of goddamn jerks in the U. S. government, and the worst pricks of all are the ones at the State Department. Biggest fuckheads I've ever met. I've completely discounted the U. S. government as a market for MAC weapons."

As Rosser Scott Reeves III speaks, it's immediately apparent that the rich have an accent all their own—an inflection of strangled certainty that comes only after years of putting somebody else's money where one's mouth is. It changes the voice somehow. And, whatever the content of the message it bears, the accent conjures images of all the nice things: squash courts, beamy sloops, brocade valances, and walnut wainscoting hand-rubbed to a muted sheen. Board chairman of the Quantum Corporation and heir to one of America's largest advertising fortunes, Reeves holds forth over lunch at the New York Racquet and Tennis Club. For a prominent investment banker who shares his name with a world-famous ruby,* Scott Reeves can be a difficult man to find. According to the telephone directory, Quantum had offices in New York and Washington, D.C. Neither Reeves nor Quantum, however, could be reached at any of the numbers listed. Moreover, Quantum's prestigious Washington address (at the Rockefeller-owned L'Enfant Plaza) is similarly "unworking"; the landlord, post office, and other corporate tenants in the building claim never to have heard of the firm. In New York one is simply told that Quantum "has moved"—where, no one seems prepared to say.

Locating Reeves is necessary if one is not to write that "Quantum is shrouded in mystery"—which, as Reeves makes clear when he's finally tracked down, it would prefer to be. Its stockholders, having extracted an oath of secrecy from their chairman, have indirectly stoked rumors of a "right-wing consortium," a "Mr. Big," and even a "Third Force" (whatever that might be). Difficulties in locating Quantum's offices, coupled with its relationship to WerBell, its exotic product line, and its gun sales to both Arabs and Jews—well, one would prefer to remove the shroud. Compounding the mystery even further is the rumor that the firm has some relationship to the CIA.

---

* The 137-carat Rosser Scott Reeves ruby, donated to the Smithsonian Institution by Reeves's father, R.S.R. II.

But Reeves, however blunt and loquacious, is not helpful. While he refuses to name his coinvestors, he describes them, first, as liberals and, later, as men and women whose politics are "to the right of Attila the Hun." As it happens, the judgment is both inaccurate and harsh. A secret list of Quantum stockholders, obtained from government sources, reveals a financial coterie whose members share an affection for mutual acquaintances, the finer things in life, backgammon, and the Racquet Club. With only a few exceptions, they reside on Central Park's posh and security-conscious East Side. To describe them all as "right-wingers" would be misleading. For the most part, they're nonideological conservatives, a Quiet Minority that would salute, but never dream of waving, the flag. Prominent, but not famous.

Indeed, they're very difficult to characterize as a group. One man belongs to the John Birch Society, but another belongs to that organization's archfoe, the Council on Foreign Relations. One is the president of a hockey team and the director of an ice-cream company, while another, Charles Spofford, has served as director of a CIA conduit of historic importance.* Yet another, Edmund Lynch, is the man who shares top billing with Messrs. Merrill, Pierce, Fenner, and Smith. Others include society dames such as Hopie Ryan Gaynor, various heirs to various fortunes, a grain magnate, the former chairman of the executive committee of the Metropolitan Opera, and— rather incongruously for an investor in submachine guns—a trustee of Union Theological Seminary. It is, in other words, a hodgepodge of the rich and social, each of whom had his or her own reasons for wanting to be a secret partner of WerBell's.

---

* The reference is to the American Committee on United Europe, formed after World War II for the purpose of enabling the rearmament of Germany (considered essential to U. S. Cold War strategy). The Committee's chairman was General William J. ("Wild Bill") Donovan, founder-chief of the CIA's predecessor agency, the Office of Strategic Services (OSS). Other Committee officers included Allen Dulles (later director of the CIA), Tom Braden (a CIA officer who later became a syndicated columnist), and General Walter Bedell Smith, Dulles's predecessor as head of the CIA (1950–53). As for the Committee's rank-and-file members, they numbered more than six hundred prominent Atlanticists comprising the financial spine of America's Eastern Seaboard. Conrad Hilton was a member, and so were union leaders David Dubinsky and Arthur Goldberg. In many ways the organization functioned as an analogue of Prince Bernhard's so-called Bilderberger group. The Committee's purpose, however, was to channel CIA funds to private political groups in Europe. And it succeeded. In 1952 alone, the Committee funded nearly two thousand youth conferences, ninety film showings, twenty-one exhibitions, and the printing of nearly five million brochures and periodicals in ten languages. (For more information on this powerful lobby, see "The 'European Movement,' 1945–53," by François Xavier Rebattet, a doctoral thesis at St. Antony's College, Oxford, England [1962].)

There is yet another stockholder in Quantum, however, who seems entirely out of place. A director of the Fund for Peace, trustee of the Center for the Study of Democratic Institutions, a Rockefeller stalwart and a $250,000 McGovern campaign backer, Stewart Rawlings Mott is clearly out of context as part owner of a submachine-gun factory devoted to Studies in the Operational Negation of . . . well, anyone.

A genetic multimillionaire, having inherited a monolithic wad of General Motors stock, Mott is a fascinating fellow. Dividends on the GM stock alone (he has other millions invested elsewhere) are estimated to bring in more than $1,300,000 in annual, unearned income. Which is to say that even while Mott sleeps, his bank balance grows at the rate of about $150 per hour, seven days a week, holidays included.

Moreover, Mott isn't merely rich—he has imagination and comes about as close to being the Magic Christian as an agnostic can get. A lusty philanthropist, he's been known to hand out intrauterine coils at parties and has even published a newsletter about his daily life. A proponent of both arms control and birth control, Mott is studiously single and prides himself on having resisted what he calls "pronatal influences." Other influences, however, have proven less resistible. In recent years he labored with architects to create Manhattan's most spectacular penthouse. Located on Fifty-seventh Street, the four-story residence was to have acres of terraces planted with hundreds of trees. The trees were to be protected from the elements, as was his sky-high organic gardens, by a series of transparent canopies that were to be visible for miles around. And Mott intended to share his plastic pleasure domes with poorer folk. As a worshipful article in *Fortune* reported in March, 1974, "Mott envisages streams of impoverished school-children parading through the place, eyeing the wonders of the earth brought to the city skies." * Unfortunately, the project proved to be too much even for Mott, and it was abandoned before completion.

It would be easy to dismiss Mott as an eccentric, but that would be misguided. His vast wealth, disposable income, and determination-to-give make him one of the most influential of America's Independents. Considered a charter member of the "Counter Gridiron," Washington's anti-Establishment establishment, he has the ears of such kingmakers and dragon-slayers as *Post* editor Ben Bradlee,

---

* Irwin Ross, "Stewart Mott," *Fortune*, p. 135.

superlawyer Edward Bennett Williams, Senator Charles Percy, and newsman Dan Rather. Mott is no mere crackpot then. It was his money that funded the Committee for an Effective Congress, the group which purged so many congressional committee chairmen after Watergate; and it was his money that helped CIA critic John Marks establish the Center for National Security Studies (perhaps the most respected civilian watchdog of federal intelligence operations).

Mott's secret financial alliance with John Birchers, CIA agents, and the spooks of Georgia, then, is so out of keeping with his liberal views that news of it alarms former associates. Jim Rowan, son-in-law and campaign aide to George McGovern, recalls that "Mott rode with us on the campaign plane. . . . He sat in on the strategy meetings. Christ! It makes my blood run cold."

For his part, Mott has a simple (and ridiculous) explanation. Confronted with the fact of his bizarre partnership, he says that it in no way contradicts his commitment to peace and disarmament. On the contrary, he says, he made the decision to invest in Quantum while "on a peace mission" to Moscow. Turning to his financial advisor, for confirmation, the Magic Christian adds, "We weren't particularly interested in the military aspects anyway."

"You weren't?" I asked.

"No. Of course not."

"But what, then? That's all there was. They were making submachine guns and silencers for the 'operational negation' of—"

"Right," Mott says. "But, you see, the silencer worked so well, we thought it could be adapted to snowmobiles and lawn mowers. The investment was an environmental one. To reduce noise. I wasn't interested in its military applications."

His aide nods. "We were very surprised—completely taken aback—when we found out about the, uhh, military orientation."

"Completely taken aback," Mott says.

Oh.

5 / GUNS TO THE A-RABS, SILENCERS TO THE JEWS

If Mott's explanation is true, it appears that he was duped. There was no effort to adapt the silencer to anything other than killing, nor had there been any plans to do so. That he should have been surprised at the "military orientation" of the enterprise seems disingenuous: his advisors had visited The Farm, observed the silent destruction of the balloons and paint cans, and seen WerBell parading in what Mott's aide called his "paramilitary costume."

Admittedly, the Quantum subsidiary charged with the responsibility of manufacturing the M-10 and M-11 Ingrams was named Environmental Industries, Inc. But WerBell says that the name was, like SIONICS, an in-joke based upon the notion that the Ingrams had a great contribution to make in the area of "population control." In any case, Environmental Industries rapidly became the Military Armaments Corporation (MAC), making the firm's purpose as explicit as possible. If Mott, resident in his Manhattan aerie, was genuinely concerned about the noise of lawn mowers and snowmobiles (of which Manhattan has neither), he must have thought it strange that the president of Environmental Industries, Inc., was the newly retired head of the weapons division of the Research, Development, and Engineering Directorate of the Army's Matériel Command, Colonel John S. Wood.

Colonel Wood seems to have been a major source of enthusiasm for Quantum's investors. Before his retirement from the Army, he'd recommended that the .45 be replaced by a "small, lightweight submachine gun or machine-pistol." His successor at the Matériel Command was a longtime subordinate and golfing partner who all were certain would implement Wood's recommendation—making Quantum's stockholders vastly richer than they'd ever been. As it happened, however, Wood's successor despised his old golf mate and, rather than follow through as expected, denounced Wood's alliance with Quantum. The resulting embarrassment caused the Army to defer its decision to replace the .45, and Quantum had its first setback.*

There were alternatives to U. S. Army sales, though. Nixon's Law Enforcement Assistance Administration (LEAA) was flooding the country with billions of dollars in an effort to maximize police efficiency, and it was thought that SWAT teams might succumb to the M-11's lethal lure. Curiously, the police-sales franchise was sold to Ken Burnstine, a Fort Lauderdale spook whose air-taxi business was a prime target of federal investigators concerned with narcotics trafficking. Until his death in 1976 (the light plane he was flying solo crashed at a California air show shortly before he was to stand

---

* I'm indebted to Andrew St. George for the information concerning Colonel Wood. Readers interested in St. George's account of the affair are referred to the August, 1977, issue of *Esquire* and his article "A Significant Little Gun."

trial on smuggling charges), Burnstine was widely regarded as the most important marijuana importer on the East Coast. A big man who looked like an NFL linebacker gone to seed, Burnstine saw no contradiction, only irony, in the profits he made arming those who were trying to imprison him.

An even bigger market existed, however, among Third World countries. Their police and military forces were infatuated with American technology, of which the Ingram was a superb example. Accordingly, thousands of M-10's and M-11's were flogged to more than thirty-eight foreign nations during Quantum's first years. Most of the guns went to Chile and Saudi Arabia, but others were sold to Uganda's Idi Amin Dada and the Mossad, Israel's intelligence service. Still other quantities, packed in grease and plastic bags, made voyages to Addis Ababa, Caracas, Barranquilla, Brussels, Zagreb, and Santo Domingo in the Dominican Republic. Paraguay, South Korea, Guatemala, and even Mali found the weapons useful, as did this country's FBI, Secret Service, and CIA.

And yet the sales never approached the fabulous projections made by Quantum's Scott Reeves. In late 1972, with the Army deal shot down, the New York investors turned a critical eye upon WerBell's operation of the Military Armaments Corporation. To some it seemed as if the Georgian was running the death factory as a kind of cottage industry, a family store. His son, Mitch IV, had been installed as vice-president. His son-in-law, a fighter pilot just returned from Vietnam, took charge of quality control, though his knowledge of the field was limited. A second son worked in the finance department, while two daughters handled secretarial chores, the payroll, and personnel matters.

Had everything been going smoothly, WerBell's nepotism might not have mattered; in fact, however, MAC was experiencing severe problems of costing. No one seemed to have any idea as to how cheaply the Ingrams could be profitably sold. At first it was thought that they might be retailed for as little as forty dollars. Subsequently, the figure rose to $75, $100, and, in the end, $180.

Compounding the problem of costs was WerBell's preoccupation with "Research & Development": his fascination with death in no way ended with the Ingram. On the contrary, he seemed always to be tinkering with lethal mechanisms of his own devising, often without regard for marketing realities. How much need, for instance, was there for the last-defense, lipstick-sized, single-shot "firing tube" developed in Powder Springs, apparently with Charles Bronson in mind? While easily concealed in a gunman's pocket, the device, upon testing, proved as dangerous to the kneecaps and genitalia of the bearer as it was to any conceivable attacker. But no matter. Like Gordon Ingram, WerBell was a pure scientist, albeit one whose life was devoted to death.

Inevitably, WerBell and Quantum's New York contingent had a falling-out, blaming each other for MAC's failure to meet sales projections. "It was like slipping under a steamroller," WerBell recalled. "They were setting me up for a patsy, if and when something went wrong—well, not on yer life. I got out." Leaving in a huff, he took the factory's plans with him, dividing with MAC the unsold inventory of fourteen thousand Ingrams. With seven thousand submachine guns and silencers as his stock, he established a new corporation, Defense Systems International—a firm capable of providing not only weapons but also paramilitary counsel. Operating out of his sumptuous office at The Farm, an office lined with bearskin and military souvenirs of the Orient, WerBell began to compete with his former company and with the millionaires behind it. While unpleasant, the breakup pleased WerBell in that he was never enthusiastic about "those hot-wires in New York" and "that damned pacifist, what's-his-name, the guy who owns all the applesauce." The separation had another advantage too, in that WerBell had a large inventory of weapons that cost him nothing to manufacture. He also had the loyalty of old friends and future Ingram distributors, Cuban exiles such as Anselmo Alliegro, chief of Miami's Parabellum Corporation; Alabama arms merchant Stuart Graydon, proprietor of American-Asian Associates and Rebel Electronics; and, of course, Kenny ("the Swinger") Burnstine, head of the deceptively named Karol Investments, Inc. Other sales agents, operating from Panama to Burma, Bangui to Paraguay, would come aboard in time.

As for the patriot Scott Reeves, he bears no hostility toward WerBell, reserving it for "those idiots in the Pentagon and the State Department." The latter, in particular, infuriates him because it refuses to permit the export of silencers to those very Third World nations in which demand for them appears to be the greatest. Why the refusals? "Because," Reeves says, his voice lisping each syllable in an affectedly swish, singsong falsetto, "they're a-*fraid* of *as-sass-in-a-tion*." It's not a fear Quantum's chairman shares. His philosophy appears to be one of "live and let die."

"Have you read *The Fountainhead?*" he asks, invoking a right-wing melodrama beloved by student-council types.

"Of course."

"Well, there you are. That's me in a nutshell. I guess you'd call me sort of an Ayn-Randist." That, of course, may explain Quantum's eagerness to service the urban warfare needs of both the Arabs *and* the Jews, but it doesn't explain the libertarian Reeves's unlikely alliance with "radiclibs" such as Stewart Mott and CIA-Atlanticists such as Charles M. Spofford. It may be that mere money is the cement of their partnership, but I think not. Glamour is an even more likely glue.*

To own a piece of the Ingram is to be a part of the spook's romantic milieu. To hold the gun against a tailored sleeve, gazing through YSL sunglasses at paper silhouettes reduced to sieves by thirty shots fired in the silent space of a deep breath, is to become the star of one's own secret epic. WerBell understood that when he arranged for the investors to fire the weapon personally—who could resist its lure? And who was to say that the private fantasies of the investors-turned-death-merchants were anything less than authentic? WerBell himself was larger than life, a paramilitary consultant who wore a monocle, lived on The Farm, carried a sword cane, and thumped his calves with a swagger stick he'd converted to "a rocket launcher." He drove fast expensive cars, carried himself with the posture of a Prussian colonel, bragged of his mistresses, and traveled the world in a private jet, accompanied by a slinky Russian wolfhound called Fritz and a submachine gun that made commandos salivate. Not content with Defense Systems International and the puckishly yclept SIONICS, he had the audacity to start a private intelligence apparat which, after some thought, he named the Central Investigative Agency, referring to it by its initials. All of which suggests that the man is a mere caricature of the secret agent, albeit one who uses the CIA as a cover for his own clandestine activities. And yet WerBell's authenticity is undeniable. There is no law of nature or espionage that insists all spooks must conform to one of two complementary images: the buttoned-down *savoir-faire* of Rich-

---

* Since this was written, the Military Armaments Corporation has tossed in the financial towel. According to Reeves, the firm couldn't function under the constraints imposed by the State Department's unwillingness to allow exports of silenced Ingrams to their "natural markets" in Latin America and Africa. As a result, Reeves says, MAC was sold "in a sort of four-cornered billiards shot" to anonymous investors who've begun to manufacture the weapon in the permissive secrecy of off-shore climates.

ard Helms, or the rumpled anonymity of a John le Carré character. There are other alternatives, and WerBell isn't alone in his predilection for the openly sinister: three-fingered Lou Conein—CIA archetype, ex-Legionnaire, veteran of a thousand secret campaigns, and WerBell's best friend—was known throughout Vietnam as "Black Luigi" and bragged of his membership in the Union Corse,* hardly the sort of thing one would expect to find in a "serious" spy novel, but . . . there he is.

WerBell, moreover, has a past that in no way contradicts his bearing and demeanor. A veteran of the OSS in China, he worked under contract to the CIA in the 1960s, organizing amphibious landings against Cuba from a base in the Dominican Republic; people died. When anti-Castro activity simmered down toward the decade's end, he traveled back and forth between Atlanta and Vietnam, Thailand and Cambodia, conferring with CIA officials, Siamese princes, and Asian intelligence czars on the subject of programmatic liquidations. Nor were these the trips of a mere free lance. Provided with a high security clearance, military aides, and transport by the Army, WerBell was also given the uniform and rank of an American general—a temporary warrant, yet hardly a privilege lightly bestowed.

WerBell is unique, of course: there could hardly be anyone quite like him. And yet, as we'll see, his tangled affairs impinge upon those of so many private intelligence agents, smugglers, hit-men, and swindlers that his authenticity is beyond question, however much his flamboyance may stimulate skepticism. In WerBell's case, the cliché holds true: what you see is what you get—rocket launcher and all.

Before proceeding further with the man from Georgia, however, it will be useful to consider the haunting of America more generally. WerBell is an aberration in many ways and, in the final analysis, a mote in a much larger phenomenon. Understanding the peculiar world of private intelligence agents, their role in our secret history, and the threatened emergence of a corporate raj requires a broader comprehension of the phenomenon's size, its origins, and, of course, its players.

---

* The Union Corse is the counterpart of the Sicilian Mafia and is generally regarded as the more deadly of the two. Conein was made an honorary member of the outfit in recognition of his service with the Corsican partisans, service rendered as an OSS officer following his earlier enlistment in the French Foreign Legion.

THE PULP DOSSIER

THINKING OF SPOOKS IN METAPHYSICAL TERMS, OR STRICTLY IN TERMS of their consequences (a "haunted" America, a "multinational raj"), is likely to be misleading. At least it will be so long as it ignores their human characteristics. Like you and me, industry's spooks have their own quirks and dreams and manners. They're fathers and lovers and football fans. I know of one who writes sonnets and another who's been working twelve years on a biography of the composer Mahler. A third is obsessed with genealogy, while a fourth spends his weekends guiding retarded children on field trips through arboretums and museums. I know a few who are, by anyone's standards, burnt-out cases; they can be found in any of a handful of Washington bars at almost any hour. And then there are some who seem to be so enraptured with the lives they lead, and with their roles, that all their interests are an extension of their "tradecraft." They read espionage novels and *Security World* in search of new tricks, practice with knives and handguns, study the most obscure martial arts, fiddle with locks, and lovingly craft eavesdropping devices in much the same way that hobbyists build stereo sets from kits. They live the life. There are no outside interests.

What all these people have in common is their work and a tendency to submit, from time to time, to what might be called the

Agent's Syndrome. It affects virtually everyone who deals with secret information.

In its mildest form the Syndrome is manifested by quizzical looks, enigmatic smiles, and a penchant for taking Tae Kwan Do classes. More virulently, there is an obsession with intrigue and clandestinity, an almost professional paranoia.

To an extent the Syndrome is catching. Anyone familiar with both the intelligence community and the fraternity of investigative reporters will agree that some writers are, in manner and method, spookier than those they investigate. This isn't to say that the Syndrome is always spurious, an internal fiction maintained solely for romantic or narcissistic reasons. On the contrary, telephones do get tapped, people are occasionally followed, and threats are sometimes made. Becoming privy to a secret, one shares in the intrigue surrounding it. Indeed, in the course of writing this book, some strange things have happened. For instance: While investigating Intertel, I scheduled an interview two weeks in advance with columnist Jack Anderson. Arriving for that interview, I learned that someone impersonating me had interrogated Mr. Anderson on the same subject the day before. There was no mistake, Anderson assured me, kindly consenting to "a second" interview: the impersonator had identified himself as "Jim Hougan—with a u." Equally unnerving was litigation threatened by a private intelligence agency. Communicated to *Harper's* magazine, the threat was to the effect that if I published the contents of a long-distance conversation between myself and a source at the Battelle Memorial Institute, the agency would sue for libel. It wasn't the fear of litigation that dismayed me, but rather the fact that my telephone conversation with Battelle was still going on when the threat was phoned to *Harper's*. Inflating the Agent's Syndrome even further in my own case were the occasional threats, veiled or denuded, delivered to me in person or through a second party. In one instance, a midwestern detective of doubtful mental stability threatened to bomb my home in response to an imaginary slight. In a second instance, a reluctant source finally agreed to discuss the wiretapping of Aristotle Onassis on the condition that I bring my parents' home address to our meeting. Asked about that condition, the source replied that, after he had spoken with me, he would need to know where to ship my body. The problem with incidents of this kind is that they create an hallucinatory atmosphere in which one is tempted to invest the most routine occurrences with a special significance: normal disturbances on the telephone line hint at a third presence; ambiguous remarks are pregnant with unintended meaning; the car behind seems to have been there far too long for mere coincidence. . . . The point, however, is not just that the Agent's Syndrome is contagious but that it is alluring as well. Experience is heightened by a sense of danger, whether that danger is real or imaginary. As a result, secret agents tend to romanticize their profession. And that romanticism, supported by a genuine need for secrecy and the frequent resort to "cover," places them at an eccentric remove from the rest of society. They are, as writers Victor Marchetti and John Marks have suggested, initiates in a *cult* of intelligence.

In the realm of the federal intelligence agencies, the cult is truly a secret society, an elite in every sense. Intimate with the secrets of the empire, government spooks often regard themselves as people charged with nothing less than the preservation of Western civilization—a mission usually seen in terms of extending American hegemony and maintaining a semblance of nuclear parity.

The private agent, however, shares neither of these responsibilities. No matter how dangerous or important his work may be, it is comparatively trivial—if only because its worth can be measured in dollars. Thus, ITT hires Intertel to perform an investigation that will discredit Jack Anderson and, by extension, his criticism of Intertel's client. In New York, Fidelifacts is employed by General Motors to probe Ralph Nader's sex life and, if possible, to bring about his seduction before hidden cameras. Elsewhere, IBM, concerned by attempts to penetrate its data banks, and also by the threat of terrorist kidnappings in Latin America, virtually beheads the Drug Enforcement Administration (DEA), hiring that agency's top intelligence officers to take charge of its international security. In Virginia, Dektor Counterintelligence, led by the intrepid Colonel Bell, handles a variety of secret assignments for industry, but undertakes a few of its own as well: e.g., the analysis of the notorious eighteen-and-one-half-minute gap on the "Rose Mary Woods tapes" and the application of the PSE to the (equally notorious) "Howard Hughes press conference." Curiously, Dektor is unpaid for its work in these two cases, performing the analyses *"pro bono publico."* (The conclusions reached: the tape gap was probably accidental in origin; that was indeed Howard Hughes on the phone—or at least a man who believed he was Howard Hughes.) In other places and times, Robert Maheu and Richard Nixon take a bead on Aristotle Onassis, deploying wiretaps against a multibillion-dollar contract opposed by the Seven

Sisters and the CIA; The Wackenhut Corporation prepares a private study on "Communist Expansion in the Caribbean"; and Walt Mackem travels incognito to the Bahamas, there to assess the efficiency of a private intelligence operation designed to separate the island of Abaco from the republic to which it belongs. In Rome, Lockheed's Roger Smith hunches over a yellow pad in his suite at the Grand Hotel, scribbling a memorandum to be made public should a French consortium engineer his "death, disability, or disappearance." In London, Colonel David Sterling makes preparations for a privately financed invasion of Libya, while a luxury yacht eases out of Miami laden with a secret cargo of automatic weapons.

There is real variety in the operations of industry's secret agents. But while those operations are of importance to the public and to those directly involved, they're nevertheless inconsequential in comparison with, for instance, strategic arms limitation. As a result, private intelligence agents tend to be more cynical about their own activities than are their federal counterparts. For the most part, the stakes are financial and the agent's loyalty is secured not by patriotism but by contract. Few spooks enjoy the affluence in which Richard Bast is ensconced and few, therefore, can afford (as he can) to accept only those assignments in which they have a special interest.

Understanding the psychology of private intelligence agents is therefore something of a study in cynicism: they work for money, and, as with some of the agents assigned to Intertel's Lordstown job, they sometimes dislike the people who've hired them and the side they represent. Moreover, the private spook is often less secure than his federal counterpart. For one thing, his working conditions are more isolated; he isn't a part of a bureaucracy and so lacks the day-to-day support of colleagues engaged in what they believe is an all-important national objective. Nor does the private agent have the financial security offered by government work, and neither does he enjoy the protection of the state. The risks he takes are proportionately greater for his lack of federal authority, and in the end he may even come to fear his own client. Paul Rothermeil, for instance, a former FBI agent hired by the ultrarightist Hunt family in Texas, is convinced that Nelson Bunker Hunt was prepared to kill him after Rothermeil refused to participate in what he says was Hunt's intention to establish an American version of the Brazilian death squads.*

---

* The reference here is to vigilante groups operating in Brazil, apparently with the cooperation of authorities; their specialty is the assassination of petty hoodlums and Marxist theoreticians.

The psychology of the secret agent working for private interests, then, differs in many ways from that of federal spooks. And yet, with the exception of those writing technical books on business intelligence and on "industrial espionage," the private use of secret agents has been the exclusive province of pulp novelists and B-film makers. And these works, sensational in concept, tend to exploit the customer's romanticism more than they explore the psychology of their own characters. Nevertheless, it would be arrogant to dismiss them out of hand. Ian Fleming was not "merely" a writer of thrillers but a knowledgeable espionage buff and a friend to numerous intelligence officers in Britain and the United States. His characters (or caricatures) were often based on real figures (e.g., Goldfinger on the American tycoon Charles Englehard, James Bond on CIA officer Steve King). The spy technology he "invented" was often speculative, but at least some of it—e.g., shellfish toxin—was leaked to him in conversations with friends belonging to one intelligence service or another. And at least one of his plots, as we'll see in subsequent pages, came peculiarly close to reality.

In any event, dismissing the pulps would be an amateurish mistake. The CIA itself maintains what may be the world's largest collection of espionage literature and fiction—literally tens of thousands of volumes, ranging from Sun Tzu's *Roots of Strategy—Art of War* (Peking, 500 B.C.) to Harry Murphy's *Where's What* and Fleming's *Dr. No.** The collection, housed in the CIA's campuslike compound near Langley, Virginia, is a musty rebuke to the immaculate world surrounding it, resembling nothing so much as a large used-book store on the seedier side of Manhattan. This library, established and supervised for decades by CIA employee Walter Pforzheimer, is regularly perused by the Agency's employees, who may be looking for new technology worth inventing, a dirty trick worth resurrecting, or just a good "read." (Pforzheimer, now retired, assisted former CIA director Allen Dulles in the preparation of several books; independently wealthy, he lives in the supernally expensive Watergate complex, having purchased two apartments, one of which is devoted to housing his private collection of books and materials on the history and literature of intelligence.)

---

* Sun Tzu's book is generally regarded to be the first treatise on espionage; a Chinese military theorist, he wrote: "Knowledge of the enemy's disposition can only be obtained from other men. Hence the use of spies." *Where's What* is a 452-page "investigator's manual" expressly created by CIA agent Murphy to assist federal spooks in compiling dossiers, conducting background checks, and generally in locating hard-to-find personal information.

Obviously, novels are no substitute for experience, and little can be concluded from even the most precisely drawn *roman à clef*. Nevertheless, the books are sometimes the product of the authors' own experiences,* however exaggerated by a need to conform to commercial expectations. More importantly, perhaps, the books themselves seem to have an impact on the world they describe—the real world. That is, the mystique propounded by the pulps not only infatuates the ordinary reader, but often informs the conduct of those engaged in the kind of activities that the novelist romanticizes.

There's no need to examine any single novel in detail (though it might be fun to identify the real-life counterparts of, for instance, major characters and operations in Frederick Forsyth's *The Dogs of War* †). Even the briefest consideration of the genre reveals a set of themes and characteristics which are common to almost all the books, the good as well as the bad. With few exceptions, the hero is an ingenious, wounded loner, a master spook alienated from his employers. Usually larcenous, almost always cynical, he adheres rigidly to some private code of honor whose origins are obscure, confused, or bitter. His mystique is considerable, a product of his inscrutability and general deviousness—a product also of his ability to circumvent the laws and customs (but seldom the manners) of society, to operate beyond the constraints of ordinary men. He is, as Nietzsche would have it, beyond good and evil, moving purposefully through a world mixed with hostility and opportunity, a world that seems to exist for his use and manipulation. *He gets around things* that stop you and me: a locked door, the police, refusals of every kind. And yet the whole persona is laden with doom: we don't believe in supermen—Nietzsche's *or* Fleming's—and know that, in the end, the world will defeat them. In fiction the defeat usually comes through a trick of fate (e.g., a policeman's chance encounter or, as in *Dogs*, the sudden revelation of a terminal disease). In reality, supermen are even rarer than they are in novels, and, as we'll see, the spy's undoing comes less often through a trick of fate than it does from some very human failing.

---

* According to spokesmen for the Agency, the CIA probably has more authors among its employees than any other state-supported institution, including the largest universities.

† Forsyth, a veteran of Biafra and the mercenaries' demimonde, is as much a journalist as a novelist. Readers who admired *The Dogs of War* and who would like to know more about the people on whom the author's characters seem to be based, and the operations that eventually became his plot, are urged to read two *nonfiction* books: *Congo Mercenary* and *The Hilton Assignment*.

There are a number of parallels to be drawn between the secret agent's mystique and those of others. It has much in common with the romance of the Mafia, for instance, but even more in common with that of the cowboy. The assassin, mercenary, Godfather, secret agent, and cowboy all operate on the borders of some literal or figurative frontier, a lawless place of fabulous extremes and dangers. Indeed, if we look at the pulp book racks, noting the vast numbers of thrillers, it's obvious that spooks have succeeded to that place in the American psyche which once enthroned the cowboy,* or, in the case of secret agents who work for themselves or private interests, "the drifter." And, insofar as spooks can be looked upon as the cowboys and drifters of the twentieth century, Third World nations can be regarded as their logical frontier—wild places filled with menace, mystery, and riches.

Admittedly, this is somewhat thick. Our sophistication is such that while we may willingly suspend our disbelief when reading a novel in bed, we know at the same time that the agent's world isn't really as exciting as James Bond's. We know too that gunplay in the Old West was relatively infrequent, that the Robin Hoods of Missouri were in fact no more than common malefactors, and that the adventures of some folk heros owed more to the imagination of penny journalists than to their own daring.

It's therefore become fashionable for those who pretend to an insider's knowledge to emphasize the drudgery of intelligence work and the seediness of its practitioners. The increasing importance of spy technology has led some to conclude that the classical spook is in eclipse, a victim of automation. To an extent the clandestine agent has even become a figure of ridicule. Everyone is familiar with the notorious "ill-fitting red wig" worn by Howard Hunt during his "interview" with ITT's Dita Beard. The implication is that Hunt's shaggy mop, flame-red and jammed down upon his ears, was no more a competent disguise than Bozo the Clown's red nose and plus fours. Similarly, the bag job at Watergate, with its crudely taped locks, disconnected walkie-talkies, and flying squad of Cuban *gusanos*, is seen to be no more than another chapter in the spook's history as clown and bungler. And yet this Disney Version doesn't add up. For one thing, Hunt's "red wig" was an expensive brown toupee which, according to those who provided it, fitted perfectly. For an-

---

* Indeed, spooks themselves give explicit voice to the analogy when they refer to their paramilitary colleagues, mixing contempt with envy, as "cowboys."

other, a good deal of evidence suggests, and several of the principals believe, that the so-called bungling of the Watergate operation was far from unintentional.

But it *is* true that technology has tended to limit the number of intelligence workers employed by the federal government. Super-computers housed at the National Security Agency (NSA), for instance, can process more than three billion "bits" of information each hour, reducing the numbers of cryptanalysts who might otherwise be needed to handle even a fraction of that amount of data. Satellites have similarly limited the federal employment of some spies, especially those needed to perform high-risk "crash operations" into denied areas (e.g., Albania, North Korea, and Tibet). Generally, though, technology has merely increased the *percentage* of technicians involved in intelligence work without substantially reducing the number of actual spooks. Meanwhile, private industry's intelligence needs have ballooned, creating an expanded job market for ex-CIA, -DEA, and -NSA officers; and because industry cannot begin to compete with government in terms of capital expenditures for the technology of espionage, it necessarily relies on the tradecraft of individual agents.

Still, one cannot deny that intelligence work is sometimes boring. Most of the raw data gathered for processing derive from public sources: newspapers, speeches, government reports, technical journals, and witheringly obscure publications devoted to the most esoteric aspects of particular subjects. The most valuable information, of course, remains that small percentage of data which is, for one reason or another, regarded as a state or trade secret. But even the most academic intelligence work is frequently redeemed, and even transformed, from drudgery to a kind of intoxication by virtue of the intelligence officer's narcissistic awareness of his elite role. Whatever the nature of his task, it's performed within an environment that's charged with significance. Whoever else he may be, the intelligence officer is an initiate, constantly reminded by his surroundings and superiors of his job's special importance. When he is privileged with access to information regarded as "proprietary"— whether it's newsclips, diplomatic dispatches, or photos of Russian submarines—his sense of self-importance can be overbearing. And while there are always elites within elites, the actual nature of the intelligence officer's job is almost irrelevant to his degree of self-esteem: like the doorman at a Broadway show, he's a part of The Theater, a man behind the scenes rubbing elbows with the stars.

I emphasize the narcissism of intelligence agents because it's central to their psychology and helps to explain much that is otherwise inscrutable. As we'll see later in the book, intelligence entrepreneur Jack Holcomb is right when he says that intrigue gets in your blood. Frequently, that "intrigue" is cultivated (and projected) for its own sake. So is a demeanor of controlled, professional paranoia. And, of course, since a spook's worth is proportional to the quantity and quality of the secrets to which he has access, mysteries are routinely, *defensively* propagated—even in areas where nothing is rightfully mysterious. Dealing with spooks, one comes to recognize what might be called the Hollywood Effect, a case of life imitating art imitating life. I'll try to explain.

The day-to-day business of the television and motion-picture industries is the idealization of dramatic themes, an idealization that leads to the creation of either archetypes (when the film's good) or stereotypes (when it's bad). If the archetypes have reference to a specific occupation (e.g., journalism in *All the President's Men* and spying in *Three Days of the Condor*), those in the audience whose occupation it is will have a special interest in the film's ambiance, the mannerisms of the actors, their clothes and quirks. No matter how shamelessly the occupation may be idealized, those whose job it is will—even while repudiating the film aloud—find some detail worthy of rescue and emulation. *Being portrayed* (by Robert Redford or Peter Fonda) is a kind of flattery whose lure is almost impossible to resist; art imitates life, but life, in turn, imitates art. Examples of the Hollywood Effect are everywhere. Following the success of *Blow Up*, camera sales boomed throughout the country, just as the sale of motorcycles reached new highs upon the release of *Easy Rider*. I don't know, but strongly suspect, that *The Godfather I & II* had a strongly civilizing effect on petty hoodlums everywhere; and black exploitation flicks such as *Superfly* and *Shaft* had obvious impacts on the dress and mannerisms of youths in Harlem and Roxbury.

What's this got to do with spooks? Well, spies go to the movies too, and they're no less susceptible to the Effect than ghetto kids are. If Robert Redford, portraying a superspook, has cause to drink Metaxa during the portrayal, chances are the bars around Langley will have a run on the Greek brandy for months. Moreover, even when the flattery of being portrayed is somehow resisted, the mystique created in the film often proves useful in itself and comes to be exploited. The FBI, for instance, capitalized for decades on its

Hollywood image, even going so far as to oversee productions of *The FBI*, suggesting scripts and advising its agents to mimic the demeanor and dress of Efrem Zimbalist, Jr. The CIA capitalized even more imaginatively on the old "Mission Impossible" series, a melodrama that romanticized the tradecraft of intelligence work while emphasizing the capers of its spies. Indeed, "Mission Impossible" was so popular with CIA officers that those stationed abroad demanded, and received, tapes of shows seen in the United States. Often, the spy-tech seen on the shows would inspire the real-life spooks to file formal requests with the Agency's Records Integration Division, asking that the Agency develop the technology seen on television.

The supposed drudgery of intelligence work, then, is often redeemed by the mystique surrounding the job. In fact, the mystique is so powerful that it seems to take precedence over more rational considerations. Following Watergate, for instance, the CIA came in for a number of very damaging congressional investigations, investigations which tended to debunk the Agency's good-guy image while at the same time emphasizing its involvement in a panoply of dangerous capers involving dart guns, exploding conch shells, shellfish toxins, and so forth. Almost immediately, the effects of the bad publicity were felt on recruitment. That is, applications for employment at the Agency more than *tripled*, and according to a CIA spokesman, the applicants were of "the highest quality—kids from the very best schools." Asked why so many applied under such difficult circumstances, the spokesman shrugged and said, "A bad job market, I suppose. And patriotism." Perhaps. But a similar patriotic backlash must have swept the ghettos at about the same time. Even while Congress was closing its doors on the CIA investigations, black youths were queueing up for employment as mercenaries in Angola. While there was some spectacular pettifoggery about "coming to the rescue of our ancestral homeland," most of the would-be mercs knew little or nothing about Angolan politics or culture. They didn't seem to mind the fact that they'd be battling the majority of Angolans (who supported the MPLA), or that they'd be fighting the very black brothers they'd enlisted to "save." Indeed, those signing up in Washington, San Diego, and London didn't even seem to mind that the war had already been lost prior to their enlistment. Nor were they too worried about the inferior equipment supplied, bad pay, psychotic commanders, executions in the field, and so forth. As an operation the recruitment of mercenaries for Angola was a cynical black comedy whose cutting edge was the exploitation of vulnerabilities in the psychology of the poor. Its success (measured by the large number of applicants) can't be explained in terms of some mythical solidarity between American blacks and the minions of Holden Roberto; nor can it be explained solely in terms of ghetto unemployment and the need for jobs of any kind. Most of the blacks who sought to fight in Angola got precisely what they wanted most when they enlisted as mercenaries: a sense of pride in their manliness, a *Shaft*-like identity, and a passport to adventure on a Hollywood scale. It was the most important fringe benefit associated with the job, and it was sufficiently valuable that all were willing to risk their lives to gain it.

For both the Angolan mercs and the Yalies applying to the CIA, the war and the hearings made an opportunity obvious. The hearings, amplifying the mystique of secret agentry while exposing the foibles of agents, humanized the spooks and made intelligence work accessible in a way it had never been. Similarly, Roy Innis's * call for evidence "of the red blood in black men" made romance and Africa accessible to those languishing in the bleakness of the ghetto. Who cared which side you were on? The point was that Angola promised to release the brave from the street corners of Harlem, and the CIA promised to release adventurous college grads from the prospect of suburban monotony. Anyone could be a spook. Wield a dart gun. Die in battle. And, just maybe, *be portrayed*. It was a New Frontier all over again.

---

* Innis is chairman of the Congress on Racial Equality (CORE).

THE PALADINS

1 / PRIVATE OPS & OPERATIONS

THE OFFICES OF FIDELIFACTS/METROPOLITAN-NEW YORK ARE IN A skyscraper on Broad Street in the navel of Manhattan's financial district. The bare floors shine dully beneath a ceiling hung with fluorescent lights, and the metal desks are a dusty shade of gray. It's a seedy maze of ringing black telephones and wastepaper baskets damp with the spillage from styrofoam coffee cups and empty cans of diet soda. Occasionally, a flashcube goes nova in the vicinity of a silver slide screen that serves as a backdrop for taking I-D photos. A Polaroid camera fitted to a tripod has the look of a permanent fixture. Nearby, a poster showing a fingerprint magnified to the size of an attaché case, with "points of identification" noted, is stuck to a wall with strips of packing tape. One gets the impression that periodically the poster swings loose, startling everyone, and forcing the secretaries to search for new tape.

Tom Norton, Fidelifacts' president, notices a visitor's surprise. Smiling, he says, "It isn't like the movies, is it?" The visitor shakes his head. "Well, it doesn't have to be," Norton adds. "Ninety-five percent of our work, maybe more, is fairly routine—in the nature of background investigations for employers, marital cases . . . and like that." Frequently the work involves some sort of detection, Norton says, "but you wouldn't call us an intelligence agency. Look," he says, pointing to literally hundreds of ancient Bell Telephone books and Polk's City Directories. "That's our most important asset. We couldn't do anything without them because it's where we always begin. Let's say a guy claims he worked for Acme Sporting Goods back in 'sixty-seven. The first thing we do is check the phone book to find out if there *was* such a firm. If the book doesn't have it listed, well, the guy probably made it up; it happens all the time—and not just with blue-collar workers. You'd be surprised at the caliber of people who try to fake their past, cover up a couple of rough years, a firing or whatever. Not," he adds, "that it's all that hard to do. But most of the time they go about it in the dumbest possible way. Smart people too. I don't know what they're thinking of."

If a prospective employee wanted to pass a routine check of faked background credentials—and such checks are made in great volume at a cost of about fifteen dollars each (up to forty dollars depending on the number of leads to be assessed)—he'd do well to make use of the same directories that his investigators will. The best method would be to go through the phone books of earlier years until a firm is found that, after years of prior listings, is omitted from the current directory. Chances are it's gone out of business, and one's future employer is unlikely to authorize a more extensive search. Of course, Norton and his staff of forty investigators only begin with the phone books, but more often than not they aren't asked to go any further: an assessment of the prospective employee's past performance on the job entails interviews and as a result costs correspondingly more. For the most part, employers are interested only in the broad outlines of the applicant's résumé.*

Marital and credit investigations, traces and the search for missing persons (all staples of private investigators) sometimes involve

---

* According to Norton, another of the areas employers most often want checked is the employee's police record. Such checks, however, become increasingly expensive in proportion to the number of jurisdictions to be queried. As a result, most checks have to be confined to the court records of a single small town, borough, or even precinct. Private employers', and investigators', access to police data banks is severely restricted by law. Contrary to the impression conveyed by *The Rockford Files*, few private investigators are able to obtain comprehensive criminal records on a subject. The point is that while court proceedings are usually a matter of public record, information stored in jurisdictionally linked data-processing systems is not. A complete search of the criminal record, therefore, is theoretically possible but almost never attempted.

real spookery . . . but rarely. Nevertheless, it's worth pointing out that investigations of this sort are of enormous importance precisely because they're so routine; the Retail Credit Bureau of Atlanta, for instance, has more than ten thousand "investigators" on its staff and dossiers pertaining to *tens of millions* of Americans in its files. It is, in a sense, America's largest "private intelligence agency" and at one time or another, for better or worse, directly affects the life of virtually every American. National clearinghouses of domestic snoopery, firms such as the Retail Credit Bureau savage a right so deeply rooted in America's frontier heritage that citizens hardly ever have need to articulate it: the right to move and start anew, the right to leave your past behind.

Tom Norton understands this, but shrugs. "It's a job," he says. "Sometimes I don't like it. But look: business has a right to protect its interests. If a deadbeat or a junky goes looking for credit, or if someone applies for a job he has no business holding down—what would *you* do?" Asked about his firm's investigation of consumer advocate Ralph Nader, Norton shakes his head, swivels in his chair, and gazes out the window. "That was a mistake. A bad mistake." After a pause he adds, "That was awful, in fact." Has Fidelifacts worked labor disputes? "Yeah. A few. We've done some undercover work for management—usually when the picketers have gotten violent, or when there's sabotage at the plant." Is that all? "No. Of course not. Sometimes you'll get a situation where organized crime is involved. If one of the guys leading the strike has criminal connections, or a record, management has a need to know about it. And so do other union members. We get that intelligence for them." Does Fidelifacts ever work for the unions? "No. Not so far. I don't know what we could do for them, really. But if a union had some legitimate need for our services, we'd work for them. Hell, yes." Where does Fidelifacts get its investigators? Norton's shoulders heave. "Most of us were with the FBI. Or the Secret Service. But we get people from just about everywhere. I have a man—one of my best investigators—used to be a baker. Another guy was a newspaper reporter. I got a kid working part time who's putting himself through school; he's in criminology, and he's *good*. The thing about Fidelifacts that's unusual is that it's a franchise-type cooperative. It was started by former FBI agents and, well, it's spread. But you're right: most of us have had government experience. FBI, Secret Service, IRS, N.Y.P.D. . . . we had a guy from the CIA a while back."

Exactly: "most of us have had government experience." And while Fidelifacts hardly ever functions as a private intelligence agency (in the sophisticated sense of the term), most of its agents are graduates of the federal campus. As they are at Intertel and elsewhere.

The point is that the federal intelligence complex serves as a kind of tax-supported university for industrial spooks, a place where investigators are trained in clandestine crafts to be used against hostile nations and organized crime—but which, eventually, are brought to bear against private citizens, business competitors, and even the government itself.

Because employment figures are kept secret within the federal intelligence complex, there's no way to know how large the annual turnover is or where the retirees go when they leave government. Still, there are indications. In 1974, for instance, more than twelve hundred executive spies at the CIA were made to retire by CIA director James Schlesinger (who claimed that he wanted to make room at the top for younger officers *). In most cases, the retiring CIA officers were men in their forties and fifties who believed themselves to be near the peak of their talents. A passive retirement therefore seemed odious to many, but so did the prospect of studying a new kind of "classified" material: the want ads. Yet many of them, made nervous by mortgages, kids in college, and their own abundant energies, had no choice but to look for new work. Adrift in a declining job market which has always placed a heavy emphasis on youth, they found that their career relationships to the CIA carried a stigma in certain quarters and that, moreover, their skills were often esoteric in the extreme. Even if they'd wanted to get out of intelligence work, the transition would have been difficult for many, and in some cases impossible. Still, they tended to be well-connected men: some were able to find work as journalists, others as teachers; and a few secured jobs with such diverse government agencies as the DEA, the Library of Congress, the Law Enforcement Assistance Administration (LEAA), and the Bicentennial Commission. A substantial number, however, went into business for themselves —not as "putsch directors," "interrogators," or "propagandists," but as "management consultants," "personnel advisors," and "public

---

* Others disagreed, insisting that the retirements constituted a "purge" of those in the Agency who were opposed to "détente." Three years later, in the Carter Administration, this first wave of reluctant retirees was succeeded by a second, even larger, one ordered by CIA director Stansfield Turner.

relations" men. In doing so, they followed in a tradition of former spooks whose talents came to be incorporated. Indeed, as early as 1966, former CIA officers and FBI agents headed up almost one hundred industrial security firms,* and ten years later the number had multiplied almost exponentially. Among them were such specialists in counterespionage as Saul D. Astor, of Management Safeguards, Inc. (New York), and Allan Bell, of Dektor Counterintelligence (Virginia). Other such firms were Crest Detective Agency (Santa Monica), George L. Barnes & Associates (Los Angeles), and Norman Jaspan Associates (a New York firm with more than five hundred employees that describes itself as a "management engineering agency"); and, more notoriously, (James) McCord Associates (Maryland & Houston), Sheffield Edwards & Associates (Virginia), Robert A. Maheu Associates, Fidelity Reporting Service (New York), and Anderson Security Associates (Virginia).†

Starting one's own business can be costly, of course, and the competition is brutal. At a recent "International Security Conference" sponsored by the industry's house organ, *Security World*, there were more than a hundred exhibitors representing manufacturers of surveillance and counterintrusion equipment, ranging from Psychological Stress Evaluators to ultrasonic, infrared, ionization, and motion detectors. Amid surveillance cameras, "multiplex security polling systems," stress alarms, automatic encoders, "cloaks," and window shock alarms, thirty-six lecturers sang the praises of Tasers ‡ and "company undercover men." In many ways it was a convention of spooks. But to the thousands of industrialists, shopkeepers, and

---

* Richard M. Greene, Jr., editor, *Business Intelligence and Espionage*, Dow Jones-Irwin, Inc. (Homewood, Ill.: 1966), p. 12.

† McCord's notoriety is an historical matter. As for Fidelity, Edwards, Maheu, and Anderson, each has been part of a shape-shifting archipelago of domestic "security" firms closely associated with the CIA. Some (e.g., Fidelity) are or were proprietary fronts handling "background investigations" of Americans. Others, such as the Edwards and Anderson agencies, were incorporated as private firms—both, however, depended upon the CIA for lucrative contracts involving security and counterintelligence tasks, including the surveillance of U. S. government workers in Washington. As for the Maheu apparat, it handled top secret CIA assignments involving political dirty tricks, assignments designed to provide the Agency with maximum "deniability." What all these firms and their unnumbered counterparts had and have in common is their proprietors' loyalty to the CIA—a loyalty predicated as much upon economics as patriotism.

‡ The Taser is a supposedly nonlethal weapon that looks and handles like a flashlight. Aiming the light's beam at the enemy, one then presses an electric release button. Immediately, two barbed contacts, connected to hair-thin electrical wires, are shot at the enemy, incapacitating him with a pulsating electrical current. Uncontrollable spasms and unconsciousness usually follow within seconds, and the victim seldom recovers in less than a few minutes.

corporate executives who came to learn, it was also a celebration of the alliance between commerce and intelligence. As the conference made clear, the security industry is a massive one, with plenty of room for talented federal agents bent on private practice. Particularly in the realm of hardware, the technically inclined would have no trouble finding work at any of hundreds of firms with such names as Spectre Security Products (Orange, California), Streamlight, Inc. (King of Prussia, Pennsylvania), Omni Spectra, Inc. (Tempe, Arizona), Impossible Electronic Techniques (Ardmore, Pennsylvania), Functional Devices, Inc. (Russiaville, Indiana), Tractron (Vienna, Virginia), and Audio Intelligence Devices, Inc. (Fort Lauderdale).

This last firm is a particularly interesting one, run by a manic and balding spook with a somewhat dicey past: Jack Holcomb. An ex-policeman, Holcomb is a longtime Caribbean operator who brags that he's had "wide experience in the field of law." Indeed he has. A man who gnaws his way through dozens of cigars daily, Holcomb is an expert in electronic surveillance who has hinted at "Mission Impossible assignments" he's performed—supposedly for the FBI. He's also suffered the embarrassment of several brushes with the law. Tried on two counts of wiretapping, he was acquitted; subsequently accused of possessing barbiturates, the charges against him were ultimately dropped. His only conviction is for failure to support a minor child (whose paternity he denies).

More than anything else, except perhaps in his role as a spook, Holcomb is an opportunist of the sort with which the Caribbean is quite familiar. Burdened by illiteracy, a colonial past, and the near absence of natural resources, the smaller Caribbean islands have always been "targets of opportunity" for adventurers. And Holcomb, today the proprietor of Audio Intelligence Devices, Inc. (AID), has never been one to pass up an opportunity. Without formal training in the law, he has the distinction of having been made *the* magistrate of the Anguillan Bar Association. That honor was accorded to him in the midst of Anguilla's abortive secession from the British Commonwealth in 1967. At the time of the planned secession, Anguilla was under siege by hustlers and hasslers of every sort: there was a Chinese Jew in a kilt who wanted to establish a nudist camp under the aegis of a religious cult; a reputed New York embezzler who sought to found the First International Bank of Anguilla; a "consortium of private investors" interested in turning seawater into gold; Canadians in sixteen-ounce suits who wanted land in return for advice; assorted Mafiosi; American doctors who wanted to establish abortion clinics; a gunrunning dentist from Chicago who allegedly shipped submachine guns to the island in crates marked "GLASS"; and, of course, Holcomb himself.

The wireman-entrepreneur had risen high in the councils of rebel leader Ronald Webster, serving as that mystic's "legal advisor." In that capacity Holcomb drafted a new constitution for the island. A parody of the U. S. version, it ignored every governmental form with which the Anguillans were familiar, while including some bizarre provisos guaranteeing Anguillan citizenship for a handful of flamboyant American expatriates active in Webster's cause. The document was also distinguished by the fact that it reserved for private investors various rights ordinarily belonging to sovereign governments. Holcomb himself was given a series of monopolies and tax exemptions that, had the secession succeeded, would have provided him with a virtual lock on the island's economic development until the year 2000. As Anguilla's only magistrate, he would have held absolute sway over every developmental contract and government permission.

Fortunately for the Anguillans, the secession failed when British paratroopers and London bobbies arrived to quell the rebellion in an operation that was later dubbed "England's 'Bay of Piglets.'" With the new republic of Anguilla crushed, Holcomb was reportedly ejected as "a gangster-type element." Before long, however, he turned up in nearby Haiti precisely two weeks before an abortive coup occurred there. His timing may have been coincidental, but the Haitians thought not: he was deported as a suspected secret agent. Holcomb won't talk about any connections he may have to the CIA, but creates the impression that the ties are there, and binding.

That Holcomb will not discuss his suspected ties to the CIA is often regarded as evidence that such ties exist. Yet there is no reason to believe that they do. Among free-lance spooks and their employers it often happens that such relationships are deliberately intimated when, in fact, they don't exist. Many free-lance spooks have used their incidental or wholly imaginary ties to the CIA as a sort of cover. Not only does this increase their prestige and inflate the value of their alleged connections, but it lends an aura of special legitimacy to their otherwise questionable activities. Indeed, it's accurate to say that this particular form of mystification is epidemic within the community of adventurers and their hangers-on.

This, then, is the proprietor of AID. A manufacturer of twenty-first century electronic eavesdropping and countermeasures equipment, AID's prosperity has been linked by disgruntled former employees to its synergistic relationship with a strange entity conceived by Jack Holcomb upon his return from Haiti: the National Intelligence Academy (NIA). If that sounds distinctly "federal," it's probably not by accident. Everything about the NIA suggests that it's a secret government installation. Set amid the palms and graceful lawns of Fort Lauderdale, NIA has always shared a modernistic, two-story office building with Holcomb's AID. Passing between two green obelisks standing sentry on the lawn, a visitor is confronted by a sign reading, "U.S. Government regulations prohibit discussion of this organization or facility. Sorry, the receptionist is instructed not to answer related inquiries." Only the second sentence is true.

For most of its existence, the NIA has been a school for wiretappers, a tax-exempt foundation where state-of-the-art electronic surveillance techniques were taught to government spooks, Latin American security officials, and undercover police. According to an NIA statement, "candidates" from American police departments had to be veterans "engaged in a field of law enforcement that is related to intelligence, organized crime, narcotics or major criminal investigations."

All of that changed recently when Holcomb's patron (and NIA's benefactor) died unexpectedly earlier this year. Doug Carlton, the former president of the NIA, and head honcho at AID when Holcomb's not around, says that the "academy is no longer a tax-exempt entity."

"It's continuing," he insists, "but in a different form than what it used to be. That tax-exempt business was always clumsy." Asked what shape NIA's new form will take, Carlton declines to answer, saying only that "I've never been a strong believer in the public's right to know. Some things deserve to be secret (in the interest of national security and law enforcement)."

During its heyday, NIA gave two-week courses in which students were taught how to bug a room in less than five minutes and were instructed in the subtleties of a vast array of Orwellian equipment and James Bond devices of every kind.* There was, for instance, in

---

* The technological secrets of electronic eavesdroppers and their counterparts are necessarily closely guarded. To be in the vanguard of the art is worth a fortune. My own information and understanding is that of a near layman's, but the sort of devices

addition to the ordinary classrooms, a model city measuring 12 by 24 feet. Complete with replicas of office and residential buildings, tiny trees, buses, cars, lawns and streets, NIA's Surveillance City was a heavy-gauge nightmare to all but the most devoted Skinnerians. (I use the past tense since neither Holcomb nor Carlton is willing to discuss the NIA's new status or continuing operation—but there's no reason to believe that Surveillance City or any other part of the NIA operation has been dismantled. Indeed, Carlton says the opposite is the case.) Used as a three-dimensional model to illustrate the techniques of electronic spying, the city all but crackled with the emplacement of bugs as the spooks loomed over its structures like crew-cut gods, chattering about the tactics of surveillance.

Down the hall from Surveillance City was Classroom D. The most secret facility at NIA, its doors were locked whenever telephone company personnel were in the building on service calls, and no mention was made of its existence in NIA literature. Basically, Classroom D was a fully operative telephone system put together with materials from salvage yards and Canadian and independent phone companies. According to former NIA employees, the room contained nearly every kind of indoor and outdoor terminal block in use today, with access points identified by the instructors. Both aerial and underground transmission cables were looped and spliced in

---

the NIA would have to combat or deploy include such things as harmonica bugs, cloaks, and silver boxes. The harmonica bug is basically an infinity transmitter that can be turned on and off by remote control. Once a phone is bugged with one, the eavesdropper calls that number; just before it rings, he gives a toot on his "harmonica," a frequency-signaling device. The bug is then working and the phone will not ring, though conversations taking place in the vicinity of the bugged phone will be fully audible. When the eavesdropper is done, he gives another toot and the bug shuts off. (An important advantage of the harmonica bug, besides the fact that it allows conversations to be monitored from thousands of miles away, is that an inactive bug is extremely difficult to locate. Because the eavesdropper is able to turn the harmonica bug on and off at will, it usually escapes detection: only a continuously transmitting bug is easy to find with conventional equipment.)

A cloak is a countermeasure device. Resembling an ordinary telephone, it has an extra panel which monitors the line to detect "eavesdropping attacks" of various kinds. With both visual and aural alarm responses, it defeats all telephone bugs by canceling signals and providing automatic disconnection if desired. In continual operation, the cloak detects and classifies a broad array of bugs and taps, including radio-frequency transmitters, telephone-tap transmitters, power-line carrier transmitters, harmonica bugs, low-impedance direct taps, tape-recorder switches, and even the threat provided by someone listening in on an extension phone. Available from Dektor Counterintelligence, Inc., the cloak sells for around $3,200.

A silver-box, manufactured by the Tel-Tone Corporation (Kirkland, Washington), is installed on the switching equipment of the local telephone exchange. Once it is in place, anyone who knows the box's code can, from anywhere in the same country, dial into conversations held on any phone whose lines belong to the exchange to which the box is attached.

Classroom D by students using live lines and approved Bell Telephone procedures. Amid it all, an anomalous indoor totem, was a fully rigged telephone pole standing atop a hillock of Astro-turf; covering the walls in the background was a medley of murals, showing typical office and residential scenes.

The wiretapping taught in Classroom D, however, was only part of the students' expertise. To receive their diplomas, the apprentice spooks had also to learn the art of bugging and prove their competence at it. Before the course ended, they were divided into two-man teams and tested on their ability to bug a room conversation in which NIA instructors simulated a narcotics transaction. Given only a few minutes to accomplish that, they'd enter the room in silence, communicating with hand signals and whispers. While practicing "on-target discipline" in this way, the students proceeded to take apart and reassemble a variety of ordinary objects to be found in any room: transmitters were taped to the backs of desk and bureau drawers, secreted in drapes and radiators, keyholes and cushions. With screwdrivers and mechanical drills fitted with tiny bits, the students turned the interiors of lamps and light fixtures, hollow doors and bedposts into receptacles for bugs.*

Completing the NIA facility—at least in theory—was the $1.2 million beachfront Trade Winds Motel. It's here, at a nominal fee of $23 per day (plus $475 in tuition), that student spooks were fed and bedded down. The motel was donated to the NIA by a private foundation controlled by Leo Goodwin, Jr. Goodwin, who died in his sixties earlier this year, was a former Army parachute instructor, the ultraconservative heir to an insurance company fortune (GEICO) put together by his father. Goodwin's interest in the NIA, and in its founder, Holcomb, stemmed from his belief that the country was going down the tubes to anarchists and worse. Used to banging around in his airy, twenty-five-room Fort Lauderdale mansion, the Benefactor was convinced that only increased surveillance would keep slime at bay. Toward that end, he provided NIA with more than three million dollars (taking a write-off as he did so), while promising more. Indeed, the former paratrooper took over the academy dreamed up by Holcomb—who, for his part, has always

---

* James M. Ellison's "A Report from the Wiretap Subculture," *The Washington Monthly*, December, 1975, is an excellent source of information about the NIA. For information about Jack Holcomb, see the *not for publication* publications of the Institute of Current World Affairs (535 Fifth Avenue, New York, N.Y.): FJM-4, FJM-5, FJM-9, and FJM-10 (by Frank McDonald).

claimed to be no more than "a special consultant" to the facility.

In reality, however, Holcomb has always been the NIA's *éminence grise*, and his connections to its work seem to have been all-encompassing. His private firm, for instance, has literally worked side by side with the foundation. AID executives have doubled as NIA officers, and students at the tax-exempt academy were routinely given tours of the AID factory. Moreover, the eavesdropping techniques taught by NIA have depended upon AID products ranging from "Unitels" (complete "attack kits" concealed in a Royal Traveler attaché case) to an AID-manufactured telephone transmitter that uses the phone company's own power and is stamped "Western Electric Noise Filter." Naturally, when students finished their course at NIA, they found AID a convenient source for obtaining whatever surveillance equipment they needed.

The cozy relationship between AID and NIA has proven to be a profitable one for the former, but it's led to controversy as well. Most of NIA's original instructors, retired government operatives from the CIA, DEA, and Justice Department, left the school shortly after its beginning, charging that NIA existed solely to create a market for the surveillance devices made by Holcomb. Still others have charged that NIA works to circumvent the law rather than to help enforce it, pointing out that *a fourth* of the academy's students are from states in which wiretapping is outlawed. Finally, Senate staffers concerned about Jack Holcomb's character and his influence over NIA worry about his contacts with academy students whose police careers are spent in the most dangerous and sensitive kinds of investigations: drugs, vice, and organized crime. They find it sinister that a deportee identified by the British as "a gangster-type element" should, even remotely, preside over the training and temporary housing of police intelligence officers in the midst of Florida's biggest gay community.

Jack Holcomb, however impressive he may seem by virtue of his NIA credentials (a red-white-and-blue American shield with taloned eagle clutching lightning bolts), does not seem to be an ex-intelligence officer—just as the NIA, whatever its pretensions, does not seem to be a federal facility of any kind. Retiring government spooks, in any event, are unlikely to have Holcomb's luck in finding a patron to support them in starting their own business or intelligence "foundation." Chances are, if they lack the capital to hang out their own shingle, they'll be able to find work on a permanent or contract basis with any of the more than 4,200 private security firms mentioned earlier. Depending on their inclinations, they can pick the firm most suited to them. While many agencies are engaged in routine investigations, some are specialists, and the biggest ones provide a range of services capable of fulfilling almost any client's needs. (Sometimes, of course, they get in trouble doing so: for example, in 1971, six executives of Wackenhut, Pinkerton's, and Burns were found guilty of bribing New York City policemen to obtain confidential records of would-be employees of American and Trans-Caribbean Airlines. Why they resorted to bribes is unclear, though, since the Rand Corporation reports that Wackenhut and Pinkerton's—never mind Burns—have dossiers on more than four million Americans). Of course, the work may not be to the agent's liking, especially if he considers himself a friend of labor. Fidelifacts and Intertel aren't the only firms that have had unions as their targets. According to an annual report of the Burns Agency, for example, undercover agents are available to probe inventory losses, pilferage, theft, fraud, falsification of records, forgery, poor employee morale, willful neglect of machinery, waste of time and materials, theft of tools, unreported absenteeism, supervisory incompetence, inadequate surveillance, and something called "delicate investigatory matters." The means of undercover investigation is also described in the Burns report: "A frequent procedure," it says, "is to have the investigator obtain work in the company in a normal manner. . . . He works full days, fills an actual job and draws a regular paycheck, arousing no suspicion among fellow employees. The person who arranged the investigation is kept informed by means of secret reports. When the work is completed, the operative leaves the job in a normal way so that no one ever need know his true identity."

If private security work isn't of interest to the retiring spook, he might apply at any of a few hundred "think tanks" such as Arthur D. Little, the MITRE Corporation, and Battelle Memorial Institute (all of which hire retiring intelligence officers). If the economy happens to be in a recession and the think tanks are cutting back on personnel, he might find job security with a multinational. If, for instance, his skills are clandestine and operational in nature, he should be able to supplement IBM's task force of former DEA agents in Latin America (handling counterintrusion and counterterrorist activities); should there not be an opening down south, the ex-spook might yet find a home with IBM's shadowy Commercial Analysis Department (the CAD is generally regarded as the most important of several intelligence units internal to IBM; while the other units are preoccupied with security matters relating to data, facilities, and personnel, the CAD is devoted to strategic assessments of markets and competitors). Or the retiring CIA man could make an application for work with the manager of competitive intelligence for Citicorp (owner of the First National City Bank). Indeed, the *Fortune* 500 group is a likely source of employment for a retiring agent, especially if the firm he applies to is involved overseas or, better yet, is *considering* such an involvement. According to Harry Howe Ransom of Vanderbilt University, one of the most respected analysts of intelligence affairs, "The pattern of history suggests that aggressive, expansionist societies have the best organized intelligence systems." * Undoubtedly, Professor Ransom was thinking in terms of countries (the United States, Iran, Israel, North Korea, and the USSR) when he wrote that, but his dictum applies equally well to corporations.

Nor has the spy yet exhausted all the opportunities available to him. Like former Justice Department spook Walter Sheridan, who went to work for Senators Robert and Edward Kennedy, he might become an investigator for a politician. Or, like former FBI agent Ken Smith, currently a private eye in the employ of Bud Fensterwald and his Committee to Investigate Assassinations, he might become the secret envoy of a powerful attorney with a sense of mission, a grudge, or both. Speaking of grudges, retiring CIA officers have found a market for a service which euphemists call "aggressive protection"; that is, if a prospective client is threatened by an identifiable antagonist—for instance, an unusually forceful creditor who seems unaware of the fact that gambling debts are *not* legally collectible—it may not be necessary to hire a full-time bodyguard. Former CIA officers can be hired to "persuade" the obnoxious to desist in their threats. How? According to one spook who handles such assignments on occasion, "I scare the shit out of them, that's all. And if that doesn't work, I knock it out of them. Real scientific."

The art world is yet another milieu in which the expertise of spooks is lucratively employed, and not just in the protection of valuable *objets*. Gallery owners and collectors alike are notoriously secretive about their acquisitions and sales, requiring inviolable confidentiality in their communications. Electronic surveillance long ago became a tool of respected art dealers interested in learn-

---

* Harry H. Ransom, *The Intelligence Establishment* (Cambridge, Mass.: Harvard University Press, 1970), p. 49.

ing the terms of a rival's sale and the identity, price, and provenance of the objects being offered; accordingly, countermeasures experts are needed as much to protect the terms of important transactions as they are to protect the treasures those transactions concern. In the same milieu, "exfiltration" skills are highly regarded. In recent years the smuggling of Third World masterpieces has become a profession in its own right. From Central America to Far East Asia, Africa, and the Mediterranean, everything from Mayan friezes and Olmec heads to Hindu statuary, animist totems, Renaissance paintings, and potsherds has been looted, smuggled, and sold. The buyers are multimillionaires such as Los Angeles businessman Norton Simon, proprietor of an Asian collection whose centerpiece is a priceless tenth-century bronze Shiva stolen from a dirt-poor Indian village in Madras. Simon reportedly paid one million dollars for the statue after a fake was substituted for it in the unguarded temple from which it disappeared. Unrepentant, the art baron has been quoted by *The New York Times*: "I spent between fifteen and sixteen million dollars over the last two years on Asian art, and *most* of it was smuggled."

Other millionaire collectors, such as Nelson Rockefeller and the late J. Paul Getty, have hired former Secret Service, CIA, and FBI agents to handle a variety of sensitive assignments within their organizations, protecting not only their property and commercial secrets but their persons as well. Working for the very wealthy can be hazardous to your health, however, as former FBI agent Paul Rothermeil claims to have discovered. In conversations with reporter Peter Noyes, and subsequently with myself, Rothermeil described his peculiar past association with the fabulously wealthy Hunt family of Texas. While employed in the secret service of the patriarch, H. L. Hunt, Rothermeil said that the old man's son, Nelson Bunker Hunt, approached him in connection with a plan to form a paramilitary group for "political purposes," a killer force that would train on desert estates in the West. A connoisseur of racehorses and right-wing causes alike, Nelson Bunker Hunt is an important contributor to the John Birch Society and a confidant of its Maximum Leader, Robert Welch. He is also one of the world's richest men, having at one time held title to all the oil in Libya. According to Rothermeil, however, Hunt was not content with mere riches, and therefore organized the so-called American Volunteer Group (AVG)—organized it, that is, with supposedly lethal intent. Recounting the story, the former G-man contends that Hunt planned to recruit his private army from the ranks of General Edwin

Walker's Birch Society cell in Dallas. The weapon of choice, Rothermeil claimed, was to be a type of "gas gun" imported from Europe, a weapon whose singular virtue was that its victims would appear to have died of heart attacks.* Asked to join the paramilitary unit in a war on liberals and the Left, Rothermeil says he refused. It was then that he found his telephone had been tapped by other spooks in Hunt's employ, and began to fear for his life.†

Asked about Rothermeil's story, Hunt calls it all nonsense and makes accusations of his own. In his opinion, Rothermeil was part of a conspiracy to embezzle millions from his employer, H. L. Hunt. That was supposedly why a detective agency was hired to wiretap members of the Hunt family's own internal security forces. (An unusual course for Hunt to take, perhaps, but it was by no means the first time an employer of spooks has had to set his right hand against his left.) Denying any knowledge of paramilitary affairs or European "gas guns," Nelson Bunker Hunt urged this writer to investigate Rothermeil's government background. "I think you'll find he's CIA," the billionaire said, though he declined to elaborate on the significance of that belief, adding only that it would explain the government's failure to indict Rothermeil in connection with the embezzling plot.

Rothermeil's story is a bizarre one that may be impossible to prove or disprove. In conversations with this reporter, it's clear that the former Hunt employee remains frightened of his old boss, and there is *no* doubt that his telephone was tapped. As for the AVG itself, its short history is a bloody one that's led investigators (most notably Peter Noyes) into an extremist's Wonderland. Seeking out its origins and "training bases," Noyes had reason to interview Minuteman leader Robert DePugh, who described the group in terms of a runaway apparat whose politics were extreme even for him. Others connected to the group in one way or another included a wealthy Californian car dealer whose private arsenal of weapons is said to exceed that of some small countries; a far-right cleric whose desert ranch is surrounded by armed guards; and a defrocked Californian

---

* The "gas gun" described by Rothermeil sounds very much like the one used by KGB defector Bogdan Stashinskiy to assassinate East European anti-Communists during the 1950s.

† Hunt subsequently pleaded guilty to a misdemeanor stemming from a massive wiretapping conspiracy in which he'd hired a Houston detective agency to eavesdrop upon his own security force, a force composed largely of former FBI agents. According to Hunt, he was concerned about an embezzling plot directed against his late father, H. L. Hunt.

cop. This last individual, living in a trailer outfitted as an electronics command post, claimed that the AVG's founding leader was an ex-Marine, Captain Medrick Johnson. A Bircher and a Minuteman, Johnson became national chairman of the AVG in May, 1968, journeying from southern California to Borger, Texas, to implement the group's policies. In July of that year, however, Johnson died of supposedly "self-inflicted" gunshot wounds—though the ex-cop insisted that the AVG chief had actually been murdered. Despite the efforts of investigators, however, no connections between the Hunts and a violent underground have been established.

Going to work for ultrarightist multimillionaires can immerse agents like Rothermeil in a weird, sometimes violent universe of plots and counterplots. Most spooks, of course, will avoid such intrigues, regarding extremists as dangerous amateurs. But others, like former Green Beret officer Robert K. Brown, will be attracted to the action, even infatuated by it.* Paramilitary maneuvers on the desert? Possibly. House trailers redolent with electronics gear? Why not? Suspicious suicides, private arsenal, and wiretaps directed against one's own secret agents? Of course. Gas guns? Maybe. Whatever the truth, this is the stuff of pulp novels, and it hardly matter that the cabals border on the insane. America has become a haunted house, aping its own worst fiction, a rambling Victorian manse whose rooms contain spooks of every kind: sober art-security specialists and banker-spies, grim "protectionists," trembling ex-G-men, conspiracy theorists, and oil-dipped Texans on a paramilitary binge. For some, it's exactly what the doctor ordered—even if the doctor's last name is Drennan (see footnote below).

---

* For more than a decade, Colonel Brown has functioned near the center of America's most violent intrigues, usually as an "advisor" or "journalist." The bizarre plot attributed to Nelson Bunker Hunt may seem incredible, but Brown has been approached with even stranger notions. For instance, according to an FBI report prepared in the wake of the JFK assassination, Brown "advised that he has been active in Cuban matters for several years and during the Spring of 1963, in connection with anti-Castro activity, he was in contact with the National States Rights Party in Los Angeles, California. In connection with this, he contacted Dr. Stanley L. Drennan (of North Hollywood, a Party activist). Brown stated that once while a guest in Dr. Drennan's home, Drennan stated in general conversation that he could not do it, but what the organization needed was a group of young men to get rid of Kennedy, the Cabinet and all members of Americans for Democratic Action and maybe 10,000 other people. Brown stated that he considered the remark as being 'crackpot'; however, as Drennan continued the conversation, he gained the impression that Drennan may have been propositioning him on this matter." Currently, Colonel Brown is publisher of *Soldier of Fortune*, a quarterly review of mercenaries' activities and opportunities.

2   /   INDUSTRIAL INTRIGUES

But where else might a retiring spook go, assuming that he's unable to start his own private security firm, declines to join someone else's, or is unable or unwilling to find employment with a lawyer, a millionaire, a politician, a multinational, or somebody's private "red squad"? The answer is that he can free-lance as an industrial espionage agent—a "blackhat"—at home or abroad. By any account, it's a booming trade with a multitude of specialties. Three of the most important areas, however, have to do with:

1) Trade secrets and "proprietary information" (including inventions, special processes, marketing information, surveys, analyses, and financial data). Every industry has them and almost every competitor wants them. It may be thought that trade secrets of value are protected by patents, but, in fact, this is far from the truth. Often, trade secrets aren't patentable, and proprietary information never is. Even if a new process *can* be patented, corporations often prefer to conceal the invented method rather than submit it to the scrutiny of government officials. Not only is obtaining a patent difficult, costly, and time-consuming, but the enforcement process tends to be lax, depending upon the patent owner's surveillance of the industry and his willingness to sue for infringements. And if the patent applied for should be denied, the exclusive use of the invention is lost forever. Frequently, therefore, corporations will utilize their inventions without making a patent application, relying instead upon plant security, "compartmentalization," business counterintelligence, and the loyalty of top executives to preserve secrecy. As a result, the invented products and processes are vulnerable to the depredations of industrial spies. Virtually every industry has them, although the chemicals, computer, drug, and electronics fields seem to have been hardest hit. Indeed, they've been hit so hard and so often that despite the billions known to be at stake, thefts of proprietary information and trade secrets hardly ever make the pages of the daily newspapers. To learn about them, it becomes necessary to read such obscure trade publications as *Oil, Paint, and Drug Reporter, Chemical Week, Datamation*, and *Electronic News*. In those journals and others like them industrial espionage is a running story of profound importance to the industries involved. Peruse the headlines: "Bush's Plea: Guilty" *(attempt to sell ethylene-propylene rubber secrets);

* *Chemical Week*, 98 (April 9, 1966), p. 20.

"Du Pont Plant Snooper Flushed Out by Court"; * "Furor in Phosphoric" † (Armour & Company accuses former employees now working for Occidental Petroleum of stealing trade secrets); "Stealing Trade Secrets" ‡ (a case involving the Pleasure Products Company and a fingernail hardener); "Tetracycline Piracy: Data Theft Confessed"; § "Deciding Drug Suits" || (the Fox-Lederle case, in which a Dr. Fox is accused of selling stolen vitamin trade secrets to various Italian firms); "Lepetit Denies Purchase of Lederle Antibiotic Data" ¶ (Tetracycline case); "New Aries Whodunnit" ** (involving trade secrets and Amprolium, a poultry drug); "Trail That Led to Spy Charges" †† (a chemist is accused, by Merck & Company, Rome & Haas, and others, of stealing secret information to sell in the United States and Europe); "Vast Conspiracy, Aries Asserts"; ‡‡ "A Bug in the Bowler"; §§ "Steel Company's Telephone Line Tapped"; |||| "Mayfield Pleads Guilty in Theft of Crest Plans"; ¶¶ "Intersil Sued by Raytheon over Raids"; *** "IBM Names Memorex in Secrets Suit." ††† And so on.

Just how one goes about purloining proprietary information and trade secrets is a separate matter. For the most part, however, it involves the same processes that rival intelligence agencies use against one another. For instance, an executive is convinced, by offers of money, promotion, or sex, to "defect" from one firm to another, taking his company's secrets with him. Or, an executive is convinced by cash deposited in Swiss and Bahamian banks to remain with his original firm as an "agent in place," leaking strategic information about marketing and financial matters to his secret employer. Or, those responsible for the installation and servicing of a rival's products are convinced to file periodic reports about the product's weaknesses, customers' satisfaction, other employees, turnover, and so forth. Much can be learned, of course, from the careful monitoring

* *Oil, Paint, and Drug Reporter*, 199 (February 1, 1971), p. 5.
† *Chemical Week*, 96 (March 6, 1965), p. 24.
‡ *Advertising Age*, 35 (March 16, 1964), pp. 89–90.
§ *Oil, Paint, and Drug Reporter*, 186 (July 13, 1964), p. 4.
|| *Chemical Week,* 94 (January 18, 1964), p. 24.
¶ *Oil, Paint, and Drug Reporter*, 186 (July 27, 1964), p. 5.
** *Chemical Week*, 90 (June 2, 1962), pp. 20–21.
†† *Business Week* (November 25, 1961), pp. 28–29.
‡‡ *Chemical Week*, 89 (December 16, 1961), p. 21.
§§ *Observer* (October 20, 1968), p. 14.
|||| *The Times* (London) (August 20, 1969), p. 2.
¶¶ *Advertising Age*, 36 (August 9, 1965), p. 3.
*** *Electronics News*, 14 (February 17, 1969), p. 14.
††† *Electronics News*, 15 (December 7, 1970), p. 37.

and analysis of information published in the public domain, but the most valuable data are often available only to persons "on the inside." One of an industrial spy's most important talents, therefore, is his ability to develop and handle agents employed by the competition.

2) A second important area of industrial espionage is computer penetration. Just how important, though, is impossible to say. As with the theft of trade secrets and proprietary information, detecting penetrations of data-processing facilities is virtually beyond the expertise of police departments. Unless the penetration is carried out for clearly felonious purposes (e.g., sabotaging a competitor's facilities or manipulating financial data and payouts), it's unlikely that the police will be of much use. Moreover, the most threatening sort of computer penetration is the one *least* likely to attract attention: that is, an intrusion designed to obtain information stored in a computer without in any way interfering with either the data themselves or the normal functioning of the installation. Tapping into a computer in this way should leave no traces whatsoever of the intrusion, and the information obtained may well prove to be a bonanza, providing the intruder with a competitor's trade secrets, financial data, and such proprietary information as his plans for design and marketing, mergers and acquisitions, as well as the specifics of his pricing basis, security procedures, and overall strengths and weaknesses.

While it's impossible to obtain any meaningful statistics about computer penetrations, an indirect gauge of their importance can be gleaned from the fact that IBM alone has spent more than forty million dollars on a research project designed to prevent them.* While the results of that project are far too technical to be reported here, security recommendations have generally fallen into four major categories:

Positive unique identification of people, devices, and other named system resources.
Authorization of system activities involving interactions among people, data, programs, devices, and other named system resources.
Surveillance of system activity, including means of achieving strict personal accountability of people for their actions.
System integrity, including means of achieving hardware and software

---

* See *Data Security and Data Processing*, Volumes 1–6, published in 1974 by IBM. Contributing to the volumes, besides IBM's own Federal Systems Division, were TRW Systems, Inc., the Massachusetts Institute of Technology, and the Management Information Division of the State of Illinois.

integrity, physical security, and protection against wiretapping and electronic and acoustic eavesdropping.*

Accomplishing these objectives involves literally hundreds of mechanisms, ranging from the use of codes, passwords, and otherwise unnecessarily complicated "machine-languages" to establishing extraordinary "auditing" methods and a means of having the computer respond to unauthorized requests by issuing a casserole of true, misleading, and blank messages. While some of the suggestions are predictably banal (e.g., put a cop at the door of the computer room), others are more imaginative. Henrik de Kanter, of the international marketing staff at Douglas Aircraft's Missiles and Space Systems Division, predicts one such imaginative development: in order to counter a device that can, by sensing the electrical fields surrounding an operating computer, "read" the computer's content, IBM and Remington Rand UNIVAC, De Kanter believes, have begun hiring "decoy computer programmers" whose sole task is to produce "counterintelligence programs" designed to mislead computer eavesdroppers.†

3) A third area of industrial espionage in which a spook may easily find work has less to do with the theft of information than with the illegal transfer of various commercial products. This is, perhaps, the spookiest area of industrial espionage and one in which former intelligence agents have been most active.

Down a seemingly endless series of corridors near the center of the Commerce Department building in Washington, D.C., is a warren of seedy offices, badly lighted by a mixture of fluorescent and incandescent bulbs. The sign on the door reads "EXPORT CONTROL SYSTEM" (a section of the Department's Bureau of East–West Trade). Inside, twenty-seven people handle as many telephones with that peculiar combination of giddiness and anger appropriate to workers who've been charged with performing an impossible task in a windowless, claustrophobic environment.

Charles B. Clements, director of the Export Control System, explains that its purpose is to process more than twelve thousand export licenses each month while preventing the export of eleven hundred categories of "strategic commodities" to a clutch of countries considered hostile to the United States. Clements attempts to

---

* "Security Risk Assessment in Electronic Data Processing Systems," by Robert H. Courtney (1975), an IBM publication. Courtney's report is a working document produced under the auspices of the National Bureau of Standards.
† Greene, *op. cit.,* p. 224.

do this by running what amounts to an international intelligence service. His office is, as they say, a hot one. (The term "hot office" is used in Washington to designate rooms to which entry is retricted on national-security grounds.)

The trouble is that Clements has neither the funds nor the manpower needed to succeed. Moreover, relations with other government agencies are less than ideal. On my first visit to his office, I found Clements barking to his secretary, "Screw the CIA! Tell 'em to do it themselves! Tell 'em I'm busy! How many people do they think I have? And where were *they* when I needed *them*?"

The real problem, though, is with the ingenuity of the opposition and its relative immunity to sanctions. While the United States proscribes the transfer of a vast number of commodities to a variety of countries, few U. S. trading partners have similar laws. Thus, a "retiring" spook can set himself up in an import-export business (just an office address will do) in a country known to be understanding—Austria, for example. He may then place orders with U. S. firms for strategically rated oscilloscopes, computer consoles, and similar gear, certifying in an "end-user" certificate that the products will be resold for final use to a country or firm that is authorized (by the Commerce Department) to have them. A legitimate deal of this sort can be profitable in itself (if the business is well run), but windfall profits are virtually assured if the export-import agent is able to circumvent the end-user certificate and sell the products on the black market. This he may do by altering the certificate, disguising the real identity of his clients, or simply ignoring the certificate's force. Once that's accomplished, any number of deals are possible.

For instance: following the imposition of an all-out trade embargo by the United States against Cuba (1959), a massive black market came into being in Europe and Latin America. Because Cuba had been virtually a colony of the United States for decades, almost all its industrial plant was stamped with the words "Made in the U.S.A." With limited capital and a desperate need to keep the economy running, Castro had little choice but to rely upon American manufacturers to produce the spare parts required. And yet, because of the embargo, he was unable to buy those parts directly from the people who made them. Obtaining the parts therefore became a matter of using intermediaries. And this itself was not quite so easy as establishing a corporate front in Liechtenstein because Clements, with an assist from the CIA and Cuban exiles, had prepared a list of spare parts needed for (he says) "every American-made machine in Cuba."

These parts were then incorporated by serial number into a Commerce Department "watch list" and their export (and end use) monitored meticulously. To obtain the parts, the Cubans had to rely upon a phalanx of black marketeers who (for an extortionate fee) would violate the end-user certificate, accept the consequences, and go out of business (only to incorporate again under a different name).

Still, Cuba's mechanical needs could never be entirely satisfied by the black market, and the Cuban economy wound down accordingly. Similar prohibitions against other countries (e.g., Rhodesia) have been evaded in much the same way that the Cuban embargo has, and with similar results. In 1973, for instance, three Boeing 720 aircraft were delivered to Salisbury, Rhodesia, in contravention of U. S. and United Nations sanctions against that country. The offending firm, innocuously named Overseas Holidays and Aircraft Hire, Ltd., was identified by Clements' agents and suffered the loss of its U. S. export privileges. In 1974 the same thing happened again, with the Compagnie Gabonaise d'Affrètement Aérien (Affrétair).

Indeed, the evidence is overwhelming that Clements' hot shoppe loses battles daily. The purpose of the Export Control System, however, is strategic rather than tactical. "Of *course*, the Russians can get this stuff," Clements says, with a deliberate pause. "*In small quantities.* It isn't so much a matter of denying the Soviets (or the Cubans or the Rhodesians) a look at secret technology as it is of forcing them to make the goods themselves. In Russia's case, the prohibitions serve to make the Soviets divert rubles and research expertise away from their military effort. Every little bit helps, you know."

Clements realizes that the black marketeers can live with the System. In fact, they couldn't live without it. The biggest threats to their illegal profits are not the efforts of Clements and his spies, but détente and the easing of trade restrictions. Every embargo lifted and every reduction in the list of prohibited commodities represent a constriction of (black) markets for people such as Montreal's Joe Lewo (a/k/a Joseph Levos and Joseph Liebow) and Hong Kong's Hsiu Kuang Li (alias S. K. Kai, I. K. Lai, and Shu Ko Rei).

The System's battles, then, are fought with individuals and trading firms, but the real targets of the war are the military capabilities and economies of countries toward which the United States is hostile. Partly because of this, and because the trading firms are usually beyond the reach of U. S. enforcement agencies, the penalties for violating provisions of the Export Control System are minimal. In some cases a black marketeer is apprehended by customs officials (as happened to Antoine George Saab when he sought to smuggle a strategically rated oscilloscope out of the United States to Beirut). More typically, the smuggler is exposed by means of an anonymous tip from a business rival or a bounty hunter (Clements is authorized to pay a "moiety in law," usually a percentage of the prohibited commodity's value, to anyone providing such information). What happens then can border on farce. After notifying the accused that he's violated the Export Administration Act, Commerce officials may bring criminal charges that provide for a maximum of one year in jail and/or a ten-thousand-dollar fine for each offense. This course, however, is almost never pursued. Instead, the black marketeer is subjected to an administrative proceeding held behind closed doors in the Commerce Department. In these Star Chamber proceedings, ordinary rules of evidence don't apply: "classified" materials may be submitted into evidence but withheld from the defense, the accused is virtually without benefit of ordinary due process of law, and the hearing record is sealed in perpetuity from public view. Few defendants complain, however, since the penalties—revocation of export privileges—are of little import to those whose business is black. And if those privileges are revoked, the impact needn't be all bad. The offender can simply do business under another name unknown to the Commerce Department (or Customs Bureau or CIA). Or, more typically, he can operate through front men in a shell corporation that's been newly established for his purposes in a country such as Panama, Liechtenstein, or Switzerland, where corporate ownership is easily disguised by limp disclosure laws.

The fact of the matter is that few countries recognize the Export Administration law, and violating it is therefore not considered a crime outside the United States—just good business. Moreover, as Clements points out, the "Table of Denial and Probation Orders Currently in Effect" (like the list of commodities proscribed for certain countries),* "is nothing less than an up-to-date shopping list for those in the black market. For some of these guys," Clements adds, "getting listed is like having a free advertisement. If someone wants something he's not supposed to have, all he's got to do is check the 'Table' for our most serious offenders, and before you know it he's got an agent who can get him almost anything."

And there are hundreds of such agents, from Argentina to Zaire.

---

* For those who want to find out what's marketable in black, who needs it, and who can probably get it, the Commerce Department sells subscriptions to its Export Administration Bulletins ($35 in the United States, $43.75 abroad).

In New York City alone, there are more than twenty individuals and firms subject to denial and probation orders. New York, however, is one of the worst places to conduct illegal transfers, if only because it's within the jurisdiction of U. S. law. While some fly-by-night U. S. firms have knowingly carried out illegal transshipments abroad, a far safer procedure is for a foreign-based firm to assume all responsibility for violating the end-user certificate: that way everyone gets paid, and only American foreign policy is damaged. In Zurich, for instance, the number of firms against which sanctions have been issued is twenty-three, though Zurich is much smaller than New York; in Paris, the number is twenty-nine; in Hong Kong, twenty-four; and in Vaduz, Liechtenstein's tiny capital, there are nineteen. In London and Vienna, though, which have seventy and sixty orders outstanding against "local" businessmen, illegal transfers approach the status of an industry.* According to Clements, London is "the Number One stopping-off point" for illegal transshipments of American products to Cuba, whereas in Vienna the traffic goes the other way —to the Soviet bloc countries of Eastern Europe.

And, while Clements says that used-computer vendors are probably the worst (and most consistent) offenders, the traffic can include almost anything . . . including a double cross. In Germany, for instance, a former Lockheed employee and onetime U. S. intelligence agent secured four surplus airplane wings for illegal shipment to Israel. After coping imaginatively with the problem of secretly transporting the giant appendages out of Germany, the spook received payment in full from the Israelis. Rather than reimburse those from whom he'd bought the wings, however, he took the cash to the German government and turned it over to them, with his apologies. All that was missing (besides the wings) was the smuggler's "commission," which he'd earlier subtracted from the Israeli payment. It was not a deal that he could repeat—at least, not with the same sources—but he'd managed the profitable trick of having his cake and eating it too. As we'll see in pages devoted to the Lockheed and Northrop affairs, that gastronomical feat is far from uncommon.

More recently, and more mysteriously, a well-organized ring of industrial spies and crooked ex-im agents set out to break the (data) bank at IBM. Operating in Frankfurt am Main (another hot spot for illegal transfers, with sixteen firms on Clements' black list), the pri-

---

* All figures are taken from "Denial and Probation Orders Currently Affecting Export Privileges," a reprint of Supplement Nos. 1 & 2 to Part 388 of the Export Administration Regulations (June 1, 1975), U. S. Department of Commerce.

vate spooks had been under suspicion for years without ever making a mistake. Then, in 1974, they made an outrageous offer to a small mail-order house. In return for camera-ready layout plans of an IBM 370 computer, the group would pay DM 25,000 (about $8,000)—*ten times the going rate* for the plans. Alerted to the extraordinary offer, U. S. and West German agents placed the group under round-the-clock surveillance. Then, on a freezing night three days before Christmas, police burst into the offices of a small commercial firm in Frankfurt. There they found two of the men bent over IBM 370 maintenance manuals; while one man turned the pages at a pace some spooks would recognize instantly, the other methodically clicked away with a Minox camera. Ordered at pistol point to drop the camera and empty their pockets, one of the spies withdrew fistfuls of German currency from his suit—more than $35,000 in all. Taken to the police station for intensive questioning, the men implicated eleven others in their ring, including an IBM maintenance-man and several contact agents for the KGB. Moreover, the agents admitted spending more than DM 1,000,000 on the operation—a fabulous sum for an industrial espionage effort.

And yet none of it made much sense. The plans they'd bought were *commercially* available at a fraction of the amount they'd paid. What's more, the group, or their employers, could have *rented* one of the computers for about half the amount which the spies eventually spent.* In any case, an IBM 370 computer was already in operation in Hungary and was therefore certainly available to the KGB. Moreover, the IBM 370 series varies from one installation to another, such that if a spy wanted to assemble a schematic dossier on the series as a whole, he would have to examine the manuals for many different installations rather than a single one.

What, then, was the group up to? The only possibilities seem to be that the ring sought to acquire an understanding of an IBM innovation common to every computer in the series—or else that the ring wanted information contained in the computers themselves. In regard to the latter possibility, there were reports from unidentified sources that the spies had smuggled "magnetic tape discs" to the USSR. Yet that would be a crude means of obtaining secret information since the thefts would almost certainly be noted immediately and the information rendered valueless. Far more likely is the possibility that the group was looking for something common to all the computers in the series. In this category there are two candidates.

---

* In Germany the IBM 370 series rents for about $200,000 per month.

The first is an IBM 370 feature, newly invented, which is responsible for carrying out security and monitoring functions. That invention is one which allows the computer, while engaged in its normal operations, to "diagnose" itself and determine the origin of all errors and disturbances. Disturbances might include unauthorized entries to the computer as well as environmental anomalies (sophisticated computers require "clean rooms," with constant temperatures and other invariables, for their proper operation; this is, in fact, the area in which the Soviet Union lags furthest behind the United States in data processing—for some reason, the USSR has been unable to construct computer environments sufficiently "clean" to allow the most sophisticated computers to function properly). If this security feature could be analyzed and "engineered backward," a means of overriding it might be found. And this, of course, would be more valuable than any other single piece of information, since it would provide the USSR with secret access to all the data contained in IBM computers everywhere.

There is a second possibility, though, and it may relate to the first. As mentioned earlier, NSA and CIA scientists have developed a novel means of bugging computers: by monitoring the noise computers make while operating, the spooks are able to "read" the machine's contents. Mechanisms for thwarting such penetrations include counterprogrammers' feeding false programs into the machine and/or constructing a series of architectural baffles around the computer in such a way that its noise can't be monitored from the outside. The problem with counterintelligence programs, though, is that those who use the computer must be able to distinguish between real and phony data, and must therefore have one kind or the other coded for identification. And that, of course, leaves open the possibility that the code may someday be compromised and the computer invaded with impunity. While it's much more expensive, the more prudent course is to invest in low-noise computers and elaborate architectural baffles (this is the course that governments usually take when it comes to protecting the "integrity" of data-processing installations belonging to the military and intelligence agencies). The difficulty here—and this may be what the German spies were working on—is that computers are still subject to penetration. Even if the workers at the installation are completely loyal, or are otherwise prevented from compromising security, and even if the most extravagant architectural precautions are taken, *the computer itself may be a spy*. IBM has a virtual monopoly on advanced data-processing equipment, a monopoly that's worldwide. And as Tom Mechling, former executive assistant to IBM chief Tom Watson, commented, "IBM considers itself an extension of the U. S. government—and it is." An internal mechanism capable of monitoring all functioning aspects of an IBM 370 computer might also be able to transmit, *from within the computer*, all information flowing through it. It seems quite possible that the German ring was engaged in a *counter*intelligence effort on behalf of the KGB, seeking to identify the mechanism responsible for data-processing leaks behind the Iron Curtain.

The eventual fate of the spy ring tends to corroborate this hypothesis. While its members were mostly independents, the involvement of KGB agents makes it clear that this was not a routine case of industrial espionage. So do the large sums of money involved and—most importantly of all—the fact that, after the group was caught in the act, successfully interrogated, and held for months, all thirteen members were released from jail and charges against them were dropped. Why? There was no explanation forthcoming from IBM, the police, the prosecutors, or anyone else. The group was simply let go. In view of the *prima facie* evidence against the ring's members, it can only be concluded that the authorities feared the publicity and information that might emerge during a trial. Perhaps U. S. and West German officials learned that the ring had breached the security of NATO computer installations—and worried about the effect *this* would have on the public's confidence. It is at least as likely, however, that IBM, brainstem of the military-industrial complex, was suspected by the KGB of having bugged the computers it manufactures for sale to governments abroad—and that a trial of the spy ring would expose this possibility to the press and IBM's competitors. In acquiescing to the release of the spooks, IBM proved it had reason to fear an open trial. Preventing that trial might leave the USSR with its suspicions in place. But it would also leave the hypothetical bugs in place in IBM computers operating worldwide.

And from the German ring's experience a retiring spook contemplating industrial espionage as a new trade can learn an important lesson: if the information sought is sufficiently consequential, getting caught may have no consequences at all.

3 / THE MERCS

WANTED: Employment as Mercenary on Full-Time or Job Contract basis. Preferably in South or Central America, but anywhere in the world, if you pay transportation. Contact Gearhart, Box 1457, Wheaton, MD 20902.

FORMER GREEN BERET, offers extensive military experience to interested parties. S.F.F., Box 1408, Brownsville, TX 78520.

Young Greek National seeks employment as mercenary on full-time or job contract basis. Write SVSV, P.O. Box 564, Athens, Greece.

Former Airborne, Ranger, Special Forces, RA Officer seeks military employment anywhere; all offers considered. Write KJG, 3470 Ever-green Road, Pittsburgh, PA 15237, or call collect: (412) 364-6228.*

The ads have an edge of pathos to them. One can imagine the intensity with which Gearheart, living in Wheaton, a sun-bleached bedroom community moored to a constellation of seedy shopping centers, yearns to fight abroad.† And KJG advertises a similar des-peration when he urges interested parties to call him collect, leaving himself and his bank account open to every crank with access to a newsstand.

Mercenaries are not, of course, secret agents—only their tools. And while secret agents tend to enter private practice after years of work-ing in the federal intelligence community, mercenaries may come from anywhere, even Wheaton. Every affluent society has its pools of would-be and incipient mercs. Refugee groups (e.g., the Cubans and, more recently, the South Vietnamese) are rife with unemployed sol-diers looking for work—any work. Demobilized GI's (Viet vets here, ex-Legionnaires in France), itinerant thugs, failing college students, unhappy husbands, and romantics of every description fill the mer-cenaries' ranks to overflowing. Because governments monopolize war to the best of their abilities, and because coups are almost always carried out by ideologues on the Left or militarists on the Right (neither of whom have much use or need for mercenaries), it's in-evitable that there are a thousand mercs waiting in line for every job that comes along. Inevitable, too, that the mercenary's days are steeped more in beer and braggadocio than blood and guts.

This isn't to say that there aren't any jobs for America's soldiers of fortune. Occasionally, someone with great wealth and a profound sense of personal immunity will organize a paramilitary operation requiring the use of mercs. Take Mitch WerBell's friend David Sterling as an instance. A political extremist and British war hero, Sterling is the founder of England's deadly commando elite, the

---

* All ads are taken from *Soldier of Fortune*, Vol. 1, No. 2.
† Since this was written, Gearhart has been executed by a firing squad in Angola.

Special Air Services. Retiring behind the smoked glass of a Rolls-Royce Silver Shadow after a shopping spree at Harrods in London, Colonel Sterling has an aristocratic air that seems at odds with his propensity for bloody intrigues. In the late 1960s, however, he undertook to overthrow the government of Libya in behalf of a deposed sheik then resident in a Swiss castle. For his expertise Sterling stood to earn millions of pounds should the operation succeed. In its simplest outlines, the plot had Sterling make contact with a motley crew of right-wing European mercs who'd be paid to storm the beaches of Tripoli. Wading ashore from rubber rafts, the mercenaries were to proceed with their assault rifles to a Tripoli prison sarcastically code-named "the Hilton." Bursting through its gates, the mercs would blast their way past the guards, freeing the country's most dangerous "political prisoners." The escapees would then serve as the inner cadre of urban guerrilla units assigned to depose the country's ruler, Muammar Qaddafi. The mercs would fight their way back to the waiting mother ship, where the second half of their contracts would be paid. The entire operation was to begin at dawn and end by noon, earning Sterling roughly $200,000 an hour. With all the preparations made, the mercs engaged, and the mother ship ready to set sail with its cargo of free-lance commandos, rafts, and machine-pistols, British and American intelligence services intervened, warning Sterling not to proceed. On good terms with both services, Sterling reluctantly scratched the operation at the last minute.

In yet another, even more bizarre, instance, four moonlighting Dade County deputy sheriffs attempted single-handedly to topple the government of Haiti in 1960. Shooting their way into the Palace in Port au Prince, the deputies successfully took control of one wing and most of the Palace's exits. Unfortunately, they were unable to grab Papa Doc (who'd barricaded himself in another wing) and could do no more than hold the fort, tour the torture chambers, and pray that the dictator would die of a heart attack. Outside, battalions of Haitian soldiers and Ton-Ton Macoutes massed behind flame trees and tanks, waiting to learn the fate of their leader. The stalemate might still be going on had not the deputies dispatched a servant from the Palace to buy cigarettes. On his way back the youth was questioned by a group of frightened generals who wanted to know how many companies were holding the Palace. Told that there were only four guys from Miami, the generals rallied their forces to the sticking point, stormed the Palace, and retook it. The

fate of the deputies has never been learned, though they've achieved
a kind of immortality at the State Department: whenever officials
gather to discuss options for resolving conflicts with intransigent
dictators, someone invariably jokes that "it may be time to call out
the Dade County sheriff's department deputies."

The brave and foolhardly, whatever their cynical veneer, have
always been in redundant supply. Desperate for "action," they're
easily exploited. That's why Colonel Robert K. Brown, a free-lance
paramilitary instructor living in Colorado, indulges his colleagues'
well-deserved self-pity by referring to them in private as "soldiers
of *mis*fortune." It's not so much the havoc that mercenaries wreak
on civilian populations that makes the phrase so apt, but rather
their own pathetic circumstances. While Colonel Sterling might receive a million pounds or more (plus expenses) for organizing a
private invasion, those who carry the guns, do the fighting, and get
killed will be lucky if they're paid $1,500 per month. In good times
Sterling and WerBell move from mansion to manor house in automobiles that cost more than most people's houses. Yet those who
carry out their plots are usually mired in the sleaziest of circumstances, living in rooming houses or relying upon the always "temporary" hospitality of friends. A few months before the Bay of Pigs
invasion, for instance, the operation was nearly blown when Miami
police ordered the "evacuation" of a rooming house on West Flagler
Street. At the time of the raid, the house was serving as a barracks
for soldiers of fortune in the pay of Rolando Masferrer.* According
to police, the invaders were rousted because they'd become notorious in the neighborhood for shoplifting and other acts of petty
thievery.

It wasn't kleptomania that drove some of the mercs to boost jars
of peanut butter from the Seven/Eleven, but simple necessity. For
the most part, life on West Flagler Street consisted of all-night
arm-wrestling contests and bloodcurdling fictions narrated to the
sound of beer cans popping like small-arms fire. The mercs' support
depended less upon Rolando Masferrer, for whose standard they
seemed prepared to die, than it did upon promises and dreams—
promises of the rich loot to be taken from Havana's dimmed casinos

---

* Mentioned earlier in connection with WerBell and the CBS Invasion, Masferrer
was a Cuban exile leader who'd earlier functioned as an executioner for Batista. An
unregenerate plotter, he was reputed to be an intellectual, a self-proclaimed socialist,
and a great admirer of French existentialist Albert Camus. In 1975, Masferrer was
assassinated by a car bomb in Miami. His murder has yet to be solved.

and dreams of paramilitary glory. The same sensibility prevails today in the "Jobs Wanted" columns of *Soldier of Fortune*. And at El Kamas Enterprises, one of many firms hiring mercenaries for work in Africa and the Mideast during 1975, recruiters were virtually swamped with applications from teen-age toughs, aging jarheads, unemployed blacks, dreamers, and ex-commandos of every skill and psychopathology known to war. In complete contradiction to the hard-nosed image that he'd like to project, the American mercenary's obsession with money is no more than the usual preoccupation of the chronically unemployed—plus a means of rationalizing a deeper romanticism of which he's ashamed. Far more important than money to the would-be soldier of fortune is the prospect of action, the quick fix afforded by the prospect of combat in a tropical land—preferably combat providing the opportunity to subdue members of a despised race.

"Dollars are," as a gambler said, "only markers. You can't play without 'em, but . . . they aren't *the thing*, the thing itself."

Admittedly, there are exceptions to the rule but, even at the top, money is almost always secondary. Mike Hoare, "Black Jack" Schramme, and Rolf Steiner, for instance, seem to have been guided in their African Adventures by political ambitions that teetered between the Napoleonic and the merely larcenous—depending on how the war was going. Others, such as the Swedish Count von Rosen, the American Hank Wharton, and Alastair Wicks, an Englishman, flew planes for the secessionist Biafrans partly because they needed the money, and largely because they liked flying dangerously in the Ibos' lost cause.* Still others, such as "Les Affreux" leader Robert Denard, a Frenchman, and Kostas Georghiu, a Greek, appear to have been motivated by nothing less than necrophilia. Certainly, Georghiu killed for the fun of it, executing other mercenaries for a variety of misdemeanors and sending his men plunging suicidally through their own minefields in loony "surprise attacks" upon the Angolan enemy.

Ed Arthur's experience may be the most typical, though his credentials are more impressive than most. A soldier of fortune and dedicated anti-Communist, Arthur has seen combat in more countries than most people ever visit; indeed, most of his adult life has

---

* The different motivations of mercenaries are incisively discussed in Mohamed Omer Beshir's *The Mercenaries and Africa*, Khartoum University Press (Democratic Republic of the Sudan), 1972.

been spent in a context of killing—either as an instructor of commando elites at the Fort Carson, Colorado, Recondo * School or as a principal in paramilitary incursions. And often Arthur's assignments have been accepted on spec, or for nothing more than hotel expenses. A big man who looks like Conway Twitty and talks with a southern-fried, life-or-death clarity ("That's affirmative, Hougan; call me back on toooo, zay-ro, sex, nanner, nanner, fo-wah, nanner"), Arthur smuggled guns cross-country for the Cubans' "Commandos L," receiving little more than pocket money. Nor did he get rich sailing into Havana's harbor with a boatload of Cuban exiles determined to sink the Russian freighter *Uluf* (they came close).

Living quietly today in the small town of Cardington, Ohio, convinced that both the CIA and the Mafia "would like to see me buried," Arthur sums up his career as a soldier of fortune: "The last thirteen years of my life," he told me, "have been a trash bin, that's all. Just a damn trash bin." The same could be said for many other mercenaries, though not, as we'll see, for all.

---

* "Recondo" is a portmanteau word combining *recon*naissance and comman*do*, specifying the kinds of training given to Rangers, Green Berets, SEAL's, and other paramilitary elites.

"IS THAT YOU, BOINIE?"

1 / TONGUE TWISTER

THERE WERE YET A FEW MINUTES BEFORE WERBELL, ST. GEORGE, AND I had to depart for the airport, and the conversation was loosening up.

"I never did understand what the hell a goddamn pacifist was doing with a lotta dough in MAC." WerBell shook his head. "Probably," he said, thinking about it, "probably he didn't even know it."

"Of course he knew it," I said.

"Nah. Those guys"—WerBell made a sweeping gesture with his hand, rocking a bottle of Budweiser—"those guys got a whole platoon of counselors who invest all their dough for them. All they have to do is clip coupons. Mott wouldn't know if his money was in AT&T or Mexican whorehouses. It's all the same."

Contradicting WerBell is like yelling at a wave, but I tried it anyway. "He knew all about it, Mitch. Mott keeps track of his investments; he's not just a coupon clipper."

"Yeah?"

"Yeah. I asked him about it."

"And what'd he say?"

"He admitted it."

WerBell grunted.

"He said he remembered the investment in MAC because it seemed ironic to him at the time."

"What was *ironic* about it? It was a damn good gun. It should have made a mint."

"The irony was that he gave the go-ahead while he was on a 'peace mission'—that's what he called it—a peace mission in Moscow."

"*Mahhh*-scow!" The word was bellowed, and heads turned.

"Yeah. That's how he remembered it."

WerBell thought about it while he finished his beer. "That still doesn't explain a damn pacifist's—"

"I asked him about that."

"What'd he say?"

"He said he invested in MAC because he thought your silencer could be adapted and that it would be perfect for, uh, snowmobiles. And lawn mowers."

WerBell didn't blink. "He said that?"

"Yeah."

"He wanted to put my suppressor on *snowmobiles and lawn mowers!*" The waitress cast a cold glance toward us as WerBell's voice rose. It occurred to me that others in the bar, rocked by snippets of WerBell's conversation, probably thought we were engaged in a weird variety of international trade negotiations. Lawn mowers for Moscow, or something. "That's the stupidest thing I've ever heard," WerBell said.

"The reason I brought it up was, I wanted to ask if you ever tried to adapt the silencer for other uses."

"Yeah. I once adapted some poor sonofabitch over the head with one. Adapted the hell out of it."

"I mean, for lawn mowers, snowmobiles, that sort of thing."

"That question is so dumb, I'm not even going to dignify it with an answer. *Of course, we didn't!* Stupidest thing I ever heard. How you gonna adapt a helical suppressor for a forty-five-caliber submachine gun to work on a goddamn grass cutter? We didn't have time to fart around like that!"

Andrew returned, smiling, from his *n*th phone call. "We'd better go or we'll miss the last flight."

To my amazement, WerBell stood and dropped a twenty on the table. "Keep the change, honey. I won't need it where I'm going."

For the first time the waitress smiled. "Come back soon," she said.

"Hear me now?" WerBell nodded and reached for her fanny.

Outside, Andrew and I had WerBell flanked as we walked down to the parking lot. There was still some grumbling about the "*federales* running me out of town," about WerBell's desire to remain with his girl friend, but it was clear that he was ready to go home. At the car, however, WerBell balked.

"What the hell is *this*?" he asked.

"My car. It's a Volkswagen."

"I know it's a Volkswagen. What'd it have, an accident?"

"No. They all look like this, after a while."

"Get in, Mitch," said Andrew. "We'll miss the plane."

He got in, pulled the door shut, locked it, and fumbled with the seat belt. The car started with a pop, and we began rolling out of the lot toward I-95. After a few minutes he said, "I drive a Porsche."

I was not certain what this had to do with anything, so I just kept driving. Andrew, however, was still hostile, and with WerBell strapped into the front seat of a speeding car, there was no need for him to be polite, not until we reached the airport. "Shut up, Mitch," he said wearily. "You're drunk. You don't make any sense."

WerBell began to hum bars from "Get Me to the Church on Time," finally breaking into song: "Ding dong the bells're gonna chime . . . just get me to the plane on time!" Andrew withdrew deeper into his suit as WerBell chuckled. "I make perfect sense," the man from Georgia said. "Listen to this: rubber baby buggy bumpers. Rubber baby buggy bumpers. RUBBERBABYBUGGY-BUMPERS! Can you say that? *Can* you?" Andrew kept his silence, so WerBell turned the question to me with a look.

"I don't think so," I said.

"Course you can't. No one can." Slowly the smile faded from his face and he turned to look out the window at the Maryland darkness rolling by, his body slumping in its seat. "Rugger baggy boos," sighed The Wizard of Whispering Death.

2 / THE "HIT PARADE": NUMBER ONE WITH A BULLET

Nineteen seventy-four began auspiciously for Mitch WerBell. Ousted two years earlier as head of the Military Armaments Corporation, he was surviving splendidly as chief of a new firm, Defense Services, Inc. Operated from offices on The Farm, DSI was blessed with limited overhead, little capital debt, and a whacking inventory of silenced submachine guns given to WerBell in exchange for his interest in the Quantum Corporation. Selling the guns in competition with his former firm was a lucrative business, with American "collectors" * and Third World intelligence services providing fairly regular custom. But arms dealing was far from WerBell's only interest at the time. Paramilitary advice was one of the "services" offered by DSI, and the firm had acquired a most interesting client. Michael Oliver, a displaced Lithuanian with a "Vere-are-you-papuhs?" accent and right-wing ideology to match, was a Nevada resident with a dream—and the money to make it come true. What Oliver wanted was nothing less than his own country, a land governed according to libertarian principles. Money would be minted privately and backed by gold, with a contract government performing only the most minimal services (e.g., countersubversion and janitorial tasks). There would be no taxes, the schools would be private, and the State would be subject to dismissal at any time that its client-citizens wished. Oliver had tried it before, and failed. In 1972, while WerBell was arguing with Scott Reeves and other Quantum investors, Oliver had formed the Ocean Life Research Foundation with the intention of building a new country. The site of choice was the Minerva Reef, a barely submerged coral rock on the South Fiji Ridge. Two hundred and sixty miles east of Tonga, the reef was an unclaimed boil in the path of the baleen whales' annual migration. Sharks surrounded it, and flying fish flung themselves across its length and breadth. Located in the navel of the earth's most tremulous seismic belt, the reef was a serrated crust that might disappear at any moment. In the making for millennia, its only significance was as a menace to navigation: a decade earlier, sixteen Tongan fishermen had foundered on its rocks and remained there, knee-deep in ocean waters, for a hundred days, awaiting rescue.

To Oliver and a consortium of wealthy libertarians the reef was

---

* That silenced Ingram submachine guns (or, for that matter, cannons) should be available on the retail market to ordinary citizens may come as a surprise to most Americans. As it happens, though, "gun collectors" may acquire such weapons upon approval by the Treasury Department's Bureau of Alcohol, Tobacco, and Firearms (ATF). The process entails application to ATF and submission to a rather cursory investigation designed to learn if the collector is a revolutionary, a drunk, a felon, a drug addict, or a maniac. If the applicant is none of these, he'll usually be given approval to buy his weapon of choice, though a two-hundred-dollar tax will be imposed upon the sale of both the silencer and the submachine gun. Other countries are even less strict: in England, for instance, the Parker-Hale Corporation advertises silencers for sale to hunters who wish to minimize "disturbance to game."

a thing of beauty, the future "Republic of Minerva." Using the foundation as their conduit, the group poured hundreds of thousands of dollars into an effort to create a four-hundred-acre island on the reef's highest points. While doing so, they sent a written declaration to the world's governments, declaring sovereignty for their oceanic landfill. Immediately, Tonga's 325-pound patriarch, King Taufa'ahau, leaped into action. Promising unconditional amnesty to the inmates of Tonga's jail, Taufa'ahau ordered his Polynesian miscreants to invade the new domain, evict the libertarians, and plant the flag of Tonga in the coral.

Oliver was embittered by the loss, but there was nothing he could do about it. That the Republic of Minerva had been a country without land was an obstacle he'd been prepared to overcome. But a nation without an army, confronted by scores of flag-waving Tongan felons armed with spears, stood no chance. Accordingly, the consortium abandoned the motherland, returning to an enforced exile in Orange County, California.

Dreams die hard, though, and Oliver was not about to give up. In 1968 he'd published a right-wing *cri de coeur* entitled *A New Constitution for a New Country*. Written at the zenith of antiwar demonstrations, when Dow Chemical was turning out napalm by the ton and the Dow Jones was screaming like a teakettle on boil, Oliver's tract was riddled with angst. Anticipating the imminent financial collapse of the West, with resultant bloodshed and the emergence of iron rule in America, Oliver urged his readers to emigrate without ever telling them where. The closest he came to doing so was to write that "One has but to look at the western hemisphere to find that places for establishing a new, fair-sized country still exist."

Infatuated with the goldbug theories of crank economist Ludwig von Mises and with the stern "positivism" of Ayn Rand, Oliver fixed upon the Bahamas' Abaco as the site for his future utopia. Having learned his lesson on the Minerva Reef, the libertarian resolved that revolution rather than landfill was the best means to a new republic. Abaco seemed the logical choice. The Bahamas had gained their independence from Britain in 1973, and conditions there were less than wholly stable. Abaco itself was dominated by the pay-for-play resorts of Nassau and Freeport, and a compulsory languor prevailed over the island. A real estate chunk of 300,000 acres, formerly crown lands, became the property of the Bahamian government (but not of the Abaconians) and was left fallow by decree. With only six thousand residents on the island, that added up to fifty acres per person—a sequestered birthright of enormous potential. Deprived, then, of their heritage by the minions of Nassau and Freeport, Abaconians languished in the midst of under-development that seemed to have been imposed from above. To Oliver, rebellion and secession constituted the logical answer. An independent Abaco, organized in conformity with the libertarian principles enunciated in his book, might become a tropical Zurich, attracting flight capital from throughout the hemisphere. Casino gambling, resorts, schools, sewers, roads, and housing developments for wealthy American emigrants would come as well, enriching both the natives and investors alike. Oliver's tract would become the new country's constitution, and he would himself begin minting money in a denomination called the rand. In gold pieces named for the novelist, the rand would be the world's hardest currency.

The problem, of course, was to convince the rather relaxed Aba-conians that they should throw off the yoke of their "collectivist masters"—a probably bloody task—and embrace the disciples of Von Mises and Ayn Rand. Accordingly, Oliver retained WerBell's para-military counsel and an operation was begun.

Seemingly overnight, a supposedly native claque called the Abaco Independence Movement (AIM) was formed. And immediately the island appeared to be a hotbed of revolutionary sentiment. Bumper stickers hostile to the regime of Premier Lynden Pindling were affixed to the island's few cars, pro-independence leaflets began to circulate, and clandestine radio broadcasts were beamed from Flor-ida to the Bahamas, touting an Abaconian republic. Most incongru-ously, given the prevailing illiteracy of the island's natives, hundreds of smuggled copies of Ayn Rand's treatise *For the New Intellectual* were passed out to any Abaconian who said he could read. Mean-while, WerBell dispatched former CIA officer Walt Mackem to an undercover assignment on the island: his job was to gather intelli-gence while posing as a tourist, serve as island contact for the "New Country Project," and gauge the natives' changing attitudes toward independence. In Britain, WerBell made contact with Colonel Colin ("Mad Mitch") Mitchell, a Scottish commando who was also a Mem-ber of Parliament and an authority on sapper attacks. It was Mad Mitch's job, and the task of the suave Robert Hamilton, Baron of Belhaven and Stenton, to wrest a promise from the House of Lords that England would not intervene in Abaco's impending secession. Already, the *appearance* of Abaconian discontent had been created, and with England persuaded to remain neutral—Lord Belhaven succeeded beautifully in finessing that vow from his aristocratic brethren—few obstacles to utopia remained. Pindling's pathetic gendarmerie would be no match for WerBell's platoons of mercenaries and killer-Dixie thugs (especially if they should be armed with Ingrams). In meetings at Duke Ziebert's restaurant, the Class Reunion bar, and WerBell's ninety-five-dollar-a-day suite at Washington's Hay-Adams Hotel, CIA veterans, free-lance spooks, and libertarian idealists agreed upon a New Year's revolution to begin January 1, 1975.

It would never happen. Between the spring of 1974 and the D-Day planned for the Bahamas, WerBell would become enmeshed in a nest of apparently related intrigues whose exposure would bring the wrath of the Senate and the CIA down upon him. Subpoenaed to testify about his meetings with Robert Vesco in Costa Rica (of which more later) and his plans to sell two thousand silenced Ingrams to Vesco, Mitchell Livingston WerBell III would demur before the Congress, remarking to St. George, "From now on, call me Mitch *the Fifth*." It was not that WerBell didn't want to talk; he simply couldn't. On the very day in which the Senate issued its subpoena, his son (Mitch IV), a business associate, and Defense Services, Inc., were named in a hasty indictment by the Treasury Department. Alleging a conspiracy to make an illegal transfer of two thousand submachine guns to an ATF undercover agent at the Travellodge Motel near Powder Springs, the indictment was the product of a noninvestigation that yielded virtually no evidence. It was due to be laughed out of court, but it served its purpose nevertheless. *Sub judice*, WerBell could not be made to talk, even if he wanted to (which he did). As WerBell did, Senate staffers believed the indictment to be a hastily contrived frame designed to obscure the affairs of Robert Vesco and the Drug Enforcement Administration (DEA). Those were the targets of the Senate probe, and the subjects of WerBell's never-to-be-given testimony. Coming as it did only three months before the "liberation" of Abaco, the indictment and Senate subpoena effectively put the invasion on the back burner. WerBell was just too hot. Besides the New Country Project, the Georgian appeared to be dabbling in DEA "wet jobs," * and the Senate had learned of that as well.

In early 1974, when the Abaco scheme was getting under way, WerBell received an electronics catalog in the mail. It was sent to him by Washington attorney Mike Morrisscy, whose firm, the

---

* A "wet job" is slang for intelligence work involving bloodshed or assassination.

B. R. Fox Company, shared an office with WerBell's Central Investigative Agency. Accompanying the catalog was a note that read:

> Mitch—enclosed is a catalog which was put together only after we started working together with Lou Conein. I wrote out this line of "ASTRO" equipment with you and Lou in mind, and because of the nature of the devices, it is not being given to anyone else. . . . Some of this equipment was demonstrated to Lou in this office about 3 weeks ago. . . . It is a listing of equipment that is available and planned for Lou up here.
>
> Mike

As we'll see, Mike Morrissey was at that time the business partner of Barbara Fox Spindel, founder and co-owner of the B. R. Fox Company. The catalog to which his note referred would soon generate a Senate investigation, devastate what might have been the DEA's most important intelligence operation, and implicate Wer-Bell in what many—including Barbara Fox Spindel and a number of DEA officials—believe to have been the establishment of a new "Murder, Inc." To understand those events, and the terrible ironies they embodied, it's important to know the origins of the B. R. Fox Company and, in particular, the identity of the widow Spindel's deceased husband.

Bernard R. Spindel is a legend within the spooks' milieu, a wireman of unequaled genius. He was, by all accounts, the Nikola Tesla of electronic eavesdropping, an inventor whose seemingly magical breadboards and conceptual leaps revolutionized the state of the art —time and again. Had Spindel devoted his talents to more banal technologies, it's likely that he'd be alive and prosperous today. Instead, he was obsessed with intrigue, and like the wireman in Francis Ford Coppola's *The Conversation*, he approached his work with the reverent intensity and painful doubts of a man imprisoned by his craft. He died in 1971.

There are things about Bernard Spindel that everyone agrees upon, and things about him that defy consensus. Everyone agrees, for instance, that Spindel was a big man with exceptional strength and quickness. But his wife remembers also that the speed and strength were unpredictable; a sick man whose suitcases rattled with the click of pill bottles, Spindel's metabolism surged uncontrollably, alternating between near-Olympian powers and utter exhaustion. He blamed it on a heart and thyroid condition that he'd had since childhood.

In the Sixties, Spindel, his wife, seven children, two dogs, and four horses lived on a small estate in Holmes, New York. Their house was a large and beautiful one on the sunny side of the Putnam County foothills. If you stood before the fieldstone fireplace in the living room, antiques and thick carpeting would surround you. Against the far wall, incongruous by their sheer immensity, were a pair of stereo speakers built by Spindel, each of them the size of an ordinary refrigerator. And, if you looked out the picture window, you'd see a pair of Lincoln Continentals in the drive, an outsized swimming pool behind them and, farther off, a quiet woods leading down to a small stream.

All of this—like the B. R. Fox Company—was held in the name of Mrs. Spindel, her husband owning the shirt on his back and not much more. Despite that precaution, almost nothing is left. Today his otherwise chic widow lives in a small house in one of Alexandria, Virginia's more run-down neighborhoods. The house needs repairs that she can't afford to make, and furniture that she can't afford to buy. In her tiny living room, guests are offered the choice between a sagging couch covered with a worn bedspread, or an easy chair covered by an Army blanket. The couch, as it happens, is a better bargain since the chair's legs have been removed, reducing anyone who sits in it to the perspective of a six-year-old. All that's left from "Bernie's time" are the stereo speakers, which have, in this terribly small room and from the vantage of the easy chair, assumed the proportions of skyscrapers.

One of the things about Bernard Spindel on which there seems to be no consensus is who he *really* was. A former FBI agent who encountered Spindel on a number of assignments says flatly, "He was the Mafia's wireman. A counterintelligence agent for the Mob." A reporter who knew Spindel shakes his head at the assessment: "He was that, all right, but he was something else too. I always thought he was CIA." Mrs. Spindel herself says, "I'll probably never know who my husband was. I've always thought he was some sort of government agent, but Bernie—well, he hardly ever said anything about his work. Sometimes he'd disappear for weeks on end and turn up in . . . the strangest countries. He always said that it was better I didn't know, that it was for my own protection that I didn't know what he was doing. And I'd say to him, 'Well, what if something happens to you, Bernie? What about the children?' And he'd say that I shouldn't worry, that everything was taken care of—when the time came, he said, 'The right people will come around,' and there wouldn't be anything to worry about. Well, it's been five years and they haven't come around yet." Her son Eliot, a lean and almost theatrically handsome young man, nods and puffs on a pipe. Then he laughs. "My father was supposed to have some money—a lot of money—in the Caribbean. In some banks down there. But we've never been able to find it. All we've really been able to locate is a P-T boat that he owned in Haiti—God knows why he owned it. Anyway, the Haitian government won't let us put a hand on it. (Though actually, I don't know what we'd do with it if we got it. Sell it, I suppose.)"

"Bernie," Mrs. Spindel says, "was too trusting. I know that sounds silly, but it's true. He trusted people. He trusted Jimmy Hoffa, for instance, and when Bernie went to jail, Hoffa wouldn't lift a finger. And when Bernie died, Hoffa—well, he owed Bernie a lot of money, and he just wouldn't pay. (I mention this because everybody thought Bernie and Hoffa were good friends. They weren't. Hoffa was Bernie's client and that's all.)

"It's been hard," she continues. "We had a father-oriented family, and the kids . . . well, after their father died, two of the children attempted suicide. . . ." Her mind wanders for a moment, and then she says: "You know, we were told that Bernie was entitled to a military funeral. I can't tell you who told us that, but it was a very good authority. But they said they couldn't bury him that way. They said it would shake up too many things."

According to Barbara Spindel, her husband was framed by the Justice Department and, then, institutionally murdered. The "assassination"—that is how she views it—began in 1969 when Spindel was convicted of "conspiring to provide technical information about electronic eavesdropping techniques" to private detectives working for A&P heir Huntington Hartford. The conviction came about in connection with a messy divorce case in which the grocery lord's detectives bugged his wife's apartment. Spindel's only involvement in the episode was his having gone to the building's basement with the detectives. There he told them that one of the bugs couldn't possibly work because the installation had been improperly made. That seemed to be the end of it, until, a few weeks later, twenty-eight people were arrested in a crackdown on illicit eavesdropping in the New York area. Spindel was one of those twenty-eight, charged in connection with the Hartford episode. One of the detectives who'd solicited Spindel's advice provided evidence against him, and as a result Spindel was the only one of the twenty-eight to be convicted (and sent to jail). The detectives who'd placed the bugs against Mrs. Hartford, and monitored her conversations for months, were never brought to trial.

The conviction almost certainly cost Spindel his life.

"Bernie served fourteen months in Dannemora," his widow says. "And for the first few months we couldn't even see him. They had him in isolation in the Tombs, then they put him in isolation on Rikers Island, then there was another transfer and another two weeks of isolation—this time at Sing Sing—and then they transferred him to Dannemora, way up by the Canadian border, and held him in isolation there. He had a severe heart condition, and some other things as well, but the prison officials refused to give him any medication whatsoever. Finally, after a year and I-don't-know-how-many telegrams from Bernie's private doctor, they gave him some of the medication he needed. After eighteen months in prison, he was paroled. Because he was dying. You could see it when he got out. He looked like he was dying and . . . he did. Right afterwards."

Just as those who knew him still wonder "who Bernie *really* was," they also wonder about "the real reason" he was sent to jail. "They wanted something out of him," Mrs. Spindel says. "They offered to let him out if he'd cooperate with them. They thought he knew something, and maybe he did, but he wouldn't tell them. I *know* it had something to do with Bobby Kennedy. And maybe . . . sometimes I think it went all the way back to Bernie's father's days: his dad was involved with Joe Kennedy and the Chicago Trade Mart and all that Mafia business in the Thirties, but . . . it's all a mystery."

Indeed. We may be tempted to believe that Mrs. Spindel's search for her husband's "real" identity, and her efforts to understand the "real" reasons for his incarceration, are merely the delusions of a widow who can't face the truth. But I don't think so. Bernard Spindel was arrested and indicted *207 times*. And the *only* conviction he suffered in all his forty-seven years was the one alleging that he *intended* to provide information that *others intended to use* in the commission of a crime. It's obvious that someone wanted Spindel badly.

When I wrote that Spindel's conviction was ironic, I did so because he was responsible for eliminating more bugs and wiretaps than anyone in history. Trained by the Army Signal Corps as a wireman *extraordinaire* during World War II, he served as an intelligence officer until the end of the conflict. Turned down in his application for employment with the CIA, he became a private detective. In 1955 he joined the New York City Anti-Crime Commission as a technical advisor and very quickly infuriated New York City police. The commission, established in the wake of sensational revelations about police shakedowns and "protected" rackets, was an *ad hoc* citizens' organization established to fight corruption.* Spindel contributed in two areas. First, he showed how corrupt police were making *private* purchases of eavesdropping equipment and using it during off-duty hours to extort money and services from prostitutes, pimps, bookies, and heroin traffickers. Secondly, Spindel led an investigation that established the existence of a massive wiretapping operation which blanketed the entire East Side of New York City; and that, moreover, police and special agents of the telephone company were *selling* the information obtained from it. More than 125,000 subscribers were involved, including the United Nations, various consulates, socialites, corporations, and businessmen (though the actual purpose behind the meta-tap was never fathomed).

Having become the Serpico of both the N.Y.P.D. and Bell Telephone Company—a dangerous move for a wireman—Spindel plunged into the intrigues of the Dominican Republic. In the late 1950s, when Spindel arrived upon the scene, the island had been ruled for more than twenty-five years by General Rafael Leonidas Trujillo Molina, a dictator of such perverse and monstrous proportions that State Department officials, notorious for their circumlocution, saw fit to compare him with Dracula in their secret communications.† A vain and vicious mulatto who affected blond face powder and resorted to "conking" his hair, Trujillo was the acknowledged inventor of the pornographic "snuff flick." Until his assassination in May, 1961, he was reputed to be the world's most barbaric torturer,

* The board of directors of the Anti-Crime Commission was a prestigious one, and included former ambassador Spruille Braden, General William Donovan (of the OSS and CIA), Sloan S. Colt, Alex Lewyt, Mrs. Julius Ochs Adler (of the *Times*), Harold Stern, Major Benjamin Namm, and William Zeckendorf. John O'Mara was its executive director and William Keating its chief legal counsel. Despite the commission's sensational revelations, only Keating actually went to jail, sent there on a contempt citation for refusing to reveal his sources. (He was subsequently burned to death in a freak accident.)

† "If you recall Dracula, you will remember it was necessary to drive a stake through his heart to prevent a continuation of his crimes. I believe sudden death would be more humane than the solution of the Nuncio who once told me he thought he should pray that Trujillo would have a long and lingering illness." (Letter from Henry Dearborn, consul general in Ciudad Trujillo, to Thomas Mann, Assistant Secretary of State for Inter-American Affairs, October 27, 1960.)

a connoisseur of other people's agonies. It was not enough to execute those who plotted against him: their eyelids must first be sewn to their brows, electric wires inserted in their ureters and colons and then pushed together so that an arc of flame passed between them. Even his sensual inclinations were skewed toward the bizarre and sadistic: a palace procurer was responsible for delivering groups of forty women to his bedroom three nights a week, receiving 10 percent of all public-works projects for his efforts—while other courtiers roamed the country in search of virgins to be deflowered.* In the wake of his assassination, heart-shaking films were found in the palace by the rebels. In these pornogons, children were made to mate with animals, and torturer-geeks were shown biting off the genitals and breasts of male and female prisoners. The films, made at the expense of political prisoners and their families, had been a source of entertainment for Trujillo and selected guests at palace soirees.† Nor is Trujillo said to have been the worst of his regime: that honor goes to Johnny Abbes Garcia, chief of the island's *Servicio Intelligencia Militar* (the Military Intelligence Service, or SIM). A Socialist and psychopath, Johnny Abbes has been described as

> an éminence gris with the operational functions of a triggerman. . . . [H]is enduring interest: the field of espionage, the darker side of police work, and political subversion. He made profound studies of this twilight world. His intelligence was not high, but in its place, to an unusual degree, he had qualities that were probably more useful for his career than mere intelligence would have been. Chief among these was a kind of evil imagination. Any destructive work carried out furtively fired his imagination and brought forth his considerable resources of malicious astuteness. Combined with this was a perverse rejection of moral principles and conduct—a rejection that expanded into genuine devotion to wickedness wherever cruelty was involved.‡

Spindel's Dominican adventures began about the time Johnny Abbes came to power there, in the late 1950s, when rebel leaders contacted him for technical advice about air drops of weapons to the island. It was a time of plots and counterplots: besides the rebels' efforts to overthrow Trujillo, the Generalissimo and his ap-

---

* Robert D. Crassweller, *Trujillo* (New York: Macmillan, 1966), p. 434.
† This is, of course, "only one side" of Trujillo. He didn't torture all his prisoners to death—perhaps because there wasn't time. He is said to have executed an average of five prisoners a day by relatively "routine" means. He was, moreover, a loving father: at nine, his son Ramses had risen through the ranks of the Dominican Army to become a general, receiving a stipend of five thousand dollars per month.
‡ Crassweller, *op. cit.*, p. 330.

paratchiks were supporting Fidel Castro's guerrilla war against Batista while also planning to assassinate Costa Rica's Pepe Figueres, Venezuela's Romulo Betancourt, and Guatemala's Carlos Castillo Armas—all heads of state. It was a bloody epoch, when killers and idealists alike roamed the Caribbean, acquiring monikers such as The Strange One, The Frenchman, Chop, and, of course, Che ("Guy"). A veteran of Mafia and Teamsters intrigues—two groups that were themselves deeply involved in the profitable business of arms smuggling—Spindel was able to win the Dominican rebels' trust by providing them with a strategy for evading Trujillo's radar installations. According to a memoir of Spindel's, the rebels were able to deliver weapons valued at $150,000 to insurgents on the island.* They'd filled the air with strips of aluminum foil, reflective "confetti" dropped from planes, and then flown in under what amounted to a radar blizzard, landing the weapons on a seldom-used military highway. Rumors of the weapons' existence terrified Trujillo. According to Spindel, the dictator contacted him through intermediaries, offering amnesty for any political prisoners that the private eye might name. All Trujillo asked was that the arms be turned over to SIM—and no questions would be asked. Each prisoner would be given five thousand dollars for the resettlement of himself and his family, a prepaid life insurance policy, and passage from the island. In addition, $150,000 would be paid for the guns.

Spindel's account is an interesting one, though as we'll see it's almost certainly false in some of its more important details. And the lies Spindel told in his own memoir go a long way toward suggesting that there was more to the burly wireman than met the eye or ear.

When the scenario Spindel describes was supposed to have been played out, the Dominican Republic was a world-class police state beset by a permanent emergency, threatened from inside and out. Besides the rebels, Trujillo and Abbes were the targets of CIA intrigues designed to overthrow them, and reprisals for Trujillo's treachery were being plotted by the governments of Cuba and Venezuela. Everywhere he looked, Trujillo found mortal enemies, and so the Dominican Republic was subject to extraordinary internal measures. Searches and roadblocks were commonplace, surveillance ubiquitous. Every telephone on the island was believed to be tapped, and it was thought that all mail was routinely opened and read by SIM. Police and military patrols roamed the cities and

* Spindel's account is contained in *The Ominous Ear*, by Bernard Spindel (New York, Award House, 1968), pp. 74–103.

countryside, while the airports were shielded by the tightest security possible. Even the CIA had a difficult time of smuggling a few handguns into the country, using diplomatic pouches lined with lead. That the rebels, through Spindel's ministrations, should have obtained an arsenal of martial dimensions is flatly incredible.

What, then, really happened? What was Spindel actually doing? The key to the affair involves the Teamsters. At about the time that the New York spook was negotiating with SIM and Trujillo's U. S. Ambassador, men called Dominic Bartone and "Jack La Rue" were trying to acquire four surplus C-74 Globemaster airplanes from Akros Dynamics, a financially troubled firm owned by friends of Jimmy Hoffa. Supposedly, these planes would be resold by Bartone and "La Rue" to the Castro regime (which, in January 1959, had just come to power). Numerous trips were made to Cuba, ostensibly to effect the sale. Meanwhile, Spindel shuttled between New York and Ciudad Trujillo, as Robert Kennedy's investigations of Hoffa and his associates proceeded apace. In the course of those investigations, Kennedy's Get Hoffa Squad, led by NSA-FBI grad Walter Sheridan, learned of a proposed Teamsters loan sought by Akros Dynamics, and intervened. In late May, Bartone was arrested by Miami customs agents. According to Customs, Bartone was stockpiling surplus arms and ammunition in a Miami warehouse. At the same time that he'd been negotiating to sell the planes to Cuba, he'd reached an agreement with the Dominican Republic's ambassador to sell the weapons to Trujillo. The arms and ammo were to be secreted aboard one of the planes bought from Akros Dynamics, and a flight plan would be filed with Puerto Rico as the destination. Over the Dominican Republic, however, the plane would experience "engine trouble" and make a "forced landing" in a remote region. Then the guns would be sold to Trujillo. Had Kennedy's agents not intervened, the deal would have gone through.

What Kennedy and the others didn't know, however, was that "Jack La Rue"—whom Sheridan today describes as "a mystery man" —was Bernard Spindel's favorite alias. "Bernie often used a phony name," his widow recalls. "Jack La Rue was one of his favorites." Thus, while Spindel was negotiating for the release of Dominican prisoners in return for supposed "rebel arms," his secret partner, Bartone, was stockpiling those very weapons *in Miami*. With the help of a Teamsters loan needed to acquire a plane from Akros Dynamics, the pair would then fly the surplus guns to the Dominican Republic. There they would be passed off to Trujillo as weapons that had been cached in the country all along. Among the many beauties of the scheme is that Trujillo seems himself to have unwittingly financed it: letters in the possession of the former Dominican ambassador, described as "forgeries" by Spindel, suggest that the New York detective was paid $75,000 in advance on the deal. Spindel claims that the money was actually pocketed by the ambassador, but the truth is probably that Bartone and "La Rue" used it to buy the surplus guns that they intended to sell for *150* grand to Trujillo. Once the down payment was spent, and the weapons confiscated by customs, there was no way that Spindel could make good on either. The deal collapsed.

On its surface the deal may seem only an artful fraud intended to bilk a hated dictator. But that it was much more is made apparent by otherwise unnecessary conditions attaching to the trade Spindel sought to make. If he only wanted Trujillo's money, why negotiate for the release of political prisoners and their families? Surely, Spindel and Bartone could have sold the weapons to Trujillo for an even larger amount had they ignored the plight of the Generalissimo's imprisoned enemies. But they didn't. Moreover, why should the new Castro regime become a party to such a plot and why should the Teamsters become involved? The answers are necessarily speculative. But it appears that Mrs. Spindel may be correct when she suggests that her husband was a "government agent" of some sort. At the time of Bernie's Dominican adventure, the CIA was actively plotting Trujillo's assassination. At the same time the Agency was on good terms with the Castro regime, having supported Fidel's bid to oust Batista. For their part, Teamsters members associated with Jimmy Hoffa—including Grady Partin, the man who would send his old friend to jail—had for years run guns to Castro and others in the Caribbean. The interests of all these groups, then, appear to have converged: certainly a plan to free Trujillo's imprisoned political enemies would have been a central part of any CIA plot to replace the dictator. The prospect, then, is one of the CIA using Teamsters agents such as Spindel to accomplish precisely that. Since relations with the Trujillo regime were ostensibly friendly even while the Agency was planning the dictator's murder, the CIA could hardly have used its own officers to dupe Trujillo into releasing a *de facto* opposition party. "Deniability" would have been paramount to any such scheme; Spindel and the Teamsters were able to provide it. As for the meetings in Cuba, Havana was an excellent rendezvous for the plot's unfolding: the war ended, vast numbers of surplus weapons were available, and Castro himself was sympathetic to the Dominican dissidents' cause.

If this is, in fact, what happened, then Bobby Kennedy's intervention in the scheme could only have outraged all who were involved. As for Spindel, he took the plot's last-minute failure with characteristic equanimity: "Based on information I had overheard," he wrote, "Trujillo would not live to see his next birthday."

Spindel was correct (as he so often was when it came to having "overheard" something), though his involvement in the scheme was not without repercussions. He became the first American ever to be placed on what the FBI called Trujillo's "Hit Parade," a list of some forty individuals on whom the dictator had placed an open contract. According to Barbara Spindel, there were at least two attempts made to collect on that contract, but neither succeeded.* Trujillo was shot to death on the last day of May, 1961, detonating a financial avalanche in Switzerland, where he had in excess of $840,000,000 on deposit.†

It's most unlikely that the Dominican affair had anything to do with Spindel's persecution by federal authorities, or with his ultimate conviction in 1969. But Barbara Spindel is certainly correct when she blames "the troubles" on Robert Kennedy.

Throughout most of the 1950s and 1960s, Teamsters boss Jimmy Hoffa was Spindel's foremost client. As early as 1953, the private detective neutralized seven bugs from the offices and pay phones in the vicinity of Teamsters headquarters. In addition, he installed a series of "tap testers" to eliminate the likelihood of future bugs succeeding and assisted Hoffa in establishing a variety of countermeasures and other security procedures. Because Hoffa was at that time under investigation by federal agencies and congressional committees, Spindel was, in effect, aligned against the legislative and enforcement branches of government.

More particularly, he was up against Bobby Kennedy, a politically ambitious government attorney who'd staked his career on finding a way to jail Hoffa. For a decade Spindel's countermeasures effec-

---

* An estimated 140 others, who made the list during Trujillo's thirty-year reign, were not so lucky. One of those assassinations, that of Jesus de Galindez, is discussed in a later chapter.

† This is the amount that the Trujillo family acknowledged owning. Reporters estimated that Trujillo's total horde actually exceeded twice this sum, being concentrated in stockpiles of gold, industrial diamonds, foreign currency, stocks, bonds, and a succession of dummy corporations owning real estate throughout the world. After the dictator's death, many of these assets are said to have been secretly looted.

tively neutralized FBI and Justice Department efforts at round-the-clock surveillance and monitoring of his client. While both Hoffa and Spindel were indicted on many occasions, convictions were elusive. In one case the two men were charged with having bugged a secret grand jury proceeding by having Teamsters lieutenants wired before they gave their testimony. Bobby Kennedy, as chief counsel for the McClellan Committee, attempted to prove the charge by showing that scores of miniature tape recorders (Minifons) were acquired by Spindel and distributed by Hoffa to all his lieutenants in the Midwest. Spindel rebutted the charge when he proved that the recorders were not sent to the Teamsters' headquarters until the grand jury proceedings were over.

As in all such protracted relationships, the enmity became a personal matter. After one congressional hearing in which Spindel made a liar of Bobby Kennedy and a fool of his staff, Kennedy loyalist Carmine Bellino rushed after the departing Spindel and took a swing at him. The private detective ducked the punch and left Bellino supine in the halls of Congress. Then too FBI agents were continually baiting Spindel about his being Jewish, questioning his neighbors, maintaining surveillance on his movements, and bugging his conversations. For his part Spindel took to making unnecessary U-turns in his car, "plugging" his desk drawers with spitballs when he left the office, and, on occasion, entering hotels at the bottom of a laundry basket. Moreover, he practiced countersurveillance against the FBI and sometimes intercepted their communications. On one such tape FBI agents are heard engaging in the following dialogue:

> "Twenty-three, are you trying to transmit [to] me?"
> "Not me, Chief."
> "What's all that noise?"
> "I think we're tuned in."
> "That's probably Bernard."
> "Hi-ya, Boinie."
> "Ha ha, maybe there is a hanky-panky, huh?"
> "Could be."
> "Hi-ya, Boin. Doing fine, making lots of money working for Mr. H? He's a good boy."
> "Go home, Bernard."

At this point on the tape an FBI technician breaks into the conversation, claiming responsibility for the unwanted "noise," and warns: "There is a good chance that if this fellow is listening to all you said, there is another good chance he is recording it, so you might consider that, ten-four."

"Seven, I presume he knows if he is that that's a violation of Federal statutes over which we have jurisdiction."

"I'm sure he knows that." *

In 1957, however, Spindel undertook what he referred to as "a counterintelligence job" against Kennedy and the McClellan Committee. Faking a dispute with Hoffa, he led Kennedy to believe that he would cooperate, and as a result the pressure against the detective was temporarily relieved. But, according to Spindel, "I was actually working as a double agent. I tried to determine what possible information Kennedy wanted me to provide and, at the same time, I was able to analyze which information he did not have in his possession." †

3 / THE KENNEDY-MONROE TAPES

Robert Kennedy's feud with Jimmy Hoffa, the Teamsters union, and the mob is notorious. It dated back to investigations conducted by Kennedy and Carmine Bellino in 1955. At the time Kennedy and Bellino were chief counsel and staff accountant for Senator John McClellan's Permanent Subcommittee on Investigations. Their first breakthrough implicated Teamsters president Dave Beck in a succession of embezzlements involving the union's pension funds. As a result of that investigation Beck was forced to step aside, and Hoffa assumed the union's presidency. Kennedy was convinced, however, that only the names had changed, and so he continued to focus on the Teamsters and its new leader. Because the McClellan Committee lacked jurisdiction over labor affairs—and because Kennedy had staked his reputation on eradicating criminal influences in the Teamsters union—the Senate Select Committee on Improper Activities in the Labor or Management Field was created. Senator McClellan was its chairman. Senator John Kennedy was a member. And Robert Kennedy was its chief counsel. Despite its formal title, the committee and those who worked with it were colloquially known as the Get Hoffa Squad.

---

* Spindel, *op cit.*, p. 172. In fact, the agents were wrong about there being a violation. As Spindel knew (and often raged against), intercepting private communications (without the use of a wiretap) becomes a crime only if and when their contents are divulged. It's this loophole that allowed federal agents to bug anyone with absolute impunity, since the contents of the monitored conversations would not be divulged but used for "pressure dossiers," surveillance purposes, and leads.

† *Ibid.*, pp. 204–205.

Even before the new committee was established, a pattern of intrigue and double cross had developed—one that seems to haunt us still. It was Hoffa, for instance, who, while a supporter of Dave Beck, arranged for one of Beck's attorneys to provide Kennedy and the McClellan Committee with the information that forced Beck to abdicate. A year later, Hoffa allegedly planted a spy on the new subcommittee. Unfortunately for the Teamsters, the spy (an attorney named John C. Cheasty) quickly became a double agent—if he was not one from the very beginning. In early 1957, Hoffa was arrested by the FBI for attempting to bribe Cheasty with eighteen thousand dollars in return for secret subcommittee documents. At the time of his arrest, the Teamsters president was literally holding the bag —an attaché case filled with secret Senate memoranda. Despite this evidence, and Cheasty's testimony for the prosecution, Hoffa would eventually be acquitted of the charge.

It was only the first in a series of indictments brought against Hoffa by Kennedy, who in later years would use his power as Attorney General to have upward of forty grand juries working simultaneously to indict the labor leader and his associates. Besides the grand juries he would also bring to bear the combined forces of the FBI, the IRS, and a consortium of Justice Department Strike Forces. There would be, in addition to a coordinated anti-Hoffa campaign in the press, an elite unit of investigator spooks, intelligence community veterans led by Walter Sheridan. All of these forces would be targeted against the Teamsters. It was no wonder, then, that Hoffa was eventually indicted on a panoply of charges ranging from bribery to wiretapping, profiteering to perjury. The evidence unearthed in these investigations makes it clear that Hoffa was an unethical man, a ruthless wheeler-dealer who used his union's pension funds for his own financial gain, making alliances with petty criminals, and in some cases negotiating "sweetheart" contracts for his private advantage. What the evidence does not make clear, however, is that many of the crimes allegedly committed by Hoffa—bribery, wiretapping, and even perjury—were *defensive* responses to the ruthlessness of Robert Kennedy and his legions of ambitious investigators and government attorneys. Indeed, it almost seems as if Kennedy's unrelenting pressure caused Hoffa to change from the mildly corrupt labor leader that he was in the early Fifties to the authentic villain he eventually became. Virtually at war with the United States government—and betrayed on every front—Hoffa's survival dictated that he respond in kind. There is a degree of scrutiny that no one can survive, no matter how ethical and honest he might be. (Hoffa, of course, was neither.) The slightest deviation in one's testimony before a never-ending succession of grand juries becomes, in the absence of governmental good faith, *perjury*. The slightest error in computing one's income tax becomes *tax evasion*. An offhanded remark to a friend is interpreted as a *conspiracy to bribe*. The purchase of tape recorders for the purpose of recording union meetings is evidence of *wiretapping*. And so on: that was the position Hoffa found himself in by virtue of his feud with Robert Kennedy.

Actually, the situation was even worse, Kennedy's ruthlessness expanded as his hatred of Hoffa increased, resulting finally in his resort to dirty tricks involving the CIA. Those who testified against Hoffa—people such as Grady Partin—were often more vicious and corrupt than the man they sought to have jailed. In exchange for Kennedy's political protection, they proved willing to say whatever the Get Hoffa Squad wanted to hear. It therefore became an easy matter for a thug such as Partin, facing more than a century in prison, to manufacture conversations that may never have taken place (as indeed, from time to time, Partin claimed to have done). The point is that Robert Kennedy's perspective was warped into an obsession by his vendetta with the Teamsters, finally overturning both justice and common sense. The drive against organized crime, for which he became famous, was in actuality a campaign directed against *a single wing* of the syndicate—that part which had common cause with Hoffa. Thus, for instance, Louisiana crime boss Carlos Marcello, a partisan of Hoffa's, became one of RFK's priority targets. There was nothing wrong with that, except for the manner in which Kennedy went about it. Not content to let justice take its course, Kennedy circumvented all due process by having the CIA kidnap Marcello as he made a quarterly visit to the New Orleans Immigration Office. The target of deportation proceedings, Marcello was grabbed by two CIA agents posing as Justice Department officials, driven in a black limousine to the airport, and placed aboard an Agency jet bound for Guatemala. He was its only passenger. Delivered to the banana republic, he was apparently held captive by the CIA until six weeks after the Bay of Pigs invasion. (Released in June, 1961, Marcello was reportedly returned to the United States by his private pilot, David Ferrie, the eccentric homosexual who was later to figure so notoriously in the New Orleans assassination probe conducted by District Attorney Jim Garrison.) We may speculate about the timing of Marcello's deportation, and about his involvement in the Bay of Pigs invasion and subsequent

attempts to topple Castro, but what is not in doubt is the almost
sovereign sense of immunity that Robert Kennedy must have felt at
the time. Named U. S. Attorney General by his brother less than
three months earlier, RFK had already carried out a capital crime
in the supposed interests of justice and fair play. That he did not
choose to act so forcefully against other elements of organized crime
is attested to by the fact that his brother Jack and the agencies that
Robert Kennedy controlled—both the Justice Department and the
CIA—became *de facto* partners in sex and attempted murder with
such Mafia capos as Sam Giancana, John Roselli, and Santos Trafficante. It's this apparent bias against a wing of organized crime that
makes the Hoffa feud of continuing relevance—despite the assassination and disappearance of the vendetta's principals. Those who investigated and prosecuted Hoffa have risen to positions of considerable
power; moreover, many of them came to play strategic roles in the
Watergate affair.*

According to Spindel's widow, Robert Kennedy was prepared to

---

* *Walter Sheridan*, whom we'll see is a top candidate for "Deep Throat" honors,
continues to work for the Kennedy family, serving as the surviving Senator's personal
spook; Sheridan is presently on the staff of the Senate Committee on Administrative
Practices and Procedures (the so-called Ad-Prac Committee), chaired by Senator Edward
Kennedy. *Carmine Bellino* became the chief investigator for the Senate Watergate
Committee and is now in a comparable position on the Ad-Prac Committee. *Robert
Peloquin*, an important member of the Get Hoffa Squad and credited with helping to
obtain Partin's damning testimony, is now president of Intertel—described by White
House spy Jack Caulfield as "an intelligence-gun-for-hire" and a Kennedy apparat.
William Hundley, another veteran of the Get Hoffa Squad, was a cofounder of Intertel with Peloquin; Hundley later formed his own law practice. Among Hundley's
partners is Henry Peterson, Attorney General during the Watergate investigation;
among his clients is John Mitchell. *Jim Neal*, one of Hoffa's prosecutors, later prosecuted both John Mitchell and Maurice Stans in connection with the illegal contribution
by Robert Vesco to the Committee to Re-Elect the President. *William O. Bittman*, who
also prosecuted Hoffa, went on to defend E. Howard Hunt, self-avowed enemy of the
Kennedy family; Bittman was later disgraced by revelations that he'd received his
attorney's fees in the form of cash delivered in a paper bag to a public telephone booth
by White House agent Anthony Ulasewicz. *Rufus King*, who'd defended Hoffa, later
represented both Howard Hunt and James McCord. So did *Gerald Alch*, a parter of
F. Lee Bailey; according to Walter Sheridan, Bailey was a Hoffa proponent who sought
to make Partin retract his testimony and who, moreover, accused Robert Kennedy of
paying $200,000 for allegations against the Teamsters boss. Alch was eventually accused
by McCord of attempting to introduce false testimony implicating the CIA in the
Watergate burglary. *Bernard ("Bud") Fensterwald* was McCord's third attorney. Founder
of the Committee to Investigate Assassinations, Fensterwald's other clients have included
Martin Luther King's convicted assassin, James Earl Ray, and Mitchell WerBell.
Fensterwald is also a veteran of the Ad-Prac Committee, which, under the chairmanship
of Senator Edward Long, was regarded by Sheridan and the Kennedys as a sort of *Pro-
Hoffa Squad*. (Senator Edward Kennedy replaced Long as the committee's chairman
after the latter's demise.) *Edward Bennett Williams*, who served as Hoffa's attorney until
1964, when their relationship ended in mutual acrimony, represented *The Washington
Post* throughout the Watergate period. It was Williams who handled the sensitive

do "anything" to convict Hoffa and, ultimately, her husband. Certainly this included extraordinary surveillance procedures: Hoffa and those in his entourage were the subjects of Justice Department "pressure dossiers" of unprecedented depth, round-the-clock visual surveillance, and, as Bernard Spindel showed, widespread electronic eavesdropping. It was to combat this that the detective was hired as a countermeasures technician. Immediately, the spooks who comprised the Get Hoffa Squad realized that their efforts to "jail Jimmy" would benefit immeasurably if they could turn Spindel into a double agent. And they tried. On one occasion, when Spindel gave Kennedy a ride to the airport, the future Attorney General is reported to have promised Spindel whatever he might ask in return for testimony against the Teamsters boss. Spindel jokingly replied that what he'd *really* like was a $750,000 "loan" to set up an electronics factory in Puerto Rico. Not realizing that the detective was playing with him, Kennedy replied: "Now, Bernie, you know my brother is going to be the next President. You don't have to worry about anything." *

The Kennedys' courtship of Spindel, however, came to an abrupt end when the detective unexpectedly invoked the Fifth Amendment during a Senate appearance, refusing at the last moment to testify against his client Hoffa. What else he may have done in his "counterintelligence job," as Spindel called it, is uncertain, but there are rumors that may well explain the persecution of the detective long after his boss, Jimmy Hoffa, was imprisoned in 1967. According to his wife and son, Bernie claimed to have obtained tape recordings of intimate conversations between then Attorney General Robert Kennedy and actress Marilyn Monroe. (Some writers have claimed that President Kennedy was also having an affair with the movie star.) The suggestion is that Spindel bugged Bobby Kennedy. That seems a dangerous undertaking—though, as Spindel himself pointed out, it could have been accomplished without breaking the law. As early as 1955, Spindel was experimenting with the use of lasers to record conversations by "reading" the vibrations on windowpanes; a few years later he was using the same technology to make visual recordings. In a letter to Senator Russell Long, written in

---

assignment as intermediary between *Post* reporter Bob Woodward and Robert Bennett, president of the Robert R. Mullen Company, a CIA front that also represented the interests of Howard Hughes.

* Testimony of James P. Kelly, taken in an IRS proceeding against Spindel, March 11–12, 1965 (Tax Proceedings Docket 3102-63, 2668-64, p. 121).

1967, he said, "It would *not be illegal* for me to take one of the advanced [laser] beams or techniques, turn off the sound portion, and take a picture of what is going on in someone's office or bedroom. Then, *using a professional lip reader to interpret the lip movements on the video tape* thus obtained, I can make a tape recording of what went on and what was *said* without violating [the law]." (Spindel's emphasis. Interestingly, the detective charged that Robert Kennedy employed a professional lip-reader during his 1968 presidential campaign, using the woman for "eavesdropping" purposes.) And, should Spindel have been willing to break the law, he certainly could have done so without detection: at the apex of the Kennedy-Hoffa feud, he was perfecting an eavesdropping device of uncommon ingenuity. The device was inspired by the recognition that water is an excellent conductor of sound. Spindel maintained that sounds entering a water system at point *A* could be retrieved at point *B—miles away.* Capitalizing on that principle, he was experimenting with a miniature invention that could be concealed in a building's plumbing system; it would be powered by the water flowing over it and, isolated from the rooms to be bugged, it would escape detection. Signals transmitted by the mechanism would be filtered by the eavesdropper until nothing but the desired conversation remained. Theoretically, it would be possible to record the conversations taking place in every room of a building, using this single bug.

Bugging Robert Kennedy, however, would have been a thoroughly dangerous proceeding no matter how it was accomplished. It seems more likely that Spindel obtained the tape recordings in a more open way—from Monroe herself.

"Marilyn was a very frightened woman," says Barbara Spindel, "and I think she had reason to be. It's possible that she made those tapes herself, or that she had Bernie do it for her. There was so much going on then. The assassination attempts against Castro—all that stuff with Giancana and Sinatra, the Kennedys' affairs with what's-her-name, Judith Exner, the Hoffa feud . . . I think Marilyn was afraid for her life. And, of course, Bernie was right in the middle of it."

According to Mrs. Spindel, the tapes—or copies of them—were seized during a joint raid on Spindel's home, a raid carried out by the New York City District Attorney's office and agents of the Bell Telephone Company. During that raid Mrs. Spindel suffered a heart attack as her husband was handcuffed and led off to jail. Charged with unlawful possession of equipment belonging to the telephone company, Bernard Spindel was subsequently acquitted on all counts. The materials confiscated by the D.A.'s men, however, were never returned to Spindel. According to the private eye's widow, those materials almost certainly included the Kennedy/Monroe tapes. In 1977, Mrs. Spindel told this reporter that she is planning to sue for the seized materials' return.

Could there be other copies of the tapes elsewhere? "I don't know," the widow says. "I've looked everywhere and . . . The only place I haven't looked is in the walls of the house we owned. I had to sell it after Bernie died and maybe . . . maybe he had copies buried in the walls. I don't know."

What the purpose of those recordings may have been is open to speculation. Perhaps, as Mrs. Spindel believes, Monroe had them made as a form of "insurance." But that seems unlikely. What use could she have made of them? A more plausible explanation is that Monroe may have been coerced into allowing the tapes to be made. The fact that *Spindel* claims to have had the tapes suggests that they were made for one of his clients—either Hoffa or members of organized crime. Given Robert Kennedy's pursuit of Spindel's clients, it's not unreasonable that they would have considered blackmail. That Monroe may have allowed the tapes to be made is explained by the fact that Hollywood studios exist more or less at the discretion of the unions that dominate them. Some of those unions were themselves subject to the influence of both Jimmy Hoffa and Hollywood labor racketeers such as John Roselli. It's worth noting that Monroe —an unstable woman in even the happiest of times—was under enormous pressure from the studios during the last year of her life. Fired from the set of what was to be her last film, and sued for damages by the movie moguls, she was suddenly and mysteriously restored to grace. Returning to the set for a time, she consumed a fatal overdose of sleeping pills on the night of August 5, 1962. Somewhere in the course of that evening, in a terminal haze of Nembutals, she's reported to have telephoned one of the Kennedy brothers, vacationing at the time with singer Frank Sinatra. The content of that call is unknown, though it might be retrieved should Spindel's tapes ever be recovered from the musty labyrinths of the New York City D.A.'s office.

Undoubtedly, those tapes could have been used effectively in a political blackmail scheme. The Kennedys' strongest trump was their wholesome family image. And yet we know that this image, in the case of both Bobby and Jack, was no more than a charade. The unchallenged revelations of Judith Exner—who carried out nearly simultaneous affairs with Mafioso Sam Giancana and President Kennedy between 1960 and 1963—and the confessions of numerous socialites and "starlets," bragging of their flings with the Kennedys, make it clear that Jack, at least, was a compulsive satyr. It may be important to note that Exner's relationship with Kennedy came about through the introduction provided by singer-swinger Frank Sinatra. And that, moreover, Exner was herself a creature of John Roselli, a mob-connected racketeer who came to serve three years in prison for extorting money from the Hollywood studios by threatening them with *labor* difficulties. That Roselli, Exner, and Sinatra were very close to Giancana is a matter of fact. That they should all be in bed with the President, literally or figuratively, makes the possibility of blackmail real to all but the most naïve.

But even with Old Blue Eyes doing his level best for the President on the West Coast, the sexual jetsam of Las Vegas and Hollywood was not enough. Kennedy bedded the wives, ex-wives, and girl friends of employees and friends as well, risking scandal with every encounter.* What was at stake with the Monroe tapes, therefore, was the political future of the Kennedy family. The American voter, while tolerant of human failings, would have been outraged by the promiscuity of the brothers, a promiscuity involving organized-crime figures as well as Hollywood decadents. It was, in short, a seamy and volatile situation brought about by an almost Hellenic character flaw in two brothers who were destined for both tragedy and legend.

If, despite the sharing of intimacies with Sinatra's stable, Giancana, Roselli, and the others did *not* try to blackmail the Kennedys with recordings made of their trysts and conversations, one has to ask: *Why not?* They had the means, the motive, and the opportunity. Are we to believe that the Mafiosi abstained from doing so because they had a distaste for blackmail or a well-developed sense of fair play? Or that they abstained because they simply had too much respect for the offices of the President and the Attorney Gen-

* One such encounter that ultimately led to headlines involved the ex-wife of Cord Meyer, a high-ranking CIA officer in the Clandestine Services. In 1962, Mary Meyer is said to have had a pot-smoking affair with JFK in the White House. A diary kept by the divorcee at the time of the affair was later burned by James Angleton, the since-retired CIA Counter-intelligence chief. The diary was burned shortly after Mrs. Meyer was found shot to death beside a Georgetown canal, the victim of an apparent mugging.

eral? It seems unlikely. Nor does it seem likely that they feared the Kennedys' wrath—since that wrath was already focused in full upon various elements of the Mob.

The questions raised by these speculations are many, but a few matters ought not to be in doubt. For instance: Spindel claimed, while having no reason to lie on that subject, to have made recordings of the Monroe-Kennedy liaison. The recordings, then, almost certainly existed. Secondly, it's very likely that they were made in a way that was legal—that is, with Monroe's consent; Spindel was not so reckless that he would have bugged the Attorney General of the United States without having established a proper defense beforehand. For similar reasons, it's unlikely that Spindel concerned himself either with Monroe's motives for permitting her home to be bugged or with the probable use to which the tapes would be put: his task was a technician's and nothing more.

There are some other likelihoods as well. For example: In interviews shortly before his disappearance in 1975, Jimmy Hoffa bragged that he had or had had information that might critically embarrass the Kennedys—but that, in deference to family sensibilities, he'd never used it: the information was too "seamy." It seems possible that Spindel and his client Hoffa were referring to the same material (though Hoffa's demurral has a self-serving air, reminiscent in its way of Jack Ruby's excuse for executing Lee Harvey Oswald: he did it to prevent Jackie from having to testify at Oswald's expected trial). Another likelihood is that the Bureau, which cautioned the President on his relationship with Sinatra and Exner, regarded Jack and Bobby Kennedy as compromised by their dalliances. In effect, the brothers became security risks.

It is here that the larger uncertainty enters. Were the Kennedys blackmailed or not? At present, there is no evidence to suggest that they were, at least not by Jimmy Hoffa. The Kennedys' pursuit of him was relentless. And yet there is an anomaly of the time which admits the possibility that blackmail may have occurred. The relationship between the CIA and the Mafia leaders Giancana and Roselli has always been an enigma. As we'll see, their roles in the 1960–63 CIA plots to assassinate Castro were almost wholly superfluous. Moreover, Senate testimony on the origin of those plots is ambiguous when it is not contradictory: no one, at least none of the survivors, has been willing or able to recall whose idea it was to use the Mafia to kill the Cuban Communist. *May it not have been the Mafia's idea?* A way of forging a political alliance so sensitive that the participants would forever after escape prosecution? It is generally believed, without much reason, that the CIA conceived the plot to kill Castro and then, always indirectly, approached Giancana, Roselli, and Santos Trafficante to carry out the hit. May it not have been the other way around? While most Americans think instantly of the Mob when contract murder is mentioned, the CIA does not and never has: the Agency has its own "assets" for wet jobs. Might not Giancana & Company, by blackmailing a presidential candidate and/or his brother, have made the CIA *their* instrument, rather than the CIA's having made the Mob *its* instrument? The testimonial uncertainty of the plot's origins, coupled with the perversity of the Kennedys' sexual alliances with hoodlums and the hoodlums' lethal alliances with the CIA, makes the specter real. With virtually all of the principals themselves having been assassinated, however, it's unlikely that the truth will ever be known.

There is one other possibility concerning the fate of the Kennedy-Monroe tapes, and it is in no way incompatible with the hypothesis advanced above. According to Barbara Spindel, "If Bernie made those tapes for Jimmy Hoffa, they wouldn't have belonged to him but to his client. And my husband was a stickler for things like that: he would have turned the originals over to Hoffa or have given them to Hoffa's lawyer." Obviously, though, Hoffa exercised no influence over the Kennedys, who were hounding him unremittingly. He could not, therefore, have benefited from the tapes. But that Spindel made those tapes we know by his own admission, and that they were probably made for Hoffa is an opinion of his widow. What could have happened to them?

One intriguing theory holds that Hoffa instructed Spindel to deliver the tapes to his attorney, Edward Bennett Williams. Already a successful criminal lawyer, Williams would later go on to even greater achievements, becoming president of the Washington Redskins, a member of the Foreign Intelligence Advisory Board, and a power within the Democratic Party.* In 1957, Williams had successfully argued for Hoffa's acquittal on charges of having bribed McClellan Committee staffer John Cheasty. In late 1962, however, Hoffa and his attorney had a furious fight. The nature

---

* Besides Hoffa and Robert Vesco, Williams' clients have included red-baiting Senator Joseph McCarthy, hoodlum Frank Costello, influence peddler Bobby Baker, former CIA director Richard Helms, John Connally, *The Washington Post*, various FBI agents under investigation for bag jobs in the Big Apple, and Aldo Icardi, an OSS officer accused of assassinating his commander-in-chief.

of the dispute has never been made public, though Washington lobbyist Irv Davidson, a friend of Williams', says that "Hoffa tried to tell Williams how to run his office, and Williams wouldn't have it." The final break occurred in 1964, when Williams ruled that he would no longer represent the Teamsters chief and that, moreover, Hoffa was not entitled to any more Teamsters funds to continue his defense. The blow was a shattering one to Hoffa. Three years later he'd go to jail.

If, as Mrs. Spindel suspects, her husband provided Williams with the Kennedy-Monroe tapes, it might be that the lawyer refused to exploit them, infuriating his client and precipitating the break between them. One notes in this regard that in the wake of Senator Robert Kennedy's assassination in 1968, Williams persuaded the slain Senator's executive secretary—and one of his closest confidantes—to become his own personal secretary. A Kennedy loyalist who was aware of what she called "the feud" between Robert Kennedy and E. B. Williams, she accepted the new job only upon the condition that Williams swear to her that the enmity had ceased before the Senator's death. Williams reportedly said that it had.

4 / BUGGING CAPITOL HILL

It would be an exaggeration to say that Barbara Spindel and her family live in fear. The truth is more nearly that the family lives with a measure of controlled trepidation, an ongoing cautiousness that finds its expression in guarded telephone conversations and a habit of questioning appearances. The family telephone is tapped by the FBI—at Mrs. Spindel's request. "We were being threatened," she says. "We'd get harassing calls at four in the morning. People who didn't like Bernie, and others who—I don't know who they were. A friend of ours, an FBI agent, was worried that someone might throw a fire bomb through the window. And so we signed a consent order with the local FBI office, allowing them to wiretap the phone. Maybe they'll find out who's been doing it."

The widow of the Mafia's wireman, elegant despite the hard times that have fallen upon her, manages to seem astute even while pleading ignorance. "When they had Bernie in Dannemora," she says, "the Justice Department arranged a few conferences with us. They'd have us in separate rooms and the agents would tell us how easy it would be to have Bernie released, if only he'd cooperate. They pleaded with me, they begged Bernie. But they never said what they wanted, and to tell you the truth, I'm not sure they knew. I think they thought that Bernie knew and Bobby Kennedy knew, but the agents themselves . . . nothing."

Up against Robert Kennedy, the Justice Department, the police, and the phone company, a survivor of the Dominican Hit Parade, Spindel lived in a reality made up of Orwellian resonances. Uncovering wiretaps and countersurveillance agents in a score of cities, faking double agentry while presiding over a family of eight dependents and a half-dozen domestic beasts, he resembled one of those Spanish figurines carved from wood—the kinds that contain smaller versions of themselves, one inside another, a succession of doppelgängers receding toward the subminiature. Eventually, Spindel was forced to shed one such skin after another, until in the end he was reduced to sickness and poverty, stripped of everything but his family and the mysteries implicit in some yet-undiscovered aliases. He died with his secrets because, he told his wife, it was safer that way.

The harassment of Spindel—207 indictments, ending in the single petty conviction that cost him his life—may be understood in terms of his effectiveness on Hoffa's behalf. But that the harassment continued after Hoffa was jailed is less easily explained. It may be that the elusive Kennedy-Monroe tapes were responsible; even though Spindel's copies seem to have been seized by New York City officials, he was privy to their contents and may therefore have been deemed a threat. I think, however, that Spindel's continued persecution had more to do with his encyclopedic knowledge of the Kennedy family as a whole. And that his ultimate downfall can be traced to his discovery of an electronic anomaly on Capitol Hill.

A few months prior to his fated encounter with Huntington Hartford's detectives, Spindel provided secret testimony to Senator Long's "Ad-Prac" committee, then interested in electronic eavesdropping. In that testimony Spindel shocked the Senators and staff by revealing that the telephone cable servicing the offices and hearing rooms of the Senate and House of Representatives had a second cable spliced into it. This second cable ran underground from the Capitol to the Esso Building * on Third Street, Northwest. While the phone company occasionally splices one cable into another for purposes of economy, the sensitivity of Capitol Hill's communications ought to have precluded their doing so in this case. Because such splices make wiretapping a very simple matter, the existence of the second cable threatened the secrecy of sensitive Senate hearings, national-security

---

* The building has since been demolished.

discussions, and privileged congressional communications. Moreover, Spindel pointed out another anomaly of the putative cable: rather than terminating in the basement of the Esso Building, which would conform to the standard procedures of the Chesapeake & Potomac Telephone Company, the cable ran to the top floor of the building, ending in a locked room leased to the Justice Department's Bureau of Prisons. That room was itself a "restricted area" into which only a few government agents were allowed; all others, including repairmen for the telephone company, were denied access. In addition, Spindel reported, "government agents were constantly working on the cable," according to tenants in the building. The implication was clear: Capitol Hill might very well be bugged. The room leased to the Bureau of Prisons seemed the most likely candidate for investigation, though the cable's track through the building made each of the offices it passed through suspect. Among those offices were several leased to "campaign committees" seeking to elect former Attorney General Robert Kennedy as the Senator from New York. Before the detective could perform a countermeasures investigation, however, Long Committee staffer Bernard Fensterwald committed a blunder. Concerned about the possibility of the Hill's being tapped, Fensterwald requested cable information from the telephone company supervisor responsible for handling government wiretaps. Since a countermeasures investigation would require days to complete, whereas it would take only an hour to dismantle any wiretap that may have existed, Spindel's probe was doomed by leaks even before he could have started .

Because the FBI is a part of the Justice Department, and because FBI director J. Edgar Hoover was known to have compiled extensive dossiers on members of Congress, it was suspected that if a tap did exist, it must belong to Hoover. The Bureau of Prisons, then, would have been providing the FBI with cover for its operations against the Hill. Others, however, suspected that the cable was Kennedy's doing, with information obtained from it being used to consolidate the family's political power.

The suspicion was far from outlandish. Since the racket investigations of the early Fifties, and more recently Robert Kennedy's reign over Justice Department Task Forces and CIA assassination plots, the Kennedys have shown an inclination for spookery. Their personal staff is studded with former intelligence agents and investigators from a host of government agencies, including the FBI, NSA, Secret Service, and CIA. Moreover, the family has been linked by rumor and by White House intelligence reports to a number of private detective agencies, including Intertel. Walter Sheridan, considered Senator Edward Kennedy's most trusted advisor, is an alumnus of the National Security Agency, the federal intelligence unit responsible for the most technically sophisticated eavesdropping and surveillance operations carried out by any government in the world. Obviously the Kennedys have a real need for security and countermeasures personnel; the family has been plagued by assassinations and death threats and has been the subject of round-the-clock surveillance by such diverse institutions as the Nixon White House and the *National Enquirer*. No one could blame them for employing counterintelligence practices unusual even in politics. But the suspicion raised by the supposed Capitol Hill wiretap is that family head Robert Kennedy was using *offensive* intelligence methods that had nothing to do with his office or public responsibilities.

According to a former Senate investigator who worked with Senator Long's committee on eavesdropping, "Bobby Kennedy had a lot of problems with Hoover. There were things Hoover simply wouldn't do for him—usually because they were illegal. So Bobby created I-don't-know-how-many proprietaries, including a couple of detective agencies, basing them in big cities down South and in the Midwest. Places like Milwaukee and Detroit. Anyway, they were the Kennedys' babies, and they did what they were told; sometimes they worked against Hoffa or organized crime, and other times they did political stuff. Actually, they're supposed to have been set up with discretionary funds from the White House, but there's no way to be sure. You had a unique situation back in 'sixty and 'sixty-one. You had one brother controlling the Presidency, and the other brother, Bobby, wearing a *couple* of hats. He was Attorney General, sure, but he was also overseeing the CIA: I mean he *ran* it. What I never understood was all that stuff about Jack's supposedly wanting 'to smash the CIA into a thousand pieces.' Hell, it was his brother's operation! Anyhow, they had a thing called 'the Five Eyes' or 'the Three Eyes'—I swear it was owned lock, stock, and barrel by the CIA. And it was a Kennedy enterprise—not *legally*, but in fact. They got their orders from Bobby, and they carried them out. They were all over Hoffa and Spindel. . . ."

The source asks not to be identified, fearing retribution. But, as it happens, there's another man who's knowledgeable about the Five Eyes: Sidney Goldberg.

Thirty miles west of Washington, Goldberg lives alone in a small house situated among farms and woods. A slight man with a crippled hand, a shock of white hair, and a deeply distracted air, he says, "All that—the Five Eyes—it ruined my life. That's who they are. Look," he says, gesturing at the dilapidated furniture. "Would you believe I had a half-million-dollar business a few years ago? A maid?" Goldberg leans forward on the couch and struggles to light a cigarette with his one good hand. "I have a nervous condition," he says, referring to his case of tremors. "As soon as I got involved in that stuff, everything began to fall apart. We had a small newspaper—the *Government Employees Exchange*—a paper for the Hill, you know. And then one day in [1968]—I don't remember exactly when—things started coming in over the transom, so to speak. About the Five Eyes, or Three Eyes. And I did a little investigation. It all seemed tied up with Otto Otepka and, later on, George Ball. But suddenly we lost all of our advertising. Overnight. And we couldn't get anyone to return our calls."

Was that all?

"No. Some guys from the FTC came in one day and said, 'We want to look at your subscription list and your books.' I told them go right ahead. Then Bud Fensterwald walked in—I'd never seen him before in my life—and said he was a lawyer and that he'd heard I needed help. Then he told the FTC boys to get the hell out, get a warrant, they hadn't any right to look at my books. So they did. But that led to a lot of other things. There was a long legal case and I wasn't getting any advertising. Finally, I signed a consent order admitting there were seven subscribers to the *Exchange* who hadn't been getting their papers. I never should have signed it, but I did. I gave up. What the hell, there wasn't any money coming in. And I had a terrible case of nerves about it all. For months there was this white Cadillac following me—conspicuous as hell, you couldn't miss it out in the countryside. And then it got worse. I was driving with my wife and somebody shot at us. Then, after that, the Cadillac drove me off the road. I quit."

Does he still have the material that came in over the transom?

"I suppose so. But I'm not going to look for it. It ruined my life. I want to forget about it. I hope I never find it. Another guy asked me about it only a couple of weeks ago. A man from the State Department. And I told him the same thing. But I'll tell you something else. I can't believe Jack Kennedy was behind all this. I must have talked to the man on ten occasions—in the White House! Just me and him. And I think he was one of the greatest people I've ever met in my life." On the mantel next to the picture window are a pair of busts, kitsch renderings of the former President and his wife.

As it happens, the "Three Eyes" stood for International Investigators, Incorporated. Chartered in Indianapolis, Indiana, its home office was referred to as the Five Eyes. The firm's formal incorporation took place on October 3, 1966. But files in the Indiana Secretary of State's office show that, more than five years earlier, three retiring FBI agents were granted licenses to work as private investigators for International Investigators, Inc. This seems strange in view of the fact that in February, 1961, when the licenses were granted, the firm had no legal existence. The three detectives were George C. Miller, treasurer; George W. Ryan, president; and Thomas A. Everson, secretary. Among them, they had thirty-four years of FBI experience.

Within two years the still imaginary firm expanded throughout the Midwest, opening offices in Chicago, Detroit, Louisville, Nashville, Memphis, and Minneapolis—coincidentally the same cities in which Hoffa experienced intensive surveillance, including a great deal of illegal wiretapping. In 1965 the firm was taken over by a mysterious former CIA officer named Beurt Ser Vaas (later to become owner and publisher of the *Saturday Evening Post*). By this time the branch offices were deemed unnecessary (perhaps because Hoffa's legal situation had moved beyond the investigative stage to that of an appeals phase). Nevertheless, Ser Vaas added six new investigators to his Indianapolis staff, making each of them a director; of these, at least three had come from the FBI. Two of the firm's original managers, however, had left for other work. George Miller became a safety officer of the Agency for International Development in Saigon, and George Ryan became an executive of the Creole Petroleum Company in Venezuela. Both organizations have provided cover for the CIA.

Despite these new recruits, Ser Vaas claimed that the firm (which had yet to be chartered) was virtually "defunct" by the middle of 1965. Indeed, it consisted only of Ser Vaas himself and another ex-CIA officer, James Hannon Meyer, formerly district commander of the CIA's Office of Special Intelligence on Formosa. After the arrival of the new recruits, Ser Vaas changed the firm's name to the less conspicuous 904 Realty Company, conducting its operations from a seemingly private residence in a suburban neighborhood. In fact, the house was the new company's offices, and according to one of the firm's former employees, it was filled with sophisticated electronics equipment of every kind. Finally receiving its charter in 1966, Ser Vaas's investigative agency was liquidated in the following year. The timing is suggestive: created only a few weeks after JFK's inaugura-tion, the firm was finally dissolved the year Hoffa entered the pen.

There are some strange coincidences—probably no more than that—but they deserve mention. It's interesting, for instance, that the Indianapolis firm should have been referred to (with some confusion) as both the Five Eyes and the Three Eyes. Interesting too that its dis-solution coincided in time with the *de facto* establishment of another apparat composed of Get Hoffa veterans, *International Intelligence, Incorporated*—another "Three Eyes." And, like its predecessor, this latter apparat would exist for more than two years before formally incorporating.* Indianapolis may seem a strange base for an inter-national investigative agency, but the town has in fact generated more than its share of spooks. Tom Charles Huston, who prepared the Nixon Administration's White Paper for the domestic repression of the antiwar movement by U. S. intelligence agencies, practices law there. Richard Helms, former director of the CIA under Kennedy, Johnson, and Nixon, married an Indianapolis girl and worked for a while as a reporter in that town. Bill Harvey, the CIA spook who conceived the Berlin tunnel and took charge of the Castro assassina-tion efforts, was an Indianapolis native who, upon retiring from the Agency, returned there to die. The city is not without its secrets.

Still, the activities of the Five Eyes must have given the Hoosiers pause. While Sidney Goldberg is unwilling to unearth materials he received "over the transom" about the firm, he refers the stubborn to two issues of his former paper, the *Exchange*. Finding the *Ex-change* is no easy matter. A transient product of limited circulation, it has all but passed from the face of the earth. The Library of Con-gress, which maintained microfilm of the newspaper's issues from 1947 until its closure, states that the microfilm has been "misplaced" and can't be found.

But what Goldberg described in the *Exchange* was a top-secret private intelligence agency with contracts from the CIA, IRS, and other government agencies. Walter Sheridan was described as "the chief contact" between the Five Eyes and Senator Robert Kennedy. As an index of the firm's circumspect operational methods and compartmentalization, its employees were said to identify them-selves by means of "doodlegrams," casual scribblings that usually included a "pentagon with five dots surrounding it at each apex.

---

* International Intelligence, Incorporated, first mentioned here in the Introduction, is discussed extensively in subsequent pages.

The 'doodlegram' was drawn in the presence of the other person with successive small 'i' letters arranged [to] form [the] pentagram. In addition, a code number or a second 'doodle' was inserted in the center of the figure to identify the project actually involved." Moreover, claimed the *Exchange*'s source, wiretap operations ordered by Kennedy were "contracted out" to "investigative," "reference," and "industrial security" firms such as the Five Eyes, firms that were paid with "unvouchered funds." According to the same source, Walter Sheridan "disposed over the personnel and currency of whole units of the Central Intelligence Agency," working out of the White House. In addition, "Wire tap tapes including . . . 'voice profiles' made at the White House by the Secret Service . . . were passed on to him and maintained in a separate facility." Supposedly, the White House tapes were processed in a State Department "electronics laboratory" before being forwarded to Sheridan. The facility to which Sheridan sent the tapes, the source maintained, was outwardly disguised as a weather station. Asked about Goldberg's allegations, Sheridan ridicules the story, calling it "nonsense from beginning to end."

Not done, the source provided Goldberg with Senate and CIA reports relating to his charges, and with copies of personal correspondence between Time-Life editors Hank Suydam and Edward K. Thompson. The letters purported to document a "special relationship" between Kennedy and Time-Life, Inc., and between Sheridan and "The Huntley-Brinkley Report." Supposedly, intelligence obtained from the wiretaps "was used to provide Robert Kennedy and Walter Sheridan material for 'plants with the press.'" And, indeed, a letter from Suydam to Thompson describes a peculiar encounter between the Time-Life editor and the Kennedy group. "At any rate," Suydam wrote, "here's the story, as related to me by this fellow after a cloak-and-dagger shift of scenery, involving Kennedy slipping us out through back corridors, a drive by a roundabout route to the guy's home in Virginia, and the assigning to me of the code name 'Brown.'" As it happened, the fellow Suydam referred to was Sam Baron, an apostate member of the Hoffa brain trust. The purpose of the meeting was to have Suydam arrange for a Time-Life ghostwriter to collaborate with Baron on an exposé of Hoffa and the Teamsters.

Despite the unusual clandestinity of the arrangement, it may not seem particularly sinister; after all, Kennedy was only serving as a middleman between a publishing company and a budding author.

But the incident was by no means unique, as the allegation about "plants with the press" suggests. It was always Hoffa's contention that Kennedy and Sheridan, having difficulty convicting him in court, sought to have him tried by headline. And there is a great deal of evidence that this was so: *Life* magazine, in particular, was used by the Kennedy spy trust to expose or condemn the family's enemies. Ostensibly objective reports, the articles were calculated in their insinuations, in some cases descending to the level of the smear. In a few instances, reporters who became sympathetic with the subjects of their stories complained that the articles under their by-lines had been grossly rewritten and packed with unjustifiable innuendo. Others griped that the photographic illustrations accompanying their reports were deliberately calculated to make the merely interesting appear sinister and sociopathic.* But, mostly, *Life* reporters accepted the Kennedys' secret handouts with unquestioning enthusiasm, in some cases winning national prizes for having done little more than opening their mail and rephrasing its contents. It was no wonder, then, that the attitude of the press toward the Kennedys approached sycophancy. With few exceptions, the family played reporters, editors, and publishers with the facility of Van Cliburn plinking away at a baby grand. Bonhomie governed the relationship between the country's most powerful political family and watchdogs of the Fourth Estate. To say that the press became a tool of the Kennedys from the very inception of the JFK Presidency is no exaggeration: on the night of his inauguration, the new President took pains to attend a 2 A.M. cocktail party at columnist Joe Alsop's house. Thereafter, friendships were cultivated (stories stimulated and stories killed) with a league of influential newsmen, including Ben Bradlee, today editor of *The Washington Post*.

The pattern that emerges from a study of Robert Kennedy's relationship to Hoffa, Spindel, the CIA, and the press is one in which illicit electronic eavesdropping and surveillance carried out by private apparats is everywhere alleged. If there is any consistent thread running through it all, it is the Kennedys' reliance upon intelligence community veterans, most notably those from the National Security Agency (NSA). Robert Peloquin, Tom McKeon, and David Belisle, all of them top executives with International Intelligence, Incorporated (Intertel), are three such graduates. Walter Sheridan is a fourth

---

* For an example of the practice, see *Life* magazine's nightmarish depiction of Bernard Spindel in its May 20, 1966, issue.

NSA grad and considers himself a good friend of the others. Indeed, it was Sheridan who allegedly preserved Belisle's job in the State Department after pressure had been put upon the spook to resign. The pressure resulted from conflicting testimony Belisle gave to the Senate in the Otepka case. In that matter Otto Otepka, a super-grade State Department security evaluator, had provided information under subpoena to the ultraconservative Senate Internal Security Subcommittee. When that information was contradicted by Otepka's superiors, he returned to the subcommittee with documents suggesting that his superiors had lied. Infuriated by these "leaks," Kennedy loyalists placed an infinity-transmitter in Otepka's telephone, in effect converting it into a miniature broadcasting station. The tapes obtained from that tap were sent to the CIA, where technicians used special filters to eliminate all background noise. Returned to John F. Reilly, Belisle's superior, the tapes were then passed to an unidentified man in the corridors of the State Department. Shortly thereafter, Otepka was transferred from his post and placed in bureaucratic purdah—an isolated office where, though he continued to be paid, he was given no work to do. Discontent with this enforced leisure, Otepka filed an administrative appeal. In the course of that inquiry, and a related probe begun in the Senate, the wiretap was revealed. Belisle, Reilly, and the technician responsible for the tap's installation at first denied knowledge of it. In late 1963, however, the technician confessed to having made the technical installation. Belisle and Reilly then admitted their involvement in planning the wiretap operation. Because their sworn testimony had undergone a polar evolution, Belisle and Reilly were referred to the Justice Department for possible indictments for perjury. Controlled by Attorney General Kennedy—in whose behalf the infinity-transmitter may be said to have been placed—the Justice Department declined to prosecute. Reilly and the technician, however, were made to resign their posts at State. Belisle, on the other hand, was simply transferred to Bonn, Germany. Over Sheridan's denials, Goldberg claims that the transfer was arranged by Sheridan and that, moreover, Sheridan was the mysterious man in the corridor of State who became the custodian of the tapes. Belisle's influence with the Kennedys is reported to stem from "favors" he performed for the family while at the NSA with Sheridan during the 1950s.

Otepka confirms Goldberg's recitation of events, though he emphasizes that Sheridan's involvement in the affair has never been proven, only suspected. As for the Five Eyes, Otepka states, "There's no question that they carried out wiretaps—not only against Hoffa and organized crime, but here in Washington, against government employees. A friend of mine, an ex-FBI agent who became chief security officer for one of the telephone company's southwestern divisions, told me about it. He'd been approached in his job at the phone company by a vice-president of the Five Eyes—also an ex-FBI agent—who wanted his cooperation in placing taps on a number of individuals. He told him that the Five Eyes was working on a Justice Department contract, and that it had contracts with other government agencies—the IRS was mentioned, as I recall. He said they'd already installed taps in the Midwest and Washington, and that some of those taps were against government employees. What we didn't find out was whether the Five Eyes was involved in my case or not; maybe they were tapping somebody else." As for the strange reference to "voice profiles," which Goldberg claims were made by the Kennedy White House, Otepka said they were used to identify sources of leaks to the press. Allegedly, ninety-five journalists ranging from Evans and Novak to Mary McGrory and the *Times'* Washington staff had their voices taped and analyzed without their knowledge. Since voice profiles are as unique as fingerprints, it was thought that unauthorized leaks could be attributed to specific sources by "monitoring" the telephones of suspected government employees. With voice profiles of the most well-informed journalists in hand, it wouldn't be necessary to overhear the entirety of each conversation (a time-consuming task) but merely to obtain *a fragment* of each call. That fragment would then be compared to available profiles, and it would soon be known to whom the employee had spoken, and to whom he had not.

The obvious illegality of such wiretaps and the invasions of privacy they entail are clear. But what is even more threatening is the general practice of "subcontracting" illegal government operations to private firms secretly supported by public monies. Under the protection of the Attorney General or the President, but not directly in their employ, private apparats have virtual carte blanche and needn't consider constitutional niceties. They're simultaneously immune both to prosecution for misdeeds and to the ordinary constraints of the marketplace. Unlike federal agencies, which tend to resist demagoguery by virtue of an entrenched bipartisanship, private intelligence agencies in the employ of a powerful politician are beyond the control of all but their creator. And because their work is done for a single man or clique, with virtually no institutional or legal restraint beyond the dictum "Don't get caught," it cannot be said that their work is ever "in the public interest."

Robert Kennedy, of course, wasn't alone in his affection for spookery and the creation of private apparats. The Nixon Administration was similarly inclined. Jack Caulfield, Nixon's spook in the White House, sought to establish Corporate Security Consultants International—a private CIA set up to "penetrate" the opposition, carry out surveillance, smear opponents, handle "black bag" operations, and, as he put it, perform "any other offensive requirement" in behalf of supposed "Republican interests." The firm's "operating cover" would have been to "posture itself" as a specialist in defensive security operations. In reality, the firm would have been a criminal apparat masterminded from New York by a cabal of spooks operating in what he called "extreme clandestine fashion." *Nothing* would have been ruled out in pursuit of the political interests of the firm's clients. Caulfield's prototype, used as a justification for creating a secret-security group, was Intertel, which he described ambiguously as "Kennedy mafia dominated." Clearly, the outrages committed by the Plumbers were motivated in large measure by the Nixon Administration's fear of the Kennedy family and its associates. In the ethical vacuum subtended by Caulfield, Ulasewicz, Liddy, and Hunt, the pattern of political espionage and dirty tricks established during earlier administrations could only be imitated and, when possible, improved upon. Spooks beget spooks, impacting the democratic process with the incubi of intelligence—that's what the phrase "haunting of America" means. And while Nixon's activities were blatantly criminal, his paranoia, and that of his staff, may not have been unjustified. When one recalls the putative tap on Capitol Hill, the bugging of Otepka, the activities of the Five Eyes, the total surveillance of Jimmy Hoffa, the background of Intertel's principals, the CIA's dalliance with the syndicate, Kennedy ties to *Time, Newsweek*, and *The Washington Post*, CIA Director Helms's known allegiance to the Kennedys—not to mention Spindel's imbroglio with the Monroe tapes—Nixon's paranoia is understandable. It should not be forgotten that the leaks that inspired the Plumbers to covert action were thought to be politically motivated, the work of double agents in the White House and, perhaps, of offensive wiretaps. That these suspicions, and the crimes they led to, destroyed the Nixon Administration is true. And while we should be grateful for that exorcism, even *it* should be suspect. To spooks and reporters alike, the Watergate burglary appears to have been willfully botched. Perhaps it was. Similarly, the strategic role of the highly anonymous "Deep Throat" is much wondered about, though the consensus holds that he must have been a White House insider of the highest rank. But in view of all this wiretapping, the archipelago of politicized apparats, and the conflicting loyalties of those within the federal bureaucracy, might not "Deep Throat" have been an outsider? A Secret Service, CIA, or Kennedy spy with access to the White House tapes that, three years after the first newspaper reports, would constitute the Administration's *coup de grâce?* This is at least as plausible as the image of the concerned closet-liberal purveyed by *Washington Post* reporter Bob Woodward. The White House taping system that yielded Nixon's deleted obscenities was, after all, begun under the Kennedy Presidency. It doesn't require a leap of faith, or even much cynicism, to imagine that Kennedy loyalists might have retained some control over the system after leaving the White House. And that, of course, would explain "Deep Throat's" encyclopedic knowledge of the crimes and cash flow of the Nixon junta. Moreover, it would explain "Deep Throat's" continued bashfulness in the face of a grateful nation's cries of "Author! Author!" If he divulged the contents of the White House tapes, whether for partisan or patriotic reasons, it would likely be treated as a crime. And if his reasons were partisan, and made known as such through the discovery of his identity, Nixon would certainly not be absolved —but Watergate would be understood in its larger dimensions.

Bernard Spindel, buried a year prior to the Watergate burglary, anticipated the crime's outlines. For more than a decade the man known as "the Mafia's wireman" warned of federal lawlessness in the areas of surveillance and eavesdropping. The invasions of privacy directed against his clients and the harassment he himself suffered at the hands and ears of the Justice Department were, in his mind, no more than a prelude. It seemed almost inevitable that, through apathy, ignorance, or expediency, Orwell's timetable would be met. Out of frustration and an unwillingness to participate in that timetable's acceleration, he began sealing his inventions in lead and passed up an easy fortune by refusing to sell any device either to law-enforcement agencies or the telephone company. Thus, his inventions were available only to private citizens and could not be copied. What Spindel could not have anticipated, however, was the fate of the B. R. Fox Company itself, or the expediency of his posthumous partner, Mike Morrissey.

The man beside me in the Volkswagen, muttering to himself

about "rubber baby buggy bumpers," had a great deal to do with the ultimate fate of the B. R. Fox Company—but he was in no shape to talk about it then. Beyond a certain point, liquor loses its utility: WerBell's tongue had been "loosened" so much that it was nearly unhinged, and the sense of his speech was lost in irrelevance and disconnection. This seemed to suit the stout St. George, who, wedged uncomfortably in the back seat, rode in silence with his eyes closed, sighing grumpily from time to time.

Except for its context, the ride was an uneventful one. We rolled along the virtually unlighted Baltimore-Washington Parkway in a haze of cigar smoke and solitude. Each of us was submerged in his own reflections: St. George was no doubt contemplating his next move in the effort to unravel the complicated universe of Mitch WerBell—while WerBell himself was a man in crisis, federally indicted and beginning to doubt his own myth. As for me, my biggest worry was that we'd be stopped for speeding, and so, while the road seemed engineered to be taken at sixty-five, I slowed down to the high forties, a few miles per hour beneath the posted limit. Other cars whizzed past with such regularity that I feared we must be conspicuous—on the other hand, Maryland Governor Marvin Mandel had just inaugurated a sort of counterinsurgency war against speeders. According to the newspapers, the parkway was aswarm with undercover police driving battered pickup trucks and unmarked "muscle cars." Taking WerBell to the airport, then, was an adventure even if nothing happened: the possibility that we'd be stopped and WerBell would be recognized was real. Too bad for WerBell, of course, but too bad for me too.

Yet nothing happened. We arrived at the airport with perfect timing: the flight to Atlanta had just been announced as ready for boarding, which meant there would not be time for Mitch to insist upon having a drink. With great efficiency, St. George obtained the necessary ticket, and, with the spook gliding along between us, we marched through the airport to the departure gate. The bright lights and the presence of airport security guards had a mildly sobering effect on WerBell—which is to say that his sense of humor returned with what threatened to be a vengeance. Nodding toward one of those X-ray devices, metal passageways designed to detect weapons, WerBell muttered, "I walk through *that* sonofabitch and the whole joint lights up like Rockefeller Center, heh heh."

St. George sighed and, without breaking step, reminded his friend that this was not the time, and it was certainly not the place, for hijacking jokes.

" 'S-afuckin' kidnap," WerBell answered. "I don't wanta go. Whattaya say we have a drink and I'll take off in the morning?"

The journalist shook his head resolutely. "You can have a drink on the plane."

WerBell shrugged and began to hum, "Show me the way to go ho-oome, I'm tired an' I wanna go to bed—I had a little drink about an hour ago, and it went. right. to. my he-ead!"

At the departure gate St. George was a model of courteous efficiency. Distinguished in a vested tweed suit, portly and urbane, he withdrew the airline ticket from his pocket and proferred it to the attendant with a brief and ingratiating burst of apologies for WerBell's condition. Mitch himself stood beside his biographer with a wild, Cheshire-like grin on his face, rocking backward and forward on his heels, staring up into the attendant's face.

I understood the grin well enough. WerBell was in the process of getting away with something—specifically, getting away from under the weight of federal prosecutors—and it pleased him enormously that the attendant should accept St. George's charm at face value. The attendant smiled solicitously and said that he understood, which tugged the corners of WerBell's mouth even higher. The attendant understood nothing, a fact that WerBell enjoyed immensely. Nearby, an airport policeman smiled benignly at the scene, returning the spook's happy nod in his direction.

After scribbling something on WerBell's ticket, the attendant promised to escort the new passenger to the waiting plane. Then it was time to leave. There were handshakes and invitations to visit The Farm, grateful thanks and promises. Indeed, WerBell began to get quite sentimental about the whole affair and the good-byes became so effulgent that the attendant checked his watch conspicuously while I began to fear that we might have that drink in the lounge after all.

St. George, however, had no intention of nursing his friend through another night and so disengaged with promises to telephone Hildegarde and inform her of her husband's impending arrival. Relieved to see that the Wizard did not light up any lights he shouldn't have when passing through the security equipment, St. George and I decided to have a nightcap in the lounge ourselves.

Leaning against the bar, we ordered a pair of drafts and lapsed into the silence that a feeling of relief brings. Normally one who can turn any venue into a corner of London's Hyde Park, St. George was curiously quiet. After a spell he said, "Well, what do you think of the great Mitch WerBell?" His voice was a lard of tired sarcasm.

What indeed? I found him likable, even charming, in a perverse way. But he was a bully, too, and petulant. I knew that he enjoyed the company of dictators, that he could rationalize the most deadly forms of commerce, that he was intelligent and yet showed no aversion to the prospect of spilling blood in a venal and even hopeless cause. He was self-indulgent and more than content to simmer in the juices of his ego. He was a hard-guy in the old, corny sense of the term, and he was vulnerable too: it was impossible not to sympathize with a man whom the government was determined to destroy. He was an actor in his own B movie.

What did I think of him? *Why was he framed? Was* he framed?

"It's complicated," I said. "He's a very strange man."

St. George threw a couple of bills on the bar and nuzzled his goatee with the edge of his glass. "Very," he said.

It occurred to me (I'd already had a number of drinks) that the question he'd asked—"What do you think of the great Mitch WerBell?"—deserved to be in a Zen text. The correct answer had nothing to do with words because WerBell defied them: he was a master of contradictions. Properly, then, I should have responded with an action, wordlessly leaving the bar and disappearing into the night. Or I should have begun sweeping the floor, or spun the channels on the television set . . . *something*. Instead, we had another beer and talked about assassination plots.

ASSASSINATION, INC.

1 / BLACK LUIGI'S SAFE-HOUSE

WHEN SPINDEL DIED, HIS WIFE ENTERED INTO A PARTNERSHIP WITH Michael Morrissey, a former Westinghouse employee who'd met her husband and worked with him for a few weeks. According to Barbara Spindel, "Morrissey didn't have the talent Bernie did. He couldn't invent, but he was a good copier. There were a lot of things that Bernie left behind, things that were still years ahead of their time. And, of course, we needed the money: the B. R. Fox Company was all I had."

Morrissey was certainly no Spindel. In a letter to Defense Systems International, New Orleans arms dealer Ken Phillips wrote:

Dear Mitch . . .

You promised to let me have that suppressor for the .308. Please send it down to New Orleans this week; I have some police demonstrations coming up.

Just tried to give some business to Mike Morrissey and he let me down again. He said he would send a transmitter and receiver right away. I had the head of intelligence for one South American country here as a guest and another friend that is head of all security for his country—no bullshitters—I have known and done business with both. I had told

them it was being flown down that day and a week later when I got
Mike on the phone he said, "Oh well the old stuff in the lab didn't
work."

Do you have a reliable source for this stuff?

The letter is dated July 26, 1974, which probably explains Morrissey's apparent incompetence: since he had only a few weeks earlier forwarded the newly developed ASTRO catalog ("a listing of
equipment that is available and planned for Lou up here") to Wer-
Bell, it's likely that he was just too busy to bother with the occasional transmitter.

The B. R. Fox Company was located in a duplex apartment on
Connecticut Avenue in downtown Washington, D.C. While B. R.
Fox was supposedly the only tenant, the apartment in fact served
a number of purposes and housed a bizarre assortment of intriguing
characters. For one thing, it was used by Lou Conein as a safe-house
for the vanguard of the DEA's Special Operations Group (DEA-
SOG). That group numbered a baker's dozen of handpicked Latino
CIA officers transferred at "Black Luigi's" behest to the DEA. Appointed to the DEA post by Nixon,* Conein's task was to establish
an international intelligence network capable of destroying the narcotics traffic. Accomplishing this would be no easy matter. The DEA
suffered from internal corruption, and its best agents were consistently outmaneuvered by Oriental, French, and Cuban smugglers
trained in intelligence techniques by their own countries and the
CIA. Lacking sophistication in spookery, the DEA compiled a stunning record of failures and desperately required the expertise available in Langley. The CIA, however, was reluctant to participate in
any serious effort to destroy the heroin trade, regarding its own
mission as more important. Moreover, many of those involved in
the trade as financiers and couriers were themselves valuable CIA
agents. Conein resolved the dilemma of DEA impotence and CIA
recalcitrance by having the Dirty Dozen transferred from one agency
to the other. His orders were to create a clandestine service within
the DEA, and each of the dozen agents was regarded as a future
DEA "chief of station" in a foreign country. There they'd establish
their own apparats, run agents, and carry out a *de facto* guerrilla

* Retired from the CIA in 1972, Conein was persuaded by Nixon apparatchik Charles
Colson to implicate President Kennedy in the Diem assassinations by suggesting to the
press that Kennedy knew in advance of a plot to execute the South Vietnamese leader.
Conein, having monitored those plots while a CIA officer in Saigon, did as Colson asked
and received his DEA post as a reward.

war on dope, all of it masterminded by Lou Conein. And, because he distrusted the DEA itself, Conein chose to isolate his protégés from other agents at DEA headquarters. He did this by having them rendezvous in the LaSalle Building apartment leased to B. R. Fox— but paid for, in large part, by the DEA.

Besides harboring the Fox Company and the Dirty Dozen, the apartment was also headquarters for Security Consultants International ("SECOIN"). Conceived by WerBell (already the proprietor of the Central Investigative Agency), SECOIN was run by John Muldoon, who viewed Washington's huge embassy population as a likely clientele for debugging services. Finally, the LaSalle Building duplex served as a kind of crash pad for free-lance spooks.

"It was bizarre," Eliot Spindel says. "Muldoon would show up every day with a stack of cards about three inches high. He'd sit down at his desk and, one by one, make phone calls to the numbers printed on the cards. He'd do that until noon or so, then he'd go out with Conein for lunch, drink beer for a couple of hours, and come back to make more phone calls till five o'clock. . . . That's all he ever did—it was unnerving! I still don't know what it was all about. But the place really jumped when WerBell came through on one of his missions. It was like a visit from the general, you know?"

It must have been. At the time, WerBell was simultaneously wired into deals involving the "liberation" of Abaco, the establishment of a submachine gun factory in Costa Rica, the sale of his arsenal to Robert Vesco, and a variety of more "routine" transactions, described earlier. He was, in addition, under pressure from the CIA to leave the country, and according to Eliot Spindel, he was preparing to establish an offshore version of the B. R. Fox Company on Abaco. It's entirely possible that the CIA pressure and the off-shore plan were related. Since the 1969 Omnibus Crime Bill, manufacturers of clandestine weapons and surveillance devices have shifted their bases to locations in the Caribbean, establishing factories and shops in mini-nations that have neither the motives nor the funds needed to regulate the export of these products. According to WerBell, the CIA and DEA wanted him in an offshore position so that he could make and sell clandestine weapons in near-absolute secrecy.

The ASTRO line of B. R. Fox's equipment was WerBell's contribution to Conein's DEA program, and he was responsible for bringing Conein and Morrissey together. In the preface to the Fox catalog, stamped "CLASSIFIED," it's explained that "B. R. Fox Laboratories . . . manufactures explosive devices in various configurations and with various trigger mechanisms. These are described under our code-name of 'ASTRO' equipment. The devices have been designed and manufactured for sale to authorized agencies of the United States Government, *specifically intended for application outside of this country*." (Emphasis mine.)

"The items offered," it continues, "are either concealed into everyday type objects, or packaged simply as 'black box' pieces of equipment with no labels or indication on the outside other than the necessary actuator switches and sensors. Upon request, this equipment can be delivered in a 'sterile' condition for foreign use.

"Actuator mechanisms available are as follows:
(1) movement (anti-disturbance)
(2) fixed time period
(3) mechanical pressure release
(4) light (either presence or absence of)
(5) audio, be it voice or noise level

"The devices offered are complete in their operation, with the exception of the explosive charge which is added by the user. All equipment in our 'ASTRO' category is manufactured to the highest standards in terms of reliability, dependability, lifetime, and performance under most weather variations. Highest grade electronic components are selected and all controls are permanently cemented into sub-miniaturized modules. . . . We welcome your inquiries."

It is a remarkable catalog, a Hammacher Schlemmer of assassination. Some of its offerings:

Telephone Handset Insert, Miniature Activator with Time Delay:
Size: 1.25" × 0.75" × 0.5"
Use inside telephone handset. Automatic charge fired at x-seconds following lifting of instrument handpiece. Easy and quick installation to underside of mouthpiece. Any desired time delay . . . no switches . . . hand-wired . . . unlimited lifetime.*

With it an assassin could install the device, telephone his victim and inform him that his face would self-destruct in three seconds.

Modified Flashlight:
Standard Everready. . . flashlight has anti-disturbance electronics concealed inside where batteries have been removed. Remainder of the battery space is packed with explosive. The flashlight's normal On/Off

---

* This and succeeding descriptions of ASTRO devices are quoted from the B. R. Fox catalog.

switch on the side activates the operation. . . . An automatic timer . . . is normally factory-set for 90 seconds, unless specified otherwise. If at any time during the 'count' period of 90 seconds the flashlight is moved, the count recycles back to zero and starts over. Once it reaches the end of its cycle without any disturbance, the electronic charge circuitry automatically becomes active and armed. Any slight movement of the unit after that time sets off the explosive charge.

Cigarette Pack—Anti-Disturbance Explosive:
Electronics and explosive module packed inside cigarette pack. When the pack is lifted or moved in any manner, the explosive is set off. . . . Once the delay interval has been reached without disturbance of the cigarette pack, the electronic charge mechanism becomes armed. Any movement after that point will set off the explosive.

Fragmentation Ball—Anti-Disturbance Unit:
Unit is similar in its operation as the anti-disturbance flashlight. The exception is in the type of explosive charge. A fragmentation ball is attached on top of the electronics box. This is packed with explosive. . . .

(It is, in other words, designed to maim rather than to kill. It's a people-shredder.)

Booby-Trapped, M16 Explosive Clip:
A mechanically activated electronic charge circuit is built into a common military item. Upon removal of the single round in the magazine, either by firing or by hand removal, the explosive concealed in the magazine is detonated.

Most interesting, perhaps, is the *"Remote-Controlled, Light-Activated Sensor"*:

Unit delivers a pre-determined charge across its output terminals when activated from a remote location according to its pre-set code. Use with explosive for firing upon the occurrence of certain conditions relating to light intensity. . . . This unit can be activated remotely in many possible ways, since it is light controlled, by either the presence or absence of the light as well as its intensity. Some examples of activation are: indoor light turned on/off, laser light beams—invisible beams at distances up to 8 miles are presently available—day/night cycle, and flashlight or automobile headlights. This list is only suggestive, for there can be many other light variations.

Indeed, the variations were practically limitless. Had Conein wanted to, he could have received explosive devices capable of being triggered by virtually any identifiable signal, including changes in humidity, altitude, room tone, or barometric pressure. Morrissey's selection, however, was sufficient for the DEA's needs, since its solution to the drug problem was one of biblical simplicity: "If thine eye offend thee, pluck it out." Because the anti-Castro Cubans were applying CIA tradecraft to the art of smuggling heroin, Black Luigi enlisted the Dirty Dozen to counter the Cubans with even more recent tradecraft. Each of the men chosen by Conein had recently served as a paramilitary case officer in Vietnam, running crash operations and deep reconnaissance missions across the Demilitarized Zone. They were brave and talented—more than equal to the task of identifying the sources of heroin, the couriers and the routes. This, however, seems to have been only a part of the solution. For years the DEA had wasted time and tax dollars in an effort to slow the flow of heroin into the United States by concentrating their efforts on low-level "mules" and small-time dealers. While arrests soared, so did the use of heroin: dealers and couriers proved to be infinitely replaceable. Failing at the retail level, DEA swung its attention to the wholesalers, joining with the IRS in the Narcotics Traffickers Project (NTP). That project sought to interrupt heroin supplies by creating a cash-flow problem for the biggest dealers: but confiscating the cash of "selected narcotics targets," with an eye toward eventual IRS prosecution, proved to be costly and ineffective. The targets were all residents of the United States, with apparently unlimited access to secret credit; on the other hand, many of the most important financiers lived abroad. The DEA thus found itself in the position of having failed across the entire spectrum of heroin trafficking: whether they struck at the upper or lower echelons of the trade, the dope poured in. And no wonder: poppies were the source of heroin and they grew almost everywhere—in great abundance. While Turkey, Burma, Laos, Thailand, and Mexico seemed to be the greatest exporters, narcotics officials estimated that no more than a ten-square-mile region would be sufficient to satisfy the cravings of all the junkies in the world. The most efficient way to interdict the heroin traffic appeared to be one that would attack the trade at its sources abroad. That, however, seemed to be a near impossibility. The narcotics brokers included some of the most influential members of their societies. Gangsters were involved, but so were foreign generals and CIA agents such as Puttaporn Khramkhruan, a dapper Thai busted in Chicago with fifty-nine pounds of pure opium contained in twenty-five film cans. At the time, Khramkhruan was a contract CIA agent supposedly engaged in narcotics intelligence work under the cover of a handicrafts business set up for him by Joseph Z. Taylor & Associates (an Agency proprietary). At the request of the CIA, the Justice Department declined to prosecute the agent, convinced that an open trial would breach national security. The Taylor front was engaged in top-secret projects whose "flap-potentials" were considered enormous. Khramkhruan might, for instance, contradict U. S. assertions that the Agency for International Development (AID) was no longer serving as a CIA cover in any country except Laos. In fact, Taylor & Associates was using AID as a cover for training Thai border police. But gangsters, generals, and CIA agents such as Khramkhruan weren't the only ones involved in heroin trafficking. DEA and White House files implicated a host of people who gave new meaning to the word "Untouchables"—among the suspected financiers of the heroin trade were prominent Latin-American industrialists, diplomats, foreign ministers, landed aristocrats, a former President of Mexico, and the heads of at least two foreign intelligence services. Convicting them in the courts of their homelands would probably be impossible, even in the unlikely event that U. S. authorities could obtain conclusive evidence. If the Justice Department couldn't prosecute a thirty-one-year-old Thai student in Chicago, what chance did it have of convicting a former head of state in Mexico City, the Napoleonic Code notwithstanding? Frustrated by what amounted to the immunity of the drug trade's elite, DEA and White House officials contemplated murder. U. S. Ambassador (to Thailand, Italy, and later to South Vietnam) Graham Martin suggested that assassination teams might be sent out to slay known traffickers. The suggestion was made to Nelson Gross, an unsuccessful Senatorial candidate regarded as the political boss of New Jersey's Bergen County. At the time Martin's suggestion was made, Gross was director of the working committee of the Cabinet Committee on International Narcotics Control.* His immediate superior was the group's executive director, Egil ("Bud") Krogh, who as head of the Plumbers certainly had the personnel available to carry out Ambassador Martin's suggestion. And the suggestion got around. E. Howard

---

* Members of the Cabinet Committee were Attorney General John Mitchell, Secretary of the Treasury John Connally, Secretary of Defense Melvin Laird, Secretary of Agriculture Earl Butz, Secretary of State William Rogers, and CIA director Richard Helms. Interestingly, the law-enforcement committee had a unique criminal record of its own. Connally and Mitchell were both indicted in subsequent years, and a substantial number of its working staff—including Krogh, Gross, Hunt, and Liddy—later went to jail.

Hunt, for instance, reportedly contacted Bay of Pigs veteran Manuel Artime, seeking to organize assassination teams composed of Cuban exiles—who would, presumably, have operated in Latin America. In addition, the proposal for a "killer force" was made to members of the National Commission on Marijuana and Drug Abuse in September, 1972. A memo written by Dr. J. Thomas Ungerleider, one of the commission's members, states: "There was some talk about establishing 'hit squads,' as they are said to have in a South American country. It was stated that with 100–150 key assassinations, the entire heroin-refining operation can be thrown into chaos. 'Officials' say it is known exactly who is involved in these operations, but can't prove it."

Implementation of the final solution to the drug traffic, however, is believed by many (including Barbara Spindel, co-owner of the B. R. Fox Company) to have fallen to Lou Conein, perhaps because Krogh and the Plumbers were preoccupied with more important matters (such as burglarizing the Democratic National Committee and other sites of interest). Conein was no ingenue where wet-jobs were concerned. In Vietnam, the story is told how Black Luigi saved the life of Daniel Ellsberg by threatening to spark a murderous war between the CIA and the *Union Corse*. According to John Muldoon, who recounts the tale with glee, the Pentagon Papers need never have been made public had Conein not intervened in a romantic affair involving Ellsberg and the mistress of a *capo* in the *Union Corse*. Sitting down with the *capo* in a Saigon bar, Conein was informed by the Corsican that he would have Ellsberg killed if Ellsberg persisted in his courtship of the Corsican's girl friend, a beautiful Eurasian. Conein reasoned with the gangster that, if he took such a step, Conein would then have *him* killed. When the Corsican raised his eyebrows to suggest the obvious, Conein went on to add that, if the *Union Corse* should then do away with Black Luigi himself, the CIA would have no choice but to assassinate *three* of the *Union Corse* for every officer the Agency lost to the *Union*'s hit-men. Sounding almost like a booster, Conein went on to point out the Agency's superiority vis-à-vis the *Union Corse,* noting that the CIA has offices world-wide, more than 10,000 employees, and a multi-*billion*-dollar budget—not to mention satellites, mercenary armies, and a secret air force at its command. While respectful of the Corsican organization (of which he claimed to have been made an honorary member while serving in the OSS), Black Luigi made it more than clear that his own agency could hardly be challenged in the area of assassination. Was a romantic interlude worth the prospect of so much bloodshed? The Corsican shook his head. Conein smiled. Years afterward, when the Pentagon Papers were released, Conein regretted having said anything at all.

In any event, Conein left the White House in 1972 to organize a Special Operations Group (SOG) within the DEA—this at about the same time that Dr. Ungerlieder reported that some in government circles were considering the establishment of "hit-squads" to eliminate drug traffickers. Whether Conein intended to create an analogue to the Phoenix Program, with narcotics financiers as its targets, is uncertain. He says he did not. John Muldoon, Conein's friend, denies it too (though he admits that Conein might not have told him everything, might even have lied to him). WerBell also chimes in with a denial, but adds that he might not have known the entire story behind the LaSalle Building enterprise. "Besides," he says, "it's a dumb question. Even if I knew, you don't think I'd say so, do you?" It's a good point. Any such operation would necessarily yield denials once its cover was compromised. And yet the circumstantial evidence for the existence of such an operation is considerable. Besides the presence of WerBell, an expert on assassination methods, there were the twelve CIA paramilitarists, the Central Investigative Agency/SECOIN nexus, the operation's secretness and separateness from the other DEA affairs and, of course, Morrissey's plans for explosive light bulbs and self-detonating telephone receivers—not to mention Graham Martin's proposal for assassination teams and Dr. Ungerleider's report about "hit-squads." However much we might like to believe the denials of Conein and the others, the circumstances that surrounded the LaSalle Building apartment are morbid to contemplate. Those inside were hardly your Hawaiian-Punch-for-lunch bunch.

Despite the denials, however, there are a number of DEA officials and others besides Mrs. Spindel who are convinced that there was indeed an assassination plot. George Crile, writing in *The Washington Post* (June 13, 1976), quotes one DEA official who comments, "When you get down to it, Conein was organizing an assassination program. He was frustrated by the big-time operators who were just too insulated to get to." Moreover, Crile wrote, "According to these (DEA) officials, meetings were held to decide whom to target and what method of assassination to employ. Conein then assigned the task to three of the former CIA operatives assigned to the Connecticut Avenue safe house." It's possible, of course, that

Conein's rivals in the DEA were passing off speculation as fact, hoping to force Black Luigi into resignation. If so, they failed: Conein remains at the DEA. My own sources, however, tend to confirm Crile's. The scenario they describe is one in which some members of the Dirty Dozen would assist their boss in selecting targets for assassination. Once those targets were approved, booby traps obtained from the B. R. Fox Company would be issued and—there is no other word—contracts put out. Wary of creating a nest of international incidents, and worried as well about their own culpability before the law, Conein and his men would do no killing themselves. They would select the target and the assassin, providing the latter with sterile devices manufactured by Morrissey under WerBell's supervision. The killers would themselves be nationals of the countries in which the murders were to occur. Picked from dossiers of DEA informants, the hit-men would be offered a variety of inducements to perform their jobs: money, U. S. citizenship, the quashing of indictments pending against them—whatever it took. And if, somehow, the assassins were to be caught, there would be nothing to link them with either the DEA or Conein. Their contacts would have disappeared into a fog of aliases and false addresses, leaving the apprehended assassins with no more than an improbable tale that could never be verified.

In its daring and ruthlessness, the scenario bears a remarkable likeness to *The Parallax View*, a pulp thriller whose plot turns upon the premise of a corporation organized to carry out assassinations. In other ways, the scenario is an Americanized version of the South American "death squads" established by the police and security forces of Argentina and Brazil. The difference, of course, is that both the Parallax Corporation and the death squads are politically motivated. Conein, so far as we know, was not. It doesn't take much imagination, however, to speculate how long it would have taken for the offshore killing to come home—assuming that it did not.

Once again Conein has denied that he intended to create a star-spangled death squad. "It's bullshit," he growled, pouring another beer at Tony's. "I didn't know anything about it. I had no idea what Morrissey was going to show me. I thought it would be eavesdropping equipment." DEA officials and sources within the B. R. Fox Company scoff at that denial, though they do so with a measure of prudence. "I don't want my name used," one of them told me, "because Conein—well, he's a helluva guy and all that, but he's the last man in the world that I want pissed off at me. But of course he knew about it. That whole line, the ASTRO stuff, was designed for him. He was working with those people." Indeed, it's hard to believe otherwise: Morrissey was in frequent contact with WerBell, a friend and business partner of Conein's. Conein was paying half the rent on the LaSalle Building duplex used by the DEA and B. R. Fox. The Dirty Dozen were using the apartment as a "safe-house" and planning headquarters. Conein's friend John Muldoon was there every day, doing whatever it was that he did for WerBell's SECOIN. At any given time there were upward of fourteen ex-CIA officers wandering around the place, every one of them a trained spy. Secrecy among them was virtually impossible. As Eliot Spindel says, "We all had the run of the place, though we had our own work areas. The only thing that was off limits was a room, a sort of attic, that was always kept locked. I don't know what it held. I was ordered never to go in there."

That "attic," according to Muldoon, was the site of the DEA agents' "planning sessions" and of their meetings with men Muldoon believes to have been narcotics informants. If there was an assassination conspiracy, its headquarters would have been in the federal attic rather than in the lower half of the duplex reserved for the use of the B. R. Fox Company and SECOIN. Morrissey, after all, was only a technician and Muldoon says that he was himself engaged in nothing more interesting than seeking out clients for SECOIN.*

---

* SECOIN, or Security Consultants International, was a short-lived detective agency that WerBell says was virtually identical with his Atlanta-based Central Investigative Agency. According to John Muldoon, who headed up SECOIN on WerBell's behalf, the firm was created to compete with Intertel. Muldoon himself has taken assignments from Intertel and says that SECOIN was patterned after that firm. What makes this interesting is a curious coincidence: White House spy Jack Caulfield's "Operation Sandwedge" proposal (detailed in subsequent pages) urged the creation of a Republican-oriented private intelligence agency that he planned to call Corporate Security Consultants International (or COSECOIN). To justify the funding of the proposed apparat and the illegal operations he planned for it to carry out, Caulfield cited Intertel, describing it ambiguously as "Kennedy mafia dominated." It may be that the similarity between the names (SECOIN and COSECOIN) is no more than a coincidence. So too might be the invocation of the rival Intertel as the *raison d'être* for the Caulfield and WerBell agencies. I think, however, that coincidence played little part in the matter. Caulfield's "Operation Sandwedge" proposal was under consideration by John Mitchell and others during Lou Conein's tenure in the White House. Recruited in 1970 by E. Howard Hunt, Conein handled various assignments for Charles Colson and, later, for Egil "Bud" Krogh—chief of the Plumbers. It's by no means unlikely, then, that Conein learned of Caulfield's proposal and, in the athletic jargon of that place and time, "took the ball and ran with it." Conein's association with the White House Plumbers, among whom COSECOIN was discussed, and his subsequent role at the LaSalle Building where SECOIN was a reality (and one whose rent was subsidized by covert DEA monies), suggests that SECOIN may have been a creation of the Plumbers. In which case, the reports of hit-squads being discussed by government officials, and of assassination teams actu-

Though the nature of Morrissey's inventions were homicidal on their face, it's by no means certain that he, Muldoon, or even WerBell was privy to whatever plans Conein may have had for his enemies. On the contrary, application of the "need-to-know" principle suggests that all of the civilians should have been kept in the dark as much as possible concerning Conein's intentions.

With the exception of the attic, though, the safe-house was open to the spooks and technicians who inhabited the apartment. Obviously, in view of Morrissey's designs, there were some in the safehouse who believed that there was a conspiracy under way to murder for the public good. As for Conein, he is utterly unconvincing when he attempts to dismiss the ASTRO equipment as nothing more than a fantasy with which Morrissey surprised him.

That Conein should have conceived of such a plot is, on the other hand, in no way surprising: most of his life has been spent in an atmosphere of blood and mud and beer. In Vietnam, to CIA officers like Conein, assassination was a part of the environment, a hazard to endure and an opportunity for advantage.

That the alleged scheme died aborning owes nothing to the common sense of those involved. In the midst of Watergate, and in advance of congressional inquiries into the CIA's "executive action" efforts abroad, a Xerox copy of the Fox catalog was provided to Senator Lowell Weicker. He in turn accused the DEA of planning to use the ASTRO equipment. It was then that Conein reported his surprise at being shown the devices. Because the DEA operation had been compromised, if not exposed, it appears to have been abandoned. Subsequently, Conein was subpoenaed to testify before the Senate Permanent Subcommittee on Investigations. That subcommittee had already subpoenaed WerBell (as earlier described) in its investigation of the DEA and Robert Vesco. But even as WerBell was prevented from testifying by the precipitous indictment of his son and his company, Conein's testimony was never taken. Before he could be brought before the microphones, the probe was aborted without explanation.

---

ally heading south, become more credible. For his part, WerBell becomes uncharacteristically quiet when asked about SECOIN and any connection it may have had to the White House and to the Plumbers. All he'll say in this regard is that "the statute of limitations has been running nine years" (as of 1978), and that SECOIN was the brainchild of himself and a former associate, Col. Robert Bayard. Almost parenthetically, he adds that Bayard, who was shot to death in an Atlanta parking lot July 3, 1975, was "assassinated." That was almost two years after the B. R. Fox Company took residence in the LaSalle Building during the fall of 1972. But as for any connection between SECOIN and the White House, WerBell declines to say.

2 / THE OFFSHORE SOLUTION

Did the operation ever get off the ground? DEA sources suggest that it may have. According to a DEA official and reporter Crile, Conein's agents made several trips to Mexico in an effort to target suspected dealers. That accomplished, an assassin was found among the DEA's ranks of informants; that man, however, never received the B. R. Fox devices intended for him—Senator Weicker intervened with his charges against the DEA, forcing the assassination program to a halt.

And just in time, it seems. Reporters who've accepted Conein's dismissal of the B. R. Fox affair point out that the explosive devices designed by Morrissey were never manufactured—only breadboarded. As Eliot Spindel says, "It was mostly on paper. We designed a slew of things, whatever we thought might work. But we never made any of it. We never got that far." In view of that, it's not unreasonable to conclude that the whole affair, the exploding light bulbs and mysterious phone calls, was no more than a pipe dream. Thinking about it in that way, we can look upon the mélange of Fox technicians, DEA agents, WerBell, and the Central Investigative Agency—that whole apartment—as a bedlam of intriguers. Interesting, but unimportant.

Had the Senate looked deeper, however, they would likely have arrived at a different conclusion. The salient facts are two. First, Eliot Spindel recalls that WerBell intended to establish an offshore version of the B. R. Fox Company in the Caribbean. Second, Barbara Spindel was forced to sue Mike Morrissey for what she claimed was his deceptive handling of B. R. Fox accounts, his secrecy and refusal to confide in her about the operations of the firm she owned. According to Mrs. Spindel, concerned that she may have been cheated out of monies owed to her, Morrissey made large disbursements of company funds for foreign travels that he insisted were of a business nature. Nevertheless, he has so far refused to elaborate further on the actual nature of those "business trips." If we put these two facts together—WerBell's offshore intentions and Morrissey's secret trips—the combination is suggestive.

Any assassination plot concocted by Conein could never have succeeded had he relied upon booby traps manufactured in Washington, D.C. To have used explosive devices (however "sterile") that were made in the U.S.A. would have been an invitation to disaster. Just as the program would have relied upon foreign nationals for the actual commission of murder, it would also, and for similar reasons, have depended upon weapons produced outside the United States. Not only could such devices, manufactured abroad, never be traced to Washington, but they would not be subject to the scrutiny of the State Department, ATF, local police, and other agencies. Conein's solution to the drug problem could not be carried out within the leaky Washington bureaucracy; neither could it depend upon the approval of the DEA as a whole. It could only succeed as an isolated operation, a breakaway group hermeticized by secret budgets and an immunity to review. It made sense, therefore, to reestablish the B. R. Fox Company, or its successor, on some remote Caribbean isle where customs were lax and the law sleepy. This is precisely what Morrissey and WerBell intended to do. There was never any intention of providing Conein with exploding flashlights, light bulbs, and telephone receivers. All he needed was a *description* of these devices, gizmos that would later be manufactured abroad and made available to agents as needed. Thus the B. R. Fox *catalog.*

WerBell's role in this was an important one. It was no accident that Fox and the DEA shared its LaSalle Building offices with SECOIN. When we think of covers, conduits, and fronts, we tend to think also of the CIA. But the CIA is not the only government agency that resorts to these devices. The NSA, DIA,* DEA and many other agencies routinely make use of them. The evidence, then, suggests that WerBell's SECOIN may have been established to serve as a DEA cover. Sharing its space with the B. R. Fox Company, while making its attic available to the Dirty Dozen, SECOIN would have been an excellent cover for clandestine government operations, such as those of Conein, that required plausible denial. That WerBell should be the owner of the "detective agency," and the proposed co-owner of the offshore version of B. R. Fox, makes sense. Conein needed someone he could trust, someone outside the DEA, who could be held publicly accountable for the private firms' operations. If the DEA operations were exposed, SECOIN and B. R. Fox would have gotten the blame. The retired CIA agents who belonged to the Dirty Dozen would, if exposed, have appeared to be employees of SECOIN or B. R. Fox—rather than of the DEA. That one man should be the proprietor of both firms was desirable:

* Defense Intelligence Agency.

it would provide him with reasons for shuttling back and forth between the two. It would be understandable that he, as their owner, should have commerce with both firms, overseeing each. It made sense as well for the owner of the firms to be a friend of Conein's. Meetings between the two men could be explained as merely "social." WerBell, in short, was an ideal choice for the assignment. Not only was he a close friend of Conein's, but his known interests made any investment in the B. R. Fox Company or a "detective agency" seem perfectly natural. Moreover, should the scheme actually backfire, WerBell made an excellent fall guy. A specialist in the assassin's art, and one who bragged of his achievements in the field, WerBell could hardly play the innocent. So far as Conein was concerned, the B. R. Fox-WerBell setup was perfect. Looking at WerBell, we can imagine Conein's thoughts: "The bullet stops there."

THE WORLD OF BOBBY V.

1 / THE MAN IN THE COMPOUND

IN EARLY 1974 IT SEEMED TO MITCH WERBELL THAT HE WAS THE central element in a Caribbean metaplot, a complex intrigue whose related elements were the CIA/DEA nexus surrounding Conein, the right-wing invasion plot targeted for Abaco, and the arsenal of silenced Ingrams. Before the month of April was over, he would add other elements to the intrigue—most notably those of Robert Vesco and organized crime. To some people WerBell's role might have been a daunting one. But to Mitch himself it was merely proof that he'd finally arrived: great things were in the works, invasions and wet jobs, multimillionaires, hoodlums, spooks, and British lords. Appeasing his appetite with mounds of steak tartare washed down with Scotch, he jetted from one capital to another, exhilarated by the overlapping intrigues.

Discussing this period with him, one notices an unmistakable change: subdued and caustic in its aftermath, he recounts the events of 1974 with a sly twinkle, enthusiasm and paranoia wrestling in his speech. To WerBell everything was related: Abaco, Conein, the weapons deals, and, most importantly, Robert Vesco. Precisely how they were related, he won't say, except to suggest that the CIA was their common denominator, the Caribbean their target. To suspect WerBell of paranoia, however, is somewhat misleading. Undoubtedly the man, seeing himself as the world's foremost secret agent, has delusions of grandeur; and unquestionably he perceives connections between events that may only be coincidental, tending to believe the most sinister explanation of each. And thinking all these things to be part of some grand conspiracy hatched at Langley, he may be thought—well, crankish at best. But WerBell's so-called paranoia is not at all unreasonable. A free-lance spook specializing in paramilitary affairs and secret invasions, his suspicion is a kind of professional tic, a survival trait which in the course of his career has proven more useful than incapacitating. More than reporters or political extremists, intelligence agents are inclined toward baleful explanations that emphasize conspiracy and ulterior motives. Nothing is too banal to escape a dark interpretation. And, quite often, the interpretation is correct.

WerBell's "paranoia," however, was not only a matter of professional discipline. There were reasons for his suspicions. With his somewhat overweening respect for the CIA, he found it difficult to believe that a lifelong spy of Conein's stature could ever really *leave* the Agency. Accustomed to the use of other government agencies as CIA covers, WerBell quite naturally held open the possibility that Conein's DEA job was no more than an exercise in "sheep-dipping"; the backgrounds and identities of the Dirty Dozen, all of whom were CIA veterans, did nothing to alleviate that suspicion. In a similar way WerBell, like any free-lance agent, was used to a certain ambiguity in the identity of his *own* employer; it did not seem unusual to him that the CIA would place its officers under DEA cover and, through their chief, engage WerBell's private services on what was, he thought, a CIA operation. In fact, it would have been standard procedure.

Perhaps equally important to WerBell's perception of a metaplot were the frequent "suggestions" he received from CIA officers and agents, suggestions to the effect that, in the wake of Watergate, it would be best if he moved his operations abroad. To WerBell those suggestions were the Agency's way of discreetly conveying its approval of, and its authority for, his involvement with B. R. Fox and the proposed offshore facility. What convinced him of the Agency's ultimate responsibility, however, was the sudden involvement of Robert Vesco, the fugitive financier accused of the largest fraud in the history of money.

In April, 1974, WerBell sat down to lunch in Miami with Stuart Graydon and Martí Figueres. Graydon is an international arms dealer based in Birmingham, Alabama. Figueres is the son of Don Pepe Figueres, formerly President of Costa Rica. Present in spirit at the meeting, but not in body, was Robert Vesco. Having flown the United States on charges that he'd sought to influence an SEC investigation by making an illegal donation of $200,000 to Nixon's 1972 reelection campaign, Vesco had found tropical sanctuary in San José, Costa Rica. He could not return to the United States without being arrested, and if he should be, his bail would be high: the SEC accused the fugitive of having masterminded the diversion of at least $224,000,000 in liquid assets from Investors' Overseas Services (IOS), funneling the money into scores of remote and sometimes phony corporations controlled by himself and his cronies.

Vesco's entrance into WerBell's affairs began in late 1973. In a letter to WerBell, Graydon reported that a "private party" in Costa Rica wanted to buy the entire arsenal of Defense Services, Inc.— two thousand silenced submachine guns. (A year earlier, Vesco had acquired a silenced Ingram from the son-in-law of Paraguay's President; obviously, he'd been impressed with the weapon.) While WerBell was more than willing to sell the guns, his application for export was turned down by the State Department: with no Army of its own, Costa Rica could ill afford to have two thousand Ingrams in the hands of an unidentified private citizen.* Undaunted by this logic, WerBell, Figueres, and Graydon met to discuss a proposal that they establish an Ingram factory in Costa Rica. Whether Vesco's name was mentioned is unknown, but it must certainly have been on the minds of some of the participants. Martí, a suave and witty Tico, was regarded in the Caribbean press as Vesco's personal emissary and boon companion. A constant passenger on the fugitive's private 707, a Boeing jet described by its pilot as a combination "command post/bordello," Figueres was also Vesco's business partner. Before fleeing to San José, the flying financier had smoothed the way with a $2,150,000 investment of IOS monies in Papa Figueres' family business, the *Sociedad Agrícola e Industrial San Cristóbal, S.A.* ("San Cristóbal"). The money came in the form of an un-

---

* The "showcase of Latin American democracy," Costa Rica has not had an Army since the 1948 counterrevolution led by Don Pepe Figueres. After ousting the Communists from power, Figueres abolished the Army on the grounds that Costa Rica had no enemies. The President, however, is protected by an elite palace guard, and the national police force receives military training. In a sense, Figueres "interiorized" the Army, providing it with a different name and mostly domestic responsibilities.

secured loan from the International Investment Trust (IIT), an
IOS mutual fund managed by Richard ("Pistol Dick") Pistell, a
confidant and business associate of Vesco's. Fast-talking, ebullient,
and built like an icebox, Pistol Dick skimmed a $150,000 "finder's
fee" off the top of the IIT loan to San Cristóbal. The SEC would
later sue Pistell for recovery of that money—plus another three million dollars of IIT funds that the happy-go-lucky fund manager
had loaned to himself for subsequent investment in companies he
owned in places as far apart as Turkey, the Cameroons, and the
Caribbean. At the time of the loan to San Cristóbal, the Figueres
company was in financial crisis, largely as a result of its black-
market activities. In 1969, San Cristóbal was rocked by the disappearance of $600,000 in black-market payments that were supposed
to have been paid to Martí Figueres but which, he swore, had not
been. The IIT loan saved the firm from disaster—but at the expense
of IOS shareholders: there was no market for San Cristóbal's paper,
and no one could say when, if ever, IOS victims would be able to
reclaim their supposedly "liquid" capital.

As if these associations were not enough, there was yet another
clue to Vesco's involvement in the submachine-gun scheme. While
the factory could not be established without a meeting of "principals" in San José, Martí Figueres asked WerBell to take care of
some relatively trivial business for him. His patron required six
AR-15 semi-automatic rifles and eighteen thousand rounds of ammunition. Could Mitch get them right away, perhaps filing the application for export at some later date? WerBell assured him there
would be no problem. In that case, Figueres said, they should be
delivered to the Mini-Bay-U warehouse in Miami and held for
Alberto Abreu, Robert Vesco's confidential agent. The keys to the
storage facility should be delivered to Costa Rica by WerBell, and
there, if all went well, they would arrange financing of the Ingram
factory.

While Vesco could not safely enter the United States, his aides
and flunkies could. For years the financier had surrounded himself
with "go-fers," and now that he found himself in an imposed tropical
exile, nothing had really changed: the go-fers merely had to travel
farther to satisfy their boss's wants. Indeed, the whole matter of
exile, the SEC investigation, and the notoriety seemed, at times,
to be no more than an inconvenience. So it was that Martí Figueres
arranged for the purchase of the AR-15's and ammo, instructing
WerBell to bring the keys for the Miami storage locker to San José;

what happened with the guns after that, WerBell was told, was none of his concern.

Although WerBell didn't have an export permit for the weapons, he nevertheless filled the order within hours. Wally Gillis, a handyman at The Farm, rented a truck in Atlanta, and drove the guns and ammunition to Miami. On the way, however, Gillis was flagged down after failing to stop at a truck-inspection station. Finding the cargo of rifles and bullets, the inspectors summoned local police, who in turn contacted agents at the Bureau of Alcohol, Tobacco, and Firearms in Atlanta. According to Hamilton County sheriff Charles Tompkins, ATF's Atlanta supervisor ordered the release of Gillis and the truck, noting cryptically that WerBell was engaged in "special work" for the government.

In Miami, Gillis transferred the weapons to a station wagon and then, as instructed, delivered them to the Mini-Bay-U warehouse. There he rented a space in the name of Albert Abreu (omitting the concluding vowel in the Latino's first name). After signing Abreu's misspelled signature to the storage documents and supplying a phony address, Gillis rushed to meet WerBell at the airport bar. Handing him the keys to the warehouse space and accepting a drink, Gillis told his boss of his near-arrest outside Atlanta. WerBell thanked the handyman, promised to reimburse him, and left to board the flight to San José. He was glad to know that he was doing "special work" for the government, but he wondered what it could be. Vesco? Abaco? Conein? There were a half-dozen possibilities and it must have occurred to WerBell that, no matter what he did, he was covered. Any involvement with the CIA provided a kind of blanket immunity: the Agency couldn't afford to let him be arrested for fear that his "special work"—whatever it was—would be exposed. The realization was intoxicating: it was almost as if WerBell had diplomatic immunity in his own country.

The flight to San José was unspectacular. As the plane landed, WerBell put the finishing touches to his tourist card, indicating that the trip was for the purpose of "recreation." Arriving by taxi at the city's best hotel, he marched inside with the keys to the Mini-Bay-U warehouse in his jacket pocket. Until he received a phone call from Graydon, Figueres, or Vesco, there was nothing for him to do but order a bottle of Scotch, send out his blue jeans to be starched (a curious habit), and wait. Which is what he did. Things seemed to be going perfectly.

* * *

There's no way to know what WerBell was thinking about as he sat in his hotel room, but he certainly must have wondered, at some time, about the meaning of the Vesco proposition. Not that there was any mystery about the AR-15's, however mysteriously the transaction was designed: one of Vesco's aides—probably Abreu—would be given the keys to the warehouse, fly to Miami, remove the guns from storage, and take them out of the United States aboard a fifty-four-foot yacht Vesco was negotiating to buy. Nor was there any mystery about why he wanted six semi-automatic rifles. Rumors had been circulating for months that the financier was having crates of weapons secretly delivered to him in San José; a private jet owned by the exile's since-imprisoned friend, Los Angeles stockbroker Tom Richardson, was most frequently cited as the arms carrier. Obviously, Vesco wanted to arm the score of bodyguards surrounding his estate. As for the large quantity of ammunition, the guards would need to become practiced with the guns. But what use would the swindler have for more than *two thousand silenced Ingram submachine guns?* It was enough to start a war. It occurred to WerBell that Vesco intended to do just that. And with the Ingram deal quashed by a worried State Department, the notion of establishing a submachine-gun factory in Costa Rica took on a fascinating aspect: it must have seemed to Vesco that if he couldn't buy the guns outright, he might just as easily make them himself. Whatever he intended to do with them, and whatever it took to get them, he clearly wanted an arsenal capable of offensive use. The millionaire's explanation, that he needed the Ingrams "for the protection of my family," was preposterous. A private war appeared to be in the making, and not just another CBS Invasion: this one had all the loot of IOS behind it and, if Gillis's immunity on the highway was any indication, the blessings of the CIA as well. WerBell must have rubbed his hands together with anticipatory glee as he gazed out across the San José skyline: a few miles away, on the outskirts of the snoozing capital, was a compound surrounded by private soldiers and, inside, a man with all the resources and ambition necessary to make WerBell a legend in his time.

Robert Vesco, the man in the compound, was probably not oblivious to WerBell's arrival. But neither is he likely to have been especially preoccupied with the paramilitarist's presence in San José. To Vesco, WerBell was only a single element in a complicated equation that included some of the most exotic figures in the worlds of crime, espionage, politics, and finance.

Consider the man: * His origins were modest to the point of prudery. The son of a Detroit factory worker, he grew up despising the fact that his last name ended in a vowel, a circumstance that seemed to hint at recent immigration, garlic, and accented speech. By all accounts he chafed at the economies forced upon his family, the fading picture tubes and chuck steak, though "Bobby V." did not himself seem destined to transcend them. In 1952, at sixteen, he left high school to work in an auto-body shop, having already ac- quired a minor police record for piloting a stolen car (the charges against him were never pressed). A year later he married Pat, a sixteen-year-old from Bad Axe, Michigan, and shortly thereafter fathered his first son.

Vesco, however, was vastly more ambitious than his circumstances could suggest. Over the next few years he moved through a succes- sion of jobs with different companies, lying about his education and experience until, at twenty-four, he'd doubled his salary several times and held the title of Project Engineer. The middle class, however, was too large to hold him, and exhibiting the *chutzpah* for which he was becoming famous, he struck out on his own. Within a year he'd become a minority partner in a number of nearly insolvent companies whose stock he'd acquired through defaults of one kind and another. Acting as a "consultant" to these firms, he sought buyers and bank

* The history of IOS, of which Vesco's story is a part, can be divided into three periods: the Cornfeld years, Vesco's takeover, and Vesco's fugitive period in Costa Rica. In my discussion of these periods I've relied upon a number of different sources. Besides inter- views with Bernie Cornfeld, SEC investigators, Intertel executives, Senate sleuths, and others, I've depended heavily upon the legal proceedings that have resulted and the briefs filed by both sides. With respect to the Cornfeld years and Vesco's later dominance of IOS, I've gleaned a great deal of anecdotal material from two books: *Do You Sin- cerely Want to Be Rich* (by the London *Sunday Times'* investigative team) and *Vesco* (by Robert Hutchison). Both books are footnoted elsewhere and are highly recom- mended. Information concerning Vesco's fugitive years derives from interviews with Vesco-watchers in the Senate and SEC, from business associates of his, from "The Robert Vesco Investigation" (*Hearings* before the Permanent Subcommittee on Investigations of the Committee on Government Operations, U. S. Senate, U. S. Government Printing Office, Washington, 1974), and from occasional articles in a number of Latin American periodicals, most notably the *Tico Times, La Nación, La República,* and *La Prensa Libre.* While letters written by Vesco to the U. S. Embassy in San José have also been made available to me and proven useful, neither Vesco nor his attorney, Edward Bennett Williams, has been willing to be interviewed by me. After protracted negotiations with Vesco's aide, Alberto Abreu, a promised interview was canceled after Vesco asked for and received a sampling of some sixty-five questions I intended to ask. According to Abreu, the questions offended his employer, who commented, "If I answer this stuff, I might as well talk to the SEC."

loans for them. While this was tactically unsuccessful, it proved strategic to Vesco's phenomenal rise: expanding his circle of acquaintances to include U. S. and foreign bankers, Vesco was able to ingratiate the older men, winning their confidence in his abilities. Before long they were lending him money to buy out the very firms for which he'd been consulting. Not yet thirty years old, he merged these small companies into a new corporate vehicle he'd created, the ambitiously named International Controls Corporation (ICC). That accomplished, he negotiated yet another merger, this time with a nearly bankrupt firm (Cryogenics, Inc.) whose single virtue was that its stock was traded over the counter. This meant that Vesco's ICC was permitted to sell its stock over the counter without having to submit itself to the SEC's meticulous registration procedure. Thus he had sudden access to a variety of new capital sources: mutual funds, investment houses, trusts, etc.

Making use of those sources, Vesco continued to conglomerate—though the word is rather large for a firm which in 1965 had fewer than twenty employees. Acquiring the stock of larger firms was no problem, however. A pygmy such as ICC might swallow giants four times its size so long as ICC shares were more highly regarded by investors; the key to that regard, of course, was evidence of ICC's growth. Through continual mergers, Vesco was able to demonstrate undeniable growth to prospective investors—ICC was doubling its size almost annually. Moreover, Vesco's credit rating was spectacular. While his firms were only marginally profitable, if that, their boss was able to use the capital of *newly* acquired firms to repay loans *made to finance their acquisition.*

So it went, as one company after another joined ICC's family: Century-Special, Fairfield Aviation, Kenyon Electronics, Intercontinental Industries, Golden West Airlines, and, most importantly, Electronic Specialties, Incorporated (ESI)—this last firm ten times larger than International Controls itself. In less than three years, then, Vesco had climbed from being a consultant to a handful of small New Jersey manufacturers that were on the edge of insolvency to become the Maximum Leader of a $100,000,000 conglomerate employing thousands—a conglomerate almost literally created out of thin air. Not bad for a high-school dropout from Motor City.

Had he wanted to, Vesco might have sold his controlling interest in ICC, retiring as a thirty-two-year-old multimillionaire. His ambition, however, seems to have been of comic-strip dimensions. Having blitzed the scene of domestic finance, he turned to the world of offshore mutual funds, glimpsing in Investors' Overseas Services (IOS) the possibility of multiplying his millions *a thousandfold*.

2 / TO COX'S BAZAR AND BACK

At the time IOS was an intriguing and vulnerable entity. It had been created by Bernard Cornfeld in the last years of the Eisenhower Administration. A middle-aged hippie, Cornfeld was a mass of contradictions: an admirer of socialism who professed a deep concern for the poor, he spent his time pursuing the interests one associates with playboys and financiers. In some ways he resembled Glenn ("Dare To Be Great") Turner, mesmerizing his salesmen and subordinates with a casserole of dreams and schemes; in other ways he resembled his friend Hugh Hefner, self-consciously surrounding himself with the status symbols of sex, power, and affluence. To some Cornfeld was a hustler, to others a poet. While he might be awesome in boardrooms and executive suites, alternately raging about "bankers' plots" and spieling eloquently on the subject of "People's Capitalism," he seemed privately insecure. A connoisseur of proxies, he was an ingenue in other ways, incapable of reading a balance sheet, gauche in his tastes, at times a schlepp. And while he was the tenant of castles and manor houses in a half-dozen countries at once, Cornfeld always seemed a Flatbush sort of tycoon. A paragon of the *nouveau riche,* his tastes in clothes, women, furnishings, recreation, and art seemed to have been dictated by researchers at *Playboy* magazine. In Geneva he purchased the Villa Elma, a mansion built by Napoleon for the Empress Josephine. Determined to impress his own personality on the historic edifice, he swathed its walls in acres of velvet (which wasn't surprising since Cornfeld tended to swath everything in velvet, at least everything that didn't move). Its halls were lined with marble busts and the most masterful canvas forgeries that money could buy. As for the toilets, they were disguised as Louis XVI wicker armchairs. In automobiles his taste ran to the most expensive and racy available: Maseratis, Lamborghinis, and Ferraris. But he drove them at such a slow and cautious speed that they were forever in need of tune-ups. Undoubtedly, this caution pleased his mother, Sophie, an octogenarian Brooklyn girl ensconced on the villa's third floor, but it irritated others in his entourage.

And what an entourage: within its ranks was Seymour ("The Head") Lazare, a pigtailed financial advisor who described himself

as "the world's only hippie arbitrage expert." * In addition to
Lazare was a phalanx of other loyalists: IOS salesmen detoxifying
from their unappointed rounds; backgammon junkies; aristocratic
pretenders; self-annealing sycophants, and, of course, *the girls*. Most
of them seemed to have come, by birth or Pan Am, from southern
California; they included knife-thin groupies in diaphanous dresses
and wraparound shades, *Playboy* bunnies on sabbatical, used models,
dropouts from UCLA's drama school, and "free-lance writers" who'd
come to Europe on vacation and remained. What they had in common was their beauty and a claim to being oh, so laid-back. Indeed,
even the secretaries were beautiful and, in their IOS uniforms designed by Cardin, seemed like Vegas chorines—leggy, sumptuous,
and chic, valkyries of the Smith-Corona.

IOS, Cornfeld's dream-spawn, was neither less interesting nor less
bizarre than its master and his entourage. A holding company that
owned banks, mutual funds, insurance companies, natural resources,
real estate, and a lot more, its operational style blended characteristics that seemed to have been culled from studies of the CIA,
Banque de Rothschild, and Tupamaros. There has never been an
organization quite like IOS. It was at once a rumor and an ideal,
an underground network with operatives everywhere and regulators
nowhere. It pretended to be the most modern financial institution
of the times, but depended for its existence upon geopolitical
anachronisms whose origins dated back to the Holy Roman Empire
and, more recently, to Europe's quest for Incan gold. IOS called
itself "the Moneycatcher" and prided itself upon having "all the
financial expertise that two billion dollars can buy"—yet the firm's
destruction was a direct result of its experts' having hallucinated a
severe cash shortage when, in fact, there was none.

IOS was founded in the late 1950s, when Cornfeld was a mutual-
fund salesman, working the military bases around Paris. Initially,
IOS salesmen (always referred to as "Associates") did no more than
sell shares in the reputable, U. S.-based Dreyfus Fund. By every
account the early operation was a family affair, with Cornfeld recruiting salesmen through ads in the *International Herald Tribune*,
providing them with loans, the use of his car and, when needed, a
couch to sleep on. Selling shares in the Dreyfus Fund, however, was
not where the big money lay: enough of a socialist to understand
the weaknesses and strengths of free enterprise, Cornfeld realized

---

* Robert A. Hutchison, *Vesco* (New York: Praeger, 1974), p. 139.

that few people ever get rich working for someone else. Accordingly, he decided to create and sell his own mutual funds, using the Investors' Overseas Services imprimatur and the sales force he'd already created. In 1960, IOS was formally incorporated in the offshore jungles of Panama, where nonresident corporations are virtually untaxed and unregulated.

That, in fact, was the nature of "offshoreness": a lack of regulation and taxation. Just as different countries have different geographical features, their concerns also vary, and so do their laws. In Panama, the regulation of *los mutual funds* has a very low priority. And yet, while Panama was a convenient place to incorporate IOS, Ltd. (S.A.), it was not a home that was likely to inspire much confidence in potential investors. What IOS needed, in effect, was a country that would front for it, covering its Panamanian roots with a veneer of respectability. Switzerland was the logical choice, especially in the wake of harassment from the French (concerned that IOS was selling its shares not only to expatriate Americans and GI's but to Frenchmen as well). So it was that Bernie moved his Moneycatcher to Geneva, trumpeting his arrival in the Alps while at the same time ignoring its natal home beside the Canal. Eventually, IOS made use of nearly every medieval enclave and colonial bastion whose archaic laws and fiscal indifference provided an edge. The International Investment Trust (IIT), IOS's first fund (and not, incidentally, a trust in any legal sense), was incorporated in the Grand Duchy of Luxembourg. Other corporate vehicles emerged in the postal redoubts of Liechtenstein, Andorra, Monaco, Singapore, Hong Kong, San Marino, the Bahamas, and the Netherlands Antilles —only Macao and the Vatican seem to have been spared, though the latter was blessed on at least one occasion by Cornfeld and his mom, descending through the night in a pitch-black IOS jet, there to have an audience with the Pope.

That IOS was everywhere is literally true. While the company itself was deliberately obscured in the jurisdictional fogs of the mini-nations, its salesmen/Associates were never hard to find. Indeed, they wandered the earth and all its seas in search of business, visiting nuclear installations in the Arctic, drilling rigs in the Persian Gulf, NSA facilities in Thailand, tents in the Sudan, mines in the Amazon, huts in Samoa, condos in Sardinia, and aircraft carriers in the Indian Ocean—not to mention whorehouses, embassies, the shrine of Lourdes, and social clubs in every capital and backwater on the planet. In a phrase: *they went where the money was.* And it was everywhere. Lou Ellenport, a former IOS salesman, ticked off one of his itineraries for reporters from the London Sunday *Times*: Glyphada, Alexandria, El Alamein, Tobruk, Tripoli, Tunis, Madrid, Lisbon, Ankara, Izmir, Iskenderun, Beirut, Latakia—not the most comfortable places. And from there to Jerusalem, Tel Aviv, Marseilles, Algiers, The Hague, Brussels, Manila, Singapore, Djakarta, and Tokyo (where Cornfeld gave him a gold Patek Philippe watch and stock options for having flogged a million dollars in securities). Armed with the correct time and the need to exercise his options, Ellenport continued on his hegira to Sydney, Christchurch, Samoa, Pago Pago, Khartoum, Addis Ababa, Kabul, Dacca, Chittagong, Cox's Bazar, Karachi, Zanzibar—and from there without rest to Bangui, Somalia, Mahé, and Mombasa. It was an itinerary that would have reduced Diogenes to a burnt-out case, and, inevitably, IOS Associates came to reflect the exhaustion of contemporary Cains, compelled to wander forever in search of dollars (rials, bolivars, cruzeiros, and krugerrands). In Zanzibar, en route to Bangui, Ellenport recalled, he replied to a group of American technicians who'd asked for a day to think over his proposition: "Whattaya think I am, the Good Humor man?" *

Nor was Ellenport a one-man band. There were more than ten thousand IOS salesmen at the organization's peak, and what drove them all was their sincere desire to make Bernie's dream come true—that is, to strike it rich for themselves and their boss. The path to those riches seemed clear. Among IOS's founding premises, three were most important. The first was that the value of stocks would inevitably rise. The second was that pooling the resources of many small investors would enable "the little guy" to take advantage of the same advice that had formerly been available only to millionaires. The third premise was that IOS's greatest asset was its own salesmen. It was they who found the money for the fund managers to invest. To motivate the salesmen (and Ellenport's efforts are an index of the plan's success) Cornfeld provided a brilliant package of double-bind incentives.

Because IOS grew so rapidly, and with such apparent success, it seemed clear that its own stock was among the most valuable that anyone could hold. It was not, however, traded on any exchange (not at first) but was instead held closely by Cornfeld and a few others, its

* Charles Raw, Bruce Page, and Godfrey Hodgson, *"Do You Sincerely Want to Be Rich?"* (New York: Viking Press, 1971), p. 73.

transfer limited by a number of artful restrictions and Cornfeld's own enigmatic intentions. Among the incentives Cornfeld offered to his salesmen was a series of annual stock options that promised to make them wealthy. When an Associate brought in a particular amount of sales, he'd be given the opportunity of purchasing IOS shares at a greatly reduced rate. If, for instance, the Associate delivered one million dollars in business, he might be offered an option to buy one thousand shares of IOS at, say, twenty dollars apiece. Since the value of these shares would be much higher—perhaps one hundred dollars per share—the Associate stood to make a (paper) profit of eighty thousand dollars by exercising his option. Still, twenty thousand dollars is a lot of cash, and some Associates protested that they couldn't afford to exercise their options. To this Cornfeld always replied that everyone could afford to become rich; after all, they were being offered (as a reward for services rendered) $100,000 in stock for a mere $20,000 in cash—the only proviso being that they could not sell their stock until such a time as Cornfeld (whose own holdings were estimated at more than $150,000,000) did also. "When Bernie cashes in, we all do" was the refrain of IOS.

Since they couldn't afford *not* to exercise their options, the salesmen borrowed the necessary cash from friendly banks (including banks owned by IOS), repaying the principal and interest over a period of years by setting aside large parts of the commissions they'd earned selling the mutual funds. It became an endless circle for many IOS Associates. To pay their expenses and make a living, they had to sell increasingly large quantities of mutual funds under often trying circumstances. If successful, they'd be given stock options, which, while making them wealthy on paper, strained their resources. The more mutual funds they sold, the more they earned in commissions; the more they earned in commissions, the more they invested in stock options. In effect, they were prisoners of Bernie's company store—albeit a store whose only hold over them was the greed they mistook for a vision. But what proved nightmarish for the salesmen was for IOS a dream. The firm's largest expenses were the commissions it paid to its ever-expanding sales force. Those commissions, however, were returned in substantial measure, sometimes (and literally) with interest. Through its banking subsidiaries IOS made loans to its salesmen enabling them to exercise their options. If the cost of an option (worth $100,000) was $20,000, a salesman might be able to spare only $10,000 from his commissions; an IOS bank, therefore, would lend him the remainder

needed to exercise the option, charging him interest on the loan
and accepting the IOS stock as collateral. Illegal in the United
States, the practice of accepting stock as collateral on a loan used
to buy more stock is virtually S.O.P., "standard offshore procedure."
(What makes the practice illegal in the United States is the fact that
banks are allowed to lend amounts equal to a percentage of the
collateral stock—usually 60 percent. This limitation guards the
lenders' money by providing a safe margin within which the stock's
value may decline without its becoming necessary to call in the
loan. If, however, the borrower is permitted to use his loan to purchase *more* stock—which he may then use as collateral on yet *another*
loan—the margin may eventually be reduced to near zero. Thus, if
the offshore practice were permitted in the United States, a declining stock market would inevitably trigger an avalanche of foreclosures that would force the borrowers to sell their stock at a loss,
depressing the market even further. If unchecked, the pattern leads
directly to bankruptcy and depression.)

Obviously, a day of reckoning had to come for the IOS salesmen
—and they looked forward to it. On that day, they imagined, IOS
would have become such an attractive property that the public
would clamor for a piece of the action, exchanging its cash for the
salesmen's equity. When Bernie cashed in, everyone would.

There were variations on the salesmen's theme, of course. Those
who did particularly well became area supervisors in charge of other
salesmen, winning an override, or percentage, of the commissions
that their subordinates earned. Area supervisors who succeeded in
meeting their sales quotas, or who developed new territories, became regional overseers, winning overrides on the overrides of the
supervisors. It was even more complicated than that, but the point
is made: the more one succeeded and the more one earned, the larger
the stock options one would be offered. And because those options
were practically irresistible, the deeper an associate was likely to go
into debt on the way toward becoming a paper millionaire.

As for IOS, its commissions and operating expenses were kept circulating, to the greatest extent imaginable, within the firm and its
subsidiaries. Moreover, as it refined the concept of offshoreness, the
firm underwent continual transformations, increasing its slice of
the pie at every step. One of the first of these transformations was the
creation of its own proprietary funds. Initially, IOS served only as
a middleman, selling shares in mutual funds owned and managed

by other companies. As an offshore entity beyond the regulations of the SEC, IOS had a number of advantages: it could, for instance, charge higher commissions than those permitted in the United States. In addition, it could extract its charges more rapidly than U. S.-based firms. This it could do by establishing a "front-end load" that would never have been allowed in the United States. For instance: an IOS salesman might persuade an investor to commit $1000 per year for ten years to an investment program. The sales charges on such a program might amount to $1000. Rather than spreading those fees over a ten-year period, charging $100 per year, IOS would load them all onto the "front end," removing the entire amount within the first two years. If an investor should after only two years decide to redeem his shares and withdraw from the program, he'd find that only half of his money had been invested, the other half having been deducted by IOS as the cost of the ten-year program. Like the salesmen, once investors became a "partner" of IOS, they were in for the duration.

3 / AND DEWI SUKARNO TOO

But even this wasn't enough. By selling other firms' mutual funds IOS gained only fleeting control of investors' money, while at the same time losing out on an array of fees charged by the mutual funds themselves. By creating its own proprietary funds (incorporated in Liechtenstein, Luxembourg, and other medieval redoubts) IOS took *direct* control of investors' money for long periods of time; this transformed the firm into a financial power in its own right while generating additional income in the form of performance and management fees. And once again the offshore concept provided advantages. For example: When IOS created the Fund of Funds (FOF), it established two classes of stock, common and preferred. In the United States mutual funds are prohibited from issuing more than one class of stock; the prohibition was created as a protection for investors. Because mutual funds are highly liquid, it's important that shareholders retain direct control over their management. By creating *two* classes of stock, Cornfeld gained control of more than $600,000,000 in investments at a cost to himself of only a few thousand dollars. This he accomplished by selling preferred shares to investors while retaining nearly all of the common stock as his own. Since only the common stock bore voting privileges, Cornfeld had virtually dictatorial control over the structure and investment policy of the Fund as a whole. The shareholders had no say in the way that their money was invested.

And while the Fund of Funds, as its name implies, originally invested its shareholders' money in other mutual funds, it gradually shifted its emphasis to newer markets, creating proprietary funds of its own. These funds, in turn, were invested in an exotic array of issues and instruments. And while the Fund of Funds and its proprietary funds were all owned by the parent IOS, the parent and its offspring took a fee *each time* shareholders' cash was shifted from one fund to another. In this way as much as 18 percent of a shareholder's investment would be devoured before so much as a penny was actually invested. Making this greedy equation even more catastrophic were the "performance fees" IOS charged. Forbidden to American mutual funds, the fees were yet another offshore perquisite. Very simply, they permitted IOS and its fund managers to take 10 percent per quarter of any increases in the value of the investments they'd made on behalf of the shareholders. To earn a performance fee, it wasn't necessary that a stock be sold. On the contrary, it need only increase in value *on paper,* and then only during the relevant time period. Thus, IOS and its fund managers would divvy up 10 percent of all paper profits at the end of each quarter or year. If the stock subsequently declined, too bad for the investors; IOS retained its percentage of even the most transient profits. Naturally (and disastrously for shareholders) this performance setup encouraged the fund managers to invest speculatively rather than prudently—to shoot for quick profits rather than the long-term capital gain that is typically the goal of a mutual fund. But by this time, 1968, the Fund of Funds wasn't what its name implied. Mutual funds were a very small part of the action (though few shareholders were aware of that fact). Among FOF's proprietary funds were holdings that included some of the market's most dicey propositions. Indeed, one such fund seems to have been set up for the express purpose of "selling short"—hardly a position geared to the investment needs of the "widows and orphans" which IOS pretended were its major customers. Other fund managers showed a preference for investing money (other people's) in boom-or-bust operations of the worst kind. And while IOS stressed the supposed liquidity of its investors' assets, enormous sums were poured into unregistered "letter stocks," which, while they couldn't be publicly traded in any foreseeable future, had a tendency to show dramatic gains on paper, gains that were subject to the dread performance fees. (Resorts International, the parent of Intertel, was one such investment, reaping millions from private placements of IOS funds during 1967 and 1968.)

One would be hard put to describe all the ways in which IOS and its managers profited from their offshore position. The firm's executives took advantage of every opportunity available: "finder's fees" proliferated, deceptively incomplete "performance records" were published, and several IOS executives used their position to invest in companies in which they themselves had an interest. Still, under Cornfeld, IOS and its employees seem to have stayed within the letter of the law; we may question the firm's deceptive practices, rapaciousness, and ethical laxity, yet it would be a mistake to suggest that IOS was organized or managed by Cornfeld and his cronies with the intention to defraud. On the contrary, Cornfeld seems to have believed that he would make everyone rich—including the benighted shareholders. Only after Vesco seized control of the firm did it become a genuinely felonious enterprise.

And yet even before Vesco's advent on the scene, IOS bordered on the bizarre. It was an underground institution, the financial equivalent of Thomas Pynchon's *V*. As we've seen, its agents were literally everywhere, from Cox's Bazar to Somaliland. And if the word "agents" suggests intrigue and skullduggery, the innuendo is apt. In Latin America, Africa, and Asia, IOS was organized in a compartmentalized, clandestine fashion. The big money that it sought did not come from millions of small investors, as it pretended; it came instead from wealthy expatriates, the bourgeoisie of politically fragile countries such as Italy and Brazil, and from the tax-evasive elites of Third World dictatorships such as Haiti and Nicaragua. And, of course, enormous amounts of cash were received from members of organized-crime syndicates the world over. In conversation, Cornfeld confirmed that perhaps 10 percent of all IOS funds belonged to people that might be described as "organized-crime types." That money, IOS staffers believed, could never be redeemed in its place of origin; in that sense, IOS served as a laundry for the mob and some of its investments must therefore be looked upon with a new sort of suspicion. But this $250,000,000 in "black money" was small compared to the merely "hot money," funds smuggled out of various countries in an effort to evade taxes. And while IOS persistently hyped its image as a firm made great by the small savings of widows, orphans, and retirees, the truth was that fewer than 1 percent of all IOS customers were the beneficiaries of more than 25 percent (about $750,000,000) of all the cash in the funds. In fact, the number of IOS clients with more than forty thousand dollars in the proprietary funds during 1969 was roughly 8,600—hardly your typical group of widows and orphans.

Because IOS was in the business of giving wings to flight capital, it necessarily came to operate as an underground bank, emulating many of the practices of an intelligence agency. Its salesmen were given aliases such as "Victor Hugo," while "area desks" were established at IOS headquarters in much the same way that the State Department and CIA have area desks at Foggy Bottom and McLean. Clients were contacted in code from secret communications centers set up in a number of unlikely places: the busy Middle East, for instance, was serviced by means of a covert facility located in the Swiss ski resort of Flims-Waldhaus. Often clients' accounts were identified only by a number, and in some instances communication between IOS and its customers was entirely *verboten*. In those cases the clients' names and numbers were placed on a so-called Hold Mail List. The List, kept in a vault at IOS's Overseas Development Bank in Luxembourg (ODB-Lux), contained the names of clients who under no circumstances should receive mail from IOS or its subsidiaries. The List was a carefully guarded one—fewer than twelve IOS executives had access to it—because it represented a sort of "pigeon list." That is, it identified those clients who could not afford to have their investments in IOS discovered. SEC officials claim that the List represented investments made by organized-crime figures, corrupt government officials, dictators, white-collar criminals, and tax evaders. More than $150,000,000 belonging to those on the List had been sunk into the proprietary funds of IOS. Should it ever be looted (as it came to be), these clients would be unable to make any public complaint: it was "mugs' money."

Nor was this all. IOS couldn't rely upon its clients' ingenuity in smuggling funds out of their homelands. As a result the firm established a variety of subterranean routes, offering yet another service to its customers. Along the Italian-Swiss border, for instance, there sprang up a clutch of tiny banks whose entire income derived from taking a middleman's share of the flight capital which IOS attracted. Elsewhere, IOS used safe-houses to process the illicit cash, "mules" to carry it, and "covers" to disguise its flow. In Brazil the firm had safe-houses in every major city—apartments that were used as secret banks where cruzeiros could be exchanged for dollars, deutsche marks, or francs. Once the money was converted into European currency, the hoard would be turned over to an airline pilot who would carry it with him to Rio de Janeiro. In Rio the pilot would take the cash to the staff lavatory, where it would be hidden in the water tank of a toilet. Another courier, also an employee of an airline, would retrieve the dough and take it to yet another safe-house, where-upon it would be handed over to still *another* pilot—one who had a scheduled run to Geneva that same evening.

And, of course, there were other ploys. In some countries controls on outward-bound currency were suspended in the case of "philan-thropic contributions." IOS therefore provided its customers with a means of making phony donations to an Israeli charity. The money went to Israel, all right, but it stayed there only long enough to be cabled on to Geneva. Another ploy used with considerable success involved the client's purchase of first-class, round-trip airline tickets to faraway places. After buying the expensive tickets for himself and his family, the client would have an IOS salesman take them to another country where, unused, the tickets would be redeemed for cash. The cash would then be sent to Switzerland for deposit in the client's account. A third ploy consisted of making bogus loans, capitalizing on the fact that few countries object to their citizens' *borrowing* money abroad. In this scheme an IOS salesman would draft a sham agreement showing that an IOS bank had loaned the client a large sum of money—to remain on deposit in Switzerland. The client would then proceed to pay off the principal and interest on the "loan," making monthly payments to Geneva. The beauty of this scheme was that the client was able to make regular payments into his secret IOS account, while at the same time securing a tax deduction on the "interest" he was supposed to be paying.* It was a classic case of having one's cake and eating it too.

The genius behind all these ploys does not seem to have been Cornfield himself but a banker-spook called Tibor Rosenbaum, head of the International Credit Bank of Switzerland. A friend of Cornfeld's whose bank was later used to handle IOS's "black" transactions in smuggled cash, Rosenbaum is a Hungarian Jew whose parents disappeared into the caldron of Auschwitz. During the Second World War he became a hero of the resistance through his underground activities in behalf of the Jews. Using "Istvan Lukacs"

---

* This same scheme has been employed by other offshore banks, most infamously the Castle Bank & Trust of the Bahamas and Cayman Islands.

as a *nom de guerre*, he carried out a series of Mission Impossible rescues. In one instance he posed as a high-ranking Nazi officer, entered a concentration camp, and under an "administrative pretext" obtained the release of thirty doomed prisoners. After the war he became a delegate to the World Zionist Congress in Basel, where plans were made for the creation of Israel, and worked in various European capitals for the Palestine Liberation Office (forerunner of the Jewish Agency). This was at the height of Zionist terrorist attacks in Palestine. A superb clandestine operator, Rosenbaum is said to have been instrumental in providing weapons to the Haganah and Stern Gang. That would tend to explain why the International Credit Bank, "Rosenbaum's Baby," became gambling czar Meyer Lansky's Number One conduit abroad. (As we'll see some pages hence, Lansky was also a gunrunner to the Haganah.) Rosenbaum was more than a friend to the Jews, however. When his bank was rocked with scandal after the collapse of IOS, the newspaper *Ha'aretz* solemnly declared, "Tibor Rosenbaum *is* Israel." And the paper wasn't far from wrong. While Rosenbaum's bank facilitated the flight-capital schemes worked by IOS, it also served as a source of secret funds for the Mossad, Israel's intelligence service, and as one of the country's primary weapons brokers. At one point "as much as ninety percent of the Israeli Defense Ministry's external budget flowed . . . through Rosenbaum's bank on the Rue de Conseil General." * In economic matters he was equally important, founding the Israel Corporation with the help of Baron Edmond de Rothschild, a French aristocrat committed to the Zionist cause. The *raison d'être* of the Israel Corporation was to raise money among the world's Jews, money to be invested in a variety of public and semipublic Israeli enterprises; by finding money abroad to fund development projects in "the homeland," Rosenbaum and Rothschild freed Israeli tax monies to be spent on the country's critical military needs. Accordingly, "Istvan Lukacs" became the "Mr. Fixit" of Israeli finance, cementing friendships with the country's most important military and political leaders.

The mix of Mob, Mossad, IOS, and Rothschild monies was an intoxicating one in which the common denominator appears to have been a love of Israel. Certainly Rosenbaum and Cornfeld shared that affection with Lansky and the French baron. But how can one

---

* The *Sunday Times* of London, an article by Richard Milner and Eric Marsden, June 5, 1975.

be certain of anything involving a naturalized Swiss Zionist who
served, like Rosenbaum, as black Liberia's ambassador to Austria?
The possibilities are too many.

In any case, IOS formed its own banks toward the end of the
1960s, phasing out the need for Rosenbaum's couriers and the facilities of the International Credit Bank. It had its own. If a Brazilian
general or an Indonesian minister wanted to take out a (phony)
loan or make a "charitable donation" to a "school for Hebrew
studies," he could go directly to any of several IOS banks. It may
seem strange, of course, that a two-billion-dollar financial institution
should depend upon such methods for its success, but it could hardly
have been otherwise. IOS's entire purpose was to facilitate the ebb
and flow of flight capital. And that quite naturally put it up against
the police and intelligence services of every country in the world
that could not afford to have its limited capital reserves exported to
Switzerland for investment in Israel or the United States. In effect,
IOS existed to bleed the Third World and, to a lesser extent, the
European Economic Community (EEC) of their financial resources,
transferring the money from the poorer nations to the suites of
venture capitalists in New York and Tel Aviv. In a sense, it was an
institutional force for perpetual underdevelopment. And because it
threatened the economic vitality of nearly every country in which it
sold funds, it was logical that IOS should function covertly, almost
as a hostile nation, a phantom country whose borders were marked
not by the positions of streams and mountains, but by the erosion
of capital. At its peak IOS probably employed more "secret agents"
than any other private firm in the world. A debilitating and clandestine operation, it compensated by taking pains to appear above-
board, enlisting the most respected names-for-hire to serve on its
board of directors. FDR's son James, for instance, was appointed
ambassador-at-large for IOS and rode the jet stream in its behalf,
extolling the firm. In fact, Jimmy Roosevelt would likely have become chairman of IOS had it not been for an unfortunate *faux pas*.
During an argument with his wife concerning their son's former
teacher, Roosevelt was taken aback when his spouse sank a ten-inch
Marine Corps bayonet into that very place. As his wife shrieked at
the gore, the former President's son rushed from the garden into
the quiet streets of suburban Geneva. "I've been stabbed!" he
screamed, running through the street. "She stabbed me!" It was
hardly the sort of P-R that IOS needed.

And yet while some IOS employees could brag of paragraphs

in *Burke's Peerage* and *Who's Who*, there were others less eminent. Within the sales force were some financial comers, but there were down-and-outers as well: defrocked priests, con men, expatriate drifters, smugglers, and at least one former Congo mercenary. Indeed, at a London convention honoring IOS's ninety-seven top salesmen in 1970, *more than half* of the celebrated crew were present under assumed names—including the Associate who'd sold the most mutual funds during the preceding year. Not that IOS was entirely devious: its clients did, in fact, include widows, if not orphans. As one IOS executive told me, "I know for a fact we had at least one widow—Dewi Sukarno. I know because I was sitting beside the pool at the Villa Elma when she showed up one day and demanded to see Bernie. When he came out, she reached down into her cleavage and pulled out fistfuls of loose diamonds, emeralds, and pearls, begging him to invest it for her. I tell you, my eyes almost fell out. . . . How much was it? I don't know. Figure out how many carats two thirty-eight-D cups will hold if they're filled not quite to the brim, and you'll be right on target."

4 / THE TAKEOVER

By 1970 the thirty-four-year-old Robert Vesco presided over an empire that had a great deal in common with malignant cancer: if it didn't grow, it would die. This fact of life made it necessary for the head of International Controls to search continuously for larger corporations vulnerable to takeover. He might, of course, have chosen to satiate the need for growth by devouring many smaller companies. It seemed easier, however, to stalk a wounded giant than to rush helter-skelter after a score of elusive pygmies. In this way Vesco resembled a financial jackal testing the reflexes of lions, waiting to find one that moved too slowly.

And by this time he himself had changed. A deliberate effort had been made to polish his demeanor, eliminating from his manner all traces of the delinquent from Detroit. As Cornfeld did, he surrounded himself with the evidence of wealth and power. No connoisseur, he preferred pizza, Coke, and "Mary Tyler Moore" in his private moments; but when an important deal was in the offing, château wines and caviar were served by caterers with BBC accents. He flew the world in a private jet whose interior design owed much to Hugh Hefner's aircraft: mirrored bed, bar, and sauna were available to his in-flight guests, though Vesco himself appears to have suffered a most literal fear of flying.

And the trips were whirlwinds, transatlantic hops from one world capital to another, with little time to notice anything. Remote behind his Foster-Grants, Vesco strode from jet to limousine to boardroom and back again, with no inclination for sight-seeing or chat. Frequently his pilot was instructed not to file a flight plan or else to file a false one. Passengers came and went in anonymity, or resorted to assumed names. On several occasions, when it was necessary to impress a banker, bureaucrat, or businessman, call girls were brought on board for a flying party. When that happened, the jet would take to the air destination-less, circling England aimlessly for the convenience of its passengers. And when everyone was spent and sobering, the plane would return to its point of departure, causing some to wonder if the entire evening had not been an hallucination. It was a robber baron's entertainment, an ostentatious mix of business and pleasure.

Vesco's search for a wounded lion larger than International Controls, but vulnerable to his depredations, was quickly satisfied. His attention had already been called to IOS by its multimillion-dollar investments in his flagship, ICC. Since that time a declining stock market had triggered a wave of redemptions at IOS, constricting the firm's cash position. Moreover, a number of lucrative markets in Latin America closed in the wake of police raids on IOS offices there. In addition, there were rumors of mismanagement and scandal, while at the same time IOS investments were faring catastrophically in the emerging bear market. All these things—the bears, the redemptions, the cops, and the bad publicity—combined to give IOS executives a bad case of nerves. And with that loss of confidence the firm became very fragile indeed: essentially a sales organization, it could not survive self-doubt.

Vesco understood IOS very well; he'd studied it for years. When the opportunity came for him to step in, he did so subtly and with what appeared to be the best of intentions. At the time IOS managers incorrectly believed that the firm was on the brink of insolvency and that within a short while it would not have enough cash available to support even its bookkeeping operations. In fact, IOS was in no real danger of collapse: it controlled upward of a *half-billion* dollars in investments which for all practical purposes could never be redeemed—the black money and the hot money were more than enough to pull the firm through any crisis short of a depression. Moreover, there were additional millions in cash deposited with a number of subsidiaries and banks, a liquid hoard which IOS executives seem to have lost track of completely.

Over Cornfeld's protestations that the "crisis" was temporary and that Vesco was "nothing more than a hoodlum," IOS directors accepted the terms of a loan offered by International Controls. The amount loaned by ICC was five million dollars and the conditions attached to it gave Vesco the leverage he wanted over IOS. Among the many conditions were provisions that barred Cornfeld from holding any IOS office without Vesco's approval; should any one of the more than fifty lending conditions be violated, Vesco would have the power to put IOS into liquidation and collect three million dollars in damages. With Cornfeld, the hip Svengali of transnational finance, removed from the scene, it was a relatively simple matter for Vesco to work his own magic upon the remaining executives, purging those loyal to Bernie and promoting his own hacks to positions of authority in Geneva. What made the loan truly unusual, however, was the financing that lay behind it: in effect, Vesco took over one of the world's largest financial institutions for absolutely nothing. It worked this way:

A newly created Bahamian subsidiary of International Controls—ICC Investments, Inc.—was the lender to IOS. But as we've seen, International Controls was itself top-heavy with debt and therefore in no position to lend what little cash it had on hand. What Vesco did was to have ICC Investments borrow five million dollars from a Wall Street brokerage house, the money to be repaid within six weeks. He then convinced the owner of Butler's Bank in the Bahamas (also undergoing a liquidity crisis) to lend ICC Investments five million dollars to repay the six-week loan. The *quid pro quo* for Butler's cooperation was the promise of increased deposits from IOS once Vesco took control. Now, as it happened, one of the fifty-two conditions attached to the loan made to IOS was that IOS would receive $350,000 *less* than the face value of the five million dollars extended to it. Hence it would only get $4,650,000. The difference, Vesco explained, was being deducted as a "front-end load" to cover legal expenses and other costs incurred in making the financial arrangements. What he did not point out was that the $350,000 would also cover the costs, and then some, of the six weeks' interim financing arranged with the Wall Street investment house. But where, one

asks, did Butler's get the cash it loaned to ICC Investments, enabling
the latter to lend the money to IOS? The answer to that question is
the proof of Vesco's cunning: the money came from IOS itself. Once
in control of IOS—a takeover which occurred simultaneously with,
and by virtue of, execution of the interim loan agreement—Vesco
forced IOS to deposit $5,500,000 in cash with Butler's Bank *as
collateral for the loan made by ICC Investments.* Thus, IOS, in
order to solve its "liquidity crisis," put up $5,500,000 in cash so as
to borrow $4,650,000—and for this privilege turned over the man-
agement of IOS to Vesco and his flunkies from New Jersey! It was
an extraordinary coup: IOS had, in effect, put up $850,000 which it
thought it couldn't afford for the privilege of being raped by the
Detroit Kid.

The actual looting of IOS was a masterpiece of unarmed robbery,
following the same something-for-nothing pattern that characterized
virtually all of Vesco's maneuvers. The first stage of the looting
scheme required Cornfeld's removal from the scene and the quashing of all dissidence within the firm. It wasn't enough to bar Cornfeld from IOS office, as the terms of the ICC loan had provided for.
It was essential to Vesco's scheme that Cornfeld disengage entirely
from the firm he'd created; so long as he remained a stockholder,
with literally millions of votes, he was dangerous. Accordingly, Vesco
made an offer which Cornfeld couldn't refuse: $5,500,000 for six
million shares of IOS stock worth about thirty cents each. Not only
was the price wildly inflated, but Vesco created the impression that
the buyer of the stock would be the prestigious Union Bank of
Switzerland, one of the few institutions genuinely capable of IOS's
salvation. That Cornfeld did not look more closely at the transaction
may seem reprehensible, but it's also understandable. At the time
his personal debts to IOS banks amounted to two million dollars—
a sum equal to the real value of all his IOS shares. By accepting
Vesco's once-in-a-lifetime offer, Cornfeld might pay off his debts and
still retire as a multimillionaire. The alternative, should IOS fail
to recover, was bankruptcy. And so Cornfeld appears to have lost
his nerve, though a face-saving gesture was made whereby he demanded, and received, assurances that the money paid to him for
his shares derived in no way from IOS's own coffers. In fact, the
money *did* come from IOS, albeit by a circuitous route. The swing
money for the deal was advanced by a Wall Street investment house
to Butler's Bank. Butler's then loaned the money to a Panamanian

shell yclept Linkink Progressive Corp., S.A. It was to Linkink that Cornfeld sold his stock, incorrectly believing it to be a front for the Union Bank of Switzerland. In fact, Linkink was owned by another Panamanian shell, one with an even more romantic name: Red Pearl Bay, S.A. (Neither corporation seems to have had any assets prior to the loan extended to them by Butler's Bank.) As for the owners of Red Pearl Bay, their identity remains unknown—though Cornfeld is reported to have cracked that "it'll probably turn out to be owned by Vesco's grandmother." Not that it mattered. What Cornfeld dreaded might happen, did: within a few months of the stock sale, the swing money was returned to Wall Street, from whence it had come. Replacing it in Butler's Bank were monies provided by subsidiaries of IOS. IOS therefore was the ultimate source of the funds Linkink borrowed to purchase Cornfeld's shares, and, naturally, IOS had the most to lose from the deal.

And it lost quite a bit. Immediately after IOS replaced the Wall Street cash in Butler's Bank with its own money, Red Pearl Bay sold Linkink (and the "Cornfeld shares," its only assets) to a subsidiary of International Controls—a Canadian corporation called American Interland, Ltd. Since Linkink had borrowed $5,500,000 a few months earlier to purchase Bernie's IOS stock, one would have expected Red Pearl Bay to have been paid at least that much. Actually, the price paid to Red Pearl Bay for Linkink and its assets was less than one-half of 1 percent of American Interland's outstanding stock. How much was that worth? Well, six months later, in December, 1971, International Controls bought back the American Interland stock from Red Pearl Bay, paying only fifty thousand dollars. In effect, that was the bottom line, the price International Controls paid for all of Cornfeld's six million shares—fifty thousand dollars. Clearly, Vesco was not taking prisoners.

While the above transaction was in progress, Vesco instituted what some IOS executives described as "a reign of terror" in Geneva. In fact, it was a rain of foreclosures. As the new head of IOS, Vesco ordered the firm's banking subsidiaries to call in all loans and overdrafts previously extended to Cornfeld's supporters. Since most of those opposing Vesco within IOS were former sales executives, they tended also to be the same people who'd borrowed most heavily to invest in once-attractive IOS stock options, collateralizing their loans with the purchased stock. By 1971, however, IOS shares had withered in value; indeed, by year's end three shares would have been needed

to buy a single New York City subway token. The selective foreclosures ordered by Vesco, therefore, came at the worst of times,
and bankrupted many of those who refused to toe the line.

With Cornfeld *hors de combat*, and the dissidents threatened with
ruin, Vesco was in control. The physical looting of IOS might take
place at any time, but first Vesco sought to insulate himself (on
paper) from the actual rape of the funds. It seemed to the Detroit
Kid, judging from his maneuvers, that a large portion of the funds
could be ripped off *with impunity*, providing that proper precautions were taken. This required several things. First, he must gain
some hold over the Nixon Administration, leverage that would
enable him to derail the onrushing investigation by the Securities
and Exchange Commission.* Money was the obvious means, and a
campaign donation the obvious mechanism. A simple donation,
however, no matter how large, would provide no *guarantee* that the
Administration would do his bidding. Accordingly, Vesco laid a
trap. The new law regulating donations to presidential campaigns
provided that all such gifts and their donors be publicly identified.
Because the law did not go into effect until April 7, 1972, a month
after the old law expired, there was a thirty-day period during which
secret donations could be made anonymously and in any amount.
It would have been a simple matter for Vesco to have made his
$200,000 donation during those thirty days: the cash was available
in any of several repositories around the globe. Moreover, he had
on several occasions (for instance, in Geneva when he'd needed bail)
demonstrated his ability to raise literally millions in cash on less
than forty-eight hours' notice. Punctuality and compliance with the
law, however, were not his intentions. On the contrary, the donation
was to be made in such a way that it would implicate Attorney
General John Mitchell and other Administration honchos in a
criminal violation of the law. This would give Vesco the hold upon
the Administration that the cash alone could never guarantee: by
making GOP leaders his supposed *accomplices* as well as his beneficiaries, he might hope to later blackmail them into sabotaging the
SEC probe.

So it was that Vesco, lolling on Paradise Island, waited until
April 6 to raise the $200,000, allegedly obtaining the cash by using

* As *Spooks* goes to press, the author has learned that the SEC investigation of IOS
was itself the product of the rather superb IRS intelligence operation masterminded by
the since persecuted IRS agent, Richard Jaffe—of whom more later.

his practically unlimited line of credit at the Paradise Island casino. While casinos do not usually lend such amounts for nongaming purposes, Paradise is a special place and Vesco a special customer. A high roller who sometimes lost fifty thousand dollars in the course of an evening's play, Vesco was a close friend of James Crosby's, president of Resorts International. Crosby was himself uniquely situated in Republican circles: a sometime guest at the White House, he'd donated $100,000 to Nixon's 1968 campaign. He was also a friend of, and frequent host to, Bebe Rebozo (with whom he banked). Moreover, Crosby's private intelligence agency, Intertel, was even then working with White House aides and ITT executives to discredit Jack Anderson's revelations anent ITT and Chile. At the same time, Intertel was the *de facto* custodian of the demented billionaire Howard Hughes (whose own $100,000 donation would later result in two volumes of Senate testimony in the Watergate affair). Indeed, the ties between Paradise Island and Richard Nixon's Administration were of the sort that bind: Allan Butler, owner of the failing bank that was his namesake, claims that Nixon was a silent partner of Crosby's in his Bahamian ventures, sharing a healthy chunk of Paradise Island bridge revenues with yet another secret partner, Bebe Rebozo. And by no means finally, James O. Golden, Resorts' vice-president and one of Intertel's founding spooks, had formerly served as Nixon's Secret Service shield, later taking charge of security for the Nixon forces at the GOP's 1968 convention in Miami Beach. That Paradise Island was a special place, and had a special place in the heart (or what passed for a heart) of the Nixon regime, is abundantly clear. That Vesco was a special customer of the casino is equally clear. His staggering losses at craps alone would have been enough to accord him extraordinary privileges; but even more compelling was the fact that throughout 1972 Vesco was negotiating with Crosby for the purchase of the casino and virtually all the assets of Resorts International.

Raising the two hundred grand, therefore, was no problem. Nor could there have been any difficulty in delivering the money on time, taking *legal* advantage of the campaign law's loophole; Vesco had two jet planes, a jet helicopter, and at least six twin-engined aircraft at his disposal. That the cash was not delivered until April 10 (four days after the deadline permitting anonymity) was no accident. Vesco wanted it that way. It was a part of his looting scheme.

Less certain is whether Vesco knew that his cash would be used to help finance the Plumbers' burglaries at the Watergate and points west. Certainly there's circumstantial evidence that he was witting. One of the first tasks that he'd undertaken at IOS was to have a study made of the firm's internal-security force. It's possible that he did this defensively, in anticipation of his looting scheme. But Vesco's real interest in the IOS spooks is suggested by the fact that he ordered a copy of the study to be forwarded to then-Attorney General Mitchell. There could have been no reason for his having done this except to offer the services of IOS spooks to the Nixon Administration. And this suggests that Vesco must have known of Mitchell's desire for an offensive intelligence capability—one which would necessarily have relied upon secret cash contributions like his own. That the White House was interested in IOS is a matter of fact: a CIA investigation of the IOS network was carried out in 1971, nominally upon the orders of John Dean. As it was supposedly conducted in an effort to learn whether Vesco's stewardship of the President's nephew, Donald Nixon, Jr., was likely to result in any embarrassment to the Administration, it's difficult to imagine that the CIA study failed to uncover any improprieties. Besides the financial irregularities piling up at the firm, Vesco's plane (on which the junior Nixon was a constant passenger) was serving as an airborne rendezvous and sometime shooting gallery for British call girls and defrocked Latin diplomats implicated in smuggling activities and financial frauds. And yet Don-Don remained the financier's factotum, suggesting that the White House had an interest in the affairs of Vesco and IOS that was independent of the President's nephew. It cannot be that the CIA failed to learn of the financier's irregular activities: a former CIA employee estimates that the Agency's "201 file" on Vesco is more than *six inches thick.* The likelihood arises, therefore, that Mitchell and Dean were using the CIA to check out the politics and expertise of the IOS security force—with an eye toward using them against the Democrats. The IOS spooks were capable of Plumberlike assignments, and this was demonstrated for Vesco on a number of occasions. Headed by former Army intelligence officers, the IOS apparat was without corporate parallel in the politically vital area of currency smuggling. And sometimes it undertook juicier assignments. During Vesco's bid for control over IOS, the security force proved of strategic use against the dissidents. And when two SEC investigators arrived in Europe to gather evidence against Vesco,

---

* "The CIA's Corporate Shell Game," by John Marks, a publication of the Center for National Security Studies (Washington, D.C., 1976). "201 files" are said to be dossiers kept by the Agency on important U. S. and foreign businessmen.

the IOS spooks wired a pair of hookers with miniature tape recorders and sent them after the investigators in an effort to compromise them. (The attempt failed.)

Gaining political influence with the Nixon Administration was only one of Vesco's preparations for insulating himself from the law. To get away with his plot, he needed to sever his connections to IOS prior to the actual removal of its millions. Moreover, he had to limit the impact of the looting, minimizing its effect on U. S. citizens and American corporations. This meant that International Controls would have to show a paper profit from its relationship with IOS—and that the looting should concentrate, as much as possible, on funds that couldn't be redeemed and whose owners could not scream "Rape!"

In short, his target was the Hold Mail List. (Plus.)

The plan he created was code-named "ABC-NV." The principle behind it was a simple one: to "close-end" the proprietary funds by selling off their blue-chip holdings in American stocks, investing the cash in a newly formed corporation that would engage in "world-wide investment banking activities." In return for the use (and abuse) of their cash, IOS investors would be given a wad of non-voting, unmarketable stock in the new firm—in a phrase, they'd get a lot of paper, but no voice in what was to be done with their money. Obviously, no sane investor would willingly go along with such a deal, yet Vesco knew that many IOS investors would have no choice; because their investments were made illegally, or represented funny money of one kind or another, they had to accept Vesco's bad paper or risk exposure of their IOS hoards and the misdeeds that stood behind them.

Before ABC-NV could be put into operation, however, Vesco had to resign all positions at IOS while at the same time arranging for the withdrawal of his flagship, ICC, from IOS's affairs. Accordingly, on April 1, 1972, he announced that ICC's controlling interest in IOS had been sold and that in the future he would serve only as an unpaid "consultant" to the ailing firm. The insulation provided by these maneuvers seemed adequate at the time: not only had Vesco bought his way into the inner councils of the Nixon Administration, but he might argue that the looting of IOS occurred *after* his tenure there, and that in any case the SEC had no jurisdiction over matters that did not involve any American firms. Vesco was out, and ICC was too.

The purchaser of ICC's massive position in IOS stock was a Bahamian shell called Kilmorey Investments, Ltd. Kilmorey was controlled by four of Vesco's closest cronies, each of them a top executive at IOS. The price Kilmorey paid was $200,000, loaned to it by the Bahamas Commonwealth Bank (BCB), and about $2,600,000 in unsecured promissory notes. At the time the Bahamas Commonwealth Bank was a subsidiary of International Bancorp, Ltd., an IOS dividend company. ICC owned 22 percent of International Bancorp, a fact which would appear to have placed it firmly within Vesco's control. Looking at the Kilmorey purchase, we can admire Vesco's financial magic: once again, IOS's own money was used to buy control of IOS itself.

Still, ICC was not wholly detached from IOS affairs: it owned large chunks of two IOS dividend companies—International Bancorp and Value Capital, Ltd.—and it was holding a few million dollars' worth of promises issued by Kilmorey Investments, promises secured by nothing more than the word of Vesco's partner in crime Norman LeBlanc. Should those notes fail to be honored, the SEC (whose investigation was by now so hot that it seemed on the verge of going nova) would have a good excuse to intervene.

ICC therefore sold its investment in International Bancorp and Value Capital, Ltd., along with the Kilmorey notes, to another shell, Global Financial, Ltd. This last firm was a subsidiary of something called Global Holdings, Ltd., which, as it happened, was wholly owned by Norman LeBlanc (Kilmorey's proprietor). The price paid by the two Globals was $7,350,000, all of it in five-year promissory notes bearing an interest rate so low that it would have to be serviced by Dr. Scholl's. Admittedly, the mind boggles in contemplation of so many shells arranged in tiers, each of them insubstantial and each of them writing paper for millions of dollars. If the reader is baffled, however, then he's gotten the point: the looting of IOS required that enormous distance be placed, on paper, between IOS investors and their money. A succession of dummies and conduits, each with an impressive name, served that purpose. To understand what Vesco did, it's only necessary to compare the looting of IOS to a child's game in which he who's It seeks to learn which of his friends—standing in a row with their hands behind their backs—has got the prize. As he seizes each one in turn, the friend passes the prize behind his back to the person next to him. The game's rules forbid the person who's It from looking behind the backs of the other players; all he can do is demand that each of them, one at a time, show him his hands. And, in every case, the hands are empty. And yet one of them has the prize. But who? This is the game that Vesco played upon SEC investigators and IOS shareholders. The prize was $224,000,000 and the investors were It. Bank secrecy laws in Switzerland, Panama, and the Bahamas constituted the game's only rules and prevented investigators and the SEC from learning what lay behind the various fronts assembled before them. And making the game even harder, there was by no means a finite number of players: the Vesco group could create and dismantle corporations with such speed that one imagined a sonic boom accompanying each transaction. So it was that the investors, playing It, found themselves confronted by a line of Ltd.'s, S.A.'s, and Inc.'s that receded into the distance, disappearing into the financial swamps of Panama. Only God and Robert Vesco knew the number of players in the game, let alone who had what at any given time.

During the two months between the Kilmorey and Global transactions, the IOS proprietary funds had been made to sell off more than half of their blue-chip investments, converting the stock into cash. In the case of the Venture Fund, 75 percent of its portfolio was liquidated in a matter of days, yielding an estimated $20,000,000 in cash. This money was then "invested" in the twin Globals belonging to LeBlanc. For its money the Venture Fund got an unsecured, fifteen-and-one-half-year low-interest debenture with a face value of $10,000,000, plus four million shares of (nonvoting) stock in Global Holdings. That is to say, IOS investors in the Venture Fund were made to exchange a portfolio of AT&T, GM, and Western Union shares for what amounted to Caribbean wallpaper. Flushed with success, Global Financial paid off its $7,350,000 debt to ICC—five years ahead of schedule—and Vesco proudly announced that ICC's seventeen-month relationship with IOS had yielded a two-million-dollar profit for the American firm. How could the SEC complain?

And so it went. IOS's Fund of Funds found itself exchanging $60,000,000 in cash for six million preferred shares in a Costa Rican entity called Inter-American Capital (perhaps to be confused with Canada's American Interland). Inter-American Capital promptly reinvested the $60,000,000 in a Panamanian vortex entitled Phoenix Financial. Phoenix Financial, in a kind of turnaround jumpshot, pumped the money back north toward the Bahamas, providing Nassau's Trident Bank with a contract to "administer" it. Trident, owned by Vector, Ltd. (itself nominally owned by Norman LeBlanc), may have been unique among world financial institutions in that it was later found to have no auditors—not even a crooked one.

As with the Fund of Funds and the Venture Fund, so with the International Investment Trust, until, by the time the SEC intervened with a civil suit in November, 1972, at least $224,000,000 had vanished and Vesco was taking Spanish lessons.

CHAPTER

 VII

"ICH BIN EIN COSTA RICAN!"

1 / "DID HE SAY 'GORILLAS' OR 'GUERRILLAS'?"

MITCH WERBELL, STUART GRAYDON, AND GORDON INGRAM DIDN'T have long to wait for the man in the compound to send for them. It was a beautiful spring afternoon in the highlands surrounding San José, and the fugitive financier had been kind enough to provide his prospective partners with a chauffeured limousine and a body-guard riding shotgun. WerBell appreciated the attention, and with a late-morning Scotch under his belt found it easy to admire the Tyrolean beauty of suburban San José, the groves of flowers, the crisp mountain air.

There was no way of knowing precisely where the car was taking them. Vesco had a half-dozen houses in Costa Rica, as well as farms and beachfront property. His first acquisition in San José had been a mansion formerly owned by the American Ambassador. Called Tara, the structure was an exact replica of the southern manse seen in the film "Gone With the Wind," having been built by a Tico tycoon during the 1930s. Beautiful to look at, Tara was nevertheless somewhat flawed. According to Jack Blum, a former Senate investigator whose probes have frequently taken him to "Costa," "The place is riddled with tropical termites. I talked with the U. S. Ambassador's wife when I was down there, and she said they had to get

rid of the joint because whenever they dropped something—a fork
or whatever—the floor would start swaying. As if it were an earthquake. Anyway, the rooms just undulated up and down, and it was
getting to be an embarrassment. You can imagine what this was like
at a state dinner—people were afraid they'd fall through the floor.
And there was nothing anyone could do about it. The only way to
get rid of tropical termites is to flash-freeze the entire building.
You lower the temperature about a hundred degrees in less than a
second . . . and the termites will die. Simple. On the other hand,
do you have any idea what it'd be like to flash-freeze a twenty-room
southern mansion in Costa Rica? I don't think NASA could do that,
let alone Vesco. The truth of the matter is that your boy got taken
by some Tican real estate agent who knew a mark when he saw one.
'Nothing but the best, señor? The bigger the better? How about
the American Ambassador's house? Very pretty. ¿*Te gusta* "Gone
with *El Vente*"?' And so Vesco got it. You might say that he paid
through the nose to get it in the neck."

WerBell wasn't taken to Tara, but to a more modern house, a
sprawling villa on the outskirts of town. Surrounding it was a high
wall topped with shards of broken glass. Armed sentries and burly
gardeners, some of them known to WerBell as Cuban exiles and
veterans of the Bay of Pigs, paced amid the bougainvillea and flame
trees. It occurred to WerBell that he could have improved upon
the compound's security. His own estate in Powder Springs resembled an electronic battlefield of sorts, with all manner of counterintrusion devices, cameras and trip wires, concealed in the local flora.
Vesco seemed to rely entirely on the loyalty of goons who, WerBell
noticed, were commanded by a colonel whose name he couldn't remember but who, he recalled, had been married to Fidel Castro's
sister—herself an agent of the CIA.

To enter the villa was a startling experience. The home's interior
seemed to have been transported whole from the middle-class sub-
urbs of New Jersey. With the exception of some sisal baskets in a
corner of the living room, there was nothing to suggest that Wer-
Bell and the others had left the United States. Vesco had made every
effort to furnish the house in such a way that there would be no
reminders around of his exile.

More than anything else, Vesco is an American, a multimillion-
dollar hard-hat who's an *aficionado* of T formations, T-bone steaks,
and all the brand names that you and I recognize. Weekly flights
from Miami and Nassau deliver cases of the best and most ordinary

American products: Wild Turkey bourbon, Tide, Levi's, Ovaltine, Adidas tennis shoes, and cases of Dial soap. The same flights have carried footballs, burp guns, bubble gum, six Amana ovens, Pampers for the baby, Hi-Standard shotguns, first-run films, Hershey bars, and prime-time television shows. "Kojak," "Mary Tyler Moore," "Mary Hartman," and Howard Cosell are all there on the color TV, playing through the Costa Rican night. In many ways the Vescos are a caricature of the American middle-class family, albeit a family that's on the lam. Having ripped off an emperor's ransom and escaped the jurisdictions of a half-dozen countries, Poppa Vesco sits with Pat and the kids, sawing at Pfaelzer steaks, drinking Budweiser, and groaning at Howard Cosell's pomposity—while, outside, an army of right-wing Cuban exiles stands guard through the tropical night. A fugitive bourgeois, Vesco is at ease in San José. Not only has he applied for Costa Rican citizenship, declaring that he's a Tico in his heart, but he and Pat have become philanthropists, forming the Patricia Vesco Benevolent Fund to assist the poor. Periodically, the Detroit Kid visits one or another of San José's high schools, appearing before classes of aspiring teen-age journalists; with investigative reporters from scores of countries tracking his every move and trying to penetrate his cordon of surly guards, Vesco delights in holding press conferences with the Latin American teenies.

It isn't all philanthropy and PTA sessions, of course. Having absconded with the illicit fortunes of Mafiosi, black marketeers, and corrupt politicians, Vesco is a hunted man and knows it. Since 1973 he's been the target of repeated kidnapping attempts organized by mercenaries and adventurers. SEC investigator Tom von Stein admits that he's received "several propositions" from people who've offered to deliver Vesco to Washington in exchange for a sizable fee. "Some of the offers," Von Stein says, "are made by obvious cranks. Not that the SEC is interested. We won't even listen to such a thing. But we've heard of other plots. Bernie Cornfeld, for instance, has apparently received several proposals—and not all of them from nuts. One scheme came from a team of British mercenaries—spooks, commandos, the lot—who were quite serious about the idea and had a plan mapped out that involved . . . well, it had what they call 'military precision.' I guess they figured Cornfeld would pay to get his hands on Vesco. But Bernie doesn't have that kind of money. Besides, what the hell would he do with Vesco if he got him? Turn him upside down and shake him?" Cornfeld certainly wouldn't pay to have Vesco abducted, no matter how much he hates him. But the fugitive financier is still a very attractive target. While law-enforcement officials would be unlikely to participate directly in such a scheme, an ambitious prosecutor in the G. Gordon Liddy mold might well be tempted to arrange a reduced sentence or early pardon for someone who promised to "produce" Vesco in the United States—with no questions asked. But the biggest kidnapping threat that Vesco faces is one in which he's held hostage to himself. That is, he could be snatched, flown to a remote spot in the Caribbean, and threatened with forcible return to the United States should he fail to come up with, say, five million dollars in cash. The kidnappers would have numerous advantages unavailable to ordinary body snatchers. Most importantly, the victim in this case would have no recourse to the police—especially if he was taken to a hideout in a jurisdiction, such as Mexico, from which his extradition would be a real possibility. In such a situation both the kidnappers and Vesco, their victim, would have equal reason to protect the secrecy of their whereabouts. Vesco, in other words, would be made an accomplice to his own abduction. Instructions for the ransom money could provide for its delivery in a neutral country such as Switzerland, where businessmen are free to come and go with enormous sums of cash. Or, even more simply, Vesco could order his minions to arrange the money's transfer by telex to a numbered Swiss account belonging to the kidnappers. Once returned to Costa Rica, Vesco would still be unable to inform the police of his ordeal: any search for the kidnappers and their loot would require the fugitive financier to reveal how the money had been raised—and that would alert the SEC to his new financial vehicles and receptacles. Even if Vesco were willing to risk such revelations, the Costa Rican police would not be much of a threat; and it's most unlikely that they'd be given much cooperation by U. S. or European agencies. So far as the law is concerned, Vesco has chosen to live outside it and must take his chances.

There's nothing mysterious, then, in the financier's extraordinary security precautions. His home in San José is, however pleasant on the inside, an armed camp capable of withstanding both sieges and sapper attacks. A jet helicopter is available at all times to remove him and his family from the city at a moment's notice. A small island off the coast of Costa Rica has been equipped with a tiny air-strip, a beach house, and radio communications equipment, should Vesco have to flee San José unexpectedly and require a safe location for the night. An enormous arsenal has been assembled, containing Russian burp guns, Gerling submachine guns, silencers, night-vision devices, AR-180 semi-automatic rifles, riot-control shotguns, and, in the words of Senate sleuths, an assortment of "James Bond weapons" suitable "for clandestine operations." The scope and character of Vesco's armory go beyond "pistolmania" and self-defense. The preferred combat-assault weapons of paramilitary teams and S.W.A.T. (Special Weapons and Tactics) forces, the arms provide the financier with a devastating offensive capability. Obviously, the former IOS chief is unwilling to become the prisoner of his own affluence.

Indeed, even his supposedly "recreational" pursuits are enameled with paramilitary trappings. Shortly after WerBell arrived in San José, a $135,000 welded aluminum Stryker yacht roared out of Miami's harbor for modifications in Panama. The yacht was Vesco's new toy—fifty-four feet of aquatic lightning purchased with a six-inch stack of hundred-dollar bills and registered to a dummy corporation in the Canal Zone. Investigators believe that when the boat left Miami, it carried an illicit cargo which included the automatic rifles WerBell had earlier had transported to the city's Mini-Bay-U warehouse. Certainly the weapons disappeared shortly after WerBell delivered the keys to the storage facility to the Vesco group in San José. In any case, it's a minor matter. The yacht itself was considerably more sinister. In Panama it was converted into a sort of flying bomb. Governors that would have regulated its speed were removed, making it perhaps the fastest power yacht afloat. A machine gun was fixed into its bow and crates of automatic weapons were stored below. Supersophisticated electronics gear, the kind that's usually found only on the largest commercial ships, was installed at fabulous expense, permitting the vessel to navigate its way through the most rockbound passages and inlets. Indeed, the navigational equipment routinely compensated for drift, permitting the boat's passengers to know their exact position at any moment. According to the boat's former captain, Jay Powell Cook, the gear would be most useful for locating objects, natural or man-made, that had been left in the water. And that worried Cook a lot. Vesco had given him explicit instructions not to keep any log of his voyages. A peculiar request to make of a boat's captain, it led Cook to wonder precisely what use Vesco intended to make of the navigational equipment. Rumors that the millionaire planned to install missiles on the boat, the readiness of the machine gun, the absence of a log, and the constant talk of future confrontations with government authorities suggested that the boat might be part of an elaborate smuggling plan. Whether that was so or not, it was apparent to Captain Cook that bloodshed was in the offing. Not only were the Detroit Kid and his bodyguards constantly armed, but Cook overheard conversations aboard the boat suggesting that murder was being contemplated. In one such discussion Vesco's sons lamented the fate of their father's former pilot, "Ike" Eisenhauer, who'd "sold out" to the other side. According to Cook, Vesco's heirs remarked that the pilot would be given "a deal he couldn't refuse," and that the matter would be "taken care of in Sicily." Frightened at the direction his job seemed to be taking, Cook decided to quit when he realized that Vesco was keeping him under constant surveillance. On the thirteenth of May, 1974 (a Friday), Cook left the yacht and returned to the United States by plane. Disembarking in Los Angeles, he was given a message by the stewardess that a man wanted to see him. In the baggage area he was approached by a man in "a sort of uniform," wearing a gun and what appeared to be a badge. Confirming the fact that he was Captain Jay Cook, the man told him to "Go right on through—we're with you all the way." Cook had little choice but to "go right on through," since his baggage had disappeared from the plane. The next day, however, the suitcases arrived at his home with their contents in utter disarray. Recalling the strange encounter at the airport, Cook feared that his life was in danger and went to the police with his story of Caribbean intrigue.

Cook wasn't the only employee Vesco threatened. Ike Eisenhauer, his pilot, was berated by the Detroit Kid for having failed to notify him of an alleged suggestion made by the SEC. According to Eisenhauer, an SEC investigator raised the possibility of bringing Vesco back to the United States aboard his own private plane. Eisenhauer shrugged off the suggestion as a frivolous one, but Vesco, learning of it, was angered by his pilot's calm.

"Ike, you should have told that guy that you wouldn't try anything like that, because you value your life," Vesco said.

"What the hell does that mean, Bob?"

"Exactly what I said. . . . There are a lot of Costa Rican gorillas who would be very unhappy with you." *

Costa Rican *gorillas*? It's an interesting turn of phrase. Did Vesco mean gorillas (in the sense of common thugs)? Or did Eisenhauer misunderstand the remark? Might Vesco not have meant guerrillas (in the sense of revolutionaries or rebels)? The ambiguity is in-

---

* A. L. ("Ike") Eisenhauer, *The Flying Carpetbagger* (New York, Pinnacle Books, 1976), p. 364.

triguing in view of the fact that WerBell's April meeting with Vesco took place less than a month after the threat to Eisenhauer was made. Indeed, Vesco had just made an offer, through Martí Figueres, for the more than two thousand submachine guns in WerBell's Georgia arsenal. Obviously, the Detroit Kid was planning *some* sort of paramilitary action. That WerBell knew something of this was to be made explicit six months later when his attorney filed a motion for dismissal of federal charges filed against WerBell's son, Mitch IV, and Defense Services, Inc. (DSI). In September, virtually without investigation, the Treasury Department indicted the younger Mitch and DSI for their alleged attempt to sell two thousand silenced Ingrams to an undercover agent at Powder Spring's Travellodge Motel. The charges were spurious and, according to WerBell, calculated in effect. The defendants would be acquitted on all counts, but the indictment would ensure the WerBells silence before the Senate's Permanent Subcommittee on Investigations. In the motion for dismissal, it was sworn that

> . . . There is memorandum and correspondence exchanged between agents of the United States Treasury Department, the Central Intelligence Agency, Department of State, Securities and Exchange Commission and other agencies and departments of the United States concerning Mr. Robert Vesco, the country of Costa Rica and the island of Abaco. Further . . . this memorandum and correspondence will show involvement of . . . these agencies and certain United States and foreign corporations in planned clandestine guerrilla activities on the continent of South America and on islands located in the territorial waters . . . of the Southern Hemisphere.
>
> This defendant would expect to show . . . by these documents that the United States Treasury and other named and unnamed . . . government . . . agencies, and corporations . . . feared that their activities would become public knowledge, by and through the investigative efforts of the [Senate Permanent Investigations] Subcommittee. Therefore, to prevent this information from becoming public knowledge, agents of the United States Treasury Department planned, instigated and executed the arrest and immediate indictment of this defendant . . . to prevent him from freely and voluntarily testifying before the . . . Subcommittee.*

The motion is both pointed and circumspect, a warning shot rather than a full barrage. The promise of great revelations is contained

---

* Criminal indictment No. CR 74-471A, U. S. District Court, Northern District of Georgia, Atlanta Division.

within its two pages, but few secrets are actually betrayed. In it WerBell appears to be threatening the Treasury Department, the CIA, and others with a whistle-blowing defense that might only be precluded by a dismissal of charges or sudden acquittal. And, in fact, the case was quickly disposed of in the wake of his motion, eliminating the need for the defense he'd planned. With the motion mooted by acquittal, the government was not required to produce the "memorandum and correspondence" being sought. So it was that only the bare outline of the Caribbean plot WerBell alleged was let to surface. And yet conversations with WerBell, combined with facts about Vesco and those around him, tend to put flesh upon the outline. For instance: WerBell confides to friends that Vesco told him "he was working for the Company—he was part of the Agency." The remark was said to have been made by Vesco in an effort to obtain WerBell's cooperation. Whether it is true is difficult to say, though as we'll see in subsequent pages, Vesco does in fact have numerous connections to the CIA, its officers and agents. It may be that WerBell was deceived by Vesco and the Figueres family into thinking that a *private* plot of theirs was sponsored by the CIA. That wouldn't have been hard to accomplish. Vesco's staff is festooned with former CIA operatives who could lend great credibility to the notion. His lawyer, Edward Bennett Williams, is also the attorney of former CIA director Richard Helms and has, of recent, served on the President's Foreign Intelligence Advisory Board (FIAB). Moreover, it was the CIA that effected Vesco's release from a Swiss prison; and in Costa Rica his protector and closest associate, Don Pepe Figueres, was himself a CIA agent of some fame. The fugitive's staff of bodyguards was packed with Cuban exiles, many of whom claimed past employment by the Agency. By no means finally, but perhaps sufficiently, WerBell had seen his handyman, Wally Gillis, released from police custody while transporting weapons destined for the Detroit Kid—the message going out that WerBell was doing "government work." None of which proves that Vesco is, as he claimed to WerBell, "working for the Company." But certainly there was enough circumstantial evidence available to make the story credible. Used to the ways of spooks, WerBell did not find it odd that the Agency might use a fugitive such as Vesco to further its hemispheric designs—perhaps in exchange for secret immunity to extradiction. After all, the CIA had made similar deals with equally notorious men, including gangsters such as Sam Giancana and Johnny Roselli.

That WerBell *believed* Vesco to be an agent of the CIA (whether he is one or not) is made explicit in the defence motion quoted above. In that motion Vesco and the CIA are linked to the plot to separate Abaco from the Bahamas, as well as to a larger Caribbean conspiracy involving guerrilla activities in South America and elsewhere. It may be, of course, that WerBell was duped by Vesco into believing that the fugitive represented the CIA. In that case he may have been wrong to name the Agency, and other government departments, as principals in the Caribbean conspiracy he alleged. Whether duped or not, however, he could not have been mistaken about Vesco's role in the Abaco matter: WerBell was the plot's mastermind, and he certainly knew the individuals involved (though he may have been wrong about their institutional affiliations). Nor is he likely to have been mistaken concerning the existence of the larger plot involving South America and the Caribbean. Vesco wanted to buy *thousands* of silenced submachine guns suitable for clandestine operations—and if he could not import them, he would manufacture them abroad. It may be that some of those weapons were intended for use on Abaco (the timing of WerBell's involvements with Vesco and the Abaco matter suggests this). But two thousand guns would certainly not be needed to repel Pindling's pitiful gendarmerie: a confrontation involving so many submachine guns on a single side would amount to an all-out war, rather than the limited paramilitary affair under contemplation. The majority of the guns sought by Vesco, then, had destinations besides Abaco— thus the larger plot described in the defense motion.

That permission for the guns' export from Georgia to Costa Rica was not obtained strongly suggests that Vesco is not the CIA agent he pretends to be. Whatever operation he had (or has) in mind was therefore a private one. And there are many clues to its real nature.

The presence of anti-Castro Cubans on Vesco's staff is one: for many of them, the spread of socialism (to Chile and elsewhere) has become as anathematic as the situation in Cuba itself. A second clue has to do with the arrival in San José of Santos Trafficante, Mafia wizard of the Southern Rim. A central figure in the 1961 CIA plots to assassinate Fidel Castro, Trafficante departed from his Florida home for an eighteen-month-long Costa Rica visit that began in January, 1974—the month in which Vesco made his tender for WerBell's submachine guns. Ever since his Havana casinos were expropriated by the Cuban regime, Trafficante has been closely identified with the exiles' cause. He's given money for paramilitary incursions against Cuba and has, according to law-enforcement authorities, employed numerous Bay of Pigs veterans in his underworld enterprises. As we've seen, the Cuban vets have made expert use of their CIA-taught tradecraft to smuggle heroin and other drugs, apparently using some of the proceeds to finance the never-ending counterrevolution. If anything, Trafficante is a hero of "La Causa," and his extended visit to San José, commencing when it did, seems more a matter of synchronicity than coincidence. Neither does it seem a coincidence that Vesco, like Trafficante, should be named by DEA informants as a financier behind the heroin trade (more of which later).

A further dimension to the affair, multiplying the number of relevant "coincidences," involves a man named Orlando Bosch and the dramatic change that took place in anti-Castro activities about the time WerBell and Trafficante arrived in Costa Rica. A fugitive pediatrician and reputed assassin, Bosch's dossier is neatly summed up by writer Taylor Branch:

> Bosch has been a political terrorist—what they call an action man— ever since the late Forties in Cuba. He worked for Castro, then for the CIA, and then he denounced the CIA. He's been an anti-Castro outlaw since the mid-Sixties, always telling the Miami Cubans not to trust the CIA in their war against Castro. Now most of the hard-line Cubans believe him. Bosch is the patriarch of Cuban terrorism. . . . In general, Bosch had a threefold operation: first, political terror against Castro sympathizers; second, ordinary crimes like extortion from rich people and companies to finance the political terror; and third, all kinds of wars and feuds with his terrorist rivals. Finally, Bosch got nailed in 1968 for shelling a Polish freighter in Miami harbor. He got ten years, but he was paroled in 1972. That brings us to his international period. . . . Bosch went underground [in 1974] and the pace of Miami bombings escalated. So did terrorist bombings against Castro's embassies all over the world. Then, in 1974, important Cubans started getting knocked off in gangland-style murders. . . . He got arrested in Venezuela about two years ago. The Justice Department decided not to ask for his return to the United States despite all he's wanted for. That's weird. Then the Venezuelans turned him loose and he left with a bunch of Chilean bodyguards and a big pile of money. . . . [In February, 1976] Bosch got arrested in Costa Rica right before Kissinger visited. . . . Bosch got out of Costa Rica somehow, and pretty soon there was a secret meeting in the Dominican Republic of all the major Cuban terrorist groups, which the Dominicans allowed, of course. There was a

negotiated truce, and the terrorists united under Bosch in an umbrella group called CORU, supposedly with the support of several juntas in Latin America.*

So . . . WerBell's and Trafficante's visits to Costa Rica, the proposed submachine-gun sale to Vesco, Bosch's "international period" of terrorism, the wave of car bombings among rival Cuban exile leaders in Miami, the plot to seize Abaco, and the larger conspiracy alleged by WerBell in his defense motion all began at about the same time. The possibility, then, is real that the putative "CIA plot" described by WerBell was in actuality the very plan put into motion by Orlando Bosch and perhaps by Robert Vesco. The purpose of that plot, at least insofar as the Cubans are concerned, is to eliminate socialism *from the hemisphere as a whole*—rather than the narrower goal of ousting Castro. Feeling betrayed by the CIA, and convinced that the State Department is "soft on communism," Bosch & Company have chosen a geopolitical theater for their terrorist assaults. In this connection it's interesting to note that the alleged DEA assassination project was put together by WerBell and Conein at the same time as the events mentioned above. That scheme would have used *cubano* CIA veterans to liquidate Latino narcotics traffickers with links, in many cases, to the Mafia and CIA. Clearly, the timing of these events, and the milieu they comprised, are claustrophobic with coincidence. The Miami bombings, after all, were accomplished with explosive devices that were similar to those invented for Conein. In several of those bombings (as well as in the subsequent destruction of an in-flight Cuban airliner and the Washington murder of former Chilean ambassador Orlando Letelier) Bosch's faction is considered a prime suspect. Admittedly, there is no known direct evidence linking Bosch to either Vesco or WerBell—merely a remarkable parallelism to their intrigues. As for Trafficante, his clandestine business affairs impinge on the same areas we've come to associate with Bosch, Vesco, and WerBell: exile politics, smuggling, and the CIA. But again, there is no tangible link, no known recorded meetings, no canceled checks between them. The problem with understanding what all these things may have to do with one another is not, of course, a matter of direct evidence: we'd hardly expect terrorists, mobsters, and the Detroit Kid to conduct their affairs in public. On the con-

---

* Taylor Branch, "The Incident," *Esquire* (March, 1977), p. 57.

trary, the problem is one of understanding motive. In the case of Bosch and Trafficante, that's not difficult. Their interests, however shaded, converge in the arena of exile politics. As for WerBell, he was interested in selling guns for money and appears to have been duped by Vesco into believing that the financier was an agent of the CIA. As for Vesco himself, his motives may well have had to do with heroin profits, and certainly had to do with his determination (of which more later) to establish a financial principality in the Caribbean—a task which Bosch might easily have helped him to accomplish. But what of Lou Conein? There is no evidence that he's corrupt, and I believe him when he says, "My price keeps going up, what with inflation, and no one's ever met it." Why would he, or the DEA, participate in Bosch's scheme?—if indeed Bosch's scheme is the one alleged by WerBell. Political sympathy is unlikely in Conein's case: he's a pragmatist, not an ideologue. And the DEA would certainly not abet Orlando Bosch in his intrigues. Eliminating money and politics, then, leaves Conein without a motive. And yet there may still be an explanation: specifically, Conein's top-secret intelligence group may have been *penetrated*—not by the Mafia, as has sometimes happened with the DEA, but by Cuban exiles sympathetic to Bosch. Prior to the creation of the LaSalle Building safe-house, Conein established a DEA intelligence operation directed against the heroin traffic, conducted by Cuban exiles who were veterans of CIA training camps. Code-named "Deacon 1," the operation employed thirty former CIA officers—all of them from the Clandestine Services, and all of them Cubans. Later, Deacon 1 would be compressed into the project being mounted at the LaSalle Building offices of the B. R. Fox Company. Is it unreasonable to consider that some of these secret agents may have felt greater loyalty to the politics of Orlando Bosch than to the goals of the DEA? Bosch, after all, reflects the views of some Cuban exiles, particularly those of a paramilitary bent. It may be, then, that Conein's DEA operation became the secret instrument of exile extremists concerned more with the defeat of Caribbean socialism than with the War on Drugs. It would not, after all, have been a difficult matter to skew the DEA operation from its avowed targets: Conein relied upon his agents, and their informants, to identify the enemy. What if, among the drug dealers, some of Bosch's enemies should be included? In this regard, one ought not to overestimate the character or sensibilities of Conein's spooks. For instance: One of those most active in Deacon 1 was Carlos Hernandez Rumbaut, a narcotics trafficker arrested in 1969 with nearly five hundred pounds of smoke in his possession. Hernandez became one of Conein's most important agents, supposedly working with the other Cubans against the "Miami Connection." In 1972, however, Hernandez decamped from the United States when the DEA proved unable to neutralize the twelve-year prison sentence he'd earlier received and fruitlessly appealed. Moving to Costa Rica, he was made an honorary member of that country's Narcotics Division—despite his previous conviction and a history of mental instability. While a fugitive from the United States, Hernandez rose to become second-in-command of the Costa Rican Narcotics Division —joining, according to confidential DEA reports, a death squad responsible for at least one local assassination. Currently, Hernandez is the personal bodyguard of Vesco's patron, former President Pepe Figueres.

If, as I've suggested, the Caribbean conspiracy described by Wer-Bell was in fact a DEA operation taken over by Cuban exile extremists, then it's not hard to understand how WerBell may have been fooled into believing that the "Vesco plot" had CIA sanction. Conein and his Cuban CIA veterans would have left no doubt in his mind.

In any event, San José was a Gordian knot of mysteries when WerBell paid his visit to the Detroit Kid in April, 1974. Up until that time Vesco's paramilitary needs had been satisfied by Los Angeles stockbroker Tommy Richardson, whose private jet had delivered crates of automatic weapons to his mentor in San José. Vesco wanted a steadier supply, however, and WerBell appeared to be the answer. While the U. S. State Department would not permit him to export his arsenal of Ingrams to the Army-less Costa Rica, WerBell might be induced to manufacture the guns in that country. According to Stuart Graydon, the proposed factory was to be a joint venture with the Costa Rican government—at least, that's the impression Martí and Pepe Figueres conveyed. Inside Vesco's fortress, however, they and Gordon Ingram learned that the government's role would be nominal. And Vesco's role, contrary to what they'd expected, would be huge. The financier, brusque and condescending, made it clear that he was to be more than a backer: he intended to run the operation, supervise the weapons' manufacture, handle sales, control inventory, and select the firm's representatives. WerBell, Ingram, and the others would be technician-cogs, financially involved but otherwise redundant. "He gave the impression,"

Graydon said, "that he knew everything about everything." When WerBell began to explain the advantages of the Ingram and its silencer, Vesco insulted him, cutting him off with a wave of the hand.

According to WerBell, he was infuriated by the financier's demeanor, and stalked out. "I called the sonofabitch a fat-faced fucking crook and got out of there. I needed him like a hole in the head."

That may be. But it's also true that Vesco didn't need WerBell. Rights to the Ingram and the silencer belonged to the Scott Reeves group—a fact that Vesco may very well not have known prior to WerBell's arrival in San José. Vesco's sudden coldness, then, after so many negotiations between Martí Figueres and the others, can probably be explained in terms of that realization. It was Reeves he needed, and not the Georgian, if he wanted to manufacture the Ingram.

In this regard it seems appropriate to mention that Reeves has since sold the rights to foreign manufacture of the Ingram. While he won't say where it's being made, or who's making it, he describes the transaction as "sort of a four-cornered billiards shot involving several foreign countries." The possibility is very real that Vesco, always indirectly, bought those rights—with or without Reeves's knowledge. Making your own submachine guns is inevitably better than buying someone else's. Making them abroad is even better: Third World countries tend not to be as restrictive in their export policies as the United States is. Moreover, the manufacture of submachine guns in the United States is rigidly overseen. Each weapon proceeds through the factory with its own identity card and serial number, making unauthorized or extra manufactures extremely difficult. (Nevertheless, Treasury agents have found Ingrams *with identical serial numbers* in the inventories of the rival Military Armaments Corporation and Defense Services, Inc. MAC executives suggested very strongly that WerBell was to blame, intimating that he'd employed a "Cuban night shift" to manufacture the doppelgänger guns secretly for illicit sale.) Having one's own submachine-gun factory in a tropical land such as Costa Rica, while being the partner of the country's President, suggests enormous possibilities that would not be present in the United States.

The big question, however, remains. Why would Robert Vesco —a venal man if there ever was one—become involved in the Caribbean's paramilitary intrigues? As we'll see, the most likely explanation for his support of right-wing extremism in the tropics has to

do with his Napoleonic bent. At some time prior to the rape of
IOS, he began to dream of having his own kingdom, a principality
of world finance in which he alone would rule. While the Detroit
Kid's chief accomplice, Norman LeBlanc, executed the actual looting of Cornfeld's baby, Vesco himself was immersed in a desperate
search for Kingdom Come and the realization of his wildest dreams.
That was two years before his meeting with WerBell.

2 / THE SEARCH FOR KINGDOM COME

It's hard to imagine a busier man than Robert Vesco was in
1972. It had taken a year to seize control of IOS and another three
months to devise a detailed scheme for its eventual looting. In laying this groundwork Vesco came to rely upon spooks. IOS security
agents spun their webs around the rival Cornfeld's supporters,
harassing them with surveillances and threats, while SEC investigators were targeted for sexual blackmail. Moreover, Vesco used the
spooks at IOS to put him in contact with employees of the secret
services of France and West Germany. Similar connections were
made by his donations to the Nixon campaign. Jailed by Switzerland in 1971, Vesco obtained a release overnight through the personal intervention of Richard D. Vine, the CIA's acting chief of
station in Berne. Supposedly, Vine was acting on vague orders telephoned by then Attorney General Mitchell, who was reportedly
distressed to learn of an American's—*any* American's—incarceration
abroad. (If Mitchell expressed similar humanitarian concerns about
any of the thousands of other Americans in foreign jails, it hasn't
been reported.) In any event, IOS couriers recall that "a fat brown
envelope" was delivered to Vine after Vesco's release; what it contained, however, is unknown. Further interventions by CIA operatives on Vesco's behalf have been alleged in connection with events
leading to the subsequent censure, and removal from the IOS case,
of the Swiss magistrate responsible for the Detroit Kid's night in
the joint. If these allegations are correct, then the CIA ought to
be added to the list of forty-two defendants named in the SEC's
civil suit against Robert Vesco et al. When the CIA sprang Vesco
from Geneva's Antoine Prison, it enabled him to proceed apace
with the looting scheme. Moreover, in bringing about the financier's
release—regardless of whatever else it may have done in Vesco's
cause—the CIA contributed directly to the dismissal of Judge Robert
Pagan, the magistrate presiding over the incipient IOS case at the

time. Because Pagan was replaced by a young and inexperienced judge who could not even read IOS documents written in English, Swiss efforts that might have prevented IOS's looting were stalled. Curiously, a freedom-of-information request made by the author to the CIA, concerning Vine's actions and the Agency's secret study of IOS, was turned down on a host of interesting grounds. According to the CIA, release of the information would have damaged "national security," revealed policy recommendations made by the Agency, and disclosed "intelligence sources and methods, as well as the organization, functions, names, official titles, salaries, or numbers of personnel employed by the Agency." It's difficult to understand how information about Robert Vesco and/or an offshore mutual fund could damage national security—unless, perhaps, one or the other is performing some service for the U. S. intelligence community. In this regard one notes that the CIA was unwilling to honor the FOI request on other grounds as well, including its fear that satisfying the request would require the disclosure of "sources . . . methods . . . *or numbers of personnel employed by the Agency.*" (Italics mine.) Considering the clandestine nature of IOS activities—its underground banks, secret couriers, and Hold Mail List—the likelihood arises that IOS was being used by the CIA as a cover for agents and officers abroad. Indeed, what better cover could have been imagined for an agent than to have been one of IOS's more than fifteen thousand globe-trotting, highly independent Associates? As journalists do, IOS salesmen had an occupational excuse to knock on any door at any time. Their irregular hours, resort to aliases, and unusual itineraries might similarly have been excused as the curiosities of an offshore mutual-fund salesman's job. As an intelligence cover IOS was ideal—in its secretiveness and ubiquity it was probably rivaled only by the CIA itself. Asked about this, the SEC's Tom von Stein agrees. "Sure, IOS would have been a good cover," he says, "but only if the agents were able to turn out some work-product." Perhaps. And perhaps not: according to a 1969 IOS corporate report, fifteen hundred of the firm's Associates were responsible for about *90 percent of all sales.* The remaining 13,500 salesmen produced very little—and some even managed to generate a negative cash flow, costing IOS an estimated five hundred dollars per year in paper work. They were useless to IOS; they might as well have been agents. Still, it wouldn't have been difficult for agents under cover to generate some business. The CIA is awash in cash that needs to be invested. Besides payments to foreign agents (which often can't be made directly), the Agency earns an annual fortune from its proprietaries (airlines, insurance companies, banks, and so forth). Other money comes from the CIA's own staff of more than fifteen thousand full-time employees; since many of these employees cannot prudently reveal the identity of "the firm" for which they work, they must rely upon in-house proprietaries to serve even the most banal needs (for example, bank loans and insurance policies). Additionally, should a spook in the Clandestine Services get in financial difficulty, the Agency is unlikely to be compromised if the problem can be contained "in house." Deciding how to invest all these millions is the problem of the suggestively named MH-MUTUAL. Group within the CIA. And, of course, it would have been a simple matter for MH-MUTUAL to have invested in IOS through agents using the firm as a cover. Not only would this have ensured secrecy for the CIA's offshore investments, it would also have protected the spooks' cover as productive IOS salesmen—while at the same time rewarding IOS for the cloak it provided. Richard Vine's intervention in Vesco's affairs, therefore, and the Agency's strange response to a routine FOI request suggest some extravagant possibilities. Did Vesco threaten the Agency's covers if it failed to win his release from prison? Did the Agency in fact have any part of its extensive portfolio invested in IOS funds? If so, did Vesco rip off the CIA even as he ripped off the Mob? Did the so-called mugs' money belong as much to U. S. taxpayers as it did to organized-crime figures and white-collar bandits? Or was Vine's intervention no more than what it was made to seem on its surface—the product of influence peddled in Washington? The answers are in Langley. And, of course, in San José.

Vine wasn't the only spook to serve Vesco, of course. When the financier went after the Paradise Island casino and other holdings of Resorts', he availed himself of an odd consortium of agents: the IOS internal-security apparat, the Mafia, and the son of Morocco's Sûreté chief. Similarly, when Vesco made a bid for the Casino du Liban, he was helped by a *Walpurgisnacht* of spies that included the CIA's former chief of station in Baghdad, Harry Neill, and industrial espionage agents working out of Beirut. In both his casino bids, described further on, Vesco made full use of the standard cloak-and-dagger procedures: false passports, safe-houses, phony flight plans, cutouts, and so forth. Moreover, when Vesco realized that he was himself the target of investigations conducted by a plurality of U. S. government agencies, foreign jurisdictions, and

private eyes, he arranged for moonlighting U. S. narcs to perform
an electronic "countermeasures sweep" of his home and offices in
New Jersey.* (The federal wiremen reportedly found no evidence
of electronic surveillance at either location.) Even in the seemingly
simple matter of arranging the anonymous donation to Nixon's
campaign, Vesco saw fit to employ the services of Phillip Beck, a
270-pound private eye whose account of the money's transfer is
flatly contradicted by Vesco's former pilot. Besides the Moroccan,
Beck, Neill, Vine, and the IOS spooks, Vesco's own lawyers, Howard
Cerny and Robert Foglia, were themselves veterans of the OSS and
CIA. Indeed, it's clear that in the course of looting IOS, Vesco acquired a gourmet's taste for intrigue. As we'll see, from 1972 on,
things became increasingly mysterious—even, or especially, after the
fugitive financier settled into his supposed "retirement" beneath
the volcanoes of San José.

Costa Rica wasn't his first choice among the world's havens. By
the time it became clear that the SEC and IRS agent Richard Jaffe
could be neither bought nor outsmarted, Vesco had already studied
the extradition treaties and tax laws of a half-dozen nations. Argentina, Brazil, Venezuela, Paraguay, Panama, and Haiti were each
considered as a potential home. Dictators such as Franco, Stroessner,
and Peron were assiduously courted, their relatives and friends
treated with exotic gifts, guns, and girls. Had Vesco sought a hideout
and nothing more, he'd have had a dozen willing hosts. But it was
never his intention to take the money and run, or only that. The
idea of spending the remainder of his life attending Paraguayan
soirees with escaped Nazi war criminals was repugnant. A haven
was the *sine qua non*, but the financier's ambitions went beyond
simple refuge: he wanted a fiefdom, a principality—an empire, if
possible. It's uncertain where Vesco's dream of Kingdom Come
originated, but the presence of Richard V. Allen on his staff is suggestive.

---

* Vesco's premises were debugged in June, 1972, ten days before the Watergate
burglary, by agents of the then Bureau of Narcotics and Dangerous Drugs (now a part
of the Drug Enforcement Administration). The since-retired agents Sergio Borquez and
Robert Saunders took the assignment from John L. Kelly, then regional director of the
narcotics agency's Los Angeles office. Kelly was picked for the sweep by his friend and
business associate Thomas P. Richardson. Since convicted in a multimillion-dollar
securities swindle, stockbroker Richardson has been identified as one of Vesco's weapons
suppliers in Costa Rica. According to Richardson, Vesco reimbursed him for the debugging expenses by giving him forty-five black one-hundred-dollar chips at the Paradise
Island casino. A year after the narcotics agents debugged his offices, Vesco was himself
the target of a DEA heroin-smuggling investigation.

One of Washington's most masterful political operatives, Allen is a suave and erudite ultraconservative, a Notre Dame graduate with seven children and charm to spare. A veteran of the Hoover Institute on War, Peace and Revolution, as well as the Georgetown Institute for Strategic Studies, he was an early supporter of Richard Nixon. Strangely, he was also the target of a 1968 CIA investigation that has proven mysterious on several counts. In that episode CIA operative Franklin R. Geraty posed as a private eye in the employ of the Fidelity Reporting Service (in actuality a CIA proprietary). Inquiring about Allen's financial affairs and associations, Geraty had his cover destroyed when a suspicious banker reported his inquiries to White House factotum Rose Mary Woods. Woods informed the banker that contrary to Geraty's pretext, neither the Republicans nor Nixon's own staff had ordered background checks on Allen or anyone else. For seven years the story went unreported until in the midst of Senate investigations of the intelligence community *The New York Times* made brief mention of it. The *Times* article was itself curious—appearing years after the incident occurred. Not only did it fail to explain why Geraty had made the historic inquiries, but it neglected to mention the illegality of CIA operations at home. Nor did the *Times* point out the obvious: that Fidelity Reporting Service was part of an archipelago of private detective agencies run by the CIA.

A year after the Fidelity probe, Allen became a member of the National Security Council. His ardor for the Cold War, however, attracted Henry Kissinger's ire, and after nine months of presiding over the same intelligence community which had earlier investigated him, Allen resigned. From the NSC Allen went on to join former astronauts Wally Schirra and Frank Borman as "consultants" to the (since bankrupted) natural-resources magnate John M. King. In that capacity, Allen says, he witnessed King's abortive attempt during 1970 to take control of Cornfeld's IOS. "I was in Geneva during a part of that time," Allen says, "and it was chaos, absolute chaos." When King's bid failed, preparing the way for Vesco's successful capture of the mutual-funds colossus, Allen returned to politics. In June, 1971—the same month in which John Dean began to receive CIA reports about IOS—Allen was appointed to a White House commission on East–West trade. A conservative theoretician, he brought an unusual combination of expertise to the White House: as a former NSC member he had a stratospheric "Q clearance" that made him privy to the inner workings of both the State Department and the intelligence community; at the same time he was an authority on the subject of tax avoidance and offshore havens. While we don't know what Allen did for the Nixon White House during this time, his spare hours seem to have been spent in nurturing a dream that he would later share with Robert Vesco. That is, Allen became enamoured of a plan to establish an international financial district, a commercial enclave within which a "specialized fiscal regime" would prevail. Unlike Michael Oliver's utopian scheme, Allen's plan excluded the participation of individuals (as such). Only corporations would be permitted to take advantage of the district's hermetic banking provisions, its tax vacuum and trade allowances. Ruling the district would be a presidium composed entirely of multinational corporations, banks, brokerages, and insurance companies. What the plan amounted to, then, was the centralization of the world's offshore tax havens in a single place, a financial mecca where business transactions would be carried out in Rosicrucian secrecy. It would be a mini-nation of transient executives ruled by corporate abstractions in the interests of profit alone. To a right-winger, it would be nothing less than Kingdom Come.

The difficulty with the plan was that it required a host country, one that would exchange a part of its sovereignty for promises of rapid development. One of the first countries Allen approached, after leaving the White House for the second time, was Rumania. And, surprisingly, the commissars proved enthusiastic. The idea of a corporate principality, a sort of "Fourth World buffer" to mediate financial transactions between East and West, appealed to them. Unfortunately, they explained, Allen lacked the financial clout necessary for the scheme to succeed. A massive capital investment would be needed to guarantee the promises of development, and Allen alone couldn't make it. Accordingly, the treacherous bolsheviks misappropriated Allen's fantasy, taking it to the Manufacturers Hanover Trust for the bank's consideration.

It was obvious to Allen that what he required was the support of an institution or, failing that, of an individual with a cash reserve equal to that of a major bank. It's not surprising, then, that with his White House contacts and sources within the intelligence community Allen discovered Robert Vesco. Precisely when that discovery took place is unknown. It was not until August, 1972, that Allen moved into the offices of Vesco's attorney spook Howard Cerny, and began drawing ten thousand dollars per month as a "consultant" to the worried financier. Months prior to that, however, Vesco had been showing signs of having dipped into Michael Oliver's utopian tract, *A New Constitution for a New Country*. To his closest associates—since immortalized by the SEC as "LeBlanc *et al*."—he spoke of the advantages to be gained by the creation of an international financial district such as the one Allen had in mind. It seems likely, then, that Allen was the original source of this financial vision and that his services as a consultant had to do with formulating the financial framework of the district and finding a suitable host country.

In June, 1972, with the SEC investigation at fever pitch, Vesco entered into negotiations with Jean-Claude ("Baby Doc") Duvalier, Haiti's President-for-Life. What Vesco sought to acquire was the island of Gonâve, a sweltering paradise larger than Manhattan and infinitely more beautiful. And while Gonâve is afflicted with varietals of the dread mansion elm, a tree whose sap will scorch the skin and blind, Vesco proposed to make the island his dominion. In exchange for virtual sovereignty over the island Vesco would transform it into a tropical Wall Street, in conformity with Allen's plan. In addition, the island would be developed as a resort, with casinos, convention centers, and "new towns," while mainland Haiti would benefit from its proximity to Gonâve, and from its "special relationship" to the island. Naturally, Vesco argued, a financial district is only as good as its reputation: accordingly, he would create a kind of "offshore SEC" to regulate the zone—and to ensure that there would be no hanky-panky with investors' money, he or his closest associate, Norman LeBlanc, would head up the regulatory body. From an entertainment point of view, the world is a poorer place for the scheme's failure. The notion of King Vesco and Prince LeBlanc administering an offshore SEC among the mansion elms and voodoo drums of Haiti is worth the price of admission. Unfortunately, "the Gonâve proposition" failed to win the approval of Baby Doc and his Ton-Ton aides. According to his pilot, Vesco departed from the island referring to its young President as "Baskethead" and "that shit-ass kid." His mistake seems to have been in thinking that he could impress the Duvalier family with his wealth and with promises of "development." In fact, the Duvaliers have been raking in an estimated $16,000,000 per year for the past twenty years, the money deriving from an unreported tax on tobacco products. And as for development, the political power (and safety) of the Duvaliers depends upon the country's continued immiserization; new schools, roads, and jobs would only lead to a political awakening with potentially bloody consequences for the Duvaliers. Baby Doc already had a "specialized fiscal regime": why should he share it with the Detroit Kid?

The search for Kingdom Come continued, however, as Vesco bounded from one banana republic to another. Finally, with the SEC poised to cast its net of litigation, Dick Pistell stabbed his finger at a map of Costa Rica, extolling the country's virtues. A swashbuckling financier, Pistell met Vesco in the ambiance of Paradise Island (where both men maintain mansions) and impressed him with his international contacts and daring. An importer of Turkish wines and an operator of gold mines in Canada and the Cameroons, Pistell is a full-time enthusiast who's reported to be equally at ease in tropical and corporate jungles. It was Pistell who convinced Vesco that Costa Rica should be his future haven and who arranged (in return for a $100,000 "finder's fee") the $2,100,000 "loan" to San Cristóbal, S.A.—the floundering business of Costa Rica's former President, Don Pepe Figueres.* Not surprisingly, Figueres was enthusiastic about Vesco's projected residence in Costa Rica and about the plan for an international financial district. Accordingly, he drew up legislation to create the free-trade zone Vesco wanted, including provisions that would have given diplomatic status to employees of the district. Figueres, however, was a lame-duck President who could not by law succeed himself for another term. This, and the fact that he was obviously laboring under the baleful influence of the fugitive *norteamericano*, led the Tico congress to reject the plan. To many Ticos the proposed financial district resembled a kind of Panama Canal Zone, through whose locks bearers' checks rather than ships would float to sea. The loss of sovereignty entailed by the plan, and the near-certainty of its attraction to terrorists and racketeers, made the financial district a dangerous proposition. And yet, should Don Pepe become President in the future, or should his son Martí achieve that office, we may yet see Vesco on a free-zone

---

* In addition to the finder's fee, Pistell was the beneficiary of a disputed three-million-dollar investment made by one of the IOS funds in Vencap, Ltd., Pistell's flagship enterprise. Pistell placed one million dollars of that investment in a time deposit at a Swiss bank. The bank then loaned $700,000 back to "Intercapital N.V.," a company controlled by Pistell. Registered in the Netherlands Antilles, Intercapital N.V. then made a $590,000 loan to Pistell himself. Most of this last sum was used to satisfy an IRS lien against Pistell. Another $55,000 loaned to Pistell by Intervent, a subsidiary of Vencap, was used to remodel his house on Paradise Island. Court-appointed liquidators of the IOS funds are suing for the return of the entire three million dollars, arguing that the IOS investment was a *quid pro quo* for Pistell's services to Vesco in Costa Rica. Pistell denies the claim, insisting that the loans are fully collateralized, and that moreover IOS stands to make a fortune through Vencap's holdings in the Cameroons.

throne. Everything suggests that he still cherishes the dream of having his own principality of finance. The only question is whether or not he's prepared to help others—such as Orlando Bosch—kill for it.

3 / THE INTRA BANK AND MR. SPECTOR

It's difficult to overestimate Robert Vesco's love of intrigue. As an employer of spooks his only rivals in the private sector would seem to be Paradise Island's James Crosby and the late, demented Howard Hughes. If there is any single pattern in the complicated career of the Detroit Kid, however, it's the way in which he so often finds himself in the company of organized-crime figures and CIA officers. In view of that, one may be tempted to conclude that Vesco is himself a creature of the Mob or Agency.

On the other hand, Vesco claims that the Agency tried to kidnap him and, failing at that, sent out an assassination team to kill him. "They will," he says, "stop at nothing to bring me back to the United States—dead or alive." There is also the possibility that Vesco destroyed IOS as a cover for the Agency—which would not ingratiate him—and that a part of the money he diverted to his own use may have been the CIA's, or that of its employees. Which would also not ingratiate him.

The evidence, then, is on each side: Vesco appears to be both a friend and an enemy of the CIA. But surely the evidence is stronger for friendship than it is for enmity. His partner and host in Costa Rica, Pepe Figueres, is a man whose political popularity and heroic reputation owe themselves in large measure to Agency support. It seems unlikely that Figueres would betray his old friends at the CIA for money alone, or that he would support Vesco's unpopular cause in exchange for a needed loan. Presidents of Latin American countries seldom have any difficulty in arranging financing, especially if they have ties to the CIA; nor do they go out of their way to offend an Agency which can make or break them. Perhaps Vesco's activities *are* sanctioned by the CIA. Certainly his immunity to extradition is suggestive, as is the presence of so many retired CIA officers and agents on his staff. And as for the Detroit Kid's allegations against the Agency, they seem implausible, a smoke screen: if the CIA wanted him as badly as he says it does, the CIA would have him. And if Vesco believes that the Agency would not even stop at murder to bring about his return to the United States, it's most unlikely that he would continue to retain Richard Helms' lawyer, Edward Bennett Williams, a member of the Foreign Intelligence Advisory Board (FIAB), as his attorney for criminal matters. As for CIA investments in IOS that Vesco may have "close-ended," the Agency could afford to bury the loss in its budget—just as it could afford to find new covers for its employees abroad.

But let's leave this question up in the air for now, contending only that Vesco's relationship to the U. S. intelligence community is ambiguous.

As for Vesco and organized crime, the evidence is also ambiguous. We know that a major portion of the money looted from IOS represented the proceeds from loan-sharking, casino skims, prostitution, tax evasion, numbers, and narcotics: at least, that's what IOS employees claim. We know also that Vesco sought to finesse his way into control of Mob-connected casinos in different parts of the world, using the same methods of financial hocus-pocus that led to IOS's destruction. In short, Vesco *moved in* on organized crime and would therefore seem likely to occupy a prestigious place on the Mob's hit-list. And yet, and yet . . . virtually his entire career has been spent in association with men who stand convicted of, or who are fugitives from, charges of swindling securities: men such as S. Mort Zimmerman and Norman LeBlanc. As we'll see, Vesco has also been named as the financier of a Mafia-inspired heroin deal; and, not least of all, is known to have concluded a verbal contract in a secret meeting at Rome's Fiumicino Airport with Eddie and Dino Cellini—the latter a fugitive described by Senate witnesses and others as "Meyer Lansky's right-hand man." That contract, agreed upon in mid-1972, while Vesco was in the midst of negotiations for the purchase of the Nassau casino owned by Resorts International, is believed to have been one in which the Cellinis and Vesco divided the offshore gambling world into spheres of mutual interest.

As with the CIA, so with the Mob: Vesco appears to be as much a partner of organized crime as he is its enemy. The explanation may be that the fugitive financier has allied himself with *factions* that would seem to exist within both the Agency and the underworld. Certainly this would explain the ambiguities in his relationships to both institutions. It might also explain Vesco's astonishing ability to raise large amounts of cash to finance his early mergers and acquisitions. As we've seen, IOS provided some of that money; financial institutions such as the Chase Manhattan Bank and the Prudential Life Insurance Company provided more; and private investors came up with some of the rest. But even beyond this, Vesco seems always to have been able to acquire the odd million when interest payments fell due, or when interim financing was required. The specter, then, is one of Vesco's having borrowed money from organized-crime figures to finance mergers that needed to be made; and of his having called upon the woollier of his associates in the securities business, buying stolen or counterfeit stocks to collateralize loans made to him by banks that were "captive," or easily duped. Admittedly, the deliberate murkiness of the Detroit Kid's offshore transactions makes it impossible to do more than speculate in this regard. There is no evidence that he did this. And yet such practices are not uncommon. No less a banker than Nixon's own Bebe Rebozo was himself unwittingly stuck with a wad of stolen IBM securities in 1968. According to Senate testimony provided by the Securities Validation Corporation, $11.1 *billion* in securities was *identified* as stolen, counterfeit, or missing in 1974. The Senate itself estimates that stolen or lost securities worth some fifty billion dollars "are floating around in our economy." * Taken from the Railway Express Agency, from the cashiers' cages of brokerages, from airports and from individuals, the pilfered stock is easily fenced for about 1 percent of it face value. The stock may then be taken abroad for resale, placed in banks as collateral, or used to establish trust accounts, which can in turn be used to create letters of credit or certificates of deposit. All that's necessary for the scheme to succeed is for the banker to neglect to check the stock's origins— a commonplace. If the banker has no reason to suspect that the stock is stolen or counterfeit, he'll probably take it at face value—especially if he knows the person with whom he's dealing. He may then lend up to 80 percent of the hot stock's "worth" at current market prices. Once accepted as collateral, the stock gathers dust in the vault until the loan is repaid (at which point the stock can be used again), or until a foreclosure on the loan forces the bank to try to sell the stock itself. All of the risk, of course, is eliminated if the person fencing the stock owns his own bank or has an "understanding" with a crooked one. If he does own a bank, he can list the stolen stock as a part of its assets; since auditors are not usually required to investigate the origins of such collateral, they will certify the bank's inflated statement of its worth. The bank's own credit is thereby

---

* Hearings Before the Permanent Subcommittee on Investigations of the Committee on Government Operations, Part 4, p. 483, June 25 and 26, 1974, G.P.O., Washington, D.C.

increased, permitting it to make more loans than it can legitimately afford. According to Frank Peroff, a specialist in passing bad paper, "Practically the entire Costa del Sol was financed that way."

In view of Vesco's remarkable facility at raising large sums quickly, it's suggestive that he bought a controlling interest in the Standard Commerz Bank of Switzerland in 1969, barely two years prior to his take-over of IOS. We don't know what he did with that bank: secrecy laws shroud its transactions. But it was not a casual acquisition. A few months earlier he'd done his best to acquire control of Geneva's Exchange and Investment Bank, about which rather more is known. Howard Cerny handled the negotiations. S. Mort Zimmerman, a convicted securities swindler and business associate of influence peddler Bobby Baker, is credited with having "found" the bank for Vesco. (At the time, Zimmerman held a large block of International Controls stock, having obtained it in return for his interest in one of Vesco's earliest acquisitions, a Texas firm that manufactured bombs.)

In some ways the bank was a dicey proposition. Its owners were anonymous and its customers invisible. Still, the premises were posh and the bank manager reported a cash flow of about four million dollars per week—all of it out of Vesco's favorite wateringholes, Miami and Nassau. In addition, the bank had a proprietary mutual fund with more than seven million dollars in assets. The biggest problem, however, was that the U. S. Attorney for the Southern District of New York, Robert Morgenthau,* had identified it as a "laundromat" for associates of organized-crime wizard Meyer Lansky. According to Morgenthau, more than two million dollars per month was skimmed from the Flamingo Hotel and Casino in Las Vegas, funneled through the Miami National Bank, and then delivered to the Exchange and Investment Bank in Geneva—whereupon it disappeared from view.

Cerny's negotiations failed, but the principals in the deal were interesting: in effect, Vesco had used the good offices of a securities swindler to effect a merger between himself and the Lansky crowd. Had that deal been unique, it might be discounted. But it wasn't. Two years later Vesco began negotiations for control of a much larger, but in other ways similar, property: the Middle East's Intra Bank.

Intra owed its existence, in a negative way, to the terrorist suc-

---

* Morgenthau is today District Attorney for the City of New York

cesses of the Haganah and Stern Gang, paramilitary organizations dedicated to the creation of Israel. Among the Palestinian refugees who fled the Haganah after World War II was Youssef Beidas, an Arab moneylender. Beidas founded the Intra Bank in Beirut during 1951, in all likelihood cursing the Israelis in the very act of incorporation. From its earliest beginnings Intra was alleged to be deeply involved in the traditional intrigues of the Middle East—narcotics, gunrunning, terrorism, and the *coup d'état*. And the bank became enormous, with investments in more than a dozen countries and assets in excess of a billion Lebanese pounds. Among its holdings were sections of Beirut Port, Lebanon's national television network, Geneva and Paris real estate, a thriving Marseilles shipyard called La Ciotat, the biggest refrigerated warehouses in the Middle East, two smaller banks, Middle East Airlines, the Casino du Liban, and more than forty-five other subsidiaries, many of them immensely profitable. The casino alone was worth a large forutne and was said to be the biggest gambling emporium in the world—dwarfing the Sands, the Dunes, the Flamingo, and Monte Carlo. Moreover, its affiliation with Middle East Airlines enabled the casino to bring in junkets from every part of the Arab world; sheiks, princes, financiers, and the *nouveau riche* of the OPEC countries flocked to its tables, as did the cosmopolites of Beirut itself. Predictably, the casino became a focal point of Holy Land spookery. The Palestine Liberation Organization (PLO) was said to extract a percentage of the casino's skim to finance terrorist operations against Israel, and law-enforcement authorities contended that the gaming tables and the Intra Bank itself were used to launder the proceeds from heroin transactions conducted by the casino's manager, Marcel Paul Francisi.

And yet despite its far-flung assets and enormous cash flow, the Intra Bank went bust a few months prior to the Arab-Israeli War in 1967. A mysterious run on the bank's deposits was credited with forcing it into receivership, and not even a 150-million-pound loan from the Lebanese government could prevent the catastrophe. The responsibility for the run on the bank has never been determined with certainty, but DEA and State Department officials privately suspect that a man named Paul Louis Weiller was the cause.

Stephen McClintic, a career State Department official attached to the Drug Enforcement Administration prior to his recent retirement, describes Weiller as "A French mixture of great wealth and mouldering aristocracy—a combination of Henry Ford and Mickey

Cohen, half industrialist and half gangster." Weiller is credited within the DEA as being "the man who moved against the Intra Bank." His financial holdings are vast and transcontinental, including interests in shipping, real estate, hotels, mines, factories, and the Bahamas Port Authority, Ltd. A yachting visitor to the Caribbean, he divides most of his time between the world's financial centers and his magnificent villa on the French Riviera, overlooking the Mediterranean Sea. A friend and dinner companion of Richard Nixon's, Weiller is reported to have bragged of donating two million dollars to the former President's campaign chest between the years 1968 and 1972. Why Weiller should have moved against the Intra Bank is unknown. DEA officials say only that it's a persistent rumor, adding that Weiller has frequently been accused of financing heroin transactions.

Whoever was responsible for Intra's collapse, Youssef Beidas, the bank's founder and managing director, took the secret to his grave. The bank was Beidas' creation and it was he who was responsible for the casino's operations—including the employment of Marcel Paul Francisi, described by senior DEA officials as "one of the richest and most influential men in the Union Corse." When the bank failed, Beidas was indicted for fraud in three countries. Rather than face charges, he went underground, surfacing finally in Brazil. And while Brazil refused to extradite him, Beidas nevertheless felt compelled to visit one of the countries in which he was under indictment. Using a forged Brazilian passport, he entered Switzerland in the aftermath of the Arab-Israeli War. In the course of his visit there in November, 1967, he was arrested while driving a car with New Jersey license plates. The charge was only a traffic violation, and Beidas might have escaped. The Swiss, however, were courteous enough to find a Portuguese translator to explain the offense to him. Beidas' blank stare gave the lie to his Brazilian passport, and it was only a matter of moments before his real identity was discovered. At the time of his arrest he was carrying $37,000 in cash and the keys to safety-deposit boxes in several European countries. Released on bail, Beidas added to the mystery by dying unexpectedly. The cause of death is a matter of dispute. Initial reports stated that he committed suicide in a Swiss hotel. The Swiss government contends that he died of cancer in a Geneva hospital. And according to Leonard Saffir, administrative assistant to former New York Senator James L. Buckley, "CIA reports list Beidas's death as a possible murder."

The key to the affair rests with one of the world's most beautiful women, Patricia Richardson Martinson. A leggy native of St. Martin, in the Netherlands Antilles, she's been the protégé of some of the world's richest men. Paul Louis Weiller discovered her on a yachting cruise when she was only fourteen (she looked older) and served as her "protector" from then until her marriage to New York business-man John Martinson. In the intervening years, she appears to have become the friend or protégé of one multimillionaire after another, winning the affections of a constellation of financial barons, hit-men, gunrunners, gamblers, and heroin marketeers. Besides her affairs with Paul Louis Weiller and Youssef Beidas, she could claim friend-ships with:

Sir Charles Clore, Britain's seventy-three-year-old "Ambassador to the Pound Itself." Immensely rich, Sir Charles is one of the sceptered isle's great industrialists, presiding over a clutch of com-panies, including the directorates of the Ritz Hotel, Sears, Self-ridge's, and Bentley Motor Cars. Allegations that Sir Charles is somewhat less than free-spending would seem to be rebutted by the fact that he treated Patricia to a St. Martin apartment whose annual rent was $24,000.

Eduardo Baroudi, described by Senate sources as one of the world's most successful traffickers in guns and drugs. A paramour of Patricia's, Baroudi was suspected by DEA officials of having "arranged" the mysterious death of Youssef Beidas in Switzerland. Patricia herself has admitted that she, too, suspects "one of [her] friends" of having murdered Beidas.

Weiller, Clore, Beidas, and Baroudi seem to have hit some of the highest notes in Patricia's heart, but through them she made other friends:

Christian David, an international narcotics trafficker and spook, he was arrested in 1972 by Brazilian police and charged with having headed a smuggling ring that delivered more than three hundred pounds of heroin per year to the Western Hemisphere. Tortured by the Brazilians, David confessed to having participated in the (as yet unsolved) assassination of Moroccan socialist Ben Barka. Luring Ben Barka to France, David said he was paid $150,000 to assist in the leftist's transmigration and subsequent burial in an unmarked grave filled with lime.

Conrad Bouchard, a Canadian crooner and heroin trafficker asso-ciated with Giuseppe ("Pepe") Cotroni, reputed Mafia leader in Montreal. Bouchard's notoriety expanded in 1973, when an undercover DEA informant charged the DEA with deliberately sabotaging the investigation of a multimillion-dollar heroin deal planned by himself and Bouchard. According to Frank Peroff, the informant, DEA officials with whom he'd been working caused him to be arrested, stripped of his cover, and abandoned to the likelihood of assassination immediately after Bouchard had named Norman Le-Blanc and Robert Vesco as the financiers behind the heroin deal. Bouchard's assertion that Vesco and LeBlanc would provide $350,000 in "front money" for the transaction was secretly taped by Peroff for DEA officials. But rather than continuing the operation, Peroff said, the DEA destroyed it overnight. (As we'll see, Peroff isn't the only informant to charge investigative sabotage in cases involving Vesco and people linked to him: William Spector and, in a separate matter, Norman Casper allege the same thing.)

Marcel ("Flokky") Boucon, skipper of the *Caprice du Temps*, a Caribbean-based tuna boat seized off the French Riviera in March, 1972, with *935 pounds* of pure heroin on board. Two weeks before the bust occurred, the boat had been at St. Martin. And what a bust. For perhaps the first time in their careers, police were at a loss to estimate the value of drugs seized in the course of an arrest, pointing out that the *Caprice du Temps* held enough smack in her hold to service the Western world for months. Conservatively, the haul was worth hundreds of millions of dollars and represented a corner on the market. In any case, the police could hardly have taken credit for the seizure, having stumbled upon the heroin hoard when they came aboard to help put out a fire in the craft's hold. To this day the case has the status of a major unsolved crime: Patricia's friend Flokky Boucon attempted suicide when placed under arrest, and, though that attempt failed, he's since refused to answer any questions about the affair. Presently, he's serving a twenty-year sentence.

Henri Helle, Boucon's employer, and another friend of Patricia's, described in French police reports as "a smuggler of stock certificates, cigarettes, and narcotics." According to those same reports, Helle brought Boucon to St. Martin, where "a network of drug traffickers . . . exist[s] in the Dutch Zone . . . which is directed toward the United States from France via Philipsburg, St. Martin." (St. Martin is an island divided into French and Dutch sectors.)

Obviously, Patricia Richardson Martinson got around. A contemporary "Carolyn Cherie"—10 percent ingenue and 90 percent bombshell—she gravitated toward geriatric men of great wealth who employed servants of great daring. She became accustomed to yachts, marriage proposals, the plush interiors of chauffeured Bentleys, and long weekends on the flagstones beside Riviera pools. An occasional model for Christian Dior, infinitely changeable with her wigs and lashes and makeup kits, she dieted on vitamin pills washed down with champagne and orange juice. And, according to her first husband, William Spector, she became an accomplice in the intrigues of her "sugar daddies." That, however, has never been proven.

Spector is a former Army intelligence agent who turned down a career with the CIA after serving as U. S. liaison to the former King of Rumania during World War II. A resident of Ogdensburg, New York, hard by the Canadian border, Spector is consumed by what he regards as Patricia's betrayal of him. The fury of a woman scorned is well-known, but Spector is proof that a cuckold's ire is at least as energetic (albeit decidedly more dangerous). Since 1971 he's devoted all his time and nearly a million dollars to prove that his ex-wife, acting on behalf of Paul Louis Weiller, smuggled tons of heroin into the United States from Canada and France. "Weiller is the French Connection," he says flatly.

Spector encountered Patricia in 1967 and spent a torrid weekend with her in New York. Twenty years younger than Spector, Patricia evidently regarded the affair as trivial, and when Monday came around she decamped for Hollywood. There she lived with the swashbuckling actor Gardner McKay, former star of the television series "Adventures in Paradise." Spector didn't hear from her for more than a year, but then, in mid-1969, a letter arrived describing the misfortunes befalling Patricia. According to the letter, she'd given birth to Spector's child, was penniless and in failing health. Apparently, she'd been injured in an accident which, DEA officials later explained, occurred at McKay's Hollywood house, where Patricia is said to have taken a high dive into a dry swimming pool.

To his ongoing regret, Spector did the decent thing. Rescuing Patricia and her two children (she'd since had another) from the miseries of Paris, to which she'd moved after her Hollywood sojourn, Spector brought them to his home in Ogdensburg. Looking back on it, Spector is convinced that the letter describing Patricia's supposedly miserable circumstances was written by Patricia herself— and not by the sympathetic nun whose signature it contained. Moreover, he believes that Patricia married him, at least in part, as a favor to Paul Louis Weiller who, Spector claims, saw a unique opportunity in the nuptials. That opportunity had to do with

Spector's respectable Cadillac dealership, Patricia's alleged loyalty to Weiller, and Ogdensburg's proximity to the Canadian border. According to Spector, Patricia admitted to him that she assisted Weiller by receiving literally hundreds of toy animals stuffed with dope; and that, in addition, she helped Weiller's "mules" enter the United States from Canada in new cars whose bodies concealed heroin.

Patricia herself has denied this vigorously, claiming that her ex-husband is paranoid and vengeful, determined to ruin her life. While admitting to having known Boucon, Baroudi, David, and the others she pleads ignorance of any criminal activities. Her life in Ogdensburg, she reports, was not a happy one; a child of the Caribbean, and a worldly woman, she dreaded the long frozen winters of upstate New York, the small-town gossips, and suburban monotony. As a high-fashion model, she found it essential to her career that she travel often to such places as Paris, Chicago, New York, Hong Kong, and Montreal. Contrary to what her possessive husband says, there was nothing sinister in this, and she couldn't help it if her exotic meanderings fed the fantasies of their neighbors. Of heroin, she knew nothing: "I don't even take aspirin."

Spector has called his ex-wife's story a pack of lies and pointed to a lurid manuscript of hers, a memoir, according to Spector, that describes a young woman's stormy affairs with a host of sugar daddies, smugglers, and thugs. Other "evidence" unearthed by Spector includes a cache of snow-white powder that he discovered in a basement hole beneath his house; the alleged statements of Patricia's friends recalling conversations in which she supposedly talked of having Spector murdered on contract; and photos of Weiller taken with Richard Nixon, photos that bear the autograph of heroin trafficker "Flokky Boucon." By no means finally, Spector claims that, in the course of a visit to St. Martin, he elicted affidavits from relatives of Patricia and from a former boyfriend of hers as well, affidavits that allege her involvement in drug smuggling. While on St. Martin, Spector says, the proprietors of a resort called Le Pirate made an attempt on his life.

Tearfully, Patricia has denied as much of her former husband's story as the evidence will allow. The "memoir" she'd written was only a clumsy attempt at a novel, according to its author. The stories owed more to her imagination than they did to her experiences. She hadn't placed a contract on her husband's life and, as for the affidavits against her, she says they were obtained by coercion. There is no truth to the story Spector tells, she claims, just a horrible framework of coincidence played upon by her jilted spouse.

And in fact Spector's story has a way of coming together only to fall apart. The white powder found in his basement yielded an ambiguous police report. The officer who tested it says it wasn't heroin and yet is unable to explain why his police report lists the test as having been "positive." Spector believes the discrepancy to be evidence of a larger conspiracy to cover up the affair, a conspiracy which includes elements of the local and state police, the DEA and Nixon White House. Police searches of automobiles crossing the Canadian border, searches that were inspired by Spector's demands, found nothing, he says, because the smugglers were tipped off in advance, perhaps by the authorities themselves. In this connection Spector points to the mysterious suicide of Ogdensburg police chief David Bell, hinting that he may have been a victim of foul play.

Spector, however, is nothing if not intrepid. When local police failed him, he sought out investigators attached to the state police. Again the results were ambiguous—if only in Spector's mind. A telling interview with a young associate of Patricia's, who bragged of his connections to the Nixon family and to organized crime, was secretly tape-recorded by Spector and an undercover policeman. The interview, Spector says, might have proven his case but for the fact that the recording later disappeared. Taking his tale to DEA agents in New York and to the New York City police, Spector intrigued the cops with the recitation of names (Boucon, Baroudi, David, Bouchard, and so forth) in his wife's manuscript—names well-known to narcotics authorities, but not to the public. New York's Finest were sufficiently interested in Spector's story to put him under surveillance. Their interest was piqued even further when the policemen following the Cadillac dealer reported that Spector was *already* being shadowed by what they described as "a professional surveillance team," consisting of three unidentified men. For their part, the DEA agents were less helpful despite the fact that Bouchard and Boucon were at that time two of the highest-priority investigative targets known to the agency. Apparently, New York's DEA contingent confined their inquiries to asking the state police if Spector's narrative was well founded. The state police said no, and the DEA went no further. By this time Spector had branched onward and upward, contacting highly placed DEA officials in Washington, the Democratic National Committee, and the White House. There the affair took on nightmarish proportions. Spector's contact at the White House turned out to be Egil ("Bud") Krogh, task-master of the Plumbers and executive director of the Cabinet Committee on International Narcotics Control—the group credited with having detailed Lou Conein to the DEA—with what strange effects we've seen. Besides his Watergate involvements (Krogh engineered the bag job carried out against Daniel Ellsberg's psychiatrist), Krogh had participated in what DEA agents describe as "the mishandling" of André Ricord. A resident of Paraguay, Ricord was identified as a kingpin in the international heroin trade. Attempts to extradite him from South America to the United States were unsuccessful until the State Department, under White House pressure, threatened to eliminate foreign aid to Paraguay's dictatorship. At that point Ricord was turned over to U. S. authorities. DEA officials who accompanied the aging smuggler from Asunción to New York later claimed that Ricord was confident that he wouldn't spend much time in prison. "You had to be there in Asunción to realize what it was like," one DEA official said. "We thought for sure that when we arrived at the airport with Ricord, someone would assassinate him on the way to the plane. When that didn't happen, Ricord became almost cheerful. He said he intended to turn state's evidence and cop out on the people above him. He was confident that we could protect him. But then, God knows why, nobody seemed interested in what he had to say. He was never questioned. They just put him away for twenty years and forgot about it. He'll never live that long." According to the same DEA official, Ricord's case was orchestrated by the White House—partly because Nixon wanted to take credit for the bust, and partly because of its foreign policy implications. Whatever its reasons, the DEA's McClintic thinks that the White House botched the case. "They should have interrogated Ricord," he complains. "They should have gone as high as they could."

Throughout it all, the Watergate saga was unfolding as Nixon drove toward reelection By Any Means Necessary. Spector's tale could hardly have appealed to Bud Krogh or any of the President's staffers. Besides the two-million-dollar donation allegedly made by Weiller to Nixon's campaign, the two men had dined together in New York's plush Côte Basque—not in itself a crime, but evidence of their relationship. In addition, Nixon's campaign headquarters had been located in the Hotel Pierre, believed to be owned by Weiller. If Spector was right about the French industrialist, the President of the United States owed a substantial political debt to one of the world's most important financiers of the heroin traffic.

Moreover, as Spector pointed out, Robert Vesco had taken an active role in Nixon's overseas fund-raising campaign, and may well have encountered Weiller in that capacity. At the time he made his charges to Krogh, Spector could not have known that, a year later, Vesco and Norman LeBlanc would be named by a top-secret under-cover informant of the DEA as the financiers of a heroin transaction organized by Connie Bouchard, the Montreal singer who figured prominently in Patricia's manuscript. Nor could Spector have known that the U. S. Attorney for the Southern District of New York would choose one of Vesco's own former attorneys to press for the fugitive's extradition from the Bahamas; and that Vesco himself would be represented in the proceedings by one of Weiller's attorneys. The extradition attempt would fail so miserably that Bahamian authori-ties would later charge that the United States did not want Vesco back, that it sabotaged its own case.

Not surprisingly, the White House did nothing about Spector's charges. Or did it? After informing the chief Plumber, Krogh, of the scandal, and getting nowhere, Spector went to the Democratic National Committee (DNC) for relief, arriving there only weeks before the Liddy-led burglary of its offices. In the DNC's Watergate suite, Spector told all to DNC head Larry O'Brien's top aide, Spen-cer Oliver. And once again Spector's tangled web replicated. Oliver is the nephew of Robert Bennett, president of the Robert R. Mullen Company. The Mullen Company, of course, was E. Howard Hunt's employer (or, depending on your point of view, his cover). It was also a front for CIA officers stationed as far apart as Singapore and Amsterdam, and it held a lucrative contract with the Howard Hughes organization, a contract formerly held by the DNC's Larry O'Brien. And if this were not incestuous enough, Robert Bennett was himself playing a three-cornered game of political intrigue that has investigative reporters still guessing whether he was "Deep Throat." In his reports to his CIA case officer, Bennett discussed a variety of matters:

- the Mullen Company's role as an Agency cover;
- Howard Hunt's political espionage;
- Howard Hughes's Gordian affairs;
- and an Intertel investigation of Hughes's fired alter ego, Robert Maheu, an investigation carried out under contract to the billion-aire's flagship, the Summa Corporation.

But the CIA wasn't the only father confessor to Robert Bennett. In the wake of the Watergate bust he became a covert source of information for *Washington Post* reporters Bob Woodward and Carl Bernstein, as well as for Washington lawyer Edward Bennett Williams. According to his CIA case officer, Bennett established a "back-door entry" to Williams by feeding information to another Washington attorney, Hobart Taylor. At the time, E. B. Williams was all over the Watergate board, and before long his list of clients would prove exotic enough to satisfy the interlocking fantasies of any conspiracy theorist. Not only was he the attorney for *The Washington Post*, credited with "breaking" the Watergate story, but he was also in charge of the DNC's civil suit against the Committee to Re-Elect the President (CREEP). Sen. Edward Kennedy, *bête noir* of the Nixon White House and one of the Plumbers' primary targets, was also a client. Soon Nixon vizier John Connally would have need of Williams' services, as would FBI chieftains under investigation for "black bag" activities. Former CIA director Richard Helms would one day come aboard. And so, of course, would the Detroit Kid himself: Robert Vesco, Watergate's own Rosetta Stone. It was an interesting and lucrative practice, though we can only wonder how Vesco, a fugitive whose assets are subject to seizure in the United States, could actually manage to pay the high-priced Williams. Not that Williams always charges his clients. Helms was a *"pro bono"* case, and there have been others as well. It's Williams' firm, for example, that's been pressing the Carter Administration, the FBI, and the Justice Department to expedite their glacial investigation of the 1976 Washington car-bombing that took the lives of former Chilean Ambassador Orlando Letelier and Ronni Moffitt. In that cause, Williams' firm represents the interests of the surviving spouses, researchers at the Institute for Policy Studies (IPS). The suspects in the murder include various American adventurers, ex-CIA agents, Chilean spooks, and anti-Castro Cuban terrorists. And yet, while one can only applaud William's keen social conscience and willingness to work for nothing in special cases, it's hard to understand how his firm can represent clients whose interests seem so divergent. Helms, for instance, was at least partly responsible for the Chilean coup d'état that seems to have led to Letelier's explosive demise several years later. And while Helms did everything he could to conceal the truth about Chile, lying about it to the Senate, subsequent accusations of perjury very nearly made him a force for disclosure. That is, in plea-bargaining sessions with the Carter Justice Department, Williams and Helms made it clear that the former CIA director's defense would require massive discovery-proceedings that promised to shed both heat and light on a vast array of national security matters (including Chile). That would have conformed nicely to the hopes of Williams' other clients, the widow and widower at IPS, but it was not to be. Daunted at the prospect of so much exposure, Attorney General Griffin Bell and his fast-rising assistant, Ben Civiletti, knuckled under to Williams, permitting Helms to plead guilty to a misdemeanor at a wrist-slapping ceremony to which no reporters were invited. This isn't to say that Williams was engaged in a conflict of interest situation, but that the situation was packed with conflict and quite interesting is certainly true. Similarly, one can only wonder at the conceptual juggling required of Williams by his representation of *The Washington Post*, Vesco, and the DNC. Why he found the need, as he apparently did, to seek out Intertel's services to investigate the Watergate affair is anyone's guess. (Intertel, whose clients include Howard Hughes' Summa Corporation and ITT, reportedly rejected the offer. After all, how could they investigate the Watergate affair without also investigating their client, Hughes, and, very likely, their parent company, Resorts International, as well?) More than anyone else, Edward Bennett Williams may be said to have the keys to America's secret history. Besides Watergate, Jimmy Hoffa, and the Teamsters, Williams might shed great light upon a number of people and events, including the Kennedy family, the destruction of Sen. Joseph McCarthy, the intrigues of Robert Maheu, the secret war against Onassis, and the politically explosive murder of OSS Major William Holohan. As we'll see, several of those matters remain relevant today.

So when William Spector walked into the offices of the Democratic National Committee, there to recount his tale of woe, he had little conception of the byzantine relationships around him, the whirlpool of associations and loyalties that would prove to be ever deepening and always expanding. Talking about his wife, Nixon, Bouchard, and Weiller, the Cadillac dealer sought to convince Robert Bennett's nephew, Spencer Oliver, of the affair's political significance and what he regarded as the DEA's "cover-up" in Nixon's behalf. A few weeks after these conversations, Spencer Oliver became one of the mystery men in the Watergate burglary when CREEP wireman James McCord placed a tap on his telephone at the DNC. While it took little imagination to make sense of the Plumbers' tap on Larry O'Brien's phone—besides his trucking in general "political intelligence," he was witting of Howard Hughes's complicated internal affairs and their relationship to Nixon—no one could figure out why Hunt and the Cubans would want to bug Spencer Oliver. Spector, however, *knew* why. He'd naïvely alerted Krogh to his allegations and then laid them on the line to Oliver at the DNC. One of the purposes of the Watergate burglary was to learn what, if anything, the Democrats intended to do about Paul Louis Weiller's connection to Richard Nixon and Spector's charges of narcotics smuggling. That, at least, is Spector's opinion, and he may very well be right.

When the White House and DNC failed him, with the latter committed to making the Watergate burglary a mere campaign issue, Spector turned to the upper echelon of the DEA. There he held discussions with top DEA officials Stephen McClintic and Jacques Khiere. Both men were impressed by Spector's uncanny knowledge of the narcotics underworld, and found the evidence he offered—while inconclusive—highly promising. They also found unconscionable lapses in the intelligence-gathering of their subordinates. DEA officials in New York seemed never to have questioned Spector's wife or, in fact, anyone else involved. Reports of the French Sûreté concerning Patricia, her friends, and drug traffic on the island of St. Martin were either lost or ignored. Files pertaining to Boucon and others named by Spector were missing. No attempt was made to learn the identity of those belonging to the "professional surveillance team" that had followed Spector. And in an obvious effort to conceal its own incompetence, DEA officials alleged that the entire matter had been checked out by the FBI and found unworthy of further investigation. Asked about that, the FBI reported that it had no information on the Spector case and had certainly never investigated it. Whatever else one may think of Spector's charges, it's clear that the DEA blundered in its investigation of them, just as McClintic claimed. Whether those blunders were made purposely, perhaps at the instigation of Nixon loyalists and Plumbers at the White House, is uncertain. Failing to consider that possibility, however, would be naïve. There's just too much there:

• the Plumbers' tap on Spencer Oliver's phone following Spector's conversations with Krogh and Oliver;

• the countermeasures sweep of Vesco's offices by federal narcotics agents;

• DEA's missing reports and inactivity on the case;

• the relationship between Vesco and Nixon, and Weiller and Nixon;

• Conein's alleged creation of CIA/DEA assassination squads which shared safe-house space with Mitch WerBell, himself a prospective partner of Vesco's;

• and the deliberate destruction by the DEA of Frank Peroff's cover after he reported Bouchard's assertion that Vesco and LeBlanc were behind a three-cornered heroin transaction involving Marseilles, Montreal, and San José.

What appears to have happened is that the Nixon forces impaled themselves on both ends of the heroin syringe. On the one hand, they contemplated serial assassinations to destroy the drug traffic; and on the other hand, they themselves appeared to be the beneficiaries of narcotics profits. Either position could have destroyed the President's chances for reelection, and both therefore had to be covered up. Accordingly, the Spector and Peroff probes seem to have been sabotaged, while Vesco was protected and permitted to remain at large in exile.

4 / PARADISE LOST

Negotiations for the Intra Bank continued for months as Vesco carried out the looting of IOS. In many ways the deal was unique. Besides the bank's exotic political history and its employees' connections to the heroin trade, its collapse had delivered it into the receivership of four unlikely creditors: Lebanon, Kuwait, Qatar, and the U. S. Agriculture Department's Commodity Credits Corporation (CCC). Agriculture's interest in the bank (and therefore in the Casino du Liban, Middle East Airlines, and the rest) came about when Intra defaulted on $22,000,000 in letters of credit extended to it by the CCC in return for shiploads of wheat and butter. Following the run on the bank's assets in 1966, Intra found itself rich in real estate and other properties, but virtually without cash. Agriculture accepted stock in the Intra Investment Company in exchange for its letters of credit.

For the first time in his career, Vesco found it necessary to operate at the level of international diplomacy, negotiating not with other corporations, but with nations themselves. The offer he made to the Intra group was eminently refusable. It promised a mere $20,000,000 cash loan and five years of Vesco's "management services" in return for about 40 percent of the stock in Intra. Since that share was conservatively worth $150,000,000, the Arabs could only blink at the American's gall. Indeed, the offer was so bad that Intra's owners decided not to refuse it out of hand, asking for time to study it in the belief that they must have "missed something." In the interim, Vesco applied pressure from behind the scenes, gathering secret intelligence about skimming at the Casino du Liban and trying for the support of influential Arabs and American politicians. Harry Neill, the former CIA station chief in Baghdad, served as spear carrier for the Vesco forces, heading up Comptrol International—a Beirut-based subsidiary of International Bancorp. Some 30 percent of Comptrol's stock was owned by a group of unidentified Arabs who, it was thought, included wheeler-dealer Adnan Khashoggi and relatives of politicians in Lebanon and Kuwait. Meanwhile, back in Washington, Vesco's flunkies persuaded Attorney General Mitchell to cable the American Embassy in Beirut on behalf of the Detroit Kid. Mitchell complied, persuading the embassy's legal-affairs attaché to provide U. S. Ambassador William E. Buffum with a memo describing Vesco in glowing terms. That was deemed necessary to erase the stigma of Vesco's overnight confinement in St. Antoine Prison a few months before, and also to contradict an earlier cable sent by the State Department in the wake of Vesco's bid for Intra. The earlier cable had warned the Mideast desk of Agriculture's CCC bureau that Vesco wallah was suspected of having ties to organized crime.

The public relations effort backfired, however, when Ambassador Buffum complained of Mitchell's meddling in State Department affairs, forcing the Attorney General to recant his endorsement of the Detroit Kid. But the Intra deal was unraveling in any case. When the bank's Arab trustees proved unable to understand Vesco's bizarre lending proposal, they hired the Beirut office of Kidder, Peabody & Company to analyze it for them. Learning of that, Vesco sought to ingratiate himself with the investment analysts by providing them with a juicy contract of his own. In return for six head-scratching paragraphs "evaluating" a most dubious Caribbean transaction, Kidder, Peabody's Lebanese office was paid $100,000— about three hundred dollars per word. Despite this, Kidder, Peabody doesn't seem to have been able to bring itself to recommend Vesco's bid to take over the Intra Bank. After four months of negotiations and skullduggery, his offer was turned down.

The loss of Intra was a bitter disappointment to Vesco. His connections had failed him at the level of international diplomacy, a blow to his pride. But, much worse, he'd lost a financial opportunity of unparalleled magnitude, an opportunity perfectly tailored to his talents and tastes. To have had a controlling interest in both the Casino du Liban and Middle East Airlines would have approximated a license to print money. It would also have provided him with a large and respectable financial base to take the place of the foundering IOS; and it would have made him a partner of the oil-rich sheikdoms of Kuwait and Qatar, providing access to almost unlimited capital. Moreover, Vesco needn't have been regarded by the Arabs as a common swindler for his having looted IOS. On the contrary, he might easily have convinced the Arabs that IOS was a political instrument of Israel, pointing to its multimillion-dollar investments in Israeli bonds and properties, and its links to such noted Zionists as Cornfeld, Rosenbaum, Rothschild, and Meshulam Riklis.* With some Madison Avenue pros in his corner, Vesco could have manipulated the nationalist sentiments of the Middle East, emerging in the Arab view as a political refugee, the victim of a sinister Zionist conspiracy. After all, as the Detroit Kid was fond of pointing out, all his troubles could be traced to "those fuckin' Jew bastids at the SEC." And there would have been some poetic justice in the event had Vesco succeeded with this ploy. As a partner in Intra, he'd have been welcome in Lebanon, as well as in the arid wastes of Kuwait and Qatar. In all likelihood he would have established his headquarters in Beirut, a cosmopolitan financial center and the site of the Casino du Liban. There, rather quickly, he'd have found himself in the midst of one of the century's bloodiest wars. One wonders what he would have done, with the grenades and bullets plopping all around him. Join other American citizens in accepting evacuation by U. S. warship (thereby bringing about his own "extradition")? Or, more probably, strike overland across the desert to Kuwait, accompanied by Don-Don Nixon and LeBlanc, his fortune and frozen pizzas borne on the backs of camels?

The collapse of the Intra negotiations prevented that vision from becoming a reality. But it also imparted a new urgency to Vesco's scheme, forcing him to accelerate his search for new vehicles to absorb the loot coming in from IOS. The most promising alternative to Intra and the Casino du Liban was Resorts International and its casino on Paradise Island in the Bahamas. We'll take a closer look at Resorts' mysterious empire in subsequent pages. Here, however, it's important to outline its negotiations with Vesco because

---

* Chairman of the Rapid-American Corporation, Riklis was one of IOS's largest stockholders.

the proposed transaction, more than any other deal, alarmed the SEC and led directly to its filing suit against the Detroit Kid.

Resorts International is a mini-kingdom in the Caribbean, with powerful political connections in both the United States and the Bahamas. The favored gambling spot of Vesco, Bebe Rebozo, and Adnan Khashoggi, Resorts' casino is immensely profitable. Like Intra's Casino du Liban, the Caribbean emporium has been repeatedly alleged to be the site of laundering and skimming operations linked to political slush funds and organized crime. Like the Casino du Liban, the Paradise Island casino is also tied to a major airline, in this case, Pan American World Airways. Located a short distance from the mainland, Paradise is connected to Nassau by a toll bridge owned by a consortium that includes James Crosby, chairman of Resorts International; C. Gerry Goldsmith, chairman of Grand Bahama Development Company; and two banks acting as nominees for a silent partner believed to be Richard Nixon. The beneficiary of a $100,000 campaign contribution from Crosby in 1968, Nixon was a frequent visitor to the gambling spa. Through its private intelligence agency, Intertel, Resorts International served for years as the custodian of Howard Hughes, having engineered the billionaire's startling dash from Las Vegas in 1970—an exodus that the fired Hughes aide Robert Maheu called a kidnapping. Intertel is also responsible, under a $400,000-per-annum contract, for providing security at the casino and monitoring its gaming operations.

A friend of Crosby's, Vesco proposed to buy virtually all of Resorts' property in the Bahamas, using funds from IOS. The purchase price was $60,000,000, split in two improbable parts. The casino and toll bridge were to be sold to Gulf Stream (Bahamas), Ltd., run by Gil Straub, one of Vesco's cronies and a fellow indictee. Twenty million dollars in cash and five million dollars in promissory notes would be the price—a bargain of the first order. More than 300,000 tourists cross the bridge each year, paying two dollars apiece (or $600,000) for the privilege, and the casino reports an annual profit of about five million dollars. Even if one discounts allegations of revenue being skimmed from both the bridge and the casino, Gulf Stream could have earned back its entire purchase price in less than five years! And if the reports of skimming are true, the deal would have been even more lucrative. How much more is uncertain. According to Resorts' figures, the average tourist leaves a mere fifteen dollars on the casino's tables, little more than a sawbuck in excess of what it costs to visit the casino. That seems an awfully modest sum when one considers the affluence of Bahamian tourists on a spree and the troops of high rollers who arrive every week on subsidized gambling junkets.

In any case, the second part of the deal served as *Crosby's* incentive. While the casino is profitable, a number of related enterprises are not. These would have been sold to Property Resources, Ltd., beneficially owned by IOS shareholders, for $35,000,000. What the IOS-ers would have gotten for that sum was a golf course, a marina, two hotels, a laundry (the kind that washes shirts), a sewer works, some small shops, the Café Martinique, and thirty acres of marginal land which, taken all together, lost about one million dollars per year.

The Paradise Island deal, then, represented a two-pronged affair by which the Vesco group would have paid very little for a racehorse, and the IOS group a great deal for a cast of lepers. For his part, Jim Crosby and other stockholders in Resorts would have picked up $60,000,000. That represented about five dollars for every share in Resorts—roughly two and a half times the going price for Resorts International stock on the American Exchange during 1972. The loudest objection to the deal was made by Bernie Cornfeld, a backgammon partner of Crosby's, who warned that Vesco was "a crook" and that "Crosby was just spinning his wheels. The SEC would never let the deal happen." Vesco and Crosby, however, had a pair of aces in the hole. In June, 1972, Vesco flew to Rome's Fiumicino Airport, accompanied by the adventurous Dick Pistell, who seemed to play an important part in the negotiations for Paradise Island. No sooner had the financier's private jet transport taxied to a halt than Eddie and Dino Cellini jogged up the boarding ramp for back-slapping embraces with Pistell and the Detroit Kid. How was Nassau? they wanted to know.

The Cellinis were gambling impresarios and looked the part: they wore soft Italian shoes with impossibly thin soles, five-hundred-dollar suits, sunglasses, and gray-on-white dress shirts made for them in a fashionable boutique near the Spanish Steps. The younger Cellini, Eddie, had no criminal convictions, but he'd grown up in the shadow of his brother, Dino, acquiring his gambling expertise in the same array of joints and palaces that his brother had: the bust-out mills of Newport, Kentucky, where everyone had a "collie" on his arm and a drink in his hand and stayed until his pockets were empty; the plush emporia of pre-Castro Cuba; and the hip extravaganzas of Nassau and the Windward Islands. Dino, on the other hand, was a fugitive from justice and well-known to police intelligence officers. A friend of George Raft's, Cellini had been declared *persona non grata* in Great Britain, where he'd run a school for croupiers. He'd also arranged junkets to Raft's swank Colony Club (before the movie star was himself expelled). His special expertise was in knowing a gambler's credit limits and how to arrange collection of his debts.

That's valuable knowledge. Casinos depend on junkets of high rollers, both for the glamour they bring and the money they lose. A group of thirty inveterate gamblers flown in to a casino for a weekend can easily lose a million dollars or more—roughly 15 percent of which will be kicked back to the man who organized the junket. None of the gambling will be done with cash, partly in order to avoid taxes and partly to circumvent currency controls. Instead, the junket's organizer will advise the house of the client's financial limits, assuming responsibility for the man's losses. After the gambler has returned home to the States, collection agents will visit him to take payment. Depending on the wishes (and legitimacy) of the casino and junketeer, that money will then be declared and deposited in a bank, or it will simply go unreported. Since gambling *losses* are not deductible for income tax purposes (beyond the amount of gambling winnings), the client who's dropped a bundle has no incentive to report it. In this way, hundreds of millions of dollars—perhaps billions—are annually laundered by organized crime: the money may be lost in Lebanon or the Bahamas, but it's paid off in the U.S.A.

Knowing the limits of high rollers, therefore, is the *sine qua non* of any casino operation, particularly one that aspires to skimming and laundering money. Lifelong entrepreneurs of chance, the Cellinis are credited with having one of the world's most valuable "pigeon lists"—an up-to-the-minute financial dossier on that select group of businessmen, athletes, heirs, and entertainers who enjoy losing big bets in faraway places. How much is a pigeon list worth? In 1966, lawyer Edward Bennett Williams handled negotiations for the transfer of one such list to Lou Chesler, part owner of the Lucayan Beach casino on Grand Bahama Island—and an admitted associate of Meyer Lansky's. Chesler needed the list because three key employees * of the casino, all fugitives from the United States,

---

* Max Courtney, Charles Brudner, and Red Reed.

were about to be deported. That might have left Chesler with a sabotaged operation. Fortunately for him, however, Williams was able to put together a deal whereby the three men were paid two million dollars in exchange for the list (Williams himself reportedly received fifty thousand dollars for his services).

In 1972, the Cellinis' pigeon list might easily have been worth almost twice that amount. Moreover, Dino was in an excellent position to provide other services and advice. If the Senate testimony of various apostate gangsters (for instance, Mafia *caporegime* Vincent Teresa) can be believed, Dino was Meyer Lansky's "top man . . . [his] right-arm." According to Ike Eisenhauer, who served as Vesco's personal pilot, Dick Pistell thought the Cellinis were even more important: " 'They're the ones you have to deal with,' " Pistell is reported to have said. " 'They control every card on every table, and every table and wheel in every casino in the world. There's no action anywhere without their say-so.' " *

The conversation between Vesco, Pistell, and the Cellinis was held in the privacy of the financier's Boeing, and no minutes of the meeting were kept. Nevertheless, it appears that a bargain was struck between the men, formalizing Vesco's connection to the underworld. According to Ike Eisenhauer, quoting Pistell, Vesco and the brothers shook hands "on a deal you couldn't imagine."

It was only a figure of speech. Vesco was then nearing the peak of his negotiations for Paradise Island, bartering sessions which brought the financier together with a curious cast of outlaws and entrepreneurs. Besides Pistell and Crosby, Vesco found himself dealing with a trio of Italo-Americans who supposedly had no connection to the casino owned by Resorts. For reasons that have never been explained (largely as a result of Fifth Amendment guarantees against self-incrimination), a man called Jimmy Neal (*née* Pellegrino Loia) was given a fifty-thousand-dollar "finder's fee" in connection with the Detroit Kid's proposed take-over of Resorts. For years Neal had organized junkets to Paradise Island, a lucrative enterprise that ended when Intertel learned he was planning to run Caribbean gambling junkets in collaboration with Montreal's notorious Pepe Cotroni.† Before Neal was fired, however, he'd prevailed upon Dino Cellini to obtain jobs for his brother and brother-in-law in

---

* Eisenhauer, *op. cit.*, p. 289.
† The same man who figured so heavily in William Spector's case and in the affair involving Conrad Bouchard's assertion that Vesco had taken a bullish position on American heroin futures.

the cashier's cage at the Paradise Island casino. This Dino was able to accomplish, perhaps because his own kid brother, Eddie, was the casino's manager. At the time of Vesco's negotiations for the property, though, none of these men was associated with Resorts. Dino was a fugitive from U. S. justice, having been indicted on a tax rap with Meyer Lansky; Eddie Cellini and Jimmy Neal had been fired; and Neal's relatives had left the casino "for their health." Why Vesco, who knew Crosby personally, should have needed Mob figures such as Dino Cellini to close a deal with Resorts is unknown. But certainly the Cellini brothers knew Paradise Island (and its possibilities) *cold,* and could have served the Detroit financier in several ways. The confab at Fiumicino, however, is thought to have gone beyond the Bahamas. Those most familiar with Vesco's ambition and the Cellinis' reach speculate that the meeting yielded an agreement dividing the offshore gambling world into spheres of mutual interest and silent partnership. The SEC roadblock thrown up in November, 1972, removed Paradise Island from Vesco's grasp, but it did not recover the bulk of the monies he'd looted. Nor did it have any lasting impact on his master plan: the establishment of an "integrated conglomerate" made up of casinos, airlines, banks, and hotels, all of them anchored beyond the reach of U. S. regulating agencies. The SEC suit was more than a nuisance, but far from a deathblow. It unmasked Vesco and forced him into exile, removing him from direct participation in the world's most important financial centers. Beyond that, the SEC could go no further except, perhaps, to maintain the loosest kind of financial surveillance, a surveillance rendered ineffective by the SEC's lack of "assets" (spooks) and Vesco's own resort to a variety of corporate cut-outs and fronts. It's interesting, therefore, that Eddie Cellini is now the proprietor of a casino on St. Martin, Patricia Richardson's stomping grounds.* Called Resort of the World, the casino was purchased in 1976 from Raymond O. Parker and his family. The Parkers own the Concord Hotel in upstate Kiamesha, New York, not far from the site of William Spector's debacle. Buying the casino from the Parkers was an Italian entrepreneur and "business consultant" named Rosario Spadaro, a developer of posh resorts in the Mediterranean and casinos in two Nigerian cities, Ibadan and Kaduna.

Perhaps the most curious role in the abortive negotiations for

---

* Until recently, another casino, on the other side of the island, was owned by Henry Ford and supervised by Intertel.

Paradise Island, however, was played by Intertel. Established in 1970, the private intelligence agency was staffed by scores of former federal investigators and spies whose services were for hire to clients contemplating mergers. Its declared *raison d'être* was to prevent the infiltration of legitimate businesses by organized crime. As Intertel was a subsidiary of Resorts, it was understandable that the parent should patronize its offspring by engaging its services. Accordingly, Intertel could hardly deny having investigated the Detroit Kid when he proposed taking over virtually the entirety of Resorts International. On the other hand, the deal was only stopped at the last minute by the *SEC's* protestation—and not through any intervention of Intertel's. How, then, does Intertel explain its apparent approval of Vesco's tender? Tom McKeon, general counsel for the Caribbean apparat, ingenuously replies with a rhetorical question: "At what point does a man become suspect? Our investigation of Robert Vesco was carried out months before the SEC suit was filed. We just didn't have any idea of what he'd been up to." That reponse begs the listener's intelligence and demeans the capabilities of Intertel's agents. The nature of Intertel's work demands that "a man become suspect" immediately. Spooks operate within the framework of the Napoleonic code: the subject of investigation is assumed to be guilty until he is proven to be innocent —not the other way around. And Intertel could hardly have failed to uncover Vesco's shady associations and the manipulations at IOS. Its directorate for Intelligence Operations was headed by two men: one a veteran of the CIA, and the other a former chief of market surveillance for the SEC. Even if Intertel had chosen to ignore Bernie Cornfeld's declarations that Vesco was a crook, its Intelligence chiefs certainly had their own sources of information. McKeon's gullible posture, therefore, is clearly disingenuous. A graduate of the National Security Agency (NSA) and Bobby Kennedy's Get Hoffa Squad, he is in no way naïve. The truth of the matter is that Intertel appreciated Vesco's criminality but realized the financial bonanza to Resorts that his offer represented. It was dirty money—but there was a lot of it. Stuart Allen, an SEC enforcer who formerly served as one of Intertel's two Intelligence czars, was candid when he laughed off McKeon's explanation. "Sure, we investigated Vesco," he said, "but the offer he'd made was too good to refuse. In the end, we told Crosby that Vesco was a crook and that the SEC was preparing to cream him. What that boiled down to, though, was a recommendation that Resorts not take his paper—the promissory notes. The deal had to be cash. In a few months, Vesco's paper wouldn't be worth anything."

Intertel's probe of Vesco, then, is a clear illustration of the venality underlying private intelligence operations. Pretending to work in the private sector for the public interest, as Intertel does, the federal graduates are in fact no more than mercenaries. Their assessment of Vesco had nothing to do with the public interest. It was a matter of purely financial expediency.

5 / DIAL M FOR MILHOUS

From April Fool's Day, 1972, until the SEC civil suit blew his cover, Vesco cruised the jet stream in a frantic effort to consolidate his political alliances and to put together new financial vehicles capable of absorbing the loot coming in from the ongoing rape of IOS. Seated behind his desk in the aft section of the private Boeing's plush interior, the Mediterranean miles beneath his feet, he'd contemplate a litter of strange documents and photos while sipping from a glass of iced bourbon. Each page in front of him represented part of a jigsaw puzzle whose shape was known only to him. There were bearer shares in the mysterious Red Pearl Bay. A topographical map of Haiti's Gonâve Island. A report by the accounting firm of Coopers & Lybrand on the operation at Paradise Island. A separate report, prepared by IOS spooks, on Intertel. The incorporation papers for a half-dozen Panamanian shells and Liechtenstein *Anstalts*. Copies of lending agreements among banks in New Jersey, Luxembourg, and the Bahamas. Numbers and codes referring to Swiss accounts. A dossier on the Figueres family in Costa Rica. Translations of extradition treaties. A draft of his resignation letter to the board of IOS. A report on Kingdom Come. And more.

There were pieces missing from the puzzle, but only because Vesco wanted it that way. There was, for instance, the conspicuous absence of a receipt for his $200,000 cash donation to Richard Nixon's reelection campaign. Indeed, there was nothing in writing that would have linked the flying financier to the President of the United States. And yet the ties were there. Besides the presence of Donald Nixon, Jr., the President's nephew and Vesco's go-fer, Howard Cerny was around. And Cerny liked to brag that the President's brothers, Donald and Edward Nixon, were his clients. In fact, Cerny and Vesco had held a late-night meeting with Edward Nixon in the Fairfield offices of International Controls only a week before the $200,000 donation left Paradise Island for New Jersey. That the meeting had the character of an emergency session is clear: en route from Washington to New York, Edward was "intercepted" at the airport by Vesco's aides and spirited to Fairfield for an unscheduled discussion of the proposed cash donation.

Two months later, according to Bernie Cornfeld, Vesco would hold a clandestine meeting with the President in Salzburg, Austria. But the most interesting link between Richard Nixon and Robert Vesco is one alleged by former Howard Hughes aide Johnny Meier. A business associate of Donald Nixon Sr.'s, Meier told me that on a business trip to the Dominican Republic the President's brother confessed that Vesco was in charge of secret bank accounts belonging to himself and Richard Nixon. Admittedly, Johnny Meier is not an impartial observer. A friend of Marlon Brando's, he shares the actor's liberal views, supported Senator George McGovern for President, and was active in raising funds to defend former CIA officer Daniel Ellsberg in the wake of the Pentagon Papers' release. But Meier was also an employee of Howard Hughes's, responsible for a number of sensitive matters. Besides lobbying to eliminate nuclear testing in Nevada, he served the billionaire in a realtor's capacity, helping to arrange the purchase of abandoned mining properties.

In the performance of this latter assignment, Meier came under investigation by a number of private and federal agencies, including Intertel and the IRS. Before long, indictments were brought against him in California, charging that he'd bilked Hughes of millions in the course of buying up worthless properties. Currently in exile in Vancouver, Meier claims that he's the victim of a political frame-up and points to a campaign of dirty tricks supposedly carried out against him.

According to an affidavit written by one "Virgino Gonzalez," who purports to be a retired CIA officer, Meier was the victim of a political conspiracy involving a host of crimes by the CIA and other agencies in the United States and Canada. The affidavit alleges that Meier was the target of constant (and illegal) surveillance; that his house and hotel rooms were burglarized by authorities; that judges were suborned by the CIA; that the Agency intervened at the *Wall Street Journal*, "funding" some reporters and bringing about the transfer of others who were friendly with Meier; that the CIA manipulated the courts and the national press to destroy Meier's New Mexico campaign for the Senate; and that the Agency contemplated assassinating British reporter Robbie Robertson, who was deemed to be too witting for his own good. In short, the Gonzalez affidavit is a bombshell. Almost parenthetically, the author makes devastating accusations, *to wit*: "During 1968/1969 I had been told to drop all investigations into Sinclair Weeks and his movement of monies abroad for political funding and first came into contact with John Meier in April 1969 in Las Vegas. At about 15.00 on April 25 Sen. Edward Kennedy arrived at Las Vegas and was to give a speech that night. With other agents *I arranged with Jack Entratter of the Sands Hotel to fix a girl for Kennedy and for pictures to be taken for future use.* Kennedy fell for the situation but the full use of the operation was ruined when Meier had heard something of it. I learned later that he had contacted Bill Haddad, Larry O'Brien, Joseph Napolitan and Steve Smith and warned them of a problem." (Italics mine.)

Elsewhere: ". . . Meier [had] met with several CIA agents in Nevada. It had been thought by them that Meier was informed regarding agency cooperation with the Hughes organization and [Robert] Maheu's company. It seemed that Meier had stepped into the Ecuadorian situation as well as obtaining *a list of politicians whom we wanted funded thru Hughes.*" "October 16 Meier again called Paul Schrade in California. And when he *talked to Stan Sheinbaum at McGovern's HQ* (213) 469 9061 on October 31 *the call was traced* and we knew Meier's new home." (Italics mine.) In other places, the affidavit describes CIA meddling in Canadian political affairs and, almost incidentally, refers to CIA surveillance of *Playboy* publisher Hugh Hefner.

It's a stunning document, ten pages long, and virtually every other sentence contains a bombshell. Did the CIA tap McGovern's headquarters, as the affidavit implies? Did the Agency plan to have Senator Edward Kennedy seduced for reasons of blackmail? Did the Agency provide Howard Hughes with a list of politicians that it wanted to support—and, if so, did the money come from Hughes or, indirectly, from the Agency itself? If the Gonzalez affidavit is to be believed, the United States is a police state run by a dangerous consortium of CIA officers, private intelligence agencies, and White House entrepreneurs. And the affidavit is not entirely unconvincing. It names names, gives dates and places, and provides a flock of unlisted telephone numbers belonging to movie stars and politicians alike. It also reports the nature of conversations that were thought to have been private—and does so throughout in the first person.

In short, the affidavit is for the most part verifiable. And one would have little choice but to believe it if one could only find its author, "Virgino Gonzalez." He, however, has disappeared after delivering his affidavit to the court. Whether Gonzalez was, as he claimed to be, a fifteen-year veteran of the CIA, or someone else is uncertain. The Agency will not comment on whether it has ever had such an employee, and sources within the spooks' milieu claim never to have heard of him. "Virgino," however, is a most unusual name, even for someone who claims to have been born in Cuba. And, interestingly, the alias "Virgino Gonzalez" has been used by a sometime CIA agent—a Cuban exile whose real name is Max Gorman. Years ago, Gorman was arrested in Miami in connection with the theft of an automobile and gave his name as Virgino Gonzalez. Today, however, Gorman denies having written the document that bears his peculiar alias.

Reporters familiar with the case are themselves divided over the affidavit's authenticity. Some think that Meier may have written it himself in an effort to further his own legal cause. As a participant in many of the events described in the affidavit, Meier could easily have forged a report of his own surveillance, attributing it to a disgruntled CIA agent. On the other hand, Max Gorman is just such a fellow: a clandestine operator and a friend of Watergate burglar Frank Sturgis, Gorman is sufficiently angry at the CIA as to have filed suit against it, charging that the Agency betrayed himself and his friends on secret missions into Cuba.

If there was nothing more than Johnny Meier's report of Donald Nixon, Sr.'s, "admission" that Vesco controls offshore bank accounts belonging to Richard Nixon, one would have to ignore the charge. And yet there is other evidence of the truth of the allegation. Norman Casper, the Tums-popping private eye known to friends and foes alike as "the Friendly Ghost," discovered that evidence while investigating the Castle Bank & Trust of the Bahamas and Cayman Islands. A nervous, thickset spook with a gentle way about him, Casper earned a curious living as a sort of bounty hunter for the IRS. His quarries were illicit bank accounts and bogus loan transactions carried out in the Caribbean by vest-pocket banks in behalf of American tax evaders. Providing the IRS with proof of such accounts, Casper (or "TW-24," as his IRS contacts knew him) would receive an informant's fee. It wasn't much in proportion to the amount of money involved—Casper might get five thousand dollars on every million—but it paid the mortgage on his house in Key

Biscayne and kept him in Bloody Marys at the Jamaica Inn. Besides, there was always the possibility that he would actually "break a bank," revealing *all* its illegal transactions, and earn a million of his own. Formerly a detective with The Wackenhut Corporation, the Friendly Ghost had good contacts in the Miami and Caribbean areas. Through a banker friend he met Samuel Pierson, then president of the Castle Bank, at the Miami airport in October, 1972. Hinting that he was a DEA agent searching for evidence of narcotics trans-actions, Casper obtained Pierson's business card with a message scribbled on its back: "HMW: give this man anything he wants." HMW was H. Michael Wolstencroft, resident manager of the Castle Bank.

Why Pierson cooperated with Casper is something of a mystery, but it probably has to do with the strange nature of relationships between banks like Castle and their customers. Like many other banks in the Cayman Islands, Castle had no guards, no tellers, and no vaults. Like Vesco's Standard Commerz Bank in Switzerland, it had no need for cameras or alarms, and hardly ever were its store-front doors invaded by the physical presence of a customer. Castle Bank had neither checking accounts nor savings accounts. Virtually all of its assets were kept on deposit with other banks in the United States, its headquarters in the Caymans serving only as a repository for the bank's records. No one knows exactly how many such banks there are in the Bahamas and the Caymans, though it's been pointed out that the Cayman Islands alone have more than 14,000 telex numbers (the instrument of most banking transactions) and fewer than 13,500 residents. According to the IRS, more than fifteen billion dollars per year flows through these banks—and a good deal of it is funny money.

Understandably, the relationship between banks like Castle and their customers is uniquely one of mutual trust and discretion. To violate that relationship is to invite retaliation. And this is the most likely explanation for Castle's cooperation with Casper. The bank's own reasons for cooperating have a self-serving ring, and boil down to the assertion that the Castle Bank & Trust was a class operation. With roughly *a quarter-billion dollars* in assets (about a million dollars per customer and about one customer per square foot of office space), Castle counted among its clients such movie stars as Tony Curtis, rock groups such as the Creedence Clearwater Revival, and business dynasties such as the Pritzker family (owners of the

Hyatt chain). Accordingly, it didn't need narcotics profits and was determined to do its bit for the War on Drugs. Thus: "HMW: give this man anything he wants." I suspect, however, that Casper was accommodated because the Castle Bank was the target of a bitter lawsuit brought against it by one of its own best customers, Billy Mellon Hitchcock (heir to the Gulf Oil fortune). One of the earliest financiers of Resorts International's expansion to Paradise Island, Hitchcock was upset about the way in which Castle was voting his stock in Resorts. He didn't like it and, throwing discretion to the trade winds, resolved to sue their brains out. Shortly after that suit was initiated, Casper was provided with Pierson's business card and, within a year, Hitchcock was testifying against his friends in narcotics cases stemming from his bankrolling of members of the Brotherhood of Eternal Love—a California drug cult that resembled a vast underground pharmacy and was found to have been responsible for the manufacture and distribution of nearly half the illegal LSD available during the 1960s.

So Casper was in fact a sort of narc, but only in order to gain entree to the bank's other records. The friendly spook was by no means content to take what Pierson and Wolstencroft gave him—he wanted to break the bank, and so hung around long after Hitchcock's humiliation in the courts.

When Wolstencroft told Casper that a bookkeeping enigma required him to visit the United States, Casper offered to fix him up with a date during his layover in Miami. Wolstencroft accepted the bait—a curvy former police trainee named Sybil Kennedy, who was, in fact, a member of what Casper later called his private "spy network." While "Sybil and Mike" were out on the town, Casper retrieved Wolstencroft's attaché case from Ms. Kennedy's apartment (the banker obviously expected to return there after dinner and a show) and photographed its contents with the help of an IRS intelligence agent. A few days later, Sybil visited Wolstencroft in the Caymans, and returned with his Rolodex file to corroborate the evidence obtained earlier by Casper. Reportedly, Wolstencroft knew nothing of this espionage until, at an IRS press conference two years later, Casper's cover was destroyed by an assistant to IRS chief Donald Alexander. Alexander claimed to be upset by the intelligence-gathering activities of his subordinates, complaining that the IRS spooks threatened taxpayers' civil rights, especially their rights to privacy. Which was certainly true. But Alexander seemed an unlikely champion of civil rights, having been appointed to his high post by President Nixon—hardly a man to rule out the use of dirty tricks in "a good cause." And so, when IRS intelligence agents saw their investigation of foreign tax havens precipitously shut down, they wondered aloud whether there was any significance in the fact that Alexander's former law firm had represented one of the companies managed by the Castle Bank. Or if the damage done to the investigation had anything to do with the President's finances. The suspicions of sabotage waxed to the melting point when Burton W. Kanter, a Chicago attorney indicted as the mastermind behind many of Castle Bank's tax schemes, made a Freedom-of-Information (FOI) request of the IRS. That in itself wasn't unusual, but the IRS response was. Within a few days of making his request, Kanter received virtually the entire uncensored dossier on his case and the Castle Bank. Usually, those making FOI requests wait months before receiving even a portion of what they seek—and often they get nothing at all. The IRS attributed Kanter's strike—which may well have ruined the case against him—to "a simple bureaucratic mistake." Intelligence agents were skeptical of the explanation and suggested that it had more to do with a name discovered by the Friendly Ghost.

What Casper did was obtain access to a computer print-out of the Castle Bank's clients. One of the names on that list was Richard M. Nixon. As Casper told me, "There's no way to know if that's *the* Richard M. Nixon. I can't believe he'd be so stupid as to use his own name on an account like that, even if the Caymans' secrecy *is* supposed to be ironclad. Of course, if the middle name turns out to be Milhous—well, then I'd say we've got something that bears looking into. There aren't too many Milhouses running around."

Indubitably. The possibility of finding out whether M stood for Milhous, however, was dealt a severe blow when Casper's cover was demolished and the investigation was gutted after he came up with the Nixon name. Nevertheless, there is an intriguing memo in existence that may shed some light on the real owner of the Castle account. That memo was unearthed in 1976 by Mexican authorities who took possession of Howard Hughes's personal effects in the wake of his death. Entitled a "Reminder," the memo to Hughes states:

Chester called and wants to discuss the accounts at Castle Bank and Trust. He thinks these will be under investigation sooner than anticipated and there is no need to ask for trouble. He thinks that *there are*

> *other people dealing there who could also bring an investigation down*
> *on us by association.**

(Emphasis added.) That the billionaire maintained accounts at the Castle Bank is news in itself. But who are the "other people dealing there" who might lead investigators to Hughes? Having seen the names of perhaps sixty clients of the Castle Bank, and being familiar with the Hughes operation, I can think of only one name that investigators would be likely to associate with Howard Hughes: Richard M. Nixon.

As for Casper himself, his fate was not unique. On the contrary, it was part of a pattern of promising investigations that were grossly mishandled or otherwise destroyed when supersnitches invoked the names of very important persons. Peroff, Spector, and the Friendly Ghost—all three were placed in extreme danger by the agencies they tried to help. As in so many pulp novels, the hunters became the hunted. "It was very, very frustrating," Casper said. "I was at the point where I could have gotten more valuable information than what I'd gathered in the past. . . . Now, I'm just trying to pay my bills (the IRS is dunning me for eight hundred dollars in back taxes). And trying not to get killed."

In view of Donald Nixon, Sr.'s comment to John Meier that Vesco was in charge of Caribbean bank accounts belonging to Richard Nixon, and in view of the memo reproduced above, it would be naïve to doubt Casper's discovery at the Castle Bank. There aren't *that* many Richard M. Nixons in the world. And if to these facts we add:

- Vesco's covert financial contributions to Nixon's reelection campaign;
- Vesco's relationship to the former President's nephew;
- Cerny's work for Vesco and his claim to have represented Edward and Donald Nixon, Sr.;
- meetings between Cerny, Vesco, and Edward Nixon in Fairfield during March, 1972;
- Edward Nixon's trips to Las Vegas aboard Vesco's private jet, accompanied by the financier;
- authoritative reports that Richard Nixon is a part owner of the Paradise Island toll bridge that Vesco tried to buy;

---

* "Chester" is Hughes's chief legal counselor, Chester Davis. The memo is neither dated nor signed.

- reports of Vesco's having met secretly with President Nixon in Salzburg, Austria, one month before he met with the Cellinis in Rome;
- and the assistance rendered to Vesco by Nixon's subordinates at the White House and CIA—

it becomes inescapably obvious that Vesco is more than casually involved in the former President's business and family affairs. Accordingly, there is no reason to doubt John Meier's assertion that Vesco held RMN's financial proxy in the Caribbean. Nor is there any reason to doubt that RMN had an account at the Castle Bank & Trust, as Casper discovered. The question is, Where could the money have come from? As we'll see, there are three likely places:

- pseudo "campaign contributions" made directly to secret accounts, such as the one at the Castle Bank, by influence seekers such as Vesco and Howard Hughes;
- payments by multinational corporations, such as Lockheed, in exchange for Nixon's assistance;
- and cash culled from the Paradise Island bridge, owned by Jim Crosby and his silent partners.

Proving the existence of such contributions and accounts, however, is likely to be a difficult and dangerous task. And, unfortunately, the one man who had both the capability and the motivation for doing so is dead. He was a private eye named Robert Duke Hall, and he's not much missed.

CHAPTER

DEATH OF A DETECTIVE

LITTLE BOBBY HALL WAS A SLEAZE. YOU COULD DESCRIBE HIM IN other ways—as a private investigator, a father, a wiretapper, an informer, a dope peddler, and a double agent—but mostly he was a sleaze. A thin, bearded guy who knew how to play the angles, he dreamed of making a fortune and didn't particularly care how he did it.

In life, as much as in death, Hall's world seemed to have been ripped from the center of a Raymond Chandler novel. He lived in a modest apartment in Burbank, California, one of those sun-bleached antitowns associated with Los Angeles County. Gay bars and supermarkets, taco stands and palm trees surrounded him; at night, blue and green spotlights threw a baleful glow on the stucco walls of buildings near his own. The lights were supposed to be cheerful, Christmasy proclamations of the area's modernity and hip life-style. But they had a lifeless, insipid quality—like the huge plastic palms that line some of L.A.'s widest streets.

Bobby Hall was tough, reasonably brave, and decidedly larcenous. He worried continuously that somebody was trying to kill him, and he was right. On a sweltering night in July, 1976, Hall snapped off the television set and went into the kitchen for a midnight snack. As he stood in front of the refrigerator, munching Bing cherries, his executioner stepped up behind him. The private detective never knew what hit him. A .38 slug smacked into the back of his head, slamming him forward into the refrigerator door. When the police found him in the morning, the body was getting stale and the blood was drying on the floor. There was a cherry in his mouth and four more in his hand, and he was lying face down in an aluminum pan.

Bobby Hall had known that somebody was out to kill him. His estranged wife, Carol, told police that he "carried a concealed weapon with him every place he went." His former roommate added that Hall never answered the door without a gun in his hand, and that other guns in the apartment were always kept fully loaded and ready for use. But Hall's teen-age daughter was more specific. She said that a month before he was murdered, Hall had taken her to a picnic in celebration of Father's Day. In the course of that outing she noticed that her dad was carrying a gun, and asked him why. "Because," Bobby Hall replied, "I think Robert Vesco is trying to kill me."

It was a candid response under the circumstances, but Hall was like a lot of spooks in that way: immersed in day-to-day deceptions, pretexts, and intrigues, he allowed himself the luxury of candor with the one or two people he could be said to have loved. And yet in some ways his reply must have been a shot in the dark. Robert Vesco wasn't the only one with a motive for killing him. There were literally dozens of people who had an interest in his premature demise. So many, in fact, that they constituted a microcosm of southern California's seediest and most opulent scene. It's a special place where the has-beens of Beverly Hills, embittered comics and faded singers, embrace the never-have-beens of nearby Hollywood. Mediating the exchange is a constellation of hooker-starlets, venal cops, pimps, dealers, gamblers, and the impresarios of blood sport and porn. It's more a state of mind than anything else, a night-world of cheap thrills and animal acts, joy-juice and cocaine. Bobby Hall lived on the edge of it, and because he was both an opportunist *and* a wiretapper, there were *a lot* of people who enjoyed his passing, and even the manner of it.

Hall was a terrific wireman—the hard way. He lacked Bernard Spindel's inventive genius, but he made up for it in other ways. What placed him at a serious remove from run-of-the-mill eavesdroppers was the fact that he had the ethical disposition of a cannibal. That's how he survived. That's why he died.

When police, led by Detective Lieutenant Al Madrid, found Hall on his kitchen floor, they searched his apartment for clues to the murder, looking for some bit of evidence that might suggest a motive for the killing. What they found instead was a cornucopia of California intrigues: cases of electronic bugging and debugging equipment, a tranquilizer dart gun, drug-tipped darts, tear-gas canisters, syringes, ampules of narcotics, lock-picking devices and cartons filled with more than two hundred tapes—each one containing conversations recorded by Hall (almost all of them without the other party's knowledge). It seemed that the private eye was in the habit of bugging both his own clients and his friends, in addition to the people upon whom he'd been hired to spy. Moreover, he routinely taped incoming telephone calls to his apartment, as well as conversations that were held there. And when he went out, his leisure suit often concealed a pair of miniature Alpha recorders. You could never be certain when Bobby Hall was working and when he was not. He wasn't just a wireman. A lot of the time he was a *wired man*.

The tape recordings were a nightmare for police. They contained evidence and allegations of numerous crimes committed by VIP's. Blackmail, extortion, prostitution, narcotics, embezzlement, bribery, conspiracy—the tapes were a catalog of felonies providing Madrid and the other cops with scores of suspects. What was worse, the tapes revealed Bobby Hall's tangled relationships with a number of police officers in the top echelon of California law enforcement. His association with Beverly Hills police captain Jack Egger was particularly deep, and that presented other problems. The Beverly Hills force is a private one that works directly for the residents of America's wealthiest enclave. Their assignment is to preserve that community's tranquillity, protect its residents' property, and—above all—not make waves. Accordingly, the Beverly Hills cops are among the most courteous and least meddlesome police in the country. Victimless crimes are of little concern to them. Notoriety, however, is. And Bobby Hall's archive implicated the community's residents in a slew of retail sins. If the tapes became public in the course of a trial, or in its aftermath, careers would be ended overnight. What Beverly Hills wanted, therefore, was a quick solution to Bobby Hall's murder and the prompt destruction of his tapes. How that was to be accomplished was of little concern.

Celebrities who'd known the detective for years—Eddie Fisher, for instance—professed shock at his assassination but claimed to know nothing about it. The police, however, were able to put together some remarkable lines of investigation, most of them converging around Robert Vesco and his associates.

One of those associates was Thomas P. Richardson, a thirty-six-year-old Los Angeles stockbroker who, two months prior to the detective's murder, had received a six-year prison sentence for bilking various brokerages, banks, and Ivy League colleges of millions. It was Richardson who'd provided Vesco with the use of his executive jet and who, moreover, had ferried prostitutes and crates of weapons to San José. It was Richardson too who'd arranged for federal narcotics officer John L. Kelly to have Vesco's New Jersey offices swept for bugs. As it happened, Richardson had also employed Bobby Hall at about the same time, dispatching the private eye to the Bahamas for the supposed purpose of removing bugs from Vesco's home there. In retrospect, it was a strange countersurveillance team. Vesco, whose premises were being swept, would soon come under investigation as a suspect in an international heroin transaction. And yet, organizing the sweep in Vesco's behalf was the Los Angeles regional director of the Bureau of Narcotics and Dangerous Drugs, John Kelly. Carrying out the sweep in New Jersey were two high-ranking BNDD agents, while, in the Bahamas, Vesco's home was being swept by Bobby Hall—a private detective who specialized in selling "happy shots" (vitamins-and-speed) to the rich. Four years later John Kelly would himself be a private detective, Richardson would be in jail, and Bobby Hall would be blown away. And when that happened, Kelly would attach himself to the homicide investigation, telling reporters that he'd been called in by the police to help them out. Apprised of that, Lieutenant Al Madrid would react with astonishment and insist that he knew nothing of Kelly's efforts in the probe.

Richardson, however, proved helpful. He told police that he'd hired Bobby Hall to perform a number of delicate assignments. One of them was to obtain information that would force the government to return his confiscated Lear jet. If Hall accomplished that, he'd be paid $234,000—one-third of the aircraft's value. But Hall's other assignments for Richardson were more perilous. The stockbroker had been begging Vesco for money to pay his lawyers. Hall recorded those entreaties and Vesco's callous replies: Richardson could go to the joint, Vesco said, or jump bail and join his mentor in Costa Rica. Incensed by the refusals of aid, Richardson sent Hall to San José in November, 1975. The message he carried was simple and threatening. If Vesco didn't come up with cash, Richardson and

Hall would go to the police with information and tape recordings that would ensure his extradition from Costa Rica. While Vesco's answer to the threat is unknown, Hall did in fact pay a visit to the FBI upon his return from San José, offering to bring Vesco to the United States in exchange for a reduction of Richardson's sentence. Richardson claimed that he offered to provide information about Vesco's gunrunning exploits—information that ought to have resulted in his extradition from Costa Rica. Federal interest in Vesco was at the time running high. The Senate's Permanent Subcommittee on Investigations was probing the possibility that Vesco's extradition was deliberately sabotaged by federal officials (there were a host of theories as to why the sabotage allegedly occurred), and the Senators were particularly interested in Richardson's gunrunning role. The stockbroker, however, pleaded the Fifth before the subcommittee—at the very moment that his wireman, Hall, was negotiating with the FBI to provide that same information. Despite the legislators' known interest, however, the G-men rejected the proposal on July 10, just two weeks before Hall's assassination. The detective's reply to the feds' demurral was succinct: "That's surprising. But if that's the way it is, so be it." The Bureau's apparent disinterest in the Detroit Kid's return is indeed surprising, but Hall seems to have developed a contingency plan. A politically ambitious prosecutor might well be willing to exchange the fugitive financier for the jailed stockbroker, but Richardson's information—no matter how incriminating—could never *guarantee* Vesco's return. Hall, therefore, is said to have plotted Vesco's abduction and forcible return to the United States. Lieutenant Al Madrid acknowledges investigating the scheme but says, "We couldn't substantiate it. The evidence just wasn't there."

In fact, the evidence *was* there, but its significance was overlooked. Police seem to have regarded the tranquilizer dart gun and its accessories, found among Bobby Hall's effects, as curiosities and nothing more. And yet, a month before Hall's November, 1975, visit to Vesco, a letter was sent to the fugitive's former pilot. The writer of that letter was an adventurer and ex-Marine pilot named Larry Blaine Jividen. According to Stephen Kobakoff, a former CIA officer working for the Justice Department's Strategic Intelligence Division, Jividen was a high-level government informant. In 1972 the ex-Marine had worked on an investigation involving Morocco and narcotics smuggling (two areas in which, as we've seen, Vesco has figured). In his letter to Captain Ike Eisenhauer, Jividen established

his credentials by revealing details of that investigation, details that
were subsequently confirmed to me by Kobakoff. According to the
letter, Jividen was employed for a six-month period beginning in
September, 1972, as a bodyguard and pilot for a San Marcos, California, man. The San Marcos resident, in concert with a prominent
Las Vegas casino manager and with a sometime associate of Howard Hughes, "were putting together a deal in which a Lear 25-C
would be purchased by a phony company for the purpose of flying
heroin across the Arizona-Mexico border. At this point," Jividen
continues,

> the two words "Rosemark" and "Rosemont" entered into the planning.
> These words represent references to funds contained in the Union Bank
> of Switzerland and the Investment and Trade Exchange Central Bank
> in Zurich, Switzerland. Large amounts of money from underworld
> operations are funneled into these banks (casino skims, narcotics profits,
> prostitution income, etc.).
>
> These underworld figures claim to have loaned Hughes large amounts
> of these "Rosemark" funds. The biggest loan was for his 707 buy for
> TWA in 1961. The money came out of Switzerland and was laundered
> through the Irving Trust Company.
>
> Puerto Rico and Santo Domingo appear to have been points for
> gold bullion pickups. Although I never was involved in any gold
> pickups, I heard it discussed on several occasions.
>
> During one flight, Donald Nixon was a passenger. My employers
> claim their influence permeated the highest levels of the government.*

It's an extraordinary letter. Asked about it, the Justice Department's Kobakoff cursed briefly but confirmed its details. He said,
however, that Jividen's role in the investigation was exaggerated.
"He picked up on some names and some important code names—
like 'Rosemark'—and thought he understood everything. But he
didn't."

For his part, Jividen told Eisenhauer that he was in touch with
"three contract CIA operatives" in Latin America who would provide support, weapons, and maintenance for the kidnapping. Central to his scheme, and giving it the earmarks of a professional
operation, was the proposed use of a tranquilizer dart gun such as
the one found among Bobby Hall's effects. The gun, usually reserved for wild animals, would be used to stun the fugitive financier
into submission, permitting his kidnappers to "bring 'em back alive."

---

* Eisenhauer, *op. cit.*, pp. 404–405.

Is it only a coincidence that Jividen mentions a Lear 25 as the vehicle in a heroin-smuggling plot originating in southern California—and that Bobby Hall's employer, Hollywood stockbroker Tommy Richardson, owned a Lear 25 which he'd leased to Vesco's partner, Norman LeBlanc (at that time the subject of a DEA heroin-smuggling investigation)? Perhaps. But it strains credulity to think that Jividen's kidnapping plot was unrelated to Hall's own plans for Vesco. We know that Hall considered kidnapping Vesco and that he owned a tranquilizer dart gun. We know that Jividen recruited personnel to kidnap Vesco and that he planned to carry out the plot with a tranquilizer dart gun. Both plots evolved at the same time, had their origins in southern California, and proposed the use of the same exotic weapon. Coincidence? It seems unlikely.

Hall, then, was a triple threat to Vesco: as a police informant, a professional wiretapper, and a potential body snatcher. But that does not mean that Vesco ordered him to be killed. Hall's relationship to Tommy Richardson was a complicated one, impinging on several dangerous matters, only one of which had to do with Vesco. The indicted stockbroker had hired the private detective to learn the identity of the government's witnesses against him. Convinced that the police had inside information about his schemes, Richardson told Hall that there were several candidates for the title of snitch:

John L. Kelly, who'd left the Drug Enforcement Agency to work as a detective in the private sector. Kelly, who arranged for the debugging of Vesco's New Jersey offices, owned a piece of Richardson's troubled brokerage.

Jack Ginsburgs. A pornographer, Ginsburgs was the proprietor of XXX, Inc. The son of a White Russian émigré, he'd spent his youth inside the decadent Shanghai *Bund*—that romantic foreign colony which, in the years before Mao Tse-tung's takeover, was a meld of opium, kinky sex, and intrigue. Ginsburgs was a so-called financial consultant to Richardson and, moreover, had been a partner in Bobby Hall's detective agency.

Gene LeBell was the third candidate for the informant's role. A burly wrestler and karate master, LeBell had also been a partner in Hall's detective agency and was, with Hall, the co-owner of a Hollywood pharmacy.

The financial and emotional relationships among the men were complicated and deep. For years they'd been the best of friends, hanging around Bobby Hall's apartment as if it were an underworld salon, a clubhouse for intriguers; there they'd each bragged of schemes and dreams, hatched scams, gotten stoned, and shared one another's girls and gossip. But each of the men had trouble with the police, and that, in the end, set the friends against one another. Richardson was running guns and girls to Vesco, one of the hottest men on the planet, while embezzling from his clients. Hall was wiretapping and dealing drugs. Ginsburgs was facing obscenity charges, as well as indictments for the unlawful possession of firearms and an explosive device. And LeBell was in trouble because of a burglary at his pharmacy—a burglary he blamed upon his friends Bobby Hall and Tommy Richardson.

With the onset of Richardson's indictment and Hall's search for the informant, the friendships quickly soured. Through his police contacts (Hall was also an informant), the detective learned that Ginsburgs was double-crossing Richardson. Posing as the stockbroker's friend, the pornographer was actually gathering evidence for the police in exchange for the quashing of obscenity indictments pending against him. With Ginsburgs, LeBell was testifying before a grand jury about Richardson's multimillion-dollar rip-offs.

Hall was infuriated by the double cross, and began to harass the snitches. This was no easy matter in view of the fact that the detective weighed less than 150 pounds, while LeBell was a giant with certifiably lethal skills. The son of an Olympic Auditorium boxing promoter, LeBell was a professional wrestler whose martial skills had earned him the right to referee the debacle between heavyweight boxing champion Muhammad Ali and Japanese karate star Antonio Inoki. At forty-three, LeBell was an all-around tough guy who supplemented his income by working as a part-time stunt man in Hollywood's film studios. There was no way that Hall could threaten him directly. So the private eye played games. One night, shortly after Richardson's release from jail, the detective and his client sneaked into LeBell's driveway. Using newspapers, washcloths, and a sponge soaked in lighter fluid, they set a fire beneath LeBell's van. When the muscular entrepreneur emerged, raging, from his apartment, Hall and Richardson boiled with laughter from their vantage down the street. In fact, Hall laughed so hard that his dental retainer fell out, remaining at the scene for LeBell to find later. And there were other pranks. "Someone" bugged LeBell's telephone, and bags of garbage were delivered to his doorstep. The water, electricity, and phone services were periodically disconnected. And when LeBell was called for temporary work as a stunt man (an assignment requiring him to be at the studio by 6 A.M), it often happened that the phone would ring at three. At the other end of the line there would be a recording of the *William Tell* overture and in the background the cry "Hi-ohhhh, Silver! A-waaaaaay!" It got on LeBell's nerves, but it was hardly a life-or-death matter.

Ginsburgs suffered much the same treatment, but was later said to have told a policeman that Hall also threatened his life, and the lives of his children.

Already, then, the police had a plethora of suspects in Hall's murder: besides celebrities whom Hall may have been blackmailing, drug dealers looking for a score, and Robert Vesco looking to remain free, there were the dead detective's friends Ginsburgs and LeBell. But there was yet another sinister connection: for years Bobby Hall had handled contract work for Howard Hughes's Summa Corporation. Precisely what he did for Hughes is unknown, though we may suppose that it had to do with his primary expertise, electronic eavesdropping. His contact man with the Hughes organization was Vince Kelly, a seventeen-year veteran of the Los Angeles Police Department (LAPD). Regarded by local radicals and others as the onetime "Lord of the Glasshouse" (a glassy skyscraper that serves as Intelligence and Records headquarters for the LAPD), Kelly was reportedly enticed away from police work (three years short of pension eligibility) by a "name-your-price" offer from the Hughes people to take charge of Summa's internal security. Introduced to Hall by George H. Yocham, an ex-police lieutenant who worked at Hall's detective agency, Kelly used Hall as a police informant and, later, in his work for Summa. Yocham and Hall, interestingly enough, are said to have given Ginsburgs the .38-caliber revolver that, according to police, was later used to murder the detective. (The gun, however, has never been found, and this is therefore speculation by the police.)

What makes the connection with Summa sinister is the fact that the super-secret Hughes organization suffered a pair of mysterious burglaries in the spring of 1974. The first burglary received little public attention. It was carried out against the Encino headquarters facility that served as the nerve center for Hughes's internal-security operations. And the only office that appeared to have been burglarized was that of Vince Kelly. Occurring April 24, the burglary was later found to have been carried out by Ginsburgs and LeBell. All that was taken from Kelly's office was a telephone scrambler belonging to Summa. Scramblers, of course, are devices which encode ordinary phone conversations in such a way that eavesdroppers

overhear gibberish, while the speaker and the intended listener
(who has a scrambler on his own end of the line) are able to speak
normally with one another. According to Ginsburgs, the stolen
scrambler was delivered to Bobby Hall. Why Hall wanted a Summa
scrambler is uncertain, but one possibility is obvious: if Hall was
bugging Kelly, or other Summa officials, and recording their scram-
bled conversations on tape, those tapes could only be made intelli-
gible with the help of a Summa scrambler. In any case, having
received the scrambler from Ginsburgs and LeBell, Hall pursued a
course of deception. Two weeks after the burglary he placed a classified advertisement in the Los Angeles *Times*:

> $500 Rew. for return of voice scram-
> bler taken from ofc. of V. Kelly
> in Encino. No ? asked 769-7320.

A few days later, Hall returned the scrambler to Kelly, though no
reward was paid. In all, the device had been missing for three weeks
—more than enough time to process hundreds of garbled tapes or,
for that matter, to "engineer it backwards." No motive has ever
been discovered for what the police called a "senseless" burglary, nor
has anyone suggested how it was that Ginsburgs and LeBell penetrated Summa's elaborate security network to rifle the office of the
firm's internal-security *chief*. Asked about this, police investigating
Hall's murder could only theorize that Ginsburgs and LeBell "must
have been stoned."

A month after the scrambler was returned (with "No ? asked"),
Hughes's communications center was also burglarized. That facility
was located at 7000 Romaine Street in Hollywood.* Called "Romaine" by Hughes executives (who mention it with the same respectful intonation that spooks use when referring to "the Agency"),
the building was the central nervous system of the billionaire's
empire, serving as a clearinghouse for communications relating to
all of Hughes's affairs: aerospace, mining, gambling, transportation,
television, film, radio, sports, aviation, litigation, philanthropy,
and a lot more. By every account the facility was an electrician's
dream. The most sophisticated counterespionage devices in existence were in use throughout the building. From a third-floor reception area, security personnel monitored banks of closed-circuit
television sets trained upon every corridor and entrance. Movements

---

* Sometime after the burglary, a new communications headquarters was established
for Summa at 17000 Ventura Boulevard in the San Fernando Valley.

within the building were indicated on an electronic grid whose red buttons flared along the path taken by any visitor. Inside, the safes were lined with lead, the vaults exceeded banking specifications, and there was equipment to screen out or garble radio and laser beams that might have been used to eavesdrop on conversations or computers. Other devices surveyed the facility's air currents to detect unauthorized disturbances, and there was even an alarm mechanism to warn of "X-ray intrusions." (This last fact was brought to light during litigation between Howard Hughes and TWA. In the course of the legal proceedings, Hughes's attorneys accused their opposite numbers of attempting to read documents in the safes at Romaine by focusing X-rays upon the building from outside. Subsequently, the attorneys explained that they'd been mistaken: the alarm supporting their allegations was a false one. The device merely required a new set of batteries.)

One might think, therefore, that the Romaine headquarters was as "burglar-proof" as three billion dollars, modern technology, and armed guards could make it—and yet it was knocked over on June 5 by four heavies who displayed all the sophistication and sensitivity of teen-agers raiding Dad's liquor closet. Very simply, we're told, the burglars walked in the front door trundling a two-tank acetylene torch on a steel dolly. The four men then wrestled security guard Mike Davis to the ground. After Davis and a switchboard operator had been tied up, the intruders spent four hours torching open the vaults before fleeing without an alarm ever having been sounded. Had they been driven to the site by reindeer pulling a covered wagon, it wouldn't have mattered: the pillage wasn't discovered until the next day. By that time sheaves of top-secret files (including papers setting out the terms of the *Glomar Explorer* contract), at least sixty thousand dollars in cash, certificates of deposit, and more were missing. Precisely what else was stolen is unknown.

Following the robbery, seventeen Summa employees were asked to take a polygraph test. The security guard, Mike Davis, refused, claiming that he distrusted the method. This was suspicious to some since Davis later confessed that, while panicked, he had himself taken home a $100,000 certificate of deposit and a memo concerning the *Glomar Explorer*. The former was returned almost a year later to its owner (Hughes employee Kay Glenn), while the memo, Davis said, had been flushed down the toilet.

As for the other sixteen employees who took the lie-detector test, all passed except Vince Kelly. The polygraph examiners said that he evinced "guilty knowledge" of the burglary. Appalled, Kelly contacted his friend Yocham (at that time working with Hall as a private investigator) and asked him to arrange an "independent" exam. Yocham and Hall put Kelly in touch with Chris Gugas, a private polygrapher, who, after administering a second test, announced that Kelly passed it with "flying colors."

Months later, Donald Woolbright, a used-car salesman, was arrested and charged with trying to extort one million dollars from the Summa Corporation for return of materials taken in the Romaine Street burglary. At this writing, Woolbright has yet to go to trial, and his exact role in the robbery, if any, is unknown.

More intriguing, perhaps, is the involvement of the friends of Bobby Hall and Hall himself. How did Ginsburgs and LeBell manage to burgle Vince Kelly's office without being caught, and why did they bring the scrambler to Hall? Why, after that, did Hall return the scrambler to Kelly (rather than simply destroying it) after concocting a cover story involving a five-hundred-dollar reward? If Kelly was unwitting of Hall's deception, why is it that Hall was never reimbursed for the five hundred dollars he supposedly paid out to retrieve the device? What relationship, if any, was there between the two burglaries, and how is it that both were carried out within months of each other with never an alarm having been sounded by the world's best counterintrusion equipment? What role, if any, did Yocham play in these events—besides arranging Kelly's second polygraph examination and providing Hall's accused killer with the alleged murder weapon? If, as I've suggested, Hall used the stolen scrambler to decode taped conversations among Summa executives, Hughes, and perhaps the CIA, did any of those conversations (or documents stolen from Romaine) have to do with the "Rosemark" funds mentioned by Vesco's would-be kidnapper, Larry Jividen? Did Vesco have any relationship to those funds and, if not, how is it that both Jividen and Hall hatched seemingly identical plans to kidnap the fugitive financier? Is it a coincidence that Vesco, like several of Hughes's business "associates" and Hall, was the target of narcotics investigations?

The answers to these questions appear to have been buried in southern California with the tough, diminutive private eye. Asked about events in the case, Robert Maheu, Hughes's onetime alter ego, shook his head. "I don't know what's going on," he said. "All I can tell you is that something stinks. I promise you, no one could have ripped off Romaine unless it was an inside job."

The only other source that may be capable of answering those questions is the more than three hundred tape recordings which Bobby Hall took the precaution of making before his death. Confiscated by the police, the tapes will eventually be destroyed, according to Lieutenant Al Madrid. "It wouldn't serve any purpose to release them. Too many reputations would be ruined—maybe unjustly."

As for Gene LeBell and Jack Ginsburgs, they were charged with Hall's murder—largely on the strength of testimony provided by a former cop who admitted to police that initially he'd lied about the case. Beverly Hills police captain Jack Egger, who quit the force when LAPD sleuths learned of his association with Hall through tapes seized from Tommy Richardson's apartment, initially provided LeBell with an alibi for the night of the murder. Later, however, Egger told police that he knew who'd committed the crime and that he'd been covering up. Ginsburgs, he said, had telephoned him shortly before Hall's death to say:

"I'm at Gene's house. I'm going to get Bobby Hall."

"What do you mean?" Egger asked.

"I'm going to get the sonofabitch."

"Why tell me?"

"I thought you'd like to know," Egger said Ginsburgs told him.

An hour later, according to Egger, the obliging Ginsburgs called him once again to report success. "I'm calling from Gene's house. I think I got him. I shot him in the neck or the head."

"You're kidding."

"No, I'm not kidding. I got him right through the kitchen window."

"I don't believe you," Egger said.

"Meet me for coffee," Ginsburgs asked.

The next morning, Egger received a phone call from Hall's almost hysterical wife, telling him of the homicide. Minutes later, Ginsburgs—obviously suffering from telephonitis if Egger is to be believed—called yet again. Beginning to take the matter seriously, Egger warned the pornographer, "You really did it—I'm going to have to report it."

"Bullshit," he was told. "You want Brian to live, don't you?"

Brian is Egger's son. Fearing that Ginsburgs would murder him, the Beverly Hills police captain kept his silence—until, months later, Egger's own involvement with Bobby Hall came to light through the dead detective's tapes.

The story could not be stranger if it had been written for Marvel Comics. Why would an indicted pornographer telephone a high-ranking police official to warn him that he intended to murder a mutual friend? Why, having killed Hall, would Ginsburgs then call the same cop to brag about the murder? Why, in any case, if Ginsburgs really did it, would he say that he'd shot Hall through the kitchen window, when, as the evidence would later show, the detective had actually been shot from a distance of less than a foot? And if the testimony of experts is accurate, how could Ginsburgs, feuding with Hall, get within a foot of the paranoid detective's back? Assuming that Ginsburgs' motive for killing Hall was, as Egger later said, Hall's alleged threat to harm the pornographer's children, why would Ginsburgs deliberately incur Egger's own fury by threatening to murder his son if Egger revealed Ginsburgs' gratuitous confession? It doesn't make sense. And even if Ginsburgs made such a threat, it's difficult to believe that a career police officer would succumb to it. Was this the first time that Egger or his family had been threatened by a felon?

Whatever the answers, it was Egger's testimony that sent the Shanghai emigrant to life imprisonment. The jury ignored testimony that Hall had probably been murdered by someone he trusted well enough to let him or her stand within a foot of his turned back. It ignored as well the fact that Egger had already lied to police about the case, denying knowledge of it for months and providing Gene LeBell with an eyewitness alibi for the time of the murder—an alibi which Egger later retracted. What made the case against Ginsburgs convincing (in the absence of both a murder weapon and witnesses) was evidence Egger obtained through a peculiar charade. Once the police knew of his involvement with Hall (the exact nature of which has never been made known), Egger turned stool pigeon. Equipping the suddenly retired cop with a concealed mike and tape recorder, police sent Egger on a visit to the pornographer's heavily barricaded offices. There, in the course of a chat with Ginsburgs, Egger obtained what appeared to be a taped confession, and police broke in. Hours later, the same ploy was used successfully against Gene LeBell. According to the tape that Egger obtained, the karate expert hadn't been with him on the night of the crime: instead, he'd driven the getaway car for Ginsburgs.

Attorneys for the men charged that their clients had been set up to make phony confessions. Ginsburgs' conversation with Egger was said to have begun on a hypothetical premise: according to Ginsburgs' attorney, his client was asked to play the role of Bobby Hall's murderer so that Egger might help to figure out how the killing had been accomplished and what clues might have been left behind. Unaware that Egger was wired, Ginsburgs played along, answering questions with the first person pronoun. For example: "Where's the gun?" Answer: "I took welding tools and melted it to nothing." The same ploy was later used, again successfully, against LeBell, according to the men's attorneys.

Murray Lertzman, who represented Ginsburgs, insists upon the innocence of his client but says there was almost no way to have him acquitted. While Egger's credibility was easily attacked, the jury was forced to choose between the testimony of an ex-cop and that of a naturalized Jewish pornographer. Inevitably, the policeman's story was believed: the missing weapon was explained away with references to "welding tools"; the jury chose to disregard testimony that the shot could not have come "through the kitchen window" but was, instead, fired by someone standing next to Hall; and testimony pertaining to the multitudes of others who had both motive and opportunity for killing Bobby Hall was declared irrelevant. Ginsburgs' own alibi—that he'd been in a restaurant shortly before the killing—was found to be inadequate. While he was indeed in the restaurant prior to the murder, no one could say precisely when he'd left. As an alibi, therefore, it was a poor one to contrive (if it was contrived): all Ginsburgs needed was someone who would testify that he'd been there within twenty minutes of Hall's murder. But no one who'd been in the restaurant was able to recall, months after the fact, whether Ginsburgs left at 10 P.M., 10:15, or 10:30.

"There was nothing we could do," Lertzman said. "There was no money for a Perry Mason defense—we couldn't hire investigators to learn who actually murdered Bobby Hall. So we based our defense on Egger's lack of credibility, the ruse he used to obtain the so-called confessions, and the impossibility of the murder's having occurred the way police said it did. But they didn't believe us. I think the jury convicted Jack because he was a pornographer. He was a convenient scapegoat."

So it is that the Bobby Hall murder is officially "solved," while everything else about the case remains a mystery: the reason for stealing the Hughes scrambler, the burglaries at Summa, the kidnapping plots, the identity of politicians incriminated by Hall's tape recordings, the relationships between the supercops and their underworld friends, and the importance of the "Rosemark" funds, if any, to all of these things. For his part, Robert Vesco remains in Costa Rica, aloof from the matter. Lieutenant Madrid admits that Vesco telephoned him after Ginsburgs' arrest to thank him "personally" for his work on the case. It was the first sign that Vesco had been worried. Months before, in a secretly taped conversation between stockbroker Tommy Richardson and the Detroit Kid, Vesco reacted to news of Hall's murder with cool restraint. Told that the detective had been shot in the back of the head, Vesco replied, "No shit." And changed the subject.

THE MASTER SPOOK

1 / AND HIS MASTER

ROBERT AIME MAHEU AND I SAT IN THE DILUTED LIGHT OF THE swank Georgetown Inn, sipping red wine and discussing his former boss, Howard Hughes. Or, as Maheu often calls him, "the Old Man." (And, as the CIA calls him, "the Stockholder.") It was early in the afternoon in the summer of 1975—less than a year before Hughes's death—and Maheu had just slipped away from reporters covering the Senate's sensational investigation of CIA/Mafia plots to assassinate Fidel Castro. Along with Johnny Roselli (since slaughtered) and Sam Giancana (similarly deceased), Maheu was an authority on the subject.

For someone who'd just been grilled about a conspiracy to liquidate a head of state, America's master spook was unusually self-composed. Leaning back in his chair, he lighted a cheroot and spoke calmly in response to a question I'd asked about Howard Hughes and Intertel. "I think they've got a vegetable on their hands," he said, exhaling smoke. "Like that poor girl—Quinlan." There was bitterness in the baritone response, reflecting Maheu's hatred for the man who, almost five years earlier, had dismissed him without warning or condolences. And there was something else: the hesitancy that comes when a man speaks the truth even though it may not be in his best interests to do so.

At the time of our conversation Hughes was widely regarded as a wealthy and reclusive eccentric, a celebrity-hermit—and nothing more. There was a stubborn reluctance in the press to credit rumors that something was wildly amiss within the Hughes empire, that the Old Man was more than merely . . . odd. In part, that reluctance stemmed from Hughes's enormous wealth: between $175,000,000 and *three billion dollars*, depending on who was counting—his eventual heirs or the IRS. Whatever the amount, it was large enough so that it seemed to many that anyone so rich could not be crazy: there must be a method to his madness. Moreover, Hughes was not merely rich but influential as well: it was unthinkable that someone with his power should be insane. Too many politicians were in his debt; and as sole proprietor of one of the country's largest defense contractors, he was privy to the nation's most sensitive military secrets. Finally, if Hughes was incompetent, as sick and mentally ill as the rumors insisted, then a Pandora's box of conspiracy might be opened. If Hughes was not responsible for his decisions, then Robert Maheu may have been correct when he charged that the billionaire was "kidnapped" from Las Vegas in 1970. The implications, then, were too large. It was easier (and safer) to believe that the Old Man, inevitably described as "a genius" (in deference to his moneymaking skills and aeronautical achievements), was only a bit queer. So it was that the eyewitness report of a boat captain who'd seen Hughes in the course of a hasty "evacuation" from the Bahamas in February, 1972, was scoffed at. According to the report, "the phantom billionaire" was in monstrous condition, emaciated and obviously dying: feral and malodorous, the Abominable Hughes was said to carry no more than ninety pounds on a 6-foot, 4-inch frame. The captain claimed that fingernails curled from his hands to a length of eight inches, that an unwashed beard straggled down the front of his dirty bathrobe, that a mane of yellowing hair hung in strands to the middle of his back.

It was not the image of Howard Hughes that most Americans cherished. A captain—nay, a five-star general—of industry, he'd courted the most beautiful women in the world, dominated the glamorous arenas of Las Vegas, and piloted his way around the planet. It was inconceivable that with all his money and panache, the Stockholder should come to this. So the press winked at such reports, sneering at those who "purveyed" them. And yet, a year after my meeting with Maheu, the boat captain's report would be confirmed. For the last years of his life, Howard Hughes lived in a blend of solitary confinement and total surveillance that resembled nothing so much as Death Row. Drugged out of his senses for days at a time, he existed in a limbo of artificial light—never seeing the sun, never feeling the touch of a human hand. By most accounts he died by inches, watching random reels of B movies, sick, addicted, and insane, while his executives ruled his empire.

The hesitation in Robert Maheu's voice when he expressed the opinion that his former boss was a "vegetable" derived from bizarre and complicated circumstances. On the one hand, Maheu *knew* that the boat captain was telling the truth when he described the Old Man's outrageous and pitiful appearance. Years after the fact, he still believed that Hughes had been kidnapped and that the billionaire controlled neither his own life nor his business empire. On the other hand, Maheu's own millions were at stake. Some years earlier, in January, 1972, a man purporting to be Howard Hughes conducted a telephonic "press conference" in which he alleged that Maheu was "a no-good, dishonest sonofabitch [who] stole me blind." The accusation was untrue. Indeed, it was so palpably false that it seemed to be a deliberate provocation. (And perhaps it was.) For more than a year the fired spook was the subject of an intensive, worldwide investigation carried out by a minimum of one hundred agents working for Intertel, the IRS, and the CIA. No convincing evidence of wrongdoing was uncovered. The billionaire must have known—unless he was grossly deceived by those in his employ—that his charges against Maheu were false. And that Maheu would, as he later did, sue him for defamation and win. So it was that when Maheu expressed the opinion to me that Hughes was mentally incompetent, he toyed with the $2,500,000 recently awarded to him by the courts. There is a difference of opinion among attorneys as to whether a "vegetable," a lunatic, or the victim of a kidnapping can be held responsible for remarks attributed to them when they suffered from such duress or coercion. Thus Maheu's slight hesitation when commenting about the Old Man's condition.

Years earlier, Maheu had been the most highly paid private intelligence operative in the United States, earning more than $500,000 per annum. Presiding over a hundred silver mines and a clutch of the most lucrative casinos in the world, he was provided with an enormous mansion and almost unlimited perquisites. For all intents and purposes, he was the king of Nevada. The governor was at his beck and call. Mere millionaires fawned for his attention. All that disappeared in the wake of the 1970 "Thanksgiving Coup" when Hughes was spirited away to the Bahamas by Intertel.

As if that leave-taking was not in itself sufficiently strange, it was followed by the curious (and libelous) press conference in 1972. During the interim Maheu had been busy organizing operations to "recapture" the Old Man or, failing that, to prove that the billionaire had been kidnapped. In one such effort a task force of private detectives and wiremen was sent to the Bahamas to bug Hughes's suite and, if possible, to enable him to escape. The effort collapsed when Intertel agents discovered the electronic eavesdropping and ordered the spooks deported.

The press conference put an end to Maheu's efforts to "rescue" the Old Man. Libeling the handsome spy so blatantly, Hughes enabled Maheu to sue him for $50,000,000 in real and punitive damages. It was an open-and-shut case. Indeed, Maheu's innocence would be established in court not through his own protestations, but through the testimony of his archenemy (and Hughes's guardians), Intertel. Maheu's attorney, Morton Galane, would call Robert Peloquin to the stand and question him about Intertel's investigation of the fired spook. Peloquin would admit that more than five hundred written reports had been filed on the subject by his highly qualified agents, and that no evidence of theft was uncovered.

The catch was that Maheu must, in order to collect damages, remain silent on the question of Hughes's volition and competency. It wouldn't do to insist that the Old Man had a gun at his head when he made the defamatory statements. Neither would it do to raise the possibility that Hughes was incompetent, comatose, or the victim of an impersonation—all of which Maheu considered possible. So it was that the master spook called off his "recovery operations" in the wake of the press conference, sitting silently by while attorneys for the Summa Corporation (the holding company for virtually all of Hughes's business interests) "stipulated" that Howard Hughes made the statements that he did under his own free will.

The press conference was itself an extraordinary event. Supposedly convened to debunk the bogus autobiography of Hughes written by Clifford Irving, it seemed to serve no purpose. Conducted by telephone, it purported to be an interview with a man no one had seen in fifteen years. Present in voice alone, "Hughes" was asked eight "identifying questions"—answering only one of them correctly. Still, the reporters were somehow satisfied that the voice belonged to Howard Hughes and that he'd chosen to break his long silence out of concern for Irving's scribblings (surely one of the most trivial events to impinge upon Hughes's solitude in the past twenty years). It was an implausible course for the hermit financier, especially since his telephone call would have less weight in court than a simple letter signed by himself and declaring the book a forgery. The press conference could have no impact on the book's publication: if anything, it could only make it more popular. This was certainly known to Hughes's advisors, who had, moreover, every reason to expect that Intertel would quickly prove (as it soon did) that the book was a phony. Why, then, was the press conference held at all? It's a speculative matter, but, judging from its only practical effect, the press conference seems to have been convened for the very purpose of libeling Robert Maheu. Until that was accomplished, the master spook had no choice but to persist in his troublesome search for the missing billionaire. And that could prove embarrassing, jeopardizing a number of sensitive relationships among Hughes, the CIA, Intertel, and the Summa Corporation. But with a multimillion-dollar damage settlement reposing in the near future, Maheu had every reason to fall suddenly quiet. In doing so, he became the silent partner of his own adversaries—simultaneously the victim and the beneficiary of a masterful deception.

He didn't enjoy the role. But, then, he didn't like Hughes either. For years he'd been the billionaire's "alter ego," or, to put it less politely, his slavey. He'd put up with the Old Man's bigotry, capriciousness, and paranoia because the money was right even when Hughes was wrong. He'd tolerated the Stockholder's 3 A.M. phone calls, worked sixteen-hour days, and taken dangerous risks. Maheu wasn't complaining: for ten thousand dollars a week he'd have overlooked a lot more. And did. Sitting in the Georgetown Inn, Maheu had frost in his voice as he spoke about his years with Howard Hughes. He told of the Old Man's flag-waving anticommunism and his frequent expressions of concern for "U. S. interests" and the "American way."

"He didn't believe any of it," Maheu remarked. "It was, let us say, a crock of S-H-I-T . . . I didn't send that in code, did I?" And he spoke of Hughes's impossible demands. "The Davis Cup," he said. "You can't imagine how hard we worked to bring the Davis Cup championship to Las Vegas, and what it meant for the city. And then, the night before play started, the Old Man demanded that we cancel the tournament. He didn't care what pretext we used, but he didn't want 'that *nigger*,' Arthur Ashe, playing on his courts! Do you *know* Arthur Ashe? He's one of the finest young men I've ever met in my life. I told him, 'I won't do that. You can fire me if you like, Howard, but there are some things I just won't do.'" After a pause Maheu chuckled, and I asked him why. "I was thinking of a call I received one night—Christmas Eve, in fact. Mr. Hughes was suddenly concerned that a plague of June bugs was about to descend upon Las Vegas. You can imagine what that would be like for tourism: the city's lighting displays are world-famous, and the casinos are almost all open-air. But June bugs have never been a problem in Las Vegas: they simply aren't indigenous. Nevertheless, the Old Man was terrified at the prospect and insisted that we get a crash program started immediately to develop a contingency plan. He wanted me to locate a group of entomologists, whose names he had, and fly them out to Nevada that afternoon. It didn't matter that it was Christmas. 'Offer them anything,' he said."

"Did you get them?"

Maheu nods. "I think so . . . Mr. Hughes usually got what he wanted. He operated on the principle that everyone has his (or her) price. The few things that he couldn't buy were of no interest to him. Or else they frightened him. Like the night."

"The night?"

"Darkness frightened him. Or—not *that*—it wasn't the darkness: he just couldn't bear to see night fall. It bothered him enormously. I think—in fact, I *know*—that's part of the reason why he lived the way he did: he shut out the sunlight, shuttering his windows, because he didn't like to be reminded that it sometimes gets dark." Maheu hesitated as a waiter gestured toward him with a telephone. "You know," he said, "he was a very hard man to feel sorry for, but . . . there were times when I wanted to go up to that penthouse, throw the Mormons out, grab the Old Man by the back of his neck, and drag him downstairs and outside, into the sunlight. He needed someone to do that for him, but . . ." A small shrug.

While Maheu excused himself to answer the telephone, I wondered about his fantasy. Would it have done Hughes any good? The notion of the Old Man kicking and screaming down the stairwell of the Desert Inn, emerging at last in the hated sunshine, evoked a theater of images. Childbirth, for one, with Maheu as the midwife-spook, Hughes as the frightened babe, and the Desert Inn as a sort of air-conditioned womb. And I thought of Rapunzel, too, with her long golden hair—but the fairy tale dissolved into a more nightmarish vision as I contemplated Hughes's habits and appearance. He was not so much Rapunzel as he was a failing Dracula: beefed up with regular blood transfusions, his vitality and intelligence resembled, in the words of his former attorney, Ed Morgan, "a sine curve. There was fleeting brilliance and enthusiasm, but then they waned, they always waned into prolonged periods of stupor and depression."

Trying to understand Howard Hughes was a process that led inevitably toward comparisons with the mythic. It seemed a useful activity in view of the fact that the Old Man appears to have had a stranglehold on the country's military and political nerve centers, buying and inveigling his way into the White House, CIA, and Congress. He was the ultimate man behind the scenes, the foremost employer of private intelligence agents in the world, and, by any standard, he appears to have been mad as a hatter. If there has been a corresponding madness running through American politics over the past two decades, it may well be that Hughes deserves a measure of the blame. Understanding him, however, is necessarily an oblique effort. Having isolated himself so completely from public view, the billionaire is revealed only through the events that surrounded him—for instance, through the unraveling of mysteries such as the "Thanksgiving Coup"—and through the people in whom he placed his trust. Not surprisingly, Robert Maheu—the Old Man's alter ego for more than a decade—is the key.

2 / THE CONTRACT

Born in Waterville, Maine, Maheu was a grocer's son who dreamed of warmer and more exotic climates, while yet taking to heart the state's conservatism and traditional values. There was nothing in his upbringing to suggest that he would one day become, as he did, the linchpin in national-security struggles involving such financial titans as Howard Hughes, Stavros Niarchos, and Aristotle Onassis—while at the same time representing the interests of such seemingly inconsonant clients as the CIA, various multinational corporations, Caribbean dictators, and labor unions such as the

United Steelworkers. Not to mention such political kingmakers as Tommy ("The Cork") Corcoran and William Loeb, publisher of the Manchester (New Hampshire) *Union Leader.*

But like so many other small-town youths of great imagination, he dreamed of the day when he might return home in a private jet, enveloped by concentric auras of celebrity and intrigue. In later years, when Maheu presided over the neon desert of Las Vegas, he'd defer to his New England heritage by hosting lavish clambakes in Nevada, clambakes for which thousands of live lobsters would have to be transported across the country.

And getting there was half the fun. After College of the Holy Cross and a short stint at Georgetown Law School, Maheu joined the FBI at the outbreak of World War II. His first years as a G-man were spent at posts in Arizona and, later, in Seattle, Washington. In 1942 he returned to Washington, D.C., to handle a prolonged and mind-boggling counterespionage assignment for which his fluency in French uniquely suited him. The mission was to spy on a French aviator, Dieudonne Coste, who'd achieved celebrity twelve years earlier by making a trans-atlantic flight. Coste had been recruited by the Nazis to gather intelligence in the United States, where he was still regarded as a friend. In return for that cooperation, the Germans promised not to harm Coste's family. The plan called for the aviator to bungle an espionage caper supposedly directed against U. S. interests, thereby bringing himself to the attention of American authorities. Once he'd been caught as a spy, Coste would then offer to be "doubled" and to feed worthless information to his Nazi employers. In reality, however, the plot called for him to provide genuine intelligence to another Nazi agent who, with a secret radio transmitter, had taken up residence on Long Island. According to the plan, the Americans would regard Coste as a double agent when, in fact, he would be a more dangerous commodity: a *triple* agent.

Before the aviator could carry out his mission for the Nazis, however, he was apprehended in Spain. There he described his role in the plot, requiring very little coaxing, and offered to become an American agent. The reader will notice—as Maheu and J. Edgar Hoover did—that Coste's arrest and offer to be doubled precisely matched the steps to be taken in the plot to which he'd just confessed. It seemed to the FBI that the aviator's arrest and confession in Spain might be a diabolical twist to the very plot he described. Maheu, in other words, was made to consider a plot in which Coste would pretend to be a quadruple agent for the Americans while, in fact, serving as a *quintuple* agent for the Nazis.

Undoubtedly, American taxpayers' interests would have been best served had Coste simply been "tweeped" (terminated with extreme prejudice). Instead, Maheu was placed under deep cover and provided with a new identity in the name of Robert A. Marchand. Using that *nom de guerre,* he kept Coste under surveillance, seeing to it that the aviator fed false information to both his principals abroad *and* to the Nazi in the Hamptons. At the end of the war, the operation was declared a success, Coste was vindicated, and Maheu promoted. But the five-dimensional chess he'd played had taken a toll: only twenty-eight years old, Marchand/Maheu found himself bald.*

The end of the war brought Maheu into a mysterious last two years with the FBI. Regarded as a top agent of unusual merit, he became personal friends with J. Edgar Hoover and some of his closest aides. His assignments in the Bureau's Washington, Chicago, and New York offices were important ones, and it appeared to his colleagues that Maheu would one day sit at the right hand of Hoover himself. It was astonishing, therefore, that the counterespionage hero should be transferred in 1946 to a specially created office in Waterville, Maine. The explanation for the Siberian assignment was that Hoover created the post as a favor to Maheu, whose wife was said to be ailing. It was hoped that the Maine climate would cure Yvette's supposed tuberculosis. The same assignment was later used to explain Maheu's precipitous departure from the FBI in July 1947. The Waterville office was dull. There were no Communists or bank robbers worth tracking in the area, and Yvette had experienced a "miraculous cure." Accordingly, Maheu found himself with nothing to do and, after his wife's recovery, quit the FBI.

The scenario has all the makings of a cover story—and an implausible one at that. For one thing, Waterville, Maine, with its chills and damp, is hardly the place to which one is likely to move in order to improve the health of a tubercular loved one. Secondly, if the Waterville office was indeed created as a favor to Maheu, as he's claimed, the office could just as easily have been dissolved (and its lone staffer reassigned to a more attractive post) once his wife's

---

* The tale of Dieudonne Coste is recounted in *The Hughes Papers,* by Elaine Davenport and Paul Eddy with Mark Hurwitz (New York: Random House, 1976), pp. 43–44.

condition had improved. Instead, he seems to have acted with uncharacteristic callousness toward his benefactors, rejecting the FBI in the wake of Yvette's spontaneous cure.

Maheu's account of the Waterville assignment, then, just doesn't add up and one can only guess at the reason he was there. It may be, for instance, that the post was a punishment for his having somehow fallen into disfavor with Hoover. Certainly Maine would be regarded as a kind of banishment for any G-man used to double-agentry and metropolitan assignments. And yet Waterville was Maheu's hometown, and it's unlikely that Hoover would punish an agent by sending him home: if Maheu was to have been banished, North Dakota would have been a more probable exile.

So the Waterville post seems not to have been created as a personal accommodation for Maheu. And neither does it appear to have been created as a punishment. At the time of the assignment Hoover held Maheu in high regard. Not only was the young man advancing to increasingly more important posts within the Bureau, but, years later, when Maheu had entered "private practice," Hoover would recommend him to personal friends such as Lewis Rosenstiel, chief of the Schenley liquor empire, as a man who could be trusted with the most sensitive assignments. It's true that Hoover's opinion of Maheu underwent an apparent change in the late 1950s. In 1962, for instance, the FBI Director recounted in a memo a conversation he'd had with Robert Kennedy concerning Maheu's role in the CIA/Mafia plots to assassinate Fidel Castro: "I expressed great astonishment," he wrote, "in view of [Maheu's] bad reputation . . ." But that opinion, assuming Hoover was not being disingenuous, was a revisionist one that obviously had nothing to do with Maheu's sudden departure from the Bureau. And yet Hoover was hardly a forgiving man. How, then, did Maheu retain Hoover's friendship for so long after repaying the Director's supposed kindness to his family by quitting the FBI?

The explanation may be that Maheu's assignment to Waterville was anything but banal. In fact, the task may have been so sensitive that it required virtual isolation and therefore the creation of Maheu's own office, an office in which he could work with only the most remote supervision. If that's so, then his departure from the Bureau, perhaps upon completion of this mysterious assignment, would explain Hoover's continuing high regard for his protégé: rather than repaying a kindness with ingratitude, Maheu would have left the FBI to choruses of a job "well done."

There's no way to know just what that assignment might have been, though the timing is intriguing. That is, the period covered by the Waterville assignment coincided nicely with the planning and creation of the CIA—a matter of great concern to the jealous Hoover. Indeed, Maheu's voluntary resignation from the Bureau came about little more than one month prior to the CIA's "activation" in September, 1947. That coincidence suggests that Maheu may have left the Bureau for the Agency. According to Maheu, however, he left to organize a business called Dairy Dream Farms, moving with his wife ("miraculously cured") to New Rochelle, New York. The entrepreneurial effort failed miserably, we're told, plunging Maheu into cavernous debt. In January, 1952, he joined the Small Defense Plants Administration as an investigator: the interest on his debts nearly equaled his take-home pay.

It hadn't taken Maheu four years to lose his shirt, however. Something else seems to have been going on in the years between 1947 and 1952. A clue as to what that may have been is contained in Maheu's personnel file at the Small Business Administration (successor to the Small Defense Plants Administration). According to that file, Maheu had accumulated "10 years comp time" (government service) when he joined the SDPA in 1952. What makes this interesting is the fact that Maheu's FBI tenure was between December, 1940, and July, 1947—roughly six and a half years. Somehow he managed to acquire another three and a half years of government service—apparently after leaving the FBI in 1947. The likeliest explanation for this discrepancy is that Maheu joined the CIA. Not only would this explain the comp time itself, but it would also explain the fact that, after leaving the SDPA in February, 1954, he was immediately put on a monthly retainer by the CIA. Indeed, this was the money that got his supposedly private intelligence agency started. Maheu, then, appears to have been sheep-dipped by the Agency during his two years with the Small Defense Plants Administration. (The practice would not be uncommon in Washington, where the CIA routinely attaches some of its officers to various parts of the federal bureaucracy.) The significance of this, in part, is that Maheu has always suggested that the CIA retainer was not much more than a helping hand provided to him by former FBI associates who'd left the Bureau to join the Agency. If Maheu was in fact a CIA officer himself in the years after 1947–48, then it may well be that the Mission Impossible agency he founded in February, 1954, was itself a CIA proprietary—rather than the occasional "cover" he pretended it was. If this is so, the Agency must take responsibility for actions which were formerly "deniable" but which, in fact, constituted gross violations of its charter prohibiting domestic operations. (As we'll see, the conclusion that Maheu's agency was a proprietary carrying out the CIA's wishes is reinforced by the nature of his earliest assignments: in one case, involving a murdered OSS major, the political and intelligence implications were enormous; in a second case, the operation against Onassis, Maheu's agents were themselves in command of CIA officers detailed to assist them.)

In any event, Maheu's career as a spy-for-hire began in early spring, 1954. Forming Robert A. Maheu Associates, he found office space with Kennedy family spook Carmine Bellino, sharing Bellino's secretary and telephone. From its inception the Maheu Agency was, in the jargon of Washington, "super-connected." Besides his relationship to Hoover, Maheu's association with Bellino (many thought the two men were partners) brought him into contact with the Kennedy family.* A suave accountant who specializes in the detection of fraud, Bellino served at Robert Kennedy's side on the McClellan Investigating Committee on Labor Racketeering. Along with Walter Sheridan, he was instrumental in RFK's pursuit of Jimmy Hoffa. In later years Bellino would emerge as a zero-cool, behind-the-scenes figure in the Kennedy organization, taking a temporary leave from Senator Edward Kennedy's powerful Administrative Practices Committee to become chief investigator for the even more strategic Senate Watergate Committee. Since that last investigation skirted so many important issues, including some that pertained directly to the Kennedy family, it's fair to speculate that Bellino's role in the Watergate probe may have been one of containment.†

---

* Years later, Maheu would make use of that connection at the direction of Hughes. A few days after the assassination of Robert Kennedy, Maheu would approach Democratic superpol Larry O'Brien with an offer to hire not only O'Brien, but the Kennedy family's "key men"—all of whom, Hughes supposed, would be looking for new work. In a memo dated June 28, 1968, Maheu replied to Hughes: "Larry O'Brien—He is coming here on Wednesday next for a conference as per our request after the assination [sic] of Senator Kennedy. He is prepared to talk employment and has received a commitment (without any obligation whatsoever) from the four or five key men in the Kennedy camp that they will not become obligated until they hear from him. S/Bob."

† Among the issues glossed over by the Watergate Committee were several that seem to be of particular importance when one remembers that the Nixon forces viewed the Kennedy family with an alarm that bordered on paranoia. In particular, the motive behind the bugging operations has never been adequately explained. The general explanation that "political intelligence" was sought is inadequate. Potentially explosive operations such as the Watergate job are never undertaken by experienced spooks (or

Besides Bellino and Hoover, Maheu had another friend at the start of his new career: Washington superlawyer Edward Bennett Williams. Like Bellino (whom he considered a friend), Williams has had a long-standing, though sometimes tumultuous, relationship to the Kennedy family. As Jimmy Hoffa's principal attorney, he battled Robert Kennedy for years. The hostility between the two men healed, however, when Williams decided (in 1964) that he should no longer represent the Teamsters' president. That de-

---

politicians) without a *specific* goal. In this connection, it's interesting to note some of the more tantalizing issues that were virtually ignored by Senator Ervin's investigators:

1) The relationship between Larry O'Brien and Spencer Oliver (targets of the Watergate burglary) to the Hughes empire. O'Brien's ties to the Kennedy family are deep and long-standing, dating back to his management of John F. Kennedy's campaign to become a Massachusetts Senator. The preceding footnote in which Maheu's memo to Hughes is quoted (above) goes a long way toward explaining how it was that Larry O'Brien and top Kennedy staffers fell into the orbit of the billionaire recluse: Maheu made them an offer which they couldn't refuse. As for Spencer Oliver, a Democratic National Committee staffer, he is the nephew of Robert Bennett, proprietor of the Robert R. Mullen Company. It was the Mullen Company that succeeded, in the wake of the "Thanksgiving Coup," to the lucrative Hughes contract ($15,000 per month) negotiated with Maheu by Larry O'Brien. The Mullen Company, of course, was the CIA front that employed E. Howard Hunt. In the aftermath of Watergate, Robert Bennett left Washington to become a vice-president of Hughes's holding company, the Summa Corporation. Bugging O'Brien and Oliver, therefore, suggests that the operation's goal was to gather intelligence pertaining specifically to connections between Hughes and the Kennedy Democrats.

2) A second issue glossed over by the Watergate investigators was the belief of the Nixon White House that Intertel was a tool of the Kennedys. A memo written by White House intelligence operative John Caulfield to John Mitchell makes this clear: "The presence of Lawrence O'Brien as Chairman of the Democratic National Committee unquestionably suggests that the Democratic nominee will have a strong, covert intelligence effort mounted against us in 1972. . . . In this regard, we should be particularly concerned about the new and rapidly growing Intertel organization. Should this Kennedy mafia dominated intelligence 'gun for hire' be turned against us in '72, we would, indeed, have a dangerous and formidable foe." The remainder of the memo will be quoted in subsequent pages, but its gist is to explain the need for what Caulfield described as "a Republican Intertel" capable of handling clandestine political assignments. The White House Plumbers seem to have evolved as a direct result of the Caulfield memorandum, suggesting that their activities were *a response* to the existence of Intertel and its real or imagined work on behalf of the Kennedys and Larry O'Brien.

3) Yet another issue ignored by the Watergate investigators was the fact that the Democrats had advance warning of the Plumbers' eavesdropping operations. Three months before the Watergate burglary, on March 23, 1972, a self-described "Kennedy Democrat" named William Haddad wrote to Larry O'Brien with the news that he was "hearing some very disturbing stories about GOP sophisticated surveillance techniques now being used for campaign purposes. Later, Haddad warned John Stewart, communications director for the Democratic campaign, that the party was the target of GOP wiretapping attempts. Haddad's source for this information was A. J. Woolston-Smith, a former British intelligence agent working as a private detective in New York City. How Woolston-Smith learned of the Plumbers' efforts has never been revealed. But the fact that O'Brien and Stewart were apprised of the bugging attempts months prior to the Watergate fiasco contributes strongly to suspicions that Hunt, Liddy, and the Cubans were set up to take an embarrassing fall. Interesting, too, that Bill Haddad should be mentioned in the "Gonzalez affidavit" described earlier.

cision was a body blow to Hoffa and, as such, a boon to RFK. That the rift between the attorney and the Senator disappeared in later years is apparent from the fact that after RFK's assassination Williams hired the Senator's personal secretary, Angie Novello, to serve him in the same capacity. Emotionally attached to the Senator, Ms. Novello resisted Williams' inducements until the attorney was finally able to convince her that his feud with RFK had been healed. And, indeed, Williams had for years been on the periphery of Kennedy affairs. In the early 1950s, he defended Robert Kennedy's boss, Wisconsin Senator Joseph McCarthy, against Senate condemnation for having conducted a demagogic campaign to expose a supposed Communist conspiracy within the U. S. government and Army. Despite Williams' efforts, "Tailgunner Joe" was destroyed by his colleagues' repudiation, a repudiation that plunged him ever deeper into alcoholism, until finally he ended his career in a straitjacket at Bethesda Naval Hospital. Williams' own career burgeoned, however. In later years he became one of Washington's most powerful political figures, earning upward of one million dollars per year as an attorney while serving as president of the Washington Redskins football team and a member of the Foreign Intelligence Advisory Board (FIAB). A real estate magnate of the first order, he'd share a small office building with Intertel in the Seventies—just as, in the early Fifties, he worked side by side with Robert A. Maheu Associates. But mostly, Williams' power would come from those whose interests he represented as a lawyer.* Befriend-

---

* When one considers his clients, it's difficult to imagine any attorney who has ever been more strategically placed. For instance: among Williams' Watergate-related clients have been: 1) *The Washington Post*, considered by many to have "broken" the Watergate cover-up; 2) *Richard Helms*, the outgoing CIA Director who was said by some to have had "advance knowledge" of the Watergate burglary; 3) *Robert Vesco*, the fugitive financier whose $200,000 cash donation to the Nixon cause led to the indictment of former Attorney General John Mitchell and GOP fund-raiser Maurice Stans; 4) the *Democratic National Committee*, headed by Larry O'Brien—the target of the Watergate burglary, O'Brien and the Committee were suing the Committee to Re-Elect the President (CREEP). As if these did not cover all the Watergate bases, Williams is also said to have become the confidant of *Robert Bennett*; according to Senate staffers on the Watergate Committee, Bennett gained a "backdoor entry" to Williams' office by prevailing upon a mutual friend, attorney Hobart Taylor. More than any other figure, Bennett was strategically cited vis-à-vis Watergate: a Morman who subsequently joined Hughes's Summa Corporation, he was president of the Robert R. Mullen Company, the CIA front which employed E. Howard Hunt, Watergate's "mastermind." It was Bennett and the Mullen Company which, in 1971, replaced Larry O'Brien's Potomac Associates as Hughes's Washington spearhead. Additionally, Bennett was a close associate of White House advisor, and Watergate felon, Charles Colson. More than anyone else, therefore, Ed Williams seems to have been in a position of near-omniscience so far as

ing Ed Williams, Maheu acquired a powerful ally. In fact, it would be Williams' old law firm, Hogan & Hartson, that would recommend Robert Maheu to its client Howard Hughes. (The incestuousness of the Washington scene is indicated by the fact that Hogan & Hartson would, in 1977, receive stinging court criticism in connection with services it performed for Robert Vesco, a client the firm shared with Williams.)

But the most influential friend of all was the CIA. From the inception of Robert A. Maheu Associates, the firm was under contract to the Agency, handling "impossible missions" (the phrase is Maheu's) and providing cover for Agency operatives. Indeed, it's impossible to say just where Maheu began and the CIA ended. The founder of Robert A. Maheu Associates received a five-hundred-dollar-per-month stipend from the Agency—more than the salaries of many staff officers at that time, causing some to speculate that the firm was actually a proprietary of the CIA. Complicating the matter even further was the fact that some of Maheu's supposedly private clients—Greek shipping magnate Stavros Niarchos may be a case in point—were themselves fronting for the Agency in their relations with the Maheu firm. And then, too, Maheu's own employees included part-time investigators who, in addition to their chores for Maheu Associates and the CIA, had private clients of their own. Nevertheless, they were encouraged to use Maheu's credit cards, even on assignments that had nothing to do with either the Agency or the firm, reimbursing the boss at the end of the month. The result was extraordinary confusion. And, of course, a magnificent framework for deniability. The compartmentalization of Maheu Associates (with different employees handling different assignments on a need-to-know basis), the firm's relationship to the CIA, and the confused situations of its employees—some part-time, some undercover, and some moonlighting—makes it almost impos-

---

Watergate is concerned; as a candidate for "Deep Throat" the Washington attorney has no rivals.

Nor have his other clients been without interest. Among them: former United Mine Workers president *Tony Boyle*; the late, disgraced Congressman *Adam Clayton Powell*; Senate "fixer" *Bobby Baker*; organized-crime chief *Frank Costello*, and various aides to Meyer Lansky (Bahamian gamblers *Charles Brudner*, *Max Courtney*, and *Rex Ritter*); discredited financiers such as *Bernard Goldfine* and *Lewis Wolfson*; Navaho tribal chief *Peter MacDonald* (whose tribe controls vast uranium and coal deposits in the United States); former Secretary of the Treasury (under Nixon) *John Connally*; and FBI executive *Andrew J. Decker,* a top G-man investigated (and subsequently exonerated) in connection with a host of "black bag jobs" carried out by the FBI against New York radicals between 1971 and 1976.

sible to say who was behind anything the firm's employees did.*

As we'll see, the problems raised by this confused state of affairs are hardly academic ones: employees and former employees of Maheu's firm would become entangled in a number of sensational events ranging from wiretapping to kidnapping and murder. Learning whether the CIA may have been responsible for some of those events is essential to understanding this country's secret history.

It would, for instance, be interesting to know if Maheu was acting in behalf of the CIA when he undertook an international investigation in behalf of Edward Bennett Williams and that lawyer's client Aldo Icardi. The investigation was one of Maheu's first assignments as a private eye. Begun in 1954, when the Dairy Dream refugee was in the secret pay of the CIA, the probe was intended to *un*solve a murder.

A decade earlier, on one of those intelligence missions that seem to have been conceived with "The Late Late Show" in mind, OSS Lieutenant Icardi and four other American intelligence agents were parachuted into northern Italy's lake region, behind Nazi lines. Code-named "Operation Mangostine," the group's mission was to arrange arms drops to partisan units in the area. Commanding the operation was a former SEC attorney, Major William Holohan, whose operational cache of gold bullion, diamonds, and Italian currency was estimated to be worth $100,000. Immediately after landing, two of the team's members were killed in a fire fight with Nazi patrols. That left Holohan, Icardi, and the team's third remaining member, Rochester-born Sergeant Carl LoDolce, to play a deadly game of hide-and-seek with the Nazis. Assisted by Communist partisans, including one who later became Italy's premier, the sur-

---

* An incomplete list of those who worked for, or with, Maheu in the 1950s would include *Raymond A. Taggert,* today a gumshoe for the Agency for International Development (AID); *Rea Von Fossen,* a former Air Force intelligence officer, currently a private eye in Washington; *John J. Frank,* a onetime FBI and CIA officer, recently released from Lewisburg Penitentiary; *Louis J. Russell,* an ex-CIA officer (deceased); *Tom LaVenia,* formerly of the Secret Service and more recently a private investigator in Washington; *Allen F. Hughes,* formerly of the Counterintelligence Corps and an electronics firm called Research Products, Inc. (of Danbury, Connecticut); *William J. Staten,* former manager of information and security for Westinghouse Electric's Bettis Atomic Division in Pittsburgh; *John F. Gerrity,* currently a newspaper correspondent in Washington, D.C.; *Joe Shimon,* former Washington police detective and today a retired private eye in the nation's capital. Others who worked with Maheu but whose backgrounds remain obscure were *John W. Leon, Oliver Angelone, John J. Murphy, C. V. M. Williams, Ed Tierney, J. R. O'Leary, William Redden,* and *Charles Lyons* (a London contact for the Maheu agency). In New York, the Maheu firm was said to use the following private eyes: *Frank Bielasky, John Daley, Robert Swanson, John Bone,* and *William Seerey.*

vivors secreted themselves in a succession of hideouts, at one point eluding Nazi searchers by concealing themselves under the altar in a small church. Eventually, the three Americans found semipermanent refuge in a moldering mansion, the abandoned Villa Castelnuovo on the shores of the Lake of Orta. Major Holohan, however, was reluctant to supply the Communist partisans with arms, believing that the "Reds" would use them to wage guerrilla war in the aftermath of the inevitable Nazi surrender. Rightly, Lieutenant Icardi argued with his commander that the Communists were the largest and most effective partisan force operating in the area—and that, moreover, Major Holohan was violating his OSS orders while endangering the partisans' fragile coalition of right- and left-wing elements. Holohan was unmoved.

At least he was until the night of December 6, 1944, when he disappeared from the face of the earth. Taking over the mission, Lieutenant Icardi dramatically increased arms drops to the Communist partisans. Holohan's friend, the young and beautiful Marina Duelli, herself a secret courier for the partisan coalition, repeatedly pressed Icardi for an official report on the major's disappearance. With the Nazis in retreat, Icardi supposedly agreed to make such a report, giving Duelli a sealed envelope to be delivered to a partisan chieftain. Becoming suspicious along the way, the woman opened the letter to find that it contained her death sentence. "It was an order," she later testified, "that I be removed for 'security reasons.' But I saved myself, fleeing to Switzerland."

At war's end, Icardi described Major Holohan's death to his commanding officers in Switzerland. According to the lieutenant, he and LoDolce were dining with the major when a Nazi patrol attacked their villa with machine guns. "It sounded like a full-scale battle," Icardi said, adding that "the details are lost." All he could recall of the episode was that he escaped, firing his .45, while guns blazed around him.

The affair might have rested there had not Marina Duelli persuaded the late major's brother that the official report was a lie. Taking leave of his Wall Street brokerage, Joseph Holohan joined this formidable woman in Europe. A fashion designer in Geneva, she and the surviving Holohan journeyed to Italy in an effort to track down former partisans, priests, and businessmen who'd been close to Operation Mangostine. On the basis of information they uncovered, Italian police dredged the Lake of Orta in 1949, and the murdered major's body was recovered.

At a subsequent trial of Italian Communist partisans, Major Holohan's murder was blamed on Icardi and LoDolce. According to the partisans, Major Holohan had been poisoned with cyanide on the night of his disappearance. When that failed to kill him, Icardi and LoDolce were said to have flipped a coin to determine which of them would be his executioner. Losing the toss, Sergeant LoDolce led his sickened commander out of the villa. In the darkness, with Holohan bent over in pain, LoDolce put five bullets in the back of his head. There was no Nazi attack. According to the partisans on trial, they'd had no choice but to participate in the affair. Because the order to "tweep" the major came from the American command, they could have been executed for refusing to carry it out. Should they, upon refusing, have then tried to escape, they would have faced death from still other directions: captured by the Germans, they'd be shot as resistance figures; captured by the resistance, they'd be executed as deserters.

Convicted in absentia (American law forbade their extradition), Icardi and LoDolce at first maintained their innocence. LoDolce, however, subsequently cracked under interrogation by Defense Department investigators and a New York homicide detective. Shortly thereafter, the homicide detective was himself murdered and LoDolce retracted his confession. Again, the affair might have come to rest. At the time, however, the United States was in the midst of both the Cold War and political witch-hunts, and it appeared to many American conservatives that Major Holohan's decision not to arm the Communists had been the right one. Moreover, testimony at the Italian trial strongly suggested that Icardi was still an American intelligence officer, that the CIA was terribly interested in the matter, and that Holohan's execution had been ordered by his OSS commanders in Switzerland—Icardi and LoDolce were merely the hatchet men. So it was that Icardi was made to testify before a congressional investigating committee. Sticking to his story of the supposed Nazi attack, Icardi was indicted for perjury.

The case was a potential bombshell, with enormous ramifications for American politics. If, as the Italians believed, Major Holohan's execution was actually ordered by OSS chieftains in Switzerland, the Icardi matter would almost certainly lead into the inner councils of the postwar CIA. With Senator Joseph McCarthy searching for Commies in the American military and foreign policy establishments, nothing could have delighted his supporters more than to have proved that those presiding over the CIA (in 1953) were the same men who'd ordered the brutal assassination (in 1944) of an American anti-Communist fighting for his country behind Nazi lines. To the Right, Major Holohan had been treacherously martyred for what they believed to be his prescience. And the blame, it was whispered, might go all the way to the top: CIA director Allen Dulles, after all, had been responsible for directing the most sensitive OSS operations from his headquarters in Switzerland. Might it not have been he who'd ordered Holohan hit for refusing to follow orders?

Faced with a maximum sentence of thirty years if convicted, Icardi turned to Senator Joe McCarthy's old lawyer, Edward Bennett Williams, for help. In his turn, Williams engaged Maheu's investigative talents, and the two men set out to prove their client innocent. After scores of interviews in four European countries, the pair announced that it had the proof it sought. To many it sounded like whistling in the dark, however: there were eighteen Italian witnesses who were ready to testify for the prosecution, and few facts seemed in doubt. As it happened, though, the Icardi matter was never fully aired in an American court, despite the alleged readiness of both sides. Shortly after the trial began, the presiding judge, in response to a preliminary motion made by Williams, shocked the courtroom by calling for a directed verdict of not guilty. According to the judge, Icardi's constitutional rights had earlier been violated by what he described as the "legislative trial" conducted by the House Armed Services Committee. The Congress had no authority, the judge said, to investigate matters (such as murder) which could not, in some direct way, lead to the creation of legislation. Icardi was off the hook.

It was a peculiar affair. Williams, Icardi's attorney, had (unsuccessfully) defended Tailgunner Joe against Senate censure little more than a year before. Prior to the condemnation that ruined him, McCarthy had let it be known that he was considering an investigation of the CIA; Richard Nixon, then Vice President, was said to be in charge of a White House operation to forestall the McCarthy probe (according to former Senate aide Roy Cohn). And now, with McCarthy broken, Williams was (successfully) defending a man on whose guilt McCarthy's supporters might easily have pinned their political hopes. Assisting Williams in this effort was Robert Maheu, himself a contract agent of the CIA—which, as we've seen, had a large stake in Aldo Icardi's acquittal. According to Maheu, he received no compensation for his services (not even expenses), despite the fact that he was near bankruptcy at the time. Williams confirms that Maheu was unpaid, saying that he undertook the assignment "out of the goodness of his great heart." If so, it would seem to be the *only* philanthropic probe the master spook has ever undertaken. As it happens, God appears to have rewarded Maheu's largesse tenfold: during the course of the Icardi case, and afterward, he came increasingly and lucratively into the orbit of Attorney Williams and Richard Nixon. Together, and at about the time of the Icardi investigation, the three men would become part of a multibillion-dollar plot to ruin Aristotle Onassis. The point here, however, is that Maheu's strange involvement in the Icardi matter suggests very strongly that the CIA intervened in the case. At the time, and for decades afterward, Maheu's employment by the CIA was one of the country's best-kept state secrets. That he supposedly handled the matter *gratis* suggests that his labors in Icardi's behalf were undertaken at the behest of his secret patrons in Langley. If so, one can only wonder whether the Agency intervened in any other way against Senator Joseph McCarthy—the man who, precisely twenty years before Watergate, would have investigated the sacrosanct Agency.

4 / THE CIA VERSUS ONASSIS

Organized in 1954, Robert A. Maheu Associates became the prototype for the "Mission Impossible" television series, handling CIA assignments so sensitive that the federal spooks dared not perform them themselves. In short, it was dirty work, involving prostitution, pornography, illegal wiretaps, assassination, and a lot more, most of it planned and carried out on American soil. According to Joe Shimon, one of Maheu's oldest friends, "Bob was a pimp for the Cookie Factory. What I mean is, the Agency would call him up when Sukarno or Hussein * was coming to town, and ask him to get some girls. To keep 'em happy, y'know? And Bob did a good job. Sukarno, for instance, never had a clue that the girls were pros. He thought they were All-American kids who loved him for his body." (More exotic requests by visiting heads of state were handled by the CIA's own Office of Security. That office ran a "sex shop" through its field offices, requiring chiefs of station to compile dossiers

---

* Sukarno was the late President of Indonesia. Hussein, of course, is the Jordanian king, who's been on the CIA payroll for more than a decade.

on the sex habits of male and female vice offenders. Such "black books" were compiled in liaison with local police chiefs who allowed Agency employees to photocopy relevant documents. The offenders —whose interests reportedly ranged from S&M to pedophilia—were later approached by the Agency to service the kinky needs of kings, presidents, defectors, and lonely agents in safe-houses that were sometimes equipped with two-way mirrors, microphones, and hidden cameras.)

The former chief of detectives for Washington's classy Northwest quadrant, and therefore responsible for almost all of the capital's embassies, Shimon is a Runyonesque figure. A topnotch wireman, he was also close friends with both Sam Giancana and Johnny Roselli (whom he describes as "fine fellows—the nicest guys you'd ever wanta meet"). Indeed, Shimon says it was he who introduced Giancana and Roselli to each other and who, moreover, served as the "cut-out" between the hoodlums and the CIA in the 1961 plot to murder Fidel Castro. And although Shimon accompanied Maheu on assignments to Tucson and Los Angeles for Howard Hughes in the late Fifties, even he did not know all that Maheu Associates was up to.

The firm was a busy and highly profitable one. As Maheu later told reporters, "I didn't get rich overnight—but I did very well overnight." Besides providing cover for the CIA, and prostitutes for the Agency's clients, he earned his monthly retainer handling various odd jobs that were too seamy for the Agency to undertake itself. And sometimes the jobs were very odd. In one case Maheu served as the "producer" of a pornographic film purporting to show a communist leader (said to have been Yugoslavia's Marshal Tito) cavorting in the nude with a big-bosomed bimbo of unusual appetites. "Tito" was impersonated by a Maheu employee whose boss had prepared for the assignment by taking a crash course in the fine arts of makeup and disguise. The woman, the wife of Maheu's employee, was made to resemble an attractive KGB agent with whom the communist leader was reliably reported to have had an affair in Moscow. The CIA goal in the operation was to release prints from the film in the leader's homeland—not so much in an effort to embarrass him, but to make him think that the Russians were responsible for the film and the exposé of his dalliance. For whatever reasons, however, the pornflick was never released and presumably remains in the CIA's vaults —a prime candidate for one of Senator William Proxmire's "Golden Fleece" awards.

CIA covers, call girls, and porn films, however, provided only a small portion of the revenues earned by Maheu's "Mission Impossible" agency. Other clients, associated in various ways with Edward Bennett Williams, Carmine Bellino, and J. Edgar Hoover, had different needs and came to his door with larger contracts. Lewis Rosenstiel, head of the Schenley Corporation, was one of the first; so were the Teamsters, the Dominican Republic, the New York Central Railroad, the Steelworkers, El Paso Natural Gas, and the Senate Banking and Currency Committee, among others. As mentioned earlier, Maheu acquired Howard Hughes as a client upon the recommendation of Hogan & Hartson, Williams' former firm. One of his first assignments for Hughes was in connection with the billionaire's peripatetic sex life. According to Maheu, he was asked to determine whether a love rival of Hughes was an undercover CIA officer. Maheu learned that the rival was indeed a spook and so advised his client.

Subsequently Maheu undertook other assignments for Hughes, and began to apply his expertise to Republican politics. Hired by William Loeb, gun-toting publisher of New Hampshire's Manchester *Union Leader*, Maheu was entrusted with the task of destroying Harold Stassen's bid to oust Richard Nixon as the GOP vice-presidential candidate in 1956. At the time Stassen was the aging whiz-kid of the Republican Party, though still quite influential and a man of unquestioned integrity. Nixon, on the other hand, appeared increasingly untrustworthy to a growing number of voters. A Stassen poll, conducted just before the 1956 Republican convention, showed Nixon to be a liability to the party's ticket—until Maheu hurriedly put together a "counter-poll" purporting to show that Nixon would be an asset. Thereafter, Stassen's fortunes went into catastrophic decline, never to recover; in later years he'd become a perennial presidential candidate, a political curiosity whose losses rendered him pathetic and the butt of endless jokes. What else Maheu did to start Stassen on his long slide toward oblivion remains a secret. But that the spook's role was more than one of a pollster is clear. As he told me, "There was a 'cover' placed on Mr. Stassen's wastepaper basket, and the results of that cover . . . well, let's just say it turned the tide." Asked what had been found inside the basket, Maheu just shook his head. "It wouldn't be in anyone's best interests to discuss it," he said.

Each of these assignments added to Maheu's reputation as a man behind the (Washington) scene. His firm was comparatively small, but his connections were almost unlimited. Besides his friends at the Bureau and the Agency, he availed himself at a very early date of an unusual group of investigative mercenaries: the Society of Former Special Agents of the FBI. This was, and is, an alumni association of ex-G-men who are available to handle private assignments for a fee (and sometimes at great risk: Allen Baldwin, for instance, was recruited for the Watergate burglary by James McCord, who chose him from the Society's membership list). As a former FBI agent, Maheu knew that he could make use of the Society's roster, splitting fees with the agents that he hired. A sort of Manpower outfit for surveillance "temps," the Society permitted Maheu to claim that he had thousands of experienced agents at his command twenty-four hours a day in offices worldwide. No assignment, therefore, was too big. Maheu could take on anyone. And he did.

In 1954, even as the Icardi case and so much else was happening, Maheu set out to ruin one of the world's wealthiest and most glamorous men: Aristotle Onassis, the Greek shipping tycoon and part owner of the Monte Carlo casino in Monaco. In the struggle between the two men, the future protector of Jacqueline Kennedy was threatened with the prospect of bankruptcy in a bizarre intrigue, a prelude to Watergate in which foreign and domestic wiretaps, a Nazi collaborator, surveillance teams, the press, the CIA, and even the Peruvian Air Force were arrayed against him. Beleaguered on every side, and oblivious to the fact that the conspiracy against him was being orchestrated by Vice President Richard Nixon, Onassis could only watch as bombs and machine-gun fire rained down upon his ships, his tankers were seized, and a boycott was organized against him—all to the distant applause of the multinational oil companies. In the end, Maheu's future would be assured by Onassis's competitors, notably Stavros Niarchos, and a grateful intelligence community.

The incident began, somewhat obliquely, in April, 1953. Stavros Niarchos, related by marriage to Aristotle Onassis and a shipping tycoon in his own right, was indicted by the Justice Department for what appeared to be violations of the Ship Sales Act of 1946. This legislation was enacted in the wake of World War II, as the U. S. government sought to unload its supply of surplus military equipment. Niarchos was accused of circumventing provisions of the act in order to gain control of tankers forbidden from sale to foreigners. To represent him in the matter, Niarchos retained Mudge, Rose, Guthrie, and Alexander, the law firm in which Vice President Nixon would later become a partner.

The indictment was a direct threat to both the livelihood and liberty of the shipowner; if convicted, Niarchos might see his American interests decimated, and there was even the possibility of a long prison term. The indictment, however, was even more sinister than that: a secret document, it was not to be unsealed until February, 1954—almost a year after it was drawn. The effect of this was to keep Niarchos stationary on a financial gallows, waiting for the floor to drop out beneath him. That tactic, of course, is a familiar one to police who use pending indictments to blackmail recalcitrant felons into cooperation on other, more important investigations.

While Niarchos stewed with dread over the indictment, his brother-in-law, Onassis, was celebrating in Saudi Arabia. On January 20, 1954, he finalized a secret contract of such immense financial implications that it might, in the space of a few years, make him wealthier and more powerful than some nations. Called "the Jiddah Agreement," the contract permitted Onassis to establish and operate an Arabian maritime fleet that would be guaranteed the right to ship between 10 percent and 100 percent of all Arabian oil.

As such, it was a direct threat to the stability of the International Petroleum Cartel (IPC), whose monopoly of world oil reserves depended upon its members' absolute control over each and every process having to do with petroleum: its discovery, production, storage, refinement, shipment, and local distribution. The workings of that integrated monopoly, in which seven multinational companies controlled virtually all of the world's energy supply, were as finely tuned as an *Apollo* launching. And the linchpin to the entire boodle was Saudi Arabia, whose enormous reserves were under the domination of the Arabian American Oil Corporation (Aramco). Aramco was itself a consortium dominated by four American firms: Standard Oil Company of California (Socal), Texaco, Mobil, and Exxon. Essential to the maximization of profits was a financial strategy which, for tax reasons, saw to it that most of the profits made were gained "upstream"—at the point of production, rather than at the point of distribution. If Onassis were permitted to intervene by acquiring a monopoly of his own on the *shipment* of Arabian oil, the elaborate price structure of fifty years' devising might collapse. And while Onassis sought only a 10-percent interest in one phase of a single country's oil industry, the proposed intervention was regarded by the IPC as about as welcome as equipping a Rolls-Royce with a whoopee cushion.

At the time, Onassis and Niarchos were on cantankerous speaking terms, though sharing the same wealthy father-in-law and working in partnership on a number of ventures. The relationship, however, would come unstuck very soon, as Niarchos joined forces with Maheu, Nixon, and the oil giants, betraying his partner and relative. In later years the feud between the tycoons would assume the proportions of Greek tragedy. At first, the pair would compete in business and with symbols, each seeking to undo the other with bigger boats and more ostentatious displays. Later, the vendetta would become increasingly personal, and Niarchos would infect the feud with a hint of incest, wedding and bedding Onassis's ex-wife—his own former sister-in-law, the fragile and disintegrating Tina.

The principals in the drama were suitably mythic. In the eyes of the public, Onassis had already replaced Croesus as a metonym for immense wealth. He was a romantic figure, dark and sybaritic, a Levantine version of Horatio Alger. He'd been born in Smyrna, when that city was both great and Greek. As a youth he'd seen the city ruined and its population raped in the course of a barbaric military campaign waged by the Turks, and he'd fled (with a small stake) to Argentina. There he'd made his first million while in his twenties, importing tobacco beneath the Southern Cross. Becoming an Argentine citizen, he made successful investments in other people's misfortunes, acquiring a dilapidated tanker fleet at a bankruptcy auction. Pioneering the concept of "flags of convenience," Onassis saved millions in taxes while employing nonunion labor at cut-rate wages. During World War II, his fortune grew to immensity as its owner's ships carried Allied supplies back and forth across the sub-infested Atlantic. At the end of the war one could speak of an "Onassis empire," an oceanic triangle whose vertexes were London, Buenos Aires, and New York. The handsome Greek commuted among these cities, maintaining quarters in each, but his imagination exceeded the possibilities of even these world capitals: in many ways he was a man with a poor boy's fantasies, albeit one who'd amassed sufficient wealth to make his dreams come true. His real homes were Monte Carlo, inner sanctum of the jet set, in which he'd bought a controlling interest from Prince Rainier; Scorpios, the faintly sinister Ionian island which he'd transformed from barren desert to a paradise worthy of a hashishin's most ecstatic dreams; and *Christina*, the sixteen-hundred-ton frigate he'd converted into a floating mansion. Buying control of Monte Carlo, Onassis appropriated to himself all the legends and glamour attendant on that principality. In a single stroke he became landlord and croupier to the dragomen and lords of high society: deposed dictators, exiled kings, playboys, arms merchants, and international financiers. Becoming the man who owned the bank at Monte Carlo, he invited others to break him, knowing that it couldn't be done. With Scorpios he acquired a private world, a sea-locked demesne of transcendent bleakness—until Onassis improved upon nature by importing fresh water, tropical flora, scores of servants, sentries, and, of course, the ultimate amenity: Jacqueline Kennedy, arguably the world's most glamorous woman. And *Christina* was equally mythic. Where some yachts have staterooms, she had suites, an El Greco, a hospital, a movie theater, and a vast sunken bath of Siena marble with mosaic tiling that recapitulated images found in the Minos Palace at Knossos. There were *nine* guest suites on the yacht, each with gold fixtures and private telephones, some with fireplaces of lapis lazuli. And—by no means finally—there was a swimming pool which, at the touch of a button, rose from belowdecks to become a dance floor. Fifty crewmen and two chefs ministered to whoever was aboard.

Another player in the drama that unfolded among Onassis, Niarchos, and Maheu was equally mythic. That was Hjalmar Horace Greeley Schacht—the man Onassis relied upon to seal the Jiddah Agreement with the Arabs. Schacht was something of a notorious figure in world finance. The son of a Danish countess and a German merchant (who'd idolized Horace Greeley), he'd been raised in Brooklyn, New York, returning to the Rhineland while an adolescent. A brilliant and faintly imperious youth, he became one of Germany's first Ph.D.'s, winning a reputation as a prodigy for his economic insights and linguistic talents. And Schacht was also a handsome man. At 6 feet, 3 inches, he sported four-inch celluloid collars, a thin moustache, and steel-rimmed spectacles; women are said to have found him charming, and in later years he was described in the press as an "aristocratic Clark Gable." In 1923, Schacht was named Reich Currency Commissioner and given dictatorial powers to end the postwar inflation that was destroying Germany. It took him precisely a week, where others had failed for years, and he became famous as the man who'd literally *saved the mark*. Subsequently, he made successful forays into politics, switching allegiances to make the most of every opportunity; of his private views, nothing was certain except that he was an anti-Communist and a defender of the German aristocracy. In the wake of the Reichstag fire, however, Schacht became an avowed Hitlerian, raising money in the Führer's behalf and persuading foreign industrialists of the Nazis' "good intentions." More than anyone else, perhaps, he made Germany's rearmament possible, establishing a policy of "Barter or Ersatz." Through that policy Germany was able to trade cheap toys and cameras for oil and war-essential materials, thereby subverting the economies of the very countries that it intended to conquer. As the Second World War loomed closer, Schacht traveled to London with a scheme that would have permitted the Jews to flee Germany if Britain and the United States would have cooperated in boosting Germany's exports. The plan was rebuffed. During the war itself the financier played a smoky role behind the scenes. "Indispensable," according to Göring (who detested him), Schacht was responsible for devising a master plan for the economic reconstruction of postwar Europe—a reconstruction, of course, that was to be carried out in accordance with Nazi ideals. He was, in other words, Hitler's appointed architect for the creation of a Nazi millennium. And yet, toward the war's end, Schacht left Germany for Zurich, apparently to press plans for a peace that would be favorable to Germany. By this time he was himself a multimillionaire, the owner of large estates, and a collector of great paintings. His ambiguous role toward the war's end permitted him, as critics said, "to brush the swastikas from his sleeves," and emerge with his own power intact after his country's military defeat.

Onassis and Schacht, therefore, amounted to an awesome team. One controlled huge fleets of tankers. The other held the keys to the institutional wealth of the Ruhr: as a private banker, Schacht's influence and resources could not be overestimated.

With the signing of the Jiddah Agreement, a great celebration took place in Saudi Arabia, with Onassis exchanging presents with the king, and his wife paying court to the monarch's four wives. The agreement, however, was kept secret at the shipowner's request. As he did with most of his business deals, he preferred not to inform the public of his plans until they were a *fait accompli*; that way his rivals would be unable to protest or otherwise intervene until it was too late. In this case, "too late" meant the delivery date of seven huge new tankers, including the world's biggest, commissioned earlier in German shipyards. Their delivery was months away, and until they were in the water, the Saudi contract was vulnerable.

Keeping the Jiddah Agreement secret, however, was a near-impossibility. The government of Saudi Arabia is largely an American creation, a convenience for Aramco and the CIA. The royal household numbered more than ten thousand dependents, and no information could be kept hidden from the Americans for long.

On February 1, 1954, Onassis returned to New York. Rumors of a sealed indictment pending against him were rife, and twelve of his ships had already been seized by the U. S. government. The nature of the dispute was similar to the one in which Niarchos found himself embroiled: their acquisition of surplus tankers in 1947 was supposedly in violation of U. S. law. The charge infuriated Onassis because the clandestine indictment originated in the Justice Department, which at the time was headed by his former lawyer, Attorney General Herbert Brownell, Jr. For years Onassis had paid Brownell's law firm royally for its legal advice; indeed, it was Brownell who'd analyzed the 1947 transactions, pronouncing them lawful. Seven years later, Brownell was going to charge Onassis with criminal fraud for having followed his own legal advice! It seemed to Onassis that a double cross was in the works, albeit a subtle one. The seizure of the T-2 tankers would have little impact on Ari's affairs. The ships had already earned a $12,000,000 profit while moving along the road to obsolescence, and their contemporary value barely exceeded the mortgages outstanding on them. The bad publicity, however, could prove disastrous. Both his lenders and his customers were conservative men who would tolerate almost anything—with the exception of a partner whose reputation was that of a crooked wheeler-dealer.

So it was that Onassis sought to defuse the simmering scandal by returning to the United States, against his lawyers' advice, and confronting the Justice Department directly. And so it was that on February 5, 1954, he was arrested in New York while having lunch in the exclusive Colony Restaurant. Three days later he was booked, mugged, fingerprinted, and publicly charged in Washington, D.C. According to his attorney, Ed Ross, the procedure was an ignominious one. "They wouldn't let me in the same cell with Ari while he was being fingerprinted," Ross said, "so I was locked in another cell with some of the wildest-looking creatures you'd ever seen. As it turned out, they were the Puerto Ricans who'd just shot up Congress that day. On the flight back to New York, I talked to Ari about all the problems he'd begun to have at about this time, and I told him, 'You know, for someone as wealthy as you, you've certainly got enemies.' 'I know,' he said, 'and it's beginning to worry me.'" For its part, the press made the most of the indictment. Described by reporters as "the *King* of Monte Carlo"—a reference that was unlikely to endear him to his partner, *Prince* Rainier—Onassis found himself shifted from the financial and society columns of the daily newspapers to those pages reserved for pix of manacled men with raincoats pulled over their heads.

What Onassis didn't know at the time, however, was that his arrest was only the first salvo in a campaign to destroy his reputation and wealth. The man behind the conspiracy was Richard Nixon, assisted by a platoon of spooks from the CIA and Maheu Associates —all of them no doubt mistakenly convinced that their assignments had to do with "national security." Others, including such political comers as Edward Bennett Williams and the future Chief Justice of the United States, Warren Burger, would play important roles in the affair. But behind them all, according to Costa Gratsos (a confidant of Onassis) and John Gerrity (a nemesis of Onassis), were the multinational oil companies. "They didn't understand what Onassis was trying to do," Gratsos told me, "so they prepared to bankrupt him—and they almost succeeded. Later, of course, the oil companies were his best friends. An understanding had been reached." Gerrity concurs. "Nixon ran the thing, but he was never more than a front man for the multinational oil companies. He loved these kinds of private intelligence operations because there was always a lot of money at stake. And you have to remember, one of his main jobs was to raise campaign contributions for the Republicans. The oil companies had a lot of dough, and the only string tied to it was Aristotle Onassis."

Just when the conspiracy got under way is unknown. The Maheu firm was a highly compartmentalized one, and those employed there worked on a "need-to-know" basis. Nevertheless, the plot was well under way in May, 1954, when Maheu's Washington "office manager," Ray Taggart, received a mysterious telephone call. The caller was Niarchos' London solicitor, a Mr. L. E. P. Taylor, and he was telephoning from the New York office of a private eye on whom Maheu often relied for surveillances, Bill Seerey. Taylor, who was in charge of the Niarchos negotiations with Warren Burger and the Justice Department, said he had an assignment and that Taggart should not leave his office. Within minutes a Niarchos messenger arrived at Maheu Associates with a photograph of Onassis and an extensive dossier on both the shipping magnate and his most important employees.

Taggart's task was to arrange for the placement of a wiretap on Ari's New York offices. The man he entrusted with that job was

Maheu employee Lou Russell, a hard-drinking spook who would eventually be borne to his grave by an all-star squad of private investigators, including pallbearers James McCord and Ken Smith (chief sleuth of the Committee to Investigate Assassinations).* A former government investigator who had worked the Alger Hiss case, Russell stayed in a Maheu "safe suite" at the National Republican Club on New York's West Fortieth Street, sharing its rooms with other private investigators targeted against Onassis. Placing the tap, however, was no easy matter: Russell didn't have the contacts to get the job done, and retired New York City police detectives who were supposed to help proved unreliable. Russell finally gave up, returning to Washington when it appeared that the tap was going to be placed on a Western Union cable—effectively wiring a great deal of Manhattan. Russell wanted no part of that.

Sharing the suite at the National Republican Club, however, was a former CIA officer who is said to have gotten the job done. That was John J. Frank, who figures in even darker episodes of America's secret history. A Maheu employee, Frank was shuttling among Washington, the Dominican Republic, and New York on a number of different assignments. According to all sources, "J.J." was close

---

* Shortly before his death, which occurred a few months after the Watergate break-in, Russell was hired by James McCord to work for the latter's private security firm. Supposedly, Russell handled matters relating to the security and investigative needs of the Republican National Committee (RNC). Whether that is so or not, he was paid by McCord with checks that Russell apparently had difficulty cashing. According to Ken Smith, first interviewed on the subject by investigative historian Carl Oglesby (see Oglesby's *The Yankee and Cowboy War*, Sheed, Andrews, & McMeel [Mission, Kansas], 1976), Russell cashed his checks at the Committee to Investigate Assassinations. That accommodation came about through Russell's longtime friendship with the Committee's founder, Washington attorney Bernard "Bud" Fensterwald. The checks were signed over to the Committee by Russell, after which he was reimbursed. Russell's last few months were even more mysterious, however. After leaving McCord's firm, he accepted work from General Security Services Company, responsible for protecting the Watergate complex into which McCord subsequently broke. According to a source of Oglesby's at the Committee to Investigate Assassinations, Russell was present in the Howard Johnson Motel (from whose rooms Gordon Liddy and Howard Hunt coordinated the political break-in) at the time the burglary occurred. After Russell's death, Kennedy in-law Sargent Shriver, writing in a Paris paper, compared Russell to "*les barbouzes*," French gangsters and mercenaries, describing the death as mysterious and suggesting that it might be linked to the Watergate burglary. Former State Department official Alger ?. Hiss has also demonstrated an interest in Russell's demise. "We tried for more than a year to get a copy of Russell's death certificate," Hiss told me, "but we couldn't. That's very strange. The certificate is a public record but, when I say '*we* tried,' I mean Covington & Burling tried—and if they couldn't get it, I don't know who can." (Hiss's brother is a partner in Covington & Burling, a large and prestigious law firm.) Hiss's interest in Russell, of course, has to do with Russell's investigation of his case, an investigation conducted in the 1940s on behalf of Richard Nixon and the House Un-American Activities Committee (HUAC), for which Russell worked.

to Manhattan detectives on the "Red Squad" and, perhaps most importantly, to a burly private eye named Horace Schmahl. The proprietor of a detective agency called the National Railways Security Bureau, Inc., a fifteen-man outfit that was highly successful and widely regarded as the New York counterpart of Maheu's Washington firm, German-born Schmahl was a naturalized American whose life seems always to have been enveloped with intrigue. A private eye in Manhattan during the city's brutal Depression years, he was said to have blistered Hitler's ego near the beginning of World War II, purloining a sheaf of embarrassing photographs from the Führer's private files in Berlin. With the outbreak of the war, it is thought, he played a double agent's role—though accounts of his auspices differ. Some say he worked for Military Intelligence, others for the OSS, and others for the FBI. Whichever's the case, he joined the Central Intelligence Group (CIG) * after the war, and subsequently went to work for the dapper John Broady, a legendary private op who was later to be convicted of maintaining a wire-tapping nest that had access to the phones of about 125,000 subscribers on New York City's East Side. (The wiremen weren't listening to all of those subscribers, of course, but they were monitoring the phones of two drug companies, Bristol-Myers and E. R. Squibb, Knoedler Art Galleries, and many other firms whose profits often depend upon their ability to keep trade secrets. The United Nations, and the residences of numerous diplomats, were also available to the wiretappers, but it's unknown whether their conversations were actually monitored.) In 1948 Schmahl was retained by the Alger Hiss defense team, only to be discharged the following year for his failure to discover useful information. In later years Schmahl's role in the Hiss matter would come to be regarded by many as sinister rather than merely ineffectual. Hiss's proponents would learn that Schmahl believed his client to be guilty and, for that reason, kept the FBI secretly informed of his work for the defense. That smacked of an FBI "penetration" of the Hiss team and may well have been a violation of the accused spy's rights. Others, notably investigative reporter Fred Cook, would go even further, suggesting that Schmahl may have been instrumental in the alleged manufacture of evidence which Richard Nixon used to ruin Hiss. (At issue is the existence of a typewriter that may have been manu-

---

* The CIG was the transitional organization between the wartime OSS and the CIA (activated in September, 1947).

factured by an acquaintance of Schmahl's, the machine's characteristics to have duplicated those of one formerly owed by Hiss.) *

Whatever Schmahl's actual role in the Hiss matter, intrigue and controversy would follow him all his life. In the mid-Fifties he'd be questioned, along with Johnny Frank, in connection with the 1956 disappearance and murder of Columbia University professor

---

* The story of Alger Hiss is an immensely complicated one filled with uncertainty. Though the case is old, Hiss himself continues in what appears to be a never-ending quest for exoneration. Since the case bears very heavily upon Richard Nixon's rise to power, and because new information continues to be released under the Freedom of Information Act, a brief summation of the case may be in order. Hiss was a retired State Department official in 1946 when Whittaker Chambers, then a senior editor at *Time*, secretly began accusing him of having been a Soviet espionage agent in the years before World War II. Chambers' accusations were investigated by the FBI and subsequently by the pungent House Un-American Activities Committee [HUAC]. In 1948 Chambers (a self-confessed traitor and apostate Communist spy) accused Hiss in HUAC hearings of having been a Soviet mole who'd smuggled secret State Department documents to the Reds. Hiss filed a libel suit against Chambers—whom he said he'd known casually a decade before (and then under a different name)—and denied the charges before HUAC. For a while it was one man's word against another's, but Hiss hadn't reckoned on either the political climate of the times or the ambitions of his foremost inquisitor, a fledgling congressman named Nixon. A year earlier, HUAC had pilloried the Hollywood Ten, 1948 was itself an election year, and fighting the Communist Menace seemed a certain way to higher office. (Nixon himself had reached Congress on the crest of a calculated smear campaign in which he'd defamed his rival as a Communist sympathizer.) Accordingly, the Hiss matter represented an extraordinary opportunity, and neither Nixon nor his investigators were found wonting. Depending on your point of view, the case broke open, or the frame-up was sealed, when HUAC investigators were led by Chambers to a cache of pre-war documents and microfilm which he'd recently secreted in a pumpkin on his Maryland farm. The materials, he said, had rested untouched for ten years in an unused dumbwaiter shaft in the home of his nephew. They'd been meant to be his "insurance" against Communist reprisals for his testimony, but Chambers was making them public in order to prove his case. The event caused a predictable sensation in the press: among the "Pumpkin Papers" were secret State Department reports which Chambers claimed Mrs. Hiss had retyped on the family typewriter, and specimens of Alger Hiss's handwriting as well. Indicted for perjury, Hiss was convicted in 1950 (after the first trial ended in a hung jury) and was sentenced to five years' imprisonment.

The Pumpkin Papers, however, have always been dubious. The envelope in which they were supposed to have been kept was too small to hold all the materials which Chambers claimed it had; lab tests showed that stains inside the envelope did not match those on the papers it was said to contain; and so on, through a host of inconsistencies which the jury chose to ignore. Chambers' own testimony was similarly odd, filled with sworn contradictions and accounts of events which the defense was able to prove had never occurred. The press, however, had been thoroughly manipulated by Nixon and the HUAC spooks so that Hiss never really had a chance.

Today those sympathetic to Hiss are investigating the roles played by Horace Schmahl and Lou Russell, the HUAC sleuth who later went on to work for Robert Maheu and James McCord. Central to their investigation is the theory that the Pumpkin Papers were either forged on a typewriter that was later foisted upon Hiss, or that the papers were forged on a typewriter that was itself created to duplicate the characteristics of the one owned by Hiss. An excellent account of the byzantine affair is contained in *Alger Hiss: The True Story*, by John C. Smith (New York: Holt, Rinehart and Winston, 1976).

Jesus de Galindez. Still later Schmahl would move his shop to Fort Lauderdale where, in time for the Bay of Pigs and subsequent adventures, he'd become enmeshed in a host of CIA intrigues.

According to FBI reports, Schmahl was suspected by his peers of having arranged the Onassis tap for Johnny Frank and his rival, Maheu.

In any event, Schmahl is given credit for having placed Frank and Maheu in contact with telephone company employees who established the wiretapping nest in the East Sixty-second Street offices of the Schenk & Schenk insurance company. Use of the offices was secured through Maheu's friendship with Robert Judge, a prominent New York Republican financier, and William Price, a vice-president of the insurance company and—like Judge—a sometime resident of the National Republican Club. Bill Staten, a former FBI agent currently in charge of the Westinghouse Corporation's security department, handled the legwork supporting the tap. Late one night in August, Staten was told to meet three men outside a drugstore on East Sixty-second Street. The men, all of them clean-cut and in their thirties, identified themselves as

"William Remson."

"William Remson."

And "William Remson."

Admitting "the Remson brothers" to the Schenk offices, Staten watched as they unloaded their equipment. "They asked me to go out for sandwiches and Q-Tips," Staten recalls. "I couldn't figure out what the hell they intended to do with tips for pool cues . . . but then they explained." (Q-Tips are cotton-tipped swabs sometimes used with alcohol to clean the magnetic heads of tape recorders.) With the tap in operation on two of Onassis's five office lines, Staten joined with other Maheu operatives Bill Seerey and John Murphy in surveilling the shipping magnate's office manager. "The guy had very regular hours," Staten recalls. "He'd go to the office early and a few hours later I'd 'take him to lunch.' Then back to the office until nightfall, then home to his apartment a few blocks away. He never went anywhere at all."

The surveillance, however, was only one of Staten's tasks. While he never saw the Remsons again, the wiretap was in operation for months and it was Staten's job to open and close the Schenk offices, picking up packages of tapes. "After the first time I never saw anyone in the offices. There were three rooms and whenever I showed up, the package would be waiting for me on a desk. I'd pick it up and take it back to the National Republican Club." There Taggart, today an employee of the State Department's Agency for International Development (AID), would "edit" the tapes while Staten—who was paid four dollars per hour for his services—would visit Niarchos' offices. "I had to pick up money from Niarchos' man, a guy we called Ambi.* It amounted to one thousand five hundred dollars per week, and I'd bring it back to J.J. at the Club." Since Frank was thought to be the personal contact with the Remsons, it was assumed that "Ambi's cash" was meant for them. But that was never certain. Frank was also being paid large sums by Ray Taggart—who thought the tap cost $1,200 per week. Maheu partner Tom LaVenia, however, was told that Maheu was being paid only $1,800 *per month* by Niarchos. Straightening out the financial details of the operation, though, seems an impossible task. FBI sources stated flatly that the taps cost Niarchos $750 *per day*, and that the total cost of the wiretap was $187,000. Additionally, the same FBI sources reported that Maheu received checks in the amounts of $5,000, $10,000, and $20,000 drawn on Niarchos' Bermuda account and cashed by Maheu at the Liberty National Bank in the nation's capital.

Whatever the sum, Maheu's men were busy. Since only two of Onassis's five lines were tapped, Taggart was responsible for acquiring the Greek's telephone toll slips to check out calls made on the three lines that were "clean." Using "city directories" (for example, *Polk's*), consecutive lists of telephone numbers with the subscribers' names beside, Taggart was able to identify whom Onassis had called on the clean lines.

Throughout this time Onassis was conferring with his lawyers concerning negotiations with Justice Department attorney Warren Burger. Nicknamed "the Admiral" for the fact that he'd seized a dozen ships belonging to Onassis, Burger was in overall charge of the civil case pending against the tycoon. Whether the tap compromised his defense strategy is uncertain. Meanwhile, though, other conferences were taking place on Capitol Hill in the offices of Vice President Richard Nixon. Conferring with Nixon were Maheu and a journalist-spook named John Gerrity. A florid and beefy Irishman from Boston, Gerrity recalls that "Nixon gave us the whole bit— you know, the 'Your assignment, John, should you choose to accept it . . .' sort of thing. He kept saying that this was a top-secret, highly sensitive national-security matter, and that if we took the assignment

* "Ambi" was Niarchos aide Ambrose Kaparis.

and got caught—well, the government couldn't be of any help. They'd deny all involvement. Well, I told him I thought that was standard procedure, and he said, 'Of course, of course it is: I just want to be sure you understand.' " After that, Gerrity says, Nixon insisted on regular briefings, and on occasion the spook conferred with Burger as well. (Gerrity is currently the Washington Editor of the *Daily Bond Buyer*.)

Ray Taggart, Bill Staten, and the others agree that the operation was regarded by them as "national-security work."

"Maheu was always talking about how the CIA was involved and everything. He kept giving us national-security pep talks about how it was all for the country's good," Taggart recalled. And that may have been the case, but the truth is that the CIA became involved only after the operation was under way. "The wiretap," Maheu says, "was useful. But my most important contribution was getting the CIA involved. You can't imagine how hard it was to convince them that the national interest was at stake." The Agency, then, gave its sanction to the operation *after the fact*.

Gerrity remembers that he personally had two CIA officers at his command as he and Maheu traveled through Europe, searching for a way to undo the Jiddah Agreement. "They [the CIA men] were supposed to be my 'mentors,' and they were right out of the book: trench coats, white-flannel pants, the whole bit. They played their cards awfully close to their chests, if you know what I mean, and they were always calling me from pay phones—you know, at six o'clock in the morning. I'd be in the rack at some Paris hotel and they'd start ringing at dawn, saying, 'Meet us at the Arc de Triomphe' or wherever. Well, I wasn't going to meet anyone *any*where at six A.M. I remember, though, one of them was named DiMaggio and he looked a helluva lot like the ballplayer. I asked him one time if he was any relation, and he just smiled. They did that a lot: ask them a question, and they'd smile. Spooky pair, no question about it."

Just when the Agency first became involved in the plot is unknown, though it must certainly have been prior to the wiretap's installation in August. As far back as February, only a few days after Ari's arrest in New York, Gerrity and Maheu had arranged publication of the Jiddah Agreement's contents in an Italian newspaper secretly owned by the CIA. That, along with Ari's arrest and the resulting scandal, made up the initial assault on the shipping magnate. Thereafter, it was a simple matter to coordinate hostile publicity: in rapid succession the Greek tycoon was blasted in the world's press by his competitors, by Stavros Niarchos, and by spokesmen for Aramco and other multinationals.

As Onassis put it, "All hell broke loose." Thanks to Gerrity's purchase of editorial space abroad, newspapers editorialized that the contract was the key to an international plot designed to wrest control of Arabian oil from American interests. According to this conspiracy theory, the Arabs intended to nationalize Aramco's holdings once Onassis's ships were in a position to guarantee an outlet for their oil. German technicians, it was said, would replace the Americans. In fact, some papers hinted, the "plot" represented the reawakening of German militance. Schacht's role in the affair was ominous in itself, conjuring visions of a neo-Nazi renaissance. Suddenly, Onassis's Argentinian citizenship appeared sinister—sympathetic to Hitler during the Second World War, the Peron dictatorship was a notorious haven for war criminals. By association with Schacht and the gauchos, Onassis came to be seen as a dangerous character, and newspapers were quick to point out that his construction contracts were responsible for the rebirth of the German shipbuilding industry—an essential component in "any future war."

To this xenophobia the oil companies added their own criticisms, pointing out that the Jiddah Agreement posed a threat to the American way of life: by inveigling a share of the multinationals' monopoly in Saudi Arabia, they reasoned, Onassis somehow jeopardized the free enterprise system itself. The reasoning was loony but, at the height of the Korean war, it sufficed.

And still the campaign against Onassis was only getting under way. With some of his ships seized, the remainder boycotted, and criminal charges pending against him, the Greek was suddenly branded "anti-American" by none other than J. Edgar Hoover. Coming in 1954, at the height of the Cold War, the accusation had all the force of a financial death penalty. It was delivered in the pages of the New York *Daily News*, which quoted a secret letter supposedly written years earlier by the FBI's legendary director. In it, Hoover accused Onassis of having expressed "sentiments inimical to the United States war effort"—a charge that infuriated Onassis, who had, in fact, placed himself and his entire fleet at the disposal of the Secretary of the Navy upon the outbreak of hostilities in Korea. By this time, however, Onassis realized that the campaign against him was well organized and spearheaded by his former partner, Niarchos. "What I'd like to know," he raged, "is how my brother-in-law can get such a government document." The answer, of course, is that the resources of the American intelligence community had been placed at the disposal of Maheu and Niarchos. The secret letter was leaked to the *Daily News* in much the same way that details of the Jiddah Agreement were leaked to European papers. The multinationals, with Nixon, Maheu, Niarchos, and Gerrity as their flunkies, were preparing to destroy the "Glamorous Greek" with every dirty trick at their disposal. And Onassis could expect little sympathy: to most Americans, "the King of Monte Carlo" was made to appear as an anti-American crook in league with former Nazis to destroy the free enterprise system.

Still, Onassis was not one to capitulate in the face of legal threats and smears. He'd survived the sack of Smyrna, prospered in Patagonia, and forged an empire by taking risks that no one else would dare. He'd bootlegged arak to the Turks and he knew how to stand his ground. And yet the ground he stood upon kept shifting beneath his feet: Maheu was no ordinary opponent. On the contrary, he fought with the advantage of an invisible man.

In April, the Saudi contract was finally implemented by royal decree, solemnizing the Jiddah Agreement arrived at three months earlier. With the contract a *fait accompli*, it appeared to Onassis that he'd weathered the storm. In June, the *Al-Malik Saud Al Awal*, largest supertanker of its time, would be christened with holy water from Zemzem, the sacred spring of Mecca. And yet before that could happen, a bizarre incident occurred at Nice Airport. There Onassis was confronted by a middleman with whom he'd had some earlier dealings. That was Spyridon Catapodis, a stocky Greek who made a profession of brokering deals in the eastern Mediterranean. Catapodis had been present in Saudi Arabia in January for the celebration honoring the Jiddah Agreement, and it's apparent that he played some role in the earliest stages of negotiations between Onassis and the Arabs. For whom he worked, however, would later become a matter of dispute.

In any case, the meeting in Nice was an unpleasant one. As Onassis prepared to embark upon a flight to London, Catapodis rushed across the tarmac with a flurry of curses, spit in his face, and proceeded to strangle him. While spectators gasped and Ari O. sank to his knees with the color draining from his face, Catapodis issued the ultimate insult to a Greek, calling him a Turk. With that extraordinary scene played out, the middleman released his victim and strode off. There were scores of witnesses, and news of the confrontation swept the Riviera.

Onassis, then, had another enemy besides those forces represented by Niarchos, and this one had the advantage of being privy to details of how the Jiddah Agreement was reached. The news could not have escaped Maheu's attention, Onassis having earlier been placed under surveillance. Indeed, it's likely that Catapodis was working with Maheu all along. Costa Gratsos, a longtime Onassis confidant, states flatly that this was so. "Catapodis was a legendary gambler, always in debt," Gratsos told me. "I'm sure he was bribed. He had to have been." What makes this seem probable are the circumstances surrounding Maheu's emplacement of a bug in Ari's Paris quarters. That Maheu did, in fact, bug Onassis in Paris he admits—but leaves to our imagination precisely how "the technical installation" was accomplished. In this regard an earlier confrontation between Onassis and Catapodis, which took place on January 30, 1954, is worth mentioning. Accompanying Catapodis to Ari's Paris apartment was Leon ("Lou") Turrou, ostensibly an employee of J. Paul Getty, arguably the world's richest man and one of Onassis's most important clients. Turrou, like Maheu, was an ex-FBI man. During the war he'd risen to the rank of colonel, serving as an Army intelligence officer. Reliable sources report that after the war he enlisted with the CIA as a deep-cover operative in Paris, using the Getty organization as a front. A personal friend of Getty's, Onassis had every reason to trust those who seemed to be in the billionaire's employ. Accordingly, there was no reason for him to suspect anything might be amiss when Catapodis and Turrou visited him. And yet within days of that meeting the Maheu team would leak details of the Jiddah Agreement to a CIA newspaper in Italy and eleven commercial papers in London. While it's a matter of speculation, it seems *very* likely that Maheu's "technical installation" was placed in Onassis's apartment during the tycoon's meeting with the mysterious Lou Turrou and Spyridon Catapodis. A few months later, of course, the once friendly Catapodis would go beserk at the Nice airport, cursing and attacking his friend in front of witnesses.

The two events seem to be related. Both the Paris bug and the assault would pay strategic parts in the war against Onassis. In September, only a few months after his violent confrontation on the Riviera, Catapodis filed a sixteen-page affidavit in Paris. The document charged Onassis with a most egregious fraud. According to Catapodis, the original inspiration for what became the Jiddah Agreement was his. He had acted, moreover, on Onassis's behalf throughout the deal, arranging to bribe an assortment of Arab sheiks. Onassis, however, is said to have double-crossed Catapodis, cheating him out of multimillion-dollar commissions that he'd been promised. Hjalmar Schacht, Catapodis said, was only brought into the negotiations to finalize the deal over the heads of those Arabs with whom Catapodis had already reached agreement. He could prove this, Catapodis alleged, except for a diabolical trick supposedly carried out by Onassis. The contract between himself and Ari, he claimed, spelled out the details of his own commissions, but Onassis had signed it in *disappearing* ink. In January, Catapodis had withdrawn his private contract from his personal safe, to refresh his memory of those details. To his horror, he said, Ari's signature on the contract was faded beyond recognition. Immediately, he'd contacted Lou Turrou and, accompanied by him, rushed to the Onassis apartment. There, with Turrou as a witness, he'd discussed the peculiar happenstance of the vanishing ink, winning Onassis's promise of a new contract, properly signed. Alas, Catapodis said, the wily Onassis had casually slipped the original contract into his jacket, failing to return it. Neither he nor Turrou had objected to the supposed sleight of hand, and thus the only "evidence" of his alleged employment by Onassis was missing and presumed destroyed. When, after two months, Onassis failed to replace the agreement (Catapodis continued), he'd realized that he'd been tricked, and in a fury, he'd confronted his "former employer" at the airport.

Not surprisingly, the Catapodis story, with its glamorous principals and sensational details, was widely reported in the international press. Amazingly, though, it was also *believed*—partly because people preferred to think that Onassis was capable of such bizarre tricks, and partly because Catapodis claimed to have evidence that Saudi officials were bribed to facilitate the so-called Mystery Pact. For his part, Onassis was agape, and he denied virtually every detail of the convoluted story. Schacht was his representative, Onassis said, and not Catapodis. There was never any contract between himself and Catapodis, nor had the latter ever been his employee. On the contrary—Onassis knew him only as "a peddler of deals." As for the missing signature on the alleged contract, the story was absurd: "What do they think I do—go around with disappearing ink in my pen?"

In fact, that was precisely what the public thought.

And still the assault against Onassis wasn't over. The boycott against him was beginning to take a multimillion-dollar toll as scores of ships remained at anchor, charterless. Niarchos and the presidents of U. S. oil companies took every opportunity to attack the ostracized Greek in public, delivering diatribes before the Los Angeles World Affairs Council and other prestigious groups. Catapodis retained Maheu's friend, attorney Edward Bennett Williams, and filed lawsuits on two continents, seeking millions in damages, and no less a luminary than Assistant Attorney General Warren Burger was placed in charge of the federal case against Onassis. Meanwhile, a fifth front was opened. For years Onassis had been operating one of the world's largest whaling operations, a sea hunt in which his ships sailed the icy Humboldt Current beside the western coast of South America. In the midst of his dispute with the oil companies, however, the government of Peru embarked upon a peculiar diplomatic course. Henceforth, it said, Peru would enforce its 1952 declaration extending its territorial waters 200 miles offshore. Obviously, the small nation had no expectation of securing world approval for this decision, but that was hardly its intention. The enforcement of a two-hundred-mile limit was a passing contrivance that allowed Peru, perhaps at the behest of the CIA, to attack Onassis in the multinationals' behalf. And attack it did. On November 15, Peruvian destroyers sailed 180 miles off the coast to surprise and capture four Onassis whalers. Shortly after dawn on the following day, the fleet's mother ship, *Olympic Challenger*, was circled by a Peruvian fighter plane, which ordered it to "Proceed immediately toward the coast." Ignoring that order, the mother ship went full speed ahead in the direction of Japan. Immediately, the Peruvian fighter rained bombs on the vessel, ripping apart its hull beneath the waterline. When the *Challenger* began to limp, the fighter swooped down upon it, strafing its decks with machine-gun fire and scattering its crew. Before the ship's radio went dead, its position was reported as 380 miles off the Peruvian coast—hardly an aggressive proximity to the Land of the Llamas. The following day, two more Onassis whalers were captured, though a half-dozen smaller ships were able to scatter in fog and heavy weather, straggling into Panama a few days later.

The war against Onassis was suddenly a literal one, and the pressure was almost crushing. His operations were being devastated, with a dozen tankers under seizure in the United States, half his whaling fleet impounded in Peru, and his supertankers (including the recently launched *Al-Malik Saud Al Awal*) boycotted at a cost of ten thousand dollars per day. In addition, his reputation was in ruins, he remained under indictment, and the word was out that doing business with Onassis meant trouble.

And still Maheu persisted in his work behind the scenes. In addition to his other problems, Onassis was hit with a $1,600,000 libel suit filed by Maheu's friend Williams on behalf of Catapodis. The suit charged Onassis with having defamed Catapodis by implying that he, Catapodis, had forged the "contracts" upon which Onassis's signature had supposedly "disappeared." Meanwhile, as Williams kept the home fires burning, Maheu traveled incognito to Saudi Arabia with alleged evidence that the Jiddah Agreement was a product of bribery. Shortly before Maheu's arrival in the desert kingdom, however, old King Ibn Saud passed away (some thought the passage to have been expedited with arsenic) and his eldest son, Emir Saud, assumed the burdens of the throne. Rioting had broken out in the oil fields (a unique incident in the annals of Arabia), and there was talk of Communist subversion, a coup, and worse. All this worked in Maheu's favor. While in the private employment of Niarchos, he had the full backing of the U. S. government and, more particularly, of the CIA. Accordingly, he encountered little difficulty in convincing the new king that his situation was parlous and that his hold upon the throne might depend upon his cooperation with Aramco and the United States. Lacking American support, Emir Saud might well find himself out of a job.

What evidence of bribery was presented to the new king is unknown. But shortly after Maheu left, Sheik Abdullah Al Sulaiman, Minister of Finance and the architect of Saudi Arabia's economic infrastructure, was purged from office. Sheik Sulaiman was the late King Ibn Saud's major-domo, having signed the original oil concession with Aramco in 1933, and it was he who'd negotiated the Jiddah Agreement with Hjalmar Schacht. Sulaiman's departure, then, placed the Onassis contract in a precarious position, and his replacement made that position clear: Onassis was ordered to discuss the Jiddah Agreement with Aramco executives in Cairo. Unless Aramco approved the agreement and a settlement between Onassis and the multinationals was reached, the deal would never be implemented. The Arabs could not afford to lose American support, and the new Minister of Finance threatened to invalidate the contract if détente with the multinationals couldn't be reached.

Meanwhile, back in the Andes, the Peruvians found themselves outgunned by a stratagem of the Greek's. Days before Onassis had sent his ships into the Humboldt Current in search of whales, he'd secured five million pounds of insurance from Lloyd's of London, indemnifying himself against virtually any loss. That amount (roughly $15,000,000 at the time) was twice the worth of his entire whaling fleet. Should the Peruvians fail to release the ships, or impose exorbitant fines upon them, Lloyd's would suffer the loss rather than Onassis. Indeed, he might even profit from the punishment. Alarmed by this turn of events, the Peruvians backed down when confronted by a financial S.W.A.T. team of Etonian dragoons in pinstriped suits and lead-gray foulards.

The affair was finally coming to a close. The criminal and civil litigation against Onassis was easily settled once the embattled tycoon agreed to meet in Cairo with representatives of Aramco. That meeting took place on schedule, in June, 1956, the same month in which Warren Burger was appointed to the country's second most important court: the District of Columbia Court of Appeals. The out-of-court agreement reached by Burger and Onassis was a complicated one that left the tycoon's attorneys grinning. "Ari was supposed to pay seven million dollars," the shipping magnate's attorney, Ed Ross, told me, "but the whole thing was done with mirrors. It was all set up to make Burger look good, but the fact of the matter is we beat him everywhere. We even got a better deal than Niarchos." Meanwhile, the Catapodis suits wasted away (for lack of jurisdiction and lack of evidence), finally dying, while the Jiddah Agreement itself was abandoned with the consent of both parties. In July, the Onassis supertanker *King Saud I* set sail from Saudi Arabia to Philadelphia, carrying a monumental load of oil under contract to the Socony-Vacuum Corporation. Only a few months earlier, that firm's president, B. Brewster Jennings, had publicly deplored Onassis, claiming that the shipowner was on a course that would wreck the economies of several small countries. Then, the *King Saud I* had been languishing in Hamburg's harbor, a victim of the oil companies' boycott, and one that reportedly cost Onassis $10,000 per day. Obviously, the rift between the multinationals and Onassis had healed. Even the bellicose Peruvians, premature 200-mile-limiters that they were, had come to see the light (thanks to the Brits).

Not that Onassis's troubles were entirely over. The boycott against him had permitted his rivals to snap up contracts that he himself would have liked to have had—as a result, a large number of his ships remained idle and without work, costing money rather than making it. Almost as bad was a controversy relating to another of his operations: a whaler of the first rank, Onassis would soon be accused in the press of having violated an array of laws having to do with the beasts' protection. Photostatic copies of his whaling firm's secret records, including kill-tables and the logs of several ships, would be revealed, showing that Onassis ignored the season imposed upon the slaughter of whales; that he encouraged his fleet to kill protected species for higher profits; that he caused the ships' records to be faked in order to disguise the fact that hunters were decimating the dwindling population of humpback whales; and that Latin American inspectors responsible for overseeing the international whaling conventions had been bribed to cover up Onassis's financial and ecological peccadilloes. The resulting furor made "the King of Monte Carlo" even more notorious, though he claimed that some of the documents had been forged. Whether they were or were not is uncertain, though anything seems possible in view of Maheu's earlier machinations against the tycoon. In any case, the source of the incriminating documents deserved to be suspect. He was an expatriate Norwegian turncoat living in Argentina, a World War II supporter of the Nazi puppet Vidkun Quisling. Onassis had given him a job some years before, and he'd repaid the shipping magnate's kindness (if kindness it was) by betraying him as well. Perhaps, however, he merely wanted to make amends to his homeland: Onassis's Olympic Whaling Company was in partnership with a second organization, the First German Whaling Company, and the private combine was cutting deeply into the fishing economy of Norway, Scandinavia's poorest country. In any case, the turncoat was rewarded for his "whistle-blowing," returning home from the pampas to a new job in Norway. There, he would not be prosecuted for his wartime collaboration, and neither would he suffer any personal retribution.

Still, none of this did Onassis any permanent harm. Sick of the whaling controversy, he eloped from it, selling his fleet to the Japanese (at an excellent price). Even the boycott against his oil tankers ultimately worked to his advantage. While the boycott was in place against him, and his ships lay idle, he suffered, watching Niarchos snap up every long-term contract available. In the summer of 1956, however, history intervened to save Onassis from disaster and to make him wealthier than he'd ever been or ever expected to be. The event that saved him was Egypt's decision to nationalize the Suez Canal. In the brief skirmish that followed, Egypt was crushed but used that trump card so unique to Middle East diplomacy: that is, it cut off its nose to spite its face, deliberately immobilizing the canal by sinking ships in its center. The effect of this was to force those shipping oil from the Mideast to send it around Cape Horn, doubling the number of tankers needed to carry it. Suddenly, Onassis was able to dictate terms to his former persecutors. Thanks to the boycott, his fleet was the only one available to fill the gap created by the wreckage of Suez. This advantage he used to compensate for his recent difficulties, hammering out contracts at rates that staggered the industry. Whereas his ships formerly broke even carrying oil at four dollars per ton, "the King of Monte Carlo" (let them *eat* that) escalated the price to *sixty dollars per ton*. He had upward of a hundred ships at his command, and all of a sudden even his smallest tankers were making a million-dollar profit every time they left the Persian Gulf. The same benefits, of course, did not accrue to Niarchos or to his other competitors—who had, through the boycott, taken advantage of the ostracized Onassis to sign long-term contracts at what soon became "the old rates."

None of which was Maheu's concern. He'd already been handsomely rewarded for his deployment of dirty tricks, and the operation might just as well be forgotten. And yet the operation ought not to be forgotten: it was a prelude to Watergate whose importance was larger than any contract, more substantial than the financial fate of a single man. In the Onassis caper, the CIA became the financial instrument of a private consortium led by Vice President Richard Nixon—who would later use the Plumbers in similar ways for ostensibly political ends. Clearly, the Onassis affair constituted an early and historic abuse of the CIA's charter, perhaps establishing a pattern for years to come. According to Harold Stassen, privy to the National Security Council (NSC) meetings that occurred at that time, there was no discussion of the Jiddah Agreement, nor was there any discussion at NSC meetings of using the CIA against Onassis. Nixon's "Mission Impossible" speech to Gerrity, therefore, appears to have been his own idea—foreshadowing not only his later use of the Plumbers, but also the way in which he would conspire to deceive the NSC about Chile in 1972, setting the murderous "Track Two" in motion outside all government channels. Whether President Eisenhower (or the new CIA director, Allen Dulles) knew of his conspiracy against Onassis is a moot point—as is the question of whether Nixon and/or the GOP received a *quid pro quo* from the oil companies. Laws pertaining to campaign contributions hardly favored disclosure in the mid-Fifties, though John Gerrity for one has always suspected that the oil companies did indeed reward Nixon and the GOP.

Warren Burger's role, like Nixon's, is opaque and disquieting. According to Gerrity, who says he reported "regularly" on the plot to the Vice President, Burger was also kept informed of the operation against Onassis. The reporter-spook says he met with Burger on more than one occasion, including once at a private house in Washington, and discussed the Onassis affair with him. If so (and Gerrity is one who seems no longer to have any reason to dissemble in the matter), then Burger seems to have been party to a conspiracy in which the Justice Department was used as a tool of private and political interests. It wouldn't have been the first time that the future Chief Justice was linked to improprieties at the Justice Department. During his tenure as head of the Civil Division, he apparently participated in the legal cover-up that resulted when a tennis pro, hospitalized for depression in New York, was poisoned with a mescaline derivative in a secret Army experiment conducted without his knowledge or consent. It was Burger's signature on the letter to the man's survivors, masking details of the athlete's death, and preparing the way for a pitiful (and entirely unjust) settlement.

As for Edward Bennett Williams, his involvement in the affair is almost as murky as Burger's. Besides his representation of Catapodis, Williams is said to have spoken with Gerrity on several occasions. The subject of those discussions, according to Gerrity, were details of Saudi Arabian shipping contracts; the reporter had sought out the lawyer's advice, and Williams had been forthcoming. In view of those conversations, the lawyer's efforts in behalf of Catapodis, and Williams' travels abroad with Maheu at the height of the Onassis affair, it seems likely that Williams' role in the affair was larger than has so far been revealed. Admittedly, it's difficult to imagine a Democrat of Williams' stature occupying a central place in Richard Nixon's schemes, but, as we've seen, Williams was counsel to the right-wing Senator Joseph McCarthy at the same time (the Senate's deliberation on the censure of McCarthy began in August, 1954, the same month in which the three "William Remsons" met to wiretap Onassis). Twenty years later, according to John Dean, Nixon would blame Williams for his Watergate troubles and swear to "go after" him. And H. R. Haldeman would agree, saying ". . . that is a guy we've got to ruin." * But, in the Fifties, Williams represented Hoffa and the Teamsters, and feuded with Nixon's own arch-enemies, the Kennedys. If anything, Nixon and Williams had a great commonality of interest in the mid-Fifties, and might easily have collaborated on various projects.

It would be nice, of course, to ask Williams, Nixon, and Burger about their version of these events, but all three have repeatedly declined to be interviewed on the subject. Maheu is only somewhat more forthcoming, discounting the importance of the wiretap. In his view, the key elements in the affair were his ability to acquire evidence that a bribe had been paid to Saudi officials and, earlier, his success in persuading government officials to take an adverse, "national security" stance on the Jiddah Agreement. This persuasion, Maheu claims, paved the way for the CIA's involvement and, ultimately, for the Agreement's undoing. Behind it all, however, was Nixon, and behind him the oil companies. Along with "Tailgunner Joe," Nixon had been a member of the Senate investigative subcommittee led by Senator Clyde Hoey during 1951 and 1952. It was that subcommittee which conducted the initial investigation of the surplus ship sales, holding that a fraud had been committed and urging the Justice Department to conduct its own investigation. That, of course, led to the Niarchos and Onassis indictments. In the meantime, Nixon had been picked as the GOP's Vice Presidential candidate: Herbert Brownell, Jr., later Attorney General and Burger's boss at the Justice Department during the anti-Onassis operation, is credited with having selected Nixon for the second highest position in the government. Whether the oil companies had any say in that selection is unknown. Investigative reporter Drew Pearson, however, wrote in his diaries that his sources were convinced that the petroleum giants had actually bankrolled the Nixon candidacy—but he couldn't prove it. Certainly Nixon was helpful to Big Oil, though. Besides destroying the Jiddah Agreement, he joined in those National Security Council (NSC) deliberations that led to the gutting of an antitrust case brought by the Justice Department against the "Seven Sisters." That case was at its most critical point in 1953–54 when (as we'll see in Chapter XII) the NSC invoked "national security" in the oil giants' behalf, classifying reams of Aramco documents "Top Secret." That effectively prevented their use in or out of court, crippling the suit. Ultimately,

---

* John Dean, *Blind Ambition* (New York: Simon and Schuster, 1976), p. 134.

consent orders agreed to by exhausted and betrayed Justice Department attorneys would serve only to sanction the very practices which their antitrust suit had sought to remedy. It would be astonishing, therefore, if the oil companies had *not* rewarded Nixon and the GOP for their efforts in the multinationals' behalf: their very existence, let alone their profitability, was owed to Ike's minions.

Through it all, one theme seems to have been dominant, and to have echoed historically: the abuse of the "national security" rubric to provide a quasi-legal facade for private operations carried out in violation of the CIA's charter. So it was that Ray Taggart, Bill Staten, and the other private spooks had no compunctions about the wiretaps: like the Cubans at Watergate, they believed themselves to be carrying out a sensitive government assignment ordained by the CIA. As Vice President, Richard Nixon was able to define the caper as one that was essential to American defense—without, of course, it ever actually being so. Still, the legality of it all was more apparent than real. The CIA's charter has always forbidden it to carry out domestic operations. The Onassis caper clearly violated that injunction. It matters very little that the domestic aspect was handled by a supposedly private operative: Maheu was at that time in the pay of the Agency, his men relied upon his assurances that they were participating in a CIA endeavor, and, what's more, the domestic and international phases of the operation were closely coordinated at the highest levels of government by the spook Gerrity. According to Ray Taggart, Maheu and Gerrity became "inseparable" during the operation, working together on the plot's every aspect. Robert A. Maheu Associates, therefore, seems to have been from its very inception a mechanism for Nixon and the CIA to circumvent the Agency's charter against domestic operations. We may well wonder if there were other such firms established for the same purposes. Whether that is so, the war against Onassis illustrates very clearly how the country's most powerful institutions—the press, the courts, the CIA, and even the telephone company—can be manipulated and compromised by a powerful few determined to maximize their political and financial fortunes.

Finally, Onassis's side of the story remains to be told, though it's unlikely that it ever will be. While his imbroglios with Catapodis, Peru, and the oil companies were reported in the world's press at the time of their occurrence, Onassis was alone in his belief that these events were related to one another. Lacking proof (and knowledge of Maheu's involvement), the beleaguered billionaire was unable to persuade the world that he was the victim of an extravagant plot masterminded by his brother-in-law. Not until the waning months of 1975, after the shipping magnate had died, was Maheu's shady role in the so-called "Mystery Pact" revealed. Whether Onassis some-how learned of Maheu's work* before his death is uncertain, but there can be no doubt that the billionaire had lately had spooks on his mind. Shortly after his son, Alexander, was killed in a small-plane crash in 1973, Onassis charged that the death was a homicide. There was evidence that the plane had been sabotaged, though Onassis couldn't be sure whether the target of the plot was himself or his son. Accordingly, he offered a one-million-dollar reward to anyone who could prove the identity of the alleged saboteur, and he spent a fortune on private investigators. He told reporters that he thought he knew who was responsible for the assassination and who the man's agent was. His suspicion, however, had yet to be proven at the time of his death in 1975, and so far no reliable sources have come forward to identify the hit-man or his paymaster.

---

* Maheu's role was sketched in a footnote to Senate Report No. 94-465 ("Alleged Assassination Plots involving Foreign Leaders"), p. 74, November 20, 1975.

HOWARD'S MAN

1 / A THEORY OF KIDNAPPING

I WAS THINKING ABOUT MAHEU'S EARLY SUCCESSES AS HE CHATTED ON the telephone in the bar of the Georgetown Inn. Many of the cases that he'd worked in the 1950s—the Onassis affair was only one—had received extensive (but ultimately insubstantial) press coverage. Usually, the public was misled about the substance of the issues involved: ignorant of Maheu's part (and of the CIA's), reporters tended to accept events at face value—while the real game, of course, was played out behind the scenes. Naïvely, the catastrophes befalling Onassis were regarded as somehow independent of one another: always wary of conspiracy theories, reporters disdained the shipping magnate's explanations and denials, giving credence to the most preposterous allegations (for example, Catapodis' charges about the disappearing signature). Had the press understood Maheu's role (or known of his employment by the CIA), it would have become obvious that the new Agency had dangerously exceeded its authority, conspiring with one group of private businessmen to ruin a rival— all the while manipulating the U. S. press and courts to achieve that end. As we've seen, it was Nixon and Maheu who enlisted the CIA in the scheme to ruin Onassis. And not the other way around. Years later, Maheu would become involved in a plot to destroy an-

other man, Fidel Castro. And in the wake of that murder plot, some
journalists, hoodlums, and spooks would charge that the scheme backfired, leading to the assassination of President John F. Kennedy.* Investigating the Castro plot, the Senate would be disturbed in 1975
to find that "lines of authority" between the CIA and its agents
were deliberately blurred—and that the scheme's origins were therefore obscure. No one could say precisely whose idea it was, though
everyone assumed that the plan originated within the Agency. As
the Onassis affair demonstrated, however, the CIA is sometimes
a tool of its agents, rather than vice versa. There is, therefore, a
possibility that the plot to kill Castro was dreamed up by the Mafia—
as represented by Santos Trafficante, Sam Giancana, and Johnny
Roselli—who then prevailed upon their friend Maheu to obtain
the Agency's cooperation and assistance. Admittedly, while the
Onassis caper provides a precedent for such a reversal of authority,
there is yet but little evidence to support the possibility that I've
raised (and just as little to deny it). Giancana and Roselli have been
brutally murdered. Trafficante absented himself from the United
States during the Senate's investigation of the Castro assassination
plot, returning only to take the Fifth in connection with the JFK
hit. Maheu's testimony, and that of the CIA officers with whom he
worked, is vague on the question of whose idea it was to knock off
Castro—but then, one would hardly expect the Agency or its representatives (or, for that matter, the Senate) to willingly acknowledge
that this country's intelligence service has, at times, been a pawn of
organized crime. To use the Mob is one thing; to be used by it is
quite another.

The point is that we're only beginning to understand the complex workings and significance of *having* a national intelligence
agency. American reporters working in the early Fifties could not
have easily questioned or revealed the CIA's role in then-current
events. To have done so would have placed their loyalty in question.
Moreover, the CIA was then so new (only seven years old when the
Jiddah Agreement was signed) that few gave it much consideration,
and *no* reporter dared to publicly criticize it. As a result, the Agency
was for decades left alone to conceal its transgressions—to the detri-
ment of both itself and the country which it's supposed to serve.

---

* George Crile, a Washington editor of *Harper's* magazine, has alleged this in a
Washington Post article. John Roselli, the hoodlum, and Joe Shimon, Maheu's friend
and cut-out man in the plot to kill Castro, have both put forward theories supporting
that view.

During the same period, the Agency's graduates (some retired, some expelled) came to play almost as large a role in business as they had in secret politics. They were, therefore, twice removed from scrutiny: few knew where they'd come from, and fewer knew what they'd come to do. And while the federal intelligence community has lately become the object of intensive scrutiny by the press, its commercial counterpart has remained almost invisible, with the result that our understanding of events in the private sector tends to be superficial when it's not entirely misguided. If there is a lesson, it is this: merely knowing that Robert Maheu or his colleagues are involved in a transaction should cause us to examine it with the same suspicion that we might formerly have reserved for acts of war. The clandestine expertise that constitutes the stock-in-trade of every spook is, in fact, a martial art. And whether it's applied to geopolitics or geocommerce, the means are often the same: deception, deniability, and dirty tricks.

"Where were we?" Maheu settled himself into his armchair, relighting the thin brown cigar which he'd extinguished while talking on the phone.

"I think—we were talking about Hughes. About his having been kidnapped."

"Impossible to prove," he said. "But the Old Man was a perfect target, isolated like that. Whoever controlled the palace guard, the Mormon Mafia, controlled him. And he knew it. He didn't trust them, whatever anyone else may say. Howard and I knew they were manipulating him: I'd send him messages, or he'd send them to me, and they'd never be received. The Mormons were censoring our communications: they'd tell me the Old Man was 'out'—when I knew that he'd just had a [blood] transfusion and that he was fully conscious. Eventually, we began timing our messages. We knew it took so many minutes and so many seconds for something to be delivered from here to there—and we'd give instructions for the communiqué to be delivered *immediately*. Sometimes it never arrived. More often, there was a delay—a few minutes here and there. We suspected that the letters were being copied by the palace guard.

"Listen," he said, leaning forward. "No one will ever prove anything about Howard Hughes. In fact, I doubt that he'll ever be seen by anyone again—assuming he's still alive."

"In the press conference—"

"I know. He promised a return to public life." Maheu laughed, reaching for his glass of wine. "It will never happen," he said. "He should—at best—he should be in a hospital. What kind of hospital, I'm not sure. You know—this kidnapping business . . . It was very well planned. Peloquin and Crosby, the Intertel people, came through Las Vegas months before Mr. Hughes disappeared. They wanted to look at our security system, supposedly to compare it with the Resorts' [International] operation in the Bahamas. What they were actually doing, of course, was casing the place. They were going to take over, and they wanted to know our weak points. And we showed them. That was a mistake. There had been indications— well, Bill Gay * was on the outs with the Old Man. Hughes hated him for having ruined his marriage with Jean Peters. (It wasn't Bill's fault, actually, but Hughes blamed him anyway.) And Chester Davis † had fallen from grace. He nearly cost us half-a-billion dollars. They were both on the edge of being fired—and both of them are very ambitious men. Gay wants to be an elder of the Mormon Church and Davis—you never met a more Machiavellian pair. And Nadine Henley: Hughes didn't even know she was still working for him until I mentioned her. And he was shocked. 'That bitch?' he said. 'Is she still on the payroll?' And now look who's running the show: Gay, Davis, and Henley. It's incredible. It's also incredible that Hughes would have placed himself and his affairs in the hands of an outfit owned by business rivals. But I should have seen it coming. Bill Gay approached me on several occasions, suggesting that we take over the Hughes operation from the Old Man. I have witnesses to that proposal—but I never took it very seriously. Now, of course, I wonder."

"You think Hughes is being held against his will?"

Maheu shrugged. "What will? I doubt that he even knows he's in the Bahamas. I suspect that he's either unconscious or deceived. It wouldn't be so hard. One hotel room is very like another—or can be made to seem so. His notion of time is terribly distorted: he can lose an entire week without knowing it. It would be a simple matter to provide the Old Man with day-old copies of the Las Vegas *Sun*, day-old video tapes of Las Vegas television shows, and so on. I'm not saying this has happened. I doubt that anything so elaborate would be necessary. Howard Hughes could be in a hotel room on Mars, and so long as the television worked and the news came from Vegas,

---

* Frank Bill Gay is a top executive of Hughes's Summa Corporation.
† Chester Davis is chief counsel for Summa.

he'd have no reason to suspect that he was anywhere other than nine floors above the Strip. You have to realize, the Mormons controlled every input and output involving the Old Man. He never looked out the window. Time was meaningless."

To Robert Maheu, the possibility that his former boss was kidnapped from Las Vegas in November, 1970, will always be real. The notion is a shocking one, of course—but no more shocking than revelations concerning Hughes's physical condition, appearance, and the circumstances of his last years. A dying drug addict, he was effectively *entombed* from 1971 until his biological death in 1975 in a succession of heavily guarded penthouses whose windows were blacked out and shuttered against the sun. Like a corpse in an air-conditioned coffin, Hughes's body underwent a slow deterioration, with only the hair and nails exhibiting any ordinary vitality—and they, of course, grew to Ripleyan lengths, emphasizing his grotesque emaciation. Weaving in and out of narcotic comas, he is said to have spent his waking moments picking at geometric desserts while staring through the darkness at segments of old B movies. Bemused personal aides who've subsequently written self-serving accounts about Hughes make it clear that the painfully constipated and malnourished Old Man was treated by his male nurses with the spiteful contempt reserved by some for the senile and incontinent.

That Hughes may have been kidnapped is a possibility that is no more improbable than the facts so far revealed about the man. Nor is Maheu alone in suggesting that possibility. An IRS memorandum written in February, 1972, by a special agent of that service states: "It is my belief that Howard Hughes died in Las Vegas in 1970 and that key officials in charge of running his empire concealed this fact at the time in order to prevent a catastrophic dissolution of his holdings." The memo goes on to suggest that a "double" was substituted for the billionaire and "schooled in Hughes' speech, mannerisms, and eccentricities." * Removing Hughes to a foreign country, the memo suggests, was necessary "to obviate the possibility of a government intrusion by search warrant." † Maheu and some IRS agents, therefore, shared similar suspicions about Hughes's dis-

---

* In fact, Hughes *did* have a double who impersonated him on occasion during the 1960s. That was Hollywood actor Brooks Randall, who was apparently hired by Maheu to serve as a decoy in an effort to keep photographers, reporters, process servers, and private detectives away from the Old Man himself.
† The memo was obtained from the IRS by Jack Anderson and Les Whitten.

appearance, differing only on the question of whether or not the billionaire left Vegas *in vivo*. And while this disagreement would appear to have been resolved by Hughes's autopsy in 1975—suggesting that he was indeed alive when he left Las Vegas in 1970— medical definitions of death vary. The possibility has been raised (by Maheu when he referred to Karen Quinlan) that the billionaire was kept *technically* alive by means of extraordinary medical measures. If we are to believe this, however, then we must disbelieve the testimony of those who guarded him during his last five years of "life"—a skepticism that is not difficult to achieve if we also believe that Hughes was taken from Las Vegas against (or in the absence of) his will.

We may wonder if such things can happen in the United States. And yet, one needn't go far to find a precedent. In fact, Hughes's disappearance from Las Vegas may well have given Maheu a sense of *déjà vu*. In 1957, while running his "Mission Impossible" agency in Washington, Maheu was hauled before a grand jury to explain what role, if any, he or his firm had played in a contract kidnapping carried out the year before. The man asking questions of Maheu was Justice Department attorney William Hundley, who, with Robert Peloquin, would one day establish Intertel. One of Maheu's employees—John Frank, the man credited with arranging the wiretap against Onassis—was a prime suspect in the kidnapping. The victim was Jesus de Galindez, and his disappearance would change the course of Caribbean history.

2 / CONTRACT KIDNAPPING

Galindez was a Spanish Basque who'd emigrated to the Dominican Republic in the 1930s and risen to a position of influence among that country's intelligentsia—only to find himself sickened by the dictator's rule. Abandoning Hispaniola for Manhattan, he took with him a detailed knowledge of Dominican intrigue. As Galindez knew, the Trujillo dictatorship was one of the richest and cruelest in modern times. Its headman, Rafael, was a decadent paranoid whose sensual appetites were rivaled only by the sadistic excesses of his favorite son, Ramfis, a psychopath who relished other people's pain. Galindez was able to document the Trujillos' crimes, and while teaching at Columbia University, he did just that.

Throughout the winter of 1955 and into the first months of 1956, the aspiring professor worked in his Greenwich Village apartment at Tenth Street and Fifth Avenue, putting the finishing touches on a dissertation * that would describe no fewer than 140 political assassinations instigated by Trujillo over the preceding twenty-five years—almost one such murder every two months for a quarter of a century. It was the most dangerous form of scholarship possible, and Galindez knew, perhaps better than anyone else, that it would place him at the top of the charts on Trujillo's "Hit Parade." Which it did. There was no way to keep a secret from the dictator's agents in New York's Dominican exile community, and it was inevitable that news of the dissertation would reach Ciudad Trujillo. A fund-raiser for the Basque nationalists who was also a controlled agent of the FBI, Galindez was not without protection and friends. But he had no way of knowing, as the spring approached, how many spooks and spies and hit-men had converged to get him killed, or who they were.

Moving between Miami and New York were Beauty and the Beast: Ana Gloria Viera and "El Cojo." Ana Gloria was a *zaftig* Puerto Rican whore who'd cast her lot with Trujillo, becoming his personal Mata Hari. She was beautiful, and according to all accounts, a woman of marginal sophistication and few scruples. El Cojo was a short, squat man of indeterminate nationality: it was said that he spoke Spanish with a Castilian accent, and yet he claimed American citizenship by insisting that he'd been born in Puerto Rico. The FBI knew him as a Dominican agent of Trujillo's, compiling a thick dossier upon him under the name "Felix Hernandez Marques." Whether that was his real name or not, no one knew: he had at least two aliases, and perhaps as many passports, for every year of his life and there could be no certainty about his origins. What was indisputable, however, was the aptness of his moniker, El Cojo, or "the Lame One." He had a withered arm, a glass eye, a toupee, and a painful limp that invited comparisons with the movements of a crab. His voice, they say, was a ruined, menacing whisper. He and Ana Gloria had come to the United States together, bearing a twenty-thousand-dollar contract on Galindez.

Besides this pair, however, there were others with an interest in the Basque professor.† Johnny Frank, alias "John Kane" and "Jason Fort," was one. Frank was a forty-two-year-old spook, ex-FBI and ex-CIA, who worked on contract to Maheu Associates as early

---

* Published posthumously as *The Era of Trujillo*.
† The honorific was bestowed posthumously by Columbia University.

as 1954. Bright and athletic, he was a tight-lipped anti-Communist who divided his leisure time between sets of tennis with other spies and reading Voltaire in French. Not that he had much leisure time. At the recommendation of the State Department, he'd served as Trujillo's bodyguard on a trip through Europe. The two men had gotten along famously, and subsequently Frank found himself embroiled in the dictator's affairs. A resident of Washington, employed by Maheu, he nevertheless had an office in Trujillo's National Palace. At the same time, he found himself spending two months a year in New York, working out of Maheu's "safe suite" at the National Republican Club in midtown Manhattan, and using Horace Schmahl's offices in the Wall Street area. Together, Frank and Schmahl, veterans of so many secret campaigns, made quite a pair. Having served in the FBI's New York office during World War II, Frank was superbly well-connected with the Big Apple's police forces, and in particular with spooks at the city's Bureau of Special Services (BOSS-y). That was Manhattan's investigative elite, with responsibility for political surveillance, counterespionage, and the diplomatic community. A "Red Squad," and much more, BOSS-y's ranks included some of the best wiremen in the country, causing detectives such as Frank and Schmahl to make a point of their acquaintance.

In 1954, Frank was thought to have arranged a tap on the New York offices of Aristotle Onassis for Robert Maheu, the CIA, and the shipping magnate's relative, Stavros Niarchos. That job had gone off well and Frank's colleagues at Robert A. Maheu Associates credited the successful "installation" to Frank's contacts with New York police and, in particular, to a mysterious "Mr. Small." Since then Frank had become increasingly busy, commuting regularly among Washington, New York, Miami, and the Dominican Republic. Along with Maheu and Tom LaVenia, a onetime Secret Service man who was a partner in the former's "Mission Impossible" agency, Frank was engaged in negotiating with Trujillo for the establishment of a school for spies in the Dominican Republic. And while that proposition would eventually come to naught, perhaps as a result of the scandal surrounding the Galindez case, Maheu Associates would be paid $81,000 by the dictator during 1956—supposedly in return for electronic security equipment ("Grey audographs," used for bugging, and "inspectographs," X-ray devices commonly used at airports). And there was other business too. One of Frank's assignments in New York was to conduct an "investigation" of Galindez, supposedly to learn whether the professor was implicated in an alleged plot to assassinate "El Caudillo" or other members of the Trujillo family. Yet another assignment of Frank's, which he used to explain his presence in New York and his frequent contacts with Manhattan police and BOSS-y staffers, was to obtain call girls willing to service Indonesia's President Sukarno on his impending visit to the United States.

An examination of Frank's telephone toll slips at the National Republican Club suggests that he might have been involved in still other matters during 1956. Besides calls to spooks at BOSS-y, Frank repeatedly telephoned Democratic campaign committees.* Since the Maheu firm was then working for New Hampshire publisher William Loeb, helping Nixon to a place on the GOP's national ticket, it was thought that Frank was part of the Maheu team that destroyed the vice-presidential candidacy of Nixon rival Christian Herter, Harold Stassen's candidate.

Cataloging all these secret operations, one can easily understand why another Maheu Associate, Raymond Taggart, found it necessary to leave the firm after two years, complaining that the work turned him into "a nervous wreck." Frank, however, seems to have had steelier nerves and even to have enjoyed his labors behind the scenes. Outwitting men such as Onassis, impinging on U. S. elections, and dabbling in the secret affairs of foreign dictators—all of it accomplished in high style, with suites in a Manhattan club and a Caribbean palace—confer a sense of power and immunity. As one looks at Frank across the distance of years, it's easy to see in him the perfect model of a clandestine operator destined by his own hubris to take a fall. And, of course, that destiny would be fulfilled: Frank would take a series of falls. His involvement in the Galindez case would leave his covert reputation in ruins, forcing him to supplement his income as a private eye by working as a "Fifth Street lawyer." (The phrase refers to any criminal defense attorney in Wash-

---

* Interestingly, several of the BOSS-y calls went to Anthony Ulasewicz. A portly and wisecracking tough guy, Ulasewicz later achieved notoriety by serving as White House bagman to the Watergate burglars. Handling political investigations for the Nixon junta in the early 1970s, Ulasewicz was picked by Herbert Kalmbach (finance chairman for the Committee to Re-Elect the President) to make under-the-table payments to representatives of the indicted Watergate burglars and their attorneys. Carrying hundreds of thousands of dollars in a brown paper bag, and wearing a bus driver's coin changer to facilitate his many calls from public phone booths, Ulasewicz disbursed a fortune in one-hundred-dollar bills to Mrs. Dorothy Hunt (chief negotiator for the Plumbers), Hunt's attorney William Bittman, and White House mystery man Fred LaRue.

ington whose clientele is a marginal one, consisting largely of indigent burglars, punks, drunks, and junkies.) And then, along with other veterans of the Maheu agency, he'd be convicted in an industrial espionage case in 1963, going to jail for his role in what came to be called "the Mayflower Affair" (the incident is described in later pages). After that, having become the archetype of an ex-CIA officer gone bad, he'd be jailed again, in 1972, this time for embezzling a cool million dollars from Trujillo's daughter. Finally, he'd be disbarred. And in the autumn of 1977 he'd walk out of the Lewisburg pen, sixty-three years old, his life a ruin. A sad man, certainly, but there are many who say he deserved it.

In the mid-Fifties, though, Johnny Frank was on top of the world. He was running operations for Maheu out of Horace Schmahl's New York office, and there was the possibility that Trujillo might one day make him a very wealthy man indeed. How far Frank was willing to go for Trujillo is a matter of conjecture, but, as we'll see, there is ample reason to believe that he went all the way. With Ana Gloria Viera and El Cojo, Frank would emerge as one of the prime suspects in the disappearance of Jesus de Galindez.

That vanishing act took place in the freezing night air of March 12 at one of Manhattan's busiest intersections. About 9:30 P.M., Galindez left a student at Columbus Circle, telling her that he intended to take the subway home to his apartment in the Village. It was the last time that he was ever seen by a friend.

For nearly a week the absence went uncommented. Then worried students and friends reported their teacher missing. Searching his apartment, police found that Galindez hadn't been there for some time and that, moreover, he'd obviously made no plans to take the trip that (equally obviously) he'd taken. The closets were full, there was food in the refrigerator, and the mail had piled up, unopened. The latest newspaper was a morning edition dated six days earlier, the twelfth.

The outcry was furious, foreshadowing the shock expressed at the assassination of former Chilean ambassador Orlando Letelier, twenty years later in Washington. It wasn't so much that Galindez and Letelier were popular figures, which they were, but that the assassins had dared to strike in America's largest cities. As news of the Galindez book leaked out—he'd given a copy of his dissertation to a publisher only days before the disappearance—*Times'* editorialists thundered, rewards were offered, and rumors abounded about the snatch. Rummaging through the Basque's personal effects, New

York police found a note urging them, in the eventuality of his death or disappearance, to seek out his enemies in the Dominican Republic. There had been threats upon his life.

Ciudad Trujillo, however, was beyond the jurisdiction of New York police, and as for Dominican embassy employees who might be expected to have some knowledge of the affair, they were protected by diplomatic immunity. Having a motive, but no clues and no one to question, New York's Finest were left to sift gossip. As for the FBI, it shrank from the controversy, refusing appeals that it join the investigation; in later months, however, it would undertake an intensive, top-secret probe. The reasons for the Bureau's demurral, and subsequent change of heart, are easy to understand. In the absence of a ransom note or other evidence, it was convenient for the G-men to regard Galindez as a "missing person" and no more: knowing that the case would be a difficult, and perhaps impossible, one to solve, Hoover's minions had little reason to risk their reputation by committing themselves to its solution despite the fact that Galindez was himself an FBI informant. Moreover, Trujillo was regarded by Hoover and others as *the* bastion of anticommunism in the Caribbean. As "the enemy of our enemy," he was a friend. In fact, Trujillo had no politics beyond that of *"personalismo"*: he was the Maximum Leader and his friendship toward the United States was purely a matter of expedience. For years the dictator had taken pains to ingratiate the U. S. Congress, bribing (some of) its members with cash, medals, women, and presents—much as the present-day Korean regime has done. And while those outlays by Trujillo were generous, they were also easily recovered: Congress routinely appropriated more than $25,000,000 per annum as "aid" to the slave-state—much of which seems to have ended up in the Trujillo family's Liechtenstein and Swiss accounts. In addition, the Dominican leader had hired influential lobbyists outside Congress, not the least of whom was Franklin Delano Roosevelt, Jr., the former President's son and Trujillo's most conspicuous apologist. Solving the Galindez case, therefore, was a matter of low priority to many of those in high office: not only would such a solution weaken an American ally, but it would also cause an "embarrassment by association" to those who'd been honored by Trujillo. Only upon discovery of the fact that an American had also been murdered, and that a former FBI agent seemed to be behind it all, would the Bureau reverse itself and plunge into the investigation.

In the meantime, Trujillo's public relations squad embarked

upon a disinformation campaign to discredit Galindez and throw investigators off the track. Falsely smearing the professor as a Communist—comparable in the Fifties to calling someone a child-pornographer today—it then suggested that Galindez had been murdered by "fellow Marxists" in an attempt to discredit Trujillo by casting him in the role of assassin. When these efforts failed, a clumsy attempt was made to suggest that Galindez was alive and well in South America, supposedly having fled there after embezzling funds raised in behalf of the Basques. Sightings were reported, though never confirmed, in a host of countries: he was in Paraguay, Colombia, Mexico, and the Philippines—often at the same time. A letter arrived in the United States purportedly from Galindez, causing some Congressmen to trumpet the case's "solution." A congressional researcher, however, submitted the so-called Galindez letter to police experts in Washington, who pronounced it a forgery. And not just a forgery, but one that appeared to have been written by an American. Meanwhile, Basque exile leaders denied that any money had been embezzled and called the IRS probe of the missing professor "useless and defamatory."

It's part of the contemporary relevance of the Galindez case that the disinformation which attended his kidnapping directly parallels incidents occurring in the Onassis affair and, more recently, in the assassination of Orlando Letelier. It seems that whom the gods would destroy, they would also slander. Like Galindez, Onassis appears to have been the victim of convenient forgeries. So too an ambitious effort was made to depict the Greek tycoon as a criminal. And while the billionaire could hardly have been made to seem a Communist, J. Edgar Hoover's letter leaked to the New York *Daily News* accomplished a similar purpose, branding Onassis as "anti-American." As with Galindez and Onassis, so with Letelier. In the wake of the latter's dramatic assassination in 1976 (he and an American companion were shredded by a car bomb while driving to work at Washington's Institute for Policy Studies), it was suggested that Letelier had been murdered by Communists in an effort to embarrass the right-wing dictatorship of Chile's Augusto Pinochet. When that effort failed, Pinochet's media flunkies exhausted themselves in attempts to depict Letelier as a spy for Castro. As if that were not enough, IRS investigators were dispatched to investigate the murdered statesman's finances amid new rumors that he'd been corrupt. Again, the charges were false, but the pattern was the same. In all three cases, a disinformation campaign was used to defame

the victim of a private intelligence operation * by raising doubts
about his honesty and his friendship toward the United States. The
real target of those campaigns, of course, was the American people:
by slandering Onassis, Galindez, and Letelier, their enemies hoped
that public opinion would shrug off whatever actions had been taken
against them—whether bankruptcy, kidnapping, or murder.

What finally drew the FBI into the Galindez case was the disappearance of a twenty-three-year-old pilot named Gerald L. Murphy.
Murphy was a barrel-chested Oregonian whose passion for flying was
frustrated by severe astigmatism. Unable to find work as a commercial airline pilot, he was forced to free-lance, compensating for his
poor eyesight by accepting dangerous assignments. Flying guns and
cash to Castro, he'd become a fixture in that Miami milieu which
gave the world Frank Sturgis, Jack Holcomb, Loran Hall, and
others.

The very month that Galindez disappeared, Murphy was suddenly
blessed with the job of his dreams, going to work as a pilot for
Dominican Airlines. The pay was good, but more than that, the pilot
seemed somehow to have acquired an independent source of cash
beyond his salary. Taking an apartment in Ciudad Trujillo, he began to live ostentatiously, bragging of his connections to shadowy
figures in the Trujillo regime, and hinting pointedly that he knew
more than a little about the fate of Professor Galindez.

The idyll was short-lived, however. Months after the vanishing
act performed on Galindez, the American pilot disappeared as well.
Suspicions of foul play had hardly been raised when this second disappearance was "solved" by a dead man, Octavio de la Maza. De la
Maza was Murphy's copilot for Dominican Airlines. Two years
earlier he'd been a Dominican air attaché in London, returning
home in disgrace after submachine-gunning another embassy staffer
in the course of a drunken brawl. De la Maza's solution to Murphy's
disappearance came in the form of a suicide note—supposedly his
own. Just before "hanging himself" in a Dominican jail, De la Maza
was said to have written a note in which he claimed to have murdered Murphy after the American had made a homosexual pass at
him. This news outraged Murphy's parents, friends, and fiancée, all

* While the campaign against Onassis was carried out with the approval and
assistance of the CIA, it was first and foremost a private operation undertaken by
Maheu on behalf of Niarchos and the multinational oil companies. And while neither
the Galindez nor Letelier killings have been officially solved, there is overwhelming
evidence that both murders involved the services of contract spooks from the private
sphere.

of whom agreed that, whatever else the pilot may have been, he was not gay. Drawn into the case by the report of an American's death, State Department sleuths examined De la Maza's "suicide note," and after comparing it to other samples of the dead man's writing, declared it a forgery. Obviously, both Murphy and De la Maza had been murdered. Not that the American's body was ever likely to be found. Investigators reported that the young flier's car was found abandoned on a cliff overlooking the Caribbean—a beautiful spot if you could somehow ignore the stench of blood and guts wafting toward it from a nearby slaughterhouse. In the waters below the car, sharks swarmed to feed upon the offal regularly dumped there by workers at the abattoir. According to State Department officials, Gerald Murphy was one day included among that offal: he'd literally been fed to the sharks. The only question is whether he was dead or alive when the fish began feeding.

Assassinating Murphy must have seemed a good idea to Trujillo: the flier knew too much—as his "legacy" proved. Among the Oregonian's personal effects in his Ciudad Trujillo apartment was a locked tin box, containing an address book, a pilot's log, and, most importantly, a yellow piece of paper filled with tantalizing notes. This last page, torn from a legal pad, was an outline composed of people's names, some dates, and references to airports. Less than a sworn confession, it appeared to serve not so much as Murphy's "insurance" but rather as his revenge in the event that "something happened to him." Obviously, the pilot was scared, realizing some time before his death that he was a marked man. The notes he left, therefore, were meant to be deliberately obscure: on the one hand, they must provide all the clues necessary to the solution of the Galindez caper; on the other hand, they must appear cryptic. He had no way of knowing who would take possession of them in the wake of his death: Trujillo's agents, the State Department, or his next of kin.

In the exact middle of the page, however, he wrote the name "Jesus de Galindez," perhaps to suggest—in a literal way—that Galindez was at the center of it all. So that no mistake could be made about this, and so that his next of kin would understand the context of his notes, Murphy's last reference on the page is to the "Miami Herald, Westbrook Pegler, April 11, 1956, Lines 1–3." Anyone finding Murphy's notes and becoming curious about them would, upon looking up that reference, learn that Professor Galindez had been kidnapped from New York. Understanding that, the rest of the notes would elaborate the means of that kidnapping.

For the most part the yellow page is a list of names, places, firms, and dates. The first name it mentions is that of Horace W. Schmahl, and so that there could be no mistake, Schmahl's address is given and his connection to Murphy established by notations referring to a flight that the two men had taken together a month before the disappearance of Galindez. The second name mentioned is that of John Frank, and the third is Frank's favorite alias, "John Kane." After the private detectives, Schmahl and Frank, comes Arturo Espaillat, the Dominican minister of state security, Trujillo's hatchet man, and one of Frank's most important connections in "the D.R." Besides references to these men there were others to Murphy's mechanic, Hal French, airports in New York and Florida, names of hotels, an aircraft-rental business, and a firm in New Jersey that specialized in the manufacture of steel drums. The significance of all these nouns was unstated on the yellow sheet. But the name Galindez and the reference to Pegler's column alerted investigators to the page's probable importance.

Immediately, FBI agents set out to question the living. Horace Schmahl remembered Murphy but said that his only connection with the pilot was to have taken a flight with him in February. That flight, he said, had nothing to do with Galindez; it concerned a private investigation involving a contested will. Johnny Frank had rather less to say. Told by interviewing FBI agents that Murphy had "disappeared," having apparently been murdered, Frank is reported to have "blanched and then clammed up."

Hal French was more helpful. He recalled a Miami meeting in late February among himself, Murphy, and three other men—two of whom he identified as Espaillat and Frank (who used the alias "John Kane"). Espaillat (having just been appointed Dominican consul general in New York) denied having been in the United States at that time, but his passport proved him to be a liar. According to French, the meeting concerned the rental of a light plane from the aircraft-leasing service mentioned on the yellow page left by Murphy. Investigating the tête-à-tête, FBI agents confirmed the report. Executives of the rental company recalled the transaction and remembered that Murphy had insisted that a receipt for eight hundred dollars be made out to his employer, "John Kane." Checking further, they were able to learn that Espaillat, Schmahl, and Frank had conferred earlier that same month in the New York area, and that Frank was virtually commuting between the United States and the Dominican Republic's National Palace. The case began to unravel.

Inquiries at New Jersey's Atlantic Steel Drum & Barrel Corporation, mentioned in Murphy's notes, were especially fruitful: a few
days before the disappearance of Galindez, Murphy had bought four
steel drums. According to Hal French, he'd helped Murphy install
the drums on the rented Beechcraft, ripping out the plane's rear
seats; they were used, he said, as auxiliary tanks to extend the plane's
range, permitting it to fly from New York to Florida before having
to refuel. And French had assisted Murphy in other ways as well:
besides helping him to plot a course from Amityville, Long Island,
to Monte Cristi Airport in the Dominican Republic, he'd undertaken an unusual assignment. For some reason Murphy wanted
French to find out precisely how long it took to drive from midtown
Manhattan to the Amityville airport. Timing the trip, the mechanic
informed the pilot that it required an hour and forty minutes. That
information would be useful to a flier whose comatose passenger
would have to be delivered from the Big Apple to Amityville by car
or ambulance: until he knew how long it would take to get Galindez
to the airport, Murphy would be unable to plan the time of his departure for the Dominican Republic.

The flight log, recovered along with the mysterious yellow page
from Murphy's apartment, describes such a flight—though the log
falsely indicates that it occurred on March 5, exactly one week *before*
Galindez disappeared. The discrepancy is annoying, but there is a
simple explanation. That is, Murphy deliberately falsified the log
to outwit Trujillo agents who, had they discovered the document
after his own liquidation, might have had orders to destroy anything
relating to Murphy's movements on March 12 (the actual evening
of the Galindez snatch). The deception was transparent, however,
and easily revealed. French told investigators that he'd been with
Murphy in Washington on March 5, later traveling with him to
New York to make final preparations for the following week's flight
to the Dominican Republic. According to French, Murphy refused
to say what this mysterious flight was about, except to remark that it
was a "national-security matter" * which involved flying a "wealthy
invalid" to the Dominican Republic. And while some investigators
have doubted that French told all that he knew, he does not seem
to have lied about the things he did say. His meeting with Murphy
in Washington and other movements he described have all been
confirmed. Moreover, other witnesses have verified the fact that

* The reader has heard this before. . . . ?

Murphy's night flight to Monte Cristi Airport occurred late in the evening of March 12.

That night Murphy took off from Amityville at eleven-thirty—almost two hours after Galindez disappeared—refueling near dawn at an out-of-the-way airport in southern Florida. Donald Jackson, a worker at the airport, told the FBI that Murphy wouldn't let him fill the interior tanks, insisting that Jackson hand him the hose so that he might do it himself. But, Jackson said, he did glance through the plane's windows. Inside, he said, were Murphy and two others: "a recumbent figure" on the floor of the plane, almost entirely covered by blankets, and another person who was seated beside him. While he couldn't identify either passenger, Jackson reported that an "incredible stench" came from the plane's interior cabin, an overpowering odor he'd never encountered before. Asked if it might have been a combination of vomit and anesthetic, the worker said he couldn't be sure. "Maybe."

There is reason to speculate that Donald Jackson wasn't the only one to watch Murphy and his "wealthy invalid" arrive in and depart from Florida. John Frank had left New York for Miami a few hours before Murphy did, buying a commercial airline ticket (and, not incidentally, paying for it with Robert Maheu's airline credit card). In Miami, Frank rented a car, using a phony driver's license which identified him as "Jason Fort," a New York lawyer. FBI agents were unable to discover precisely where Frank went in that car on the morning of March 13, but they speculated that he may have visited the airport to observe Murphy's arrival and departure—it was Frank, after all, who'd paid for the plane's rental. And the car's odometer bore out that possibility, conforming to the round trip exactly.

What happened to Galindez after his arrival in the Dominican Republic is uncertain. Nor is it certain how he came to be put aboard Murphy's plane in the first place. Those investigators most familiar with the case are convinced that he was dragged or lured into a car at Columbus Circle immediately after leaving his student friend. How this was accomplished is a matter of speculation. For a time it was thought that the professor had been taken into a rented or stolen ambulance and driven to the Amityville airport. A complete check of ambulance services in the New York area, however, ruled out every one, and no witnesses could recall any ambulance at either Columbus Circle or Amityville Airport. If Galindez was put into an ordinary car, then—and Murphy's request that French time the trip by automobile bears out this likelihood—the question is, How? No one recalls any struggle near the subway station, and so one may suppose that Galindez entered the car willingly or, at the very least, with a routine air. Given Frank's connections with New York police, it's possible that the professor's kidnappers used some form of police inquiry as a pretext for getting Galindez into the car that would drive him to his death. He may have been told that a friend was injured or in trouble, and that he'd asked for Galindez's help. And since Galindez was an FBI informant, he may have been prevailed upon in that capacity. Or he may simply have been grabbed at gunpoint, or lured into the car by Ana Gloria Viera's many charms. The possibilities are too many.

Investigators agree, however, that once the professor entered the car, he was drugged. The mysterious second passenger in Murphy's plane, glimpsed through the window by Donald Jackson, is thought by many to have been Ana Gloria; acting as a "nurse" to the "wealthy invalid," she'd have kept Galindez comatose throughout the flight. If so, one can imagine his feelings when, hung over from the drug, he felt a blast of tropical air in his face and suddenly realized that he was no longer in New York.

Verifying Ana Gloria's role, however, was impossible. Like Murphy and De la Maza, she was murdered in the Dominican Republic. In mid-August her mangled body was found in a car at the bottom of a ravine in the Dominican mountains. She appeared to be the victim of an automobile crash in which she and her car had gone over the edge of a cliff. This was surprising, though, in view of the fact that Ana Gloria Viera had never learned to drive and had therefore never gotten behind the wheel of any car. Ever.

What El Cojo might have said to police about his former companion's role is also a matter of speculation: about the time of Ana Gloria's death, the twisted assassin vanished, along with his wife and two children. He's never been seen since, a fact which—in view of his bizarre appearance—leads investigators to believe that he *and* his family were murdered en masse.

Donald Jackson, the airline worker who peeked, died a few months later in a small-plane crash that was blamed on pilot's error. While Jackson had earlier provided FBI agents with a sworn statement of what he'd seen the morning of March 13, he didn't live to testify before the grand jury investigating the Galindez disappearance.

Others did, but their testimony was of little use. Under subpoena Robert Maheu testified about his employment of Frank, emphasizing that the detective's connection to Murphy had nothing to do with the firm. As for the electronics deal, which bracketed the period before and after the kidnapping, it was a straightforward affair arranged by Frank and another Associate, former Secret Service man Tom LaVenia. Frank's use of the firm's credit card was an embarrassment, but routine: virtually all of Maheu's employees had access to those cards, reimbursing him for their use in private matters.

Unable to prove Frank's alleged guilt in the Galindez snatch, Justice Department attorneys William Hundley and Plato Cacheris indicted him for failure to register as a foreign agent (of Trujillo). In the course of the trial Arturo Espaillat approached the State Department with dossiers incriminating American embassy officials in a variety of scandalous matters. His offer was a blunt one: if the Justice Department would drop charges against Frank, the dossiers would be destroyed. "Otherwise . . ." But there was no "otherwise." The State Department reacted to the blackmail attempt with fury, causing Trujillo to capitulate and Espaillat to return home in disgrace. Subsequently, Frank changed his plea from not guilty to no contest, and a verdict of guilty was entered against him. The conviction, however, was overturned on appeal as Frank's lawyer successfully argued that his client's case had been prejudiced by references to the Galindez matter.

So Johnny Frank "walked."

But downhill.

The Galindez case had destroyed support for Trujillo in the Congress and press. The professor's book, highlighted against his own dramatic disappearance from the streets of New York, made "the Dominican horror" apparent to all. Espaillat's blackmail attempt caused whatever support there was for the dictator within the foreign-policy establishment to shrivel. Relations between the two countries drifted from friendship to enmity until, finally, the CIA began plotting against the Caudillo's life. In 1961, five years after Galindez, Viera, Murphy, and El Cojo had met their fates, Trujillo was torn apart by shotgun blasts. Antonio de la Maza, brother of the hanged Octavio, is credited with having fired the fatal shots, paying for the privilege with his own life. Today a statue stands in the renamed Dominican capital honoring Antonio de la Maza, but only hinting at the blood that underlies the statue's form.

Trujillo's decline and fall rippled through the Caribbean, consuming many of those who'd been close to him. The dictator's psychopathic son, Ramfis, suddenly deprived of a citizenry to torment, sought escape in booze and sport cars—a happy combination in that it one day delivered him at high speed to the base of a large Spanish oak. Arturo Espaillat, also an exile, ended his own life with a shotgun blast to the tonsils. And Johnny Frank lost his luck. Unlike some spooks, he was never able to make celebrity, or notoriety, work for him. As the court-appointed lawyer of indigent misdemeanants and petty crooks, the welfare cases of the underworld, he made a modest living, taking investigative assignments whenever he could get them. No longer a Maheu Associate, with all that implied, he became one of the "black hats." Joe Shimon, the Washington detective who counted Frank, Giancana, Roselli, and Maheu as his friends, recalled some of those assignments.

"We had a lot of propositions going," Shimon said. "Some of them worked out, some of them didn't. I remember Johnny and Maheu had a job, a sorta 'repossession.' Involved a little kid whose old man had taken her to Spain, and her mother wanted the kid back. Fifty grand to bring her back. So Bob and Johnny got all excited: they found out that the kid went to the beach every day, and the idea was to, uhh, snatch her. So Johnny sent a guy over to rent a motorboat, one of those high-speed jobs, and the idea was to, you know, hit the beach, grab the kid, and fly. . . . Well, for chrissake, they'd already spent ten grand setting it up, but none of them had even bothered to see what the kid's situation was. So I had someone check it out, and he sent back pictures. It was a lovely scene: the little girl sittin' on the beach, playing with her shovel and sand pail, and right behind her—what's this?—one of those guys with the Mickey Mouse ears holding a submachine gun! The kid was guarded round the clock. Johnny Frank hits the beach and he ain't gonna leave it. Well, it was typical of their fuck-ups. They were lucky they had me around." Did they go ahead with it anyway? "Nah. We told the mother about the problem—the guy with the gun. We could have solved it. But it would have cost a lot of dough. You hadda buy off the guy's boss in the *Guardia Civil*. So the price got too high. We needed a hundred grand to do it right, and Mommy had already shelled out quite a bit, thanks to Frank, and received nothin' in return. She thought we were crooks. Well, we could have done it. No sweat. No fuss. It was just a matter of money. But she backed out."

In 1962, Frank and Shimon found themselves in the middle of

an even more lucrative "proposition"—a two-billion-dollar dispute that saw veterans from the Maheu agency pitted against one another on behalf of rival utility firms. The issue involved the El Paso Natural Gas Company and the Tennessee Gas Transmission Company. Both firms wanted to build gas pipelines to serve the southern California region. The Federal Power Commission (FPC) was to decide which of the utility giants would prevail. The arguments before the commission were reasoned and highly technical, with batteries of attorneys vying against one another. Behind the scenes, however, both utilities were relying on spooks. Tom LaVenia, Maheu's former partner, was engaged by Hogan & Hartson,* the law firm representing El Paso Natural Gas. According to Shimon, the utility company bought a house for LaVenia, conveniently located next door to one owned by a principal attorney for El Paso's rival. LaVenia and the attorney became good friends, with the latter unaware that his neighbor was working for the competition. In the course of outdoor barbeques in the backyard and drinks together after work, LaVenia is said to have plumbed Tennessee's legal strategy on an almost daily basis reporting to Hogan & Hartson. More seriously, though, Shimon insists (but cannot prove) that one of the FPC commissioners was bribed to support El Paso's petition for the right to build its pipeline to Los Angeles.

Whether that suspicion was shared by the Tennessee Gas Transmission Company is uncertain. Shimon claims that it was and cites it as the reason for the industrial espionage that took place. As a high-ranking Washington police detective, Shimon was in an ideal position to bug conferences taking place in the capital's posh Mayflower Hotel. He knew the doormen, the switchboard operators, and the hoteliers, all of whom respected his official position. What's more, he was something of a master of tradecraft. "There was a time," he says, "when I had master keys to just about every hotel room in the city. Getting them wasn't a problem: you rented a suite with adjoining rooms, you know? And then you took out the lock between the rooms. Then you'd take it to a locksmith—not any locksmith, of course, you hadda know your man—and get a master key made for the whole hotel. Then you took the lock back and put it in again. The part you hadda be careful about was installing the bug. You

* In the parlance, Hogan & Hartson can be said to "swing." It was Hogan & Hartson, Edward Bennett Williams' natal home as a lawyer, that came to handle many of Robert Vesco's business intrigues—before Williams handled his criminal litigation. And it was Hogan & Hartson that recommended Maheu to Howard Hughes.

didn't want to get caught with the master key, you know? So what we did was, we gave one of the guys a pint of whiskey. Splashed some on his clothes, made him take a couple of swigs, and sent him into the room. As soon as he opened the door, he'd give the key back. So if he got caught, he wouldn't have it on him. If he got caught, it'd just be some drunk who'd wandered into the wrong room, you know? Because he'd be registered down the hall. Whenever we went into a place, we registered. If you haven't registered, you haven't covered your ass."

Johnny Frank and another veteran of the Maheu agency monitored the bug Shimon provided, taking an expensive suite down the hall from the room in which El Paso's attorneys were conferring. It was a good bug, providing great reception. So good, in fact, that commercial airliners making their descent to National Airport complained that when flying over the Mayflower, their radio communications were interrupted by mysterious legal discussions. In the long run that might have been a threat, but an even larger threat was boredom. Few things are duller than eavesdropping on the conversations of attorneys. Accordingly, Frank and his partner convinced two friends, a belly dancer and a blond Swedish stewardess, to entertain them in the hotel. There the men were said to have been rebuked by the girls who reportedly complained that the headphones scratched their thighs. Always gentlemanly, the industrial spies accommodated the women by removing the headsets. On company time, however, they still had a duty to monitor the conversation taking place down the hall. To satisfy both their clients and their lovers, then, the men turned up the volume on the tape recorders so that they might listen to the lawyers talking while at the same time they ministered to the girls. This was a mistake, though. El Paso executives, coming and going from their suite, were surprised while standing in front of the elevator to hear their own conversation emanating from a room in which they'd never been. Within hours Hogan & Hartson obtained a subpoena for the tapes, delivering it in person to Frank's nude partner and bedmate. And while Tennessee and El Paso both hoped to settle the matter privately, a criminal prosecution developed against their will. After years of haggling in the District Attorney's office, Shimon pleaded guilty to "operating an illegal radio station." Others who were involved pled to similar misdemeanors. But only John Frank went to jail, receiving a six-month sentence.

When he got out, Frank returned to his law practice and private investigations, staying out of the news until the winter of 1972, when the Trujillo family returned to curse him once again. Prevailing upon his old association with the dictator's family, Frank convinced Trujillo's daughter, Maria, an exile in Florida, to invest in Canadian real estate. The investments he recommended included two lots that he and his partners had secretly purchased for themselves. Providing the gullible Maria with inflated estimates of the property's worth, Frank and the others sold the lots to her for a reported $1,114,000. Their actual worth was about one-tenth of that amount, leaving Frank & Company with a million-dollar profit. The transaction seems not to have been questioned until Maria Trujillo married and her husband sat down to study the family books. Again, a civil action was begun, with Maria and her spouse seeking recovery of the lost cash. And again, the action degenerated into a criminal suit that sent the former CIA officer Johnny Frank back to jail—this time for years.

In the autumn of 1977 the disbarred Frank walked, blinking, out of the federal penitentiary at Lewisburg, Pennsylvania. There was no way of knowing what his next move would be, though his friends predicted that he'd visit the Bahamas: the cool million has never been recovered.*

3 / JOHNNY ROSELLI REDUCED TO GAS

By the middle Fifties, Maheu's work had made him famous in a special way: along with Horace Schmahl, Bernard Spindel, John Broady, and a handful of other spooks, he was regarded by those in the know as one of the world's premiere clandestine operatives for hire. The key phrase, of course, is "in the know."

New Hampshire publisher William Loeb and vice-presidential candidate Richard Nixon were in the know. So was United Steelworkers president Larry MacDonald. In fact, MacDonald was in the know to the tune of $7,500 *per month*—supposedly for "public relations work." Joe Shimon confirms that characterization with a wolfish smile. "Yeah," he says, "it *was* public relations work. I handled some of it for Bob myself. What it involved was, I used to have to deliver

---

* And his friends' predictions have so far been proven wrong. When I visited him in his modest Falls Church home, Frank arrived at his font door, pajama'd in the afternoon, hands trembling, eyes bloodshot—seemingly frightened by the specter of an unexpected suit. He didn't want to talk. "I've had some hard times," was all he'd say—about Onassis, Galindez, or anything else.

these packages to strange guys in hotels. I think they musta been the *public*, those guys. What I'd do is, I'd give 'em a call from the lobby and have 'em meet me at the bar. We never knew each other, so I'd make 'em identify themselves—you know, I'd have 'em carry somethin'. Then I'd go in, hand 'em the package, tip my hat, and get out as fast as I could. Public relations is a good word for it because whenever I left those guys, they were smilin'." Asked what was in the packages, Shimon grins. "Gee," he says. "I never looked. Probably brochures. Felt like some kinda paper, anyway. *Musta been brochures.*"

And, of course, Howard Hughes was in the know. By 1956 Maheu's agency had already handled a number of sensitive assignments for the billionaire. An angry landlord of Hughes's, who apparently wanted to evict the billionaire, was placed under what Maheu's partner Tom LaVenia euphemistically called "microphone surveillance." The landlord soon relented. So did a man who tried to blackmail Hughes: meeting with LaVenia and another Maheu Associate, Allen F. ("No Relation") Hughes, in a New York hotel suite (Maheu Associates seems never to have rented a single room), the man spelled out how much he wanted to keep his bad news secret. That was a mistake, of course, since the Maheu team had earlier wired everything from the plants to the lamps. Hopelessly incriminated, the blackmailer agreed to keep silent. Even more sensitively, Maheu plunged into Hughes's sex life. In 1954, a North Carolinian named Stuart Cramer III was courting Jean Peters, an actress who resembled Grace Kelly and with whom Hughes was infatuated. The billionaire asked Maheu to find out if Cramer, a Lockheed employee, was also an undercover CIA officer or agent. Maheu made some phone calls and reported in the affirmative. A few months later Peters and Cramer were wed, honeymooning aboard a fishing yacht on which Hughes had infiltrated a spy. Shortly afterward, the newlyweds separated. In the meantime Hughes had the CIA man placed under surveillance so that he, Hughes, might plead his own cause with the actress while her husband toiled in Washington. Described as "painfully shy" (a euphemism for paranoid), Hughes could not have been expected to enjoy a confrontation with the southern spook should he be caught asking for Mrs. Cramer's hand in marriage. With Maheu's help such a confrontation was averted, and the mission was pronounced successful. In December, 1956, Mrs. Cramer was divorced, becoming Mrs. Hughes in the spring of 1957. The couple left the United States for a six-month honeymoon in the

Bahamas, a time that Hughes spent flying lazy circles over the archipelago, day after day, in an enormous TWA passenger plane which he'd diverted to his private use.

Not that Maheu was Hughes's only love-spook. Beginning in the 1940s, and until the billionaire's marriage, a small task force of private eyes, including a detective called "Mike Conrad" (né Gerald Chouinard), was retained by the billionaire to handle what might be called his "sexspionage." It cost Hughes millions, but more than a hundred beautiful women were placed under electronic and visual surveillance. Elizabeth Taylor, Ava Gardner, Sophia Loren, Janet Leigh, Anne Bancroft, and others, lesser known and unknown, seen in films or glimpsed in passing cars, were shadowed at bullfights, ball games, and in department stores. Photographers worked round the clock providing Hughes with blowups of the women leaving their apartments—and sometimes, using observers who clung to telephone poles near the women's rooms, Hughes was provided with reports of their doings at home.

By 1958, however, Maheu had become the billionaire's spook of choice, commuting fortnightly between his home in Virginia and Hughes's residence in Los Angeles. His assignments were diverse. Dossiers were compiled on foreign governments and corporations, detailing who had influence over whom. This sort of business intelligence was essential to an operator such as Hughes, who, according to Maheu, worked on the assumption that everyone has his price. Contracts—whether for helicopters, missiles, or electronic warfare systems—often depended on whom one knew . . . or owned. In addition, Hughes had need of security services, which Maheu provided, to protect a bizarre assortment of properties which he'd acquired over the years. These ranged from documents and memorabilia (old letters, films, and trinkets) to a score of empty houses in Arizona and a gargantuan "flying boat" hangared in Long Beach.*

---

* The Arizona homes were supposed to house Hughes Aircraft executives when that firm moved its headquarters from California to the Sunshine State. In fact, the firm never moved anywhere—nor was it intended to. Hughes bought the houses as a public-relations ploy to disguise the fact that his purchase of a massive land tract near Tucson was no more than a real estate deal. Hughes's attorney Edward Morgan explains, "Howard never really built anything. He never put a spade into the ground. The hotels, the casinos, the Tool Company—he didn't build any of it, no matter how much he was always talking about the construction of new industries, airports, and resorts. Basically, Hughes's wealth was tied to real estate. He bought huge tracts of land near rapidly growing cities (Tucson, Los Angeles, Las Vegas) and held onto it. He could always borrow money on the land—Christ, its value increased faster than the interest that he had to pay."
As for the flying boat, the *Spruce Goose* is a ten-story-high amphibious aircraft with

In addition, Maheu conducted surveillances and investigations of
Hughes's executives; deployed Hughes's doubles to lead process
servers astray; introduced ciphering to the Hughes organization, cod-
ing the accounts; handled the billionaire's byzantine contributions
to politicians; and established a sort of in-house "Export Control
System" to prevent Hughes products from reaching Communist Bloc
nations. It was during this time, between 1957 and the next decade,
that Hughes's penchant for secrecy became a commitment to hermitage. By 1960 he hadn't been seen in public for a year and a half; he
was accessible by telephone to only a handful; and he'd begun to
look with a curious eye at the Mormon assistants who worked so
diligently in his Romaine communications center. Before long the
Mormons would be Hughes's only direct contact with the human
race.

Indeed, the beginning of the Sixties was a watershed for Hughes,
Maheu, the United States, and even the hemisphere. In the Caribbean, the dictators of Cuba, Haiti, and the Dominican Republic
were ousted, dead or doomed by CIA decree. In the United States,
the Republican Administration was on its way out, with Hughes's
candidate, Richard Nixon, engaged in a downhill battle with the
charismatic Jack Kennedy. Cuban exiles were beginning their long
apprenticeship to the CIA's JM/WAVE station in Miami, and a
comparative handful of CIA advisors were joining Lou Conein in
Vietnam. The economy was moving from recession to boom, and
Hughes had finally arranged financing for $345,000,000 in passenger
jets that would make TWA the world's first all-jet airline. As for
Maheu, his "Mission Impossible" agency was on the verge of becoming "the Hughes Apparat." While he still had a few clients other
than the billionaire and continued to live in Virginia, Maheu came
increasingly within the Hughes orbit. Within a year he'd cut his
other clients loose and move to California to be nearer to his boss.

One of the clients that still remained to be served, however, was
the one that had gotten him started: the CIA. In August, 1960, according to Maheu, his Agency case officer, Jim O'Connell, approached him with a proposition: $150,000 to anyone "tough
enough" to assassinate Fidel Castro. The notion of "eliminating"

---

a wingspread longer than a football field. Capable, in theory, of carrying seven hundred combat-ready troops, it arrived too late for World War II. That delay, coupled
with Hughes's failure to deliver on $60,000,000 in other wartime contracts, led to his
1947 interrogation by Senator Owen Brewster, investigating those who'd profited from
the war.

the Cuban Communist had been floating around the Agency for nearly a year, and several plots to accomplish that end had already gotten under way. During the spring and summer of 1960 a box of Castro's favorite cigars was doctored with a botulism toxin by the Agency's Technical Services Division (TSD): the result was biological stogies so lethal that any smoker putting one of the cigars in his mouth would have keeled over even before lighting it. Other plots in the works, or soon developed, included one that would have caused the Cuban leader to go berserk in the course of a radio address (the recording studio having been sprayed with what one spook called "super-acid," a refinement of LSD). Another plan would have had a secret agent dust the insteps of Castro's shoes with thallium salts, a powerful depilatory that would have caused Castro's beard, pubic hair, and eyebrows to fall out (destroying the image if not the man). Yet other fantasies involved transmission of the dread disease Madura foot; Castro's use of a skin diver's wet suit that had been treated with a virulent strain of tuberculosis; a ballpoint pen with a poisoned needle in the clicking mechanism; an explosive conch shell; and, of course, neither last nor least, General Edward Lansdale's scheme to foment a messianic counterrevolution that would have had a (presumably pro-capitalist) Christ arrive in Cuban waters aboard an American submarine with star-shell flares exploding across the skies; having earlier identified Castro as the Anti-Christ, Lansdale's proposal would have had the Cubans overthrow their leader in the interests of the Second Coming.

Explaining such perversity is a hopeless task. Perhaps institutions, like individuals, undergo a "change of life," with attendant eccentricities: if so, 1960–62 may be described as the CIA's menopausal years. Besides the plots against Castro, agents and officers were bustling around the Caribbean and Africa with guns, explosives, and biological murder kits intended for the assassination of Rafael Trujillo, Patrice Lumumba, and, we may suppose, lesser lights who stood in the way of Agency objectives.*

The CIA plan to assassinate Castro, using Maheu and organized-crime figures associated with Havana's casinos, seems initially to

---

* It is a curious circumstance of the Church Report that upon reading it one may come away with the impression that the CIA has never assassinated anyone. Discussing what it calls "alleged assassination plots involving foreign leaders," the report finds no *conclusive* evidence that the Agency's plots led *directly* to the death of any foreign leader. As for the deaths of others, with the exception of Chile's General Rene Schneider, the report does not concern itself with them.

have contemplated the Cuban leader's death in a sort of "gangland killing." That is, Fidel would get bushwhacked—perhaps while getting a haircurt (à la Albert Anastasia). That plan, however, was impractical, and for obvious reasons: Castro was not a common hoodlum but a head of state. His security guards carried sub-machine guns, and as the country's premier, Castro was unlikely to be caught alone and unaware in a Havana barbershop. Anyone willing to hit him in the style of Murder, Inc., would have to be as crazy as he was tough—because he'd never escape to collect the 150 grand. The Agency was undaunted by these observations, however. The gambling syndicate had other "assets," specifically those personnel who'd remained in Cuba after Castro's take-over, operating the Havana casinos. It was thought that among this group someone might be found to slay Fidel by subtler means than those suggested earlier. Accordingly, the TSD prepared a package of poisoned pills. These, however, were rejected by Colonel Sheffield Edwards when he noticed that they neither dissolved nor sank when placed in water. Abashed, the TSD scientists returned to their labs to manufacture botulism capsules that would liquify in coffee, highballs, or gazpacho.

Meanwhile, Robert Maheu was meeting with his friend Johnny Roselli in Hollywood's Brown Derby Restaurant (a favorite meeting place of celebrities, the restaurant gets its name from its architecture). By anyone's standards, Roselli was tough enough for the job. A racketeer with ambassadorial good looks, he's remembered by Washington detective Joe Shimon as "a stand-up guy. Johnny was all alone in the world," Shimon recalls. "He didn't have anybody —no family to speak of. He stayed away from his mother and his sisters until he retired. Before that, though, he helped put them through college. Anyway, you couldn't scare Johnny. There was no way to threaten him. If you put a gun at his head, he'd just smile and tell ya to shoot. He had nothing to lose."

In fact, Roselli *was* a romantic figure—the so-called Don Giovanni of the Mafia. Born Filippo Sacco in Italy, he came to the United States as a child, though in later years a birth certificate would describe him as a native American, Chicago-born on the Fourth of July. In fact, Sacco/Roselli grew up in Boston the hard way, running numbers as a teen-ager and, later, helping his stepfather burn down the family home for the insurance. At twenty-two he changed his name to Roselli, leaving Boston with his proverbial shirttail on fire. He'd be sixty-five years old before he'd see any of his family again—and yet, in the best Hollywood tradition of the gangster with the heart of gold, he'd helped put his sisters through college, using an intermediary to send money home. In Chicago, Roselli found work with Al Capone, running liquor for the Mob. What else he may have done is a matter of conjecture: charged with selling morphine to an undercover cop, he was acquitted when both the arresting officer and the informant disappeared—forever, as it turned out. By the time World War II began, Roselli was established even further west, in Beverly Hills. There he became a fixture in the movie colony, and best friends with Harry Cohn, head of Columbia Pictures. Cohn lent Roselli money to buy a quarter of the Tijuana racetrack, a loan Johnny paid back in a matter of months. When the studio chieftain tore up a check for interest on the loan, Roselli went out and bought a pair of twin star rubies. Setting the gems in two rings, he gave one to Cohn and put the other on his own hand. Cohn wore his until his death. In Hollywood, Roselli had a reputation as a man who could always get a bet placed; women were attracted to him and he could claim the friendship of such stars as Dean Martin and Frank Sinatra. Despite this clout, 1943 saw him indicted in connection with a labor racketeering case in which the film studios were victims of extortion. Despite the testimony of Harry Cohn, who insisted that Roselli was a moderating influence who'd ended the strike against his own studio, Don Giovanni got ten years. And when he came out, he found it impossible to shed the notoriety he'd acquired. Publicity surrounding a supposedly secret appearance before the Kefauver crime committee established his association with a constellation of racketeers ranging from Meyer Lansky to Bugsy Siegel, Tony Accardo, and Lucky Luciano. This squelched an offer from Harry Cohn that would have permitted him to go straight in style, making films about prisons and crime. Unwilling to change his name again, and bitter, he re-upped with the Mob, helping out with its Las Vegas and Havana gambling operations. It was at about this time that he took up with Judith Campbell Exner, the party girl whose friendship he would share with Sam Giancana and President John Kennedy.

In 1960 Roselli was one of a handful of operators (Dino Cellini was another) responsible for managing the Mob's investments in Cuba. According to the FBI, these operations were owned by Santos Trafficante and Meyer Lansky, with New Orleans' Carlos Marcello and Chicago's Sam "Momo" Giancana having smaller pieces of the action. The Mob's relationship to the *arrivista* Castro regime was a stormy one. On the one hand, some of its members had been active in the revolution, ferrying guns to Castro's guerrillas. On the other hand, the new Cuban premier seemed determined to eradicate those social evils that the Mob found most profitable: drugs, prostitution, and gambling. Castro had, moreover, jailed both Trafficante and Meyer Lansky's brother Jake in the wake of his triumphal march upon Havana. It was a reflection of this ambivalence, perhaps, that caused Castro to close the casinos after taking power, subsequently to reopen them—only to close them some months after the Bay of Pigs invasion.

The relationship between the Cuban Marxist and the American criminals, then, was a hesitant one. While Meyer Lansky's position was clear—he's reputed to have placed a one-million-dollar contract on the Cuban leader—others in the Mob thought that the multimillion-dollar investment in Havana might be saved. So it was that while Lansky looked toward the Bahamas as a substitute for Cuba, others hoped that a deal might still be made. Trafficante's role in all this was a particularly unusual one. As he was a friend of Batista's and a notorious figure, it was perhaps natural that Castro would have him arrested upon taking power. Trafficante, however, does not seem to fit the right-wing stereotypes which other organized-crime figures have adopted. José Aleman, a Cuban exile leader who was also an FBI informant, has recalled conversations with Trafficante in which the mobster "spoke almost poetically about democracy and civil liberties," * complaining that Attorney General Robert Kennedy's attacks on Teamsters leader Jimmy Hoffa amounted to attacks upon "the blue-collars," the working class. Whether Trafficante's remarks were self-serving is uncertain, though it's hard to imagine why they would have been. Aleman was asking Trafficante to assist him in getting a loan from Hoffa's Teamsters union. Trafficante therefore had no reason to impress his Cuban supplicant. In any event, I mention Trafficante's remarks only because the suspicion has recently emerged (in *The Washington Post* and elsewhere) that he may have become a secret agent of Castro's during his confinement in the Havana prison. The basis for that suspicion seems to be that Castro's intelligence agents in the Miami community are believed to have received their funding through illegal activities said to be under Trafficante's control. The numbers game, for instance, as it's played in Miami, selects its winner ac-

---

* *Washington Post,* article by George Crile, May 16, 1976.

cording to a formula based upon the winning numbers in the Havana lottery. That lottery is said to be fixed so that the winning numbers conform to those which have been played *the least* during that week in Miami; provided with the winning numbers in advance, Castro's Miami agents are able to depend upon regular winnings—while Trafficante's own profits are maximized. In addition, these agents arc thought to obtain other funds through the importation of heroin, another activity in which Trafficante is believed to figure heavily. The beauty of the scheme, of course, is that Castro's intelligence network is supported in large part by the Cuban exile community itself; the funds cannot be traced; and Trafficante's own profits are guaranteed by his advance knowledge of the winning numbers.

So CIA agent Maheu was entering murky waters when he prevailed upon Johnny Roselli's patriotism to contact Trafficante and Sam Giancana for the purpose of assassinating Castro. There was a distinct possibility that the killer force contained a double agent (Trafficante) from its inception. If so, that may explain how it is that Castro managed to survive an almost endless succession of attempts upon his life. Following Maheu's September meeting with Roselli in the Brown Derby, the two men met with O'Connell in New York's elegant Plaza Hotel, informing him that the contract was accepted. From there the trio traveled to Miami to work out details of the operation during a stay at the Kennilworth Hotel. There Roselli (using the alias "John Rawlston") introduced Maheu to Giancana ("Sam Gold") and Trafficante ("Joe"). O'Connell called himself "Jim Olds." *

Giancana was then at the height of his power, crime boss of all Chicago and, less happily, one of the FBI's Ten Most Wanted Criminals. He had a record of some sixty arrests (including three for murder while still a teen-ager). As Roselli did, he had financial interests in Las Vegas and counted Frank Sinatra as one of his closest friends. Giancana was Trafficante's backup man in the assassination plot. He was supposed to find a potential assassin from among his Cuban contacts, but those efforts seem to have been unsuccessful: "Momo's" biggest contribution to the scheme was his

---

* Within the intelligence community, it's standard procedure for agents to use aliases that include their first name, or nickname, and correct initials. This is thought to lessen the likelihood of embarrassing memory failures and also to minimize losses incurred through unexpected encounters with old friends hailing the undercover agent by his first name.

sense of humor, a contribution that was somewhat lessened by his anxiety that Las Vegas singer Phyllis McGuire might not be constant to him. Before long, that would cause problems. In the meantime, however, Trafficante would serve as courier to Cuba, selecting the actual agents who'd be used to carry out the murder attempts.

Moving in October to Miami's premiere wedding-cake hotel, the Fontainebleau, the plotters aimed for a November deadline on Castro's demise. Whether that early deadline was intended to affect the presidential elections, improving Nixon's chances over Kennedy, is a matter of speculation.* In any case, the deadline would never be met. The plot moved forward at an evolutionary pace, enervating the men. In Los Angeles, Howard Hughes chafed at the absence of his secret operative, telephoning Miami with demands that Maheu return to work. Faced with the likelihood of losing his most important client, Maheu says, he informed Hughes of his CIA assignment, winning the billionaire's forbearance. And Giancana was restless too, worrying that Phyllis McGuire was having a love affair in Las Vegas with comedian Dan Rowan. To prevent Momo from suddenly flying west to wipe the smile off the funnyman's face, it was decided to bug Rowan's hotel room. Edward DuBois, a Florida detective, was paid one thousand dollars by Maheu (using CIA funds) to make the installation. DuBois then assigned the task to one of his employees, Arthur Balletti, who flew to Vegas with the necessary equipment. There he proceeded to install a wiretap—rather than the requested bug—in Rowan's room. Halfway through the job, however, Balletti got a severe case of the munchies. Thinking that the maid would not return that day (the place was quite tidy and she'd already *been*), the Florida wireman went out for lunch, leaving his greasy tools, spliced wires, and microphones on a table in the neat room. As it happened, the maid *did* return. And called the sheriff. Who busted Balletti. Who compounded his luncheon mistake even further by calling Maheu for help. Which, as Jim O'Connell put it, "tied [him] into this thing up to his ears."

Maheu was furious. Not only had Balletti botched the assignment,

---

* During the 1960 election campaign, Kennedy preempted Nixon on the Cuban issue, scoring heavily with the American public. In speeches and debates the young Senator made it clear that, if elected, he'd support direct action against Castro. This infuriated Nixon, who as Vice President presided over the planning process that led to the Bay of Pigs. Nixon, however, was constrained by secrecy from revealing his own Administration's plans for settling "the Cuban question." Had Castro been eliminated before the U. S. elections, then, the issue might have been defused, regaining Nixon some badly needed votes.

but he'd done so three times over. Getting caught was bad enough. Calling "home" was worse. Attempting to install a wiretap was the final blow: Maheu had wanted Rowan bugged, not tapped. A "spike-mike" would have served as well, and less dramatically.* Now Maheu would have to ask the Agency to intervene in any felony trials that the Las Vegas police were certain to contemplate. This would complicate things even further because the eavesdropping assignment had had a more sensitive purpose than Giancana knew. There had been a leak. Within weeks of the plotters' arrival in Miami, J. Edgar Hoover had written to Dick Bissell, head of the Agency's Clandestine Services. "During recent conversations with several friends," Hoover's memo advised, "Giancana stated that Fidel Castro was to be done away with very shortly. . . . Moreover, he allegedly indicated that he had already met with the assassin-to-be on three occasions. . . . Giancana claimed that everything had been perfected for the killing of Castro, and that the 'assassin' had arranged with a girl . . . to drop a 'pill' in some drink or food of Castro's." The information was attributed to "a source whose reliability has not been tested"—in other words, to a new informant. To Maheu and Giancana, who'd discussed the rivalry over Phyllis McGuire, Dan Rowan was the most likely suspect. The question is, if they had determined that it was indeed Rowan who'd told the FBI of their assassination plot, what would they have done about it? Or, more precisely, what would Giancana have done? Killed him?

So the tap on Rowan was more serious than the comedian's friendship with a sexy singer. The leak raised important questions about the operation's security. Even more important, perhaps, was the trouble that would result when the Bureau learned that with Maheu's help the CIA had become entangled in the affairs of organized crime—compromising criminal investigations that had the highest priority. And the Bureau *would* learn of the entanglement: the Agency would have to intervene with the FBI to prevent Maheu's prosecution in "the Balletti incident."

To Roselli, Giancana's sexual escapades were nightmarish. Not only had the Chicago gangster unbalanced the plot through his affection for Ms. McGuire, but he'd also become entangled in an

---

* A spike-mike is a nail-shaped microphone which can be driven into a wall, permitting those in one room to monitor conversations in an adjoining one. Since it is not, strictly speaking, a transmitter—but only an eavesdropping device—its use was not covered by wiretapping statutes.

affair with the President's mistress—Judith Exner, to whom singer
Frank Sinatra introduced both John Kennedy and Sam Giancana.*
So far as Roselli was concerned, the events in Florida were becoming awfully claustrophobic. A professional, he was outraged at Giancana's peccadilloes, haranguing the Chicago mobster to the effect
that Momo's pillow talk may have saved Castro's life. And that, he
added, in a fit of patriotism, put the future of democracy up for
grabs. Giancana burst out laughing. According to Roselli, "I remember his expression. Smoking a cigar—he almost swallowed it, laughing about it." This infuriated Roselli even more. Balletti's *faux pas*
"was blowing everything, blowing every kind of cover that I'd tried
to arrange. . . ."

Actually, the plot's cover story had been concocted by Jim
O'Connell. Maheu and he were supposed to represent a consortium
of Wall Street businessmen and multinational corporations who'd
pooled their cash for the assassination of Fidel. The CIA, despite its
intensive activity in the Miami area at the time, was not to be connected with the plot. And the story wasn't an implausible one. Many
American businessmen whose Cuban properties had been national-
ized were supporting invasion efforts that may well have included
attempts on Castro's life. (One of the most flamboyant of these
businessmen was William D. Pawley, one of Richard Nixon's most
avid supporters. A counterrevolutionary of legendary stature, Pawley
had organized the Flying Tigers, American "volunteers" who supported Chiang Kai-shek in his battle for mainland China. A multimillionaire many times over, Pawley owned the Havana Bus
Company and had large investments in Cuba's mineral and sugar
industries. Supporting the extreme-right wing of the Cuban exile

---

* As a result of Giancana's untimely demise in 1975, a few days before he was to be
subpoenaed before the Church Committee, and as a result of that committee's perverse
unwillingness to subpoena Sinatra, there is some uncertainty about precisely when
Ms. Exner met the President and the gangster. It appears, however, that Sinatra introduced Kennedy to Exner at the singer's Palm Springs estate in the spring of 1960, when
then-Senator Kennedy was campaigning against Nixon for the Presidency. Sinatra's
introduction of Giancana to Exner occurred in Miami sometime in the fall—in other
words, Giancana's relationship with Exner began at the same time that he was plotting
the Castro assassination. The question of timing is of more than academic interest. How
much did Exner know of the plot, and how much of that knowledge did she convey to
Kennedy? What, if anything, did she tell Giancana of her relationship with the soon-
to-be President? What did Sinatra himself know of the Castro assassination plot? And
regarding the introduction to Exner of both Kennedy *and* Giancana, was this mere
gaucherie on the part of the middle-aged singer—or was there something more to it?
The Church Committee's unwillingness to subpoena Sinatra (and Exner) suggests an
almost criminal malfeasance on its part.

movement in Miami, Pawley was a Daddy Warbucks figure who while in his sixties insisted upon accompanying mercenaries and exiles on midnight raids against Havana's harbor.)

Still, the Wall Street cover story was a failure. Roselli learned of the CIA's role at his first meeting with Maheu in the Brown Derby. And Giancana learned about it from Roselli. As for the Cubans, they'd had enough experience to recognize a CIA plot when they saw one—and this one was almost obvious.

Indeed, it was so obvious as to invite suspicion. How is it that experienced spooks such as Maheu and O'Connell, backed by Sheffield Edwards and Dick Bissell in Washington, proceeded with their plans even after their cover had been blown, the FBI had become involved, and indictments were being prepared in Nevada? It didn't make sense. To explain the operation's continuation we must rely upon the "menopausal theory," which holds that the CIA, in its 1960–62 operations against Cuba, was an institution that had lost its reason. There is considerable evidence for that besides the continuation of the Maheu/Roselli plot: the supposedly secret training of Cuban exiles that culminated in the April, 1961, Bay of Pigs fiasco was, in fact, something of an extravaganza. As early as October, 1960, Castro had placed his troops at "ready-alert" and broadcast a speech warning that an invasion was "imminent." Newspaper articles in Miami, New York, and foreign papers corroborated the Cuban's analysis, detailing exiles' training sessions in Florida and Central America. Still, the invasion took place (with what results we know), and it may be that Maheu and Roselli shared the Agency's attitude of "Damn the torpedos, full speed ahead!" Or it may be that *greed* was a motivation. While none of the plotters was paid for his work against Castro, and while the promised $150,000 CIA reward was payable only to the actual killer, a much larger reward was also in the offing: the one million dollars proffered by Meyer Lansky. Certainly Roselli, Trafficante, and Giancana knew of that contract. They were Lansky's friends. And had they killed Castro, they certainly could not have been blamed if they'd staked a claim to the money on the premise that "a contract is a contract." The CIA's involvement, then, can be looked upon as a convenient excuse for the plotters to neutralize the Neutrality Act.*

---

* Or to put it more succinctly, it may be that Maheu's "cover story" about the assassination plot having been organized by multinational corporations and private parties *was true*—and that the real cover story was the one that emerged a decade later, attributing his conspiracy to the CIA.

Whether it was greed or menopausal madness, the plot proceeded. Trafficante had found a Cuban exile leader (believed to have been Rolando Masferrer) who agreed to help. Whatever his identity, the CIA later concluded that the leader may have been receiving funds from Trafficante and other racketeers interested in winning "gambling, prostitution, and dope monopolies" following the overthrow of Castro. If the leader *was* on Trafficante's payroll, then the possibility must be raised that he too may have been a double agent in Castro's employ.* In any event, the exile leader persuaded the Agency that his primary interest in Castro's assassination was to obtain the $150,000 reward, which he intended to use for the purchase of arms and other equipment that would come in handy for an invasion of Cuba. Killing Fidel, the Cuban said, would be accomplished with poison. He had a contact, a woman, in Castro's favorite restaurant. *She* would put the botulism in his food, and two days later the Cuban premier would sicken and die. An autopsy would attribute the death to "natural causes." All the Cuban asked, in return for his cooperation, were the pills, some cash, and communications equipment.

And having asked, he received. The radio equipment was sent down to Miami with a CIA officer. He turned it over to Maheu, who delivered it, in a "sanitized" automobile, to a vacant lot, where the Cuban picked it up. Meanwhile, back in Langley, Sheffield Edwards rejoiced at the death throes of monkeys who'd been fed the new batch of poison, glimpsing Castro's agony in the simians' demise. Along with an estimated ten thousand dollars in cash, the poison capsules were dispatched to the Fontainebleau. By this time it was early March, a month before the scheduled invasion. Joe Shimon, the Washington cop and confidant of Giancana and Roselli, had joined his friends in time to see the Patterson-Johansson heavyweight title fight. Informed of the plot, Shimon became a sort of fifth wheel in Maheu's fifth column, serving as a cut-out. According to Shimon, the poisoned capsules were passed by Maheu to an odd-looking Cuban who stood in the doorway to the Fontaine-

---

* A Cuban exile leader in Castro's employ is an obvious contradiction in terms—as any double agent's situation would be. That Castro may have established an actual supporter of his cause as a supposed "exile leader" in Miami is quite possible. The counterintelligence value of such an agent would be enormous: besides providing intelligence, he might also act as an *agent provocateur,* sapping the exile movement of its strength and sabotaging its plans. In this regard it should be noted that Masferrer was once a supporter of Castro and that his Miami operations were uniformly unsuccessful in their attacks upon Fidel's regime.

bleau's appropriately named Boom Boom Room. Maheu disputes that account, but Shimon says that he remembers it well: "The Cuban was so out of place! He had orange hair and he was sweating. Listen: the Fontainebleau was a class hotel—the Cuban just didn't belong there. He stood out like a sore thumb. I'll never forget it: it was funny."

The Bay of Pigs invasion was by this time only a few weeks away, and it takes little imagination to envision what might have happened had Castro sickened and died at this crucial time. While the invasion was unlikely to succeed in any case—the marauding exiles being too few in number and bereft of meaningful air support—there is a chance that Fidel's demise would have dispirited and perhaps divided the young regime in its most fragile moment. Certainly, this was the intention of the CIA. As it happened, however, Castro was saved by what we're told was a fortuitous change in his dining habits. According to Senate testimony, the Cuban premier suddenly stopped eating at his favorite restaurant. And this put him beyond the reach of the woman who was to have poisoned his food. Obviously, such things happen: other nations have been saved, and still others lost, through seeming happenstance—the want of a horse to seat a king in battle, a President's decision to see a famous actor on the stage, and so forth. But given the rumors and suspicions concerning Trafficante's alleged role as a double agent, there is every reason to speculate that Castro may have been warned of the plot even as it unfolded. This appears to have been Johnny Roselli's view. In later years he would confide in his friend Joe Shimon, and in his attorneys Ed Morgan and Tom Wadden, that he had reason to believe that the assassination force had been betrayed—and that, moreover, the hit-men targeted against Castro were later used to carry out a retaliatory assassination against President John Kennedy.*

Of course, neither those who plotted against Castro nor Castro himself would have wanted the double agent's role exposed—especially if, as Roselli later told his attorneys, the plot led directly to the murder of an American President. It was safer for everyone concerned to support the notion that the plot had come unstuck from its own deficiencies, rather than from the presence of a double agent. In that way the exploding conch shells, poisoned cigars, and

---

* Ed Morgan is also a close friend of Maheu's and formerly an attorney representing Howard Hughes. Tom Wadden is a criminal lawyer who was formerly the partner of Edward Bennett Williams.

tubercular wet suits might be seen not as diabolical, but as comical. Reducing these operations to their least threatening aspect (much as the Watergate burglary has been made to seem a Keystone Kops affair), the would-be assassins escape intensive scrutiny (and perhaps punishment) even as the double agent remains protected. Obviously, if the Agency's plot against Castro led to the liquidation of Jack Kennedy, neither the Agency nor Castro would want that fact revealed. Neither would the individual plotters against the Cuban premier, nor any double agent who may have been involved. In that sense, then, we can imagine a conspiracy to cover up details of the "CIA/Mafia plot," a tacit conspiracy between otherwise deadly enemies.

With the failure of the plot, the men went their separate ways:

- Joe Shimon returned to Washington to become enmeshed in the Mayflower Hotel bugging, described earlier. A disgraced cop thereafter, he became a private investigator, subsequently testifying before the Church Committee concerning his knowledge of the Castro plot.
- Santos Trafficante went back to Tampa and the rackets he controls from there. In 1963 he became the subject of intensive scrutiny by the FBI for his having predicted, during a 1962 conversation with Cuban exile leader José Aleman, that Jack Kennedy "is going to be hit." Today such predictions are less than remarkable: political assassination has become, if not a commonplace, at least an obvious possibility in any presidential campaign. In 1962, however, the prediction had a fantastic quality, so long had it been since murder had invaded American politics. Accordingly, CIA, FBI, and private investigators interested in the Kennedy case looked for connections between Trafficante and those associated with the events in Dealey Plaza. The results were meager but provocative. It was learned, for instance, that Trafficante's closest associate among organized-crime figures is Carlos Marcello, the New Orleans don kidnapped by the CIA (at Robert Kennedy's orders) a bare two weeks before the Bay of Pigs invasion. Flown to Guatemala and supposedly held there against his wishes, Marcello returned to the United States in the wake of the Cuban invasion; the means of his reentry was afforded by his private pilot, David Ferrie—who later figured so dramatically in New Orleans District Attorney Jim Garrison's investigation of the Dallas assassination. In addi-

tion, it was learned that Trafficante, while a prisoner of Castro in 1959, was "frequently visited" by "an American gangster" named "Ruby." * Whether that Ruby was the same Ruby who killed Lee Harvey Oswald, Kennedy's alleged assassin,† is uncertain. But it seems likely. As David Ferrie had (and, for that matter, Teamsters stoolie Grady Partin, wireman Bernard Spindel, and Galindez pilot Gerald Murphy), Ruby had smuggled guns from the Miami area to Castro's troops in the Sierra Maestra. He was, moreover, a close associate and friend of Lewis McWillie, Trafficante's casino manager at the Tropicana Hotel in Havana. Linked in FBI reports to Havana gambling czars Meyer Lansky and Dino Cellini (later an associate of both Robert Vesco and the top employees of Resorts International), McWillie was visited in Havana by Jack Ruby on at least two occasions during 1959 ‡—the same year in which the jailed Trafficante was visited by the "American gangster" named Ruby. According to the Warren Commission (which failed to interview either Trafficante or McWillie), Ruby "idolized" the Tropicana's casino manager.§ It seems very likely, then, that the Rubys who visited Trafficante and his employee McWillie were the same. And this likelihood, given Roselli's belief that Trafficante was a double agent of Castro's raises the specter that Ruby's liquidation of Lee Harvey Oswald was carried out *in behalf* of Trafficante—that it was not the spontaneous act of a man who grieved for Jacqueline Kennedy, as Ruby himself sometimes suggested, but the elimination of a dangerous scapegoat.

The man who might dispel the mysteries surrounding the apparent links between the attempted assassination of Fidel Castro and the actual murder of John Kennedy is, of course, Santos Trafficante. But he isn't talking. During the Senate's 1975 investigation of plots against Castro, Trafficante was conveniently out of reach, having joined Vesco in Costa Rican exile. Returning to the United States immediately after the Senate hearings were completed, Trafficante subsequently found himself sub-

---

* CIA memorandum of November 28, 1963, Warren Commission Document #206-83.
† Not only had Oswald never been convicted of killing John F. Kennedy, he was never booked on the charge. His detention in the Dallas jail that became his killing floor was on a charge relating to the murder of Dallas patrolman J. D. Tippit.
‡ March 26, 1964, memorandum entitled "Jack L. Ruby, Lee Harvey Oswald—Victim."
§ Warren Commission Report, p. 708, and Warren Commission Exhibit 1697.

poenaed to testify before the House committee investigating
the tweeping of JFK. To every question asked, including those
concerning his relationship to Jack Ruby, Trafficante's response
was the same: he took the Fifth.

- If Trafficante has prospered in the years after the intrigues led
by Maheu, San Giancana did not. The Chicago mobster fell
into bad odor with his criminal associates as a result of his
ostentatious life-style. Always one for a good time, he paid a
fateful visit to the swank Cal-Neva Lodge and gambling casino
in 1963, visiting with headliner Phyllis McGuire there. What
made the visit fateful was the fact that Giancana had been
banned from Nevada's resorts, his notoriety having preceded
him. Even worse, news of his visit became the subject of headlines to articles exploring his close friendship with Frank
Sinatra, at that time the casino's ostensible owner (and always
good copy). Sinatra's friendship with the Kennedys and his
affection for Mafiosi such as Giancana were an embarrassment
—not only to the Hyannis Port bluebloods, but to organized-
crime figures as well. Giancana's sin was one of indiscretion—
and it could not have helped matters that Lewis McWillie,
Ruby's idol and a refugee from Castro's Havana, had found
new employment at the same Cal-Neva Lodge. So it was that
Giancana suddenly fled the United States at about the time of
the Kennedy assassination, taking refuge in Mexico City and
later in the Argentine. Returning years later to Chicago, his
powers were considerably diminished. Finally, on June 19,
1975, he was slain in his home by an extremely competent
killer who used a sawed-off .22-caliber pistol whose silencer
was made doubly effective by the killer's having drilled *forty-
two* holes in the gun's barrel. Indeed, the killer left nothing
to chance: no fewer than seven shots were stitched in a tidy
circle around Giancana's mouth—suggesting to police that
someone was concerned that Giancana might be talking and
that, moreover, that same someone wanted to warn others
against the practice. At the time of his death Giancana was
under two subpoenas (and round-the-clock police surveillance
as well). One subpoena would have had him testify anent the
laundering of money through banks in the Bahamas. The other
subpoena (undelivered at the time of his death) would have
had him tell the Senate's Church Committee what he knew
about the plot to murder Castro. Giancana was the only Senate

witness ever to be murdered just prior to giving testimony, and police agree his murder is unlikely to be solved. Neither the FBI nor the Chicago police is openly involved in the investigation (both plead lack of jurisdiction), and the only clue seems to be the origin of the gun: Florida.

- If Giancana's ending was a brutal one, Roselli's was barbaric. When the initial plot against Castro failed for the premier's having changed restaurants, the Mob's Don Giovanni didn't give up. Though Maheu and the others were removed from the assignment, Roselli was soon teamed with the CIA's top gun, Bill Harvey. Following the Bay of Pigs debacle, Harvey was placed in charge of a CIA "assassination bureau" code-named "ZR/RIFLE." So secret was this bureau that the Agency's own director, John McCone, didn't know of it. Still, Castro eluded the Agency's hit-men until Jack Kennedy's own death —after which the CIA ceased in its efforts to murder the Cuban leader.* These plots ended, Roselli trekked westward, helping Maheu to negotiate the sale of the Desert Inn to Howard Hughes, paving the way for Hughes's domination of what became a Nevada fiefdom. And, always, Johnny Roselli had his scams. Between 1962 and 1968 he participated in rigging card games at the Friars' Club, a world-class wateringhole for Hollywood's greatest celebrities. With holes in the ceiling, mirrors strategically deployed, and electric buzzers on the calves of the gamblers, Roselli and his accomplices bilked moviedom's biggest stars of millions at gin rummy. The affair was a distinct embarrassment to the ubiquitous Frank Sinatra and his chum Dean Martin, who'd sponsored Roselli for membership in the club. Just as the Cal-Neva incident sent Giancana into a mandatory retirement from the rackets, Roselli's gaff at the Friars' Club finished his own criminal career. Retiring to Florida to live with his sister and her husband, Roselli planned to spend his golden years golfing in the sun. In 1976, however, those years were cut short some two weeks after he dined with Santos Trafficante. Leaving home one afternoon to play a round or

---

* Indeed, the Agency went even further, informing Castro in 1968 of an assassination plot led by Cuban exiles. The exiles, believing themselves to be in the employ of the Agency at the time of the projected hit, were killed or captured. One who escaped, interestingly enough, was Max Gorman Gonzalez—a/k/a "Virgino Gonzales," the Cuban thought by some reporters to have authored the so-called Gonzalez Memorandum, detailing CIA and Intertel surveillance of former Hughes employee Johnny Meier and *Playboy* publisher Hugh Hefner.

two, Roselli temporarily disappeared. That the disappearance was supposed to be permanent is clear: the handsome hood's automobile was found at the airport, a circumstance that was clearly meant to suggest that Roselli had, perhaps in fear of deportation proceedings pending against him, flown to parts unknown. In fact, however, Roselli surfaced—literally—only a few weeks after he'd vanished. An oil drum containing his body had floated to the surface in Miami's Biscayne Bay. Loaded down with chains, the fifty-five gallon drum was stippled with holes intended to provide escape for the gases emanating from the decomposing body within. But somehow the chains and holes failed in their purpose. Johnny's tomb floated onto the front pages of newspapers everywhere. Emptying the oilcan's contents, police found that the racketeer had been garroted and stabbed. His legs had been sawed off and jammed into the can with his torso and the weighting chains. Only the sequence of these brutalities, and the identity of the killers, remain in doubt.

- As for Robert Maheu, the Castro plot seems to have diminished his influence with the CIA—perhaps because, as Joe Shimon suggests, he was unwilling to take the rap for the Agency when Senate investigators tried to probe his eavesdropping activities. And while the Agency aborted several such investigations into Maheu's career, it could not have been happy about it: the CIA resents those who have leverage over it.

In fairness, though, Maheu could not have cared too much about his disintegrating relationship with the forces at Langley. By 1961 he'd become the grand vizier of the man whom *Fortune* called, with more wit than it knew, "the spook of American capitalism." Moving to Los Angeles to be closer to his boss, Maheu began to play a real-life J. Beresford Tipton to the billionaire's demented Scrooge.

4 / THE STOCKHOLDER

Howard Hughes's career is so well-known that any summary of it must seem superfluous. And yet, so large is the concentration of wealth that's become synonymous with the initials *H.R.H.* (His Royal Highness Howard Robard Hughes), and so enormous has the power of his empire become, a brief review may be excused. His holdings, after all, have so far remained intact after his death in 1976.

Those holdings are as wide as one can imagine. As heir to the Houston-based Hughes Tool Company, young Howard found himself in possession of a monopoly upon a drill bit that was virtually essential to removing oil from the ground. That was in the Roaring Twenties, at the very inception of the fifty-year boom during which the search for petroleum would be at its height. During that time "Toolco" would earn its sole owner nearly $800,000,000 in profits. This alone would have made Hughes wealthier than most millionaires ever dream of becoming. To the young Texan, though, Toolco was merely a capital base, a place of departure. Abandoning Houston to let the firm run itself (he would visit its offices only once in his life), he went to Hollywood. There he made a series of artless B movies, many of them bombs, some of them successes. But his interest in Hollywood owed more to his sexual drive than to any schemes of financial glory. While gaunt and shy, he was nevertheless tall, dark, and handsome—not to mention absurdly rich and even, at times, rather charming. Admittedly, he was also weird: on occasion he'd greet important guests wearing only a pair of empty Kleenex boxes on his feet; at other times, in deference to his nocturnal habits, he'd order bellboys to place ham sandwiches at 2 A.M. in the boughs of trees outside his rooms at the Beverly Hills Hotel. His friends and girl friends attributed these "eccentricities" to a puckish sense of humor, finding this early evidence of madness to be nothing more than the idiosyncrasies one is supposed to associate with "genius."

Hughes's claim to that last appellation derived from his aeronautical exploits. In 1938 he set a round-the-world flight record, winning the sort of acclaim achieved earlier by Charles Lindbergh. A shy man, he found himself the hero of ticker-tape parades, the occupant of a fantastic place in the American mythology: undeniably rich and reputedly brilliant, he was also an acknowledged hero, Hollywood's sexual commandant, and, not least of all, a Texan. Wealth, aviation, sex, films, and Texas proved an irresistible combination to a public suffering through the economic abscess of depression, and they gave him their heart because in a real sense Hughes lived for all of them. If ever a man seemed to have been one of the elect, it was Howard Hughes.

"Genius" was certainly an excessive evaluation of his inventive talents, but Hughes figured so hugely in the imaginations of Depression era Americans that few newspapers could bring themselves to describe him in anything less than mythic terms. So it was that the talented tinkerer was characterized by the same word that had earlier been reserved for the likes of Michelangelo, inviting comparisons between the Sistine Chapel and *Scarface,* one of Hughes's better films.

And still the money came rolling in, permitting Hughes to expand both his economic ventures and the stable of starlets whom he'd signed to contracts that would deliver some of them from adolescence to menopause without ever having made a film. In 1938 he began buying TWA stock with the proceeds from Toolco, while at about the same time establishing Hughes Aircraft as a subsidiary of the Texas firm. His contribution to the war effort during the 1940s was sufficiently questionable that Hughes became the subject of Senate scrutiny. It was the first time that truly hostile publicity had been directed against him. Brought to Washington against his will, he was depicted in the press as a war profiteer, a man of dubious loyalty: he'd received $60,000,000 in Air Force contracts during the war and yet he'd failed to deliver a single plane. Watching old film clips of the painfully private Hughes seated amid the klieg lights and hostile questions of the U. S. Senate, one gets the impression of a man submerging his panic in paranoia, treating each question as if it were his last, evaluating his interrogators with an almost reptilian stare. The Senate hearings were a terrible fall from grace for a man who was used to being worshipped from afar. And they were made even more painful (and highly personal) by the sarcastic questions directed at the development of his pride and joy: the ten-story-high *Spruce Goose,* an amphibian colossus which Hughes claimed could carry seven hundred combat-ready troops thousands of miles. He swore it would fly, contradicting the skepticism of his interrogators, and millions of dollars and two years later it did. He flew it himself for a distance of a mile, at an altitude less than the plane's own height. And then he locked it away in a hangar, out of public view.

It was at about this time that Hughes's shyness veered toward the extremities of personal secrecy. While not yet a recluse, he became increasingly less accessible. Believing himself the victim of a Communist conspiracy—and believing too that he was under the constant surveillance of his enemies—he participated enthusiastically in the infamous blacklisting of Hollywood writers, actors, and directors. Despite his right-wing enthusiasms, and his firm place in American culture as the inventor of actress Jane Russell's canti-levered bra, he continued to anger those responsible for America's military preparedness. In particular, his whimsical direction of Hughes Aircraft, a bastion of high-technology expertise, led his most talented employees to desert the firm amid charges that his eccentric behavior was a danger to national security.

By 1955 Hughes had sold RKO Studios and placed Hughes Air-craft in trusteeship, naming the Howard Hughes Medical Institute as sole beneficiary. This largesse, however, seems less than genuine when one considers that Hughes remained as president of the air-craft company while at the same time serving as the Institute's sole director: his control over both was total. The Institute, moreover, has been less than generous in its contributions to medical research. During the 1960s it doled out about $2,500,000 annually—a paltry sum in view of its holdings: an estimated $154,000,000 in stock, paying an abysmal dividend of about 2 percent. Had the Institute sold that stock and placed the proceeds in an ordinary savings ac-count, at least twice as much cash would have been available for philanthropy. But, of course, Hughes's real interest had more to do with tax avoidance than with medicine. And by that standard his philanthropy was a success. Becoming a billionaire, he found him-self with a personal tax liability which in some years was less than $25,000.

And his life had become a closed book: disappearing into a cocoon of secrecy, he directed his empire by remote control. Inaccessible to all but a few, he conducted business by telephone in the bleakest hours of the night, traveling from one imperial hideout to another in anonymous old Chevrolets. His security needs and his insatiable appetite for secret intelligence rivaled those of embattled kings surrounded by a poisonous court. In 1956 he hired Robert Maheu as a prelude to taking Jean Peters to wife the year after. And then, in 1958, he vanished forever from public view, entering an un-broken hermitage until the time of his death, eighteen years later. When the Sixties dawned, Hughes's "eccentricities" had evolved into full-blown manias of a sort seldom encountered beyond the confines of a padded cell. Judging by his memoranda to Maheu, the billionaire retained a measure of clarity and cunning where his business affairs were concerned. In other areas, however, he was a study in the pathology of terminal greed. His secretiveness and fortresslike security precautions can only be explained with reference to clinical terms describing extreme paranoiac states. With the exception of a half-dozen Mormon aides, whose only qualifications appear to have been plodding rectitude and tractability coupled with what Hughes's attorney Edward Morgan has called "almost supernatural mediocrity," virtually *no one* saw Howard Hughes. His phobia of germs was similarly extreme: secretaries typing correspondence to be handled by the billionaire were made to wear white gloves, while Hughes himself observed his Mormon retainers from behind a perimeter of plate glass which surrounded his rank inner sanctum. The severe mood-swings described by those few who knew him can be explained in terms of his regular blood transfusions—but they can also be seen as evidence of a powerful, even consumptive, manic depression. As for his having sometimes dictated a single sentence or phrase to a stenographer, repeating it over and over, during the course of an entire evening, insisting that she write the words each time they were spoken, we may resort to a variety of explanations: senility, brain damage, or the cruelest sort of compulsion. The evidence, however, is clear: Hughes was starkers.

Interestingly, gross insanity was no obstacle to the billionaire's continuing success in the fields of American commerce. In an effort to make TWA the world's first all-jet airline, he found it necessary to acquire a temporary partner in the form of an eastern banking consortium. In return for hundreds of millions in loans needed to finance the acquisition of jet airliners, Hughes agreed to place his 78-percent holding of TWA stock in trust for ten years, control of the airline passing temporarily to a management team appointed by the banks. (It was this loan to which DEA informer Larry Jividen had reference when he wrote that organized crime provided Hughes with the capital for TWA's expansion, supposedly laundering the "Rosemark" funds through Swiss banks and New York's Irving Trust.) Surprisingly, one of the first acts taken by the airline's caretaker government was to sue TWA's owner in July, 1961, for "atrocious mismanagement." This, then, became Robert Maheu's first assignment for Hughes upon his return from the wars against Castro. A manhunt was on for the Stockholder, with process servers and private detectives trying desperately to serve him with a subpoena, demanding his appearance in court. Besides coordinating an offensive intelligence operation, Maheu was under orders from Hughes to prevent service of the subpoena at almost any cost: the Old Man had declared his willingness to suffer an anticipated judgment of $150,000,000 rather than make a personal appearance in court. To prevent service, Maheu waged a counterintelligence operation worthy of his talents, deploying Hughesian doubles, renting Mexican hideaways, and sowing red herrings throughout the West Coast and Latin America. Hughes was here, he was there, he was everywhere—but he was nowhere to be found.

The suit itself was an amazing one, a corporate double cross of historical dimensions. Had the billionaire lost the case, he'd have been made to pay most of the judgment to himself as the firm's largest stockholder. Before this could happen, though, Hughes sold his TWA stock to the public in 1966, getting seventy-eight dollars per share—*almost seven times what the same stock would be worth ten years later.* Had he wanted to, Hughes could have repurchased his TWA holdings a few years later for less than the interest due him on the amount received from the 1966 sale. The TWA bailout, then, was perhaps the smartest stock transaction in the history of paper, earning Hughes more than one-half billion dollars in cash.

With a check for $546,000,000 in hand, he journeyed by train to Nevada in all the secrecy that could be mustered to surround twin-diesel locomotives dragging a chain of heavily guarded pullmans across the Continental Divide to America's gaudiest city. Bundled into the Desert Inn's top floor on Thanksgiving Day, 1966—Johnny Roselli interceded with the owners to get Hughes the space he wanted—the billionaire issued orders that Maheu reinvest the proceeds from the TWA sale in order to minimize his tax liability. Overnight, the Las Vegas establishment began to receive offers that couldn't be refused. Within a year of his arrival in Nevada, Hughes had made the state his personal province, expanding his holdings to include vast expanses of western real estate, mining claims, casinos, shops, hotels, airports, airlines, broadcasting and cable-television firms—not to mention Hughes Helicopter, Mother Toolco, and the control he exercised over the Hughes Aircraft Company and the Medical Institute. By 1970, when the spooks went to war for control of Hughes's protoplasm, he was unquestionably one of the most powerful men in the world, with huge investments in a kaleidoscope of industries whose common denominators were glamour and risk.

Getting there was a predictably controversial task, requiring not merely large sums of cash, but a Machiavellian knowledge of how they should best be applied. Accordingly, Hughes long ago set out to acquire as much influence as possible in all branches and parties of government. Republican and Democratic politicians on local, state, and federal levels were bought with gifts, loans, campaign contributions, and secret cash payments. In both the Johnson and Nixon White Houses, Hughes's bagmen made their presence felt, delivering satchels filled with cash to candidates and aides waiting in parked limousines or lolling beside Florida pools. Neither the Civil Service bureaucracy nor the staffs of influential politicians were ignored: former employees of the IRS, FBI, CIA, NSA, GSA, HEW, HUD, FAA—the entire alphabet soup of Washington rule—found jobs with Hughes's enterprises. In the nation's capital it was understood that the Stockholder took care of civil servants who took care of him. And they took *good* care of him. Between 1965 and 1975 Hughes companies were awarded more than six billion dollars in defense contracts alone—the majority of the awards having been made without competitive bids. Today Hughes enterprises are approaching the two-billion-dollar *per year* mark (again, in defense contracts alone). The significance of this for the taxpayers is spectacular since the federal government itself estimates that noncompetitive bids tend to be 25 percent higher than bids awarded in competition.

If the federal government, paying Hughes upward of five million dollars per day, can be said to have been his partner, it's been his only one. For the most part, Hughes's enterprises were wholly owned by him; and on those few occasions when having partners was unavoidable, as with TWA, the billionaire retained a majority of the stock. So it was that Hughes exercised totalitarian control over his empire, limiting federal regulation and SEC scrutiny to a minimum. There was, of course, another advantage to sole proprietorship: answerable to no stockholders, Hughes was an ideal contractor for CIA projects requiring both secrecy and public deception. In fact, according to Nixon staffer Charles Colson, Hughes was the Agency's single largest contractor. Just how much he reaped from the Agency is uncertain, though, since so many of its contracts have been disguised within the budgets of other departments.

Despite his friends at the Agency, Hughes was in almost constant trouble with other businessmen whose firms he manipulated and with a variety of federal institutions. If greed were a disease, Hughes would have died in infancy: not since the heyday of hot-blooded madams traveling through the frozen wastes of Yukon boomtowns in search of fortune has there been a businessman of such rapaciousness. Accordingly, he had need of a phalanx of attorneys, the best that money could buy. And he used them magnificently: in one case he gave three separate attorneys his "full authority" to pursue the case in three opposite directions—one was to negotiate for an out-of-court settlement, another was to fight the case in court, and a third was to delay the litigation until its death. The effect of this, of course, was to confuse and paralyze the opposition. And it succeeded. With more legal talent at his disposal than all the law faculties within the Ivy League, Hughes waged a war of legal attrition against his enemies, his victims, and the cranks * who flocked toward his wealth. Authors who sought to write about him were sued or bought off. Cost overruns on government contracts demanded frequent explanation, sometimes in the courts. Brutal take-overs, such as that of Air West in 1968, often resulted in litigation on several fronts, involving both stockholders and the SEC. Former employees were eternally suing him; the Justice Department was ever on the brink of antitrust action; IRS attorneys seemed constantly to be taking depositions in preparation for litigation; and two Air West stockholders were even suing to have an administrator appointed for Hughes's estate, contending in 1975 that Hughes was already dead and had been dead "for a considerable period," the "fiction" of his vitality having been maintained "for the personal profit of various and sundry persons." And, of course, the TWA suit crept along for more than a decade in the manner of Charles Dickens' *Jarndyce v. Jarndyce*. Its resolution was a bad joke. After twelve years of tedious debate, lawyers for both sides expressed astonishment at the Supreme Court's 1973 ruling in support of Hughes, overturning a 1969 judgment awarding TWA more than $137,000,000

---

* It was natural that Hughes's wealth would attract cranks of every psychological shade, but some were more interesting than others. Richard R. Hughes, for instance. In 1976, Richard Hughes (formerly Joseph Michael Brown) claimed in the New Mexico courts to be Howard's long-lost son. He also claimed, however, to be in constant contact with "his father" by means of a secret communications device which unnamed surgeons had implanted in his brain. A bizarre case, it was eventually dismissed by the courts when a document allegedly signed by Howard Hughes, admitting his paternity, could not be gotten verified. What made the incident even more peculiar, however, were the following facts: Richard Hughes's claim was supported by one Grover Walker, an acknowledged employee of Howard Hughes's since 1971. Walker swore that he'd been hired by the billionaire to handle communications between the putative father and his supposed son. It was Walker, moreover, who claimed to have met Howard Hughes in New Mexico and to have received the document purporting to admit Hughes's paternity. This in itself might suggest no more than a cheap conspiracy but for the following fact: Howard Hughes was represented in this case—that is, denying the paternity—by one William Durden, a Hughes lawyer. What makes *this* peculiar is the fact that earlier, in 1975, Durden had represented *Richard* Hughes in a $50,000,000 lawsuit filed against *Howard* Hughes. What all this means is uncertain, but Richard's claim to have a communications implant in his head *does* make him sound like a chip off the old block.

356 /   SPOOKS

in damages. The Supreme Court's decision ignored virtually the entirety of the voluminous briefs submitted by both sides, relying instead upon a "fleeting" argument that seemed to have been abandoned by the Hughes forces years before. Briefly, that argument held that the Civil Aeronautics Board (CAB) had effectively "immunized" Hughes against litigation involving charges of mismanagement. Regulating Hughes's management of TWA, and approving each of his decisions as a part of its oversight responsibilities, the CAB had in fact certified his management as sound. Accordingly, Hughes could not be held liable in court for the effect of decisions that the appropriate regulatory commission had found, by virtue of its approval, to be in the public interest.

In many ways the identities of those involved in the Court's decision were more interesting than the decision itself. In its earliest years, when the dispositive argument had been so badly neglected, James Lee Rankin (formerly general counsel to the Warren Commission and later corporation counsel to New York City) served as special master in the case. Taking over from Rankin in 1966, when Hughes sold his TWA stock, was Herbert Brownell, the former Attorney General who'd indicted Aristotle Onassis for having taken advice that Brownell's own law firm had propounded. As special master, Brownell virtually devastated Hughes's defense, reversing decisions favorable to Hughes and generally bolstering TWA's position against the billionaire. Deciding the case *en fin* was the Supreme Court whose Chief Justice, Warren Burger, was also a figure in the Onassis affair. Burger's presence on the Supreme Court was owed to Richard Nixon, who'd appointed him to that post in 1969, and Nixon too had been a principal in the plot against Ari O.

All of this could only have worried Hughes. Like Onassis, he was a man whose enormous wealth had been leeched from the oil industry—though, like Onassis, he'd never been a part of it. For the past fifty years, that industry has been dominated by a consortium of multinational corporations which, while needing Hughes's toolbit and the Greek's ships, never had much use for the men who owned them. They were rich and flamboyant, cowboy-egotists who could never be depended upon to go along—and so threatened the industry that had made them as wealthy as kings. Like Onassis, whose Jiddah Agreement promised to upset the distribution system established for mutual profit decades before, Hughes might bite the hand that fed him. Admittedly, there were some common interests among the families that ran and owned the multinationals and the men, like Hughes, who serviced them (or like H. L. Hunt, the "independents" who were never content with their tiny percentages). To the league of multinationals, such men, by flaunting their wealth in egregious displays, attracted the attention of reformers. Few things could be worse. As for those who ran the multinationals, they embodied a corporate style in the service of the corporate goal. They tended to owe their allegiance to families belonging to the Main Line of the eastern Establishment, families with ties to the largest banks in the world and to the foundation and foreign policy apparatus associated with the Rockefeller name. Onassis, Hughes, and the others had no such ties, or were (like Onassis) capable of severing them at a moment's notice. So these men were seen as interlopers, potential rivals strung out on free enterprise: they threatened to unhinge cartels that had been a century in the making. So Hughes could not have applauded the appointment of the brahmin Herbert Brownell as Special Master in the TWA case. Neither could he have delighted in the appointment of Warren Burger to head the Supreme Court. Burger was the creation of Harold Stassen, an Atlanticist in the same eastern establishment mold as Brownell, Burger's former boss in the Justice Department. In his war with the big banks, Hughes could expect little comfort from either man. (Nor would he get any. Brownell, as has been said, nearly devastated Hughes's case by means of his rulings as Special Master. And subsequently, Burger would decide against the Hughes interests in an opinion dissenting from the majority.)

So it was that Hughes saw a special kind of leverage in the person of Robert Maheu. The spook held the keys to some of the Nixon Administration's darkest secrets. He'd been a part of the Onassis plot, helped to unseat Stassen and, more recently, held responsibility for Hughes's political contributions, including secret cash donations to the President's friend, Bebe Rebozo. Nixon's corruption might, with Maheu's help, save Hughes from the fate the banks had planned for him in open court.

A different kind of "NixonBurger" * than that of a decade earlier

---

* In 1957, Vice President Nixon's mother received a virtually unsecured loan of $205,000 from Howard Hughes. The money was used by Nixon's brother Donald to beef up a rapidly failing fast-food franchise in southern California—a franchise which specialized in the sale of a gastronomic bomb which Donald, in his hubris, called "the Nixonburger." The incident nearly ended Nixon's career since it appeared to many that Hughes had received extraordinary *quids pro quo* in return for the loan. Shortly after it was granted, earlier government decisions unfavorable to Hughes were reversed by a host of agencies, including the CAB, IRS, SEC, and Justice Department. New routes were granted, lending proposals approved, refunds extended, questioned stock transfers permitted, and antitrust suits dropped. The value of the reversals to Hughes has been estimated in the tens of millions of dollars.

seemed to be in the works, and so Hughes elevated Maheu above every attorney on his staff, giving him complete responsibility for the TWA matter—as he made clear in the following memo to his private spy.

> Bob, please understand one thing which I do not think you have understood heretofore: You have the ball on the TWA situation. You do not need further approval from me until such time as you are prepared to recommend to me a specific sum of money. About legal representation is up to you.
>
> If I am to hold you responsible for the overall outcome of the litigation, I must give you complete authority to decide which law firm you want to handle each phase of it.
>
> I repeat, Bob, you have *full* authority. [Emphasis in original.]

Chester Davis, Hughes's main attorney, appeared to be out; Maheu believed that the only way to save the case was to argue that Hughes had not had adequate representation in the lower courts. It was not an argument that Davis could advance himself, so Maheu began a search for Davis's successor, infuriating the lawyer whose position in the Hughes empire was deteriorating. At that point, the summer of 1970, Maheu seemed to be all-powerful within the Hughes camp. Even Charles Alan Wright, the brilliant constitutional lawyer who would soon become Richard Nixon's defender in the Watergate scandal, and who would also argue Hughes's case before the Burger Court, would have no more authority in the TWA matter than Maheu—providing, of course, that Maheu remained in Hughes's employ. But that was not to be. At the most strategic point in the TWA suit, immediately prior to its entry into Burger's Supreme Court, Maheu was purged from power. Taking his place at the top was Chester Davis, whose legal strategy in the TWA case had met with successive rebuffs in the courts, adverse decisions that threatened to wreck the empire.

The significance of all these maneuvers, and of the personalities making them, is occluded by the conflicting loyalties and complex relationships among those involved. It may be that the anti-Onassis caper held no significance for the TWA matter. Yet, as we've seen, those who were crucial to the Onassis affair subsequently presided over the TWA case: Brownell as special master, Burger as Chief Justice, Nixon as President, Maheu as *éminence grise*. While more than a decade had passed between the two affairs, the same men could be found playing essentially the same roles in each. A coincidence? Perhaps. But one notes also the similarity between the campaign against Onassis and the subsequent Watergate intelligence operation (undertaken, not incidentally, while the TWA case was before the Burger Court). In each affair, Onassis as much as Watergate, spooks were deployed on behalf of Richard Nixon, with "national security" coming to be invoked as a protective rubric, an afterthought. (In the Onassis incident, Maheu claims that the CIA became involved only *after* the private intelligence operation was well under way.) This isn't to say that the TWA case had any direct connection to Watergate, or that either conundrum bore a direct relationship to the problems of Onassis a decade before. The players, however, were the same. Fronting for Niarchos, Maheu intervened against Onassis on behalf of Nixon in an effort to preserve the profits and monopolies of Big Oil. In that connection, a 1952 entry in the diaries of Drew Pearson is provocative. According to the late columnist, "(a source) telephoned me from Texas . . . to tell me about a conspiracy which began about two years ago by H. L. Hunt, the big oil man, and a publicity firm called Watson Associates, to put Nixon into the Vice Presidency. He claims an untold amount of oil money had been behind Nixon for some time, and that all this was put over on Eisenhower without his knowing it. Later, some calls to Texas indicated the story is probably true . . ." *

Just as Maheu intervened for Nixon in the Onassis matter, he intervened for Hughes in the TWA suit, hiring super-Dem Larry O'Brien, eventual target of the Watergate burglary. Whatever else Maheu may have done in relation to TWA is unknown: his handling of Hughes's political contributions to Nixon and others might have been related to the case, and then again they might not have. But certainly Hughes was up to his fingernails in the Watergate affair. Besides the suspicious cache of one-hundred-dollar bills delivered to Rebozo by Hughes's secret agents, another of the billionaire's spooks, Ralph Winte, discussed with White House Plumbers E. Howard Hunt and Gordon Liddy how to invade the safe of Las Vegas *Sun* publisher Hank Greenspun (a Maheu loyalist believed

---

* Tyler Abell, ed., *Drew Pearson Diaries, 1949–1959* (New York: Holt, Rinehart and Winston, 1974), pp. 228–229. Actually, Hunt seems to have supported the presidential candidacy of General Douglas MacArthur, opposing Eisenhower. Pearson's source, however, may still have been right. The billionaire may have supported Nixon for Vice President, accepting Eisenhower only reluctantly. As I wrote earlier, the multinational oil companies and independents such as Hunt have little in common. But what they do have in common (e.g., the oil depletion allowance) might easily unite them behind a political candidate favorable to their mutual interests.

to have numerous Hughes memoranda). Moreover, Hunt's espionage activities were carried out under cover of the Robert R. Mullen Company, a CIA front which had taken over the Hughes "public-relations" account from Larry O'Brien and his Kennedy brain trust.

The significance of all this is elusive, and the most one can say is that there is a distinct style to certain historical events, and that many of the same people have played crucial roles in some matters that have yet to be fully explained. From the Onassis operation to the assassination in Dallas to the resolution of the TWA case * and, perhaps finally, to Watergate, the same people slink across one another's path. Dallas? Well, it's difficult not to note that Nixon sought (unsuccessfully) to have J. Lee Rankin, Warren Commission counsel and Brownell's predecessor as special master in the TWA case, edit the so-called Watergate Tapes impartially to delete "national-security" information from them. Difficult also to neglect mention of Jacqueline Kennedy's surprising marriage to Onassis, of Hughes's decision in that same year to establish an alliance with Kennedy strategists in the wake of the Senator's murder, and of Leon Jaworski's role as counsel to the Warren Commission and special prosecutor in the Watergate scandal. Of such stuff are conspiracy theories made. We can imagine all these events to be linked by some common thread of malignancy, a malignancy whose proportions remain just out of view, kept hidden by silent witnesses and shredded facts. Or we may regard such imaginative acts as the trivial preoccupations of political paranoids. And yet, if *Spooks* proves nothing else with its discussions of Robert Maheu, Johnny Frank, Mitch WerBell, Robert Vesco, Howard Hughes, and others, it does prove that conspiracy is a commonplace of contemporary politics and finance. Indeed, that would seem to be the message of the Watergate scandal alone, and to think otherwise is to ignore the obvious. Still, the thread that runs from Scorpios to Dallas, Washington, and San Clemente remains occluded and only half-glimpsed, like a wall running into and under the sea. The most that can be said at present is that Washington is, at the very least, an incestuous town.

While Hughes's lawyers were a keystone of his empire, its first line of defense against the TWA wrecking ball, they were only one source of his power. The Hughes empire was built upon the muck of secret intelligence, the operations needed to acquire it, and the

---

* On January 10, 1973, with Chief Justice Burger and Associate Justice Harry A. Blackmun dissenting, the Supreme Court ruled 6 to 2 in Hughes's favor, finding him not guilty of antitrust violations charged by TWA.

purchase of political influence needed to exploit it. No event was unworthy of being reported to Hughes, nor was any anticipated action by any public body so insignificant as to escape his attempted influence and control. Tom Bell, an attorney of Hughes's, revealed just one employee's responsibilities:

"I have a file concerning Nevada government—state, county, and municipal. I have a file that reflects my efforts to avoid the personal appearance of Hughes before any governmental agency in Nevada. I have . . ." Just getting started, Bell went on to enumerate scores of such files involving the executive, legislative, and judicial branches of Nevada and Clark County governments; AEC tests; legal action against the construction of a local hotel; "every single bill introduced into the Nevada legislature"; files pertaining to sales, gaming, gasoline, cigarette, inheritance, and keno taxes; special sessions of the state legislature; files relating to Hughes's opposition to local school-integration plans, his resistance to legislation that would have made gambling debts legally collectible, his disapproval of anti-pornography, obscenity, and censorship laws, and his desire to prohibit the realignment of any streets in Clark County "with his personal views being first had or given." And still Bell was not done. He had files on "the qualifications and background of everyone running for political office and who he should support in various political races"; files on proposed changes in local convention facilities, changes in the rules of roulette; and files in support of his decision to "discourage appropriate state officials from permitting communist bloc entertainers or shows from appearing in the Las Vegas casinos and hotels." And more. The list went on, with Hughes's informational demands taking on an aspect of inexhaustibility. And Tom Bell was certainly not unique. His bailiwick was a carefully defined one, limited to the internal politics of Nevada. Other Tom Bells monitored aspects of the national scene, U. S. presidential politics, the politics of France and Japan, and, we may presume, anything else that impinged on Hughes's widespread interests in aviation, military technology, real estate, recreation, *ad infinitum*. Curiously, Hughes himself apprehended all these matters as abstractions: he was concerned about the realignment of streets whose pavements he never walked, about the backgrounds of people he'd never meet, and the outcomes of elections in which he had no intention of voting. His interest in all these matters was purely a function of his quest for power. And he didn't care how he acquired his information. As he told Robert Maheu in a memo concerning atomic testing in Nevada, "my confidantes in the H.A.C. [Hughes Aircraft Corporation] and H.T. Co. [Hughes Tool Company] organizations put their very lives in jeopardy with some of the disclosures they make to me. . . ." He wasn't exaggerating. In March, 1968, a Japanese Air Force colonel, Kenkichi Kawasaki, was arrested for leaking classified information to Hughes Aircraft's Far East representative. The leaked data represented the secret electronics defense plan for all of Japan—information of strategic value both to Japan's enemies and to military contractors (such as Hughes) who sought an edge on rival bidders. At the time of his arrest Colonel Kawasaki was vice-principal of the Japanese Air Self-Defense Force's School of Military Science. Rumors of multimillion-dollar payoffs to Japanese militarists and politicians, including the country's premier, became impossible to prove when two of Colonel Kawasaki's colleagues died violently and unexpectedly, alleged suicides. (A few years later, during the Lockheed bribery scandals, these two would be joined by a host of other Japanese officials, also suicides.)

To understand Hughes—who he was and what he was after—two different approaches may be taken. The first approach requires an analysis of the minutiae: Why did Hughes oppose integration? Why did he oppose antipornography laws. Why, more than a decade after the McCarthy hearings and two decades after his own inquisition by the Senate, did he continue to maintain a blacklist against entertainers of the Marxist persuasion? Why did he fight those who would have made gambling debts legally collectible?* Why his

---

* Gambling debts are not, of course, legally collectible—though the most lucrative legal gambling tends to be done on credit. This seeming paradox is the nutriment upon which loan sharks feed. Opposing legislation to make such debts binding in law, Hughes was aligned with a peculiar consortium of IRS agents and underworld figures. The latter oppose such laws because they would destroy one of organized crime's most lucrative enterprises: the organization of gambling junkets. While all such junkets are not put together by hoodlums, many are, and they depend upon legal *un*collectibility of gambling debts for their profits. Briefly, the junket's organizer assumes responsibility for making good the debts of "his" gamblers, retaining (by agreement with the casino) a percentage of the money they lose. Occasionally, collections involve strong-arm tactics. Occasionally, too, the gambler is unable to pay—in which case his losses may be treated by the junket's organizer as a personal loan, the interest on which may vary between 10 and 80 percent *per week*. Additionally, the legal uncollectibility of gambling debts provides other advantages. It allows casinos, for instance, to write off a large number of markers (the gamblers' IOU's) as bad debts—even though the money may have actually been collected. Moreover, existing law facilitates the laundering of money between countries: for example, gambling debts incurred in the Bahamas (or Austria, Italy, Africa, etc.) may be secretly collected in the United States without any record of the transaction having been completed. Since the debts are legally uncollectible, and mostly undeductible for income tax purposes, the gambler has no incentive to report the payments he's made to the casino or the junketeer.

phobia of germs, his intensive seclusion, his fear of light? Understanding Hughes in this way, however, is less than necessary. All of these questions can be answered, with absolute or near certainty, drawing upon the resources and recall of shrinks, spooks, accountants, and bagmen. But the simpler approach to understanding Hughes is to accept the Man at face value: like a character in a child's comic book, he was an unimaginably wealthy paranoiac who seemed bent upon ruling the world from the vantage of his secret aerie above Las Vegas. Unfortunately for the real world, there seems to have been no compensating Superman to check his progress.

And Hughes was a busy man. Having arrived in Las Vegas in 1966 with about a half-billion dollars in proceeds from his sale of TWA stock, he'd set about wrapping up the state and the town, buying casinos, real estate, and people at a breakneck pace. He'd picked up Larry O'Brien for fifteen thousand dollars per month, eviscerated Air West in the course of making it his captive, and he'd even seen to it that AEC explosions would take place nearer to Arctic igloos than to southwestern craps tables.

Predictably, accomplishing these ends left some blood upon the floor, and Hughes was in no way satisfied with the state of his empire. As 1970 dawned, things were moving too fast for the Stockholder. And most of them were going downhill. *Viz:*

On the last business day of 1969 Hughes's empire came under threat of dismemberment as TWA was awarded $137,000,000 in triple damages. Suddenly, a severe cash-flow problem loomed on the horizon, with only the Supreme Court standing between the billionaire and a forced sale of assets. Placing Maheu in charge of the litigation, Hughes must have felt as though Chester Davis had failed him.

The take-over of Air West, while successful, had been so brutal that criminal indictments against Hughes and several of his aides, including Maheu, were under preparation. Reviewing the take-over, the SEC charged that Hughes and others engaged in a conspiracy to defraud Air West's shareholders by manipulating the airline's stock, issuing false proxies, intimidating the directors through covertly financed lawsuits, and more.

Squeezed for cash and on the brink of indictment, Hughes was devastated in his private world by the loss of his wife, Jean Peters, who divorced him in 1970. A seemingly personal matter, the divorce had strong implications for the internal politics of the Hughes organization. Frank Bill Gay, a top Toolco executive, had been responsible for maintaining the loyalty of Hughes's wife, and his failure was bitterly evident. In response to a Maheu request made in behalf of Gay, Hughes wrote: ". . . apparently you are not aware that the path of true friendship in this case has not been a bilateral affair. I thought that when we came here and I told you not to invite Bill up here and not permit him to be privy to our activities you realized that I no longer trusted him. . . . My bill of complaints against Bill's conduct goes back a long way and cuts very deep. . . ." Brooding on the temper of that memo, Hughes emphasized his ire against Gay in another note, written a few hours later: "Bob, I have read your message about Bill again, and the more I read it the more angry I get. I certainly cannot get very sympathetic . . . when Bill's total indifference and laxity to my pleas for help in the domestic area, voiced urgently to him, week by week through the past 7 to 8 years, have resulted in a complete, I'm afraid irrevocable, loss of my wife. I am sorry, but I blame Bill completely for this unnecessary debacle. . . . I don't usually discuss this subject, but . . . I feel he let me down—utterly, totally, completely." One might think that Hughes, having so little regard for Bill Gay, would have fired him. But according to Maheu, the billionaire didn't think he had that option. An influential (and ambitious) Mormon, Gay had the loyalty of Hughes's retainers, the palace guard. Like Nadine Henley, the so-called Queen of Romaine, whom Maheu claims Hughes also abhorred, Gay "knew too much about Hughes's private life" to be fired.

The Hughes empire, therefore, was threatening to fly apart in 1970. The Nevada Operations had mushroomed in the short space of four years, and Maheu had become the empire's most dominant and highly visible figure. To the public, and many of the organization's own executives, Maheu had *become* Howard Hughes: "My mail was unbelievable," he recalls. "The mail was delivered to the office *in sacks*. At one time we kept track of the telephone calls that I could not return and they averaged, over a period of ninety days, one hundred and four telephone calls *a day* that I could not return." The ascendancy of the Nevada Operations and Maheu himself entailed a corresponding decline in the influence wielded by Toolco and its top executives. Besides the fall from grace of Henley and Gay, Davis's authority had been undercut in the TWA case, an action that seemed to reflect an even deeper dissatisfaction with Toolco's general counsel. According to Maheu, Hughes did not want Davis to come within a hundred miles of Las Vegas. And when the super-spook suggested to his employer that Davis might handle some special legal work in Nevada, the billionaire is said to have screamed: "Goddamn it, Bob, you must be losing your mind. If we allow this man to come to Las Vegas, in twenty-four hours the whole city will be devastated, and in forty-eight hours the entire state of Nevada will be in chaos."

As it turned out, that assessment was prophetic: before the year was out, Davis *would* come to Las Vegas, and, within forty-eight hours of his arrival, Nevada *would* be in chaos. In 1970, then, both the financial and private worlds of Howard Hughes were approaching a point of disintegration. The adverse TWA judgment pending against him, the painful divorce, the pending Air West indictments, and the factional split within his empire had placed Hughes under an intolerable strain. Making the strain even worse was the threat of antitrust proceedings under contemplation by the Justice Department, whose antitrust staff tended to view Hughes's acquisition of so many Nevada casinos as a bid for a monopoly. And while Hughes could count upon a degree of cooperation from the Nixon Administration and Attorney General John Mitchell, his alliance with Larry O'Brien and the Kennedys threatened to backfire: Nixon & Company, programmatically paranoid in their own right, regarded O'Brien's new employment with Hughes as both a political betrayal by Hughes and a direct threat to their White House tenure. A loyal and powerful Democrat, O'Brien was feared to have become privy to the Nixon Administration's secrets, including its cash receipts from Hughes. To those in the know, it appeared that the billionaire's clandestine use of the Rebozo conduit may have been "a setup."

It was no wonder, then, that Hughes was looking for an escape route in 1970. Accordingly, he contemplated two strategies: flee the country and enmesh the CIA in his affairs.

To further the first strategy, he commissioned a secret report, code-named "Downhill Racer." The report was a study of the Bahamas, which, unhappily for Hughes, described the archipelago in apocalyptic terms, predicting racial and political "cataclysm" in the islands' near future. And while getting embroiled in a post-colonial race war was the last thing Hughes needed at the time, he was nevertheless determined, as he told Maheu, to "wrap that government up down there to a point where it could be—well, a captive entity in every way." It wasn't the first government Hughes had sought to package. According to Maheu, the billionaire had long sought to "own the President" of the United States and "to choose his successor"—that was the purpose, he said, of Hughes's donations to the

Nixon and Humphrey campaigns. (Not that Maheu always went along with Hughes's requests. On one occasion the Stockholder prevailed upon his majordomo to bribe Lyndon Johnson in an effort to end nuclear testing in Nevada. Recalling that incident, Maheu said, "I showed [Toolco executive Raymond] Holliday a handwritten memorandum from Mr. Hughes where Mr. Hughes was asking me to make a million-dollar payoff to a President of the United States. Mr. Holliday fainted, dropped the yellow sheet of paper on the floor, and requested of me whether or not his fingerprints could be taken off the piece of paper."

The second strategy—to enmesh the CIA in his affairs—was equally bluntly put. Hughes simply ordered Maheu to use his supposed influence at the Agency to turn the Hughes empire into a CIA front so as to give the billionaire leverage in future court cases and regulatory proceedings. According to Maheu, he refused to comply with the demand, citing all the right and noble reasons for demurring. That account seems a self-serving one, however, since, as we've seen, Maheu had himself escaped legal jeopardy on several occasions by pointedly reminding the Agency of his involvement in its past affairs. His refusal of Hughes's request, then, probably had more to do with his own lack of influence at the CIA (in 1970) than it did with any moral or patriotic objections which he may have felt.

Hughes's problems in 1970 must have seemed almost insurmountable to him. His empire was factionalized at a time when it was being threatened by financial dismemberment; his influence with the Nixon Administration was qualified by that Administration's mistrust of him; his wife had shuffled off her marital coil; and a phalanx of government agencies was preparing lawsuits. As if this were not enough, his escape routes were obscured by political uncertainties and Maheu's unwillingness or inability to ensnare the CIA in the Stockholder's meshes. Not surprisingly, then, Hughes's health broke, undergoing a catastrophic decline in the summer of 1970. To Hughes's personal physician in Las Vegas, it appeared that Maheu's boss might be dying. He had anemia, complicated by pneumonia and chronic constipation. His red blood count could be tallied on the fingers of a single hand, necessitating regular transfusions in an effort to supply his brain with an adequate amount of oxygen. Equally ominous was the billionaire's loss of weight: a big man, 6 feet, 4 inches tall, he'd lost upward of sixty pounds in the course of the summer, his weight toppling to ninety pounds in the fall. Doubting that the Old Man's remaining health could survive the trip to a nearby hospital, his physicians equipped the penthouse at the Desert Inn with enough medical equipment to supply an intensive-care ward—in effect, moving the hospital to him. And still he languished, unimproving.

It was at about this time that Maheu moved against Davis in what in retrospect appears to have been an attempt to consolidate his own power at the expense of the faction led by the Toolco lawyer. Using the "full authority" granted to him by Hughes, Maheu decided to remove Davis from the appeal of the TWA case. Davis's strategy throughout the litigation had been to offer no defense to TWA's charges against Hughes, insisting that the airline had no case against its former owner. Since that strategy led directly to the 1969 default judgment against the billionaire, Maheu wanted to base Hughes's Supreme Court appeal on the grounds that he'd lacked competent representation. To do that, of course, required that Davis be removed from the case, since the Houston attorney could hardly allege his own incompetence. Predictably, Davis eyed the plan with undisguised horror. His own strategy had not been fully tested—only the Supreme Court could do that—and his career could hardly be expected to advance should he become the scapegoat of the TWA judgment that was costing Hughes *one million dollars per month in interest*. To Davis it looked as though Maheu had set him up for a fall. And with the Old Man on what seemed to be his deathbed, it appeared to the Davis faction that Maheu was grabbing for control of the empire as a whole.

Whether that was so or not, the Davis faction had its own plans for ridding the empire of its ambitious spook. Beginning in the summer of 1970, the Davis faction held a series of meetings with a private intelligence agency that had been formed only a few months before. The nature of those meetings between the Davis faction and Intertel is disputed by the principals, but there can be little doubt as to what was involved. Tom McKeon, general counsel and senior vice-president of the then-fledgling apparat, told this writer that the meetings were devoted to planning the removal of Hughes from Las Vegas. "We developed a plan this thick," McKeon says, indicating a dictionary-sized space between his thumb and index finger. "We'd worked on it for months." According to McKeon, the plan provided for Maheu's firing, Hughes's shift to the Bahamas, and the orderly transition of Nevada properties from Maheu's oversight to that of Intertel's—all of this, McKeon said, in accordance with Hughes's wishes. (Though no one at Intertel, he said, had actually met

Hughes.) Subsequently, the existence of the plan described by Mc-Keon was denied by Intertel's president, Robert ("The Needle") Peloquin. That such a plan existed, however, is certain. Peloquin's denial seems designed to muddle the nature of the meetings held between Intertel and the Davis faction during 1970, to suggest instead that the apparat's removal of Hughes to the Bahamas in November of that year was an act of near spontaneity. Peloquin would have us believe—contrary to his general counsel's earlier statements —that the summer meetings with the Davis faction concerned a "bomb threat" to one of Air West's planes. After handling the supposed bomb threat to the satisfaction of Davis et al., Peloquin says, Intertel began receiving future assignments, culminating in the Hughes exodus from the Desert Inn. The disputed facts may appear to be trivial, but they probably contain the key to understanding exactly what happened when Hughes vanished in the course of what's come to be called the Thanksgiving Coup.

Peloquin's contradiction of his general counsel's statements about the existence of a plan seems designed to obscure the origins of his firm's relationship to the Davis faction during 1970. At the time it was hired by that faction, Intertel could not have been in existence for more than a few months: its Delaware incorporation had taken place only in the beginning of the year. Nevertheless, while yet in its infancy the private intelligence agency was entrusted with perhaps the most sensitive assignment imaginable—Hughes's exodus from Las Vegas while apparently dying, and the supplanting of Maheu in Nevada. That such an important assignment should be given to a firm that had no track record is passing strange. Even more bizarre, however, is the fact that Intertel is a subsidiary of Resorts International, a Bahamas-based rival of Hughes's in the cutthroat casino business. How is it that Hughes would willingly entrust himself and his affairs—assuming that he had any say in the matter—to such an organization?

Indeed, it doesn't seem to make much sense unless one realizes that in the summer of 1970 the Davis faction was engaged with yet another subject—one that may well explain the choice of Intertel for its assignment. Two years earlier, a Russian submarine had sunk in the Pacific Ocean northwest of Hawaii. Besides the missiles it contained, the sub held the key to Russian military codes, which, if cracked, would provide the United States with a decided military advantage. Accordingly, the federal intelligence community resolved to recover the submarine and its code books. Accomplishing that required the construction of an extraordinary ship capable of precision retrieval of relatively small objects from great oceanic depths. Since the operation—code-named "Project Jennifer"—demanded the utmost secrecy, the vessel would have to be constructed under the aegis of a private corporation, using a cover story to disguise the vessel's real mission. The ship, of course, was the *Glomar Explorer,* subsequently built by the Global Marine Corporation under contract to the Hughes organization. The cover story was that the vessel would be used in oceanic research and, more particularly, in the retrieval of manganese nodules from the ocean floor. Supposedly, the ship would be owned by Hughes. The point here, however, is that the Project Jennifer discussions with the Hughes organization began in 1970—after Maheu had already refused to entangle the CIA in his master's web. In fact, according to Maheu, he had no knowledge of these discussions, which must have been carried out with the Davis faction alone. Why Maheu should have been excluded from participation in discussions of such a monumental project is uncertain—perhaps it had to do with the CIA's alleged mistrust of the spook, or it may have been a condition imposed upon the talks by the Davis faction itself. As for Hughes himself, his own knowledge, or ignorance, of the discussions is unknown: it's entirely possible that ill health precluded his awareness of the project.

What Project Jennifer may have had to do with the choice of Intertel as the instrument of Hughes's removal from Las Vegas is this: discussions pertaining to both Project Jennifer and the Thanksgiving Coup took place at about the same time. News of both projects, moreover, was confined to a single faction of the Hughes organization—the Davis group. The possibility arises, then, that the two projects were part and parcel of each other. If so, then Intertel would have to have represented either the National Security Agency (NSA) or the CIA, or both. That, of course, would explain the choice of Intertel for its sensitive assignment: the fact that it lacked a track record would certainly have been outweighed by its representation of the federal intelligence community. Indeed, it may be that Intertel's formation in 1970 was itself a part of Project Jennifer.

This is, of course, speculative, but there are other reasons to believe that Intertel and Project Jennifer were joined—and that Hughes's removal from Las Vegas, therefore, was conceived by the federal intelligence community in conference with the Davis faction.

The responsibility for cracking Soviet codes, which is what Project Jennifer was all about, belongs to the National Security Agency (NSA). This agency is, of course, *the* inner sanctum of the intelligence community, with responsibility for some of the country's most technically oriented espionage. Operating secret communications-intercept bases located in some of the world's wildest and most remote regions, NSA captures and records the coded messages of both friendly and hostile nations, multinational corporations, and "individuals of interest." Acquiring the messages is, in many ways, the simplest part of its multibillion-dollar task. Decoding them is a more difficult matter, however, as NSA's storage of literally trainloads of tape recordings proves. Unintelligible, and yet potentially invaluable, the undeciphered messages are stored in the hope that someday NSA's computers will crack the code, or a "break" will be achieved through some other means. And yet, despite its 25,000 employees, massive budget, and futuristic hardware, the NSA has been notorious for its inability to crack Soviet military codes. David Kahn, author of *The Code Breakers*, blames that inability on the fact that "Cryptology has advanced, in the last decade or so, to systems that, though not unbreakable in the absolute, are unbreakable in practice. They consist essentially of mathematical programs for computer-like cipher machines. They engender so many possibilities that, even given torrents of intercepts, and scores of computers to batter them with, cryptanalysts could not reach a solution for thousands of years." * Cracking the codes therefore becomes an operational matter, and it's in this context that Project Jennifer ought to be understood. It seems very likely, given the nature of the project and NSA's responsibility for breaking the Soviet codes, that NSA—and not CIA —originated the scheme to recover the sunken Soviet sub (and, with it, the code books it was certain to contain). As an intelligence coup it would have been unprecedented, unlocking the mysteries manifest in all those intercepted (but so far undecipherable) Russian communiqués. Since that was the goal, then, the probability exists to a near certainty that the CIA's role in the project was purely operational and that NSA held ultimate responsibility for the project's success and its budget.

That NSA should turn to Hughes to carry out the operation is not surprising: he's one of that agency's major contractors. But the significance of NSA's relationship to the project rests with a curious

---

* *The New York Times*, June 22, 1973.

imbalance in the backgrounds of those at the top of Intertel. Among Intertel's five chief executives are Edward M. Mullin, a former CIA officer who serves as the firm's director of operations; Robert Peloquin, Intertel's president and a reserve commander in naval intelligence; William Kolar, vice-president of Intertel and formerly the director of the Intelligence and Internal Security divisions of the IRS; and, perhaps most interestingly, two vice-presidents whose careers have been spent in the National Security Agency—Tom McKeon, who created the plan for Hughes's removal to the Bahamas, and the mysterious David I. Belisle. McKeon is the former chief of the NSA's Special Projects Section, while Belisle has done triple duty, serving as a reserve commander in naval intelligence and as both deputy inspector general and deputy director of security for the NSA.* Intertel's executive echelon, therefore, is composed of spooks whose backgrounds are precisely those one would expect if Intertel represented the National Security Agency in discussions of Project Jennifer with the Davis faction: IRS, naval intelligence, CIA, NSA, and, again, NSA.

When the crunch came on November 25, 1970, Maheu didn't know what hit him. For a month he'd had no contact with Hughes, the billionaire's illness having rendered him incommunicado, according to the Mormon aides. It occurred to Maheu, who was used to receiving numerous memos and phone calls daily from Hughes, that the Old Man might be dead and that the aides, loyal to the Davis faction, might be concealing that information. But there was no way to learn if this was true: Maheu's agents, who guarded access to Hughes's penthouse at the Desert Inn, reported nothing unusual.

---

* Belisle is also the spook who, apparently at the request of the Kennedy White House, undertook a bugging operation against Otto Otepka, super-grade security evaluator for the State Department. In June, 1963, Otepka was ordered removed from office by Secretary of State Dean Rusk, supposedly for having given classified information to the Senate Subcommittee on Internal Security (in fact, Otepka had drawn the Kennedys' ire for having rejected some of their nominees to high State Department positions, regarding those nominees as security risks). Not content to remove Otepka—whom Belisle had bugged with an infinity-transmitter—Rusk also ordered his safe drilled open and his office locks changed. According to Otepka, the only "non-routine" material in the safe at that time was a half-finished study on American defectors, including one Oswald, Lee Harvey. Coincidentally, Oswald had just received a new passport from the State Department on the day Otepka was ousted. According to Otepka, the study on defectors was initiated by him because neither the CIA nor military intelligence agencies would inform the State Department which defectors to the Soviet Union were double agents working for the United States. Asked whether Oswald was "one of ours or one of theirs," Otepka recently grouched, "We had not made up our minds when my safe was drilled and we were thrown out of the office."

In fact, however, they were guarding access to an empty suite of rooms. Hughes had left the Desert Inn Thanksgiving Eve, having supposedly been carried on a stretcher past Maheu's guards and taken down nine floors to a fire exit and into the casino's parking lot. There he's said to have been bundled into a station wagon and driven to Nellis Air Force Base, where a rented Lockheed JetStar waited for him. Taken aboard the JetStar, supposedly making wise-cracks about hijackers, the sick-unto-death Hughes was flown to Albuquerque, New Mexico, where the jet refueled on its way to Nassau, the Bahamas. In Nassau some seven hours later, Hughes is said to have transferred to a helicopter which delivered him, apparently none the worse for wear, to the Britannia Beach Hotel on Paradise Island.

To Bob Maheu, learning all this a week after it was supposed to have occurred, Hughes's trip was simply incredible; the spook believed that the billionaire had been kidnapped by the Davis faction, and he had his reasons. Almost nothing about the trip made any sense. For instance:

The destination: Hughes had made it clear to Maheu, in a long conversation, that the Downhill Racer report predicting disaster for the Bahamas had disappointed him, but that "if there is deep-seated hatred there we'll just have to go somewhere else. . . . So much for the Bahamas."

His physical condition: At the very least, the arduous trip out of Las Vegas was a dangerous undertaking for a man in such fragile health, and it was by no means certain that Hughes was even cognizant of the journey. Moreover, in the apparent haste to evacuate the penthouse, Hughes's climate-control equipment, regulating humidity and hermeticizing the premises from germs, had been abandoned.

A witness: A passerby in the parking lot of the Desert Inn claimed to have seen a thin man being led away, seemingly against his will, to a phalanx of waiting automobiles on the night Hughes was supposed to have left his penthouse. According to the witness, the man pleaded aloud: "Won't someone please call Bob Maheu or Pat Hyland [chief of Hughes Aircraft]!"

Means of transportation: Hughes had not flown for nearly fifteen years and, according to Maheu, had developed a phobia against doing so. This was the reason he'd come to Las Vegas by train in 1966 —despite the publicity it had been bound to cause—and it was unlikely that he'd have agreed to the arduous jet/helicopter that took him to the Bahamas. In Maheu's opinion, the decision to make that trip, and the mode of transportation to be used, had been decided for him.

Davis faction authority: As we've seen, Hughes appeared to have lost confidence in the very people in whose hands he is said to have placed himself: Davis, Henley, and Gay.

The missing proxy: Compounding the inherent incredibility of the Davis faction's sudden ascendancy over Maheu was the fact that the faction refused for weeks to produce a proxy allegedly signed by Hughes on November 14, giving the Davis group complete authority over virtually all his affairs. When, finally, the proxy *was* produced (by Mormon aide Howard Eckersley), it turned out to be a typed document—whereas Hughes had always handwritten such instruments. Witnessed by one of Hughes's Mormon aides and notarized by Eckersley, the putative proxy became the subject of intense scrutiny. A handwriting expert for Maheu pronounced it a forgery, while another expert, hired by the Davis faction, declared it genuine.

Hughes's silence: For some reason Hughes refused to contact Maheu by telephone, informing him that he'd been fired. Instead, a man claiming to be Hughes spoke by phone with Nevada governor Paul Laxalt, who'd heard Hughes's voice on only one other occasion. According to Laxalt, he believed the man he'd spoken to was Hughes, and that the billionaire's wishes were being carried out by the Davis group.

Permitted chaos: Hughes had always been a meticulous man insofar as details were concerned. The transition in power, however, had been carried out in a manner that guaranteed chaos and which could only have damaged Hughes's enterprises. The cashiers' cages in the casinos were invaded by Intertel agents and a task force of auditors hired by Toolco, auditors Maheu described as "those Mongolian monks" who'd appeared "out of Mars." "Surprise audits" aren't unusual in Las Vegas, but the "Mongolian monks" disrupted the casinos in a dangerous way, sealing the "banking drawers" with adhesive tape, and stuffing gamblers' markers into paper bags. The disastrous possibility arose that a big winner would arrive at the cages to cash in his chips, and instead of being promptly and happily paid, he'd find the casino short of funds. News of that kind could only devastate the reputation and goodwill that Hughes had labored to create for his gaming palaces. Nor was this the only source of chaos: the operating licenses for all Hughes's casinos were in Maheu's name, and there did not seem to have been any preparations made for ensuring their orderly transfer. Intertel & Company had simply walked in and taken over. Nevada didn't like that.

Subsequently: Maheu would find even more reasons to believe that Hughes was no longer in control of his own empire. Formerly, the billionaire had insisted that his name should not be used for promotional purposes, but in the wake of the Thanksgiving Coup his name became a preface to Air West and was used in connection with a number of ventures in Las Vegas. Secondly, a handwritten memo purporting to come from Hughes, confirming Maheu's discharge, was declared by Maheu's handwriting analyst—the former chief of the FBI's documents laboratory—to have been written by someone who was "not in a natural condition." The suggestion was that Hughes had written the letter, but that he'd been drugged at the time. Interestingly, that letter had been brought to Nevada from the Bahamas by Mormon aide Howard Eckersley, who'd also notarized, and reluctantly produced, the putative Hughes proxy mentioned earlier. Indeed, Eckersley's role was another reason to believe that Hughes was not in control, or "not himself": in the wake of the struggle for control of Hughes's Nevada Operations, Eckersley was implicated in a fraudulent Canadian stock deal in which his association with Hughes was deliberately flaunted. It was obvious to Maheu that Hughes would never have tolerated that, and he certainly would not have kept Eckersley on had he known of it. And, finally, convincing Maheu to a certainty that his boss had been kidnapped, he observed that AEC testing in Nevada had resumed "without so much as a burp being heard from Hughes"— despite the fact that the billionaire abhorred the tests so much that he'd earlier tried to bribe Lyndon Johnson with a million dollars, hoping to end them.

Indeed, it all looked very fishy, but there was little Maheu could do about it. Recruiting a platoon of nine private investigators, led by his son Peter and Edward DuBois (whom Maheu had hired in 1960 to bug Dan Rowan), Maheu sent the spooks to the Bahamas. While Peter, a CIA veteran, stayed in Miami with a network television crew, the remaining spooks arrived at Paradise Island, renting rooms on the eighth floor of the Britannia Beach Hotel, directly below Hughes's suite. Their assignment was to ascertain Hughes's physical condition and learn whether he'd gone to the Bahamas under his own free will. If he hadn't, a rescue attempt would be made.

At first, the operation went well. Spike-mikes were implanted in the ceiling of the Britannia Beach, and DuBois even managed to obtain permission for the bugging operation from the Bahamas' Attorney General, who agreed that the stakes were large and that the truth concerning Hughes must be known. The operation fell apart, however, when the DuBois team persuaded a bellboy to place a bug in Hughes's room. The bug was secreted on a room-service tray being delivered by the bellboy and, of course, it was discovered. With the operation blown, it was only a matter of hours before Bahamian police, accompanied by one of Intertel's most mysterious agents, Jim Golden, came banging on the doors of Maheu's spies. Caught monitoring the spike-mikes, the team was arrested and held for twenty-four hours before being deported back to the United States. A classic among Maheu's "Mission Impossible" assignments, it had failed. And, for the first time, Maheu realized that he was up against someone else's "Mission Impossible" agency—Intertel. And he knew almost nothing about it.

1 / A NICA-RICAN CANAL

THE MAN WHO COULD HAVE TOLD MAHEU MOST ABOUT INTERTEL WAS James M. Crosby, its chairman of the board. With Henley, Davis, Gay, and other Toolco executives, Crosby had been in Las Vegas when the "Mongolian monks" stormed the cashiers' cages in Hughes's casinos. But he hadn't come to talk, and despite Maheu's surprise, he hadn't come "out of Mars" either. On the contrary, Crosby was a New Jersey businessman transplanted to the Caribbean, a thin, even frail man who looked and sounded much older than his forty-two years: despite a painful case of emphysema silting up his lungs, Crosby persisted in chain-smoking cigarettes, lending a bass and sandy tone to both his voice and his breathing.

Intertel was nurtured in the rich financial humus of the Bahamas and, more particularly, of Paradise Island. A creature of Resorts International, its history was inseparable from that of the parent firm. A corporate infant in 1970 when it burst upon the Las Vegas scene—quite literally like gangbusters—it nevertheless had a genealogy of contacts and "contradictions" that took it back to the bad old days of America's "southern sea."

Those were the early Sixties, when Robert Maheu was plotting Castro's murder, Cuban exiles trained for their invasion of the Bay of Pigs, and a group of white British colonials ruled the black Bahamas with an iron hand clenched in a velvet glove. They were the "Bay Street Boys," a tribe of wealthy whites whose most influential member was probably Sir Stafford Sands, a corrupt British lord who served as the Bahamas' Minister of Tourism and Finance. The world presided over by the Bay Street Boys was a tropical expanse composed of some 2,500 rocks and islands spread out like a fan off the coast of Florida. With the exception of a mostly illiterate black labor force, the island group could not be said to have significant natural resources—unless one took into account its crystalline waters lapping at miles of unused beaches the color of new cotton.

One of those who did take that into account was Wally Groves, an ex-con who'd served time for mail fraud. Prevailing upon an old friendship with Sands, a friendship that generated literally millions of dollars in so-called legal fees for the barrister-knight, Groves persuaded Sir Stafford to draft the Hawksbill Creek Act of 1955. Under the terms of that act, Groves was permitted to buy 211 square miles of Grand Bahama Island for less than three dollars per acre. It was as if a national fire sale had been held, because a few years later some of those acres would be sold for as much as $50,000 apiece and Groves's total holdings would be valued at more than $300,000,000.

Initially, Groves hadn't contemplated developing Grand Bahama Island for recreation. His intention was to create an industrial vehicle that would take advantage of American firms' interest in avoiding taxes while obtaining cheap labor. Accordingly, he sold the concept of a free port, with imports and exports moving duty-free across the docks of a city which Groves would have to build, virtually from scratch. To accomplish that, the ex-con established the Grand Bahama Port Authority, Ltd., a private firm which, thanks to Sir Stafford Sands, had nearly feudal powers. It was, for instance, responsible for most of the custodial functions usually performed by municipal and state governments (for example, construction of schools, sewers, and housing), but it also had the authority to deport persons it deemed "undesirable." Freeport, as the city came to be called, was therefore a "company town" in the classic sense of the phrase.

The notion of a tax-free enclave supported by a cheap labor force and American industry is one that's since appealed to a number of entrepreneurs and wheeler-dealers: the reader will recall similar plans advanced by former Nixon staffer Richard Allen and fugitive Robert Vesco. Even back in the late Fifties, however, there were those who realized that a killing could be made through such a scheme, and Groves therefore was not lacking for capital. Not at first, anyway. Fifty percent of the Port Authority was purchased by a Wall Street brokerage and a British holding company for an estimated $5,600,000. Curiously, that was the same amount spent by shipping mogul Daniel K. Ludwig to dredge the harbor needed for Groves's free port. A reclusive billionaire, Ludwig is the proprietor of National Bulk Carriers, one of the world's largest shipping fleets, and is credited with having pioneered the concept of containerization. Regarded as ruthless and astute, he's avoided public scrutiny for decades—though recently, in Brazil, he was blasted by that country's President for maintaining "slave-labor conditions" on Rhode Island-sized plantations that he owns there. Why Ludwig should have dredged the Freeport harbor for Groves is unknown, though the billionaire seems to have been recompensed in later years, becoming the owner of vast tracts of Grand Bahama real estate once held by Wally Groves.

The industrial scheme failed, however. Neither American nor British corporations were enthusiastic about what was, after all, a backwater. Accordingly, Groves readjusted his development plan to emphasize recreation and tourism, entering into yet another partnership, this time with Lou Chesler, a three-hundred-pound Canadian whose business and social connections ranged from Meyer Lansky to Wall Street and the jet set. (All three had money in common, and Chesler knew how to use it. According to Edward Wuensche, a mob-connected racketeer who specialized in fencing stolen stocks, he met with Chesler and another hoodlum in the Bahamas around 1966. There, he said, Chesler taught him to launder stolen securities through Switzerland by way of trust accounts in the Caribbean. "I personally delivered stolen securities to Chesler," Wuensche swore before the Senate, "in 1968 in the Bahamas." *) With Chesler's help, and with the assistance of the ubiquitous Stafford Sands, a new agreement was drawn up with the Port Authority, permitting Groves to sell the land he'd acquired as residential, rather than industrial, property. A condition of the new agreement, however, was that Groves would build Grand Bahama's first hotel, and that it would be a first-class facility with hundreds of rooms.

The Lucayan Beach Hotel opened in January, 1964. If you'd be-

---

* *Hearings* before the Permanent Subcommittee on Investigations of the Committee on Government Operations, United States Senate, "Organized Crime: Stolen Securities," Part 3, p. 852, U. S. Government Printing Office, Washington, 1971.

lieved the architectural plans, you'd have expected to find a handball court in its center—instead, there was a gambling casino. While the hotel had been under construction, the curly-haired Lou Chesler had visited Meyer Lansky in Florida, soliciting his advice concerning the recreational interests of tourists. Lansky was a mine of ideas, having only recently given up hope of murdering Fidel Castro to recoup his capital investments in Havana. The Bahamas were a reasonable substitute for Cuba, though the island group *did* seem to be handicapped by the fact that gambling was illegal there. This, however, was easily resolved by Sir Stafford Sands, who, after conversations with Lansky, legislated a certificate of exemption permitting the proposed handball court at the Lucayan Beach to become a casino. Just how hard this legislative feat was to achieve is a matter of speculation. If Sands's legal fees were any indication, it must have been very difficult indeed, since he was paid more than two million dollars by Groves and his associates—coincidentally, the same amount which, he later testified, Lansky offered to pay him through a Swiss bank if the British knight would assist the mobster in his plans to legalize gambling in the Bahamas. Sands, of course, did even better: he provided Groves and Lansky with a near monopoly ("near" because a certificate of exemption already existed for the Bahamian Club in Nassau, a private emporium that was no competition for the huge Lucayan Beach).

Immediately, Lansky's managers, trained in Havana, London, and the illicit roadside joints of the Bluegrass State, moved in with their credit dossiers and a hawk-eyed regard for the skim. Running the new casino were Red Reed (Frank Reiter), Max Courtney (Morris Schmertzler), Charlie Brud (Charles Brudner), and Dino Cellini, whose brother Eddie was across the channel at Nassau, running the casino in the private club mentioned earlier.

While these events were taking place at Freeport, A&P supermarkets heir Huntington Hartford was trying to transform a dilapidated islet named Hog into the Monaco of the Caribbean. Between 1959 and 1965 the eccentric heir poured $28,000,000 into Hog's 685 acres, renaming the island Paradise. Whatever its name, it was proving to be a financial catastrophe: removed from the Nassau mainland by four hundred yards of water, the island was an awkward place to visit and, once you got there, there wasn't much to do that couldn't be done better somewhere else. What the island needed was a tourist attraction—gambling—and a bridge to connect it with Nassau proper. Hartford, however, was in no position to obtain permission for either, having antagonized the Bay Street Boys with his financial support of the Progressive Liberal Party (PLP), led by black Bahamian Lynden Pindling.

While Groves and Lansky prospered a few miles to the north, Hartford watched in horror as his own investment, bolstered by additional millions, withered in value until the multimillionaire found himself without the cash to continue. Accordingly, he sought a buyer, and found one in the Mary Carter Paint Company.

Mary Carter (she never existed but the name sounded nice) was pretty much a family affair controlled by Jim Crosby, two of his brothers, and his in-laws. Based in Tampa, Florida, the firm included in its directorate James Crosby, John Crosby (a plastic surgeon in Mobile, Alabama), William Crosby (a Tampa realtor), and the Murphy brothers, Henry and Tom, who'd married the Crosby daughters. Henry owned a funeral home in Trenton, New Jersey, while Tom was board chairman of Capital Cities Communications, a successful broadcasting business founded by explorer Lowell Thomas. The explorer too was an early stockholder in Mary Carter Paint, as was Republican leader Thomas Dewey.

The paint company had already developed an interest in the Bahamas, having made a 1963 investment in Wally Groves's developmental dream for Grand Bahama Island: that investment was a 1,300-acre tract which Crosby called "Queen's Cove," intending to subdivide it for sale to wealthy and retiring Americans who might appreciate the Bahamas strict bank-secrecy laws.

The real bucks, however, were in gambling, and Crosby, bored with the paint business, labored to put together a deal that would give him entrée. Following negotiations with the panicked Huntington Hartford, Crosby's company acquired 75 percent of Paradise Island for only $3,500,000. It also acquired the legal services of Sir Stafford Sands, the man with whom Hartford had been unable or unwilling to deal. Sir Stafford, whom Crosby recalls as "a very impressive intellectual," made it clear that the path to success would need to be modeled along the lines of Freeport and that, moreover, it would be prudent to have Groves et al. in charge of the casino. Crosby agreed, giving four-ninths of the casino action to one of Groves's companies in exchange for its operational expertise. Midway through 1965, Sir Stafford arranged permission for the construction of the desired bridge connecting Paradise to Nassau, and obtained transfer of the Bahamian Club's certificate of exemption to the planned facility on Paradise.

Things were moving quickly, both before and behind the scenes. Even as Howard Hughes was chugging into Las Vegas by train in 1966, musing on his planned buy-out of organized crime in that city, Crosby was building apace in the Bahamas—a circumstance that seemed to be to Meyer Lansky's liking. According to a memorandum about the planned Paradise Island casino, a memo written in January by Justice Department gangbuster Robert Peloquin, "the atmosphere looks right for a Lansky skim. . . ." Peloquin, who would later head Intertel, knew whereof he spoke: for years he'd been investigating organized crime's domination of the Bahamas, and he had, moreover, become deeply involved in IRS's top-secret "Operation Tradewinds." Begun in 1965, Tradewinds was an ambitious and highly sensitive tax investigation of the financial dodges used by rich American racketeers, attorneys, and businessmen to launder, conceal, and skim cash in the Bahamas. Special agents of the IRS made literally hundreds of trips to Nassau and Freeport, developing informants within the business community, the police force, and the seemingly hopeless Progressive Liberal Party (PLP). So successful were the special agents that they allegedly turned Lynden Pindling, the country's next premier, into an informant—an irony of some dimension since Pindling would later become the island group's most vigorous proponent of plans to make the Bahamas a tropical Switzerland, a haven for the hemisphere's funny-money. Because Operation Tradewinds was an international project with implications for the Justice Department's own investigation, State Department matters, and SEC scrutiny of certain family trusts and corporations, liaison among the various agencies was essential. Accordingly, Peloquin found himself in a most strategic position, serving as middleman among the agencies. It was he, for instance, who informed State in 1966 of a meeting held between top IRS spooks and Peloquin's boss, Henry Petersen, then chief of the Justice Department's Organized Crime and Racketeering Section. The purpose of that meeting was to cope with the fact that Operation Tradewinds acquired its evidence in ways that violated Bahamian laws and which therefore required "special handling." Specifically, the information had to be laundered, just as the money it concerned had been laundered. The intelligence section of the IRS, it was decided, could continue securing information from bank employees in the Bahamas, using American spooks such as former Wackenhut agent Norman Casper, a/k/a "TW-24." But the data could only be used "for lead purposes" and the information would have to be delivered to IRS agents on American soil. The agent paying the informant and receiving the information could not be the same agent as the one traveling to the Bahamas for "normal liaison purposes." Indeed, the operation was highly compartmentalized—though in subsequent years it all came together under the rubric of Intertel. Many of those involved in Tradewinds —Bob Peloquin, Justice Department attorney William Hundley, assorted IRS agents, and IRS intelligence chief William Kolar—would all find jobs with Intertel, a subsidiary of the Crosby firm Peloquin once declared "ripe for a Lansky skim."

And so while Paradise Island's casino was under construction, Peloquin was shuttling between Washington and Nassau, conferring with the new U. S. consul general there, Turner B. Shelton. Shelton was a right-wing Hollywood film maker and an associate of Howard Hughes's who'd seemed, upon joining the State Department in the mid-Fifties, to be destined for a mediocre career. He'd been saved from that destiny, however, by a combination of sycophancy and good fortune. After Richard Nixon's defeat in the 1960 presidential election, he'd undertaken a world tour, supposedly to "lick his wounds." During those travels, though, Nixon became angered by the lack of enthusiasm accorded him by State Department officers in U. S. embassies abroad—except at the legation in Budapest, Hungary, where a second-echelon Foreign Service officer named Turner Shelton rolled out the burgundy carpets, the black limousines, and the flags. Nixon was uplifted by the adulation, and in 1967 Shelton found himself lavishly ensconced in the Bahamas, hobnobbing with a host of new friends including Wally Groves, Jim Crosby, and Crosby's banker, Bebe Rebozo. Indeed, Shelton's circumstances may have been too lavish: there were allegations that became the subject of an internal investigation by the State Department, allegations which suggested that Shelton's consulate was the site of "fraud, theft, [and] misappropriation of Government funds." The accusations were never proved, however, and they were probably exaggerations: Shelton has never endeared himself to his subordinates, who, in many cases, regard him as "a snob." His name, in any case, is one to remember and it may be worthwhile here to digress briefly upon his role in some extraordinary subsequent events, events that may well contribute to an understanding of his place in Paradise:

After Nixon's assumption of the Presidency in 1968, Shelton would linger in Nassau for another year before receiving an appointment as U. S. Ambassador to the newly strategic Nicaraguan dictatorship managed by the immensely rich Generalissimo Anastasio Somoza.

What made the dictatorship "newly strategic" was the saber-rattling of Nicaragua's neighbor, Panama, whose chief operating officer, General Omar Torrijos, was threatening to nationalize the Panama Canal. Nicaragua became a poker chip in that dispute since its own geography and politics would permit the construction of a new, "even better" canal. The new canal, requiring twelve years and $5.1 billion to construct, would accommodate those three thousand superships and oil tankers whose size forbids their navigation through the existing Panama Canal. The proposed Nicaraguan canal (which would actually pass through much of Costa Rica) would be superior to its Panamanian counterpart in another way as well: that is, it would permit more than 200,000 ship transits per year, *quintupling* nautical traffic through the area. Its impact on Central American commerce and, even more importantly, the redistribution of world energy supplies would be profound. And Somoza, as America's most "loyal" friend in the hemisphere, would be far more reliable than his colleagues in Panama. The problem with a "Nica-Rican" canal, however, was environmental. Unlike its counterpart in Panama, the Nicaraguan trench would be a *sea-level* canal, posing extreme ecological hazards to the Atlantic Ocean by virtue of the species exchange that was certain to take place with the Pacific. Moreover, economics dictated that Somoza's big ditch would have to be dug with thousands of nuclear explosions, irradiating the surrounding jungle and raining endless tons of mud and gravel upon its canopy. More than a half-million mestizos and rural farmers would have to be resettled and— Well, it was not a project in which the U. S. government could participate, however useful the new canal might prove.

Still, there was a possibility that the canal could be built—if not by the United States, then by some other country or private consortium. Under the Nixon Administration in 1970, the U. S. Senate unilaterally terminated the ancient Bryan-Chamorro Treaty, which had reserved to the U. S. government the exclusive right to build a sea-level canal through Nicaragua. Ending that treaty made it possible for such a canal to be constructed by others, including private parties. Three months after the treaty's termination, the Senate confirmed the nomination of Turner Shelton as America's new ambassador to Nicaragua. Almost immediately thereafter, Hughes decamped from Las Vegas, arriving at Shelton's old post in the Bahamas in December, 1970. There he entered into negotiations with shipping magnate Daniel K. Ludwig, a client of Nixon's former law firm (Mudge, Rose), and with the supernaturally wealthy Rothschild family. A year later, in February, 1972, Hughes joined Shelton and Somoza in the south, taking residence in Managua, the capital of Nicaragua. If any private consortium could build a sea-level canal through Nicaragua and Costa Rica, it would be Hughes, Somoza, the Rothschild family, and Daniel K. Ludwig. And, indeed, the intrigues were exceedingly thick during Shelton's tenure in Somoza's banana republic. In an effort to ingratiate the dictator, according to U. S. embassy officials who served under him, Ambassador Shelton provided Somoza with top-secret CIA reports on the local political situation, including materials about Somoza's pro-American adversaries as well as the Sandinist guerrillas in the mountains. That caused a total breakdown in communications between the local CIA station and its embassy, leading eventually to the station chief's *de facto* deportation at the ambassador's hands. It also led one top staffer of the Senate's Foreign Relations Committee to say, in an interview with this reporter, that Shelton's actions "amounted to treason." Whether they did or not, Shelton was immersed in political intrigues that spanned the Tropic of Cancer. With Hughes in Managua, the U. S. Ambassador served as liaison between Somoza and the billionaire, conferring daily with Paradise Island spooks led by former Nixon security chief Jim Golden. At the same time, other envoys of the Nixon White House shuttled in and out of town, including fund-raiser Maurice Stans and Watergate spook E. Howard Hunt. Indeed, if earthquakes can be triggered by the coming together of psychological platelets of money and intrigue, then the seismic devastation of Nicaragua's capital in December, 1972, can probably be explained in terms of those who had come and gone within Managua that year. Whether Hughes and the others were actually planning to construct a "Nica-Rican" canal—or merely frightening Panama's Torrijos with the appearance of doing so—is uncertain. A former high-ranking employee of Hughes's confirmed that "extensive discussions" were held on the subject but added a *caveat*. "Sure," he said, "the canal project was what Nicaragua was all about, *in a sense*. I emphasize 'in a sense' because Hughes was always promising to build the Pyramids, if you know what I mean. He was going to move Hughes Aircraft to Arizona, he was going to build an SST port near Las Vegas, he was—you get the picture. None of it ever materialized. And in this case there were a lot of uncertainties. The economics were the least of it—economically it would have worked out. But there were so many other reasons for Hughes to be in Nicaragua. With Somoza in his pocket, he owned the place. And it had fabulous communications: Managua's got a ComSat facility that Hughes was hooked into—so his communications systems was better there than if he'd been in New York, for chrissake. But I always thought the canal business was a sham. I figure what Hughes was doing, or wanted to do, was play around with minerals futures, real estate. . . . Convince people you're gonna build a new canal, jack up the rates, develop Fonseca—and you got a situation for making a lot of money without digging a single hole. But who knows? Maybe the old man was serious this time. A lot of people thought so."

Whether he was or wasn't, the Christmas earthquake smashed the negotiations, demolishing Managua and sending Hughes fleeing to London. Learning precisely what occurred during the tenure of Shelton and Hughes in Somoza's barony is no easy task, as a memo circulated on Capitol Hill by the ambassador's bitter subordinates makes clear. Among the questions asked by the normally reserved Foreign Service officers were the following:

What was the true purpose of the $100,000 that Howard Hughes purportedly gave to Bebe Rebozo as a campaign donation, and was then left in a safe-deposit box in Miami for so long? Could it have been to purchase the ambassadorship in Managua for Shelton, so that he could act as Hughes' agent in negotiations with Anastasio Somoza?

What were the results of the Foreign Service investigation of Shelton's tenure as Consul General in the Bahamas?

What were the true circumstances surrounding the death of the Consul, James Hargrove, in Managua shortly after the earthquake . . . ? [Hargrove, in charge of issuing visas, died under circumstances that were mysterious even for Nicaragua. In the wake of the quake, his body was found in the tropical garden of a house he shared with the American FBI agent stationed in Managua. Amid the city's rubble, an investigation was impossible, and the consul's death was listed as "an apparent suicide," probably brought about by "depression." What made some Foreign Service officers suspicious was the fact that the gun Hargrove was said to have used on himself had no fingerprints upon it; what's more, there were *two* bullets in his head—not one.]

What was the Hughes and Shelton relationship in Nicaragua? It should be noted that Shelton is the last man who acknowledges seeing Hughes. He was given an interview with Hughes in mid-72, after which he laid to rest press reports that Hughes was bearded, with six-inch nails, ill, incompetent, etc. Why was a distant cousin of Hughes, who mainly played polo while in Managua, assigned to the Embassy at that time? Was Shelton in the pay of Hughes during his tenure as ambassa-

dor, to act as his agent in the establishment of Hughes' business headquarters in Nicaragua?

And so on, in the same tenor, through sixteen questions. Whatever the answers, the timely quake interrupted a lot more than
Managua's architecture.

2 / TRADEWINDS & THE ACID RACKETEER

So U. S. Consul General to the Bahamas Turner Shelton was a
man whose name one would want to remember. In 1967, Shelton
was regarded as that most blessed of men—a man appreciated both
by Howard Hughes and the next President of the United States.
There was no mention of canals at that time, but Shelton was still a
busy man. The Bahamas were at their turning point, politically and
financially. The consul general's friend Jim Crosby was building a
casino that would not open until January, 1968, and Crosby had, of
necessity, made a pact with the Bay Street Boys, Wally Groves and
Sir Stafford Sands. Now, after centuries of British rule, the white
colonials were being challenged by the independence-bent Progressive Liberal Party (PLP), and the possibility existed that the British
tenure would soon be at an end. In Washington a PLP victory was
regarded as potentially advantageous to the United States in that it
would diminish British influence in the Caribbean—a circumstance
that could only increase America's own hegemony there. The problem was that Britain is an ally, and a reduction of its influence must
not be attributable to the United States: it must seem to "evolve" as
a natural outcome of its colonial history. On the one hand, then, the
removal of the Bay Street Boys was desirable. On the other hand, it
would jeopardize Crosby's new casino, the more so because those
supporting the PLP included a troika of American promoters who
sought to replace Wally Groves as the dominant gambling figure in
the archipelago. They were Mike McClaney, David Probinsky, and
Tex McCrary. The second problem, then, was how to eradicate the
Bay Street Boys, bringing Pindling to power, while at the same time
eliminating Pindling's own supporters. A dilemma, its solution rested
with Operation Tradewinds. The IRS/SEC/Justice (and, for all we
know, CIA) project contained all the elements for a "double coup."
The Bay Street Boys could be discredited by leaks to *Time, Life,* and
the *Wall Street Journal,* describing the colonials' corruption and
links to organized crime. That would likely be enough to tip the

election. As for McClaney, Probinsky, and McCrary, Tradewinds operatives could easily persuade Pindling of the troika's undesirability. In any case, the trio might be smeared in the press, wrongly identifying its members with gangster elements that PLP leader Pindling had sworn to remove. It didn't matter much that Lansky's bets were on Groves, the portly Chesler, and Sir Stafford Sands—the important thing was to give Pindling an opportunity to renege on campaign promises to his financial supporters.

Operation Tradewinds, then, became an instrument to unseat the Bay Street Boys while at the same time extricating Crosby from the dilemma presented by, on the one hand, his alliance with the slipping Brits and Wally Groves and, on the other hand, the predicted depredations of Pindling's American supporters. Just who deserves credit for arriving at this scheme is uncertain. What's clear is what happened.

As recently declassified Tradewinds memoranda make clear, Consul General Shelton repeatedly urged Tradewinds operatives to investigate the affairs of both Wally Groves and Pindling's supporters. The effect of this was to stimulate intensive federal investigations whose ambiguous results were later leaked to national magazines, damaging the men's reputations and leading to their expulsion from the Bahamas. Credit for the leaks is usually given to Peloquin.

This isn't to say that McClaney and his cohorts were sterling characters. They weren't. McClaney was an ersatz socialite, a sporting gent and sometime hustler who'd operated a casino in Havana and later in Haiti. Probinsky was a New Jersey P-R man associated with the civil rights movement in the United States; an owner of nightclubs catering to black clienteles, he had an abrasive personality and a penchant for putting together "incredible deals" that had a habit of falling through. McCrary was a fading radio personality (senior citizens will recall the "Tex and Jinx Show") who lived on the edge of other people's affluence. The point, however, is that the men seem to have been purged from influence in the Bahamas not because of who or what they were, but because it was a profitable course for those supporting Crosby.

In later years McClaney would be asked by a Senate investigating committee, "Who is behind Intertel and Resorts International?" And he'd reply, "I don't know. It's misty, shadows." Had he known, he might well have been stunned. If McClaney's "guilt" by alleged (and disputed) association with reputed organized-crime figures was sufficient justification for his removal from the Bahamas, Jim Crosby should have been made to take the same plane out. The hypocrisy behind the actions of Peloquin and the Tradewinds spooks went much deeper than their taking jobs with Resorts International after furthering that firm's interests in their federal capacities. Jim Crosby's own associations were as pungent as McClaney's, and they could not be disputed.

His brother Peter Crosby was one of the country's most notorious security swindlers, having served five years in prison for a multi-million-dollar fraud involving the criminal manipulation of nearly worthless stocks. A good-looking charmer with a ravenous appetite for the good life, Peter Crosby had been wed to a famous French actress and to organized crime. As Senate testimony and the memoirs of white-collar racketeers and Mafiosi have made clear, the black sheep of the Crosby family was better known for his association with Lansky henchmen such as Dino Cellini than he was for his relationship to the exquisite actress.

It wasn't only Jim Crosby's brother that made the proprietors of Paradise Island deserving of a second look. The moneymen who'd provided much of the capital to develop the island were themselves a bizarre lot. Among them were:

William Mellon Hitchcock. Heir to what may be America's largest family fortune, Billy Hitchcock is the great-grandson of one of the republic's most influential Secretaries of the Treasury, the grandson of Gulf Oil's founder, and the son of a world-class polo player. With an income from a family trust that's estimated to provide him with more than $15,000 *per week* in spending money, Hitchcock has never *needed* to work. That doesn't mean he hasn't been active, however. A big, athletic-looking man with a genius for mixing intrigue and high finance, Billy Hitchcock is one of those lads who, having sucked a silver spoon throughout infancy, prides himself as an adult in his willingness to "kick the Establishment in the teeth." *
In 1967, he resolved to do a José Greco on the heads of America's flower children. For some time Hitchcock had been the patron of LSD advocate Timothy Leary. After settling the silver-haired laboratory freak in a fifty-five-room mansion at Millbrook, New York, Hitchcock reportedly embarked on a score of acid trips under Leary's

---

* Mary J. Worth, "The Story of the Acid Profiteers," *The Village Voice*, August 22, 1974, p. 7.

guidance, sailing across Millbrook's 2,600 acres of private lawns and gardens, rocked by invisible breezes and hallucinations at which the mere bourgeoisie can only guess. Through his patronage of the Emperor of Psychedelia, Hitchcock became friendly with those in command of the counterculture's inner-space probe: legendary chemists, dealers, and distributors such as Owsley Stanley III, Nick Sand, Tim Scully, and Michael Boyd Randall. Through them, by means of personal loans and other forms of support, Hitchcock helped finance an acid cult called the Brotherhood of Eternal Love. California-based, the Brotherhood manufactured and distributed what may have been *most* of the illicit LSD in the United States at that time; its chemists also invented and popularized STP, a baroque psychedelic. With the Hell's Angels as its distributors, the Brotherhood's profits were enormous, hidden, and untaxed—a circumstance creating problems well known to organized-crime figures. But Hitchcock had the solution. Gulf Oil had been laundering money through Bahamian slush funds for more than a decade, and Billy knew how the cumbersome cash could be handled. With acid chemist Nick Sand the Mellon heir journeyed to the Paradise Island mansion of Sam Clapp, a Harvard lawyer associated with Investors' Overseas Services (IOS) and its stepchild, the Fiduciary Trust Company. Amid Clapp's cathedral ceilings, black lights, and the Grateful Dead's haunted rhythms, Hitchcock arranged for the Fiduciary Trust to handle proceeds from the missionary work being done by the Brotherhood of Eternal Love. That wasn't all he did, of course. While enjoying himself at Clapp's palace in Paradise, Hitchcock reportedly discussed the feasibility of establishing an offshore LSD lab on one of the Bahamas' remote cays—a notion which led some to think that the young heir "was on a Doctor No trip." Whether he was or wasn't, Hitchcock had the clarity to realize the advantages to him in gaining part ownership of an offshore gambling casino that was less than thirty minutes from Miami. At Clapp's urging, he plunged into Resorts stock. The mechanism for the plunge was his relationship to Delafield & Delafield, a brokerage by which Billy Hitchcock was technically employed; in fact, he did handle a few accounts at the firm—mostly his own and those of his relatives. During an eight-month period beginning in May, 1967, roughly ten million dollars in "private placements" of Resorts stock was made —at least half of which could be traced to Hitchcock's effort at Delafield & Delafield. This was the single biggest chunk of money made available to Resorts at that time, and it proved to be a disaster for Hitchcock. According to the testimony of Operation Trade-winds' TW-24, the informant known as the Friendly Ghost,* the manager of the vest-pocket Castle Bank & Trust Company of the Cayman Islands provided him with access to the bank's secret records in an apparent effort to destroy Billy Hitchcock. The heir and the bank were said to be quarreling over the bank's handling of Hitchcock's share of Resorts, and the dispute was sufficiently acrimonious as to lead the bank's manager to cooperate in what he thought was a narcotics investigation. As a result of TW-24's efforts, Hitchcock and the Brotherhood of Eternal Love (which had established an acid lab in, of all places, Costa Rica) were busted. It was another victory for Operation Tradewinds, reflecting its earlier triumphs over McClaney, Probinsky, and others Crosby feared.

Hitchcock wasn't the only investor in Resorts, of course. Thanks to Sam Clapp's enthusiasm, IOS poured nearly four million dollars into the firm's letter stock. Yet another investor, the American National Insurance Company (ANICO) of Galveston, Texas, was persuaded by "Pistol Dick" Pistell and a Hollywood stockbroker named Burt Kleiner to purchase $1,750,000 of the firm's convertible debentures. It was an exotic crowd. Hitchcock was the patron of those operating an international drug ring tied to Timothy Leary and the Hell's Angels. IOS would soon go bankrupt in one of the century's most notorious looting scandals. ANICO already held nine million dollars in mortgages on Las Vegas casinos, including a casino owned in part by ANICO's president and its board chairman. Both men would subsequently become the targets of a federal investigation linking them to a reputed Mob attorney and there would be charges that the pair had engaged in "self-dealing." As for Pistell, he was an importer of Turkish wines and a developer of gold mines in the African Cameroons; he'd soon be sued for millions in connection with the looted IOS. And Kleiner . . . well, Kleiner was a wheeler-dealer whose brokerage license would be lifted by the SEC on his firm's way into liquidation. In 1969, Kleiner would also serve as architect of Resorts' disastrous bid to take over Pan American World Airways, Inc., an effort which cost Resorts more than $20,000,000, and failed.

It would be wrong to give the impression that Resorts' only early investors were wheeler-dealers, IOS-ers, or persons connected with drug dealers or organized crime figures. The Chase Manhattan Bank,

---

* Norman Casper.

among others, also put up money. But the fact remains that the private financing of Resorts International depended very heavily upon a medley of characters who were bound for something less than glory. Whatever else may be said about Crosby's adventure in Paradise, his associations do not seem to have been any better than those whom he, Turner Shelton, and Bob Peloquin deposed.

The instruments used to evict McClaney et al. from the Bahamas were several. Investigations conducted by Tradewinds operatives led to sensational news articles in the American press, linking Groves's Lucayan Beach casino to Meyer Lansky. Almost incidentally, the same articles smeared McClaney and others, while offering no reason for doing so. The effect of this, and Peloquin's work with Shelton behind the scenes, convinced Pindling that he need not honor the commitments he'd made to his white supporters—commitments which would have given McClaney the right to operate existing casinos in return for a percentage of their profits. Upon Pindling's election, and the ouster of the Bay Street Boys, a royal commission of inquiry was convened by the Bahamian government in response to the newspaper exposés. Its purpose was to investigate the local gambling industry and its relationship to organized crime and the Bay Street Boys. Heading the commission was Sir Ranulph Bacon, formerly the commissioner of Scotland Yard and subsequently a director of Intertel. Bob Peloquin was an "unofficial," but influential, observer of the commission's work.

By August, 1967, that work had been completed amid great publicity. Sir Stafford Sands, disgraced by revelations of the millions that he'd made drafting legislation for Mob-connected entrepreneurs, retired to his castle in Spain. McClaney was declared "a thoroughly dangerous man" and, with David Probinsky, was ordered to leave the Bahamas. Lansky's relationship to Groves's Lucayan Beach Casino was documentarily exposed, forcing him into retirement from both the Bahamas and his deal with Jim Crosby. The managers of the Lucayan Beach Casino—Courtney, Brudner, and Reed—were declared *personae non gratae*, an unhappy circumstance in view of the fact that all of them were fugitives from indictments in the United States. Should they return, they'd likely go to jail. The men owned a sheaf of credit dossiers on the world's biggest gamblers, however, and without that, the Lucayan Beach Casino could hardly operate. It was fortunate for all concerned, therefore, that lawyer Edward Bennett Williams was able to put together a deal whereby Courtney and the others were given special residence permits in the Bahamas and *$2,100,000* in exchange for their pigeon list and retirement from the gaming industry. For his services the attorney and future president of the Washington Redskins football team reportedly received a fifty-thousand-dollar "finder's fee."

The commission, then, had accomplished its purposes. It had not, of course, investigated Jim Crosby, his brother Peter, or the financial backers of Mary Carter/Resorts: Crosby's casino would not even open its doors until the first day of 1968 and, therefore, had had no past to investigate. Instead, the commission had concentrated on Crosby's competition and upon the men who gave him worry. It was the best of possible worlds, then, and the head of Mary Carter/Resorts was delighted.

With the commission's investigations at a productive end, Peloquin decided to strike out on his own, retiring from the federal service in the company of a fellow attorney, William Hundley. Hundley was a veteran of Smith Act prosecutions who'd risen to become chief of the Justice Department's Organized Crime and Racketeering Section. He was also the government lawyer who'd harried John Frank and quizzed Robert Maheu in the wake of the Galindez kidnapping. In later years he'd defend a galaxy of incriminated political figures, including Korean spook Tongsun Park, corrupt Maryland governor Marvin Mandel, and former Attorneys General John Mitchell and Richard Kleindienst.

In 1967, though, the firm of Peloquin & Hundley was new on the Washington scene. Its first customers were the National Football League, in which Edward Bennett Williams was becoming a factor, and Time-Life, sued by Mike McClaney. It was only a matter of weeks, however, before Peloquin and Hundley were named vice-presidents of the Resorts subsidiary responsible for the new casino on Paradise Island. Jim Crosby had extricated himself from his agreement with Wally Groves (no clarification was forthcoming about that), and the casino was preparing to open its doors. Meanwhile, Resorts' chairman had grown increasingly close to Bebe Rebozo and Turner Shelton. Through them he renewed an old acquaintance with Richard Nixon, then gearing up for the New Hampshire primary, and became one of RMN's biggest supporters. Only a few weeks before his casino opened, Crosby wrote out thirty-four separate checks to Nixon campaign committees—all but one of them for three thousand dollars—and, at Maurice Stans's urging, raised a second hundred grand from friends.

Not unexpectedly, then, Nixon was delighted to attend the lavish New Year's opening of the Paradise Island casino, taking time off from campaigning to become one of the first to cross the toll bridge linking the island to Nassau. Others attending the opening included Nixon cronies Bebe Rebozo, Robert Abplanalp, and Turner Shelton, IOS millionaire Sam Clapp, the sometimes whacked-out Billy Hitchcock, jet-setters such as the Ladies Astor and Sassoon, celebrities such as Carol Channing, and, of course, the casino's manager, Eddie Cellini. Whether Robert Vesco was on hand is unknown, though Paradise would become his favorite hangout.

Indeed, it was "Hail to the Chief" and "Hail, Hail the Gang's All Here" at one and the same time, but nobody thought to ask who Eddie Cellini was or, as it happened, who really owned the toll bridge. The questions would later arise amid (as yet unproven) allegations that cash from the toll bridge was being skimmed, laundered through Rebozo's bank, and used, in part, to support President Nixon in the style to which he'd become accustomed. As for Eddie Cellini, he was a competent casino manager, but his brother Dino was a source of some embarrassment—just as Crosby's own brother Peter was. Within a short time Crosby would tire of Eddie's noisome presence, and disregarding his own sibling problems, order Peloquin to "Can him! I don't care if he's Pope Paul." The embarrassment would be compounded in later years when Dino's gambling junkets to Paradise Island would be ordered to a halt, supposedly because the elder Cellini was enmeshed in the affairs of international narcotics trafficker Giuseppe Cotroni. And the embarrassment would be compounded even further upon hearing that the two Cellinis had shaken hands "on a deal you couldn't imagine" with Robert Vesco, an erstwhile purchaser of Resorts' Paradise properties.

It was a heady mix of personalities among the roulette wheels, craps tables, and slots: the next President avoided the casino proper, but Billy Hitchcock was there, as were various IOS figures, tourists, Beautiful People, the feds, the heads, various shysters, and the future spooks of Intertel—all of it overseen by Eddie Cellini. Had someone had the foresight to throw a net over the place, America would have been saved a lot of trouble over the next few years.

3 / THE APPARAT IN PARADISE

But it would also have lost a terrific resort. The facilities at Paradise Island are deservedly esteemed: the ocean views are spectacular, the casuarina trees majestic, the beaches Oxydol-white, and the tennis courts and swimming pools superbly lighted. There are six *luxe* hotels on the island, four of them owned by Resorts International (the old name, along with the paint company, was sold in 1968 to a consortium of Italo-American businessmen in Tampa, Florida). You can dine, expensively and expansively, at any number of restaurants, attend fashion shows, "native revues," or a "junkanoo jamboree." It's an air-conditioned planet set squarely in the Bermuda Triangle and served both daily and directly by Chalk's International Airlines, a Resorts subsidiary. For the most part, though, people come to Paradise to gamble at its casino—a half-acre of blackjack tables, roulette wheels, iced drinks, British croupiers, and 350 slot machines that begin spinning at noon and don't stop until the rooster crows. And when that happens, you can usually find a high-stakes backgammon game in the vicinity, settling down with a rum punch and a set of dice across from another player whose face you can't place but whose name reminds you of the Fifth Amendment.

The company had been in operation for two years before its owners got around to incorporating Intertel in 1970. The purpose of the new subsidiary, according to a brochure it no longer issues, was to "create a management-security system designed to uncover and thwart employees with criminal backgrounds and/or intentions. . . . We provide management with the necessary intelligence service and guidance on possible exposure to organized crime through companies with whom they do business or with whom they are considering business relationships. . . ." It billed itself, in other words, as a private intelligence service "created specifically to safeguard business from the hidden risks of vulnerability to criminal elements. . . ." There's nothing wrong with that, of course, except that, as we've seen, the parent firm was itself embroiled in some very worrisome relationships. Paradise Island was a hangout not only for Eddie Cellini but also for securities swindlers of historic dimensions—indeed, in 1972 Crosby was preparing to sell the place to the king of them all, Robert Vesco, on terms electrifying to the SEC and IOS shareholders. What's more, Intertel's parent firm was prepared to pay, or *did* pay, a fifty-thousand-dollar "finder's fee" to Jimmy Neal (*né* Pellegrino Loia). The uncertainty about the payment stems from the fact that Neal, an associate of Canadian narcotics kingpin Giuseppe Cotroni, decamped to Costa Rica rather than answer questions on the subject. According to Phillip Manuel, a burly Senate investigator who looks and talks like a man whose nickname should be "Rocky," Jimmy Neal was a man of some influence at the Paradise Island casino. His brother, Adolph, and Dominic Salerno, Neal's brother-in-law, were both employed in the cashier's office at the casino—while Neal himself ran gambling junkets to the island. According to Manuel, the two men got their jobs—not through the *New York Times*' want ads—but through Dino Cellini's intercessions with his brother, Eddie. As if this weren't enough, there was also the problem of acid-angel Billy Hitchcock's involvement with the firm. Obviously, then, Intertel was in no position to cast the first stone at companies considering business relationships with members or associates of organized-crime groups.

Resorts defends itself, insofar as Vesco is concerned, by stating that "there was no way of knowing," in 1972, that Vesco was anything other than a legitimate businessman—though Intertel claims to have investigated the prospective buyer of their parent firm. That's nonsense, of course. The Detroit Kid was one step ahead of the law in mid-'72, and he was losing ground fast. The public at large may not have been aware of his criminality, but Resorts and Intertel were hardly "the public at large." The latter's staff is composed of former high-ranking federal investigators whose livelihood depends upon the acquisition of secret business intelligence and the preparation of in-depth background investigations. Moreover, Intertel's two directors of operations were uniquely situated: they were the former chief of the SEC's Market Surveillance Section, and a veteran CIA officer. The significance of this ought not to be underestimated: while *SEC* sleuths were rushing to halt the deal between Crosby and Vesco, the *CIA* was investigating the Detroit Kid for the *White House*—whose main tenant was a beneficiary of Crosby's largesse. As if this weren't enough, Operation Tradewinds had also become enmeshed in the Vesco probe, and the operation's former intelligence director, William Kolar, was an Intertel vice-president. Obviously, Resorts was wired into every institution that might have had a shred of information about Vesco's difficulties and activities.

In fact, "wired" may not be an exaggeration. In July, 1972, when the Vesco/Crosby transaction was nearing its fever point and the SEC, Intertel, and CIA investigations were rumbling toward conclusion, Operation Tradewinds agent Richard Jaffe held a supposedly secret meeting in the Britannia Beach Hotel on Paradise Island. With him were SEC and Justice Department Strike Force representatives. They were there to discuss immunity with "a very senior official" of

IOS who was prepared to give them virtually all of the company's records: according to Jaffe's notes, the man—a European—was one of the original founders of IOS, who "knows where all the money and 'bodies' are buried."

The secret meeting, however, turned out not to be a secret. Two days after it was held, Jaffe received "a complete report" of the conference from another IRS agent who'd obtained details of the meeting from "an outside source." Infuriated, the Tradewinds veteran recalled meeting Bob Peloquin at the hotel, remembered that the hotel was owned by Resorts, knew that Crosby was negotiating with Vesco, and pondered the fact that Intertel provided security for the Britannia Beach. Not surprisingly, Jaffe concluded that Intertel had bugged the meeting, and he fired off an angry memo on the subject to the new director of IRS intelligence (whose predecessor had already joined Intertel). The memo circulated within the IRS for two weeks, by which time Intertel had learned of it and sent back an angry denial. Two days after Intertel's denial was received, IRS Commissioner Johnny Walters electrified Jaffe and the others by suspending Operation Tradewinds until further notice. (A few months later, while Tradewinds was still under suspension, Walters would again intervene, ruining Jaffe's plans. In the dark hours before dawn on Christmas Eve, 1972, Howard Hughes would fly into Fort Lauderdale amid great secrecy. Despite the precautions of the Hughes team, however, Jaffe would be waiting at the airport with a subpoena for the billionaire. He would never serve it, though. With Hughes trapped in the hangared jet, Jaffe would be made to wait while one of the billionaire's aides communicated with his attorney, Chester Davis. Midnight telephone calls by Davis to IRS Commissioner Walters and his top assistant led to a decision to let Hughes proceed on his way despite the subpoena outstanding against him. The next time a public official would see Hughes in the United States would be on a mortician's table.)

The significance of Tradewinds' suspension will presently be made clear, but first the events should be placed in context. In the four years since Resorts' casino had opened, Tradewinds had become an enormously effective intelligence operation of almost as much importance to the SEC, Justice Department, and DEA as it was to the IRS. With the IOS investigation heating up, Jaffe was appalled at the operation's suspension. The longtime operational chief of Tradewinds, he was suddenly banned from traveling to the Bahamas. That order, however, held no authority over free-lance spook

Norman Casper; one of Jaffe's agents, Casper was in it for the money, and his curiosity had been piqued recently by the computer print-out from the Castle Trust showing "Richard M. Nixon" as a secret depositor. Casper, then, kept on working and, at about this time, came to the conclusion that not all was kosher at Resorts International. In congressional testimony on the subject, Casper identified one Seymour Alter, "a Resorts consultant," as the firm's "bagman." According to Casper, he was told that Resorts maintained a double accounting system for revenues from the toll bridge. "When a Bahamian two dollars goes in," he said, "it goes into a regular Bahamian bank account for regular accounting. When an American two dollars got in, it got thrown . . . into a box. . . . [J]ust kind of crammed in there, surprisingly enough." Recalling the weeks after Tradewinds' suspension on August 23, 1972, Casper said that a Resorts official removed the "box" from the bridge. "They counted it up and it was better than $200,000." Subsequently, the money was put in a vault at the Britannia Beach Hotel. It was checked daily, until one day it disappeared. "That same day," according to Casper, Seymour Alter telephoned Frank Lichtenburg, master of Resorts' fifty-five-foot speedboat, the *Orca*. Alter told Lichtenburg "to get that boat up to the Jockey Club real fast, posthaste. . . ." So, Casper says, Lichtenburg "goes up to the Jockey Club . . . and picks up Si Alter. . . . Si has a briefcase and some *stuff* on him. Whatever stuff it is, I don't know. All I am doing is repeating what Frank told me. When he says 'stuff' I can't press too closely because, once again, I was afraid of expressing too much interest. . . ." Then, Casper explained, Alter "said, 'I am going to see the Man. Get me over to the Key Biscayne Yacht Club as fast as you can get me there.' He was really nervous and in a big hurry, again according to Lichtenburg. . . . They got there and Bebe drove on the dock. He was driving a black Lincoln Continental. Si got out the box and climbed in the car real quick; but prior to that Si said, 'I am going to see the Man.'

"Nixon was in town at the time. He was in the house on Bay Lane. They headed for either Bebe's house or Nixon's house. . . . Si has been known as the bagman for Resorts International for quite some time. . . . He was the man who transferred monies for Resorts International, for what purpose who knows, via Chalk Airways. . . . They use seaplanes."

Casper's testimony about these incidents was partly hearsay. Yet other events would bear out his suspicions. In 1973, for instance, Resorts would be sued by Huntington Hartford, charging that the casino was "skimming" its revenues and, therefore, defrauding him as a stockholder. The suit was later settled out of court and Si Alter's role in the alleged skimming, if any, is unknown. But Casper wasn't alone in his belief that Alter was Resorts' bagman. An ebullient entrepreneur and glad-hander, Alter was the man who'd put Jim Crosby and Huntington Hartford together in 1965. He owned a gift shop on Paradise Island, banked with and borrowed from Rebozo, and counted Nixon, Bebe, and Bob Abplanalp as good friends. He was also the one to see if you wanted to smooth your way through Bahamian customs because he'd long ago made it a point to ingratiate local officials: sending them on trips to Las Vegas and Acapulco, the Resorts "consultant" provided the officials with booze, food, hotel rooms, and, by his own statements, girls.* Franklin S. DeBoer, a former vice-president of Rebozo's Key Biscayne Bank, shared Casper's opinion that Alter was Resorts' bagman, telling Watergate investigators that "I'm just quoting ten thousand other people" on the subject.† Richard Stearns, another veteran of the Rebozo bank, had harder information, however. In sworn statements to Florida prosecutors, Stearns recalled after-hours meetings with Alter in Rebozo's bank. During those meetings, Stearns said, he would give Alter hundred-dollar bills in exchange for tens and twenties.

None of which *proves* that Alter is a bagman or, if he is, that he's a bagman for Resorts, laundering casino skims through Rebozo's banking facility on the mainland. But certainly there's enough circumstantial evidence to give the possibility more than a passing glance. Vesco, too, was convinced that Resorts was skimming. According to Robert A. Hutchison, a biographer of Vesco:

> [Howard] Cerny and [Gil] Straub were particularly interested in the skimming procedures whereby, it was discovered, millions of dollars were diverted from the cash receipts allegedly without appearing in the books. . . . The skimming system implied the continued presence of a Mafia credit man inside the casino. According to one of Vesco's Super Group lawyers, the system centered upon the acceptance of IOU notes from known creditworthy players. The IOUs would not be cleared through the casino's accounting department but would be

---

* Denny Walsh, "Rebozo Bank and Gambling in Bahamas Attract Investigators," *The New York Times*, January 21, 1974, p. 1.
† *Ibid.*

placed aside and taken to Miami, where they were discounted for cash with a Mob-connected collection agency or bank.*

The skimming and laundering allegations were based upon more than mere suspicion: Vesco's auditors, Coopers & Lybrand, had conducted an extensive study of the casino's operations and books throughout the negotiations with Crosby. Richard Jaffe's belief that Intertel was "bugging Federal agents in Nassau" during 1972 is doubly interesting, then. At the time, $200,000 in small bills, revenues from the toll bridge, had disappeared, according to the Friendly Ghost. Alter, Resorts' alleged bagman, had held a panicky meeting with Rebozo, and perhaps with Nixon, during a time when, Dick Stearns said, Alter was collecting hundred-dollar bills. This was also the period, it should be noted, when E. Howard Hunt's wife, Dorothy, was collecting cash from White House spooks on behalf of the Watergate burglars. It would be naïve to ignore the likelihood, in view of the above, that some of those payoffs may have been made with currency whose origin could be traced to Paradise. In this connection, Jaffe's allegation of Intertel bugging is of direct importance. If the cash being raised to buy the Cubans' silence came from the Bahamas, Tradewinds operatives were the most likely ones to discover that fact. So it is that Intertel's protests about Jaffe, and the immediate suspension of Tradewinds, are highly suspicious. For *five months*—the most strategic months of the Watergate cover-up—Tradewinds didn't exist. Kept in a bureaucratic holding pattern that began in August, the operation was not reactivated until January 22, 1973—exactly two days after Nixon's inauguration and a month after Dorothy Hunt's death in a Chicago plane crash.

This is not to say that Intertel bugged Jaffe's meeting, as the IRS intelligence agent believed. After all, the since-murdered private detective Bobby Hall was working for Vesco in the Bahamas at about the same time, and certainly *he'd* have had no compunctions about wiring the feds' room. But that somebody did is certain. And that it had to do with Vesco's proposed take-over of Paradise, and his looting of IOS, is clear. The bugged meeting was with an IOS turncoat who threatened ruin, not only of the lucrative deal for Paradise, but of Vesco himself. Regardless of who was responsible for the eavesdropping, however, the events it generated were far from ambiguous. A few days after Intertel's protest of Jaffe's allega-

---

* Robert A. Hutchison, *Vesco* (New York: Praeger Publishers, 1974), p. 267.

tions, Operation Tradewinds was suspended, blacking out the Bahamas in the aftermath of the Watergate burglary: without any reporting from the area, it became the most logical and attractive site for obtaining White House hush-money.

Subsequently Tradewinds was resumed—only to be terminated three years later under IRS commissioner Donald Alexander. The circumstances under which Alexander permitted the project to end were so acrimonious, and so dangerous to the informants, that Jaffe, Casper, and other agents combined to file suit against the commissioner. According to their attorney, the suit was prompted by the fact that "the intelligence community as a whole felt that there was a conspiracy to destroy them by the administration of the IRS."

While Tradewinds ended disastrously for Casper and Jaffe, Intertel prospered through the skills of some Tradewinds agents and others who'd shed their federal cloaks to join the private apparat. Even at the organization's lowest rungs there were men of considerable expertise, white-collar spooks such as *Albert Murphy*, former special intelligence investigator for Lockheed Aircraft Corporation; *Alfred Pease*, former senior instructor in investigative techniques for International Police Services; * *Lynn Sawyer*, former coordinator of research for the Los Angeles Police Department's intelligence division; and fifty-two others. At the executive level, however, Intertel's expertise and clout became positively scary. Among the government titles its top executives have held were Chief, Special Projects Section, National Security Agency (NSA); Director, Intelligence and Internal Security Divisions, Internal Revenue Service (IRS); Chief, Intelligence Division and Organized Crime Strike Forces, Bureau of Narcotics and Dangerous Drugs (BNDD); Deputy Director of Security, Department of State; Commissioner, New Scotland Yard; Supervisor of Intelligence Activities of the Federal Bureau of Investigation (FBI); Supervisor of Espionage and Internal Security Investigations, FBI; Senior Advisor, U. S. Department of State, Southeast Asia; Coordinator of Interpol Operations for the Royal Canadian Mounted Police (RCMP); Supervisor, Organized Crime

---

* International Police Services, or INPOLSE, was a supposedly private firm, similar in some ways to the National Intelligence Academy. Operating out of a sedate town house in a fashionable section of Washington, D.C., INPOLSE trained CIA officers, agents, and foreign policemen in investigative and counterinsurgency techniques. It also sold police and military hardware to foreign regimes and came to be regarded as a "graduate school" for international spooks. The film *State of Siege*, in which an American official of AID's "Public Safety" program is executed by Uruguayan Tupamaros, is apropos to INPOLSE.

and Intelligence Squads, IRS; Chief, Justice Department's Organized Crime Strike Forces; Detective Supervisor, Special Investigating Unit and Narcotics Squad, New York City Police Department (N.Y.P.D.); Director of Enforcement, U. S. Bureau of Customs; and —not least—Fred Robinette, J. Edgar Hoover's only nephew.

The firm's outside directors were equally impressive for their successes in the business world.* But there were two men at Intertel who deserved special notice.

One was James O. Golden. What made Jim Golden notable was that he was considered by many to be "Nixon's man" at Intertel. An ex-Marine interrogator, his life has been spent in almost continuous association with organizations and firms committed to intrigue. A degreed criminologist, he joined the Secret Service in 1955. Attached to the White House detail, he was one of two agents assigned to Vice President Nixon, traveling with him to countries as far apart as Russia and the Bahamas. Reportedly, the close association made the two men friends, and when Nixon left the White House, Golden departed from the Secret Service. Joining the General Mills Corporation after Kennedy's inauguration, Golden left that firm in 1962 on special assignment to an unrevealed government agency. He himself won't say much about that assignment, but he's known to have been stationed at the U. S. Embassy in the Philippines. Whatever he did there, he became the first American to be named an "honorary agent of the Philippines' National Bureau of Investigation (NBI)." In 1965, Golden found himself at the Lockheed Aircraft Corporation's Washington headquarters, holding the job title of International Representative. He doesn't like to talk about that either, except to say that "It involved a lot of embassy work, making the rounds in Washington." In 1968, Golden returned to the Nixon camp, taking leave from Lockheed to serve as staff security chief to the country's next President. After the inaugural ceremonies, however, he did not return to Lockheed. Instead, he joined Resorts International as its deputy director of security, becoming a vice-president of Intertel shortly thereafter. In 1972 he made the transition from Resorts to Howard Hughes's Summa Corporation, leading the billionaire's forces into Nicaragua. According to Foreign

---

* Among Intertel's original directors were the president of the Dreyfus Corporation and the publisher of *Life*; the president of Carte Blanche; the chairman of the board of the Royal Bank of Canada Trust Company; the vice-chairman of R. H. Macy; and a director of the Prudential Insurance Company. Crosby, Peloquin, and Sir Ranulph Bacon were also directors.

Service officer Jim Cheek, who received a commendation from Secretary of State Henry Kissinger for reports he'd written contradicting U. S. Ambassador Turner Shelton, "Shelton gave Golden the run of the embassy. We couldn't see the ambassador half the time, but Golden always got what he wanted. He never needed an appointment." Today the peripatetic spook has yet another assignment, handling intelligence matters for the Law Enforcement Assistance Administration (LEAA).

The other man at Intertel who deserves special notice, of course, is its president, Robert Peloquin.

In many ways Peloquin resembles Bob Maheu. Both are Catholic churchgoers of French-Canadian descent, the sons of New England small-business men. Both are tennis players and Sunday sailors, and, more than anything else, each is a spook. Peloquin, however, is a tall, lean man with an abundance of nervous energy. For years he smoked four packs of cigarettes a day, and though he's recently abandoned that habit, his voice retains the smoker's ragged edge. Rather more than Maheu, he's a hobbyist, a cabinetmaker and shade-tree mechanic whose Saturday afternoons * are divided between sets of tennis and restoration of a 1961 Mercedes-Benz. As Maheu's friends describe Maheu, Peloquin's describe him approvingly in terms that some people would resent but which in the agent's milieu are heard as compliments. One calls him "crafty," another "cunning." Yet a third describes him as a man "who likes that specter of mystery." †

The "specter" hasn't been insubstantial. Under Peloquin's leadership, Intertel's acquired more than two hundred clients, most of them under "oral" contracts and most of them blue-chip corporations. The oral contracts are preferred to written ones, according to Peloquin, "for security reasons." Billing itself as a "management consultancy," the firm offers an array of intelligence services, which it couches in the most recondite prose imaginable. For instance, Intertel will protect "proprietary information" (secrets), whether it's on tape, in print, or in an employee's head; perform background investigations and "employee attitude assessments"; establish industrial "intelligence systems" and guard against corporate espionage; provide "defensive electronic surveys" (debug); authenticate, or discredit, documents using state-of-the-art laboratory equipment and

---

* Tom Zito, "Peloquin of Intertel: Intelligence, Security, 'Targets of Opportunity,' " *The Washington Post,* February 20, 1977, p. 1.
† *Ibid.,* Zito.

techniques; undertake "communications integrity analyses" to learn if scrambling or cryptographic equipment is needed by a client; hermeticize the data in computers; sanitize public images; shred red tape, monitor relevant government legislation, and lobby; identify stolen stocks and bonds; prevent the theft of securities; and make "industrial site relocation surveys"—sort of what happened to Howard Hughes, whose "site" Intertel relocated only a few months after it began operations.

Predictably, Intertel refuses to identify its clients or reveal what it does for them. Nevertheless, the following selection has been put together from a variety of sources:

- *Resorts International*—of course. Security services for the casino and other properties on Paradise Island is the main responsibility. Investigations (for example, of Vesco) are also important.
- *McDonald's:* investigations of franchise holders and applicants to determine their suitability and to identify any who may be connected with organized crime. The notion of the Mob infiltrating America's biggest hamburger chain ("Over X Billion Sold!") may seem absurd, but McDonald franchises have long had secret investors and have always generated a huge cash flow—of special interest to organized crime. In 1976, with Intertel's help, McDonald's filed suit in federal court to void the franchises of two Michigan businessmen with secret holdings in thirty of its restaurants in the South. The two men protested that McDonald's was simply trying to force them out of lucrative franchises obtained more than a decade ago. In any case, both men were suspect to Intertel. One owned a fifth of a Las Vegas casino which he and partners had built on land purchased from Hughes's Summa Corporation. The casino was then leased to Allen R. Glick, target of numerous organized-crime investigations, after which the Michigan man and his partners received a ten-million-dollar loan from the Teamsters Union Welfare Fund. The second Wolverine was a forty-six-year-old pension-plan expert with close ties to Jimmy Hoffa's foster son; according to federal investigators, Hoffa told friends that he owned parts of McDonald's franchises in cities where the two Michigan men have their franchises.
- *International Telephone & Telegraph (ITT):* Following Jack Anderson's disclosure of the infamous Dita Beard memorandum (revealing *quids pro quo* between ITT and the Nixon Admin-

istration), Intertel was hired by the phone company to discredit Anderson and his stories. The discrediting attempts included efforts to prove Beard's memo a forgery and, when that failed, to suggest in the press that Beard and Anderson's secretary were alcoholic chums who conspired to embarrass the Nixon Administration. (They weren't, and they hadn't.) Reportedly, Intertel's efforts in this case were coordinated with the White House and ITT by John Martin, an attorney with the Justice Department's Internal Security Division.

- *Roger and Jules LeBlanc:* Implicated in an enormous financial scandal, the politically powerful Louisiana brothers have hired Intertel to work behind the scenes in their behalf. At issue is a series of byzantine transactions carried out by the young wheeler-dealers in Grady Partin's old stomping grounds, Baton Rouge. According to federal investigators, the brothers acquired a number of banks and insurance companies, pyramiding their assets for leverage to extend themselves even further. After gutting the assets of one such firm, the North American Life Insurance Company (NALIC), Roger LeBlanc sold it to a West Coast consortium with ties to the Teamsters union. LeBlanc's removal of the firm's assets prior to the sale was described by Mary Robinson, general counsel to the Louisiana Insurance Department, as "the rape of NALIC." SEC, Justice Department investigators, and other authorities are looking into the scandal, and a number of suits have already been filed or are contemplated. The affair is politically explosive, however. Besides the LeBlancs' ties to Louisiana Senator Russell Long and other politicians in the state, Larry O'Brien owns a large piece of a company that runs the Hilton Hotel in the LeBlancs' biggest developmental project, Baton Rouge's Corporate Square. The Hilton is the LeBlancs' most important tenant, and O'Brien's son Lawrence III, a New York attorney, has served as a director of Roger LeBlanc's holding company. Moreover, according to the SEC, the California-Arizona consortium which purchased the deflowered NALIC allegedly did so with Teamsters union insurance premiums that had been unlawfully "siphoned off." The consortium had obtained the premiums after former Attorney General Richard Kleindienst allegedly prevailed upon Teamsters president Frank Fitzsimmons. Kleindienst, then a partner of Hughes's attorney Edward Morgan, received a $125,-000 fee for his representation of the consortium. The scandal, then, is a complicated and bipartisan one, involving luminaries in both the Republican and Democratic parties, with Intertel working invisibly in the middle. How well the story will be reported is of special interest to the mod LeBlanc brothers—whose holdings have included the hip New York journalism review, *More*.

- *Summa Corporation:* Besides engineering Hughes's exodus from Las Vegas, providing security for his casinos, and compiling hundreds of investigative reports on Robert Maheu and his associates, Intertel is credited with having identified Edith Irving as the putative "Helga R. Hughes" who cashed checks made out to "H. R. Hughes" by the McGraw-Hill Publishing Company. Nailing the beautiful Edith, Peloquin put an end to the notorious Clifford Irving hoax. Other assignments for the Summa Corporation have been less dramatic, but equally intriguing. In 1973, for instance, Intertel was approached by BNDD officials who asked that it take part in "Operation Silver Dollar." This was said to be a plot to nab a guest of the Hughes-owned Frontier Hotel who was thought to be dealing drugs. The BNDD promised to infiltrate the man's milieu if Intertel would convince Summa to bankroll the narcs in their efforts to bust the unwelcome guest. The cash, upward of $100,000, was provided, and the agents dutifully gambled it away—but the guest was unimpressed by the flashing cash, and there was no sale of drugs or anything else.

- Other Intertel clients have included *Henry Ford*, whose Caribbean casino was a source of worry; *The New York Times*, which required Intertel's investigative services; *General Motors*, whose Lordstown strike threatened to explode; *Jim Piersall*, a Texas developer, whose plans for Tortuga Island were torpedoed by Haiti's government; *Detroit*, whose airport security system was designed by Intertel; *Rhode Island*, where Intertel designed a prison security system; *Illinois governor Otto Kerner*, indicted in a racetrack kickback case; *IBM*; and an unidentified American drug firm which required Intertel to locate and destroy a million dollars' worth of missing drugs, which, as it happened, had turned to poison in a small African backwater.

Not that Intertel accepts every assignment that comes its way. Two which it turned down were requests by the Democrats' Edward Bennett Williams and the GOP's Murray Chotiner to investigate the

Watergate burglary. (From opposite points of view, one supposes.)

Without knowing it, Intertel had cast a pall over the White House spooks who would later become principals in the Watergate scandal. Indeed, as the following excerpts from Jack Caulfield's "Operation Sandwedge" proposal make clear, White House espionage operations were at least partly defensive and predicated on a fear of Intertel and its relationship to the Kennedy family:

> The 1972 Presidential Campaign strongly suggests a definitive need for the creation of a political intelligence-security entity to be located within the private sector. This entity, surfacely disassociated from the Administration by virtue of an established business cover, would have the capability of performing in a highly sophisticated manner designed to ensure that the major offensive intelligence and defensive security requirements of the entire campaign . . . would be professionally structured, programmed and implemented. . . . Indicated below, therefore, are a series of considerations . . . :
>
> *OPPOSITION INTELLIGENCE EFFORT*
>
> The presence of Lawrence O'Brien as Chairman of the Democratic National Committee unquestionably suggests that the Democratic nominee will have a strong, covert intelligence effort mounted against us in 1972. . . . In this regard, we should be particularly concerned about the new and rapidly growing Intertel organization. Should this *Kennedy mafia* dominated intelligence "gun for hire" be turned against us in '72, we would, indeed, have a dangerous and formidable foe.
>
> Close scrutiny of this organization's activity has been ongoing here. Indicated below are a series of points designed to suggest the political hazards that this group represents:
>
> A) The organization was co-founded by Bill Hundley, former Special Assistant to A.G. Bobby Kennedy and Bob Peloquin, [another] Kennedy loyalist. . . .
>
> B) Other Kennedy mafia types, including the so-called mysterious David I. Belisle, former *Director Investigations* for the *National Security Agency*, are principals in the organization.
>
> C) It has been reliably determined that Stephen Smith, EMK's brother-in-law, has privately visited Intertel's New York office, headed by former FBI supervisor Jack O'Connell, known by his colleagues to have been a 'black bag' specialist while at the Bureau. Smith, unquestionably, would think Intertel should EMK go for the big prize.
>
> D) On Intertel's Board of Directors is Jerome S. Hardy, Executive Vice President of the Dreyfus Corporation which is chaired by Howard Stein. The media reports that Stein will be a heavy contributor to a Democratic-liberal or 3rd Party Presidential candidate. Shortly before this media revelation, the aforementioned Jack `O'Connell accom-

panied an electronics specialist to both Stein's and Hardy's offices for sweeping purposes.

E) It has been very reliably determined that some of Intertel's principals possess gambling weaknesses or have been quietly let go from their sensitive federal law enforcement positions because of financial improprieties. One Intertel principal, related to a known Baltimore Cosa Nostra figure and released from federal service because of an established gambling weakness, is now in charge of Hughes' security operation in Las Vegas.

F) The investigative reporter fraternity is taking a closer look at the potential for Intertel to be exposed as a mafia front or a mafia exploitable tool for its Caribbean and Vegas operations. Bill Kolar . . . and Resorts International's President I. G. (Jack) Davis recently testified before the New Jersey legislature advocating legalized gambling in that mafia-ridden state. . . .

It is recommended that consideration be given to have Intertel neutralized by Justice. . . . This can be accomplished by directing Justice (if it has not done so already) to open a case with a view towards determining if the organization has unauthorized access to sensitive government files. It most certainly has.

Among other factors supporting this contention is the consensus in the federal intelligence sector indicating that Intertel, in all likelihood, delivered the details of a reported Justice-IRS skimming investigation of Bob Maheu to Hughes causing Maheu's fall and Hughes' departure from Vegas. . . .

PROPOSED "SANDWEDGE" RESPONSIBILITIES

. . . Operation Sandwedge proposes that it be charged . . . with the following responsibilities:

OFFENSIVE (New York City based—clandestine operation)

A) Supervise penetration of nominee's entourage and headquarters with undercover personnel.

B) "Black Bag" capability (discuss privately) including all *covert* steps necessary to minimize Democratic voting violations in Illinois, Texas, etc.

C) Surveillance of Democratic primaries, convention, meetings, etc.

D) Derogatory information investigative capability, world-wide.

E) Any other offensive requirement deemed advisable.

DEFENSIVE OPERATIONS

A) Select and supervise the private security force hired in connection with the Republican National Convention. Conduct all political security investigations [there].

B) Establish and supervise nation-wide electronic countermeasures capability in connection with all non-presidential security aspects of '72 campaign.

C) Supervise all security operations at . . . [the] Republican National Committee. Conduct all security investigations (leaks, personnel, etc.). . . .

OPERATING COVER

The consensus dictates that a privately created corporate business entity would be the most effective tool to implement [the] above. The corporation would posture itself as a newly formed security consulting organization ostensibly selling itself as a group of highly talented investigator-security experts with impeccable Republican credentials who actively seek only Republican Corporations and law firms as clients.

Since the key operating principals (3 or 4 persons) in the corporate entity would be well known Nixon loyalists in the law enforcement area, the defensive involvement . . . would be plausible. . . .

The offensive involvement . . . would be *supervised* and programmed by the principals, but completely disassociated (separate foolproof financing) from the corporate structure and located in New York City in extreme clandestine fashion. My source would be charged with setting up and supervising this operation. In other words, he would not surface. Rather . . . he would be charged with setting up the clandestine operation in exactly the same fashion as he did during his career. You are aware, of course, that his expertise in this area was considered the model for police departments throughout the nation and the results certainly proved it. [All emphases are Caulfield's.]

Caulfield then went on to recommend that the "Republican Intertel" should be headed by himself, Rose Mary Woods's brother Joseph, and Vernon Acree, deputy commissioner of the IRS. The organization would be highly compartmentalized, Caulfield said, and he suggested a probably criminal means for funding it. That is, "Republican corporate giants" would pay enormous fees for security services that would not, in fact, be performed—or which would, in any case, be worth much less than the sums paid. The surplus income, then, would be used to support the clandestine political operations of what Caulfield intended to call "Corporate Security Consultants International (COSECOIN)." In effect, the "corporate giants" would be making secret contributions to Republican campaigns, laundering the money through COSECOIN under the pretext of fulfilling their own security needs.

It was a corrupt proposal, and its implementation would probably have preserved Richard Nixon's place in the White House and prevented the Watergate scandal in its entirety. What put that scandal on the front pages of American newspapers was the fact that the burglary was so easily traceable (through McCord, Liddy, and Hunt) to the Republican National Committee and the White House. Had Caulfield been allowed to found COSECOIN, the firm could have carried out the same operations that ultimately sent the White House Plumbers to jail. Even if COSECOIN agents had been caught, just as the Plumbers were caught, White House "deniability" could have been easily preserved: there would have been nothing to link Caulfield's men to Nixon or the GOP.

As it happened, of course, Caulfield was turned down, perhaps because his analysis of Intertel had been simplistic.

He was right about some things, though, particularly Intertel's involvement in "mafia-ridden" New Jersey. For some time Resorts stock had been depressed. After trading in 1968 at more than forty dollars per share, the stock took a nose dive. Most damaging, perhaps, was Resorts' effort to acquire 10 percent of Pan American World Airways stock. The transportation giant fought what seemed to be a take-over, and in the end Resorts found itself with 3 percent of the airline's shares, having paid a mind-boggling $27,000,000 for them. Very quickly, those same shares were worth less than $4,000,-000 on the open market, and the effect on Resorts' balance sheet was nearly catastrophic. Compounding the firm's difficulties were a host of Bahamian uncertainties: the Paradise Island casino, for instance, operated under a license issued by the Pindling government. That license was due to expire in December, 1977—and while Pindling promised that a new license would be issued to Resorts, it was certain that the renegotiated conditions would not be as favorable as the old. Moreover, Pindling announced that his government intended to construct a new gambling resort in Nassau, one that would compete with Crosby's own. In addition, taxes on casino revenue were rising, and some of Resorts' subsidiaries (for example, Marine World/Africa U.S.A. and the real estate division on Grand Bahama Island) were losing money. By 1976 Resorts stock was selling at little more than a buck a share.

But you could have made a killing on it.

Within a year the stock geysered from $1.50 to more than $35 per share (at this writing), as New Jersey voters approved the legalization of privately operated casinos in Atlantic City. Resorts, of course, had not been taken by surprise. On the contrary, Crosby's firm was the architect of the politically slick, million-dollar campaign which led New Jersey voters to change their minds on the subject. In 1974 a referendum to legalize state-operated gambling casinos had been roundly rebuffed by the local citizenry. Two years later, however, a new referendum, providing for privately owned casinos "in Atlantic City only," was in the works. And the man who brought it to the attention of Resorts, strangely enough, was David Probinsky (formerly of the Bahamas and one of Pindling's disappointed supporters). Probinsky convinced Crosby that the new referendum would pass if Resorts got behind it. Which Resorts did, acquiring the huge (and moldering) Chalfonte-Haddon Hall Hotel on the Boardwalk, as well as a fifty-six-acre tract that had been cleared for "urban renewal." Resorts told its stockholders that "the tract would be developed under an urban renewal plan with hotel, housing and other facilities." It didn't say what those "other facilities" would be, but it wasn't hard to guess.

Managing the casino drive for Resorts were two lawyers, Marvin Perskie and Patrick McGahn. The former was Probinsky's attorney, and it was his idea to bring McGahn aboard, remarking that his colleague "ain't the greatest brain in the world, but he's a doer." That may have been true, but what Perskie neglected to volunteer was the fact that both he and McGahn were closely related to the same New Jersey legislators who'd sponsored the legislation to legalize casino gambling: one was Perskie's nephew and the other was McGahn's brother. Confronted with this later on, they dismissed the relationships as irrelevant, irrelevantly pointing out that they'd become Resorts' lobbyists only *after* the legislation had been introduced. As for the New Jersey legislature's Joint Committee on Ethics (which, after all, has a very tough job in the Garden State), it saw no conflict of interest so long as the legislators themselves received no personal benefit from the relationship.

In any case, those who opposed casino gambling were hard put to counter the economic arguments tendered by Resorts. Atlantic City was dilapidated and tacky, decrepit and short of cash. Legalizing casino gambling was tantamount to financial renewal: huge tax revenues would be generated, unemployment eased, real estate values multiplied, and the city reborn with a fresh face. Resorts' case was optimistically presented, but it made sense. The only argument that seemed to have a chance of defeating the referendum alluded to the depredations of organized crime. And that was an argument which the greed-struck Jerseyites seemed unable to comprehend, despite the efforts of local law-enforcement officers to make them understand. The citizenry saw no reason why Nevada should have a monopoly on casino gambling. As for the companies that would likely run the casinos—firms such as Resorts, Playboy, and Caesar's World, Inc.—they seemed reputable enough. Indeed, Resorts had its own subsidiary that was *packed* with former government crime experts; Hugh Hefner was a good liberal who'd published numerous exposés of organized crime; and as for Caesar's World, it was represented by no less distinguished a law firm than Rogers & Wells, in which former Secretary of State William Rogers was a partner. So the Mafia couldn't be a problem—and even if it was, who cared? So far as many New Jersey residents were concerned, the Mob *already* owned the state. Casino gambling wouldn't make much difference to that: all it would do would be to give the place some badly needed class, cash, and action.

The pro-casino people were remarkably glib, and with only a few exceptions,* the press tended to repeat whatever it was told. Even *The New York Times*, whose own reporters† had probed Resorts International with wrinkled noses, was reserved in its reportage. It made no comment, for instance, when Resorts executives bragged that "there is no way that control [of Resorts stock] can fall into the hands of the unscrupulous or organized crime." Nor did it comment when Bob Peloquin explained that "We have intense background checks, like the secret clearance tests you'd get in the Army. We watch our stock. If a large bloc is traded we want to know who bought it." Well, one chides the *Times* with trepidation, but it would not have been wildly irresponsible of it to have pointed out that Resorts—despite its "secret clearance tests" and hawklike regard of the marketplace—had only a few years before come within a hairsbreadth of selling nearly all its assets to Robert Vesco, perhaps the biggest swindler in history. And that the firm would undoubtedly have done so had not SEC attorneys sprinted through traffic to intervene in the juridical nick of time.

But no matter. The numbers mentioned by Resorts were too large. A rejuvenated Atlantic City, it said, would be within driving

---

* Two exceptions were Bruce Locklin and Vinnie Byrne of the Bergen County *Record*.

† Most notably, Denny Walsh.

distance of sixty million eager tourists, and Resorts was ready to accommodate them. The firm intended to spend upward of $100,-000,000 upon the city's development, and other firms could be counted upon to invest precisely $844,000,000 in new construction, *providing the referendum passed.* Thirty thousand jobs would be created. About $150,000,000 in annual retail and gasoline taxes would be added to the state's budget, and—why, the show-business budget alone would hit $75,000,000 a year! If you couldn't get rich in the new Atlantic City, you couldn't get rich anywhere.

There were some who questioned the optimism of Resorts and that of the referendum's other sponsors. They argued that casino gambling had always attracted people determined to "get away from it all," people who could afford to fly to isolated resorts such as Las Vegas and the Bahamas. Atlantic City was hardly an isolated resort: located in the Bos-Washi-Delphia corridor, it suffered all the urban ills of the big cities surrounding it. Casino gambling there was hardly likely to attract a class crowd once its novelty wore off. On the contrary, it would likely become "Grind City," a magnet drawing all those who could not afford the plane fare to more distant resorts—the very people, in other words, who could least afford to gamble.

But in the end it came down to the magical numbers uttered by the pro-casino forces: 844 . . . 30,000 . . . 75,000,000 in entertainment alone! So the referendum passed by a huge margin, putting Resorts stock into an orbital trajectory matched only by Monopoly City's hopes and real estate values. From 2 it went to 5, from 5 to 10, from 10 to 20—and so far no one had even put a spade in the ground. Jim Crosby's net worth inflated to the dimensions of a weather balloon, and so did that of a lot of others.

As it happened, the referendum's passage came just in time for Intertel. The new security assignments in New Jersey's casinos would take up some of the slack anticipated by the death of an important client.

4 / THE CON IS OVER

On April 5, 1976, a cadaver identified as "J. T. Conover" was removed from a jet ambulance that had just rushed from Acapulco, Mexico, to Houston, Texas. Taken to the city's Methodist Hospital, where a suite had been reserved in Conover's name, the body was newly identified as Howard R. Hughes. So that there would be no mistake, fingerprints were taken from the shriveled corpse and compared with others to which the IRS had access.

It was Hughes. Spokesmen for the Summa Corporation announced that the billionaire had perished of a stroke, but the autopsy contradicted that: he'd died, according to pathologists, of kidney failure. The physicians attending the cadaver were properly circumspect in their replies to reporters' questions; while they confirmed that Hughes weighed only ninety pounds, they preferred not to elaborate on the matter. He was dead, and the doctors were content to let him rest in peace. They would not "fuel speculations" about the billionaire's life-style, nor would they permit reporters to view the corpse. A few days later, Hughes's body was buried, and lawyers and relatives and cranks from every part of the country began the scramble for a piece of his estate.

Since leaving Las Vegas five years before, Hughes had led an existence that was at once hermetic and peripatetic. His wanderings had taken him to Paradise Island, Nicaragua, Canada, Nicaragua once again, and then to London, the Bahamas, and finally to Mexico. The transitions were all carried out in the secrecy of night, using fire escapes, decoys, speedboats, and private planes. Despite the efforts of the world's press, with all its informants and ingenuity, no reporter was on hand to record any of the moves. Of those who claimed to have seen Hughes during this period, their accounts differed. General Somoza and Ambassador Shelton described a lean, distinguished figure with a firm handshake and a trim Vandyke beard. Others echoed the description, ridiculing the bizarre account of Hughes's appearance provided earlier by a boat captain who'd transported the billionaire from the Bahamas.

After his death, however, the personal accounts of two Hughes aides clarified the discrepancy.* The billionaire had indeed been well groomed on those few occasions when audiences with outsiders were unavoidable. The rest of the time, though, Hughes was in every way the Abominable Billionaire. His hair grew to a shaggy mane that hung in strands down his back, just as his beard straggled to his navel. His fingernails and toenails went unclipped for years, evolving into grotesque yellow horns, organic corkscrews. During the last years of his life, after breaking his hip in a fall at London's

---

* James Phelan, Melvin Stewart, and George Margulis, *Howard Hughes: The Hidden Years* (New York: Random House, 1977).

Inn on the Park, he gave up virtually all activity. Evidently preferring nudity, he lay in bed unclothed, watching B movies and shooting drugs into his groin. Using Kleenex tissues to handle inanimate objects, he "insulated" himself from the touch of virtually any other thing, including the bed in which he lay and the Mason jars he used to capture urine. Dehydrated, malnourished, emaciated, and feral-looking, he suffered agonizing bedsores, the cravings of drug addiction, and a seeping wound on the side of his head that simply would not heal. It was said that his constipation was of marathon dimensions, but others who'd seen him insisted that "He had a colostomy bag hanging from his side." All agreed, however, that the Stockholder had been held in worse than penitential circumstances, without sunlight, recreation, or communication, conditions which led to an appearance that reminded people of children who'd been locked in dark attics for years.

Those responsible for Hughes's health were four doctors, who worked in rotation, an "inner circle" of six aides, including five Mormons, and a few attendants who were forbidden to speak with the billionaire. Of the inner circle, John Holmes and Levar Myler were regarded as the most important of the aides. Both men had joined the Hughes organization as chauffeurs, and such were their talents that at their boss's death each was a member of the Summa Corporation's five-man board of directors. Holmes, a former tobacco salesman, and Myler, an ex-mechanic, had come a long way.

It was inevitable that in the wake of Hughes's death, amid revelations of his miserable living conditions and bizarre behavior, questions would be raised concerning his competency—and, by extension, the good faith of his retainers. Was Hughes a prisoner of his staff, as Maheu believed? If so, had he in fact been kidnapped from Las Vegas, or had his circumstances merely deteriorated after he left "of his own free will"? If Hughes was incompetent, as it appears, why wasn't a guardian appointed to administer his affairs while he received proper attention in a hospital or institution? The questions were not merely academic. They impinged upon control of a multi-billion-dollar empire whose operations profoundly affect virtually every area of American life, from national security to diplomacy, communications, gambling, energy, recreation, transportation, philanthropy, politics, and real estate. If Hughes was a mad puppet, who was his master? It was not as if the billionaire during his post-Vegas decline had been inactive in a corporate sense. On the contrary. Not only had the *Glomar Explorer* project been undertaken for the intelligence community, placing in question the ownership of more than $300,000,000 in assets,* but the Summa Corporation had been formed in 1972, with the Hughes Tool Company having been sold to the pubic.† These were monumental undertakings in Hughes's name and, it was presumed, with his authority. If he wasn't responsible, who was?

The Houston autopsy failed to answer any of these questions, but there were hints in Acapulco that the circumstances surrounding Hughes's presence there, and his subsequent death, were even more unusual than anyone had imagined.

The morning before Hughes died, his attending American physicians took the precaution of having a Mexican doctor brought to the scene at the Acapulco Princess Hotel. That doctor, Lieutenant Colonel Victor Manuel Montemayor, said he was "aghast" at the billionaire's condition, his "undernourishment and dehydration." Moreover, he was shocked when told that Hughes had lain that way, unconscious, for three days. The patient, he said, "should have been hospitalized immediately when he entered the coma" days before. *What was on his doctors' minds?* The American physicians, Montemayor told police, explained to him that Hughes was "a difficult patient over whose medical treatment or eating habits they sometimes had little influence." Perhaps so, Montemayor countered, but Hughes could hardly have resisted going to a hospital when he was unconscious. Why hadn't they taken him? "The doctors were vague," he said, "and did not give any credible explanation. I had a sense that the doctors weren't really in command of the situation . . . I had the sense that I was not just dealing with individuals, but with a whole corporation." ‡

Mexican police characterized Hughes's circumstances in terms of "neglect" and made no secret of the fact that they suspected foul

---

* Ownership of the *Glomar Explorer* has been long disputed. While the ship was built with federal funds, its title is believed to have been passed to Summa Corporation, raising the specter of windfall profits. The CIA has declined public comment on the issue while at the same time hampering the SEC in its investigation of the matter. Last year, however, several Summa employees held a secret meeting with California tax authorities. Falsely identifying themselves as CIA officers, they asserted CIA ownership of the vessel, hoping to save Summa millions in taxes. The hoax, however, was later exposed.

† Merrill-Lynch handled the huge transaction in which the public bought the Hughes Tool Company name, its oil-tool division, and two foreign subsidiaries. Summa kept everything else. It was a great deal for Summa because Toolco's most important patents were about to expire.

‡ "Mexicans Rain Questions on Hughes' Death," by Marlise Simons, *The Washington Post,* April 15, 1976, p. 1.

play might have been involved. The billionaire had been "virtually smuggled into the country," they said, and it appeared to them that Dr. Montemayor had been "used."

"What did they need outside witnesses for?" a police official wondered. "What were they trying to prove? It seems that their . . . interest was to show that Hughes was still alive." *

And there were yet other oddities. For instance: a search of Hughes's quarters yielded not a single fingerprint belonging to the billionaire. Though he was said to have resided at the hotel for two months, none of his prints could be found in his room, upon his wheelchair, his bed, furniture, doors, or medical equipment. It was as if he'd been taken "out of storage," put in bed, and left to die, comatose and immobile, while a Mexican witness was called. The Mexican police were also disturbed by the vast quantities of paper that had been shredded by the billionaire's aides and by the fact that Hughes's windows had been fully boarded up. In addition, they could not understand why the jet ambulance had been left idling on the runway for hours on end before Señor Hughes was taken to it. Neither could they make much sense of what the aides had to say. One of them, Eric Bundy, was said to have been in overall charge of the billionaire's day-to-day operations, and yet he told police that he hadn't spoken to Hughes in eight years "because the other assistants," his subordinates, "prevented him from doing so." Similarly perplexing was the statement that Hughes was always in the company of two aides; what made this perplexing was that it contradicted another aide's statement explaining a gash in Hughes's head. According to Clarence Waldron, Hughes "had fallen from his chair a few weeks earlier, causing the tumor on his head to open with a great loss of blood. No one saw what happened, for no one was with him at the time." Finally, the Mexican police said, it appeared that Hughes had been "kept incommunicado" and that, judging by his physical condition, it seemed unlikely that he'd been able to exercise any volition. "There is no evidence from the few people who say they saw him," concluded a lengthy report on the subject, "that Hughes made any requests or decisions or even dealt with the smallest matter." †

Except for the lawyers, the relatives, the cranks and the intelligence agencies, the con was truly and finally over.

---

* Ibid.
† Ibid.

IT STARTED WITH THE PRINCE OF PHONES, PERHAPS

CONSERVATIVE WRITER VICTOR LASKY HAS REMARKED (AND REMARKED), "It didn't start with Watergate." He's right, of course. It didn't even start with the CIA, which, as we've seen, was still in its infancy·when Nixon went for Ari's jugular. Just when it started—the pronoun may easily stand for what I've called "the haunting of America"—is hard to say. Perhaps in Paradise, with the snake's arrival on the scene—a "penetration" of cosmic significance—and with the reptile's "doubling" of the planet's first lady. Certainly it was well under way in the Age of Elizabeth, during which the dashing poet-spy Kit Marlowe was murdered in a pub, apparently for playing three royal ends against his private middle. But insofar as Americans are concerned, it may be said to have started in the twentieth century, with the emergence of multinational corporations. Which is to say, with a man named Sosthenes Behn.

The prototypical "Milo Minderbinder," Behn was a flamboyant wheeler-dealer, expert at playing every side against each other, canceling all advantages except those that accrued to himself. Founder and chairman of the International Telephone & Telegraph Corporation (ITT), Behn had global business interests. He was "the Prince of Telephones," a title neatly summing up both his power over world communications and the aristocratic éclat with which he wielded it.

He was the master of the golden mien, rolling through Europe in the back seat of a chauffeured Rolls. In his lap would be the day's stack of telegrams and memoranda from ITT offices on three continents. At his side a copy of the *Financial Times*, perhaps opened to its list of comprehensive shares. In front of him, beneath the gray smoked glass that separated the boss from his chauffeur, there might well be a magnum of fine champagne wedged in a silver bucket of shaved ice. His (French) chef would have preceded him by a day to whatever world capital Behn would be visiting. And wherever it was, it was certain that Behn would be housed in the most resplendent hospices. If not the embassy, then some private mansion—the ancestral home, perhaps, of the Duke of Alba (that was, after all, what local front men were for: to be seen with). And if not there, then the Plaza, the Ritz, the Metropole, the Grande . . .

Behn was by all accounts a brilliant man—and by some accounts an unscrupulous one as well. The empire he founded established the die from which subsequent multinationals would be struck. From the beginning he recognized that all nations demand control of their own telecommunications systems. To accommodate that demand, while yet obtaining a monopoly over those systems, Behn established a series of quasi-national phone companies, each staffed and managed by natives of the countries in which they operated, each tied through its board of directors to the country's political power center—and each owned by ITT.

Because each monopoly was responsible to the government of the country in which it operated, and because all were threatened by the possibility of expropriation, Behn's politics were those of conservative boosterism. He supported any non-Communist regime in any country in which ITT operated, and pretended to support the Communist regimes as well (while in fact sabotaging them). Thus there was no real contradiction in his enthusiasms for Franco, Peron, Roosevelt, Hitler, and the Queen of England. They all had two things in common: power and ITT.

As to where Behn's own loyalties lay—he became an American by default when the United States purchased Behn's natal home, the Virgin Islands, from Denmark—he was simply a citizen of the firm he founded. Everything else about him, and particularly his role behind the scenes during World War II, is ambiguous. What is known, however, is that Behn anticipated the war and, as early as 1933, began filing secret reports on a variety of matters to highly placed American officials, reports that remain classified to this day.

In those reports, and in long, analytical letters to cabinet officers in the Roosevelt Administration, Behn detailed his meetings with businessmen and politicians in every country serviced by ITT. He is also thought to have provided copies of supposedly private telegrams and telexes sent by governments and individuals through ITT channels. By virtue of his monopolies over the world's communications systems, the Prince of Telephones was also an aristocrat of intelligence.

All of which would seem to make Behn a secret hero of the war (he was, in fact, awarded America's highest civilian honor, the Medal of Merit). And yet there is considerable evidence * suggesting that ITT and some of its subsidiaries performed similar services for *both* sides. In South America, ITT facilities served as covers for FBI and Nazi intelligence agents alike, the latter of whom were in constant contact with Berlin, forwarding valuable economic data about the shipment of raw materials and the movement of Allied vessels. Moreover, as early as 1933 Behn met with Hitler in Berlin, seeking the Führer's advice on personnel matters. In deference to that advice, at least two top Nazi officials were placed on the directorates of ITT's European companies: Dr. Gerhardt Westrick, the envoy of General von Ribbentrop; and Kurt von Schroeder, a plutocrat who subsequently became an SS general and an important financial conduit to the Gestapo. By the time hostilities actually broke out between the United States and Germany, Behn was well regarded in the councils of both nations. Clearly vital to U. S. military and economic interests, ITT facilities had also been carefully and deliberately integrated with the Nazi war machine as well: following a series of meetings with Luftwaffe chief Hermann Göring, Behn encouraged ITT's Lorenz subsidiary to purchase 28 percent of the Focke-Wulf firm, manufacturer of the bombers that were to sink so many Allied ships during the war. ITT, in other words, by expanding into the area of armaments and ingratiating itself with belligerents on every side, became virtually immune to expropriation by anyone. From this vantage ITT subsidiaries were able to function without threat of political intervention, reaping fabulous profits throughout the war. In Germany, for instance, Focke-Wulf manufactured bombers

---

* Especially useful is the material contained in Record Group 259 at the National Archives and, strangely enough, a series of articles published in *Sigma*, an ITT journal, entitled "An ITT Memoir" by Maurice Deloraine (1970). I'm indebted to Anthony Sampson's excellent book *The Sovereign State of ITT* (New York: Stein & Day, 1973), for both references.

to sink American destroyers, while in the United States another ITT subsidiary produced high-frequency detection-finders designed to help those same ships to sink or evade Nazi submarines. Meanwhile, in the neutral, if elegant, ambiance of Phalangist Madrid, ITT executives from the United States, Germany, Latin America, and England were able to meet *sub rosa* on the baronial estates of Spanish aristocrats, there to discuss the fortunes of war over glasses of Jerez sherry and plates of *pâté de foie gras*. And throughout this period, ITT facilities were used to communicate intelligence to the Allies and the Axis, while Behn himself reported directly to the U. S. Secretary of War (and indirectly, it's suspected, to Göring *). Finally, while Secretary of War Henry Stimson relied upon Behn's secret communiqués for the information they contained, Behn was nevertheless placed under surveillance and mail cover by the FBI while also having a wartime tap placed on all his telephone conversations. Strategic to every side, he was trusted by no one—except, perhaps, by the stockholders.

Behn's story is extraordinary for many reasons, but mostly for the brilliant way in which he maneuvered himself and his empire to become *de facto instruments of foreign policy* for countries whose interests were diametrically opposed. Functioning as a Third Force throughout the Second World War, Behn established the prototype that would later become Milo Minderbinder in *Catch-22*. In fact, even the most straightforward newspaper accounts, detailing Behn's triumphant "repossession" of ITT facilities in France, Belgium, and Holland, have a surrealistically comic tone to them, exactly as Heller's novel does. While the German line was being rolled back, Behn and his envoys were seen to be close behind. Supposedly a communications "advisor" to the American Army, Behn arrived in Paris on the very day of its liberation, costumed in a war-torn battle jacket, riding in a battered Jeep. While the French threw flowers from their balconies, Behn toured ITT factories and labs, massaging workers' morale and reestablishing his direct authority. Elsewhere in Europe, never far behind the advancing Allied lines, other ITT executives were provided with the uniforms of American Army generals and, so garbed, went about the reamalgamation of the ITT empire under the protection of U. S. GI's. At the side of the curious "generals,"

---

* Behn's frequent meetings with Göring before the war were particularly suspicious, since at that time Göring was plotting with several European industrialists to take control of the Nazi party from Hitler.

and under their protection, were their German counterparts—ITT execs, some of whom had until recently been functionaries in the Nazi regime. And they moved quickly: in one case, two Focke-Wulf aircraft plants disappeared virtually overnight from the environs of Mühlhausen, located in the Russian sector of the newly partitioned Germany. Shortly thereafter, the plants somehow found their way to Nuremberg, and were promptly reassembled there under ITT auspices. How were such things accomplished? According to an employee of the National Archives, who's spent most of his middle age studying ITT and OSS materials, the multinational's postwar activities were enabled by Allen Dulles (OSS chief in Geneva and later head of the CIA). Besides his gratitude for the intelligence provided by Behn during the war, Dulles is said to have recognized the strategic postwar value of the multinational. Nor was Dulles alone in his estimation of the firm's importance. A year after the war, former Cabinet official James Forrestal articulated the theory that ITT represented an instrument of U. S. foreign policy. In a message to Secretary of State George Marshall, himself in charge of U. S. reconstruction efforts in Europe, Forrestal declared that it was of "the utmost importance to the national interest and security that all communications facilities in the western hemisphere be owned by hemispheric interests and, if possible, by citizens of the United States." * Forrestal had wanted the U. S. government to provide ITT with loans to buy out its competitors in Latin America. While his request was turned down, his theory seems to have been accepted: in Europe, at least, ITT was given every advantage. Indeed, more than twenty years later (in 1967), the firm was even awarded $27,000,000 in "compensation" for damages sustained by its German subsidiaries during the war; of that amount, $5,000,000 was in compensation for Allied bombings of the Focke-Wulf plants—the same factories that were manufacturing bombers for the Luftwaffe!

ITT, of course, was not unique in its corporate role as "an instrument of American foreign policy." The banks and oil companies, internationally committed for decades prior to the CIA's founding, were similarly blessed by the appellation, and it seems fair to say that every multinational of consequence has since come under the label's protection. (Just what the phrase "of consequence" means is open to debate. But certainly it includes most sizable firms engaged in finance, energy, mining, communications, transportation, data

---

* *The Guardian,* July 19, 1972.

processing, and the manufacture of arms—all strategic industries in one way and another.)

Nevertheless, the International Petroleum Cartel (IPC) was probably the first group of American corporations that had reason to call upon the protection of that label. In 1952 the IPC was faced with a massive antitrust suit brought against it by the Justice Department at the urging of outgoing President Truman. The suit charged that the world's largest oil companies were engaged in a global conspiracy to divide world markets among themselves, garrot all competition, and monopolize the production and distribution of the world's primary energy source. As soon as the suit commenced, however, the trustbusters found that opposition to their efforts was by no means confined to oil companies themselves. Besides political pressures brought to bear by foreign governments (notably Saudi Arabia, England, France, and Holland), Justice Department attorneys found themselves blocked by opposition concentrated at the highest levels of the State Department, the Defense Department, the Joint Chiefs of Staff, and the CIA. Repeatedly, oil company documents originating with subsidiaries abroad were subpoenaed only to be blocked for reasons of "national security." What made these documents particularly useful to the trustbusters was the candor found in them, a candor based on the subsidiaries' belief that they were not subject to antitrust law and could therefore speak openly about their conspiracies to demolish competition and unfriendly governments (such as the conspiracy in Iran prior to the CIA coup which brought the Shah to power).

Time and again, IPC documents were stamped "Secret" and "Top Secret" after they'd been subpoenaed; at one point, a blanket refusal to allow Leonard J. Emmerglick, responsible for the Justice Department's case, to examine the documents was defended on the basis that Emmerglick had flunked his security clearance—not the clearance provided by the FBI, but rather that of King Ibn Saud. Without access to the evidence available in the subsidiaries' documents, the case was virtually eviscerated from its inception. Nevertheless, Emmerglick continued the fight.

"The assumption always present in the national security arguments [against the antitrust case]," Emmerglick later testified, "was that the five major American oil companies * *were the instruments*

---

* Standard Oil of New Jersey, Socony-Vacuum Oil Company, Inc., Standard Oil Company of California, the Texas Company, and Gulf Oil Corporation. Referred to as Exxon, Mobil, Socal, Texaco, and Gulf in subsequent pages.

of U. S. foreign policy." * (Emphasis mine.) The Justice Department did not, however, agree. In a message to the National Security Council written by Attorney General James McGranery in 1954, the A.G. wrote, "No hazard to national or company interests will result from disclosure of the facts to the primary guardian of the national security, the government itself. . . . For a year and a half the defendant companies have obstructed the production of documentary information, such production being a commonplace of antitrust law enforcement, and further obstruction will do a disservice to the manifold national security interests which dictate that this government be fully informed on any matter so vital to national defense [as petroleum is]." †

Later, Emmerglick (today a professor of law at the University of Miami) told the Senate Foreign Relations Committee:

We argued that our country's national security lay in the early dissolution of the existing international petroleum cartel. Attorney General James P. McGranery submitted a major policy statement to the National Security Council at the time, in which he stated, "The Sherman Act was described by Chief Justice Hughes as our charter of economic freedom. The Supreme Court has repeatedly rejected proof of public benefit and business necessity as justification for cartel operations and has emphasized the primacy of economic freedom as the highest value for our economy. Our concern for an adequate future supply of petroleum is a concern ultimately for the preservation of freedom for ourselves and the free world. Free private enterprise can be preserved only by safeguarding it from excess of 'power,' governmental and private. The selective socialization of business in the ancestral home of our free institutions points to the end result of the cartels which flourished and became the outstanding characteristic of the British economy after Great Britain adopted the Import Duties Act of 1932. The world petroleum cartel is an authoritarian, dominating power over a great and vital world industry, in private hands. National security considerations dictate that the most expeditious method be employed to uncover the cartel's acts and effects and put an end to them." ‡

McGranery and the rest of the Justice Department didn't have a chance. Not because the other governmental departments were

---

* *Hearings Before the Subcommittee on Multinational Corporations* of the Committee on Foreign Relations, United States Senate, 93rd Congress, Second Session on Multinational Petroleum Companies and Foreign Policy, Part 7 (G.P.O., 1974), p. 109.
† *Ibid.*
‡ *Ibid.*, p. 106.

united in their opposition to Justice's efforts. They weren't. In the State Department, for instance, a background paper * prepared by Richard Funkhouser (later U. S. Ambassador to Gabon) noted that "State has not been able to agree on oil policy within its own walls, let alone develop substantive agreement between other agencies. Probably the major impasse comes down to whether the principles of the Sherman Anti-Trust Act are good or not good for the world and oil."

Funkhouser's paper, which predicted with extraordinary accuracy the Middle East oil embargo and inflationary price hikes twenty-four years in advance of their occurrence, called for State to consider proposals for what would amount to the dismantling of the IPC. Jack Blum, of the Multinationals Subcommittee staff, questioned Funkhouser about the policy paper he'd prepared.

"What I am especially struck by," Blum said, "is the date [September 10, 1950] because, at the same time you in the State Department, for national security reasons, are proposing these remedies, the people in the Justice Department are proposing the same remedies and in fact bringing a legal action and they are being sandbagged for national security reasons. I wonder what the explanation is."

"It was easier for me to write this," Funkhouser said, "than it was for the man who was responsible to do it. . . . It takes a command decision on high to say whether going ahead with tearing oil companies apart is really in the U. S. national interest." †

Besides the pro-IPC solidarity at the top of government, hinted at in Funkhouser's testimony, the oil companies themselves had virtually infiltrated the U. S. bureaucracy, controlling informational inputs and profoundly influencing policy. Funkhouser's own job came about through his contacts with Standard Oil's Nelson Rockefeller. After working for Rockefeller in Venezuela, Funkhouser applied for work at the State Department.

". . . After the war I went into the State Department and they said, 'What have you been doing? You are an oil specialist, aren't you?' I said, 'No, I am not an oil specialist, I—'

" 'You worked for an oil company?' and I said 'Yes.'

" 'Well, that makes you an oil specialist in the State Department.'

* *Middle East Oil* (1950), pp. 122–139. ("Middle East Oil," quoted in Part 7 of the Senate *Hearings* on multinational corporations, was a State Department Policy Paper used as a background paper for a September 11, 1950, meeting with oil executives.)
† *Ibid.,* pp. 151–152.

"So this," Funkhouser went on, "was my introduction to my Foreign Service career, why I became petroleum attaché for Western Europe, why I ended up in the Middle East, and why I became petroleum advisor to George McGhee. . . . That is like saying you are advising the Encyclopaedia Britannica about facts. George McGhee is an oil man, a brilliant man, a Rhodes Scholar, and, incidentally, made many millions of dollars after finding his own gas fields in Louisiana." *

"At that time," Funkhouser told the Senate, "we found that the problems that existed in the Middle East were so complicated that we wanted the best brains available to work on them, and a lot of those brains happened to be with oil companies. So under George McGhee's leadership, we had regular meetings with the oil companies. The oil companies, after all, command a great deal of intelligence of every sort on Middle East oil problems and we in Government, certainly, starting with myself, have a certain modesty about knowledge of the industry." †

The subservience of middle-level bureaucrats to the oil millionaires who were their superiors, and to their counterparts in private industry, was not confined to the State Department. The same pattern existed at the CIA. Established almost twenty years after the infamous Achnacarry Agreement,‡ the CIA had to develop its oil expertise virtually from scratch. And this entailed listening very closely to what the oil companies had to say on any policy matter. In addition, Agency personnel were routinely detailed to oil company "schools" where, under the Mobil and Socal banners, field officers were trained for their assignments in the oil-producing countries. Besides sharing "intelligence" with the oil companies— a part of the Agency's "mission"—the CIA also found itself having to prevail upon the larger companies both for the creation of "cover" slots and for the loan of oil company executives who could

---

* *Ibid.*, p. 140.
† *Ibid.*, p. 141.
‡ So named for its having been signed at a gathering of oil company moguls following a grouse hunt in the environs of Achnacarry Castle, England. Former antitrust lawyer David I. Haberman aptly described the agreement and its supplements when he told the Senate that "the major international oil companies in 1928 fashioned a complex of what may best be characterized as private nonaggression treaties, complete with 'spheres of influence' and 'peacekeeping machinery' for their mutual protection and defense. These 1928 arrangements became the cornerstones of a vast new supranational system whose quasi-sovereign powers, policies, and programs were for almost half a century to transcend national boundaries, and political and legal barriers." (See *ibid.*, p. 19.)

428 /   SPOOKS

assist the Agency in oil-related matters on a day-to-day basis. In
short, the State Department and the CIA were, at least from the
inception of the latter, virtually captives of the oil industry. Executives who left the major oil companies for service in government
did so, in many cases, upon the understanding that when their
low-paid stint with government ended, they would return at com-
pensatorily higher salaries with their original firms. They had, in
a sense, "penetrated" the CIA and State Department as effectively
as any KGB agent might, ostensibly serving government interests,
while in fact reserving their true allegiance for the vast supranational powers that were the oil companies.

In the end, the criminal conspiracy suit contemplated by the
Justice Department was downgraded to a mere civil suit.* "Then,"
Emmerglick remarked, "the blood was sucked out of the civil suit
by a series of decisions which could only have been brought about
by continuing presentations in Government circles by the oil companies." † Or, as antitrust lawyer David I. Haberman said, "the National Security Council ultimately came to issue policy directives
which, for all practical purposes, gutted the oil cartel case. In effect
. . . the Security Council . . . cut the very heart out of the cartel
case." ‡ As a result, the case dwindled down to a single attorney (Haberman), handling the tattered remains of a lawsuit initially designed
to break up the world petroleum cartel—*but which, in the end, served
only to institutionalize it.* "I ended up the final legatee of the case,"
Haberman said, "and signed a . . . consent decree, substantially
along the lines of the decrees entered [earlier]. . . . [Those] decrees,"
he added, "reflected all the handicaps and deficiencies of the imposed
national security constraints, and consequently *those decrees, in effect, gave carte blanche to the companies to continue salient features
of their joint venture cartel system for a period of 25 years. . . .*" §
(Emphasis mine.)

It may be thought by some that the suit was ill conceived in the
first place. After all, why demolish a meld of "great American companies"? Wasn't the Justice Department's argument that the cartel

---

* *Ibid.,* p. 103. Interestingly, Emmerglick testified that President Truman told him
during a White House meeting that he reached that decision "not on the advice of the
Cabinet officers who attended the Security Council meeting, but solely on the assurance
of Gen. Omar Bradley that the national security called for [the suit to be demoted
from a criminal to civil case] . . ."

† *Ibid.,* p. 120.

‡ *Ibid.,* p. 33.

§ *Ibid.,* p. 35.

threatened national security merely a self-serving counterfoil to the national-security arguments advanced in favor of the oil companies by State, the CIA, and (not least) the oil companies themselves? Apparently not. According to Emmerglick, "In 1952 the Secretary of the Interior commented that we did not have reserves to give us maneuverability in the opening months of a war. The Petroleum Administrator for Defense said that our reserves were about 15 percent of our actual consumption at that time, and he commented that this is too narrow a margin for safety, and, therefore, we were intent upon correcting the situation as expeditiously as possible." *
In other words, the cartel's absolute control over the production, refinement, and distribution of petroleum products presented a direct threat to the security of the United States at a time when the Cold War was hottest and the Korean conflict boiling over. (The threat was made especially direct by the fact that the oil companies connived to limit oil production in the most drastic way, thereby constraining competition and keeping prices high. In Syria, for instance, one general manager bragged to his home office by saying that he was complying with Syrian regulations by drilling exactly the number of wells they demanded—but was making sure the locations would be where no oil could be found! † Syria, as other oil-producing countries did at the time, wanted to maximize the production of oil but was thwarted in that effort by the companies to whom it had given concessions.)

There was a second bottom line to the unraveling of the Justice Department suit, besides the institutionalization of the cartel. While Justice was never formally advised of the reasons that led the National Security Council to defend the oil companies, the Department's suit indirectly led to the Council's placing the oil companies beyond the law—literally. In a letter from the National Security Council to John Foster Dulles, then Secretary of State, the Council instructs:

"It will be assumed that *the enforcement of the antitrust laws of the United States against the Western oil companies operating in the Near East may be deemed secondary* to the national security interest. . . . In the event of a conflict between any proposed relationships and the enforcement of the federal antitrust laws, the proposed solution will include, without recommendation, appropri-

---

* *Ibid.,* p. 108.
† "Remarks by Ambassador Richard Funkhouser Before the National War College, December 4, 1951—The Problem of Near Eastern Oil," pp. 160–171.

ate legislative, executive or administrative action required to remove such conflict." * (Emphasis mine.) Shortly thereafter, all matters pertaining to the oil companies and the antitrust laws were transferred by the National Security Council to the portfolio of the Secretary of State—although the authority for doing so was, at best, obscure, if it existed at all.†

What an extraordinary situation! Not only had the oil companies been placed *above* the law, the Congress, and the public, but—almost as an afterthought—the firms were placed beyond even the *scrutiny* of the law, having been delegated into the purview of the (politically appointed) Secretary of State. It must have caused the oil kings to exert themselves in high, pealing giggles over their *homus* and champagne, because what the NSC letters amounted to was a license to steal.

The failure of the antitrust case, then, demonstrated that America's foreign policy "instruments," designated by the CIA and State Department to include *at least* Exxon, Mobil, Texaco, Socal, and Gulf, take precedence over the public's will (manifested by the laws of Congress) because these so-called instruments are thought to work for a more general good (than, presumably, the law itself).‡ What we have, in effect, is a series of decisions by a handful of NSC, State Department, and CIA bureaucrats and spooks, themselves indoctrinated by Exxon seminars, to overrule the public's congressional representatives, manipulate the courts for the direct advantage of a few (in the name of the many), and generally render the practice of "free enterprise" impossible. All this, supposedly in the best interests of the public, "best interests" which (by their actions in the IPC case) the State Department and CIA pretend to know better than the public itself. It's this patriotic paternalism which gives dramatic meaning to the phrase "secret government," justifying the fears of liberals and conservatives alike, setting in motion a process of decay that can work only toward the destruction of democratic institutions. The irony, of course, is that the destruc-

* See Subcommittee on Multinational Corporations of the Senate Foreign Relations Committee, February 21, 1974, *The International Petroleum Cartel, the Iranian Consortium, and U. S. National Security*, p. 52.
† Ibid., p. 55.
‡ There would seem to be no way to know how many other firms, in what areas of international commerce, are similarly protected by NSC co-option and memoranda. The Freedom of Information (FOI) Act's first five exemptions would preclude the release of any other covenants similar to the one referred to here.

tion is justified as an effort to defend those very same institutions—an argument reminiscent of an American officer's explanation to a newsman that it was "necessary" to destroy a certain Vietnamese village "in order to save it [from communism]."

I don't want to belabor the importance of the ill-fated cartel case, but the issues and circumstances surrounding it were not unique. In many ways they spoke directly to that peculiar coincidence of circumstances that led to the emergence of the United States from its pre-war isolationism, the establishment of the CIA, and the proliferation of multinational corporations after World War II. Those events had a profound impact on the subject of this book. And, while I quote David Haberman speaking about the Big Five oil companies, his description of them may well remind the reader of other multinationals—of ITT, for instance, and Chase Manhattan, Reynolds Aluminum, Du Pont, Summa, Lockheed, IBM, Northrop, and other firms. As we'll see, there is no single "secret government" —there are dozens.

"This system," Haberman says,

[is] a kind of supranational government, a private United Nations, if you will, because its members severally and collectively possess massive wealth and resources, including an exchequer, shipping fleets, production facilities, pipelines, refineries, etc., which exceed by far the resources available to many nations of the world. Furthermore, these companies have shared for many years a broad community of interest and a functional unity of policies and actions in the disposition of such wealth and resources. This has been facilitated by the highly developed technical and diplomatic capabilities which these companies have frequently and effectively exercised *en bloc* in sophisticated high-level dealings with the governments of the world.

Like many other world government organizations, this private government emerged from a period of internecine economic warfare among these companies that was finally resolved by a series of "peace treaties." . . . In their exercise of virtually sovereign power, this bloc of companies has consistently promoted and exploited national economic needs and international differences, government ignorance, and the gaping lacunae in the fabric of international regulatory control mechanisms—in pursuit of their private commercial goals.

In some of this, of course, affected governments have not always been unwitting accomplices. Indeed, in many instances governmental policies have been lodged in the hands of officials who had themselves been involved either directly or indirectly with these same corporations. . . .

Why [Haberman asked] . . . did we, as a recognized bulwark of the post-World War II free world, virtually by executive fiat, delegate to this private corporate bloc the awesome responsibility for safeguarding U. S. and allied interests in a commodity so vital to social, economic, and military well-being of the free world? And why, also, were those private companies made our emissaries and assigned the delicate task of critical foreign negotiations?

Even assuming that some overriding national interest was to be served by having these companies act as surrogates of our foreign policy, why was this same international private cartel then given un-fettered power (unconstrained by effective countervailing supervision and control) and allowed to erect and operate a vast supernational structure . . . capable of acting against the economic interests of the several international communities, which those companies served? *

The questions are good, if unanswered. Clearly, the multi-nationals are not so much instruments of American foreign policy as American foreign policy is an instrument of the multinationals —an obvious case of the tail wagging the dog.

Haberman's language is far from recondite in his description of the oil companies' role. His remarks about "diplomatic capabilities" and the firms' manipulation of "international differences, govern-ment ignorance," and regulatory gaps in the pursuit of profit neatly define the arena of multinational spookery. And yet, the multi-nationals cannot be blamed for taking every advantage available to them. The metaphor of multinational sovereignty is quite accurate in the main, but sovereignty is not the equivalent of independence. Since the multinationals owe their primary allegiance to themselves while at the same time having to maintain complex relationships with a variety of regimes, they inevitably come to function as prin-cipalities. The intricacy of their relations with other firms and states, coupled with their need to preserve and expand their own influence, requires that they develop an intelligence capability of their own—one that can make alliances, shape *the corporation's* foreign policy, coordinate advertising/propaganda campaigns, and exploit secret information pertaining to the firms' competitors, critics, and host countries. The multinationals' intelligence needs, then, are not much different from those of the United States, France, or any other country. Nor are they any less vital; insofar as the

---

* *Op. cit., Hearings,* pp. 42–43.

corporation is concerned, competition, taxation, expropriation, and the denial of markets are threats to the very existence of the multinational "state," and must be countered . . . perhaps by any means necessary. And this entails, to a degree that depends upon the nature and operations of each firm, the use of spooks.

Of course, it would be misleading not to qualify assertions about the multinationals' self-interest. While it's true that firms such as IBM and Socal have an international character, and their own foreign policies as a result, it's undeniable that they're also peculiarly "American." We think of them as such because their success is intimately bound up with the health of the American economy, consumer expectations at home, and so forth. The same is true of other countries' multinationals: while each is, in a sense, its own sovereign state, each is also vital to the interests of its "parent" nation (for example, Mitsubishi/Japan, Shell/Holland).

It's only natural, therefore, that the multinationals should individually incline toward an alliance with their parent nations' State Departments and intelligence agencies, all of which devote a large part of their "assets" to the protection and extension of their countries' financial interests abroad. Because the multinationals share, and increasingly shape, their parent nation's foreign policy, it should come as no surprise that they also share the facilities, personnel, and other assets of the homelands' intelligence communities. Indeed, any discussion of the intelligence battles among the CIA, KGB, and their satellite agencies will be incomplete if it doesn't describe the increasingly important roles played by the apparats of Exxon, Chase Manhattan, Mitsubishi, Lockheed, Phillips, and others.

The dangers posed by these relationships, however "natural," are enormous.

There is, for instance, the danger that derives from the multinationals' perversion of U. S. foreign policy. In Venezuela, for example, Exxon's Creole subsidiary was found by the CIA to have a larger intelligence budget, and more secret assets and information, than the local CIA station (itself large). In recognition of these peculiar circumstances, but in complete disregard of the need for objective intelligence estimates, the CIA consolidated its files with those of Creole, moving them into Creole offices and, in effect, merging its assets and officers with Creole's own. American foreign policy vis-à-vis Venezuela could not, from that time on, be anything other than a reflection of the views prevailing in the boardrooms of Exxon. In Venezuela, Exxon *is* the CIA.* And vice versa.

The multinationals' distortion of American foreign policy is obvious in a number of other places, besides the Persian Gulf and Venezuela. ITT's perversion of this country's policy in Chile, by means of a covert action project supervised by former CIA director John McCone while he was employed as a director of ITT, is well-known. Offering a million-dollar campaign chest to his successor, CIA chief Richard Helms, McCone's efforts in behalf of ITT led the United States into a foreign policy disaster of such magnitude that only the catastrophes of Cuba and Vietnam seem larger. Indeed, the Chilean fiasco may represent an even greater disaster than Vietnam and the Bay of Pigs, because in these latter places misguided objectives were pursued to failure, whereas similarly wrongheaded objectives were pursued in Chile, and succeeded. Brutally. The result being that the Pinochet regime, with all its bloodlust and venality, endures for every Latin to see, a carcinoma ordained through the auspices of big business and the CIA.

Elsewhere, in Israeli Palestine, a potentially all-consuming scenario is building even now, with multinational "inputs" coming to dominate American objectives. On the one hand, the United States enjoys its access to, and diminishing control over, Arab oil. On the other hand, the U. S. national interest seems inextricably tied to that of Israel. The resulting dilemma, mediated by multinational spooks and pawns, seems certain to be resolved in the Arabs' favor. Consider: in the Middle East, both Arab and Israeli intelligence agencies owe their organization to the combined efforts of Britain's MI-5 and to the CIA. As indicated earlier, the CIA as well as the State Department, owes most of its expertise in Middle East affairs to the ministry of the multinational oil companies. In addition, Aramco has long served as a receptacle for retiring CIA and State Department officers, many of whom retain ties to their former agencies, and has also functioned as a cover for active CIA officers. Aramco's influence over the CIA has, as a result, been great. But, until recently, that influence was *not* brought to bear upon

---

* One of the largest individual stockholders in Exxon, and therefore a part owner of Creole, former Vice President Nelson Rockefeller was asked to confirm or deny the assertion that the CIA carried out investigations of all prospective employees of Creole and, moreover, that the CIA was given "veto-power" over Creole's hiring. He denied it. If the unpublished testimony of top Creole executives is true, however, Rocky lied. The testimony is part of the still-secret records of the Multinationals Subcommittee.

Israeli affairs. The mechanism for insulating Israel from multinational pressures within the CIA was the CIA's own compartmentalization. In Israel's case, that compartmentalization was most extraordinary. Virtually all CIA intelligence operations in connection with Israel were isolated from normal channels within the CIA and placed instead under the jurisdiction of superspy James Angleton, chief of the Agency's Counter-Intelligence/Counter-Espionage section (CICE, or "Sissy"). Angleton, whose task as head of CICE was to maintain the Agency's "integrity" and resist penetrations, was the logical choice for the assignment. Considered "the best friend Israel ever had," a career intelligence officer with no desire to join the directorates of any firms, Angleton was finally forced out of the Agency in 1975—leaving with a sense of great bitterness and a feeling that he'd been "double-crossed" by inquisitors attached to the President's Commission on CIA Activities in the United States. According to Angleton, that commission (headed by Exxon heir Nelson Rockefeller) turned the tables on CICE's chief when it reneged on promises it had made, delving into areas supposedly excluded from inquiry. In the end, Angleton served as "fall guy" for the domestic espionage activities carried out under Operation CHAOS, a minor and ineffective program that was both illegal and under his supervision. When Angleton left the Agency, reportedly feeling "betrayed," so did the entire second echelon of the Counter-Intelligence staff, which resigned *en masse* in support of their boss. The result was that Israeli intelligence matters were reorganized along more "conventional" lines within the Agency. That is, they devolved into the orbit of the Middle East specialists and thereby, for the first time, came under the domination of the multinationals and their pawns within the Agency. With the CIA and State Department virtual captives of the multinationals, the future of "the third temple" looks dim.

It may be argued, of course, that this is no more than pragmatism in an era of détente: after all, our allegiance to Israel is largely sentimental, whereas the importance of Arab oil is concrete. Yet the argument deserves resistance, if only because those shaping American foreign policy are so obviously in debt to, and the creatures of, private interests. Kissinger, married to a former Rockefeller aide, owner of a Georgetown mansion whose purchase was enabled only by Rockefeller gifts and loans, was always the protégé of his patron, Nelson R., even when he wasn't directly employed by him. Indeed, Rockefeller's palatial bomb shelter in Westchester County even served as a temporary repository for Kissinger's secret papers whenever the Secretary of State feared that things might be going down the tubes (a strange choice since alternative federal facilities were located closer to Washington). In view of this, it would be naïve to overlook the Rockefeller family's long-term stake in the expanding markets promised by Kissinger's détente; naïve, also, to disregard the more immediate family investments in the petroleum and banking industries—industries that will fuel and finance our *rapprochement* with old enemies.

It becomes important to ask, Can a Kissinger or Cyrus Vance distinguish between the private interest and the public interest when making foreign policy? Consider the record: besides the purge of Angleton and his Counter-Intelligence staff, the former Secretary of State appropriated to himself the names of all foreign politicians and businessmen who were the recipients of multinational bribes. Despite the fact that the continued secrecy of those names subjects the individuals to the threat of blackmail, jeopardizing the security of the NATO and SEATO alliances, the information remains buried.* In the Middle East, Kissinger did everything possible to bring the greatest pressure to bear upon Israel. Besides rearming Egypt and paving the way for its emergence as a nuclear power, Kissinger prevailed upon the Shah of Iran to sever all military supplies to the insurgent Kurdish minority in Iraq, having earlier forbidden the Kurds to engage in a timely skirmish with their enemy during the Arab-Israeli War. At one stroke, Kissinger thereby betrayed two American allies: abandoning the Kurds (after encouraging their rebellion for more than a decade) led directly to their near-annihilation as a people—while at the same time bringing increased military pressure upon Israel, permitting Iraq to ignore its ethnic problem in the north and train its tanks upon the Jews.

"We're not missionaries," Kissinger explained.

Apparently not. But what, then? If we ask who benefits from all these machinations, the only conclusion possible is that Kissinger served as neither more nor less than an agent of the multinationals.

Sosthenes Behn. Henry Kissinger. Nelson Rockefeller. They seem

---

* I'm indebted to former Lockheed agent Ernest Hauser for pointing out to me that "This works two ways. Of course the KGB might exploit the bribery information, if they knew it. But so can Kissinger. That's why he persists in covering up the names of those who were bribed. It gives him an unequaled personal advantage, a means of keeping foreign officials in line."

out of place in a book about the private use of secret agents. And yet, omitting the roles of men like Kissinger—and Kissinger is by no means unique, whatever his flacks may suggest: Cyrus Vance, John McCloy, Clark Clifford, Nicholas Katzenbach, Larry O'Brien, and some others fit the same mold—omitting mention of them would be to decapitate the study of spooks. While not spooks themselves, they preside over the milieu, and their decisions frequently have the force of fate. It would be absurd not to emphasize that the private use of secret agents is almost always at its most effective when the agent himself occupies a position of great importance in the *public* sphere; not only may his private undertakings be pursued as public policy, carried out in your name and mine, but the public itself can be made to underwrite the costs of the adventure—thus, quite often, enabling it in the first place, and, occasionally, affording it an unlimited scope.

CAVIAR'S LOCUSTS

WHEN DANIEL J. HAUGHTON FLEW INTO WASHINGTON IN THE SUMMER of 1975, arriving from the citric wastes of southern California, no one knew quite what to make of him. A paragraph in *Who's Who* described in breathless, telegraphic prose an executive of planetary stature: a director of some of the nation's largest banks, utilities, and manufacturing concerns, he'd been enshrined in the Aviation Hall of Fame, made a governor of the Red Cross, and named chairman of the National Multiple Sclerosis Society. He was, in short, a multimillionaire with Palm Leaf Clusters, a businessman whose wealth and honorary degrees gave him access to private planes, limousines, and a thousand letterheads.

It was as the Lockheed Corporation's chairman of the board, however, that Haughton came to Washington. Where, in the space of a single day, he came to be regarded by many as the "Shoeless Joe Jackson" of the aerospace industry. To most of the Senators and staff of the Subcommittee on Multinational Corporations, it was apparent that the organization Haughton masterminded had raped the treasuries of a dozen nations, corrupted the political processes of both hemispheres, jeopardized national security, screwed the taxpayer, destabilized the governments of three allies, undermined

NATO, subverted the marketplace, boosted inflation, and stimulated suicides as far apart as Tokyo and L.A.

In hearing rooms accustomed to recitations of the Fifth Amendment by witnesses with chilling monikers and paper bags over their heads, Haughton presented a strange demeanor. Because he and his organization had not, apparently, broken any American laws in the United States, Haughton and his attorneys insisted that he'd done nothing *wrong*. Senator Joseph Biden (among others) took issue with this, commenting that "Your concept of morality is very intriguing. . . . The chairman * has said [that] we have got to search for a way out of this. I am not sure I want to look with you for a way out, to be perfectly blunt about it. . . . In my mind, you may have corrupted the system completely. . . . I'm curious: I would like to hear what you didn't do. You told us what you did do. I would like to find out whether or not you in fact think there is any way—well, maybe I should drop this whole thing."

Senator Biden was not alone in his despair of arriving at a clear view or a way out. Just as he threw up his hands in frustration, so did the press. For more than a year, the subcommittee had been engaged in a series of investigations into the corrupt practices of American corporations operating abroad. With lunar regularity, silver-haired barons of commerce arrived in Washington under subpoena, shot their cuffs, swore to God, and reluctantly confirmed the pattern of bribery and intrigue revealed by the subcommittee's staff. Daylong affairs, the hearings were predictably sensational, starring a parade of Whos and an offstage cast of geographically immune characters that seemed to have slunk from the pages of pulp fiction. In the case of the Lockheed Corporation alone, the missing principals included a Dutch prince, a French socialite called "Paris Popette," a chorus of dead Luftwaffe pilots, a defrocked Spanish priest on the Hong Kong–Tokyo currency run, various heroes of the European resistance, the architect of Pearl Harbor, a survivor of Nazi medical experiments, former Manchurian spies, and a pro-fascist samurai with bags of industrial diamonds and ties to both the Ginza Mob and the Moonies—not to mention an assortment of Ivy League bagmen, Swiss gnomes, Arab sheiks, and Third World generals linked invisibly to one another by a sirocco of numbered accounts, conduits, and dummy corps.

It was too much to handle in a single day of hearings, and report

---

* Senator Frank Church.

ers' jobs were made harder, rather than easier, by the release, *en bloc*, of some few hundred pages of relevant documents. Included among them were checks, contracts, audit reports, memos, letters, telexes, receipts, and hand-scrawled notes—many of them censored and all of them couched in double-talk of one kind or another. The lawyer's recondite phrase. The spy's allusion. The bagman's euphemism. And just plain code.

The stories the documents told were of bribery and "black salesmanship." The tale was not so much a financial saga, however, as it was an epilogue to the Watergate crisis. Indeed, the hearings of which Lockheed became a target began with a suggestion from the Watergate special prosecutor's office: there seemed to be a lot of funny-money floating around in the Alps, Bahamas, and Macassar Strait—why didn't Church's subcommittee have a look at it? Complying, the subcommittee found that corporate slush funds, laundered abroad, had not only been used to fund Nixon's enormities, but that the relationship between the White House and the multinationals was central to the entire Watergate affair. The two existed in near-perfect symbiosis, forming an ecosystem of high-altitude corruption.

Once pieced together, the documentary evidence confirmed the beliefs of the most cynical among us: the corporate milieu, at its highest levels, was indeed a jungle. Some of America's most celebrated businessmen—pillars of the community—had not only paid bribes, but taken kickbacks. They'd not only stolen contracts from crooked foreign firms but from honest American ones as well. They'd cheated on taxes and, what's more, they'd made it absolutely clear that they'd stop at nothing to make a sale: even in the absence of competition, they'd paid bribes to ensure that Third World countries spent their treasuries on weapons rather than food or schools. Neither was "national security" their concern. Having need to pay off only the most respected and influential—NATO generals, defense ministers, and heads of state—the multinationals achieved with ease what hostile intelligence services had been endeavoring to accomplish for decades. Suborning and corrupting their counterparts, industry's captains rendered them susceptible to every kind of blackmail. In short, it appeared that some multinationals had evolved into genuinely criminal enterprises.

It was not a realization that many in the press were prepared to admit. With their cultural and career investments in upholding the stereotype of the Mafia as *the* vehicle of organized crime, the public and the press have generally failed to grasp the felonious nature of the outfit's WASP counterparts on the Big Board. Whereas some petty hoodlums put out contracts on individuals, the multinationals have begun to place contracts on entire *countries* (for example, ITT versus Chile). With that difference, their operational styles are similar: offshore laundries used to wash bribes paid in clandestine support of a sales effort designed to create and satisfy the potentially lethal addictions of their would-be customers. Whether the product is heroin or Starfighter jets, the result is often the same: profits that corrupt and impoverish.

Corruption, of course, is not a new phenomenon. It has always been a factor with which governments, businessmen, and the public have had to cope. What *is* new, however, is the sophistication with which the corruption is carried out and kept hidden. Members of the Church Subcommittee, contemplating that development, were at a loss to explain it except in hypothetical generalities that spoke of "moral decline" and "cynicism." Karen Lisakers, a subcommittee staffer, came closer, though, when she was asked if those involved in the scandals had anything in common. "Well, yes," she replied, "virtually every one of them—from Japan to France, Indonesia to Italy—had an intelligence background." That, of course, is the point. The chickens have come home to roost. The sophisticated corruption of the black-business sector is made possible by former government spooks whose intelligence skills have been leased to the multinationals.

Consider Lockheed. The largest defense contractor of the most heavily armed superpower in the history of the world, it has sixty thousand employees, an equal number of stockholders, and contracts in the billions. It is the Contac of the Cold War, producing passenger jets, cargo jets, fighter jets, patrol planes, helicopters, missiles, armored cars, subs, satellite systems, computer wares, and a lot more —most of it classified and all of it expensive.

The firm's sales to foreign countries are a relatively small, but not insignificant, part of the country's overall balance of trade—and a key to whatever financial success Lockheed can have. In the past, that success has been considerable. It was Lockheed, for instance, that put the Luftwaffe back in the air following World War II, flogging nine hundred Starfighter jets to the fledgling West German Air Force. That sale proved strategic to the company's subsequent growth because it led, rather directly, to the sale of still more Starfighters to the other NATO countries and Japan. Accomplishing this rearmament at a time when European industry was still rebuilding from the war meant that Lockheed's only competition came from other American companies. This, however, did not stop the firm from engaging in certain "business unorthodoxies." According to Ernest Hauser, the sometime spook and international arms merchant whose Lockheed journals have caused him to be dubbed "the Diary Man," the firm pumped $12,000,000 into West Germany's ultraconservative Christian Social Union. The money, Hauser claims, was paid to the party's right-wing leader, Franz-Josef Strauss, to influence the 1961 Starfighter transactions. Former West German Defense Minister Strauss denies the allegation, and there would seem to be no way of proving it: Defense Ministry files pertaining to the Starfighter deal have mysteriously "disappeared." Strauss, however, has an allegation of his own: according to him, West German Chancellor Helmut Schmidt offered Prince Bernhard of the Netherlands $40,000,000 in the early 1970s if the prince would urge the Dutch to purchase F-14 Cobras from the Northrop Corporation. (Schmidt denies the accusation.) A former Lockheed representative in Europe, Hauser also alleges princely greed, insisting that under-the-table Lockheed payments in excess of a million dollars were paid to Bernhard in the early Sixties.

The accusations against Bernhard are particularly scandalous and interesting, touching as they do upon family affairs that seem an aristocratic analogue to "Mary Hartman, Mary Hartman." Heir to the principality of Lippe-Biesterfeld, in Germany, Bernhard was an early member of the Hitler Youth Movement and an employee of the sinister I. G. Farben combine. The prince, however, became a hero of the Dutch resistance shortly after his wedding to Juliana (heiress to the House of Orange, future queen, and perhaps the world's richest woman). Taking an active role in Europe's reconstruction, Bernhard joined the boards of more than three hundred corporations and, by the by, founded the "Bilderburgers": regarded by both the far Right and Left as a dangerous transnational elite, the group is composed of financiers and industrialists from many nations. It meets annually, amid very tight security, to talk about money. In any case, it's widely believed that Bernhard accepted the million-dollar Lockheed bribe in order secretly to support his illegitimate daughter, and her mother, "Paris Popette," in France. Queen Juliana, patroness of a mystical right-wing disarmament cult with inclinations toward the extraterrestrial, is not thought to be tolerant of earthly wanderings.

Hauser's accusations, while convincing in many details, have yet to be proven, however. Lockheed officials admit that some of the money was paid, but their European capo, an American expatriate named Fred Meuser, claims to have pocketed the bribe himself (thereby echoing an alibi put forward by another agent in behalf of an *Arab* prince). An investigative council of "Three Wise Men," appointed by the Dutch, has issued an ambiguous report on the matter, simultaneously chastising and acquitting Bernhard in the name of reasonable doubt. For his part, Hauser insists that the prince bagged the boodle, and claims that the "Wise Men" uncovered receipts that would prove it. Alas, Hauser says, the receipts were signed by a man who is presently "locked up in a madhouse."

The Starfighter affair is an especially sensitive one. A financial bonanza, the plane was less successful in a military sense. An "unforgiving" bird at best, the jet became positively dangerous when its European purchasers converted it from a "single-mission" fighter to a "multiple-mission" aircraft. Loading it down with a vast array of special equipment, they brought the plane to the very edge of its capabilities. Getting it there was a notoriously profitable business for Lockheed and its agents, since commissions on the additional equipment and replacement parts were often two and three times as high as those on the original sale. It seemed to many, therefore, that the agents made a financial killing by rendering the plane into a kind of time bomb. Crashing with amazing frequency, it came to be called "the Widowmaker"—not because of its fighting prowess, but for its effect upon its own pilots' marriages. The outrage felt by the Dutch, the Germans, and the Japanese at learning of the bribes is consequently something of a family affair. Some of the widows and next of kin see a direct connection between their loved ones' deaths, the choice of an inferior plane,* and the licentiousness and greed of potentates.

And there are ironies, some absurd, and others terrible. The numbered Singapore accounts into which Lockheed paid its kickbacks and bribes to officers in the Indonesian Air Force (AURI) was nicknamed the "Widows and Orphans Fund." In Germany, General Gunther Rall, former commander of the Luftwaffe, has denied the Diary Man's allegation that he received, while in the hospital, a thirty-thousand-dollar bribe buried in a pot of gladiolus.

---

* In its Starfighter sales effort, Lockheed competed against the Grumman Corporation's F-11F fighter. Of 900 Starfighters sold to the Germans, 174 crashed (in peacetime), killing 96 pilots. In Japan, 60 of 230 crashed.

Another general, said to have taken a bribe in furtherance of the Starfighter's cause, lost his son in a Starfighter's crash.

Amid all the denials, one hardly knows whom to believe. Mechanisms for paying the bribes were deliberately established in such a way that the payments might never be uncovered or, if they should be, would allow the recipient room for "plausible denial." Moreover, many of the agents were themselves quite devious, in some cases peddling influence they didn't have, pocketing kickbacks intended for others, making pacts with competitors, and "discounting" their own contracts to third parties. "Double agents" were commonplace, especially at Lockheed.

Lockheed's financial success was, in any case, a temporary thing. While it organized a worldwide private intelligence network of considerable competence, the firm suffered ghastly setbacks on the domestic front. Among other things, the C-5A cargo jet, built for the Defense Department, incurred massive cost overruns. Worse, Uncle Sam insisted that the firm be held responsible for the money. To extricate Lockheed from what appeared to be financial doom in 1972, President Nixon and then-Secretary of the Treasury John Connally intervened personally and with great effectiveness in Congress. After considerable arm-twisting and cries of "corporate welfare," the Senate narrowly voted to guarantee a $250,000,000 loan to the aerospace giant. That wasn't all Nixon achieved for the firm, however. In meetings with Soviet leaders, he is reported by State Department sources to have urged the Russians to purchase an enormous number of Lockheed planes—a circumstance that would have permitted the corporation to merge with the giant Textron conglomerate. When that deal fell through, Nixon prevailed more successfully upon Japan's premier, paving the way in secret meetings for that country's major airline, All-Nippon, to purchase twenty-one Lockheed Tristars for more than $400,000,000 (less bribes).

Meanwhile, in Europe, the Orient, the Mideast, and Latin America, Lockheed's self-described "foreign intrigue channels" were ablaze. From Saudi Arabia, a coded telegram arrived with the message that the Saudis had broken the company's code. That was a serious matter. The Arabs were one of the firm's best customers, and there was considerable danger that Lockheed would lose the king's business if his intelligence service was to prove superior to the firm's own.

For years Lockheed's secret agent in the Mideast had been Adnan Khashoggi. A portly and balding Arab sophisticate whose time is divided among the royal palace in Jiddah, his own private Boeing 727, and the craps tables of Paradise Island, Khashoggi is a fabulously wealthy "consultant" who well understands the importance of "communications integrity." A sometime dinner companion of Richard Nixon's in Paris's plush Rasputin Restaurant, he has also served as the former President's personal envoy to King Faisal during the 1973 Arab oil embargo. Between 1970 and 1975, Khashoggi and his corporate fronts in Beirut, Liechtenstein, Riyadh, and Geneva were paid more than $100,000,000 by the Lockheed Corporation alone (he has other clients)—supposedly for "marketing services." With vast estates in the Sudan, banks in the United States, and boutiques in Paris, he is the consummate corporate spook whose subordinates include a clutch of former CIA officers. To keep track of it all, he has a computerized intelligence service run out of an unmarked London mansion, a service that is said to keep tabs on literally every private and governmental contract being let in the Mideast, along with their ramifications and opportunities for every Khashoggi customer.

Had the Saudis, in fact, broken the Lockheed code—in which the firm is referred to as "Caviar" and its agents as "Locusts"—they might have uncovered the secret bank accounts Khashoggi shared with Arab generals and princes in his pay. They would have unmasked Lockheed's so-called first- and second-tier subsidiaries which were used to launder the illicit millions tacked on to nearly every Lockheed sale to the Saudis. They would have learned that Khashoggi received upward of 16 percent on each of these sales—despite the fact that Saudi law forbids foreign corporations from having agents in the country. They would have learned a great deal, indeed.

But Khashoggi was far from Lockheed's only agent; Saudi Arabia was by no means its only customer; and fears of the Arabs making a cryptographic breakthrough were far from the firm's only worry. In Turkey, and later in England, Lockheed had hired veteran intelligence agents on a contract basis, paying them for industrial espionage. There were fears that the agents they'd employed might be doubles. In Italy, they'd employed Ovidio Lefebvre, a rich and well-connected Roman attorney, to serve as the aircraft firm's local cut-out in making "direct payments" to Italian ministers and politicians, using such fronts and conduits as the Ikaria Establishment (of Liechtenstein) and the Temperate Zone Research Foundation (Tezorefo, of Panama and Geneva). Lefebvre was doing a good job, but Lockheed was competing against a Franco-Germanic consortium known for its unholy pragmatism in matters economic. There were fears that the rival consortium might assassinate Lefebvre or, worse, the firm's American lawyer, Roger Smith. In a spooky letter to his superior, Smith wrote:

> Please accept my apologies for addressing you on scratch paper and in my execrable handwriting, but I am in no position to disclose to local Third Persons the contents hereof. . . .
>
> Please hold onto your seat, as what follows may be a shocker to you. . . . Lefebvre states that [we] . . . must be prepared to go as high as $120,000 *per airplane* for the cumshaw pot. He hopes it will be less . . . but says that such is a nasty part of life in the arena in which we are trying to off-set the same type tactics by a combination (this time) of both the French and the Germans. . . .
>
> Furthermore, he said that, unlike in the P-3 matter, there will not again be a face-to-face negotiation between a representative of the [Christian Democratic] "party" and Lockheed representatives, but that he will be told, probably, by the Antelope Cobbler (get out your little black book—mine is dated October 15, 1965)* just how much the "party" demands.
>
> Further, there will be the Cobbler himself, and Pun, and various others. . . .
>
> In this connection, he insists that he will only give names and figures to one person. . . . If I get the information I would propose to seal it up and deliver it, so sealed, to our Paris lawyer for safe-keeping, with instructions to deliver it to the President of Lockheed in the event of my death, disability, or disappearance. . . .

To the fears of compromised codes, double agents, and assassination was added the fear of blackmail by spies formerly in the company's pay. With the reputations—and even the lives—of NATO generals, princes, and premiers in their pockets, the company's spooks and its Ivy League bagmen could not be let go without the risk of dire consequences. Years later, they might go over to the other side if they were not well treated. Consider, for instance, the following letter written by former Lockheed agent Fred Meuser to Northrop president Tom Jones. Mailed from the elegant redoubt of Switzerland's St. Moritz, the missive reminds Jones of Meuser's past work and intimacy with the affairs of both Northrop and Lockheed.†

---

* Antelope Cobbler is a former Prime Minister of Italy. The "little black book" is a reference to the Lockheed code book, changed at regular intervals.

† The reader may find it strange that a former Lockheed agent should be on such intimate terms with the head of a rival firm. In fact, however, many agents work both

Is the letter as innocuous as its careful phrasing suggests, or does it contain the hint of something else? Whichever is the case, Tom Jones must have asked himself that same question:

> Dear Tom,
> The other day it occurred to me that it is just about 10 years ago that you and I first discussed your Company's need for a top European consultant to discreetly act as a "gray eminence."

Recalling the selection of Hubert Weisbrod for that task, the letter recapitulates Weisbrod's background.

> Hubert made a distinguished international legal career from his base in Zurich. He travelled extensively . . . and maintained the highest level contacts. . . . Both he and his wife, Mary, took out their private pilot's licenses, he was elected President of the Swiss Automobile Club, Mary became Swiss waterski champion and both are still dedicated downhill skiers, even though Hubert is 70 next year spring. Recently Mary set up a stud-farm in Gstaad to breed and train racing horses and Hubert goes as strong as ever after his legal work and associated interests. . . .
> Ever since 1954 when, as a naturalized American citizen, Lockheed transferred me to Switzerland as Director for Europe, Africa, and the Near East, Hubert was my close advisor . . . he indicated channels to follow, whom to contact, and how to go about it and how to spread the name of Lockheed. . . . Much of the success I could book for Lockheed . . . particularly the unique and highly profitable export program of the F-104 Starfighter, was in no small measure due to his expert counseling and behind the scenes pulling of strings. Hardly ever did Hubert appear in the open . . . practically all his constructive work was done discreetly, indirectly.
> Recommendations are accompanied by a certain responsibility and you know yourself . . . how unfortunate it is if [they] do not work out and so I believe you will agree that we should pause for a moment and realize that this particular one was and still is a success. Hoping to see you at Farnborough (I will arrive at Claridge's late Sunday . . .)
> *I am . . . sincerely, Fred C. Meuser.**

---

sides of the street, ensuring themselves a commission on every deal. "Defections" among corporate spooks are commonplace. Moreover, Lockheed and Northrop were not always as competitive with each other as they pretended: in Europe, for instance, they knowingly employed the same secret agents and conduits on a number of occasions.

* Letter from Meuser to Jones, August 10, 1974.

The task of choosing "agents of influence" fell to the top echelon of the corporation's international section, and knowledge of the agents' work was confined to a very few on a need-to-know basis. As often as not, the agent was courted and recruited after social encounters in the mansions of politicians, at bloodstock auctions, dog shows, wine-tastings, and confabs of the rich and powerful such as those held under the auspices of the so-called Bilderbergers. In almost every case, the agents were already wealthy at the time of their recruitment: indeed, their value was largely a function of their ability to entertain decision-makers in high style. The pay was enormous. In the case of West Germany's Christian Steinrucke, host to the military, political, and industrial elite of his country, it amounted to $100,000 per plane, plus expenses. Such agreements, however, were often illegal, and influential agents risked not only their freedom but their honor and social standing as well. In France, for instance, a French general learned that his clandestine work in behalf of Northrop was about to be exposed by the U. S. Senate. Crushed by the news, he went for a stroll with his wife through the streets of Paris: stopping at a street corner to let a racing bus pass by, he stooped over the curb, lowering his head into the path of the vehicle—and so was decapitated hours before his role was to be made known. Other agents, their roles revealed, died equally as violently in places as far apart as Tokyo and Brazil. Indeed, Lockheed's own treasurer, Robert N. Waters, was found shot to death, an apparent suicide, in Los Angeles only hours after the Church Subcommittee revealed it would subpoena him. Elsewhere, in Indonesia, Lockheed executives contacted the CIA to learn whether their local agent, "Ike" Dasaad, was scheduled to be "liquidated" by the Indonesian regime. The firm needed to know in advance so that if Dasaad was in fact about to be tweeped, the corporation might switch its custom to another agent of influence—one with a longer life expectancy.

Lockheed, of course, is only one among literally hundreds of American corporations found to have paid bribes and kickbacks amounting to billions of dollars. With so much money at stake, and most of it flowing underground, it's not surprising that the methods of international business rivals have come to resemble those employed by countries stalking one another in a cold war. Commercial agent networks traverse the planet, with the usual double-crosses abounding, their members communicating in code about greedy ministers and industrial spies; the prospective "liquidation" of an agent becomes an "economic indicator" of sorts, while top executives launder funds through medieval enclaves to bribe a general, a politician, or a prince. Meanwhile, at thoroughbred auctions in Ireland, art auctions at Christie's in London, and imperial celebrations in Teheran, corporate chieftains nod knowingly to one another across tables spread with Beluga caviar and brut champagne. The business is as polite on its surface as it is dirty and dangerous underneath.

Nowhere so much as in Japan is the criminality of those involved so clearly revealed. There Lockheed's agent of influence was a strange and dangerous man named Yoshio Kodama. A Japanese extremist with powerful links to the Park dictatorship in Korea—not to mention his own private army—Kodama has lived a life of intrigue and high melodrama that may be unmatched in the annals of nonfiction.

An orphan raised in terrible poverty by increasingly remote relatives, he was duped at eleven into the service of a Korean sweatshop. There, in an iron foundry manned by consumptive children, Kodama was held against his will, sleeping in the corporate barracks in virtually unpaid bondage to the firm for which he slaved.

Escaping this servitude, he made his way to Tokyo, having long before made the journey from childhood to adulthood without any intervening stage of adolescence. Hardened and filled with hate for those who'd exploited him, he descended into the Tokyo slums, determined to become a great man and restore Japan to its former grandeur. An ultranationalist and terrorist leader at fifteen, Kodama immersed himself in the political bedlam of Depression Japan joining an even score of conspiratorial societies with such names as the Blood Brotherhood, Holy War Execution League, Federation of Radical Patriotic Workers, and the Capital Rise Asia Academy. These societies, many of them murderous and fly-by-night affairs, provided him with a precarious living. Ostensibly political, they were often no more than street gangs manipulated for private ends by wealthy industrialists, the police, and the Army. They fought the Communists and one another with equal frequency, and underwent a continual factionalization. Often the societies consisted of no more than a dozen friends, a post office box, and stolen gelignite.

It was in this right-wing milieu, part underworld and part underground, that Kodama plotted to conduct a battue of the Emperor's entourage—a state massacre that would eliminate at one stroke all the most powerful men in the realm. A premature explosion led the plot awry, however, and Kodama found himself beginning the first in a series of prison terms meted out to him for his terrorist activities.

Molding himself into the image of a twentieth-century samurai, devoting himself to the martial arts and traditional Buddhist meditation practices, the young Kodama refined his political beliefs as well. By 1940 he'd forged a peculiar ideology, combining elements of fascism with those of Japanese feudalism. He'd also forged powerful links to Japan's military intelligence apparatus, carrying out numerous secret missions to Manchuria.

As a reward for his intelligence work, he was entrusted with the task of supplying the Japanese Navy in wartime. Establishing the Kodama Kikan, or Kodama Agency, he built a financial empire from a handful of rooms in Shanghai's Shin-Asia Hotel. According to formerly secret reports of the U. S. Army Counterintelligence Corps, Kodama accomplished the Navy's ends at gunpoint, taking hostages and forcing Chinese villagers to sell him the goods he demanded; paying a pittance to the Chinese, he then resold the goods at fabulous profit to the Imperial Navy. Systematically looting China of its raw materials, he amassed a personal fortune of colossal dimensions. To accomplish that, he acquired heroin on the black market in Tokyo, traded it for tungsten in Shanghai, sold the tungsten for yen, used the yen to buy guns, sold the guns in Borneo for gold, exchanged the gold for industrial diamonds, and in the meantime, cornered the Shanghai radium market by emptying the hospitals of their supplies. In addition, he operated salt mines, iron mines, farms, fisheries, an orphanage, a molybdenum mine, and secret munitions factories throughout central China. In his heroin deals he sometimes burned the consumer, and there were unproven allegations that the yen spent in China was counterfeit (not that it mattered, since it was useless to the Chinese in any case). He came to be regarded as "the man behind the Kempei Tai" (or "secret police"), financing its Shanghai office in return for its "physical support." Intelligence reports show that this was sometimes bloody work, revealing that Kodama was suspected of assassinating his partner and of taking part in a massacre of Chinese at the Shin-Asia Hotel.

At war's end, the thirty-four-year-old was a brigadier general, a Cabinet advisor, and the possessor of a financial horde that included half a roomful of platinum, sacks of industrial diamonds, an undetermined amount of foreign currency, and upward of 3.5 billion yen *—not including illiquid assets. Just how much Kodama was worth, however, could not be exactly ascertained. All documents of the Kodama Kikan were burned at the end of the war, and Kodama himself admits that he hid most of his wealth.

Imprisoned as a war-crimes suspect in 1946, he'd been attempting to organize a new political party for Japan, a party in naked emulation of those that governed the United States. This democratic pretense, however, failed to deceive American Occupation authorities. An intelligence assessment of Kodama concludes:

> In summary, KODAMA appears to be a man doubly dangerous. His long and fanatic involvement in ultra-nationalistic activities, violence included, and his skill in appealing to youth make him a man who, if released from internment, would surely be a grave security risk. In addition, there is the outstanding probability to be reckoned with that, as a result of his hearty cooperation with the war effort, he has a large fortune to back-up whatever activities he might see fit to undertake. His success in the difficulties of securing supplies in wartime for the Navy mark him as one who could very easily become a big-time operator in Japan's reconstruction period. Persistent rumors as to his black-market profits in his Shanghai period, plus his known opportunism, are forceful arguments that he would be as unscrupulous in trade as he was in ultra-nationalism. KODAMA's past performance indicates that he is the sort of man G-2 considers more dangerous than either the superannuated ideologists or the professional men who aided Japan's wartime effort for reasons of patriotism or survival of their professional interests. . . . Dangerous potentialities for the future. . . .†

Another report, prepared by Kodama's chief inquisitor, Lieutenant Frank O'Neill, concludes: "I am satisfied that KODAMA or his associates . . . for whom he is responsible committed numerous acts of violence in China in the acquisition by foul means or fair of commodities and goods [belonging to] the Chinese." ‡

Shortly after this assessment was made, and in spite of it, Kodama was released without trial. Walking out of prison with him was Nobusuke Kishi, a future Prime Minister, and seventeen other war-crimes suspects who would become the financial and political spine

---

* About $175,000,000 at the time.

† G-2 Report, 24 May 1947, Far East Command, marked to the attention of Colonel R. E. Rudisill. The report was quietly declassified of recent, and made a part of the records of the International Military Tribunal for the Far East, International Prosecution Section (IMTFE-IPS) at the National Archives.

‡ "Progress Report" in re Yoshio Kodama and Ryoichi Sasakawa, 7 July 1948, IMTFE-IPS.

of a new, democratic Japan. Why was Kodama released? The last pages of his diary give a clue: "Who, in this age of ideological confusion, is capable of bringing the laboring masses, influenced completely by Communist ideals, and rampaging like a wounded beast, under control? . . . The bestial roar of the Communist Party [reaches] into my cell through the barred windows of Sugamo Prison. . . . I can hear the dull thud of the marching feet of thousands of Communists advancing toward the bolshevization of Japan. . . . Who will fight the last fight with them? Behind the steel bars of Sugamo, this young life of mine, burning with the passionate ardor of a love of my country and of justice, strains against the bars that hold it in." * A few days after Kodama's release, Lieutenant Frank O'Neill was reported to have predicted: "Ten years from today this man Kodama is going to be a great leader of Japan." † He was right.

Working behind the scenes, Kodama established the Liberal Democratic Party (LDP), using funds hoarded from his Shanghai days; it soon became the most important political party in Asia, leading some to suspect that Kodama's release from Sugamo had been engineered by the fledgling CIA. Whether that is so or not, Kodama rapidly consolidated his hold over Japan's ultranationalists and reestablished contact with anti-Communist gangsters and street punks from the Tokyo Ginza. Before long, his flunkies would brag in print of his role behind the scenes, describing him as "the driving force" in Japanese politics.

Indeed, by 1958 Kodama was once again one of the most powerful men in the Orient, almost as influential in Korea as he was in Japan. In that year he signed the first of many contracts with the Lockheed Corporation, promising to reverse Japan's decision to outfit its born-again Air Force with Grumman F-11F's. To accomplish that reversal, he relied upon a bizarre cast that included an American-born espionage agent who'd lost his citizenship by working for the Japanese in occupied Manchuria; another spook who'd plied his trade in southern China; a politician who was later jailed for embezzlement; an extreme right-wing publisher; various war-crimes suspects who'd shared the anxieties of Sugamo; and the architect of Pearl Harbor, General Minoru Genda. Appointed commander-in-chief of the Japanese Air Force (through the backing

---

* *Op. cit.*, Kodama, pp. 204–212.
† *Ibid.*, pp. iii–iv.

of Kodama and Kishi, then Prime Minister and chief of the National Defense Council), Genda was wildly enthusiastic about the Lockheed Starfighter. After testing it in California, he returned to Japan with the recommendation that only the Starfighter would do. At about the same time, Genda's recommendation was echoed by a special delegation of German Air Force officers, including General Gunther Rall, who'd arrived in Tokyo to persuade recalcitrant Japanese of the Starfighter's dubious superiority. Supported, then, by Japan's most honored military figure, by its respected ally in the preceding war, by the Prime Minister, and by Kodama's political manipulations, Lockheed accomplished the impossible. Grumman's contract evaporated. A few months later, after the Lockheed contract was signed, General Genda was awarded the U. S. Legion of Merit by the American Air Force—seventeen years after he'd annihilated its planes in Hawaii.

Indeed, 1958 was a busy year for Kodama. Besides the difficulty of engineering the Lockheed sale, he was called upon to preserve the disintegrating political position of Prime Minister Kishi. Regarded by many as an American puppet for having pushed an unpopular Japanese-American security treaty through the Diet, Kishi appeared to be on the way out. Kodama, however, was able to save him, rallying the right wing to his standard and provoking street demonstrations in his behalf. Those demonstrations were countered by even larger ones organized by the Left, and it appeared that President Eisenhower's impending visit to Japan would result in widespread bloodshed. With the demos gathering force, U. S. and Japanese authorities called upon Kodama to take charge of "Operation Protect Ike." Moving with customary quiet, the former assassin pried loose an estimated $2,300,000 in "contributions" from local businessmen, ultranationalists, and racketeers. With that in hand, he hired platoons of anti-Communist street fighters, providing them with riot gear, trucks, and helicopters. At the last minute, however, Ike's visit was aborted, as American authorities contemplated what appeared to be the makings of a massacre.

Sometime after the mooting of Operation Protect Ike, Kodama seems to have joined the Unification Church, gravitating toward that organization through the auspices of Ryoichi Sasagawa. An old friend of Kodama's, a veteran of Sugamo and the Shanghai-Manchuria intrigues, Sasagawa came into enormous wealth after the war, becoming, among many other things, chairman of the Japan Shipbuilding Association. An ultranationalist whose views paralleled Kodama's, Sasagawa established himself in his friend's mold, becoming one of Japan's leading *kurumaku*.* Just as Kodama privately financed military exercises on the remote island of Choju, Sasagawa lavished money on Tokyo's "martial arts societies," a euphemism that might cover everything from karate clubs to paramilitary cabals.

Sasagawa's pet project, however, was Win Over Communism (WOC), a fund-raising subsidiary of the Unification Church. Sasagawa served as WOC's chairman, and Kodama as its chief advisor. This needn't indicate any special religiosity on the part of either man; on the contrary, the Unification Church's evangelical anticommunism is a bulwark of South Korean "stability" and, as such, protective of Kodama's investments in that country. Still, the implications of Kodama's relationship to WOC and the allegedly Reverend Sun Myung Moon are interesting to ponder. The recipient of untold Lockheed millions, Kodama was the aircraft firm's agent in both Japan and Korea. Other corporations (notably Gulf) have been shaken down for "political contributions" by Korea's Park regime, the *quid*'s *quo* being the right to do business there. It's almost incredible that Kodama, with his influence and investments in South Korea, should not have provided Park's minions with support, financial and otherwise. If he did, then his affiliation with WOC is particularly suggestive. Specifically, it raises the specter of the Lockheed Corporation subsidizing the Moonies' spread from Seoul to Savannah by means of bribes laundered through Hong Kong by an apostate Spanish missionary (see below) for delivery in so-called Bekin's boxes to the industry's *kurumaku* in Tokyo.

The Spanish-born priest was a naturalized Japanese citizen whose given name, José Gardeano, had been changed to Hoze Aramiya. Father Hoze functioned as a courier for what Japanese police officials describe as an "underground bank" based in the jet stream between Tokyo and Hong Kong. When Lockheed needed to bribe someone in Japan, it made an electronic transfer of funds from its Los Angeles office to its Hong Kong foreign-exchange dealer, Deak & Company (founded, not incidentally, by a former OSS operative with continuing links to the CIA). The sums, converted to yen, were then hand-carried aboard planes in flight bags that held upward of

---

* Literally, "black curtain": a term from the Kabuki drama which refers to someone who works behind the scenes.

9,300 ten-thousand-yen notes, weighing about twenty-seven and one-half pounds.* In Tokyo with the cash, Father Hoze would consult his instructions for delivery. Often those instructions were unusual. For instance: "To: Mr. A. H. Elliott, Okura Hotel, Tokyo Japan: Deliver on Sunday January 31st—if impossible on Sunday, deliver on Saturday Jan. 30th. Contact Mr. Elliott ONLY at hotel." † Obviously, Lockheed's Tokyo rep didn't want to be seen with Hoze at the office (even on a weekday).

The priest, however, was not the only one working in Lockheed's Chinese laundry. While Deak & Company served as middlemen in transfers amounting to $8,300,000 between 1969 and 1975, another $4,300,000 was sent by other routes, notably through Lockheed's Swiss branch. Receipts for this money came in a variety of shapes and forms. Shig Katayama, an American, provided the aircraft firm with an undetermined number of blank receipts signed by himself as proprietor of the I-D Corporation's Hong Kong office. The owner of Japan's largest coffee vending-machine company, Katayama founded I-D in the Cayman Islands in 1973. Paid $72,000 for his signatures, Katayama is a Los Angeles resident and, apparently, I-D Corporation's only employee.

Other receipts, some acknowledging the payment of what was described as "peanuts," were issued by Kodama and his friends, but the purpose was the same: to pay off upper-echelon Japanese officials and to disguise the route of payment. The ultimate goal, of course, was to sell airplanes. And in this Lockheed was successful. After years of behind-the-scenes maneuvers, involving relatively small remittances, Lockheed's breakthrough came in Hawaii on September 1, 1972. There President Nixon, accompanied by Secretary of State William Rogers and National Security Advisor Henry Kissinger, met for three days with Japanese Prime Minister Takuei Tanaka. The purpose of the summit talks was to conclude a U. S.-Japan trade agreement that called, in part, for Japan to purchase at least $320,-000,000 in civilian aircraft from an American manufacturer within the next two years. Meeting alone in a remote Hawaiian hotel, accompanied only by a Japanese translator, Nixon and Tanaka quickly

---

* The statistic, unearthed by Tokyo's *Asahi Shimbum*, is not as academic as it may seem: it explains why it is that the receipts Kodama issued to Lockheed never exceeded 93,000,000 yen. Unlike others, who were sometimes paid off in yen bearer checks, Kodama always insisted on cash. This amount, then, represents the largest that could be hand-carried aboard a commercial aircraft.

† Deak & Company, "Foreign Money Transfer Receipt" for $337,837.84, dated January 19, 1973, received from Lockheed Aircraft International, Inc.

reached accord. There were no minutes kept of the secret talks.

Within a few days, however, their effects could be felt. First, the Japanese Defense Council retracted its previous decision to produce antisubmarine patrol planes domestically—thereby opening the door to a billion-dollar sale of Lockheed P-3C Orions to Japan. Within days of that decision, Father Hoze left for the airport. Before a month was out, exactly one billion yen was delivered to Kodama in small wooden packing crates that required fifteen separate deliveries.* The last payment took place on the day Americans went to the polls to reelect Richard Nixon.

While this financial blizzard was under way, Tanaka was meeting with executives of All-Nippon Airlines (ANA). One week after a meeting with the firm's president, ANA announced that it would purchase six Lockheed Tristars, later upped to twenty-one, at a cost of $20,000,000 apiece. The man behind ANA's decision is believed to have been Kenji Osano, the firm's chairman and its largest stockholder. A confidant of Tanaka's, Osano is also the owner of the hotel in which the Nixon-Tanaka talks were held.

4 / EPILOGUE

There is no proof that Lockheed was specifically discussed during the Nixon-Tanaka summit talks. And yet, it would be feloniously naïve not to speculate about the matter. Certainly the Japanese have. In the wake of the subcommittee hearings, three ANA executives have been arrested and former Prime Minister Tanaka has been jailed. No fewer than a score of Japanese industrialists and government officials are under investigation, and indictments against them are being considered.

As for Nixon, his involvement with the Lockhood Corporation is deservedly suspect. Staffers of the defunct Subcommittee on Multinational Corporations have told me, "It's absolutely incredible that Lockheed should have been the only U. S. corporation of any size *not* to have made a contribution to Nixon's 1972 reelection campaign—and yet that's what we're told. It just doesn't make sense, not after what he did for them. I mean, he intervened *personally* to get that loan." Another staffer said, "Obviously there's something

---

* At the official exchange rate, this would be about $2,700,000; on the black market, however, a billion yen would amount to exactly $2,500,000. Whichever is the case, the deliveries required that the courier have a strong right arm; if the *Asahi Shimbum* is correct, the money weighed 412 pounds.

to the Nixon connection, but there just isn't the stomach to investigate it, not anymore. We'd never get the go-ahead." The suggestion that campaign contributions may have been sought in connection with the 1972 Nixon-Tanaka summit talks is more than mere speculation. A former executive of the Grumman Corporation (which hoped to sell its E2C aircraft to Japan) testified before the Senate that he was asked for such a campaign contribution by Richard Allen—the same Richard Allen who, in that summer of '72, went on to work for Robert Vesco. According to the Grumman exec, Thomas P. Cheatham, Jr., the donation was solicited as a *quid pro quo*: if it were made, Grumman's aircraft would be hyped at the summit talks. Asked how much the donation ought to be, Cheatham testified that Allen told him, "Oh, I think the E2C is worth about a million dollars." Asked if this amounted to a "shakedown," Cheatham waffled, then said, "Yes, something of that sort."

The absence of a Lockheed contribution to the Nixon campaign is therefore intriguing. So is the proximity of the summit talks to the Kodama payments, the decision against Japan's domestic production of patrol planes, and ANA's choice of the Tristar. But there are other reasons to wonder.

Subcommittee investigators, for instance, are curious to know if the Lockheed Corporation retained Richard Nixon in the years during which he held no public office (1963–68). A partner in the law firm of Mudge, Rose, Nixon made numerous trips to Japan, Europe, and the Middle East, conferring with foreign leaders and businessmen on behalf of his law firm's clients. Whether the Lockheed Corporation was one of those clients is unknown: Mudge, Rose refuses to comment. On one trip, however, Nixon dined with Lockheed agent Adnan Khashoggi in Paris's Rasputin Restaurant. Khashoggi, of course, later became a contributor to Nixon's presidential campaign, while also serving as the President's personal emissary to King Faisal. Nixon, moreover, went out of his way to appoint senior Lockheed executives to posts of influence in his Administration: former Lockheed vice-president James Hodgson, for example, was named ambassador to Japan in 1974, while another Lockheed exec was named to a high Air Force position.

Finally, we may recall that Jim Golden, the Intertel/Hughes spook who'd served as Nixon's friend and Secret Service protector, was himself Lockheed's international representative between 1965 and 1969. That may be a coincidence, but as we've seen, right-wing journalist Victor Lasky is righter than he knows (or tells) when he insists that "it didn't start with Watergate." On the contrary, "it" goes back to Nixon's earliest years in government when he joined with Bob Maheu, John Gerrity, Stavros Niarchos, and the multinational oil companies to destroy Aristotle Onassis by any means necessary. And it continued in his use of Maheu during the 1956 presidential campaign and, after that, in his relationship to Howard Hughes. And it continued through his involvement with Khashoggi, Intertel's Jim Crosby, and, according to Bill Spector and Norman Casper, it continued through his relationships with the mysterious French industrialist, Paul Louis Weiller, and the Cayman Islands' Castle Bank & Trust.

Nixon, however, is a mere mote in what I've called the "haunting of America." Ruthless, unlikable and corrupt, he's a convenient fall guy whose banishment to San Clemente may tempt us to believe that the worst is over. And yet Nixon was only the symptom of a much deeper malaise that respects neither party lines nor distinctions between the public and private sectors. As we've seen, the malaise of intelligence has afflicted such odd bedfellows as the liberal Kennedys, the right-wing Hunts, and others at points in between. Indeed, from presidents and billionaires to the manufacturers of cars and hamburgers, spookery has spread with a vengeance, corrupting what it touches as certainly as a cancer cell will do. Its nature is inherently corrupt: to gain advantage over others by the secret manipulation of people, products, and information, using any means necessary to accomplish whatever objective the paymaster commands. Inevitably undemocratic, the use of intelligence methods has nevertheless been tolerated as a necessary evil of foreign policy. Unfortunately those methods cannot be confined to relations between states. On the contrary, precisely because the methods are so effective, they've become an integral part of both domestic politics and the commercial sector.

In training its agents and officers, the CIA uses a curriculum of about sixty courses. But hundreds more are taught throughout the country at private schools for spooks and at industrial seminars on the practice of intelligence. As we've seen, Dektor Counterintelligence will teach the apprentice spy the secrets of the Psychological Stress Evaluator, giving him a unique advantage in contract- and collective-bargaining negotiations. The National Intelligence Academy will instruct students in the nuances of electronic eavesdropping. And the would-be spook or his employer can pick up a lot more at schools and conferences run by a host of private firms and organizations such as Federal Laboratories (of Saltsburg, Pa.), the International Association of Chiefs of Police, *Security World*, and Business International, Inc. Some of these restrict their students to those with official cachet or employment by a domestic or foreign police/intelligence organization. But most do not. Business International, for instance, recently sponsored a security conference for executives of multinational corporations. At a secret and closely guarded location in the New York City area, the execs paid $4,750 each to receive individualized instruction in counter-terrorist tactics and intelligence techniques designed to be used abroad. With the help of Business International's specialists, each exec was enabled "to create, step by step, a counterintelligence program for his company." The program showed "how to protect information about the company and its managers' movements from leaking out, and how the company should gather and process intelligence about terrorists and disseminate it within the company." Far from a generalized discussion, the program included "the use of external, published sources; the use of embassies and paid informants; what information should be gathered at the local (foreign subsidiary) level and what at headquarters; and how this information should flow within the overall company." * This, of course, was only one of twelve areas covered at a single conference devoted to the counterintelligence problems of multinational corporations. Literally hundreds of other intelligence problems—not to mention opportunities—are annually discussed in thousands of conferences, seminars, and boardrooms belonging to firms specializing in this most peculiar form of "management consulting."

The executives, however, needn't go to the spooks: the spooks will come to them. In the past few years alone, an estimated three thousand employees of the CIA's clandestine services have been discharged in an effort to rejuvenate the Agency and appease the ambitions of upwardly mobile recruits. Many of those discharged have offered their skills to employers outside government, hiring on with large corporations or forming their own small firms. Nor are the CIA vets more than the vanguard of a much larger group composed of agents from a host of federal directorates with intelligence responsibilities. Former DEA chief John Bartels, for instance, recently went into private practice with two intelligence officers who

---

* NACLA, Latin American and Empire *Report*: "The CIA: White Collar Terrorism," Vol. 8, No. 10, December, 1974 (Washington, D.C.), Institute for Policy Studies.

served under him at the DEA: George Belk and Stephen McClintic. Operating from a small Washington office near the White House, the trio intends to export police- and intelligence-related systems (including computer technology) to Third World countries such as Libya.

The effects of this invasion of the private sector have been as we've seen: both those industries that are regulated and those that are not have become increasingly remote and manipulative. The marketplace, in effect, has been subverted by an array of intelligence devices and techniques including burn-bags, codes, shredders, bugs, bagmen, PSEs, surveillance equipment, propaganda and financial laundries—so that taxes are commonly evaded, bribes, kickbacks, and industrial espionage are almost routine, the consumer is deceived, stockholders are cheated, and the government is kept in the dark. Spookery, then, has become a big business . . . one that exists *for* big business.

Admittedly none of this is new: the devious have always been among us. What *is* new, however, is that the clumsy aberrations of past years have been rationalized and streamlined by specialists using sophisticated techniques. Thus, in only the past ten years or so, those techniques have become an "invisible commonplace" of the private sector. If we take a detached, rather than a civic, view of this, a great deal of irony is apparent. It's ironic, for instance, that the tax-supported intelligence community of the United States, established to protect a democracy against a variety of alien threats, should turn inward against the public on behalf of an industrial sector that waxes increasingly totalitarian in its own right. It was, after all, your tax dollars (and a few of mine) that helped develop the PSE for the use of military intelligence agents. Today, however, the device is more likely to be applied to an American job applicant (or one who files an insurance claim) than it is to be used against a Chinese secret agent. It's ironic, too, that the public should be up in arms against those threats to privacy represented by federal surveillance and government information systems—while, at the same time, remaining nearly oblivious to the far more pervasive threats represented by *private* information systems, the telephone company's "Service Observance Bureau," and the proliferating surveillance procedures currently in use in this country's supermarkets, banks, airports, chain stores, and so on.

In this connection it should be pointed out that the Watergate scandal outraged the majority of Americans because they perceived the threats which spooks posed to the democratic process. The private use of secret agents, however, poses an even greater risk. Not only are the paladin spooks more widespread than their federal counterparts, and wholly unaccountable to the public, but their activities impinge more directly upon our daily lives than political espionage is likely to do. The public, after all, is their target, rather than a rival politician. Accordingly, their impacts are felt in the most banal—and therefore the most important—ways. They affect what we buy and how much we pay for it, how we do business and what we say. They affect our income, the jobs we hold or don't hold, the amount of taxes we pay, and even the way we feel when we walk down the street. And those things, of course, make up the real fabric of America.

As for what can be done to reverse the process, it's essential that the problem and the players be identified. In part, that's why I've included so many names in this book: in the hope that others will turn their attention to individuals and events that constitute mysteries. *Spooks* is merely one step in an investigative process that involves many reporters and others who are determined to make America's secret history public.

Disclosure, however, will be fruitless if it's not succeeded by action. This country's *kurumaku* must not only be identified but also be made to bear public responsibility for their deeds. This means, of course, an end to the kind of pardon Richard Nixon received (surely the final step in the Watergate cover-up) and an end as well to cor·rosive plea-bargains of the sort struck by Spiro Agnew, ITT agent Hal Hendrix, Richard Kleindienst, Richard Helms, and so many others.

Finally, a legislative mechanism should be established to monitor the private employment of "retired" government intelligence agents and the apparats for which they work. Like lobbyists and propagandists for foreign nations, their loyalties should be a matter of public record. Accordingly, a "Domestic Agents Registration Act" should be drafted, requiring the spooks to identify their clients and to make periodic reports concerning their activities, contracts, and contacts. There are problems with this proposal, of course, not the least of which is a definitional one: who is a former "intelligence agent," and who is not? Similarly, risk attaches to the prospect of retiring deep-cover employees making public their former connections to the federal intelligence community. Yet another problem the proposal is likely to encounter is the opposition of the spooks and their employers: they will argue, correctly, that secrecy is at the very heart of their work. While this is true, their business is often dirty business. Applying the need-to-know criterion with which the spooks are so familiar, the public's need to be informed of the paladins' activities overrides any claims they might make for the sanctity of so-called "proprietary information."

However difficult they may be to solve, the problems manifested by the private use of secret agents are fundamental to the well-being of a democratic society. If we ignore those problems, we're likely to witness the emergence of a new sort of totalitarianism, an industrial regime of secret agents and manipulators operating within the framework of a state that has become only nominally democratic.

If that happens, it will be too late for any exorcist.

ACKNOWLEDGMENTS

To SPEND FOUR YEARS INVESTIGATING THE PRIVATE USE OF SECRET agents is a task that necessarily puts the writer in debt to a great many friends and sources.

It's literally true, for instance, that *Spooks* could not have been written without the generous understanding of my wife, Carolyn, and the patient intelligence of my editor at William Morrow, James Landis. The patronage and affection of good friends were also essential and always unflagging: Mike Salzberg, Lewis Lapham, Carl and Pat Dobkin, Jon Wolman, Mary Satterlee, the Sidrans, Scott Spencer, Tom and Rena Stein . . . came through in every way.

A number of fellow journalists were helpful in providing leads, introductions, and information. Especially so were Allen Fitzgibbon, Andrew St. George, Carl Oglesby, Taylor Branch, Joe Spear, Julie Moon, Peter Noyes, Jim Steele, John Marks, and Victor Marchetti.

John Taylor, of the National Archives' Modern Military Records Branch, proved uncanny in his ability to locate intelligence documents and memoranda that others thought had been misplaced or destroyed. Ken Smith and Bud Fensterwald, of the Committee to Investigate Assassinations, were similarly helpful, as were Otto Otepka and Sidney Goldberg. Institutional help was also made available in the form of meticulously documented research, and special thanks is due to the Institute for Policy Studies and the Center for National Security Studies. Others to whom I'll always be grateful, but whose names it would be imprudent to mention here, include present and former staff members of congressional committees and subcommittees having to do with Permanent Investigations, Multinational Corporations, Intelligence Operations, and Government Operations with respect to the IRS. Others in the Executive Branch were similarly helpful and unstinting, but especially so were those agents and staffers who, by discussing various matters, jeopardized their careers in the Treasury Department, the Securities and Exchange Commission, and the Intelligence section of the Drug Enforcement Administration.

By no means finally, I owe a tremendous debt to scores of former CIA officers, military intelligence agents, private investigators, adventurers, arms dealers, and sometime mercenaries who were willing to discuss their lives and the issues raised in this book. Some of them I knew by phony names; others were merely telephone numbers whose information always checked out. Those I knew best and drank longest with are mentioned by name in *Spooks*, but they'd hardly welcome public acknowledgment of our conversations and their help.

Some, however, will not mind, and so I'd like to thank the following for their insights and anecdotes: Robert Maheu, Lou Conein, Mitch WerBell, Tom Norton, Bill Spector, Walt Mackem, Joe Shimon, Colonel Paul Routhier, Barbara and Elliott Spindel, Ed Arthur, Mike Kradz, Costa Gratsos, John Muldoon, John Gerrity, and Colonel Allan Bell—each of them at home in the twilight zone described by *Spooks*. Others such as attorneys Ed Morgan (of Washington, D.C.), Ed Ross (of New York), and Morton Galane (of Las Vegas, Nevada) provided important analyses and leads, as did Detective Lieutenant Al Madrid of the Burbank (California) Police Department's homicide squad. People talk to reporters for different reasons, some good and some bad. Those mentioned here, however, spoke candidly about their affairs even after it became obvious that our views did not always coincide and that, in several cases, my reporting would be highly critical of the sources themselves. Accordingly, they have my gratitude and my respect as well.

INDEX